Foundations for

marriage and

family relations

Dale L. Womble, *Ed.D.*

Ohio University

Foundations for marriage and family relations

The Macmillan Company, *New York*

Collier-Macmillan Limited, *London*

Library of Congress catalog card number: 66-15662

THE MACMILLAN COMPANY, NEW YORK
COLLIER-MACMILLAN CANADA, LTD., TORONTO, ONTARIO

Printed in the United States of America

Preface

Compared with much of the college curriculum, courses in functional education for marriage and family relations are still in their infancy. New ideas and concepts are constantly emerging because the body of research findings in the area of human behavior is growing and becoming better authenticated. This fact alone is sufficient to justify the writing of additional books from time to time.

This book is intended primarily for use by unmarried college students who are making their first, and possibly only, academic exploration into this area. It seeks to assist them toward the development of a basic philosophy about marriage and family relations. Although no one should anticipate becoming an authority on marriage by reading this book, every reader should feel challenged to build on this foundation a more positive attitude toward the possibilities of constantly enriching his future marriage and family life. Fundamentally functional and practical, the book is geared to the marital interests, needs, and concerns of college students as I have heard them expressed in my classrooms.

This is not a book on marital therapy, nor is it a book of recommendations or advice. Its primary theme emphasizes that freedom under our concept of democracy makes American marriages different from those in other societies, for this freedom goes far beyond merely choosing governmental leaders: it encompasses every part of the individual American's life, including his expectations within marriage. Within our society, it is possible for successful marriages to take many diversified forms, so that no one description of an American democratic family is suitable. Every reader is entitled to have his freedom of choice respected; his success in marriage will depend upon how well he formulates and implements his goals within the framework of whatever system he does adopt. *Foundations for Marriage and Family Relations* emphasizes that successful marriages depend upon our learning to exercise our freedom in this manner. And, to the extent that we establish successful marriages and families, we shall insure a strong nation.

I do not pretend to cover all phases of marriage and family relations, to treat all areas with equal intensity, or to exhaust the subject matter in those phases of marriage and family relations that are included. I do attempt to place in proper relation to contemporary living certain phases of marriage and family relations. The greatest portion of the text is devoted to the areas most important at this moment in history. Yesterday's marital conditions are dealt with when they contribute to a better understanding of today's realities. I recognize that, because tomorrow's marriages will be different from today's, the maintenance of a successful marriage in an ever-changing society is necessarily a continuing process.

At the end of each chapter there is an extensive, yet carefully selected, set of current references for further reading. These references include material on many levels of interest and ability, and are from diversified, but readily available, sources.

I want to express my gratitude to a number of persons for their encouragement and assistance in the writing of the manuscript.

I am especially indebted to the many students in the various institutions where I have taught courses in marriage and family relations. They have, through the years, contributed much to my knowledge and concepts.

Drs. Mildred Morgan, Blaine Porter, and Aaron Rutledge read different sections of the manuscript and gave invaluable critical comments and suggestions. Dr. Ruth Hoeflin, Associate Dean of Home Economics, Kansas State University, read a preliminary draft of the manuscript and contributed many helpful comments. Dr. Vladimir deLissovoy contributed a most welcome detailed analysis of the final draft.

To Dr. Henrietta Fleck, Dean of Home Economics, New York University, goes a warm, personal appreciation. It was she who first interested me in planning this book and who patiently and constructively read and criticized the many preliminary drafts, and constantly encouraged me to complete the task.

My thanks also go to Miss Anna Syarse for her editorial assistance.

Finally, words are not adequate to express my deepest gratitude to my entire family whose continuous uncomplaining support through the many versions at last makes this book a reality.

D. L. W.

Contents

Tables

Foundations for
marriage and
family relations

chapter 1

Preparing for marriage today

This is a wonderful time to be nearing readiness for marriage in democratic America. For those who are adequately prepared, there is promise within today's marriages of possibilities far beyond the wildest imaginations of most people of bygone eras. The world is constantly shrinking, which sometimes makes a successful marriage more complex, but also makes it much more exciting than ever. The rate of change in all areas of life is accelerating. As a result, many former "rules" of American marriage and family life are—and need to be—challenged. Is a marriage which was good enough for one's parents still "good enough"? To get the most out of marriage, should one still select a mate with a background as similar as possible to one's own? To get the most out of life, should one even marry? Is it moral for two people to stay married when they are no longer in love? Is it really a tragedy that about half of all brides this year will be in their teens? Why must one's marriage conform to the "traditional" model when some other pattern appears to hold forth a far greater potential? With increasing longevity, can society still reasonably demand that young men and women who marry must remain permanently yoked "until death do us part"?

It is increasingly evident that the American democratic ideal has been unique in the world. Although the United States is a republic rather than a pure democracy, the American concept of freedom is democratic for it goes far beyond the individual's privilege of choosing governmental leaders: at present, this democratic belief and practice encompasses nearly every part of his life, including his expectations within marriage. Therefore, marriage in the United States is frequently different from marriage in other societies.

1

This is not to suggest that this concept of complete freedom for the individual in all areas was as much in evidence in the early days of the republic as it is now. Although the ideal of this concept is yet to be achieved in American society, there is evidence that its success has stimulated other societies to try democratic practices with greater confidence.[1] This increasing emphasis upon the individual's freedom of choice in *all* his activities has been, and still is, in the process of evolution. It is in a state of continuous change. No other society, however, has yet exercised this concept of freedom as fully as has the United States.

In order for marriage to be considered successful within such a concept, individuals must be allowed a choice of unions in many diversified forms. Because every citizen is entitled to have his freedom of choice respected, no one description of an American marriage is necessarily suitable as a universal pattern. The concept of democracy in action has the potential of creating the healthiest marriages the world has ever known, and there is evidence of an ever-increasing number of such healthy unions in the United States. Just because a higher percentage of marriages in some societies are more permanent units than those of America today does not necessarily mean that such marriages are happier or more conducive to healthy individual emotional development. A low divorce rate is by no means positive proof of marital success or happiness. As Westermarck has pointed out, in most all societies where the laws or mores permit only separation, and no absolute divorce, it is found that many mates actually have other lovers.[2] It must be recognized, however, that democratic ideals carried over into marriage also bring the potential of greater discontent and unhappiness. In order to increase the number of healthy marriages, it is necessary for each citizen to become personally prepared for formulating, appreciating, and implementing his goals within the framework of whatever form of marriage he chooses to adopt.

It must be emphasized that the elemental part of American democracy —mutual decisions for individual personal fulfillment (the management process)—can insure a strong nation and is most meaningful when it is practiced by each citizen within his marriage and within his family life. In addition to the classic ingredients—time, money and energy—there are many other useful and valuable resources for effective democratic home management. These include all types of knowledge, interests, attitudes, abilities, skills, and the use of authoritative opinions. Such resources may be used interchangeably, conserved, or increased. This is not to suggest that management should ever be considered an end in itself, rather, it is the process through which one uses resources to achieve certain goals. In a democracy, management should play a part in every thoughtful act and decision. Through democratic management practices, the rights, privileges, and differences of all family members are considered. Such democratic practices should greatly contribute to each individual's capacity for fulfilling his highest potential. This is truly the American ideal, and—as it is achieved by more and more citizens—the nation will become even stronger and more dynamic. A satisfying home management process gives greater assurance of a strong democratic nation than do rich deposits of raw materials, a healthy capitalistic economy, or even a staunch military establishment. Wealth, a sound economy, patriotism—these are of little value to a democratic nation unless its citizens are able to think clearly and are willing to act for the benefit of all mankind. These attributes are best developed within a family framework consistent with the American ideal.

With democratic ideals shaping the criteria of a successful marriage, marital failure results in serious emotional difficulties more often than when the criteria are shaped by other ideals. These disturbances not only cause the unhappiness of countless individuals, but they also damage the democratic society itself. Counselors in all areas report clinical evidence by the ton that unsuccessful marriage is the root of much American unhappiness, and that it frequently results in both physical illness and mental breakdown.[3]

Industrial management reports that the well-adjusted family man is usually an even better producer than the maladjusted family man. Therefore the happily married man is worth more in dollars and cents to his company, to his nation's economy, and to his family.[4]

Marriage preparation is needed

Young people must make a serious effort to prepare for marriage. Many agencies are now dedicated to improving this preparation. The results, although far from perfect, are most encouraging. American marriages are becoming healthier. It is apparent that to maintain an inwardly strong democratic America, preparation for the democratic foundations of marriage is essential.

If a person lives to the age of forty-five, the chances are greater than nine out of ten that he will marry at least once.[5] Excluding the feeble-minded, the permanently insane or criminal, and those pledged to certain religious orders, almost everyone who really wishes to marry actually does so. Americans might well be described as the most marrying people on earth. Certainly in no other Western culture does so high a percentage of the population marry.[6] Yet many of those who marry do so without adequate preparation.

PREPARATION FOR EVERYTHING BUT MARRIAGE. The average American spends years in preparing for a vocation. College students spend hours with advisers planning programs of study to prepare themselves for their life's work. Yet within a very few years after commencement, many graduates change to jobs entirely unrelated to their major areas of study.[7] Many other graduates continue in their major fields, but are dissatisfied. Whatever their work choice, however, nine out of ten of them will marry. Therefore, it would seem that a course in marriage preparation is more pertinent to the needs of the student than almost any other single course.

UNREALISTIC MARRIAGE ATTITUDES. Too many Americans still believe that anyone can marry anyone else with little or no preparation and live happily ever after. Much of this casual indifference is generated by the mass communication media, which have found that romanticism and family farce are better money-makers than their serious or satirical counterparts. Presented in unreal terms for so many years, the family unit seems either too trivial or too intangible for practical study. This uninformed point of view results in complacency when marriage is smooth, and apathy when it is rocky.

The best antidote to such attitudes is a study of the dynamics of interaction within the family. It is particularly true in modern American life that more and more successful marriages are neither gifts nor accidents, but rather hard-earned achievements.

The rapidly changing culture

The need to prepare seriously for marriage has been accentuated by the rapidly changing culture. For better or worse, things have changed remarkably and will continue to do so. Modern historians have discarded almost all of the so-called laws of history, with the exception of the law of change; nothing can remain exactly the same forever. History includes many accounts of resistance by one group against the efforts of another to throw off the shackles of colonialism, or of a group attempting to defend and re-establish the status quo. In the long run, the proponents of the status quo eventually lose.[8]

A WIDE VARIETY OF SOCIAL CONTACTS. In a rural society, the individual's social contacts are quite limited. Most mates in such a society grow up in close proximity to one another,[9] and thus have similar social, economic, religious, educational, vocational, and ritualistic backgrounds. These areas, then, do not need to be explored, tested, or discussed before marriage. This understanding, of course, eases stresses and strains and helps to perpetuate many unions in such a society.

Conditions are much different in modern America. The average student has the opportunity to see, date, and have a speaking acquaintance with more individuals of different background in four years at college than his great-grandfather had in his entire life. In the year 1900, only 27 per cent of the boys and girls who had entered the first grade later entered high school, and less than 3 per cent of high school graduates attended college. Now about 89 per cent of first-graders eventually enter high school, and more than 30 per cent, in some states nearly 60 per cent, of high school graduates go on to college. Today's undergraduates have opportunities for a wider variety of social contacts before marriage than even their parents had.[10] Under these conditions, the emphasis on romanticism makes it much easier for two completely different people to fall in love and to marry. Research suggests that today's campus life, in contrast to yesterday's, encourages the associations of persons of diverse backgrounds and thus increasingly favors heterogeneous pairings.[11]

INCREASED FAMILY MOBILITY. A few decades ago an average worker in Ohio could not consider an attractive job offer in California as realistic. Today, transcontinental job-hopping is a reality. America has become a nation of movers. It is easier today for a family to move from one side of the continent to the other than it was to move from one side of a county to the other a few years ago. One out of every five families in the United States moves each year; in fact, one out of every eleven families has moved to a new state each year since World War II, and only 35 per cent of family heads are living it the state of their birth.[12]

Today's Americans have mobile homes as well as mobile families, for in many cases the house is also on wheels. Many communities have trailer parks or camps. These families live in their trailers; the children attend schools, churches, community functions, fall in love, and marry in a series of different locations as they travel from place to place. The mobile home groups today constitute the largest single expanding way of life in the United States, whereas a few years ago they represented less than 0.1 per cent of American families. At that time, most mobile home owners were retired grandfathers and grandmothers, but this is no longer the case.[13] Problems of human relationship may increase in these circumstances because the traditions of one subculture may be challenged or altered by the mores and customs of a different group. It is easy to subscribe to the American concept of individual freedom of choice when neighbors and others with whom one interacts are of quite similar background; it is quite another thing when the people are different. It is not enough to give lip service to the American ideal only when it applies to one's own situation: the ideal must apply with equal force to all individuals. The true test of the American concept of democracy may now be at hand, as Americans move often and constantly acquire new neighbors. Admittedly this constitutes a more difficult situation and may be a threat to some marriages. If the concept is adhered to seriously by all, however, this nation and its families can, in the long run, only grow stronger.

MOBILITY AND FAMILY PROBLEMS. Moving about the country can increase tensions and frustrations within the members of the moving family. Research by George Fry and his associates disclosed the fact that the average modern young junior executive moves once every two years.[14] Whenever a family moves, usually one or more of its members must sever a close friendship or attachment. Because friendships are good for mental health, it is important to make new friends, church associations, and school affiliations in the new location. Adaptation to new community traditions and patterns of behavior may take special effort. Until familiarity replaces strangeness, daily frustrations may occur that will test the tempers of all concerned. This can be a difficult period for newlyweds, who have not yet had time to establish a social pattern of their own. On the other hand, free of old associations, a young married couple may feel stronger and more adventuresome in a location other than the home town.

A LONGER LIFE TOGETHER. The chances that a young couple now entering marriage will survive until their golden wedding anniversary have more than doubled in the past sixty years. Although in the past many unhappy marriages might have been dissolved by the early death of one spouse, this prospect is not so likely in the United States today. In fact, the annual rate of marital dissolution from the total of *all* causes (divorce, desertion, and death) is actually lower today than that brought about by death alone at the turn of the century. Nowadays people are more frequently forced to choose between making a success of their marriage or dissolving it legally. The outcome is more a voluntary choice than ever before.

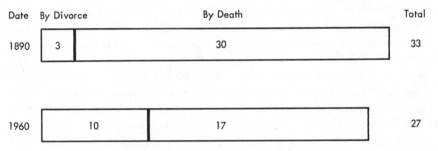

Date	By Divorce	By Death	Total
1890	3	30	33
1960	10	17	27

Figure 1-1. The annual rate of marital dissolution from all causes is lower today than that brought about by death alone at the turn of the century.

THE THREAT OF WAR. The threat of war has always seemed to induce hasty marriages. Deep social unrest has always produced general anxiety and distrust. Although the individual can do little to change the world dilemma, he can do much for himself by intelligent preparation for marriage. His personal family strength will add to his democracy's strength.

The new industrial revolution

America is experiencing an acceleration of technological change that has already surpassed that of the mid-nineteenth-century Industrial Revolution. In a predominantly agrarian society, the family worked and played as an interrelated group, and many of life's satisfactions were supplied by working together. In today's industrialized society, the paycheck is one of the few family satisfactions resulting from the nonprofessional worker's efforts. Even farming has become a big business, totally dissociated from the family as a unit. This, of course, forces the family to find a new focus for unity. In a few decades, the United States has changed from 75 per cent agrarian to more than 90 per cent industrial, and the trend continues.[15]

AUTOMATION IN THE HOME. The accelerated change called *automation* can be observed within the home as well as in industry. The new labor-saving devices cost money, and today a disproportionate amount of family income seems to be going into gadgets and their repair. The added financial burden is sufficient to cause much frustration or misery and to break up some homes. It may be true that Americans are living on a plâne never dreamed of a few generations ago, but it has not been achieved without additional cost, especially for the newly married couple. Many items totally unknown to Grandmother are regarded as absolute necessities in setting up housekeeping today. In today's home the capital outlay for the kitchen—with its blenders, mixers, washers, dryers, push-button ranges and ovens, dishwashers, garbage disposers (to say nothing of its prepared frozen and packaged foods, ice-crushers, freezers, and can-openers)—is many times greater than was the total investment for setting up housekeeping sixty years ago; Ogburn and Nimkoff[16] state that it will be even more expensive in the future.

MORE TIME FOR LEISURE. From the sixty-hour work week of a few decades ago, today's American workers now usually enjoy a work week of forty hours or less. Used in a positive manner, this shortened work week can improve many marriages; used negatively, it can precipitate the breakdown of a marriage.

The new freedoms

The ever-increasing emphasis on individual freedom is a natural outgrowth of the American concept of the democratic way of life, but it can have repercussions in marriages and families. A democratic society cannot long endure unless freedom is geared to the balance wheel of personal responsibility.

The effect upon the family (and thus, in turn, upon society) of certain freedoms without corresponding responsibilities has not always been entirely good. Freedoms from outside pressures—such as religion, public opinion, and parental wishes—has not always produced exemplary results.

INCREASED SECULARIZATION. Increased freedom has resulted from a decrease in religious pressures on personal behavior.[17] Fear has been replaced generally by logic and an insistence upon free choice. Secularism implies that when the individual questions standards which are presented to him, he is questioning man's edicts and not necessarily God's. Thus, if the individual should wish to change some standards, he may do so without fear of divine reprisal.[18] Although ethics may reach many people when threats and fear would not, the fact remains the change has not been offset by an increased "social-relationship" consciousness. Although the authority to force one to "do right" has decreased, the personal desire or ability to "do right" has not as yet increased sufficiently. This change in the approach of religion over the control of human behavior has apparently lessened its effectiveness, at this moment, as an agent in society for the support of permanent marriages.

LESSENING OF THE INFLUENCE OF PUBLIC OPINION. In former times a man's behavior was often inhibited by what his neighbors might think. Rather than face ostracism in his permanent community, he was more likely to forego temptation. Today there is less government by gossip because it is easy to move away from disapproving neighbors.

This freedom for individual action has, of course, been accompanied by a greater variety of temptations. There is still some pressure from public opinion today, but it has definitely lessened. This may actually be a step in the right direction for a democracy, but a concomitant social consciousness of equal force must evolve to temper the freedom with justice.

LESSENING OF PARENTAL CONTROL OVER MATE SELECTION. When parents made the final decision as to whom, when, and where their offspring might marry, a higher percentage of marriages remained intact. This is still the practice in some countries, and by their standards the marriages are generally successful.[19] Kapadia describes mate selection in present-day India:

> The social background provided by the authoritarian joint family with its domination in all spheres of life affords no scope for the recognition of any personal factors, individual interests, and aspirations. . . .[20]

This is not to suggest that Americans should revert to that system for, of course, the standard of marital success differs widely by cultures. In an earlier period of American life, parents took the business of mate selection seriously. Because they believed they knew best, they insisted on being responsible for the selection. Young people have rarely been as free to choose their own mates as haphazardly as the American youth of today.

PARENTAL SUPERVISION. Formerly, the young married couple was expected to take up residence in the near vicinity of parents and other relatives. Parents were then on a stand-by notice to step in if the new marriage did not get started right. Most young couples welcomed whatever aid they could get. Parental advice was not considered the interference it so often is today. Young couples respected the years of married experience of their elders and often sought out their advice. To today's parents, however, marriages seem so different from their own that they are often reluctant to step in even when requested. Then too, youngsters separated by thousands of miles from any of their relatives cannot get family advice easily even if they want it. There is also the feeling among many young couples that *any* parental intrusion or advice suppresses their own superior improvisations.

Better marriages

It is inconceivable that anyone would wish to settle for anything less than a first-rate marital relationship. Yet, the fact remains that numerous marriages lack many of the positive benefits and potential joys that are possible with adequate preparation. Situations can be minimized that might otherwise be difficult. Better balance can be achieved in an already potentially well-adjusted marriage through understanding the art of family living. Better marriages have grown from "good" ones by increased knowledge and understanding of such vital points as the relation of a satisfactory courtship process to marital success, the relative importance of various background factors in mate selection, complementary needs, adaptability, how to recognize love strong enough for marriage, measures of marriage readiness, the problem-solving process, the psychosocial as well as the anatomical aspects of sex, the psychology of spending money, methods for enriching a relationship, the establishment of responsive and complementary family roles, conception control and family planning, the physical and emotional aspects of pregnancy and birth, the maturation process of children, and concepts for keeping flexible and up with the changing times and values of life.

Specifics in preparation

Understanding the necessity for preparing for marriage is vital, but more vital still are the specific details of the task.

HOME INFLUENCE. Everyone receives some understanding or training for marriage from the home. Even the best home training, however, is often insufficient for today's marriages. Furthermore, it is inconceivable how society could expect the unhappy home to prepare its offspring adequately for a happy, successful marriage. Rebecca Liswood, who serves as executive director of the marriage-counseling services of Greater New York, pointed out that a survey of engaged couples in that area revealed that more than one half of the young men interviewed considered their home preparation for marriage as "entirely inadequate."[21] A committee of the American Medical Association, in a recent extensive survey of high school and college students, found over 70 per cent of the students expressed a need for more information than had been supplied by their homes. The report ended by suggesting as a possible solution to the dilemma that courses on marriage and the family should be offered in the schools.[22]

MARRIAGE COURSES.   As early as 1894, a course in marriage, consisting of lectures by Elsie Clews Parsons, was offered by Barnard College,[23] but it was not until February 1924, at Boston University, that the late Ernest Groves taught the first college-credit course in functional preparation for family living.[24] It is estimated today that more than 600 colleges offer at least one such course; about half these courses have been added to the curriculums since 1949.[25] There is also a growing emphasis upon family courses in the secondary schools.[26] For the most part, these had their beginnings in 1926, when the Laura Spelman Rockefeller Fund and the Progressive Education Association made grants to the American Home Economics Association to introduce such programs into high schools.[27] Many of the earlier programs in home economics have been more recently broadened to include family life as a psychological and social phenomenon.[28]

An evaluation of such courses at the college level proves their worth. Junior-college administrators have cited evidence that marriage courses, among other things, encourage students to face responsibilities, retard hasty marriages, save some marriages, and help to prevent premature marriages.[29] There are published evaluations of marriage courses at Temple University, Boston University, the University of Kansas, Michigan State University, the University of Minnesota, Syracuse University, Utah State University, San Francisco State College, and Stephens College.[30]

Although there has been little published research on the effectiveness of such courses at the secondary level, there is a growing belief in their value. One study at Tampa, Florida, found conclusive evidence that attitudes accepted by research as conducive to happier marriages resulted from a high school course on family study. The family-study students were measured against a group of similar students who had not received family-life education, and the differences were drastic enough to show the advantages of marriage-preparation courses in helping to build positive attitudes.[31]

College or high school marriage courses are no panacea, but there is certainly evidence that they help. The Stephens College survey found only twenty-eight alumnae of their functional course in marriage who had experienced divorce.[32] At the time of the survey, about 4000 girls had taken the Stephens course since its inception in 1930.[33]

BECOMING WELL INFORMED.   Another way to prepare for marriage is to keep informed by reading the facts about marriage and human behavior. Research findings in the area of marriage relationships constitute one of today's largest growing bodies of knowledge. Innumerable books, pamphlets, and articles are currently being written with professional interpretations of the new data. Such books are becoming more common on the shelves of every college, high school, and private and public library. Thus it is possible for young couples to enter marriage with common denominators of information, attitudes, and values even when they themselves come from diverse backgrounds.

TALKING WITH PEOPLE. When a young person wants to know more about the actual practice of many occupations, he is urged to seek out those who appear to be successful in the particular area of his interest and to try to learn all he can from them. The same idea holds true in preparing for marriage. Very practical suggestions can come from discussions with friends and relatives who have successful marriages.

Summary

Sooner or later marriage is likely to play a part in almost everyone's life. There are many forces at work today that can adversely affect the chances for a happy and successful marriage. These include the rapidly changing culture, technological change, and the irresponsibilities inherent in the new concepts of freedom. Furthermore, the spirit of American democracy makes success in marriage and family life difficult to achieve. Nevertheless, the family is still the backbone of the American way of life, an effective force in meeting both personal and national crises.

Notes

1. See William J. Goode, *World Revolution and Family Patterns* (New York: The Free Press of Glencoe, Inc., 1963).

2. Edward Westermarck, *The History of Human Marriage,* Vol. 3 (London: Macmillan & Co., Ltd., 1921), p. 371.

3. For research results which substantiate this mountain of clinical evidence, see, e.g.: C. Charles Burlingame, "Home-Made Mental Illness," *Psychiatric Quarterly,* **28**:102–11; Florence Kluckholm, "What's Wrong with the American Family?" *Journal of Social Hygiene,* **36**:227–36; John A. Schindler, M.D., "Family Relations: Greatest Cause of Illness," *The Progressive,* **28**:9–13.

4. Rebecca Liswood, "Raise Your Son to Be a Good Husband," *This Week Magazine* (October 2, 1960), 29.

5. U.S. Bureau of the Census, Series P–20, No. 70.

6. For details of the marriage rates of all member nations of the United Nations from 1940 onward, see the latest edition of the *United Nations Demographic Year Book* (New York: Columbia University Press).

7. Dael Wolfle, *America's Resources of Specialized Talents* (Washington, D.C.: American Council on Education Studies, 1957). Studies of all professions indicate that only about 38 per cent of college men graduates remain permanently in the field of their college major.

8. For example, since 1956, twenty-four countries in Africa have become independent from foreign rule.

9. See, e.g.: Ray H. Abrams, "Residential Propinquity as a Factor in Marriage Selection: Fifty-Year Trend in Philadelphia," *American Sociological Review,* 8:288–94; James H. S. Bossard, "Residential Propinquity as a Factor in Marriage Selection," *American Journal of Sociology,* 38:219–24; Maurice R. Davis and Ruby Jo Reeves, "Propinquity of Residence Before Marriage," *American Journal of Sociology,* 44:510–25; Alvin Katz and Reuben Hill, "Residential Propinquity and Marital Selection," *Marriage and Family Living,* 20:27–35; Thomas Monteville Coffee, "An Empirical Study of Residential Propinquity and Marital Selection, South Bend, Indiana, 1954–1958 inclusive," *Dissertation Abstracts* (October 1962), 1450–51.

10. The average American adult today has completed 1.4 more years of schooling than the average American adult of 1950. College graduates increased 39.8 per cent in 1960 over 1950; college students, by 53.6 per cent. *NEA News Release* (May 30, 1960, and March 1, 1963).

11. Gerald R. Leslie and Arthur H. Richardson, "Family Versus Campus Influences in Relation to Mate Selection," *Social Problems,* 4:117–21.

12. U.S. Bureau of the Census, Series P–20, Nos. 73, 85, and 113.

13. *Ibid.* Over one hundred thousand homes on wheels are purchased each year in the United States.

14. Lester and Irene David, "Your Wife Is Your Business Partner," *This Week Magazine* (April 15, 1956).

15. U.S. Bureau of the Census, Series P–27, No. 29. Actually only about 8.7 per cent of present families live on farms.

16. William F. Ogburn and Meyer Nimkoff, *Technology and the Changing Family* (Boston: Houghton Mifflin Company, 1955) .

17. For a fuller discussion of the growth of secularization, see Victor Obenhaub, *The Church and Faith in Mid-America* (Philadelphia: Westminister Press, 1963).

18. For a fuller discussion of the implications of this, see Howard Becker, "Sacred and Secular Societies," *Social Forces,* 28:361–76.

19. See either David and Vera Mace, *Marriage East and West,* Garden City, N.Y.: Doubleday & Company, Inc., 1960, or David Mace's article, "Marriage by Arrangement," *McCalls Magazine* (August 1959), 50–51, 101–103.

20. K. M. Kapadia, *Marriage and Family in India* (Bombay: Oxford University Press, 1958), p. 169.

21. Liswood, *op. cit.*

22. Spurgeon English, *et al.,* "Preparedness of High School and College Seniors for Parenthood," *American Medical Association Archives of Neurology and Psychiatry,* 71:469–79.

23. Lester S. Pearl, Doctoral Study, University of North Carolina, 1950.

24. Ernest R. Groves, "Memorandum of the First Credit Course in Preparation for Family Living," *Social Forces,* 20:140.

25. Judson T. Landis, "The Teaching of Marriage and Family Courses in College," *Marriage and Family Living,* 21:36–40.

26. See, e.g., Edith E. Rosenstiel and Harold E. Smith, "The Growth of Family-Life Education in Illinois," *Marriage and Family Living,* 25:109–11.

27. Lemo D. Rockwood, "Highlights of a Study of the Sources and History of Family-Life Education" (Ithaca, N.Y.: Cornell University, 1948), p. 9. Mimeographed.

28. Selma F. Lippeatt and Helen I. Brown, *Focus and Promise of Home Economics: A Family-Oriented Perspective* (New York: The Macmillan Company, 1965). Over 60,000 boys are now enrolled each year in high school home eco-

nomics courses, the titles of most such courses being "Family Living." See Beulah I. Coon, *Home Economics in the Public Secondary Schools—A Report of a National Study,* Bulletin No. 661 (Washington, D.C.: United States Department of Health, Education, and Welfare, 1962).

29. George W. Gambill, "A Survey of Marriage Education in Twenty-Nine Junior Colleges," *The Junior College Journal,* 32:97–99.

30. Donald S. Longworth, "Critique of Attempts to Evaluate Marriage Teaching," *Marriage and Family Living,* 15:308–12. See also more recent studies reported by Virginia M. Moses, "A Study of Learning Derived from a Functional Course in Marriage and Family Relations," *Marriage and Family Living,* 18:264–68; or Dorothy Dyer, "A Comparative Study Relating Marital Happiness to University Courses Helpful in Marital Adjustment," *Marriage and Family Living,* 21:230–32.

31. Dale L. Womble, Doctoral Study, Florida State University, Tallahassee, Fla., 1955. See also *Family Life Education Survey,* Indiana State Board of Health, 1960.

32. W. Clark Ellzey, "Marriage Questionnaire Report," *Marriage and Family Living,* 11:133.

33. Current Syllabus, Stephens College Marriage Course.

Questions for further thought

1. In what ways is the effort at preparing for marriage consistent with American concepts of democracy?
2. What circumstances were most instrumental in the founding of formal courses on marriage and family relations by American colleges and universities?
3. What should be the primary reasons for students enrolling in marriage- and family-relations courses? Are these the real reasons for which students take such courses?
4. What are the arguments for and against making education for marriage and family relations a required part of the curriculum in (a) elementary school? (b) high school? (c) college?
5. Should both sexes, or only women, study marriage and family relations?
6. Did those with successful marriages form a higher percentage of the population years ago than they do today?
7. Has the net effect of newer and faster means of transportation been a cohesive or disruptive factor in American marriage?
8. Would modern American marriages have more or less stability if parents exerted as much influence on mate selection as they used to do?

Recommended films

Our Changing Family Life (New York: McGraw-Hill Book Company, Inc.).
Families on the Move (Ann Arbor: University of Michigan Television Center).

Suggested supplemental readings

BOOKS

Beasley, Christine. *Democracy in the Home.* New York: Association Press, 1954.
Bulletin of the National Association of Secondary School Principles. *A New Look at Home Economics,* 48, 296 (December 1964).
Carr, L. J., and J. E. Stermer. "Life in the Trailers," in Marvin B. Sussman, *Sourcebook in Marriage and The Family,* rev. ed. Boston: Houghton Mifflin Company, 1963.

Dodson, Garner. *Making the Most of Every Move.* New York: G. P. Putnam's Sons, 1958.

George, F. H. *Automation Cybernetics and Society.* New York: Philosophical Library, Inc., 1959.

Keats, John. *The Crack in the Picture Window.* Boston: Houghton Mifflin Company, 1956.

Mace, David and Vera. *The Soviet Family.* Garden City, N.Y.: Doubleday & Company, Inc., 1963.

McGregor, Douglas. *The Human Side of Enterprise.* New York: McGraw-Hill Book Company, Inc., 1960.

Ogburn, William F., and Meyer Nimkoff. *Technology and the Changing Family.* Boston: Houghton Mifflin Company, 1955.

Packard, Vance. *The Status-Seekers.* New York: David McKay Co., Inc., 1959.

Simpson, George. *People in Families.* New York: Thomas Y. Crowell Company, 1961. Chap. 1.

Sorokin, Pitirim A. *Social and Cultural Mobility.* New York: The Free Press of Glencoe, Inc., 1959.

Thomas, John L. *The American Catholic Family.* Englewood Cliffs, N.J.: Prentice-Hall, Inc., 1956. Part I.

ARTICLES

Bardis, Panos D. "Influence of Family Life Education on Sex Knowledge," *Marriage and Family Living,* 25:85–88.

Foster, Robert G. "Effects of Mobility on the Family," *American Journal of Public Health,* 46:812–18.

Frank, Lawrence K. "The Beginnings of Child Development and Family Life Education in the Twentieth Century," *Merrill-Palmer Quarterly,* 8, 4 (October 1962).

Gordon, R. E., and K. K. Gordon. "Emotional Disorders of Children in a Rapidly Growing Suburb," *International Journal of Social Psychiatry* (Autumn 1958), 85–97.

Kolb, William L. "Family Sociology, Marriage Education, and the Romantic Complex: A Critique," *Social Forces* 29:65.

LeMasters, E. E. "Holy Deadlock: A Study of Unsuccessful Marriages," *Midwest Sociologist,* 21:86–91.

Leslie, Gerald R., and Arthur H. Richardson. "Family Versus Campus Influences in Relation to Mate Selection," *Social Problems,* 4:117–21.

Litwak, Eugene. "Geographic Mobility and Extended-Family Cohesion," *American Sociological Review,* 25:385–94.

———. "Occupational Mobility and Extended-Family Cohesion," *American Sociological Review,* 25:9–21.

National Education Association. "America on the Move," *NEA Research Bulletin,* 36:4 (1958).

Nimkoff, Meyer F. "What Do Modern Inventions Do to Family Life?" *Annals of the American Academy of Political and Social Science,* 272:53–58.

Otis, Jack. "The Use of Teacher-Student Conferences in a 'Sex-Education and Family-Life' Course," *Marriage and Family Living,* 21:369–72.

Pagent, Norman W. *Family-Life Education, Program Profiles.* San Bernardino, Calif.: Kendal Publishing Company, April 1961.

Popenoe, Paul. "Effects of Education for Family Life," *Family Life,* 14:1–2.

Salisbury, W. Seward. "Religion and Secularization," *Social Forces,* 36:197–205.

Scates, Douglas E. "Education for Personal and Family Living in Public Schools: A Sample Survey," *Social Hygiene Papers* (December 1955), 18–26.

Sirjamaki, John. "Culture Configurations in the American Family," *American Journal of Sociology,* **53**:450–56.

Tumin, Melvin M. "Some Unapplauded Consequences of Social Mobility in a Mass Society," *Social Forces,* **36**:21–37.

Meeting the
legal requirements
chapter **2** *for marriage*

Every known human society has considered the marital relationship important to both social and individual welfare. Therefore, the state—which is, in essence, the guardian of all welfare—has been generally regarded as having the right to legislate on marriage. This concern, and subsequent regulation of marriage by society, has particular significance to citizens of the United States, for constitutionally the laws governing marriage were left exclusively in the power of the separate states.

The genesis of American marital laws

Laws on marriage grew out of expressed needs of the inhabitants of each region. Thus since the problems, interests, and needs of many areas of the United States differed, the marital regulations differed also. Changes and refinements in each state's marriage laws have tended, at times, to increase the differences. It would seem logical that marriage laws would become more uniform as individual state identity blends into a stronger union, but this has not always occurred.

From time to time efforts have been made to bring the laws governing marriage in the various states into greater conformity. Unfortunately, these efforts have always failed. For almost thirty years, the late Arthur Capper, United States Senator from Kansas, tried unsuccessfully to introduce legislation pertaining to uniform marriage and divorce laws, but he was never able to muster sufficient Congressional support for this cause. The implications of the conglomeration of state marriage laws sometimes involve the innocent citizen in unexpected difficulties. It is possible, for instance, to be legally married in one state, legally divorced and remarried in another, and yet to be a bigamist under the law of a third state. This variance occurs within a fifteen-mile radius in the United States.[1]

Those contemplating marriage, as well as those already wed, would do well to become familiar with the laws governing marriage, not only in the state of current residence but in any state the couple might move to in the future. The Constitution states emphatically that full faith and credit shall be given by one state to the laws of another. In instances of variable marriage laws, however, it has not always been clear which state laws have been in effect and which ones have been yielded.[2]

Similarities of state marriage laws

In spite of the many differences between state marriage laws, the basic principles are generally similar.[3] In every state there are laws pertaining to consanguinity, prior marriage, minimum age, and physical and mental capacity. A license is required in every state, but the details of fees, waiting periods, and physical examinations vary. Common-law marriages are not permitted in some states, and interracial marriages are barred in many states.

LICENSE REQUIREMENTS. All states require a marriage license. The fee charged varies, but the license is an unvarying requirement for legal marriage. Possession of a license does not mean that a couple is married; it is simply evidence of *legal permission* to marry. Ordinarily, the license must be used within a specified number of days after issuance, or it becomes invalid. As specific as the states are about requiring a license to marry, this time limit is not always enforced. It is possible that a couple might marry without a license, provided they find an officiant who is willing to perform the ceremony under those circumstances. In most states, such a marriage is deemed legal. But if any penalty is invoked, it is imposed upon the officiant, who is fully cognizant of the license requirement.

COMMON-LAW MARRIAGE. Marriages made without benefit of license or officiant are usually of the common-law type. Such marriages are still permitted in fourteen states. In the United States, this custom undoubtedly originated during the years of territorial expansion and pioneer isolation. Circuit-rider judges and parsons were able to visit only a few of the most populated settlements; the outlying districts were seldom, if ever, visited. A couple considering marriage might have to wait years for a license, and an even longer time might pass before an officiant could be found to perform the ceremony. Under such circumstances, many marriages took place without license or officiant. Such couples usually appeared for a proper ceremony whenever the opportunity presented itself. In many instances, however, this might be years after the couple had set up housekeeping together and raised several children. Many states passed legislation exempting such couples from any penalty—declaring, in effect, that two people who identify themselves as husband and wife to others within their community of residence become so in fact. No license or officiant was ever required, and the state recognized such marriages as valid as—and carrying all the privileges and responsibilities of— every other marriage.

Although common-law marriage was once justifiable to encourage marital stability, it now serves the opposite purpose. Recognition of common-law marriage in today's society is actually detrimental to the state's interest in promoting the general welfare. Common-law marriages were abolished by the Roman Catholic Church through the Council of Trent in 1563; England followed suit in 1753. There does not appear to be a valid reason for the continuance of common-law marriage in the United States today.[4]

CIVIL CONTRACT.   Every state recognizes a marriage as a civil contract between two people. Marriage, therefore, like all other civil contracts, is subject to regulation, supervision, and registration by the state. Like other civil contracts, the marital contract implies the creation of a body hitherto nonexistent. It likewise merges the identity of the participants in legal matters: each is held responsible for the debts and civil actions of the other. One spouse cannot be forced to testify against the other in court because, legally it would be tantamount to testifying against oneself. Unlike other contracts, however, it is considered unreproachably permanent. The two parties cannot mutually agree to dissolve the partnership. One member must first be proved guilty of misconduct before the other is released from the contract, and this release can be obtained only through court action.

OFFICIANT REQUIRED.   Every state requires that someone legally responsible be in charge of the wedding. All clergymen are accepted as fulfilling the legal definition of competency to perform the wedding ceremony, and many nonclergical judicial officials are duly authorized in most states. In the case of Quakers, who have no clergy, forty-one states recognize as officiants the witnesses who sign the marriage certificate. In such ceremonies the couple publicly proclaim themselves husband and wife in front of as many witnesses of the congregation as wish to gather for the event.[5]

An authorized official is not compelled to perform the wedding ceremony for every couple possessing a valid license. He can refuse to officiate without offering any reason to the couple. Couples marry each other; officiants are merely the first to recognize the new relationship. If, for any reason, personal or professional, the official believes the marriage to be an ill-advised action, he may simply refuse to participate.

MUTUAL CONSENT.   No state considers a marriage as valid which involves force or willful misrepresentation. To represent oneself falsely is usually sufficient grounds for the consideration that no true contract has ever existed. This, of course, rests on the assumption that it was the misrepresentation that helped to entice the innocent party into contracting marriage. It must be shown that the deliberate misrepresentation was of such a nature that the knowledge of the truth before the marriage would have prevented or diverted the union.[6]

In every state, all marriage must have the free and open consent of the two parties involved; without it, no marriage has taken place.[7] This is not true in all cultures; in some, there is a direct exchange of a boy and a girl by the respective parents.[8]

THOSE OF UNSOUND MIND. Because people who are not of sound mind cannot legally make a contract of any kind, they cannot legally marry. All states have regulations prohibiting the marriage of mentally ill persons. Because, by the legal definition, insanity may be considered at times to be a temporary condition, no state permanently forbids such individuals the right of marriage. The restrictions usually apply only as long as the individual is considered legally to be of an unsound mind. Likewise, not all states recognize insanity as sufficient grounds for the dissolution of a valid marriage; in some states insanity is considered adequate grounds for the breaking of the marriage contract only after a specified length of time.

THE BIOLOGICALLY UNFIT. Individuals who have been declared feeble-minded are positively forbidden to marry in every state but three. Nebraska, South Dakota, and New Hampshire now allow the feeble-minded to marry under guardianship approval, if they first submit to sterilization.

Much has been written about the pros and cons of allowing the "biologically unfit" (in any category) to marry. There is little consistency among the several state laws regarding this subject. Much of the literature nowadays is in general agreement that such persons, if allowed to marry, should not be allowed to reproduce. Many people prefer to leave such matters to nature, and cite evidence that the so-called unfit seldom produce many children anyway. Others point to case studies which testify to the fact that, no matter how few, the offspring of the unfit are a catastrophe to society.[9] It is now generally believed that not enough evidence exists to warrant enforced celibacy or childlessness of "outwardly" healthy individuals simply because they have questionable family backgrounds. It is generally agreed, however, that those who show definite signs of retardation should be restricted.[10]

Thirty years ago few states required examination for venereal disease as a prerequisite for marriage. The few laws that were enacted pertained to males only. Connecticut, in 1935, was the first state to pass legislation requiring examinations for venereal disease for both sexes. Since that time, most of the states have followed suit. There is, however, little uniformity in the various state laws concerning this requirement. States that require an examination for venereal disease specify the number of days prior to the marriage that the examination must take place, but this period varies from as few as seven days to as many as forty; a re-examination is necessary if the marriage is not performed within the specified period. In some states, the test includes all venereal diseases; unfortunately, the majority of states require tests only for syphilis.

Only North Carolina and North Dakota prohibit marriage of tubercular persons in the infectious stage.

Much has been learned recently about epileptic seizures which suggests that prohibition of marriage on this ground is not entirely warranted. Nevertheless, seventeen states have rigid laws forbidding marriage for anyone so afflicted.

CONSANGUINITY. Every state has laws regulating marriage of blood relatives. Here again, however, there is a wide variation of degree and definition. All states appear to agree that the blood tie between siblings, parents and offspring, grandparents and grandchildren, and uncles or aunts with nieces or nephews, respectively, is too close for marriage.[11] Here the similarity ends. Twenty-nine states forbid marriages between first cousins; six states, between second cousins; and some states, even within certain degrees of in-law relationship.[12]

There is no genetic reason for the restraint of in-law marriages, but the appearance of such marriages is suspect in many subcultures, resulting in restrictions by social disapproval. By contrast, there are various religions throughout the world that decree that a widow automatically becomes the wife of her late husband's eldest surviving brother. A similar practice appeared in early Mormon tradition.[13]

There is strong genetic evidence for the restriction of marriage between close relatives. Blood relatives are likely to possess similar genes, which may transmit hereditary defects; the chances of the offspring inheriting that pattern are therefore doubled.[14] It is also true, of course, that desirable genetic traits might be perpetuated and strengthened. This is the basis of animal husbandry leading to prize stock. In-breeding for stock improvement, however, is based on the practicality of destroying defective offspring. This expediency, of course, cannot be condoned with humans.[15]

AGE. Every state has regulations regarding the minimum age at which persons may marry. The age restrictions depend upon parental consent and the sex of the applicant. Generally a couple may marry at an earlier age with parental consent, and the woman may marry at an earlier age than the man. There is more justification for variance in age requirements in different states than for many of the other variables mentioned. In a strictly rural community, where the early marriage is likely to perpetuate a pattern long in existence and the couple intends to remain in the community, a much lower minimum age might be acceptable. With today's technology, however, there is little assurance that any given community will remain static for long.

The most widespread minimum age requirement, with parental consent, is eighteen for men and sixteen for women; without parental consent, the minimum age is generally twenty-one for men and eighteen for women. Old English common law stipulated the ages of fourteen and twelve, with parental consent, for men and women, respectively; until recently that was still the law in Idaho and New Jersey. Apparently, the legal requirements and the actual practice may vary according to such circumstances as public opinion, geographic locality, and the possibility of pregnancy. Child-brides and grooms are more likely to be found in the sparsely settled rural areas of the Southern states than elsewhere in the country.

The marriages of couples who have misrepresented their ages in order to marry are almost always accepted as valid unless there is a strong protest from the parents. In such a case the falsely based marriage can be annulled. This implies that no valid marriage ever existed, and the parties (regardless of religious convictions) are free to marry—either each other or someone else—when they are more mature. In a few states, however, if such a marriage has lasted a given number of days without formal parental protest, and has been sexually consummated, the couple have every right to continue the marriage in spite of age restrictions.

INHERITANCE. All states recognize various rights of inheritance for spouses and children. Again, however, there is anything but general agreement on the extent of these rights. In some states all property is held in equal ownership by spouses, whether registered in the name of one or both. In other states, if the property is registered in one name only, the other marital partner cannot even apply for a renewal of the license tag. In some states widows automatically inherit the full estate of the deceased spouse unless a will stipulates otherwise. In others the automatic inheritance is cut to one third or one half, and the only way the wife may inherit all of it is if the husband leaves a will. Legitimate children are generally regarded as next in line to the widow for inheritance. In some states such children are automatically given from one third to one half the estate, which is held in trust until they are of age. In only four states can illegitimate children inherit property from the father.[16] In all states illegitimate children can inherit property from the mother. In a few states, one half of the groom's property automatically becomes the bride's upon marriage, but all that she owns at the time of marriage remains exclusively hers.

ILLEGITIMACY. There are many differences in state laws pertaining to the identification of illegitimate children and their legal status. Under some state laws all children born out of wedlock are considered illegitimate regardless of the circumstances. This apparently also applies to offspring from an annulled marriage, an incestuous union, a bigamous union, rape, or from a union which is of questionable legality or in any way not bonafide.

Progress in changing these laws is slow, but it must be remembered that any suggestion of sexual indulgence without the sanction of marriage has a "bad" connotation for most of American society. In case of illegitimacy, society is quite likely to penalize the innocent offspring.

Arizona and North Dakota legitimize all children. Sixteen states no longer refer to illegitimacy on the issued birth certificate.[17] It may still be recorded as such in the vital records of those states, but the children are spared the embarrassment of lifelong identification with an event over which they had no control.

When paternity is established (and this is not easy in some cases), fathers are usually held legally responsible for the financial support of the illegitimate minor child. Texas and Virginia, however, make no mention of this in their statutes.[18]

IMPETUOUS MARRIAGE.   The Roman Catholic Church has long recognized the necessity of preventing hasty marriages. Since 1215 it has been mandatory for Catholics to have published banns, ordinarily for three weeks in advance of the ceremony. Before 1930, only the state of Maine required a waiting period between the day of license application and the date of the wedding. Now, with the exception of Nevada, every state has a three- to five-day waiting period either specified by license or incurred by the venereal disease tests. These delays often serve the purpose of preventing impetuous marriages. It is possible to have the waiting period waived in some states under extenuating circumstances, such as the final stages of pregnancy.

The effects of a waiting period on the elimination of hasty marriages is a well-established fact. Baber mentions the experience of Los Angeles County, California, as evidence. In the first year after the enactment a law enforcing a three-day waiting period in that county, more than 1000 couples who had applied for marriage permits did not follow through.[19] The rate of marriage in Iowa fell off 20 per cent in 1961, after the enactment of a three-day waiting period and a raising of the minimum age level.[20]

INTERRACIAL MARRIAGE.   In spite of our democratic precepts, twenty-two states currently forbid interracial marriages. In seven of these states, a person with one eighth nonwhite blood is classified as nonwhite. The penalties for violation are often quite severe, generally including from five to ten years of imprisonment, a fine of several thousand dollars, or both. Such penalties can be imposed not only on the couple but, in some cases, on the officiant as well. Absence of such restrictions may indicate advanced democracy in action, but all too often it merely indicates a low percentage of other races within that particular state. Southern state laws usually refer specifically to a Negro-white union, whereas Western state laws restrict the union of a Mongolian with a non-Mongolian.

Such restrictions may be in violation of the United States Constitution, for the federal courts have ruled that racial discrimination is not to be condoned. Segregationists argue, however, that to marry against "public sentiment" is to commit a crime against the "general welfare." A California law forbidding interracial marriage was declared unconstitutional by that state's supreme court on the grounds that it prevented free exercise of religion. Both of the partners involved in the test case were of the same faith and contended that the law prevented them from receiving one of their religion's sacraments. The laws in other states which have been challenged, however, have so far been upheld on the grounds that, because the prohibition applies equally to all races, it does not necessarily discriminate against any one race. Nevertheless, it is encouraging to note that eight states have voluntarily eliminated such laws from their statutes since 1960, and three more have similar legislation under consideration.

Marital privileges and obligations

Both members of a marriage are guaranteed certain privileges by law in every state, but at the same time they are expected to assume certain obligations. It is considered a gross breach of contract for the marital partner to refuse, without just cause, to grant the privileges or to refuse those obligations.

COHABITATION.   The couple is expected by society to live together in a place approved by the husband. Couples may mutually agree to circumvent this rule either temporarily or permanently. This, however, is usually interpreted as desertion should one partner desire cohabitation, and the other decline for no just cause. Such refusal is considered cause enough for the contract to be broken or for the offender to be punished.

SEXUAL ACCESS.   Closely allied to the obligation of cohabitation is the right to sexual intercourse with the partner. Absolute refusal without just cause has been interpreted by the courts as a form of desertion. Inability to perform the sex act might be considered just cause for refusal. If impotency is known before marriage and concealed from the partner, however, it is usually interpreted as fraud or deliberate misrepresentation. The courts have, as a general rule, held that each partner in a marriage has an "inalienable right" to expect the other to be "healthy" at the time of marriage if not warned otherwise beforehand.

SEXUAL FIDELITY.   In most states, laws specify that each marital partner is expected to be sexually "exclusive" to the other. The interpretation of this last stipulation, however, is stricter in some states than in others.

Table 2–1. Some marital law differentials by states, as of July 1963

| State | Minimum age requirement | | | | Common-law marriage valid | Blood test required and days valid | Waiting period required | | Marriages prohibited between whites and | | |
| | With parental consent | | Without parental consent | | | | | | | | |
	Male	Female	Male	Female			Between application and issuance of license	After license issued before it can be used	Negroes	Orientals	American Indians
Alabama	17	14	21	18	Yes	Yes 30	None	None	Yes	No	No
Alaska	18	16	21	18	No	Yes 30	3	None	No	No	No
Arizona	18	16	21	18	No	Yes 30	2	None	Yes‡‡	Yes‡‡	Yes‡‡
Arkansas	18	16	21	18	No	Yes 30	3	None	Yes	No	No
California	18*	16*	21	18	No	Yes 30	None	None	No	No	No
Colorado	18	18	21	21	Yes	Yes 30	None	None	No	No	No
Connecticut	16	16	21	21	No	Yes 40	4	None	No	No	No
Delaware	18	16	21	18	No	Yes 30	None	1 or 4#	Yes	No	No
Florida	18*	16*	21	21	Yes	Yes 30	3	None	Yes	No	No
Georgia	17	14	21	18	Yes	Yes 30	3†	None	Yes	Yes	Yes
Hawaii	18	16	20	20	No	Yes 30	3	None	No	No	No
Idaho	15	15	18	18	Yes	Yes 30	None	None	No	No	No
Illinois	18	16	21	18	No	Yes 15	1	None	Yes	No	No
Indiana	18	16	21	18	No	Yes 30	3	None	No	No	No
Iowa	18	16	21	18	Yes	Yes 20	3	None	No	No	No
Kansas	18	16	21	18	Yes	Yes 30	3	None	No	No	No
Kentucky	18	16	21	21	No	Yes 15	3	None	Yes	Yes	Yes
Louisiana	18	16	21	21	No	Yes 10	None	3	Yes	Yes	Yes
Maine	16	16	21	18	No	Yes 30	5	None	No	No	No
Maryland	18	16	21	18	No	Yes 30	2	None	Yes	Yes	No
Massachusetts	18	16	21	18	No	Yes 30	3	None	No	No	No
Michigan	18	16	21	18	No	Yes 30	3	None	No	No	No

State											
Minnesota	18	16	18	No	No	No	5	None	No	No	No
Mississippi	17	15	21	18	Yes 30	No	3	None	Yes	Yes	No
Missouri	15	15	21	18	Yes 15	No	3	None	Yes	Yes	No
Montana	18	16	21	21	Yes 20	Yes‡‡	5	None	No	No	No
Nebraska	18	16	21	21	Yes 30	No	None	None	Yes‡‡	Yes‡‡	No
Nevada	18	16	21	18	No	No	None	None	No	No	No
New Hampshire	14**	13**	20	18	Yes 30	No	5	3	No	No	No
New Jersey	18	16	21	18	Yes 30	No	None	3	No	No	No
New Mexico	18	16	21	18	Yes 30	No	None	None	No	No	No
New York	16	16	21	18	Yes 30	No	None	1††	No	No	No
North Carolina	16	16	18	18	Yes 30	No	None or 2#	None	Yes	No	Yes
North Dakota	18	15	21	18	Yes 30	No	5	None	No	No	No
Ohio	18	16	21	21	Yes 30	Yes	5	None	No	No	No
Oklahoma	18	15	21	18	Yes 30	Yes	3‡	None	Yes	No	No
Oregon	18	15	21	18	Yes 30	No	3	None	No	No	No
Pennsylvania	16	16	21	21	Yes 30	Yes	3	None	No	No	No
Rhode Island	18	16	21	21	Yes 40	Yes	None	5#	No	No	Yes
South Carolina	16	14	18	18	No	Yes	1	None	Yes	No	No
South Dakota	18	15	21	21	Yes 20	No	None	None	No	No	No
Tennessee	16	16	21	21	Yes 30	No	3†	None	Yes	No	No
Texas	16	14	21	18	Yes 15	No	3‡	None	Yes	No	No
Utah	16	14	21	18	Yes 30	No	None	None	Yes‡‡	Yes‡‡	No
Vermont	18	16	21	18	Yes 30	No	None	5	No	No	No
Virginia	18*	16*	21	21	Yes 30	No	None	None	Yes	Yes	Yes
Washington	15	15	21	18	No	No	3	None	No	No	No
West Virginia	18*	16*	21	21	Yes 30	No	3	None	Yes	No	No
Wisconsin	18	16	21	18	Yes 20	No	5	None	No	No	No
Wyoming	18	16	21	21	Yes 30	No	None	None	Yes	Yes	No

* No requirement if both have been married before.
† Unless both twenty-one or older.
‡ Unless male twenty-one and female eighteen.
‡‡ Legislation is pending to eliminate this law.

\# For nonresidents.
** Provided parents and judge both consent.
†† Except that three days must elapse after blood test.

Source: Personal correspondence with Attorney Generals of all fifty states.

Flirtations not involving full sexual expression have on occasion been considered acts of infidelity by the courts in some states. As a general rule, however, the meaning of *sexual fidelity* is simply that each spouse shall remain faithful to the other in the coital relationship.

INDIVIDUAL PERSONALITY. Although the law recognizes that the marital relationship makes each partner a member of a unit bigger and more important than either individual, at the same time it insists that each person, *as a person*, shall retain some individual identity. Neither partner is expected to submerge himself into the relationship so far as to lose sight of the dignity of each as a person, with feelings separate from the marital relationship. The husband is considered the legal head of the house and, thus, of the wife—but he may not exploit this advantage in the relationship solely for his own benefit. He is to be a benevolent leader; she, a cooperative and supportive follower. Each is required to contribute to the emotional and physical needs of the other as much as possible without imposing an undue hardship on either's individuality.

Summary

Legal controls over marriage are necessary to safeguard both social and individual welfare. The laws governing marriage in the United States were left under the jurisdiction of the individual states. Because of differing conditions and subcultures, the marital laws of the several states—although agreeing in principle—frequently are varied in specifics. Basic common similarities include the requirement of a license to marry, recognition that marriage is a civil contract; requirement of an officiant; emphasis upon mutual consent; restrictions on those with unsound minds, certain diseases, and blood ties; minimum age levels for both sexes with and without parental consent; inheritance rights; and traditional privileges and obligations. It is strongly suggested that every citizen become familiar with the basic laws pertaining to marriage—not only within the state where he is married, but within any state where he might possibly reside.

Notes

1. Ray E. Baber, *Marriage and the Family* (New York: McGraw-Hill Book Company, Inc., 1953), p. 75.

2. For an extensive coverage of state marital-law differentials the reader is referred to the five-volume works of Chester G. Vernier, *American Family Laws* (Stanford, Calif.: Stanford University Press, 1931–38), plus supplements. For less detailed, but more concise information, see Harriet F. Pilpel and Theodora Zavin, *Your Marriage and the Law* (New York: Holt, Rinehart & Winston, Inc., 1952); or Morris Ploscowe and Doris Jonas Freed, *Family Law: Cases and Materials* (Boston: Little, Brown & Co., 1963).

3. See Table 1 at end of chapter.

4. Pending legislation in Montana would abolish common-law marriage in

that state, and require all couples presently living together under the system to appear in court by a specified date and testify to their status or face charges of illegal cohabitation.

5. For an account of a Quaker wedding, see James H. S. Bossard and Eleanor S. Boll, *Ritual in Family Living* (Philadelphia: University of Pennsylvania Press, 1950), pp. 16–17.

6. A case in point would be a wedding ceremony officiated by a Catholic priest for a Catholic individual and a divorced person when the previous marital status was unknown except by the divorced person.

7. The coercion of a man into marriage by threat from one of a girl's relatives (usually the father) for real or supposed premarital relationship (realistically, when the girl is found pregnant) is called a "shotgun wedding." Such a wedding is not legally a marriage in any state of the Union.

8. See, e.g., C. T. Hu, "Marriage-by-Exchange Among the Tharus," *The Eastern Anthropologist* (December–February 1956–57), 116–29.

9. See the story of the Kallikaks and Jukes in Amram Scheinfeld, *You and Heredity* (New York: Frederick Stokes, 1939), pp. 362–65. Or read the relation of feeble-mindedness to parental inheritance factors in Marian S. Olden, "Present Status of Sterilization Legislation in the United States," *Eugenic News* (March 1946), 10.

10. Aubrey Lewis, "Fertility and Mental Illness," *Eugenic Review* (July 1958), 91–105.

11. Rhode Island permits marriage between uncles and nieces, but not between aunts and nephews, provided both partners are of the Jewish faith and the wedding ceremony is to be performed by a rabbi.

12. Kentucky, Maine, Maryland, Massachusetts, Michigan, Rhode Island, South Carolina, and Vermont. For a complete listing of the jurisdictional prohibitions relating to consanguinity, see Richard V. Mackay, *Laws of Marriage and Divorce* (New York: Oceana Publications, 1959), pp. 21–25.

13. For a detailed account, the reader is referred to Kimball Young, *Isn't One Wife Enough?* (New York: Holt, Rinehart & Winston, Inc., 1954).

14. For concise data on chances of defective genes from cousin-to-cousin marriages, see C. Nash Herndon, "Medical Genetics and Marriage Counseling," *Marriage and Family Living*, **16**:207.

15. There is historical evidence to suggest that in-breeding was a quite-common practice in some societies about 300 B.C. See, e.g., Russell Middleton, "Brother-Sister and Father-Daughter Marriage in Ancient Egypt," *American Sociological Review*, **27**:603–11.

16. Arizona, Iowa, North Dakota, and Wisconsin.

17. Arizona, Arkansas, California, Colorado, Connecticut, Georgia, Idaho, Maryland, Massachusetts, Montana, Nebraska, New Hampshire, New Mexico, New York, Oklahoma, and Vermont.

18. It needs to be pointed out that attitudes toward illegitimate children vary from culture to culture, including the rights of the mother over the child, and the financial responsibilities involved. See, e.g., E. Bamberger, "The Child in an Incomplete Family Environment," *Social Welfare* (December 1958), 23–25.

19. Baber, *op. cit.*, 125–26.

20. Metropolitan Life Insurance Company, *Statistical Bulletin* (July 1962).

Questions for further thought

1. Consistent with American concepts of freedom, what legal restrictions on marriage are justified?

2. What are the pros and cons of uniform federal laws governing marriage and divorce?
3. What immediate changes should be made in some states' marriage laws?
4. What are some arguments for the continuation of common-law marriage?

Suggested supplemental readings

BOOKS

Baber, Ray E. *Marriage and the Family*. New York: McGraw-Hill Book Company, Inc., 1953.
Becker, Howard, and Reuben Hill (eds.). *Family, Marriage, and Parenthood*. Boston: D. C. Heath & Company, 1955. Chap. 19.
Clarke, Helen I. *Social Legislation*, rev. ed. New York: Appleton-Century-Crofts, Inc., 1957.
Goldstein, Joseph, and Jay Katz. *The Family and The Law*. New York: The Free Press of Glencoe, 1965.
Linton, Ralph. *Study of Man*. New York: Appleton-Century-Crofts, Inc., 1936. Chaps. 10–11.
Murdock, G. P. *Social Structure*. New York: The Macmillan Company, 1949.
Pilpel, Harriet F., and Theodora Zavin. *Your Marriage and the Law*. New York: Holt, Rinehart & Winston, Inc., 1952.
Ploscowe, Morris, and Doris Jonas Freed. *Family Law: Cases and Materials*. Boston: Little, Brown & Co., 1963.
St. John, Norman. *Life, Death and the Law*. Bloomington, Ind.: Indiana University Press, 1960.

ARTICLES

Burma, John H. "Research Note on the Measurement of Interracial Marriage," *American Journal of Sociology*, 57:587–89.
Butler, F. O. "Sterilization in the United States," *American Journal of Mental Deficiency*, 56:360–63.
Hedrich, A. W., and Charlott Silverman. "Should the Premarital Blood Test Be Compulsory?" *American Journal of Public Health* (February 1958), 125–32.
Herndon, C. Nash. "Medical Genetics and Marriage Counseling," *Marriage and Family Living*, 16:207.
"Premarital Health Examination Legislation, Analysis, and Compilation of State Laws." Washington, D.C.: U.S. Department of Health, Education, and Welfare, Publication No. 383.
Reis, Raymond H., and Robert Hoene. "A Study of Catholic Consanguineous Marriages," *American Ecclesiastical Review*, 142:145–63.
Smithburg, Mary M. "Divorce Deviations," *The Legal Aid Briefcase*, 19:7–9.

Defining marital success

chapter 3

Why do so many people get married? What do they expect from the marital relationship? What does society expect? Often it appears that today's definitions and expectations are quite inconsistent with today's realities. Too frequently, the husband and wife define their own marital relationship from diametrically opposed demands and concepts.

A relative matter

Marital success cannot be judged in any absolute terms; however, the degree of its accomplishment of particular tasks can be assessed and used as an index of marital success. Thus, marital success is a relative matter.

In very large measure, marital success is dependent upon the criteria used as standards. A given marriage might be considered relatively successful when compared by certain criteria, yet it might be considered unsuccessful when compared by different standards. A marriage which existed a hundred years ago might have been considered very successful by the usual measurements of that time, but by today's standards it might be judged an utter failure. It is not as likely, however, that a successful marriage of today would have seemed unsuccessful by earlier standards.

Two basic ways to judge marital success

There are two basic ways to measure marital success or failure: (1) The extent to which the union appears to meet the purposes for which marriage is supported in society, and (2) the degree to which the couple is satisfied with the extent to which the union fulfills their personal expectations.

Marriage evolved because of society's needs. It appears, however, that with each succeeding generation, individual expectations are superseding the interests of society. This evolutionary process is occurring now, and the purposes of tomorrow's marriages will probably differ as much from today's as those of today's marriages appear to differ from yesterday's.

The ubiquity of marriage

It is significant to note that there has never been a civilization that thrived for long without some form of marriage. Environmental influences—such as geographic location; economic, social, and political conditions; and especially previous customs—have had much influence upon the forms of marriage, but all surviving groups have marriage in some form. LaBarre states that "man has all the forms of marriage he has been able to think up."[1]

Familiar patterns of marriage can be readily identified even in remote areas of the world, and numerous modifications of the form typical of the Western culture are sometimes recognizable. In addition, there are other patterns which have no apparent connection to any of the more commonly known marriage customs. An example of this is found among the Nayars of Malabar, where all the daughters of one family are married long before puberty to one and the same man at the same time; they are then immediately divorced. The women are never permitted to remarry; they may later mate with whomsoever they choose, but such mates are never considered husbands. The legal father of their children is the divorced person.[2] Among the Mentawei of Indonesia, a man is not allowed to marry until he has become a father; a high premium is placed upon fertility in that culture.[3] Roberts states that there are so many different forms of marriage in the West Indies that it is impossible to make accurate comparison there with the Western system.[4]

POLYGAMY. Some cultures permit—and some even encourage—polygamy. The most popular form of polygamy is polygyny, which involves one husband and multiple wives. LaBarre comments that this form was quite common among most of the early tribes of North and South American Indians.[5] It was also an acceptable pattern among ancient Hebrews and Chinese, and the nineteenth-century Mormons. Polygyny (up to four wives) is still permitted in the Moslem faith, provided the husband can afford it.

Polyandry, which involves one wife and many husbands, is reported to be the practice in parts of Tibet, and also among the Todas of India.[6] Murdock reports finding more than forty different forms of this practice around the world, but cautions against classifying all of them as marriage.[7]

Even where the taking of plural spouses has been condoned, however, the majority of people do not practice it. Polygyny was most commonly practiced when it appeared that a man's first wife could not bear children.[8] Social responsibility has been a feature of marriage in all cultures; for example, a man might have more than one wife only if he could afford it, and men were encouraged to take more than one wife only where and when there was a surplus of females. A reverse policy has prevailed in some cultures with a surplus of males, or where economic conditions place limitations on the possibility of marriage; under such circumstances, men might be encouraged to share a wife.[9] In most cases, however, it was sharing by brothers, not by several unrelated males. Tylor reports finding levirate (the practice of a younger brother automatically assuming the husbandship for an older brother's widow) still the custom in some primitive societies. A more common practice today, however, is sororate, the practice of taking the first wife's younger sisters as wives upon their maturity. This is more often the practice where there is a surplus of females or where only a few men can afford marriage.[10]

MONOGAMY. Modern Western culture subscribes to monogamy, the

Figure 3-1. **Monogamy appears to offer the best opportunity for fulfilling the fundamental purposes of marriage in democratic America.** (Photo copyright © 1958, by Parke, Davis & Company.)

practice of taking one spouse for a lifetime; it is the only form legally permitted today in the United States.

A more facetious interpretation of monogamy is that it is synonymous with monotony. With the ever-changing goals and expectations for life and marriage, the concept of one spouse at a time—but not necessarily for life—has been given more serious thought. In some circles it is called *serial monogamy*. It implies that perhaps the same spouse for an entire lifetime is not the most ideal situation. The traditional Judeo-Christian concept of marriage supports the first interpretation of monogamy; and it is generally believed that one spouse for a lifetime affords the best opportunity for fulfilling the fundamental purposes of marriage for the individual, the family, and the democratic society. Several modifications have been proposed, however, including *trial marriage* (by Elsie Parsons), *companionate marriage* (by Judge Ben B. Lindsey of Denver), and *term marriage* (by E. D. Cope).[11]

A social institution

Marriage, as distinct from mating, is an entirely human relationship. Animals that mate for life do not marry; there is no legal process which recognizes the exclusive right of one animal to another. Should the animal suddenly feel that a different member of the species is more attractive, it is free to act accordingly. Then, too, the pattern of life in one animal family is much the same as that of any other mating unit of the same species; human family patterns, on the other hand, differ according to culture, personality, and geography.[12]

A PROTECTIVE UNION.   Mating is an inborn drive in man, but marriage is a formal institution. One of the major considerations in instituting the custom of marriage was probably the desire to enjoy the sex drive as fully as possible with a minimum of hazards and anxieties. The natural sexual impulse of man needed to be satisfied, and yet some responsible control over it was also necessary. Having the same woman or women at his command would simplify the man's life; having the same man or men possess her would also assure the woman of protection from other men. General promiscuity was abandoned for the comforts of stability. The pattern of control in mating thus evolved into the marriage ritual, and protection became an additional asset of cohabitation.

Today the institution of marriage serves as a special protectorate over welfare of both the individual and society. Individually, it assures females of freedom from unresponsible sexual exploitation. Without marriage, a woman would be without protection while pregnant; she would have no help in the raising of her offspring nor any security against abandonment in her later, less attractive years. For men, marriage provides a degree of freedom from extensive competition and from the loss of his mate to more attractive or stronger males. In addition, marriage provides a man a measure of freedom from doubt and exploitation regarding his obligations as a father.

Most important, however, family living affords a means for the nurture and care of the young, helpless child. Two parents are necessary for the proper rearing of the human infant because it remains helpless for a much longer period than does the offspring of other animals. Experience indicates that the emotional needs for growth and development of the child, as well as its physical needs, are best fulfilled by two parents through the institution of marriage.

EARLY WRITINGS ON MARRIAGE. Early writers appear to have had only man's mating drive in mind when they referred to the major purpose of marriage. For example, Paul and many other early Christian leaders believed that sexual impulses were too much exploited as an element of pleasure. Therefore, they wrote quite vehemently about marriage. Such writers frequently described the marital relationship as a surrender to the pleasure of the flesh. In light of the conditions of that period, this attitude is understandable. Sensual excesses were extolled as royal entertainment; decadence was the ascending rule. Then, too, the followers of Jesus were of the firm conviction that He was to return in their own lifetime. They believed man, to be properly prepared for this event, would be better off devoting his time to spiritual pursuits rather than to the desires of the flesh. Nevertheless, Paul usually chose only married men with children as his bishops, indicating his belief that fathers have a greater sense of responsibility than bachelors. Indeed, celibacy was not compulsory for most of the clergy until the fourth century of the Christian era.

Still later, even after it was commonly accepted that Christ's return was not immediately imminent, the major societal purpose of the marital relationship was to provide an acceptable outlet for man's sexual desires. The writings of Martin Luther and his contemporaries indicate that they considered marriage chiefly as a means of defense against carnal lust.

THE SEXUAL PURPOSE OF MARRIAGE. There can be little less than universal agreement that a satisfactory control and expression of man's sex drive is still one of the important focal points of a modern marriage. This fundamental concept of marriage is still valid, but today marriage offers a socially sanctioned ritual for mating. Modern couples have added their personal expectation of mutual sexual pleasure. Far more important, however, a modern marriage is also judged by the extent to which the couple are able to have the number of children they desire, but only when they desire to have them.

CULTURAL PRESERVATION. In order for a society to survive, it is necessary for its children to be inculcated early with proper behavior standards and for its adults to pass on the accepted cultural patterns to the next generation. Where better to initiate this process than in the family unit, where the newborn are "captive" for many years? Thus, a most important purpose for the institution of marriage is evident: the transmittal of the cultural heritage. This assignment makes civilization, in large measure, dependent upon marriage and family living. Of course, there are societies in which the government wishes to supplant the traditional culture with new concepts. Gradually, however, as such revolutionary governments become more self-assured, the family unit regains importance as the natural instrument for transmitting the general standards of culture to the offspring.

In a democracy, however, the government tries not to eliminate tradition but, rather, to implement those cultural patterns preferred by its citizens and proven to be most beneficial to the general welfare and to the ideals of individual freedom. Thus in the United States, although the family is not the sole instrument for perpetuating the cultural standards, the early stages of passing on these values are best served by parents through marriage. By assigning the initial responsibility for this task to the family unit, society assures itself of survival.

IMPROVEMENT OF THE HERITAGE.   It is of questionable value merely to preserve the past without exchanging, improving, or enlarging upon it. Thus, individual expectations within a free society have tended to emphasize the selection and utilization of cultural factors for the purpose of enriching all aspects of life. This has culminated in the expectation that marriage, particularly, leads to a more comfortable and stimulating way of life. Thus, from the process of preserving the past has emerged the possibility of progress, and marriage for the individual has come to mean much more than mere survival. Marriage is now expected to provide a more meaningful, richer, and fuller life for each individual. As a consequence, the marriage state itself helps to perpetuate the institution. As people experience living in the marital relationship, they become more aware of its potential and orderliness, and thus become the system's staunchest recruiters. Because of the variety of expectations in today's marriages, marital success must be judged not only by the extent to which it helps to preserve the cultural heritage, but also by the extent to which it improves that heritage and uses it for the enrichment of every facet of life.

ECONOMIC GAINS.   Because of the female's greater biological and physiological limitations, most societies have established or encouraged a division of labor through cooperation within marriage. Males were expected to devote a larger portion of their time to the gathering of life's necessities, and the females were expected to use to the greatest advantage those things which the male provided. Thus a division of labor emerged as a societal expectation within marriage. Without marriage, each sex would have had to devote a larger portion of its time to the gathering of materials and to the utilization of those materials for living. This means that each sex would be compelled to devote time to tasks for which the other was better suited. The institution of marriage offered both sexes a wider and more efficient potential than mere economic survival. It is not surprising to discover that one of society's criteria for a successful marriage today is that each partner be able to live more comfortably than if he had remained single. Traditionally, marital success was further judged by the extent to which the husband was a better-than-average provider and the wife a better-than-average homemaker.

Today, so clear-cut a division of labor is neither expected nor practiced. The advantages of greater flexibility, however, also carry the disadvantage of inherent confusion of roles within the marriage. Conflict and uncertainty on role assignments are a great problem in many young marriages today. Previously, the differing roles were largely necessitated by the exigencies of life. The man had to assume the major duties as provider, whether or not he wanted to; likewise, there was no way for a woman to avoid household tasks. The possibilities for profitable female employment outside the home were generally nonexistent, as were the possibilities for domestic employment for males, particularly in the American culture. Men had to devote long and tiresome hours to the business of providing and had little time or inclination to do household tasks. Most men were much more physically exhausted at the end of the day's work than they are today.

Because the ascribed division of labor was a necessity, it was more easily accepted. These conditions, however, are fast disappearing. Modern man no longer needs an all-day housekeeper. Except in a few remote areas, most household services are provided commercially today. In fact, many household needs—such as food, clothing, and laundry—which are now offered to the public under the supervision of trained home economists, often exceed the quality standards that could be expected from the average young wife. By the same token, it is not as essential economically for today's woman to have a husband provide for her. Respectable jobs are much more plentiful for both sexes. Generally, the average female college graduate can expect to earn more as an employee than as housewife sharing her husband's earnings. Thus, the success of modern marriage must be judged not only by the extent to which it facilitates a comfortable existence, but also by the extent to which each mate is personally satisfied with the division of labor within the marriage.

PERMANENT EMOTIONAL AND SOCIAL COMPLETENESS. Single persons, by family-unit standards, are incomplete; it is only through the marital relationship that most people discover a sense of completeness. Benjamin Franklin compared celibacy to a half-pair of scissors, many things being possible to a whole pair that neither could accomplish by itself.[13] To a degree, society expects the institution of marriage to create a union in which the whole is greater than the sum of the parts.

> In marriage alone, is the woman completed
> And fulfilled by the man, and he through her,
> Man and woman together compose the fullness
> Of humanity. . . .[14]

Therefore, successful marriage is often judged by the extent to which the two individuals become one, with the resulting entity being more important than either part. From this union, a new state of being emerges: the marital relationship—an affectional and complementary interaction between mates. A leading authority on marriage describes this as a functioning unit comparable to a lock and key: "Together they can accomplish something that neither acting alone can accomplish. Nor can it be accomplished by two locks or two keys."[15]

Democracy is based on the premise that man is essentially a social creature; therefore, the extent to which the feeling of "belonging" accompanies marriage should be evaluated in determining marital success. For many people, successful marriage is the fulfillment of a compelling need for emotional and social interdependence. It is not surprising to find research supporting this thesis. Hart, for example, reported a method for measuring happiness within human relationships; the device used was called an *euphorimeter*.[16] With it, he concluded that married couples who had never contemplated divorce or separation averaged a score of 213 points; engaged couples, 173 points; single persons who had never been engaged, 75 points; single persons who had experienced broken engagements, 62 points; and married couples on the verge of divorce, —160 points.

In spite of satirical works by American writers, such as James Thurber, who wittily point out the foibles on the battlefield of marriage, most Americans expect more comfort than conflict from their marriages. A democratic society expects marriage to foster a permanent state of security and affection between the mates, much like that protective love that exists between mother and child. Each individual seems to need the assurance of exclusiveness or monopoly in the giving and receiving of love, and nothing can fill this need as completely as the right marriage. Marriage releases a couple for the accomplishment of other important tasks for it eliminates most threats to their greatest need: love and affection. In comparing his sample of divorced and successfully married couples, Locke found the element of love and companionship significantly more often described by the successfully married.[17] Adler believed that all individual problems and conflicts were essentially social in nature.[18] Indeed, because marriage is, in its broadest sense, a social institution, its potential for solving many of the social problems of mankind is great. Although marriage of itself is no solution to universal problems, the means to happier marriages might also be applied to larger areas of human relationships, with correspondingly successful results. If mates do not take the task of understanding one another seriously enough, it is not likely that entire nations of individuals living in disharmony can negotiate a world peace.

GOAL FULFILLMENT. Today's marriages are expected to be more than a reciprocal affectional relationship. More and more people are trying to find or work out a type of marriage which contributes to the development of the full potential of each partner. This implies that the integrity of the individual personality is actually cultivated to greater distinctiveness by the state of being married. Whenever this occurred in marriages of the past, it was considered a wonderful by-product, but few people ever thought they had a right to demand, or even to expect, this from marriage. The success of today's marriages, however, should also be judged by the extent to which individual members feel that the marital relationship has contributed to the achievement of their individual goals, happiness, and development. Thus it is increasingly important that one take stock of himself and his personal goals—be they wealth, power, prestige, or status—before venturing into marriage. Can he reasonably expect to fulfill such goals more easily by marrying, or by remaining single? What about the potential mate's goals? Can each partner, without threatening his own goals, contribute to the fulfillment of the mate's goals?

It is probably safe to say that, given only the expectations of former years, many modern marriages which end in divorce or are considered unsuccessful would, in all likelihood, be permanent and successful. Conversely, many marriages judged successful by yesterday's standards would probably end in divorce or be considered unsuccessful if evaluated against today's criteria of marital success. Research by Popenoe and others at the American Institute of Family Relations, for example, reveals that before filing for divorce today, people wait only about half as long as formerly.[19] Still, the time between serious consideration and actual filing for divorce today is usually long enough to eliminate the possibility that many of today's divorced couples are simply acting in haste without much thought.

Marital happiness

In spite of the higher expectations and more numerous demands of the marital relationship today, research by Burgess and Cottrell, Terman, and Landis indicates that most couples consider their marriages to be relatively successful. The responses varied in these studies from a low of 5 per cent to a high of 22.5 per cent for persons who considered their marriages anything less than average. More than 40 per cent of the middle-class marrieds studied by Burgess and Cottrell rated their unions as "very happy." Terman, in his study, asked couples: (1) whether they would remarry if they had it to do over again; and (2) if so, would they marry the same person. Almost all agreed they would indeed remarry, and 83 per cent of the husbands and 86 per cent of the wives replied that they would marry the same person.[20]

Summary

Historically, marriage evolved into a social institution to meet certain specific needs of society. These needs included the following: (1) the establishment of responsible control over mating in order to safeguard the welfare of society and individuals; (2) the assurance of civilized survival by establishing responsibility for the transmittal of the cultural heritage; (3) the assurance of economic survival through the creation of a system of labor division between the sexes, in which each could contribute and gain more together than alone; and (4) the assurance of a measure of individual emotional and social completeness so necessary to life by encouragement and enforcement of a permanent bond based on affection between mates. To these societal purposes of marriage, individuals have from time to time added their own expectations, many of which have become almost universally accepted.

The process of defining marital success appears to be an endless one. With time, some expectations and purposes grow in relative importance while others lessen. The purposes of marriage also have different priority according to the type of union considered most useful in a particular culture at a given time. No marriage can be expected to meet all the criteria for success all the time, nor can it be expected to arrive at complete perfection. Marital success is therefore a relative matter.

Many forms of marriage are observed throughout the world, but the traditional form of monogamy appears most suitable for the purposes of marriage in a democracy.

Finally, in spite of greater demands and more numerous obstacles to a successful marriage today, most marriages are considered successful by the partners themselves.

Notes

1. W. LaBarre, *The Human Animal* (Chicago: University of Chicago Press, 1954), p. 111.
2. *Ibid.*, pp. 110–13.
3. *Ibid.*
4. J. W. Roberts, "Some Aspects of Mating and Fertility in the West Indies," *Population Studies* (March 1955), 199–227.

5. LaBarre, *op. cit.*

6. *Ibid.*

7. G. P. Murdock, *Social Structures* (New York: The Macmillan Company, 1949), p. 25.

8. Edward Westermarck, *The History of Human Marriage,* Vol. 3 (London: Macmillan and Company, Ltd., 1921), p. 2.

9. C. M. Abraham, "The Custom of Polyandry as Practiced in Travandore," *The Eastern Anthropologist* (India), 12:107–18 (December–February 1958–59).

10. E. B. Tylor, "On a Method of Investigating the Development of Institutions: Applied to Laws of Marriage and Descent," *Journal of Royal Anthropological Institute,* 18:245–72.

11. See, e.g., B. B. Lindsey and W. Evans, *The Companionate Marriage* (Garden City, N.Y.: Garden City Publishing Company, 1929).

12. See, e.g., Ruth Anshen (ed.), *The Family: Its Functions and Destiny* (New York: Harper & Row, Publishers, 1959).

13. A. S. Rosenbach, "The All-Embracing Dr. Franklin," quoted in Bernard Stern, *The Family Past and Present* (New York: Appleton-Century-Crofts, Inc., 1930), p. 208.

14. Theodor Gottlieb Von Hippel, *Über Die Ehe* (Leipzig: F. M. Brock, 1872).

15. Henry A. Bowman, *Marriage for Moderns* (New York: McGraw-Hill Book Company, Inc., 1954), p. 20.

16. Hornell Hart, *Chart for Happiness* (New York: The Macmillan Company, 1940), p. 35.

17. Harvey Locke, *Predicting Adjustment in Marriage* (New York: Holt, Rinehart & Winston, Inc., 1951), p. 98.

18. Alfred Adler, *Understanding Human Nature* (New York: Greenberg Publishers, 1927).

19. American Institute of Family Relations study, *Family Life Education,* 6:12.

20. E. W. Burgess and Leonard S. Cottrell, *Predicting Success or Failure in Marriage* (Englewood Cliffs, N.J.: Prentice-Hall, Inc., 1939), p. 32; Lewis M. Terman, *Psychological Factors in Marital Happiness* (New York: McGraw-Hill Book Company, Inc., 1938), p. 78; and Judson T. and Mary G. Landis, *Building a Successful Marriage,* 4th ed. (Englewood Cliffs, N.J.: Prentice-Hall, Inc., 1963), Chap. 1.

Questions for further thought

1. What motivations for marriage are consistent with the American concept of democracy?
2. Is it possible to achieve extreme happiness in life without marriage? Explain.
3. If both mates think they are successful in their marriage, even if it does not meet other people's standards, is it successful or not?
4. What is an (a) average successful marriage? (b) above-average successful marriage? (c) extremely successful marriage?
5. Is a successful marriage always a happy one? Is the reverse true?
6. To what extent is an ideal marriage a value judgment?
7. Does a philosophy of rugged individualism support or interfere with the possibilities of success in modern marriage?
8. In how many phases of married living must a couple be relatively successful in order to consider their marriage a success?
9. Would today's individuals be happier in marriage if they did not expect so much from it?

Recommended films

Marriage Today (McGraw-Hill Book Company, Inc.).
Family, An Approach to Peace (McGraw-Hill Book Company, Inc.).

Suggested supplemental readings

BOOKS

Anshen, Ruth N. (ed.). *The Family: Its Function and Destiny,* rev. ed. New
    York: Harper & Row, Publishers, 1959.
Briffault, Robert, and Bronislaw Malinowski. *Marriage: Past and Present.* Boston:
    Porter-Sargent, 1956.
Calhoun, Arther W. *A Social History of the American Family.* New York: Barnes
    & Noble, Inc., 1960. 3 vols.
Ditzion, Sidney. *Marriage, Morals, and Sex in America.* New York: Bookman
    Associates, 1953.
Ellis, Albert, and Robert A. Harper. *Creative Marriage.* New York: Lyle Stuart,
    1961.
Montaigne, L. *The Origins and Nature of Marriage.* New York: Citadel Press,
    1953.
Nibley, Hugh B. *Sounding Brass: An Exposé of the Book "The 27th Wife."* Salt
    Lake City, Utah: Bookcraft, 1963.
Nimkoff, Meyer F. (ed.). *Comparative Family Systems.* Boston: Houghton Mifflin
    Company, 1965.
Wallace, Irving. *The Twenty-Seventh Wife.* New York: Simon and Schuster,
    Inc., 1961.
Weingarten, Murray. *Life in a Kibbutz.* New York: Reconstruction Press, 1955.
Westermarck, Edward. *The History of Human Marriage,* 5th ed. London: Mac-
    millan & Co., Ltd., 1921. 3 vols.
Young, Kimball. *Isn't One Wife Enough?* New York: Holt, Rinehart & Winston,
    Inc., 1954.

ARTICLES

Ellis, Albert. "A Plea for Polygamy," *Eros,* 1:22–23.
Mead, Margaret. "The Contemporary American Family as an Anthropologist
    Sees It." *American Journal of Sociology,* 53:453–59.

Insuring a successful marriage through courtship

chapter 4

The practice of dating in the twentieth-century United States is a natural result of diminishing parental control of mate selection. With this "new freedom" from parental supervision, dating is at first considered by many young people to be merely a means of gaining personal popularity. Unfortunately, parents themselves are often unaware of the importance of the proper sequence of the stages of dating. They still think of it, perhaps, as a modern variation of the "calling" that Grandfather did, but Grandfather's courting was usually under the strict supervision of watchful parents and followed a pattern the elders themselves had observed in their courtship. The dating practices in the United States today, however, have broken sharply with tradition and are duplicated nowhere else in the world; for here dating has evolved into a substitute process for parental control of the youth's preparation and final selection of a marriage partner.[1]

Dating defined

It is not easy to arrive at a specific operational definition that can accurately describe dating in its entirety. Most definitions seem to agree on the fact that dating is a paired heterosexual association, a relationship between two members of the opposite sex; however, it is questionable that every heterosexual activity can be accurately called a "date." The focus of interest on a date is interpersonal. The relationship between the two individuals involved becomes a matter of great interest to them. It involves planned *companionship* within activities or entertainment of *joint* interest for the declared purpose of amusement. A date has a specific beginning and end. Ostensibly, it is free from any connection with marriage to the particular person dated. Actually, however, it is the first real step in a sequence of stages leading to an acquaintance with the opposite sex that may progress to a degree of readiness for marriage. Dating is therefore an intrinsic part of courtship. It is preparation for marriage—perhaps not to the particular person dated at the moment, but to someone, sometime, somewhere.

The advantages of dating

The outcomes of dating are as varied as its activities. In the beginning, dating may be only for fun or amusement, but it produces many secondary benefits of much greater value to total courtship than mere entertainment. It is most important that young people be made aware of the possibilities of developing these secondary by-products of dating, which include increased poise, prestige, self-understanding, ability to communicate, a broader outlook on life, a greater appreciation of the opposite sex, and deeper acquaintance for mate selection.

POISE. People actually grow toward maturity through dating. With the wide variety of activities available in campus dating, enjoyment and meaning is added to life. This, in turn, produces a more assured and socially balanced person. Research indicates that college students who seldom or never date are predominantly retiring and often show a slight tendency to be emotionally maladjusted.[2] A question arises, however, whether students do not date because they are socially or emotionally maladjusted, or whether they are maladjusted because they do not date. The author's opinion is that either situation may be operative, with the latter situation more prevalent than many have ever realized.

PEER PRESTIGE. The general peer group is more likely to accept a person who is dating; this, in turn, gives the individual new confidence in himself. When a person is doing the same things as the majority of the peer group, he feels more "normal." Dating is now one of the chief criteria used in young people's circles to judge the extent of peer acceptance.[3]

SELF-UNDERSTANDING. To understand himself, it is necessary for the individual to discover his real interests, likes and dislikes, tastes, needs, and characteristics as they relate to interaction with others. Dating offers a golden opportunity to do this in a most effective manner. By observing the reactions of others to his own behavior, the individual learns his real meaning to others; in their response he is better able to see himself as others conceive him to be. This increased self-understanding will lead to maximum improvement in all his relationships. In fact, certain aspects of this understanding are possible only through dating.

EASIER COMMUNICATION. People have been known to argue over and around a given issue for hours, only to discover in the end that they were in agreement from the beginning, that their major difference was not in ideas but in interpretations of meanings. Certain words and phrases have come to have specific meanings within one subculture and yet may have different meanings within another group. Almost every profession has its own jargon; so do young adults. Each sex also has a vocabulary that differs in interpretation as well as in specific words and phrases from the usual vocabulary of the opposite sex. Dating, therefore, can be considered as a "practice field" for communication and serves to reduce semantic misunderstandings within social situations and later within marriage itself.

A BROADER VIEWPOINT. Dating offers a genuine opportunity for learning to meet and to understand others, lessening the tendency to dislike strangers at first sight. Hostility toward others is often the result of immature attitudes. Although a person need not approve of everyone or of all standards, he should have an open mind when confronting new people and new situations; he should not live in a world that is too narrow. Concepts and ideals can be broadened without sacrificing values and standards, and dating is an excellent activity for this purpose. Furthermore, for partners to get along in even the best of marriages, considerable broadmindedness is necessary. Thus dating experience helps the individual grow in his ability to make decisions, or to stand by those previously made, when faced with possible conflict.

APPRECIATION FOR THE OPPOSITE SEX. If an individual has a few unpleasant experiences with the first few persons dated, he may feel that all members of that sex behave that way. However, upon further dating he comes to recognize that men and women often differ in their points of view. Through dating, appreciation of these differences grows, and it becomes easier to judge members of the opposite sex more sensibly. Thus dating offers the individual an opportunity to discover compatibility. Even a "bad" date helps the individual to learn better how to deal with frustrating situations.

ACQUAINTANCE FOR MATE SELECTION. Each person responds better to certain types of individuals than to others, and it is wise for him to choose a mate with whom he responds favorably. The individual, however, cannot possibly know whether certain responses are best for him until he has had the opportunity to compare a number of persons. This is a fundamental part of the dating process. Dating gives each person an opportunity to become acquainted with an unlimited variety of persons and to test his responses with them. Sometimes married people remark about the waste of time and money they experienced in dates prior to those with the person finally selected for marriage. Actually, it is money and time well spent, helping to narrow the field and thus promoting wiser mate selection. One research study found that college students living in high-prestige residence groups tended to confine their dates to others living in similar groups.[4] Such actions may be somewhat detrimental to providing proper acquaintance for mate selection.

Stages in dating

There are basically four distinct stages of dating; they are (1) casual dating, (2) periodic dating, (3) steadily dating, and (4) steady dating. The usual contemporary pattern is the sequence of all four stages before marriage. It may not be conducive to marital success, however, to remain too long (proportionately) in any one stage. The four types of dating patterns need not necessarily require equal attention or time.

CASUAL DATING.   The first stage should constitute the greater portion of all dating time. Casual dating is playing the field. It is dating whomever is available, looks interesting to know, and is willing. There need be no commitment or involvement beyond the single date.

Sometimes young people resist the next stage, periodic dating, by remaining in the casual stage. This is usually because of a fear that a more serious commitment might lead too soon to marriage, or it may be because some other goal or objective appears more important. To remain in the casual-dating stage seems to be a good defense of the goal. Motives should be re-examined very carefully under such circumstances, however, to make certain they are legitimate. A young man studying for the profession of medicine would be justified in not progressing beyond the casual-dating stage if he had a long time to go before finishing his academic work. If, however, a young man finds himself rejecting involvement after a prolonged period of casually playing the field, and he has no other goals or ambitions to interfere and he has ample opportunity for periodic dating with attractive members of the opposite sex, then he should probably seek professional help of some sort. Through counseling, his inner fears of the involvement process may be revealed and resolved.

PERIODIC DATING.   When two people have no commitment beyond each date, and have occasional dates with others but date each other at fairly regular intervals, the relationship has advanced to the second stage: periodic dating. This may be purely accidental, or it may be the narrowing of the field for one or both. As each experiences the pleasure of interacting with someone who responds to him in a more pleasing manner than others, it is only natural that he periodically seek the companionship of that person.

STEADILY DATING.   Closely resembling but not quite meeting the qualifications of going steady (the fourth stage), steadily dating occurs when (1) one of the two people dates no one else, or (2) when, without discussion or agreement to date exclusively, the two people nevertheless remain available only to each other. In the first situation, the fellow may be dating only one girl because of insufficient funds; he prefers one girl, so when he does date he confines his dating to her. In the second situation, the fellow is perhaps away at college and the girl remains at home or is still in high school. They may date only each other when both are home, but are free to date others when apart. Under these circumstances, even if neither dates any other person, it is still not the steady-dating stage. Going steady requires a mutual agreement; steadily dating does not.

Evidence suggests that steadily dating is more likely to be the pattern of modern college dating. Although many college students engage in steady dating when in high school, they seem to revert to the casual stage upon arrival at campus. Often, while in college they never again have any formal agreement of exclusiveness in dating prior to engagement. An extensive survey covering several years on one campus indicated that casual dating was the dominant pattern. Smith found that, at any given time, only 34 per cent of the students were going steady, and about one third of those had no definite dating agreement.[5]

STEADY DATING. Just as it would be hazardous to try to run before learning to sit, crawl, stand, and walk, so it would be foolhardy for anyone to start steady dating before mastering the earlier stages. To skip the casual phases is to miss the experiences that lead to the mature judgment so necessary for a happy marriage.

The author's records of college seniors enrolled in his courses on marriage and family indicate that only about 20 per cent had gone steady during the first two years on the campus. The overwhelming majority of that college group regarded such behavior by young students as "kid stuff." Apparently college students prefer to regard steady dating as a very serious fourth stage in the preparation for marriage, rather than as a form of heavy dating with many successive partners.

In contrast, the author's files on more than 1000 high school seniors in Kansas and Florida disclose that more than 80 per cent had engaged in steady dating. Many of these students indicated that they had gone steady with at least three individuals.

Herman found that steady dating was more likely in the last two years in high school than at any other time.[6] A more recent study of sixteen- to seventeen-year-olds revealed that about 75 per cent of the boys and about 50 per cent of the girls had already experienced going steady.[7]

Today's high school pattern of going steady is often (at least at first) only a variation of dating rather than a serious relationship leading to marriage. For example, when they first begin to date, high school students go steady with the same person, but only for short periods.[8] Instead of dating a dozen different persons at the same time, today's high school student frequently dates each one exclusively, in turn. A survey of the opinions of high school students shows that more than 50 per cent favor going steady as a dating pattern.[9]

Disadvantages of early steady dating

GETTING TOO INVOLVED. Young daters are not ready for the intimacies that naturally accompany the advanced stage of going steady. They are quite likely to be bored without realizing it, and so may often start seeking thrills and diversion from the physical side of the relationship. It is normal to wish to express affection; when two young people are together too much, this desire may take the form of physical familiarities which, in the American culture, are considered marital privileges only. Often young steady-daters discover too late that they have gone too far in their exchange of familiarities. When not counterbalanced with the maturity that comes from experiencing a long casual-dating period, the sex drive may lead to premature experimentation and permanent involvement.[10]

NARROWS THE CHOICE TOO SOON. Because a person marries only someone whom he has dated, going steady too soon will limit his selection considerably. He cannot tell how much he might have liked other types if he has not given himself a chance to meet them. Steady dating has definite mate-selection limitations when begun too early.[11] Thus, early steady dating sometimes leads to an unhappy marriage. Marriage might happen not only before one is ready for it, but also before one has had the opportunity to look around and to find out what is really best for him. Research shows that early and unhappy marriage is often related to going steady too soon.[12]

It is not a matter of never going steady; it is simply a problem of timing. Unfortunately, in modern American culture it is easy to start going steady too soon. All the stages of dating are necessary to the involvement, engagement, and marriage-adjustment processes. The stages, however, should be experienced in proper sequence and for long enough intervals for dating to be a screening process in successful mate selection.

TRENDS IN DATING. Research indicates that today dating begins at an earlier age and occurs more frequently and with more different people than formerly. Gilbert reported that in the United States in 1953 the average age at first date for boys was fourteen and for girls thirteen and a half, which was about one year younger on the average than in 1943.[13] Lowrie's study identified several factors that apparently influence the age that dating begins. These included:

1. [In cases of] higher parental education, girls especially start dating earlier.
2. [In cases where] parents [are] not completely assimilated into American culture, girls especially start dating later.
3. In small families, girls especially start dating earlier.
4. In higher economic and social status families, dating starts earlier.
5. Dating begins at different ages in different regions. Dating begins earliest in the South.[14]

A study in Michigan found that both sexes begin dating today at about age fourteen. The girls in the study, however, thought that they should begin dating earlier than the boys. Furthermore, it was found that the popularity of steady dating as a first pattern was beginning to fade away.[15]

Lowrie found a correlation in Ohio between earlier dating and dating frequency.[16] His more recent study, which included several cities in different regions, reaffirms these findings.[17] Koller's study, confined to Ohio (the site of Lowrie's first study), indicates that college students date more today than in former years. He found that college women who subsequently married had averaged three dates a week; their mothers, two dates a week; and their grandmothers, only one date a week.[18] He also found that today's wives, as well as their mothers, did not become acquainted with the men they eventually married until the average age of nineteen, so they probably dated many more different individuals before marriage than had the previous generations. It is reported that fraternity men date more than independents and that about three times more independent men do not date at all.[19] Dating frequency of one particular sex, however, may be curtailed or enhanced by the sex ratio on campus. For example, Ehrmann reported that men students outnumber women students at the University of Florida by a ratio of eight to one. He believes this cuts down on the frequency of dating for men students on that campus, and probably increases the frequency for women students.[20]

Usually, couples can stay out later at night than formerly, although on most campuses girls still must observe dormitory closing hours.[21] With more women attending college, the topics of discussion on dates have greatly increased.[22] Thus, coeducation also narrows the vocabulary difference between the sexes and increases mutual understandings. The proximity of the sexes on campus, however, has greatly increased the problems of rules, conduct, personal morals, and promiscuity in college.

Poor dating habits

Poor habits of conduct in any of the dating stages often give rise to later problems. Because parents no longer select mates for their offspring, dating has become a serious part of mate selection, and it is quite possible for a person to fail in marriage because he first failed in dating.

SKIPPING THE STAGES. One of the biggest failures in dating is the tendency to rush through or to skip the early stages of the dating sequence and to settle down to one person too soon. This often causes dissatisfaction within marriage and may lead to extramarital affairs. Modern American youth is given great freedom in choosing a mate. This is in keeping with democracy, but with this privilege goes the responsibility of making as sound a selection as possible.

ROMANTIC BLINDNESS. Some people date as though they were blindfolded. They have preconceived notions of what their ideal spouse should be like, and rather than dating casually until they meet someone who comes closest to their ideal, they start going steady with almost anyone. But they deny that person real identity by refusing to acknowledge his true character. The "blinded" person fictionalizes the partner and often will not take heed even when the partner attempts to dispel the delusion. The romantic fever is sustained by unrealistic dreams, but later the individual is awakened by the shock of complete disillusionment. The awakening to reality may occur only after the wedding has taken place. Many times this sad sequence of events has been related to the author by an unhappy married person. When asked whether there were clues to the spouse's true nature at any time during the courtship, the client usually admits that there were many. He was so strongly attracted by one attribute of the partner, however, that he preferred to ignore the truth about the rest. He married a person who could not satisfy his basic needs—not because of misrepresentation, but because of his stubborn indifference to reality.

PLAYING A FALSE ROLE.   Another very poor dating practice is to play a role rather than being natural while with the other person. For the dating process to be an effective means of mate selection, it should result in loving someone for what he really is and not for what he appears to be. The individual who, for the sake of courtship, makes himself more attractive on the outside without a corresponding change inside will be faced with serious consequences after marriage. He can go on with a perpetual pretense and possibly incur a disastrous personality maladjustment, or he can revert to his natural behavior pattern, which may disillusion the partner and lead to marital conflict. People should fall in love with each other for what they really are, not for pretended values. If by being one's true self an individual is unable to secure dates, it would still be wiser to avoid superficial change and perhaps even not to marry than to assume the serious responsibilities of such a relationship on the basis of a false characterization.

Some people play a dangerous game while dating: they try to find out what characteristics their dates like and then assume the role while with that particular partner. When one or both are pretending to be something they are not, both are playing a losing game. It is impossible to discover the mate who would respond best while carrying on such a defensive masquerade.

Many marriage quarrels result from one mate's attempt to force the other to behave according to the false role. A complaint that marriage counselors frequently hear is that the spouse has "changed a lot" since marriage. The truth usually is that both mates are revealing their real characteristics for the first time. For later marital success, not only must one behave naturally on dates, but he must be alert to the true character of those whom he dates.

To counteract the tendency of youths to conceal their true nature in order to become more attractive as dating partners, an engagement period is of particular value in today's society.

The beginning of engagement

When two people become seriously involved in courtship, they usually make clear to each other their intention to marry. Later on, after a period of "private" testing, they usually make this agreement public. This public announcement, however, does not necessarily mark the beginning of the engagement period in today's society. Many engagements actually begin with the private understanding. Today's society does not demand, require, or even expect a formal announcement.[23] Any couple is free not to announce their engagement if they so choose. The girl, however, usually enjoys the status of a formal fiancee. Women, as a group, take more interest in such things, and in the American culture marriage constitutes a greater change in status for women than for men.

PUBLIC REACTION. A valuable part of experience gained from the formal engagement is the reaction of friends to the announcement of the approaching wedding. When friends react as though the couple were already a "pair," this has a strengthening effect on the two partners. It helps the couple to feel the social effects of their relationship, which will have an important bearing on their own reactions to the future marriage state. Thus it is probably wise for every couple, no matter how long their informal engagement, to experience a formal engagement period also.

A WORKING AGREEMENT. The engagement is an agreement, between two persons of the opposite sex who profess great affection for one another, of their desire and intent to marry. It is the stage in their relationship at which the idea of their marriage is to be explored both as a working hypothesis and as a future life pattern. It is the time to determine whether their love is strong enough for marriage.

Most engaged couples have basic weaknesses in their relationship that could significantly affect the success of their marriage. Although somewhat aware of these weaknesses, they are more likely to be aware of their strong similarities. Sometimes the glamor of dating accentuates the positive strengths to the point of completely obscuring the weaknesses. There are always such weaknesses, and it is during the engagement period that they should be critically examined. If the couple discover their major weaknesses early and still look forward to spending their lives together, then all the compelling forces that first attracted them to each other will come surging back with new meaning. When the man proposes marriage, he is saying, in effect:

> We have been going together for quite a while, and we have had a great deal of fun. We both feel that we like each other real well as dating part-

ners, but what would it be like to be married to each other? Let us become engaged and test that possibility.

Benjamin Franklin never wrote a book on marital success, but many of his expressions made reference to marriage. In *Poor Richard*, he advised: "Keep the eyes wide open before marriage and half-shut afterward." It is still good advice.

COMPANIONSHIP TESTING.   The engagement period is a time for testing companionability as well as attitudes and values. It is sometimes easier to love one's spouse than to like him, and it is particularly necessary for the success of a marriage with democratic ideals first to ascertain the degree of understanding possible between the couple as persons as well as lovers. Is there a high degree of confidence and trust? Is there a growing willingness to share in disappointments as well as in successes? Is there a feeling of mutual responsibility for the success of the marriage? Is each partner beginning to accept the other for what he really is rather than for what each hoped he would be? A spouse should be a friend as well as a lover, for marriage in America involves the whole person, not merely his gender.

Engagement functions

There are many duties in the engagement stage that appear to be specifically masculine, feminine, or couple-oriented. This is not to say that the functions never overlap, but only that their major emphasis may be identified more readily along the lines of sex.

THE WOMAN'S ROLE.   Although dating mores have broken with tradition, the girl's pattern before engagement is not much different from the passive pattern in the past. She has usually waited to be asked out on dates. The man generally decides where they will go, and with whom. She has had to wait for a marriage proposal and could not mention her desire until the man first declared his love. After the girl is engaged, however, the situation almost reverses. The engagement period provides her with the first real opportunity to experience a woman's "new freedom." How will she react to it? Will she use her new power to benefit the total relationship, or to demand selfish favors? The pattern she establishes during engagement may well be perpetuated after marriage, so it is important for both partners to observe her responses objectively.

HER RESPONSIBILITY.   As a direct result of the new freedom of choice in mate selection, the girl now must assume a duty which was previously the responsibility of her parents. Today, it is the bride-to-be, not her parents, who determine the integrity of her future mate, and the intensity with which he intends to carry out his ambitions. She may have been well informed earlier concerning his background, his prospects, and his plans for the future, but during the engagement she must doublecheck all the facts.

FINANCES: A MUTUAL RESPONSIBILITY. The laws of most states hold the husband legally responsible for the finances of the marriage. Thus the engagement period is a time to consider seriously such things as income, expenditures, insurance, retirement, and even debts. It is also a period to test the business sense of the prospective bride. This refers not only to her insight into the groom's job, but also her sense of values regarding the spending of money. Does her judgment on what should receive top priority in budgeting concur with his? If not, how can these differences be reconciled?

THE MAN'S ROLE. Engagement offers the man the opportunity to make important decisions. Perhaps for the first time in his life his decisions will permanently involve another individual. Does he like exercising this power, or does the responsibility of implicating others affect his decision-making? For example, a man about to graduate from college has several tempting job opportunities; however, the most attractive offer from the standpoint of future advancement requires that the young couple establish a residence far from home. His future bride has always been very close to her parents, and there is a lesser position available right in her home community. No one can make this decision for him; although it should be fully discussed with his fiancee, the decision is still the man's to make.

PREPARATION FOR MARITAL LOVE. Love play does not cease during engagement, but usually increases, serving as a transition into married sexual love. During the engagement the man should begin to note the sexual responsiveness of his future wife. His understanding of her reactions can make their transition to marriage a much easier process. Normal love play should continue as before, only it should become much more meaningful during engagement. Whether from cultural conditioning, or lack of experience or vocabulary, women are less likely than men to verbalize their sexual desires. The male must therefore first instill within the woman a sense of complete trust and confidence in both his actions and his words. This requires not only keen observation, but also much reassuring and patience. Only in such a manner can he encourage his wife to become an active sexual participant after marriage.

COUPLE-CENTERED FUNCTIONS. There are some functions of the engagement period which are "couple-centered" and must be considered only in this light. These include discussions on plans as to where and how to live. Will either partner seek additional education? Can the bride work, keep house, and go to school at the same time? If she works outside the home, can she expect help from her husband or a hired person at home? How much money will there be? How does each like the other's parents? How are the parents responding to the possibility of an approaching marriage? Are there likely to be in-law problems? How intense are the feelings of each mate concerning religion? What are their attitudes about children? What kind of a wedding will they have? Where will they go for the honeymoon?

The engagement provides the first opportunity to discuss such serious problems. During the dating stages, the possibility of competition from others in providing pleasanter amusement for the partner made it necessary to relegate weighty personal discussions to the background. Now, free of fears of a rival's luring the partner to lighter pleasures, both can engage in debating their respective viewpoints. If they disagree seriously, can it be worked out? Can they remain divided in some areas? The engagement is a pilot test for marriage, but the couple must not become more critical than they would be ordinarily.

THE TESTS.   Not to be overlooked during the engagement evaluation

Figure 4-1.   What is each like without the emotional and physical glamor of dating? (Courtesy of the Warner-Lambert Pharmaceutical Company.)

is physical appearance. What is the girl like without the glamor, emotional and physical, of dating? What is she like without makeup? What is he like without a shave? Without the compelling drive of competition to stimulate his charm, what is he like? What is she like when she is tired? What is he like after a disappointment? Across the breakfast table, will she make him want to hurry home after work? After a hard irritating day, will he have the energy for romance or the patience for tenderness? During the engagement each should relax and allow the other to feel and learn his private moods.

When the couple disagree, do they usually work out the problem to the mutual satisfaction of both, or do they frequently quarrel? Quarrels indicate that basic needs are not being met. If such needs cannot be met outside the stresses of marriage, it is a safe bet that they will never be satisfied. How many times has the couple faced situations where it was necessary either to cooperate or go down to defeat? Which did they do?

How many times has the relationship been broken in the past? Or to be more honest, how many times has either partner *thought* of breaking it off? Even the secret desire to dissolve the relationship may indicate that misgivings may arise later in the marriage. If doubts persist or certain differences seem to increase, they should be worked out before the wedding—or the engagement should be broken. How many changes would each like to make in the other? Can each honestly say that he or she is a better person because of the relationship? If not, then this is not the right partner for marriage.

How does each feel about the other's friends and family? Does either partner always feel like an outsider in the company of the other's friends? How often have the couple visited in each other's home? Is there still a strained formality after several visits and overtures of friendliness from the future in-laws? There should be an easy air about the visits, with the prospective in-laws going about their regular duties and including the new member gradually in their family pattern.

How does each usually face a crisis when the other is present? Has either ever heard from others evidence contrary to this behavior pattern? How effective is his way of handling life problems? Do her reactions help or hinder? Do both naturally enjoy being together with nothing definite planned or done? If every moment must be filled with some action, marriage for the two should be postponed.

Have the two reached a simple and direct approach to discussing their sexual standards, expectations, apprehensions, and ideals? Does each feel relaxed and "pleasurable" when engaged in physical love play, or is there still a certain amount of tension? Has the couple reached an understanding on the extent of physical love before marriage, and is that limit respected by both?

How long have the couple really known each other as adults? Mar-

Figure 4-2. How effective
is his way of handling life
problems? Do her reactions
help or hinder? (Courtesy
of the B. F. Goodrich Company.)

riage is an adult status and as a standard yardstick, nothing that trans-
pired before the end of high school qualifies for consideration as adult
acquaintance.

Length of engagement

How long should an engagement be? It depends upon so many variables
that one can speak only in broad generalities or conclude by qualifying
his remarks with such phrases as *provided this* or *provided that*. The fact
that the couple are not sure about when to marry would certainly seem
to indicate basic doubts. When a couple anxiously ask about the "proper"
length of an engagement, theirs has probably not yet been long enough.
When the engagement has served all its functions adequately, the couple
will not need to inquire about its "proper" length.

TOTAL ACQUAINTANCE. If many functions of an engagement had already been fulfilled in the going-steady stage, an extended engagement
would be unnecessary. In today's society it is even possible that much of
the premarital testing might be accomplished without an engagement;

however, all functions should be re-evaluated during the actual engagement, for the situation is not the same as before. Years ago, many of the functions of engagement were performed for the couple by society and parents, but today most of the responsibility rests entirely with the couple.

If a couple knew each other rather well before the engagement period, their engagement can be relatively short. The value of the engagement, however, depends more on the quality and intensity of acquaintance than upon its actual length. It is quite possible for two individuals to date for years and never really know each other very well.

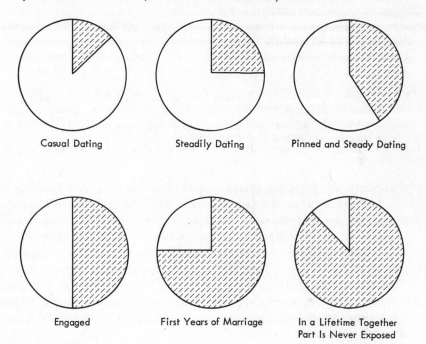

| Casual Dating | Steadily Dating | Pinned and Steady Dating |

| Engaged | First Years of Marriage | In a Lifetime Together Part Is Never Exposed |

Figure 4-3. Progressive areas of self-exposure at different stages of the relationship.

Studies of divorce cases seem to substantiate the irrelevancy of length of acquaintance or engagement if that period is not used productively by the couple. What the couple do with the time is more pertinent to marital success than mere prolongation of the engagement. The new freedom in mate selection places the responsibility for the marriage choice on the couple. If there is any fakery going on, time spent seriously together will expose it. People do not usually keep up a pretense forever; sooner or later their natural impulses will take over, revealing themselves with added force after suppression. Because of the varying backgrounds of today's citizens, each couple must earnestly try to reveal their true needs and likes before marriage.

RESEARCH FINDINGS. Research by Terman, by Burgess and Cottrell, and by a host of others, indicates that married couples with the highest adjustment ratings were engaged for two or more years.[24] These reports, however, are based on averages. Unhappy marriages have occurred where engagements were longer than two years, so it is clear enough that the length of the engagement period is important only insofar as it is impossible to pretest marriage in a short time.

Table 4–1. **Length of engagement and marital adjustment score**

Duration in months	Per cent poor	Per cent fair	Per cent good
Under 3	50	24.3	25.7
3 to 8	33	26.8	40.2
9 to 23	18	35.9	46.1
24 and over	11	26.4	62.6

Source: E. W. Burgess and Leonard S. Cottrell, *Predicting Success Or Failure In Marriage* (Englewood Cliffs, N.J.: Prentice-Hall, Inc., 1939), p. 407. Copyright © 1939, by Prentice-Hall, Inc., Englewood Cliffs, New Jersey. Reprinted by permission of publisher and authors.

Obviously, the most important consideration is how well the couple get to know each other. An acquaintance should be long enough to pass through the best and the worst displays of temperament. Falling out of love may take as much, if not more, time than falling in love. The couple should take enough time before marriage to make sure love is not fading. There may be affection or passion, but they must give themselves a chance to determine whether their love is truly strong enough for marriage. The tasks of testing, discussing, learning, quarreling, and loving—which are inherent in most successful marriages—require time to be performed and tested adequately.

THE PROLONGED ENGAGEMENT. It is unlikely that a couple can thoroughly perform all the functions of an engagement in less than six months; however, most couples can—if they try—fulfill the functions of an engagement within a year to a year and a half. This figure is, of course, an arbitrary one, offered only as an opinion, and does not apply in every case. An engagement, however, is helpful in every case. Studies by Popenoe indicate that it is more important to have even a short engagement than none at all.[25] Other research indicates that more than 90 per cent of all marriages were preceded by engagements, although of shorter duration than in former years.[26]

It is useless to continue an engagement that has little or no possibility of leading to a successful marriage. If, after a period of thorough testing, there appears to be an increasing amount of tension, anxiety, and frustration, the engagement is probably too long. In such cases there is often a growing feeling of discouragement and general indifference. Sometimes couples who have been going together too long begin to lose interest in ever being married, and begin to accept the engagement situation as "better" than marriage. None of this, however, should be construed as encouraging hasty or early marriage. Generally, however, engagement is long enough when reasonable assurance for a successful marriage has developed or, conversely, when it is evident that the relationship is likely to fail.

Confiding in the partner

There should be no feeling of compulsion to confess everything to the partner during the engagement period. It is doubtful that such an attitude will contribute anything but frustration to the already burdensome problems of every engaged person. Minute details concerning the past are probably better left unaccounted for or talked over with a clergyman or marriage counselor. Frank discussions are commendable, but nothing is to be gained by telling every detail of the past. Perhaps, however, it is more honest to reveal too much than too little.

BE HONEST. Honesty with the partner is absolutely essential before the marriage takes place. Any circumstances or conditions which might, whether hidden or revealed, affect the welfare of either the partner or the marriage should be explained before marriage. There must be no fraud to threaten the validity of the marriage.

Some things that should be told because they are bound to affect the marriage relationship, and would probably be reavealed with time anyway, include (1) a previous marriage and the circumstances under which it terminated; (2) congenital defects and the probabilities of their being inherited by the offspring; (3) general state of health, especially as it relates to bearing or siring children; (4) a history of serious infections or diseases such as tuberculosis or heart murmur; (5) citizenship record if it refers to arrests or imprisonment; (6) relatives who have been criminal, immoral, or insane; and (7) any financial, emotional, or moral debts or obligations.

PREVIOUS SEXUAL EXPERIENCE. Revealing previous sexual experience does not appear to have too much relation to the success of the marriage. If it serves no purpose to tell about it, why tell? In some cases it is perfectly all right; in others, the shock of such frankness might serve only to disillusion the partner, with a resultant loss of respect. Guilt feelings should not be unloaded gratuitously on a prospective mate. Such problems should be taken to professionals trained for that purpose.

Dating others while engaged

Apart from a situation in which the engaged couple is experiencing a prolonged and unavoidable separation, the problem of dating others should never arise. Engagement means monopoly; there is no alternative —otherwise there would be no engagement. If the couple know they must be separated, it would seem of little value for them to become engaged at that time.

Suppose a couple are engaged and separated, what then? This may occur if the man goes to college and the woman stays home, or if each attends a different college some distance apart, or if the man has already graduated and is employed some distance away, or if he is in the armed service. These are but a few of the possibilities of forced separation during an engagement. Because most social activities are paired affairs the alternatives are either to stay at home or to go out with someone else.

TEST OF DEVOTION. The problem of dating while separated from the partner would not occur if the couple were already married. Because they are engaged, the question should be considered in the same terms as though they were married. Separation might be used as a test of the couple's fidelity. If their devotion cannot withstand the test of separation, how can they meet the much bigger problems of marriage? It is true, however, that the restriction of social activities to members of the same sex can be terribly dull even for the most devoted of persons. This limitation is the expectation within today's society, so if it puts too much of a strain on an individual, there probably should be no engagement.

A few colleges have established extracurricular activities for engaged persons. Such groups sponsor forums and invite qualified leaders to discuss particular aspects of marriage. This may not be the most exciting social event on the campus, but at least it is an effort in the right direction.

In the absence of such programs, some individuals might simply find the sudden loneliness unbearable. It might be wiser for such persons to date occasionally. If there is fear of losing interest in the engaged partner by dating another, it is probably safe to say that the interest is already waning, and it might be better to discover it now. Dating others may help such people to see the weaknesses that are already there; seldom does it create them. This problem can be avoided by refusing to become engaged until the couple can be together. Only then can the functions of engagement be fulfilled.

LETTER-WRITING. The best thing the separated engaged couple can do is to correspond as frequently as possible. Their letters should include details of their day-to-day experiences and how they feel about them. This may give each a clue to any serious turn in the personality development of the other. Letters containing recent photographs keep each in constant awareness of the physical appearance of the other.

It is even possible that some couples may make greater headway in discussing certain problems by letter than when distracted by the physical nearness of each other's charms. If they are thinking of buying a home, they might exchange news items or pictures of the kind of house or location they prefer, or if he is planning a business or considering further education, she might read to become better informed on the subject. Marriage, however, is more than letter writing.

The greatest hazard of engagement by correspondence, however, is that it encourages fantasies about the partner at a time when a couple should be exploring absolute realities. Couples tend to read into and between the lines of letters exactly what they want. Thus, when they reunite they are likely to react not to each other as they are, but as they have recreated one another in dreamlike fictions. There is no substitute for being together during engagement. Without this, there is no real test at all.

GET REACQUAINTED BEFORE MARRIAGE. Separated engaged couples should allow additional time for reacquaintance before marriage. It is surprising how much people seem to change when away from each other. Nothing could be more foolhardy, for example, than for a young woman to plan to marry the day after June graduation when she has not seen the man since Christmas, and then probably for only a few days. Sadly enough, there are many such cases. Others plan to marry as soon as the man returns from two years of overseas military duty. One does not need to wonder how long the great majority of these marriages will last. The answer is one of the tragedies of the time.

OTHER PROBLEMS DURING SEPARATION. Solving problems day in and day out is an essential part of an engagement. This cannot be done if the couple are apart, even under the most favorable conditions of phones, telegrams, television, shortwave radios, and letters.

Doubts

Doubts are a natural and perfectly normal phenomenon of life. Often one meets a young adult who states his intention to enter a particular trade, profession, or business. When asked whether he has any doubts as to his success in his chosen vocation, he often admits freely that he has a few—but that is not going to stop him from going ahead with his plans. Doubts arise about almost everything one ever attempts. Why then should it not be natural for engaged couples to have some doubts about the success of their marriage? More important is to define the doubts and then to evaluate their extent. Serious persistent doubts are one thing; regular little doubts are another.

PEOPLE ARE NEVER FREE FROM PROBLEMS. Engagement, by its nature, brings doubts to mind. As the couple talk over and perhaps solve some problems, others loom on the horizon. When they settle one, two more seem to appear. Life is a constant stream of problems. Often, however, confiding doubts to the partner may reveal them as trifles, and this reassurance may strengthen the relationship. Sometimes, doubts appear as romantic dreams disappear. It is then necessary to readjust to reality as the facts of the relationship assume their true proportions. Only 59 per cent of husbands and 52 per cent of wives studied by Burgess and Wallin reported experiencing unhesitating progress without occasional doubts during their engagements.[27]

Serious doubts, however, are another matter. Problems that keep haunting the relationship must be faced. These serious doubts must be expressed openly, defined, evaluated, and resolved by both partners before marriage. Serious doubts should never be suppressed during the engagement with the intent of resolving them after the wedding.

Escapes from doubts

There are three possibilities that might be considered by a couple when many doubts, or serious ones, threaten the relationship: (1) elopement; (2) re-evaluation; and (3) breaking the engagement.

ELOPEMENT. The couple could elope, but this actually settles nothing. It does not get to the root of the problem; it merely avoids an honest solution. It is usually unfair to one or both partners. An elopement indicates the same kind of immaturity manifested by those who break their engagement by leaving the intended spouse waiting at the church. Couples who elope are not facing reality.

RE-EVALUATION OF THE RELATIONSHIP. When there are serious doubts, the couple should re-examine their total relationship. The re-evaluation must be done when any incident or clue, no matter how trivial, indicates that the original basis for the engagement has been altered. Sometimes the romantic impulse that prompted the engagement proves to be the result only of the inaccessibility of the partner. When possession of the partner becomes a living possibility, the desire for him diminishes. Usually, however, doubts are resolved as readjustment to reality becomes more attractive than the pale romantic dreams.

Breaking the engagement

If the doubts are severe, the couple might break the engagement. Today broken engagements are not the scandal of former years, nor do they incur the emotional disturbances of a divorce. Unlike some broken marriages, the results of a broken engagement are usually positive, not negative. Indeed, one of the basic functions of the modern engagement is to prevent persons from marrying who would find nothing but unhappiness together. As a matter of fact, fifteen states now have laws prohibiting breach-of-promise suits,[28] and several other states have similar legislation pending.

INCIDENCE OF ENGAGEMENT-BREAKING. There have been several studies made to determine the incidence of broken engagements today. The results show that engagement-breaking is quite common. One study reveals that at least one third of the men and one half of the women presently married had experienced at least one engagement prior to the one that led to marriage.[29] Another study indicated that only about 50 per cent of all engaged couples marry each other. Still another survey revealed that about 25 per cent of the college girls questioned had broken engagements.[30]

OUT OF EVERY 100 COLLEGE COUPLES WHO ARE ENGAGED

APPROXIMATELY

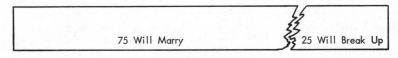

Figure 4-4.

Engagement-breaking, however, is not without problems either. There will always be embarrassing questions. A few people will always act as though the couple did not behave properly; no explanations will ever satisfy their suspicions. The prospect of social difficulties following a broken engagement must not be allowed to intimidate the couple into going through with the marriage. It is incomparably better to postpone or break an engagement full of doubts than to tolerate an uneasy marriage or to be divorced with recriminations on all sides. It is neither a favor nor a charity, Bowman states, for a person to marry anyone when he has serious doubts or reservations. Thus, it is better to break the engagement as soon as either party wishes it. In fact, Bowman suggests that the longer such a break is postponed, the greater the hurt is likely to be.[31]

THREATS. If one partner wishes to break off the engagement and the other refuses and even threatens himself or his partner with destruction, what should be done? Such threats indicate instability, and one should not marry such a person under any conditions. It must be realized that if a person has suicidal tendencies, this will be his reaction to every personal crisis unless he has strong professional help. A future family life cannot be based on threats of destruction. Actually, suicide threats are very rarely carried out. Individuals who make such threats are volatile and usually rebound in short order. One research study reported finding that only 7 per cent of males and 11 per cent of females required a year or longer for readjustment following an engagement breakup.[32] Another study reported finding that it took a year or longer for about 27 per cent of males and 30 per cent of females, however, 50 per cent of males and

49 per cent of females considered themselves fully recovered within eight weeks or less.[33]

Table 4-2. Cause of breakup of love affairs

	Per cent answering	
	230 men	*414 women*
Mutual loss of interest	46.9	38.1
Subject's interest in another person	15.1	32.2
Partner's interest in another person	29.7	15.3
Pressure from parents and friends	8.3	14.4

Source: Clifford Kirkpatrick and Theodore Caplow, "Courtship in a Group of Minnesota Students," *American Journal of Sociology,* **50**:123. Copyright © 1945, by The University of Chicago Press. Reprinted by permission.

Table 4-3. Feelings about the way love affair ended

Reactions	Per cent answering	
	230 men	*414 women*
Crushed	2	5
Angry	3	4
Bitter	6	4
Remorseful	7	7
Hurt	10	14
Mixed regret and relief	22	21
Indifferent	19	16
Relieved	15	17
Satisfied	12	8
Happy	4	4

Source: Clifford Kirkpatrick and Theodore Caplow, "Courtship in a Group of Minnesota Students," *American Journal of Sociology,* **50**:124. Copyright © 1945, by The University of Chicago Press. Reprinted by permission.

Summary

Dating is a unique but integral part of the total courtship process in modern America. Besides entertainment, there are many advantageous outcomes of dating, such as increased poise, prestige, self-understanding, communication ability, appreciation of the opposite sex, and better mate-selection possibilities. There are four basic stages of dating, and it is important for all persons to experience the four stages in their proper sequence.

Engagement was basically defined as a testing interval for determining the possibilities of a successful marriage. The major items to be tested were identified, and it was pointed out that some are better suited for the man's consideration, others for the woman's, and still other responsibilities are couple-centered. It was suggested that length of engagement is not nearly so important to marital success as the quality of the relationship; however, the importance of at least a short engagement was also reaffirmed. Some engagements may actually be too long. Suggestions were also made as to what should be told during engagement, what to do about dating others while separated, and how to face the doubts common to all engaged couples. Figures were given on the extent of engagement-breaking. It was concluded that the courtship process is a most important consideration for success in modern marriage, and that today the responsibility for successful courtship rests squarely on the couple themselves.

Notes

1. See, e.g., Howard Becker and Reuben Hill, *Family, Marriage and Parenthood* (Boston: D. C. Heath and Company, 1955), Chap. 7; or William M. Smith, Jr., "Rating and Dating: A Re-Study," *Marriage and Family Living*, 13:213–17; John F. Cuber, "Changing Courtship Customs," *Annals of the American Academy of Political and Social Science*, 229:31–34; or Samuel H. Lowrie, "Dating Theories and Student Responses," *American Sociological Review*, 16:334–40.

2. See, e.g., Meyer F. Nimkoff and Arthur L. Wood, "Courtship and Personality," *American Journal of Sociology*, 53:266–69; or E. W. Burgess and Leonard S. Cottrell, *Predicting Success or Failure in Marriage* (Englewood Cliffs, N.J.: Prentice-Hall, Inc., 1939), pp. 357–58.

3. Carson McGuire, "Family and Age-Mates in Personality Formation," *Marriage and Family Living*, 14:20.

4. Everett M. Rogers and A. Eugene Havens, "Prestige Rating and Mate Selection on a College Campus," *Marriage and Family Living*, 22:55–59.

5. Ernest A. Smith, "Dating and Courtship at Pioneer College," *Sociology and Social Research* (November–December 1955), 92–98.

6. Robert D. Herman, "The Going-Steady Complex: A Re-examination." Unpublished paper read at the Groves Family Life Conference, Purdue University, Lafayette, Indiana, 1954.

7. Samuel H. Lowrie, "Early and Late Dating: Some Conditions Associated with Them," *Marriage and Family Living*, 23:284–91.

8. *Ibid.* Lowrie reports that those who begin dating early tend to go steady earlier, but also tend to revert to playing the field again.

9. Purdue Opinion Panel, Purdue University, Lafayette, Indiana (April 1957), 15:4.

10. Both Riesman and Ehrmann reported finding that going steady often involved greater sexual intimacy for younger daters. See David Riesman, "Permissiveness and Sex Roles," *Marriage and Family Living*, 21:211–17; and Winston W. Ehrmann, *Premarital Dating Behavior* (New York: Holt, Rinehart & Winston, Inc., 1959), p. 134.

11. For a fuller discussion of this, see Phyllis McGinley, "The Fearful Aspects of Too-Early Dating," *Good Housekeeping* (April 1956), 60–61, 277–88.

12. Lowrie, *op. cit.,* pp. 284–91; and Lee G. Burchinal, "Adolescent Role Deprivation and High School Age Marriage," *Marriage and Family Living,* 20:378–84.

13. Eugene Gilbert, "Teen-Agers Turning into More Formal Boys and Girls" (New York: United Press News Release, February 4, 1954).

14. Lowrie, *op. cit.,* pp. 284–91.

15. Panos D. Bardis, "Attitudes Toward Dating Among the Students of a Michigan High School," *Sociology and Social Research* (March–April 1958), 274–77.

16. Samuel H. Lowrie, "Factors Involved in the Frequency of Dating," *Marriage and Family Living,* 18:50.

17. Lowrie, "Early and Late Dating . . .," *op. cit.,* pp. 284–91.

18. Marvin R. Koller, "Some Changes in Courtship Behavior in Three Generations of Ohio Women," *American Sociological Review,* 16:366–70.

19. Rose V. Goldsen, *et al., What College Students Think* (Princeton, N.J.: D. Van Nostrand Co., Inc., 1960), pp. 70–71.

20. Ehrmann, *op. cit.,* p. 41.

21. An examination of the rules governing women's residence halls on several campuses shows a gradual but steady lengthening of the limitations on night hours over the years.

22. Forty-five times more women attend college now as did seventy years ago. The percentage of women in college is increasing more than the percentage of men attending. See U.S. Department of Health, Education, and Welfare Bulletin *Statistical Report* (January 1962), viii.

23. Ninety-four per cent of engaged women do get engagement rings, announced engagement or not. See August B. Hollingshead, "Marital Status and Wedding Behavior," *Marriage and Family Living,* 14:307–11.

24. Lewis M. Terman, *Psychological Factors in Marital Happiness* (New York: McGraw-Hill Book Co., 1938), pp. 198–200; Burgess and Cottrell, *op. cit.,* p. 407.

25. Paul Popenoe, *Modern Marriage* (New York: The Macmillan Company, 1947), pp. 175, 222–25.

26. See, e.g., Judson T. and Mary G. Landis, *Building a Successful Marriage* (4th ed.) (Englewood Cliffs, N.J.: Prentice-Hall, Inc., 1963), Chap. 14.

27. E. W. Burgess and Paul Wallin, *Engagement and Marriage* (Philadelphia: J. B. Lippincott Co., 1953), p. 180.

28. Alabama, California, Colorado, Florida, Maryland, Indiana, Maine, Michigan, Massachusetts, Nevada, New Hampshire, New Jersey, New York, Pennsylvania, and Wyoming.

29. Burgess and Wallin, *op. cit.,* p. 273.

30. Landis and Landis, *op. cit.,* Chap. 14.

31. Henry A. Bowman, *Marriage for Moderns* (New York: McGraw-Hill Book Company, Inc., 1954), p. 209.

32. Clifford Kirkpatrick and Theodore Caplow, "Courtship in a Group of Minnesota Students," *American Journal of Sociology,* 50:125.

33. Landis and Landis, *op. cit.,* Chap. 14.

Questions for further thought

1. In what ways is dating consistent or inconsistent with American principles of democracy?
2. How could some competition for dates actually be regarded as a constructive force in personality development?
3. How could some marriage failures really be courtship failures when there is no one-and-only right person for marriage?

4. Why do so many young people of both sexes bluff and employ "cover" techniques on dates? What can be done to aid this situation?
5. Should one's choice of a marriage partner grow out of his experiences in dating, or should one decide what he wants and then systematically go about looking for it?
6. Should an exceptionally bright girl tone herself down on dates to protect the male ego? What are likely to be the results either way?
7. What is meant by the expression, "he (she) is fun to date but wouldn't do for marriage"?
8. Why is it that so many married adults who went steady as teen-agers are now so unalterably opposed to it?
9. What would be the advantages or disadvantages of reinstating the traditional meaning of *engagement*?
10. What should a happily engaged couple do who have just taken a "marital-success checklist" test in a magazine, and the results indicate that their chances of happiness in marriage are not so good?

Recommended films

It Takes All Kinds (McGraw-Hill Book Company, Inc.).
The Meaning of Engagement (Corenet).
Date Etiquette (Coronet).

Suggested supplemental readings

BOOKS

Burgess, E. W., and Paul Wallin. *Engagement and Marriage*. Philadelphia: J. B. Lippincott Co., 1953. Chaps. 3, 4, 5, 8, 9, 10.
Duvall, Evelyn M., and Joy Duvall Johnson. *The Art of Dating*. New York: Association Press, 1958.
Duvall, Sylvanus. *Before You Marry*, rev. ed. New York: Association Press, 1959.
Fortes, Meyer (ed.). *Marriage in Tribal Societies*. New York: University Press, 1962.
Glass, Esther Edy. *When You Date*. Scottdale, Pa.: Herald Press, 1952.
Mace, David and Vera. *Marriage East and West*. Garden City, N.Y.: Doubleday & Company, Inc., 1960.
McManus, William F. *Marriage Guide for Engaged Catholics*. New York: Paulist Press, 1961.
Missouri Synod and Concordia Seminary. *Engagement and Marriage*. St. Louis: Concordia Publishing Company, 1959.
Riesman, David. *The Lonely Crowd*. Garden City, N.Y.: Doubleday & Company, Inc., 1953.
Turner, E. S. *A History of Courting*. New York: E. P. Dutton & Co., Inc., 1955.
Wedeck, Harry E. *Love Potions Through the Ages: A Study of Amatory Devices and Mores*. New York: Philosophical Library, Inc., 1963.
Wenger, John C. *Clear Thinking About Courtship*. Scottdale: Herald Press, 1952.
Weyer, Edward, Jr. *Primitive Peoples Today*. Garden City, N.Y.: Doubleday & Company, Inc., 1961.

ARTICLES

Blood, Robert O. "A Retest of Waller's Rating Complex," *Marriage and Family Living*, 17:41–47.
———. "Uniformities and Diversities in Campus Dating Preferences," *Marriage and Family Living*, 18:37–45.

Bossard, James H. S. "The Engagement Ring—A Changing Symbol," *New York Times Magazine* (September 14, 1958), 32.

Christensen, Harold. "Courtship Conduct as Viewed by Youth," *Journal of Home Economics,* 50:580–86.

Connor, Ruth, and Edith Hall. "The Dating Behavior of College Freshmen and Sophomores," *Journal of Home Economics,* 44:278–81.

Cuber, John F. "Changing Courtship Customs," *Annals of the American Academy of Political and Social Science,* 229:31–34.

Delora, Jack. "Social Systems of Dating On a College Campus," *Marriage and Family Living,* 25:81–84.

Gray, Robert F. "Sonjo Bride Price and the Question of African Wife Purchase," *American Anthropologist,* 62:34–57.

Harper, Robert A. "Honesty in Courtship," *The Humanist,* 18:103–107.

Mace, David. "Marriage by Arrangement," *McCall's* (August 1959), 50.

Ojemann, Ralph H., and Eva H. Grant. "Dating—Big Business of Youth," *National Parent-Teacher,* 45:35.

Rogers, Everett M., and A. Eugene Havens. "Prestige Rating and Mate Selection on a College Campus," *Marriage and Family Living,* 22:55–59.

Schnepp, Gerald J. "Survey of Going Steady and Other Dating Practices," *American Catholic Sociological Review,* 20:238–50.

Wolford, Opal Powell. "How Early Background Affects Dating Behavior," *Journal of Home Economics,* 40:505–506.

Selecting for happiness

chapter 5

It is possible for a marriage to exist happily and successfully even though it has many differences. This is possible when the husband and wife have strength and maturity, and have followed their plans for marriage carefully through the stages of courtship. No matter how right the plans and the maturity of the couple, however, no two individuals behave consistently all the time. Because differences of background will contribute greatly to the inconsistency of the couple's behavior as man and wife, it seems important to examine and identify major differences before marriage. All studies have indicated that selecting a partner with a background similar to one's own in certain categories frequently is indeed selecting for happiness. Nothing in this discussion, however, should be interpreted as intending a denial of the importance of psychodynamic factors in mate selection. Part of the mate-selection process is conscious and rational, part is not. The part that is not is felt to be important enough to merit special consideration (see Chapter 6).

What constitutes a mixed marriage?

Whenever a difference exists, or is believed by the couple to exist, and that difference is generally regarded within the culture as being significant or quite unusual, then the couple most likely have a mixed marriage. If a couple do not recognize themselves as being different from each other, and others do not think of them as being so, it is then only an *assumed* difference by other cultures and may not be an important consideration in the culture where the couple resides.

It is possible that a person's ancestors belonged to a particular group, yet the individual may no longer consider himself within the same group, nor do other people in his culture. Negroid racial background, for instance, might be apparent only in the ancestors. Through intermarriage with Caucasians, a generation of slightly darker-skinned whites results. Unless such persons meet and mate with similar individuals, or a very dark Negro, there is no biological possibility of any offspring appearing of a darker shade than they are themselves.[1]

When persons have conscientiously, deliberately, and actively become members of a group different from their ancestral group (other than racial), theirs too may or may not be a significant enough difference to qualify as a mixed marriage. The *serious* religion convert is a prime example, as is the rise in social status of others. (Research discloses that about one fourth of all Americans experience a change in social class from the one in which they are born.[2])

Usual problems of a mixed marriage

Mixed marriages may involve special problems between (1) the mixed spouses, (2) the in-laws and the couple, (3) society and the couple, and (4) various combinations of the first three and the offspring of the couple.

The most common problems between spouses of a mixed marriage arise from an unrecognized lack of communication. Although they may try hard to understand one another, their differing rituals, attitudes, habits, and role conceptionalizations may interfere. Sometimes a hidden streak of prejudice toward the group of the other flashes through even though the spouse is found acceptable, for it has been a matter of accepting the spouse in spite of the difference. Mixed mates may find they have few common values in many areas. Sometimes they find that even their friendships have become limited to a small circle of people in much the same circumstances.[3]

Sometimes one of the two sets of parents never stop trying to break up the mixed marriage. Duvall reports that a mixed marriage is much more likely than ordinary marriages to have in-law trouble.[4] This is a very serious problem when the spouse loves his parents deeply.

Sometimes die-hards in the community continually bring pressure to bear upon the mixed couple. If it is a pronounced racial mixture, for example, certain businesses may be reluctant to trade with them when together; if it is a religious mixture, certain organizations may choose to invite only one of the couple to affairs.

For the children of a mixed marriage, the problems may become particularly acute. The children usually grow aware of the differences between the mother and father, and may find it difficult to establish absolute values in their own lives.

Why mixed marriages occur

Sometimes young persons turn to a mixed marriage in a spirit of rebellion or revenge. Their marriage to someone of a group disliked by the parents is a method of showing complete independence or rejection of their authority. Sometimes members of an ethnic group deliberately seek to marry outside the group but wish to retain the old customs. These mixed marriages are often motivated by defiance of the family hierarchy so common in such groups.[5]

Sometimes mixed marriages occur in the hope of attaining the "out-of-reach." A poor boy might marry a rich widow for her money, and the rich widow marries the poor boy in an effort to regain her lost youth. Social prestige has sometimes been a factor in mixed marriages, and has been the motivation for marriage for some of the most famous leaders in history, such as Napoleon and Disraeli.

At times an individual has intermarried with an almost instinctive belief that he was a crusader in a great movement to bring about an end to the embarrassing discrimination shown by his group toward another. He seems compelled to demonstrate through his own "generosity" that all of his group are not the same.[6]

Americans are known for their interest in the unusual. At times, for the glamor and excitement of a mysterious romance, an individual might deliberately seek a partner significantly different simply for an "adventure" into marriage.

Extreme loneliness has caused some young soldiers to ignore differences that they would not overlook in their home town.[7] On the other hand, marriage to a member of the World War II occupation forces caused many a foreign war bride tragic disappointment. There is the case of the German girl who married an American soldier thinking he was a "big oil man." She was shocked and disappointed to discover that in real life he was merely a gas-station attendant.[8]

Some mixed marriages, however, are entered into not because of the differences but in spite of them. When this happens, it is most probable that the same two individuals would have married had there been no differences. These marriages continue happily because basic needs and interests are being met for both partners; their basic similarities tend to counterbalance their differences. It is quite important that the individual examine motivations in a pending mixed marriage. If the prevailing ones appear best described as "exploitative," then the predictions for marital happiness are indeed limited.

Kinds of mixture

Some differences of background are naturally more important than others. Then, too, what may appear to be an overwhelming difference in one subculture may not be considered so in another. In selecting for happiness, it becomes necessary to distinguish the various kinds of mixture and their relative importance, if any, in a constitutionally free society.

There are many ways in which a marriage can be mixed. It should also be pointed out when there is a significant difference, other types of mixture may also exist. If there is an educational difference, there is likely to be a difference in intelligence and in social class. Differences that relate to marital adjustment include religion, race, social class, age, education, nationality, physical size, health, previous marital status, and philosophies and values.

Mixed religious marriage

Few young Americans seem to appreciate the fact that religion is still one of the most powerful forces in the world. Wars have been fought in the name of religion and people are still willing to die in its name. Purpose

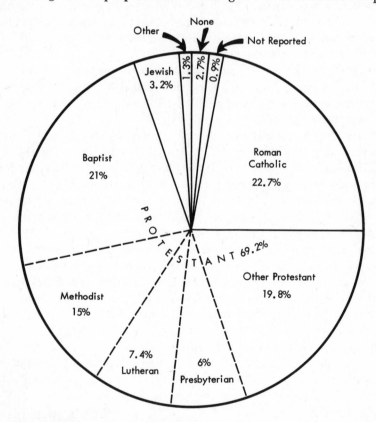

Figure 5-1. Religious affiliations reported by citizens of the United States during the 1960 census.

is given to the lives of millions through religion. Many people feel that, without it, they would have nothing. Religion can be the greatest bond between two people, or it can be a powerful disorganizing force. The common bond of religion may complete the union of two individuals. Individuals with differing religions nearly always experience some social distance, for seldom are any two religions exactly alike in their attitudes and standards. Religious practices may differ with respect to food and drink, recreation, holiday observances, in the use of tobacco, or even on when it is proper to read a newspaper. A shared religion usually helps create a common denominator of meaningful purpose in a marriage, in much the same way as it can give meaningful purpose in life to an individual.

INTERDENOMINATIONAL. Differences of denomination need as serious a consideration as the more apparent differences. Within some denominations the services are so similar that it would be difficult to differentiate one from the other without prior knowledge; others vary greatly from the more orthodox groups. In some services, the congregations are quite vocal in their emotionalism; in others, particular emphasis is placed on quoting Scripture word for word. Some observe a strict interpretation of the Bible and the keeping of the Sabbath, while others are liberal in these matters.

It is probably safe to say that there are sometimes greater theological differences between the 250 various Protestant sects than there are between some Protestants and Catholics and Orthodox Jews. These Protestants who marry members of other sects would have a mixed religious marriage; this would also apply to intermarriage among Orthodox, Conservative, and Reform Jews. There are even marked deviations in interpretation of Catholicism in various dioceses of the United States. Of all the differences, however, there is none more outstanding than between some of the Protestant sects in America. It is probably fortunate that few radical and conservative elements of these groups ever mix.[9] When they do, marital problems usually arise.

Except for a study of the rate of intermarriage between Lutherans and other groups, there has been little research on the extent of such mixtures. The study of Lutherans indicated a steady increase in interdenominational marriages over the years; the rate is currently at an all-time high, with 60 per cent of all Lutheran marriages contracted with non-Lutherans. Most of the other denominations, however, were very similar in beliefs and practice to the Lutheran sect.[10]

JEWISH-GENTILE. Statistically, one of the most difficult of mixed religious marriages is that between a Jew and a Gentile. Not only does the religious difference cause problems, but special problems of prejudice and discrimination seem likely to occur. Many of these problems are related to a mutual ignorance about the partner's religion as well as to community ignorance. Barron has reported that, in Jewish-Gentile marriages, it is more likely the man who is Jewish. Yet Jewish men usually take their religion more seriously than do Gentile men. In such a mixture, the religious problem is intensified because, among Gentiles, it is usually the women who are more religiously inclined. Jewish women appear to be more restricted than Jewish men in their associations with Gentiles, and thus have less opportunity for intermarriage. The Jewish college-trained woman intermarries at a much greater rate than the non-college student. The children of a Jewish-Gentile marriage are nearly always raised in the Jewish faith.[11] The religion of the children in such marriages appears to be less of a problem than in other mixed religious marriages. There have been few studies of Jewish-Gentile marriage, mainly because the rate is so much lower than for other types of mixed (religious) marriage. Only about 5–7 per cent of Jewish marriages involve a non-Jewish spouse[12]; rarely is the Gentile partner a Catholic.[13] Conservative and Reform rabbis will consent to perform mixed marriages even if the Gentile retains his own religion, but the Orthodox Rabbi would consent to officiate only if the Gentile converted, and that conversion proved sincere.

CATHOLIC–NON-CATHOLIC. The intermarriage of Catholics with non-Catholics is increasing. Research discloses that at least 30 per cent of all Catholic marriage ceremonies performed by priests in a given year involve a partner who is, or has lately been, a non-Catholic,[14] and that at least 15 per cent of Catholics who marry in a given year do so outside their faith.[15] The Catholic Church considers this latter group as invalid marriages.

> The Catholic's conscience has been formed from the beginning to regard matrimony as a sacrament instituted by the Son of God. . . . Since matrimony is a sacrament, the Roman Catholic Church as the guardian of the sacraments has the right and the indefectibly infallible authority to make explicit legislation binding all Catholics who wish to enter the married state. No Catholic marries contrary to that legislation without violence to his conscience, and no Catholic violates his conscience without mutilating his personality to become something that he was not before. . . .
>
> The *only* way to marry a Catholic in conscience—is to marry him before a Catholic priest. . . . If you haven't married your Catholic spouse before a priest, then you haven't married him at all, no matter how much you yourself might be in good faith about the matter, no matter what ceremonies you've gone through together.[16]

There are some communities with few such mixed marriages and others with many. According to Thomas, the rate appears to increase in a community where the proportion of Catholics is small, reaching as high as 75 per cent or more in some areas of the country.[17] Where the eligible field within their own church is limited, Catholics may be forced to marry someone outside their church or not marry at all. Locke found the same thing to be true for all religious groups. That is, the rate of interfaith marriage or of interdenominational marriage for a group increases as the percentage of that group decreases in a given community.[18] It is generally the higher-social-class and intellectual Catholic who most frequently gets involved in a mixed religious marriage performed outside his own faith, and subsequently runs the risk of excommunication.[19]

PROMISES MUST BE MADE. Before a priest is permitted to perform the marriage ceremony in a Catholic–non-Catholic union, the partners are requested to take a series of instructions together about the Catholic faith,[20] and certain promises are exacted from both parties.[21] If the partners can keep these promises, such a marriage, although perhaps not free from friction, is not nearly so complicated. Practice indicates that it is much easier to make the promises than to fulfill them. This seems to be especially true after the arrival of children. It should be pointed out that no matter how official such an agreement may appear on paper and no matter how many witnesses there are to the signing of the agreement, such agreements have not been considered by the courts to be legally binding on either party. Enforcement depends upon the faith of the Catholic and the conscience of the non-Catholic.

The Catholic Church is unalterably opposed to divorce and remarriage. A Catholic is not permitted to marry a divorced person within the church. To do so within or without the church, in knowledge or by accident, and to remain in the union, means excommunication. The only exception to this rule is the "Pauline Privilege," or special dispensation. Fundamentally, dispensation is granted when the divorced person's first spouse had never been baptized in any church. (This is so rare in the United States that it is only mentioned in passing.[22])

Some of the most serious problems in Catholic–non-Catholic marriages have been over birth-control methods and the religious training of the children. Although it may be a debatable point by both lay and clerical theologians for generations to come, the controversy over the use of some artificial method for family-planning appears to be fading away as an issue in mixed marriages. Studies by Samenfink, a Catholic, for example, suggest that some form of birth control, including artificial devices, is practiced within a large number of nonmixed Catholic marriages and in a majority of the mixed marriages.[23]

Controversy over the religious training of the offspring is perhaps the biggest point of friction. At the time of the wedding, it is difficult for either partner to project himself into the future and realize how he will feel about this point. It is only natural for both parents to wish to impart to their children some of the wisdom or ideals which they have grown to appreciate through the years; yet, in such a mixed marriage, the non-

Catholic partner has agreed not to do this in the area of religion. This is a promise that may be difficult to keep; unconsciously, the non-Catholic may venture "too far." Sometimes non-Catholics have a change of heart about this promise and develop feelings of guilt. Anyone who cares about his own religion may find it impossible to refrain forever from passing some of the teachings of his faith to his children. Conversely, if the children should begin to show signs of leaning toward the non-Catholic faith, this could easily result in the development of some deep-seated guilt feelings on the part of the Catholic mate, who may then begin to question his own religious conscience.[24] By and large, research indicates that, in the United States, children are usually reared in the faith of the mother, whatever it is. Only about 5 per cent of all children in mixed marriages grow up with no church affiliation.[25]

In general, all religious groups are opposed to mixed religious marriages. Schmiedeler, who for years served as director of the Family Life Bureau of the National Catholic Welfare Conference, states that Catholics are opposed to mixed marriage particularly because it leads in many ways to a "watered-down" type of religion.[26] All groups know from past experience that, when mixed couples are devout, the differences brought about by religion usually grow more acute with time. All groups are constantly active in attempts to discourage such affairs. The general Protestant viewpoint is perhaps best stated by the National Council of Churches through their spokesman, Leland Foster Wood:

> When intolerable conditions are introduced the young person should reject them even if it means delaying one's marriage until an equally attractive person of one's own faith can be found.[27]

Although divorce is not the only method of measuring the success or failure of a marriage, the figures from studies by Landis, Bell, Weeks, and Iowa State University are worthy of consideration.[28] In the main, the results shed considerable light on the risks of a mixed religious marriage.

Landis' study indicates that the chances of divorce in a Catholic-Protestant marriage are almost three and one half times greater for the Catholic party and two and one third times greater for the Protestant party, than if either had married within his own faith. The more recent study conducted by Iowa State University indicates the increased divorce risk to be five and one half times greater for the Catholic party and slightly over one and one half times greater for the non-Catholic. The popular misconception that one partner should convert to the other's religion or both should change to a third religion is apparently not very effective. Such a conversion is probably ineffectual because it involves only a surface change; a deep change is almost impossible for most people. Sincere conversions at the most common marriage age are scarcely a reasonable expectation in any event. No matter which partner converts to what religion, the rate of divorce is still higher for both parties than when each marries within his own faith, and the rate is about the same regardless of which one converts. Landis did find, however, a wide variation of divorce rate related to whether it is the husband or the wife who is Catholic. In his study, mixtures composed of Protestant men and Catholic women experienced fewer divorces by far than marriages of Catholic men and Protestant women. In general, a Catholic man who marries a Protestant woman increased his chances for divorce approximately five times over those of divorce in a marriage within his own faith. A Protestant woman who married a Catholic man increased her chances for a divorce by almost three and one half times over the normal rate in marriages of Protestants with Protestants. Monahan and Kephart report much the same sex differential in a Catholic-Protestant marriage.[29] The more recent study conducted by Iowa State University also supports these findings, but not to the same extent. Because it is usually the woman who files for divorce, it stands to reason that there would be less divorce in mixed marriages involving Catholic women. Divorce, however, is only one method of registering marital unhappiness.

Sometimes the factor of children creates unrest in mixed marriages. A study by Dyer and Luckey of those mixed religious marriages with no children or with only very young children, found no statistically significant differences in happiness when compared with nonmixed marriages. The findings from a study by Alfred Prince, however, did not necessarily support this conclusion.[30] Of course, all these studies are speaking of the statistical average, they do not apply, and were never intended to apply, to each individual case. As an illustration, Heiss found that many of the "more successful and happy interfaith marriages" were composed of mates who were not serious "defenders of their own faith." In fact, many came from homes in which differences of religious doctrines, theology, and practice had not been considered as being too important in relation to other considerations in life.[31]

None of these studies, however, discloses all the facts behind the facts, and until further research is possible, further discussion is highly speculative. Very likely, if Catholic-Protestant marriages could be broken down by particular Protestant denominations, it would be seen that certain mixed marriages are far better risks than others.[32] To date, there has been little published research on this subject. The Iowa State University study suggests that the risk of divorce is twice as high in Catholic-Baptist marriages as in marriages between Catholics and all Protestants together. By the same token, it is doubtful that the grouping of all Protestant marriages together gives a true picture. It is common suspicion that patrons of certain denominations experience much more divorce than others, but as yet no scientific research known to the author has been published on this subject.

Table 5–1.   **Divorce as related to both mixed and nonmixed religious marriages**

	Per cent divorced	
Condition	Landis study	Iowa State University study
Both Catholic	4.4	4.0
Both Jewish	5.2	
Both Protestant	6.0	14.0
Mixed Catholic-Protestant	14.1	22.0
Both None	17.9	
Protestant changed to Catholic	10.7	
Catholic changed to Protestant	10.6	
Protestant father and Catholic mother	6.7	20.0
Catholic father and Protestant mother	20.6	25.0
Father none and mother Catholic	9.8	
Father none and mother Protestant	19.0	

Source: Judson T. Landis, "Marriages of Mixed and Nonmixed Religious Faiths," *American Sociological Review,* 14:401–407. Copyright © 1949, by The American Sociological Association, Washington, D.C. Reprinted by permission. Lee G. Burchinal and Loren E. Chancellor, "Survival Rates Among Religiously Homogamous and Interreligious Marriages," *Research Bulletin No. 512758* (Ames, Iowa: Agricultural and Home Economics Experiment Station, Iowa State University, December 1962). Adapted by permission.

SUGGESTIONS.   It may appear to be an oversimplification to state that the problems of a mixed religious marriage are best avoided simply by abstaining from such a marriage, but perhaps such is a fact. Be that as it may, it seems apparent that some mixed religious marriages will occur each year, and the percentage will probably even increase.[33] A few suggestions are in order when such is to be the case. It is well to keep in mind, however, that the truly mixed religious marriage has not been discussed, for it would involve, for example, a Judeo-Christian–oriented individual and a non-Judeo-Christian–oriented individual, and the latter is rare in the United States. This discussion has considered mixed dogmas or theologies which are related to the Judeo-Christian tradition of marriage and religion. There are many basic similarities among all such religions. With this in mind, when considering a mixed marriage a couple should try to learn all they can about each other's theology by reading, by attending the church services, and (through discussions with other members) attempting to discover what it is that attracts his potential mate to this particular belief. Each should search his soul, with the aid of trained leaders in both religions, for reasons why he can or cannot officially, sincerely, deeply accept the other person's faith as his own as much or more than his present faith. Also, the two partners must devise mutually acceptable answers to all possible questions and problems of mixed married life, leaving nothing to chance or to be settled later. After they have made their decisions, they should go together and discuss them with both sets of clergy and parents. They should have their decisions clearly in mind and well stated so that there is not the slightest possibility for a misunderstanding later. Finally, they should increasingly and consistently pray for the strength, wisdom, and guidance that will be necessary to carry them over the rough spots.

Mixed racial marriage

Because representatives of all three races live in the United States, it is possible to have an interracial marriage without a corresponding mixture of nationalities.

SOCIAL DISAPPROVAL. There is no biological threat involved in racial mixture; however, extreme prejudices within some subcultures of the United States appear to perpetuate the myth.

One study reveals that couples wishing to contract an interracial marriage frequently have trouble finding a clergyman willing to officiate. Thus, the usual wedding ceremony in such instances is a civil one.[34] Western white culture has always had its element of enthnocentricism, but perhaps nowhere is it more pronounced than within the social attitudes regarding mixed racial marriage in parts of the United States. Many other cultures accept such marriages readily; in Puerto Rico, for example, racial prejudice is practically unknown. A research census indicated that at least 85 per cent of the people of color in that country have mixed racial ancestry.[35] It is reported that even the United States Army frequently prescribes certain procedures designed to discourage interracial marriages among its personnel. The soldier who wishes to enter such a marriage may be requested to sign an agreement to accept military assignments only in certain areas. Chaplains and commanding officers spend time conferring and explaining to the couple the difficulties they will probably face. As a delaying tactic, request for permission to marry is sometimes referred to the top-level command in the area. It is hoped that by the time a reply comes through channels, that many such affairs will have ended.[36]

LEGAL PROHIBITIONS. Not only is an interracial marriage forbidden by law in many states, but frequently severe penalties for violations are enforced upon both the couple and the officiant.[37]

Full faith and credit toward the laws of other states may make it legally acceptable for a mixed racial couple married elsewhere to abide anywhere in the United States, but social pressure and "protective" laws are not on their side in some instances. The current exception to this taboo is an American Indian-white mixture. People with a small amount of Indian ancestry are likely to brag about it and whites today think it a most romantic and wonderful heritage. Not too many years ago, such marriages had as many problems as today's Negro-white mixtures.

LOW HAPPINESS RATIO.   According to Baber, the average happiness rating for the total mixed racial group is very low. In fact, it appears lower than for the total for all marriages of mixed nationality or mixed religion. Baber also discovered that, where there is an appreciable degree of happiness, the "color" difference is usually very slight. The greater the "color" difference, the less chance of happiness.[38]

NEGRO-WHITE.   The least acceptable interracial type of marriage in the United States appears to be the Negro-white. Apparently, there are fewer of this type than the average citizen believes, for when studies have been attempted, only a few cases have been discovered. Jacobson estimates from his studies of selected areas of the United States that perhaps no more than eight out of every 10,000 marriages is interracial.[39] A survey of a twenty-five year period in Boston found only .10 per cent of marriages involving whites had also involved a Negro.[40] Even when such cases are found, however, it is difficult to obtain the cooperation of the couple in a sociological study—often they simply refuse to answer questions. The partners involved are usually of the lower socioeconomic class. (This is quite the reverse of the case in mixed religious marriages.) There is a common misconception that interracial marriage occurs frequently among theatrical people, probably because the few that do occur make headlines in American newspapers. None of the published research studies to date, however, has found this mixture prevalent enough to warrant citation.

If Baber's study has any degree of authenticity (and he is the first to caution against generalizing too much from it), it can be assumed that when a Negro-white marriage does occur, the chances are about three to one that the white person will be female.[41] Baber found only a few cases to study, but in these a majority of the whites were foreign-born.[42] Such people would, of course, be less concerned with the prejudices existing in parts of the American culture. The interracial marriage rate is considerably higher in many other countries (such as France) than in the United States, probably because of less prejudice.[43]

ORIENTAL–NON-ORIENTAL.   There are too few mixed marriages of the Oriental–non-Oriental type to draw any substantial conclusions. It is a common belief that the chances for happiness are greater when the female is of Oriental ancestry and the male white, than when it is the other way around. This appears logical when one considers that the training of the Oriental woman has usually been toward achieving happiness for her husband, even at the expense of her own. Baber's small study appears to support this thesis. He also advances the concept that because the majority of Orientals in this country have been males, many of them were forced to marry non-Orientals or not to marry at all; thus, if such individuals had a strong desire for marriage, they perhaps were less selective than they might have been.[44] A high incidence of interracial marriage is reported in Hawaii. Studies there show that native Hawaiian women like to marry white men because they consider them more energetic and, thus, better providers. Such marriages are usually quite successful, but the marriages of white women to native Hawaiian men are usually unsuccessful and do not occur as frequently.[45]

There are conflicting views and opinions regarding the effects of interracial mixtures on the offspring. More than one third of the mixed marriages studied by Baber were classified as childless.[46] This is considerably above the national average of other childless marriages. Because there is no genetic evidence to indicate a decrease in fertility in such marriages, the increase in childlessness must be considered to result from the couple's own decisions—decisions perhaps forced by increased social and parental pressure.

It may be that interracial marriage is not as hard on the children today as it was formerly, and that the idea of the "suffering" offspring has been merely part of the propaganda against such marriages. Many of the earlier writings of this subject offered only one case study or an opinion (based on little actual research) to support this thesis. Such writings sometimes contained vivid descriptions of the ridicule and ostracism suffered by the children of such mixed marriages. It is a common assumption that neither race freely accepts these offspring, but that the degree of acceptance is greater within the nonwhite community. According to Walter White, an official of the National Association for the Advancement of Colored People, about 12,000 light-skinned Negroes "disappear" into the white population each year.[47]

ON THE INCREASE. As more Negroes move North, it seems reasonable to expect that interracial marriage will increase as equal economic and educational status is achieved. The 1950 census figures reported that over 70 per cent of the Negroes in the United States lived in the South; today, less than 60 per cent do.[48] Allan Nevins, a noted historian, speculates that when the Negro attains the social, cultural, and economic rights of the whites, there will be a noted increase in intermarriage.[49] World events are showing the fallacy of the belief that any race is "superior" to another. It takes time for the significance of these implications to be understood, but certainly within a democratic society a discussion such as this on mixed interracial marriage should soon be a thing of the past.

Socioeconomic differences

At present, patterns of behavior vary greatly with socioeconomic level, even in a society that strives for equality in all things for all classes. Indeed, the "correct" standards of behavior differ in each class. Attitudes toward authority, freedom, morals, ethics, education, and many other values are markedly different. As a rule, families of lower social class are much less democratic, or else they go quite far in granting freedom without a corresponding balance of responsibility.[50] Money matters are handled differently according to social class. Although individuals have successfully married across social-class lines, research—using the Burgess and Cottrell marital-adjustment scores—reveals that the majority of such marriages show a significant number of low scores.[51] Different social classes have decided cultural and financial attitudinal differences. Attitudes toward the care of children and elders are quite different. Many lower-class families are considered by others to be quite narrow in their beliefs, but few of them recognize this and consider those who differ from them as being odd or abnormal. Middle-class people, more often than those of other classes, favor compromising measures. Lower-socio-economic-class individuals belong to few associations; in fact, when labor unions and religious affiliations are excluded, few lower-class people are found to belong or to participate in any organizations.[52] The homes of most middle-class families are filled with a variety of books and magazines, while in many lower-class families even a daily newspaper is a rarity. All of this adds up to such a different orientation toward life that a genuine togetherness in marriage between partners of different socio-economic backgrounds is almost impossible.[53]

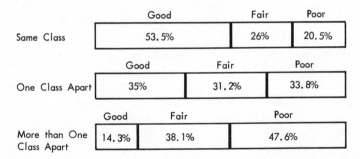

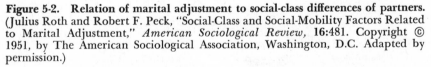

Figure 5-2.   Relation of marital adjustment to social-class differences of partners. (Julius Roth and Robert F. Peck, "Social-Class and Social-Mobility Factors Related to Marital Adjustment," *American Sociological Review*, 16:481. Copyright © 1951, by The American Sociological Association, Washington, D.C. Adapted by permission.)

If there is to be a marriage across socioeconomic classes, research suggests that it is much more satisfactory if it is the female who marries upward.[54] Even this is not without its difficulties, for the husband's relatives often refuse to accept such wives entirely. There are many things that happen as everyday occurrences to middle- and upper-class families for which lower-class individuals are totally unprepared. For example, when lower-class individuals are given the freedom of more money than they have been accustomed to, their tendency to spend it too fast and foolishly frequently appears to be irrational.

Men who marry upward are often accused of having ulterior motives for marrying. The knowledge of this charge prevents some husbands in this position from acting as freely as they might otherwise. Feelings of guilt, frustration, and anxiety are common to them. In some cases the wife agrees to live on the husband's income as a public demonstration that he did not marry her for her family's money or status. Nearly always she does not fully realize the implications of this promise. Accustomed to a high standard, she cannot entirely understand what a lower standard entails; the experience can seem romantic and adventurous for a time, but not for long.

Age differences

In American marriages the husband is usually from two to three years older than the wife. This age differential has been the general pattern for several decades. Bossard's study of 13,000 marriages in Philadelphia showed that the man was the older partner in four out of five marriages; of the same age in one out of every ten marriages; and younger in one out of every ten marriages.[55] Because the sexes do not mature at the same rate, it seems that most couples acquire a readiness for marriage with approximately the cited age differential. A few years either way does not appear to cause any marital problems, but a difference of ten or fifteen years may cause difficulties. Even then the problems may not be pronounced, for there are usually several compensating factors that brought the couple together in the first place.

SPECIFIC TROUBLE SPOTS. The specific problems connected with such marriages are quite obvious to most observers. The older person often assumes the role of parent rather than that of spouse. The wisdom that comes with the experience of living often places such a person in the position of "overseer." Sharing may never be complete; neither may trust or judgment. Impatience with the younger person's immaturity is sometimes expressed by the older person. Such a couple may find it difficult to agree on one set of mutual friends, each being attracted by those nearer his own age. Because physical deterioration usually comes with age, their shared physical activities will decrease. Public opinion is also a factor for consideration, for general social approval is often withheld from marriages with wide age differentials, particularly if there are children. Even prominent personalities have been severely criticized when marrying women younger than some of their children by former marriages. The behavior patterns of the spouses, their tastes, interests, and general attitudes toward life are likely to be at variance. It is estimated that energy directed toward certain behavior characteristics may be from five to ten times stronger in the younger partner. Thus, temperamental compatibility is much less likely.[56] The older person is more likely to be set in his ways; if there is a need for adjusting, and there usually is, it is the younger individual who must make the adaptation.

POSSIBILITY OF WIDOWHOOD. Women in general outlive men by several years. Thus a wife who is her husband's junior by about fifteen years should ordinarily expect to be widowed for at least twenty years. This is not a very pleasant thought. Coupled with the present trend for older people to live away from their offspring, it could well mean that a woman who marries a man considerably her senior has automatically sentenced herself to a very lonely existence in her later years.

WHAT RESEARCH SHOWS. Locke states, in effect, that where other things are equal, an approximate equality in age appears most conducive to good marital adjustment, but he hastens to add that his research on the subject is too inadequate to draw any complete conclusions in this regard.[57] Terman found that where the wife was from four to ten years older than the husband, the happiness score was high,[58] but he too is quick to point out that this obviously would not be the result if everyone were to follow such a pattern. Most of the happy younger husbands in such research studies have been found to possess a strong "mother complex," and their older wives demonstrated a distinctive "maternal" interest. Probably such age differences would be advisable under such circumstances, but because most people do not fall into these categories, it is doubtful that the same results would be found if all were to follow this pattern.

UNUSUAL MOTIVES. It is probably safe to say that in the great majority of successful marriages with a wide age differential, the motivation is likely to be quite out of the ordinary. It may be that a marriage with any or a combination of these motives is actually best for some people, because such special motives may well indicate a person's greatest needs in life.[59]

Educational differences

There are many meanings attached to the word *education* which might lead to the conclusion that this area could comprise one of the most significant differences in marriage. Other interpretations of the word, however, might seem to eliminate education as a possible source of marital difficulties. The fact is that where there is a wide variation in educational achievement between partners, there are more likely to be other distinctive differences as well. It may well be that the other differences, rather than the educational factor itself, lead to the failure of a marriage. Extreme differences in formal educational levels are quite likely to lead to a divergence of interests and friends; thus communication may be more difficult. The more highly educated person usually has much more reliable information, and may as a result become impatient or disgusted at the "gems of ignorance" occasionally put forth by the less-educated partner. Yet, education is also supposed to develop objectivity in social relationships and to create tolerance toward differences. If such are the marks of a truly educated person, then it would appear that different educational levels alone would not make much difference to marital success. Education consists of more than college credit hours. Furthermore, formal educational attainment may not be matched by living experience. A university professor may have many years of professional training behind him, but it is doubtful that his educational level for living is any higher than the man with a simple bachelor's degree. It is not a wide variation of vocational or professional training between husband and wife that would create a significant difference but, rather, variations in the level of achievement in learning how to live graciously.

RESEARCH INDICATIONS. Burgess and Cottrell found that the educational attainments of a couple and the degree of marital success or adjustment were closely associated.[60] There is no clear-cut distinction made in their study, however, as to educational-attainment differences between spouses. When the husband's education was far less than the wife's, the wife usually scored low on Terman's happiness-rating tests; however, in most of those instances the husbands were intellectually inferior to their wives.[61] It cannot be concluded, therefore, that it was the educational level that made the significant happiness differentiation.

Two studies by Landis and Landis are probably the most inclusive of all in this area. After an examination of 1704 cases in which the husband had more education than the wife, and 1532 cases of the reverse situation, they concluded that similarity in levels of educational attainment is only slightly favorable to good marriage adjustment.[62] A limited study of one hundred couples by Hamilton over thirty years ago found a strong correlation between marital happiness and level of formal schooling.[63] Educational differences seemed more important then, but nowadays there is much more opportunity for informal learning. The differences in formal education are not as important to a couple as their ability to observe and utilize the knowledge that each gains through living. Couples with a healthy outlook on life do not seem adversely affected by differences in formal education.

MATURITY AND INTELLIGENCE. The fact that more successful marriages are found where both partners have a high degree of educational attainment may have little actual connection with the education involved. By and large, college graduates who marry are less likely to be divorced than the rest of society, but they are usually older when they marry; they are probably more mature simply because they have lived a little longer before marriage. Wives who finish college average almost twenty-four years of age when they marry; their husbands average twenty-six years of age.[64] Both Paul Glick of the U.S. Bureau of Census, and Hugh Carter of the National Office of Vital Statistics, have said that there is a direct relationship between education and successful marriage, and that this may well be the result of better education for marriage.[65]

A 1950 study of the graduating classes from Cornell for the years 1919–21, inclusive, found 6 per cent of the graduates' first marriages had terminated in divorce and/or separation. By comparison, the rate of divorce for first marriages in the general population (with marriage dates matched to those of the Cornell students) was found to be 16 per cent, and a substantial additional percentage had ended in separation.[66]

A survey of the late 1940s indicated an over-all divorce rate of 5.8 per cent for college married men, and 11–13 per cent for the total population. The rate of divorce for college women graduates was found to be only slightly less than that for all married women, but the rate of separation was only one fourth as much.[67] The findings from that study have been supported by more recent census data.[68]

A difference in basic intelligence is probably much more significant than educational level. It is much more difficult for a marriage to be successful when there is a radical disparity in basic intelligence. Such a difference limits the area of common ties, and even becomes more significant with time. The more intelligent individual continues to grow, while the less intelligent one tends to stand still. Despondency and increasing feelings of loneliness and inferiority are then likely to be experienced by the less intelligent mate. The marriage will face more problems each year. Early romantic love should blend into a more pronounced conjugal feeling as marriage progresses, but this is next to impossible where there is a wide variation in basic intelligence. A freer exchange of ideas can counterbalance the diminishing urge for physical embraces, but if this does not happen, the couple are quite likely to drift farther and farther apart.

Intelligence is often confused with education, for crude as it may be, educational attainment is one index of basic intelligence. Because it takes a certain amount of intelligence to achieve a high level of education, people with similar education are likely to be somewhat similar in intelligence. Most individuals usually have more intelligence than they ever use, so there is really less reason for education to give rise to serious differences if the less intelligent of the two "comes alive."

Nationality and ethnic differences

Ethnic groups are those that are citizens of one country but closely identify themselves with another. Examples of such groups in the United States include Syrians, Greeks, Italians, Cubans, and Swedes. Such groups are more often than not quite ethnocentric; that is, they guard their former national heritage with extreme vigor, and many of their members sincerely believe in the supremacy of their kind over all others. In some such groups there is an organized hierarchy of elders whose duty it is to "crack the whip" over the youth. They see that the youth maintain a distance from outsiders, continue to respect the traditions and customs of the group, and select their mates from within the group. To an outsider all of this may appear to be a bit ridiculous, but most of these groups are in earnest. They know themselves to be a minority. They recognize the fact that, unless it maintains a set of hard-and-fast rules, a minority group in a country like the United States is likely to disappear. The intense belief that theirs is the "best" group often inspires severely restrictive measures upon the activities of their youth.

A marriage of mixed nationalities involves a couple with differing citizenship loyalties; a marriage of two people from different ethnic groups does not. The problems of the two types are so similar, however, that they can easily be discussed together.

The greater the contrast in nationality backgrounds, the greater the difficulty in the marriage. Customs, standards, and points of view may be at odds. The attitudes toward woman and her rights, duties, and position in the family are often extremely different. Even the question of when and how a demonstration of affection is considered acceptable is often confusing to the outsider. Family patterns of authority, distribution of wealth, or role expectations of various members is often shocking to the average young American. Sexual morality may differ, as may the "morality" regarding the responsibility for the care of elders by the younger members of the family.

The possibility of marital difficulties depends upon the actual differences between the two groups represented and the attitudes each group holds toward the other. Englishmen and Americans are not too different, but because some Irish have been conditioned to be suspicious of English, an Irish-American clan might resist accepting someone of English extraction even though they had much in common.

LIVING ABROAD. When marriage means that one spouse must leave his native country, additional problems may arise. Going to another country may appear to be adventurous, but such things as learning another language, seeing the children readily acquire strange customs, and homesickness soon cloud the picture. The drastic change of citizenship most usually must be faced by the woman. Greater in-law adjustment and severe social reorganization is also incurred by this move.

CHANCES FOR HAPPINESS. It is not known exactly how many World War II marriages of mixed nationality have subsequently failed, but according to Blood, the International Migration Service reported that more than 12,000 broke up before the end of the first year.[69] This rate would appear to be much higher than that for marriages between people of the same nationality.

Physical characteristics

Many people know husbands and wives who resemble each other physically. One theory is that a person tends to fall in love with someone who greatly resembles a past love object. This, of course, in many instances means the parent of the opposite sex, so the tendency for many husbands and wives to look somewhat alike might be explained on this basis. Burgess and Wallin found that similarities of such items as height, weight, health, and physical appearance were all correlated between mates at a rate far above chance.[70]

Society itself is a big factor in promoting similar physical characteristics between mates. When dating partners possess significant differences in physical stature, people tend to poke fun at their differences. Society expects the husband to be taller than the wife, but if he is too much taller the couple is often referred to as "Mutt and Jeff." Added to the difficulties of an already unstable marriage, the insults of society can spell disaster.

It is also much more likely that a forgive-and-forget policy can be more easily established when the partner closely resembles an earlier love object. Physical characteristics have a decided influence in mate selection, and it is probably healthy that they do.

Previous marital status

To marry someone who has been married before is rarely the same as a marriage between partners who have always been single. Sometimes the less experienced partner feels he is being compared with the previous mate, while the spouse may lack the eagerness of "the first time." If the partner's first marriage was a happy one, this fact will undoubtedly affect the new relationship at times; if unhappy, it probably left a few sensitive spots. It would certainly be wise at least to identify and understand the problems. Research conducted in the State of Iowa suggests that remarriage after widowhood is about as stable as primary marriages, but that remarriage for the divorced is significantly more risky.[71]

EXAMINE THE MOTIVES. Perhaps the best rule when marrying someone previously wed is to learn as much about the first marriage as possible. No one should become the victim of an individual on the rebound or who is simply desperate to remarry.[72] If there has been a divorce, why? How long ago? What were the circumstances surrounding the first marriage relationship? What happened? Could the second marriage possibly be motivated by a desire for revenge on the first mate? What is his expressed attitude toward the first spouse? Might the first spouse re-enter the picture? Why is marriage desired with the new person? Does the new partner resemble the first spouse in some ways and, if so, in what ways? As Becker and Hill suggest: "In remarriage where one person is widowed, the new mate may be found to be competing with an idealized ghost."[73] Does he ever compare the second with the first spouse? In what ways?

If there was a bereavement, probably the most important thing to know is how long ago it occurred. Has the individual readjusted himself from the crisis of the loss? Is he full of optimism about the future of his pending marriage, or does he sometimes seem depressed? These and many other questions should be considered before the marriage. It is also important that the uninitiated partner try to gain insight into the needs and desires of the prospective mate and the kind of relationship he is most likely to repeat.

Marital happiness can result with a spouse who has been previously married, and there are numerous cases of fine second marriages. There are also many cases with significant and unusual differences between the spouses. Such marriages therefore must be considered mixed.

SPECIAL PROBLEMS.   The special problems of marriage to a person with previous marital experience can be generally classified into three areas: social, economic, and family-centered.

Special social problems revolve around (1) in-laws and their attitude of acceptance, rejection, or comparison of the new mate with the former spouse; (2) the acceptance of the new relationship by the friends of both partners and the community in which they will live; and (3) the attitudes of the former spouse, if alive, toward the new marriage, and of the former spouse's friends and relatives. If the former partner is still in the community, it is quite likely that he or she and the new couple will be cast together socially on more than one occasion.

Special economic problems may be encountered where there was a divorce with alimony commitments. This can increase the "overhead" of a second marriage tremendously. If the proposed partner lost the first spouse through a long illness, there may be a large unpaid debt.

Special family problems arise when there are children by the first marriage. If additional children are planned in the new marriage, there may be divided loyalties on the part of parents and offspring. Children serve as a constant reminder of the former marriage. Also, there is the issue of discipline for the spouse's children. A survey of 4300 children compared those having step-parents to those from unbroken homes. Among other things it was found that "step-parent families" usually had (1) more children, especially where there was a stepmother; (2) a higher rate of geographic mobility; (3) a lower rate of church attendance by both the children and the parents; (4) a lower rating of parental happiness by the children, especially where there was a stepfather; and (5) a better adjustment between step-parent and child of the same sex than of the opposite sex.[74]

THE DIVORCE FACTS.   The real facts concerning a divorce are important to a proposed new marriage. Seldom, if ever, is a divorce a completely one-sided affair. Unless the potential partner fully understands this, and is willing to face up to the facts, the risk of repeating the same mistake is very real. As Goode points out in his study, remarriage is seldom an improvement when part of the problem is still within the divorced person.[75] In spite of all extenuating circumstances, there is a likelihood that the divorced person still has some feelings of love for the former mate. Most marriage counselors generally agree that most divorced persons never completely succeed in disestablishing themselves from some emotion toward their former spouses.

OTHER RESEARCH FINDINGS.   In general, marriages to divorced persons have more hazards than ordinary marriages. Monahan's studies indicate this type of marriage to be 50 per cent more risky; furthermore, his findings show second marriages for women to be more risky than for men. If the person has experienced only one divorce, his chances for success are greater than if he has had several marital experiences.[76] It must be re-emphasized, however, that the majority of today's remarriages following one divorce are relatively stable and happy affairs. In fact, some marriages of this type approach a degree of success much to be desired by all.

The remarriage of divorced and widowed persons is a frequent event in the United States. It is estimated that approximately 20 per cent of each year's American marriages involve persons with previous marital experience. This does not mean that the unmarried person's chances of marrying someone previously married are one in five, for there is a tendency for divorced persons to marry other divorced persons. According to the U.S. Department of Health, Education, and Welfare, 78.5 per cent of all the marriages that took place in 1959 involved single partners; 18 per cent were second marriages for at least one partner; 3 per cent were third marriages; and 0.5 per cent were fourth (or later) marriages.

Many divorced individuals remarry; in fact, age for age, the chances of remarriage for both divorced and widowed individuals is higher than for single persons. Widowers appear more likely to remarry than widows, but the difference is not great. Widowed women with small children tend to remarry very soon after bereavement or not at all. According to the U.S. Bureau of Census, at age thirty the single woman has about a fifty-to-fifty chance to marry; the widowed woman, a sixty-to-forty chance, and the divorced woman, a ninety-four-to-six chance! At age forty-five, the chances of remarriage for the divorced individual are still better than fifty to fifty, but are less than ten to ninety for single women.[77] The higher rate of remarriage for divorced persons over widowed persons may be related to the possibility that the widowed often have many pleasant memories to sustain them, while the divorced have only unpleasant memories which they hope to erase by another marriage.

Philosophy and values

What is proposed for examination is the extent to which values may be mixed within a marriage, regardless of the presence or absence of other mixtures. This is not to suggest that individuals tend toward radicalism in their values. As a matter of fact, it is probably safe to say that many individuals possess very few values. But two partners may possess defined values that are different, and this is probably the most intensely mixed marriage of all.

ATTITUDES OR VALUES? Most people have attitudes, some of which are expressed overtly and others covertly, but an attitude is not always a value. Attitudes may be correctly considered as basically stemming from religion, race, nationality, socioeconomic class, and other background factors. If one marries a partner from a similar background, he is more nearly assured of a mate with similar attitudes, but values stem from the heart of each individual. Values, to be certain, may be greatly influenced by background, but each individual makes his own values; they are not institutionalized as attitudes may be.

Just because an individual's background can be classified in a particular manner does not assure his has certain prescribed values. A potential partner may be overheard supporting a certain attitude. Does this single experience mean that the attitude is a value? Suppose later on, after some discussion, he expresses a complete reversal in attitude? Does this mean that his values are now changed? Suppose instead, that after some discussion, he re-expresses the original attitude? Does the repeated manifestation of an attitude always mean it is a value? Suppose the individual continuously repeats his original attitude, but confesses that he is unhappy with it? Is it then a value?

APPRAISAL. If a person grows up exposed to certain predetermined ideas or attitudes, but has not on his own initiative made an effort to appraise them, it is doubtful that they are *his* values. Some people give little thought to why they believe what they do. They grow up within a certain fenced-in program. They support the ideas imposed by their environmental influences, without really knowing why. Such people do not necessarily have special values, for they have not given any personal thought to why they feel as they do.

If, after a critical analysis of all the facts, the individual still supports a designated attitude, then it closely resembles a value.

CALLS FOR DEDICATED ACTION. To become a true value, the expressed attitude must be supported by the individual's actions within the society. He should be willing, for example, to join forces with those professing similar attitudes and work for their acceptance by others. His choice of friends, entertainment, education, or cash donations should be designed to support the attitude. In short, when the accepted attitude permeates the individual's life to the extent that he is willing to organize his resources to perpetuate the idea, then it is a value. Without this dedication, it is not a true value.

A value is determined by (1) a pattern of repetition; (2) an affirmation of the attitude after exposure to alternatives; and (3) a dedication to it by action. As John Dewey has stated: "Values are the things, ideas, institutions, and processes which we prize, cherish, or hold dear."[78] In this connection, it would seem possible that any form of mixed marriage might be successful if the two individuals both prize a successful marriage more than the uncommon attitudes they encourage or represent. If marital success is only an attitude, and not the highest value, then a mixed marriage should probably be avoided.

Summary

A mixed marriage has been defined as one in which the culture and the spouses consider that there are significant and unusual differences between the partners, but the partners are unable to change identification with their separate groups. Mixtures usually involve special problems in one or all of four areas of living: (1) between the spouses, (2) between the families and the couple, (3) between society and the couple, and (4) between various combinations of the first three and the offspring of the couple. The motives for many mixed marriages may be unsound. Several of the most prominent types of mixed marriages in American society were identified, and the special problems and implications of each examined.

It would seem from an examination of the facts that mixed marriages are taken too lightly in today's American society, in spite of the increased divorce risk they entail.

Second, the possibility of changing any significant difference after marriage is usually rare. If differences exist, the couple must adjust to them before marriage. In some cases, a relationship with a radically different individual should seldom progress beyond the casual-dating stage.

Third, it is well to remember that a mixed marriage includes all the problems of any marriage plus the problems evolving around the differences. At best, it may be a hazardous relationship.

Fourth, mixed marriages are not doomed to failure; some do succeed. Nevertheless, the fewer the differences between mates, the less is the strain on the relationship. Some people are able to endure more stress than others, and some mixed marriages can succeed if the partners face and solve the special problems involved. Some marriages are doomed to failure because the partners do not possess sufficient strength as persons.

Last, a word of caution: the success of any mixed marriage depends not only on solving the special problems involved, but upon total adjustment as well. The values which each partner holds dearest are a determining factor. Most cases of marriage failure or unrest arise not from a single factor but from many factors. It is easy to blame marital difficulties arising from other causes onto the obvious difference between the spouses.

PRE-NUPTIAL AGREEMENT [79]

*To be Signed by Applicants for Dispensation from Impediment of
Mixed Religion or Disparity of Cult*

Non-Catholic Party

I, the undersigned _____ of _____, not a member of the Catholic Church, desiring to contract marriage with _____ of _____, who is a member of the Catholic Church, propose to do so with the understanding that the marriage bond thus contracted can be broken only by death.

And thereupon in consideration that if the Catholic Church grants the necessary dispensation for such marriage, I, the said _____, do hereby covenant, promise, and agree to and with the said _____ that (he) (she), the said _____, shall be permitted the free exercise of religion according to the Catholic faith without hindrance or adverse comment and that all the children of either sex born of such marriage, as soon as possible after their birth, shall be baptized and carefully educated only in the faith and according to the teachings of the Roman Catholic Church by those most competent to do so, even if the said _____ shall die first. In case of dispute, I furthermore hereby agree that the custody of the children shall be given to such guardians as to assure the faithful execution of this covenant.

I hereby promise that no other marriage ceremony than by the Catholic priest shall take place.

I furthermore realize the holiness of the use of marriage according to the teaching of the Catholic Church which condemns birth control and similar abuses of marriage. I shall have due respect for the religious principles and convictions of my Catholic partner.

Witness my hand this _____ day of _____ 19_____ at _____ in the County of _____ and State of _____ signed in the presence of Rev. _____.

_____

Signature of Non-Catholic

Catholic Party

I, the undersigned _____, a member of the Catholic Church, of _____ Parish _____, wishing to contract marriage with _____, a non-Catholic, only after understanding the import of my action, do hereby solemnly promise to have all the children of either sex, born of this marriage, baptized and reared only in the Catholic faith. I understand that in the event of a dispute, the custody of all the children shall be given to such guardians as to assure the faithful execution of this covenant.

Furthermore, I promise that no other marriage ceremony than that by the Catholic priest shall take place.

I also realize my obligation in conscience to practice my religion faithfully and prudently to endeavor especially by prayer, good example, and the reception of the Sacraments, to induce my life partner to investigate seriously the teachings of the Catholic Church in the hope that such investigation may lead to conversion. I further promise to live within this marriage in conformity with the laws of the Catholic Church regarding birth control, realizing and fully understanding the attitude of the Catholic Church in this regard.

Witness my hand this _____ day of _____ 19_____ at _____ in the County of _____ and State of _____ signed in the presence of Rev. _____.

_____

Signature of Catholic
Priest

I, the undersigned, do hereby declare that I am morally certain that the promises herein made before me by both the Catholic and non-Catholic party were fully understood, freely entered into, and will be fulfilled.

_____

Signature of Priest

Notes

1. Amram Scheinfeld, *You and Heredity* (New York: Frederick Stokes, 1939), pp. 67–68.

2. Carson McGuire, "Social Stratification and Mobility Patterns," *American Sociological Review,* 15:201.

3. For example, research reported by Strauss indicates that couples in mixed race-nationality marriage associate almost entirely with similar couples. Anselm Strauss, "Strain and Harmony in American Japanese War-Bride Marriages," *Marriage and Family Living,* 16:99-106.

4. Evelyn M. Duvall, *In-Laws Pro and Con* (New York: Association Press, 1954).

5. Unpublished research from the author's counseling files.

6. See, e.g., the counseling case reviewed by M. J. Karpf, "Marriage Counseling and Psychotherapy: A Case," *Marriage and Family Living,* 13:169-78.

7. According to Cannel there have been over 60,000 marriages between American GI's and Japanese girls since the end of World War II, and Japan is presently averaging about 4000 such unions a year. Most of these Japanese brides are from the lower socioeconomic classes, but possess better education than their GI husbands. See Ward Cannel, "United States—Japanese Marriages Undisturbed by Politics," *NEA News Release* (April 1960).

8. Taken from the author's counseling files.

9. Fourteen per cent more engagements were reported to have ended before marriage where the couple represented differing religions including differing

Protestant denominations, than otherwise. E. W. Burgess and Paul Wallin, *Engagement and Marriage* (Philadelphia: J. B. Lippincott Co., 1953), p. 289.

10. James H. S. Bossard and Harold C. Letts, "Mixed Marriages Involving Lutherans—A Research Report," *Marriage and Family Living,* 18:308–10. A comprehensive study of all interdenominational marriages for the state of Iowa is reported to be nearing completion. For details of progress contact Director, Agricultural and Home Economics Experiment Station, Iowa State University, Ames, Iowa.

11. Milton L. Barron, "The Incident of Jewish Intermarriage in Europe and America," *American Sociological Review,* 11:11–12.

12. *Ibid.,* p. 11; and Ruby Jo Reeves Kennedy, "Single or Triple Melting Pot? Intermarriage Trends in New Haven, 1870–1950," *American Journal of Sociology,* 57:56; and Paul C. Glick, "Intermarriage and Fertility Pattern Among Persons in Major Religious Groups," *Eugenics Quarterly,* 7:31–38. Of course, it must be recognized that this rate would vary by communities. This figure has reference to the nation as a whole. Recent research found the rate in some communities to be over three times the normal national rate. See Lorene Chancellor, and Thomas P. Monahan, "Religious Preference and Interreligious Mixtures in Marriages and Divorces in Iowa," *American Journal of Sociology,* 61: 233–39.

13. The same comment made earlier, applies here. Exceptions like New York City must be recognized. In some areas of the United States, Protestantism is actually a minority religion. Census figures disclose that about 75 per cent of United States citizens of the Jewish faith reside in five states: New York, Pennsylvania, New Jersey, Illinois, and Massachusetts. New York State alone accounts for nearly one half of all American Jews, with over 2 million residing in New York City.

14. John L. Thomas, "The Factor of Religion in the Selection of Marriage Mates," *American Sociological Review,* 16:491.

15. Estimates based on research by Catholic authorities during the 1950s were that 15 to 25 per cent of Catholics who marry in a given year do so outside the church. John L. Thomas, *The American Catholic Family* (Englewood Cliffs, N.J.: Prentice-Hall, Inc., 1956), p. 154. A more recently published report by C. Stanley Lowell, *Protestant-Catholic Marriage* (New York: Broadman Press, 1962), estimates that in about 40 per cent of the cases of Catholic–non-Catholic marriage the ceremony takes place outside the Catholic church, that in about one third of the mixed marriages taking place in the church, the couple ultimately leave Catholicism.

16. C. A. Liederbach, *When a Catholic Marries* (Milwaukee: The Bruce Publishing Company, 1949), p. 47–48.

17. Thomas, "The Factor of Religion in the Selection of Marriage Mates," *op. cit.,* p. 491.

18. Harvey J. Locke, "Interfaith Marriages," *Social Problems,* 4:329–33. Locke found the rate-range for Catholic–non-Catholic intermarriage to be from a low of 13 per cent in New Mexico to a high of 70 per cent in North Carolina.

19. Thomas, "The Factor of Religion in the Selection of Marriage Mates," *op. cit.,* pp. 467–91.

20. See Catholic Pamphlet Publication by Fathers Rumble and Carty, *Six Premarriage Instructions for Catholics and Non-Catholics* (St. Paul, Minn.: Radio Replies Press).

21. See a typical prenuptial application request for special dispensation to be signed by parties to a mixed Catholic marriage at end of chapter; or consult

pamphlet by Warren Lilly, *The Mixed Marriage Prenuptial Contract* (New York: The Catholic Information Society).

22. For more detailed information on this possibility, see article by Father Dulou, "Pauline Privilege," *Catholic Biblical Quarterly*, 13:146–52.

23. J. Anthony Samenfink, "A Study of Some Aspects of Marital Behavior as Related to Religious Control," *Marriage and Family Living*, 20:163–67.

24. Suggestions for Catholics in this situation are discussed in John S. Banahan, *Instructions for Mixed Marriages* (Milwaukee: The Bruce Publishing Company, 1957).

25. Murrah H. Leiffer, "Mixed Marriages and Church Loyalties," *Christian Century* (January 19, 1949): 78–80. It needs to be noted that there are strong advocates among high Catholic leaders at present to eliminate some of the promises now required in a mixed marriage.

26. Edger Schmiedeler, *Marriage and the Family* (New York: McGraw-Hill Book Company, Inc., 1946), p. 111.

27. Leland Foster Wood, *If I Marry a Roman Catholic* (New York: Commission of Marriage and the Home of the Federal Council of the Churches of Christ in America, 1945).

28. See Judson T. Landis, "Marriages of Mixed and Nonmixed Religious Faiths," *American Sociological Review*, 14:401–407; Howard M. Bell, *Youth Tell Their Story* (Washington, D.C.: American Council on Education, 1938), p. 21; H. Ashley Weeks, "Differential Divorce Rates by Occupations," *Social Forces*, 21:336; Lee G. Burchinal and Lorene Chancellor, "Survival Rates Among Religiously Homogamous and Interreligious Marriages," *Research Bulletin No. 512758* (December 1962).

29. Thomas P. Monahan and William M. Kephart, "Divorces and Desertion by Religious and Mixed-Religious Groups," *American Journal of Sociology*, 59:454–65.

30. Dorothy T. Dyer and Eleanore Luckey, "Religious Affiliation and Selected Personality Scores as They Relate to Marital Happiness of a Minnesota College Sample," *Marriage and Family Living*, 23:46–47; and Alfred J. Prince, "A Study of 194 Cross-Religion Marriages," *The Family Life Coordinator*, 11:3–7.

31. Jerome S. Heiss, "Premarital Characteristics of the Religiously Intermarried in an Urban Area," *American Sociological Review*, 25:47–55. Prince reported finding that 42 per cent of spouses in interfaith marriages, and 60 per cent of those in interdenominational marriages, were themselves offspring of similar mixed marriages. See reference above.

32. Clinical Observations of the author and of many other marriage educators known to him suggest this quite strongly.

33. Over 50 per cent of Protestant students on a college campus indicated willingness to marry a person of another faith "other things being equal." See Judson T. and Mary G. Landis, *Building a Successful Marriage*, 4th ed. (Englewood Cliffs, N.J.: Prentice-Hall, Inc., 1963), Chap. 13. Over one third of Catholic students attending a Catholic college indicated willingness to enter an interfaith marriage. See Thomas, "The Factor of Religion in the Selection of Marriage Mates," *op. cit.*, p. 491. A recent survey at Rutgers found the majority of Jewish students, 40 per cent of Catholic students, and only 10 per cent of Protestant students opposed to mixed religious marriages. See Joseph Maier and William Spinrad, "Religious Convictions and Religious Behavior," *Sociological Abstracts*, 8: Report Number 7138. The increase in interfaith marriage in recent years has not been confined to the United States. For example, the increase in Canada from 1927 to 1957 amounted to 132 per cent for Protestants, 126 per cent for

Jews, and 60 per cent for Catholics. See David M. Heer, "The Trend of Inter-faith Marriages in Canada," *American Sociological Review,* 27:245–50.

34. Joseph Golden, "Pattern of Negro-White Intermarriage," *American Sociological Review,* 19:144–47.

35. Charles Rogler, "Morality of Race Mixing in Puerto Rico," *Social Forces,* 25:77–81.

36. "When Negro Servicemen Bring Home White Brides," *U.S. News & World Report,* 43 (October 11, 1957): 110–13.

37. The Chester County Court of Pennsylvania forbade intermarriage between whites and Negroes as long ago as 1698.

38. Ray E. Baber, "A Study of 325 Mixed Marriages," *American Sociological Review,* 2:705–16.

39. Paul H. Jacobson, *American Marriage and Divorce* (New York: Holt, Rinehart & Winston, Inc., 1959), p. 62.

40. Louis Wirth and Herbert Goldhamer, "The Hybrid and the Problem of Miscegenation," in Otto Klineberg (ed.), *Characteristics of the American Negro* (New York: Harper & Row, Publishers, 1944), p. 277.

41. Baber, *op. cit.,* pp. 705–16. Burma's study in Los Angeles County, California from 1948 to 1951 disclosed 445 marriages between whites and other races with the wife being white in three out of four cases. See John H. Burma, "Research Note on the Measurement of Interracial Marriages," *American Journal of Sociology,* 57:587–89.

42. *Ibid.*

43. See latest edition of *The United Nation's Demographic Year Book* (New York: Columbia University Press).

44. Baber, *op. cit.,* pp. 705–16.

45. Romanzo Adams, *Interracial Marriage in Hawaii* (New York: The Macmillan Company, 1937), p. 49; and C. K. Cheng and Douglas S. Yamaura, "Interracial Marriage and Divorce in Hawaii," *Social Forces,* 36:77–84.

46. Baber, *op. cit.,* pp. 705–16.

47. Quoted in Clement Simon Mihanovich, Gerald J. Schneep, and John L. Thomas, *A Guide to Catholic Marriage* (Milwaukee: The Bruce Publishing Company, 1954), p. 173.

48. "The New America the Census Shows," *U.S. News & World Report,* 50 (January 2, 1961): 72.

49. Allan Nevins, "A Historian Predicts Intermarriage of the Races 'Will Be Inevitable,' " *U.S. News & World Report,* 45 (November 14, 1958): 72.

50. Glen H. Elder, Jr., "Structural Variations in the Child Rearing Relationship," *Sociometry,* 25:241–62.

51. E. W. Burgess and Leonard S. Cottrell, *Predicting Success or Failure in Marriage* (Englewood Cliffs, N.J.: Prentice-Hall, Inc., 1939), pp. 354–55.

52. Howard E. Freeman and Leo G. Reeder, "Social-Class and Reference-Group Theory," *Research Studies of the State College of Washington,* 24, 2 (June 1956), 178.

53. For a concise but well-organized discussion of various attitudes associated with social-class orientation, see Ruth Shonle Cavan, *The American Family* (New York: Thomas Y. Crowell Company, 1953), pp. 119–242.

54. Julius Roth and Robert F. Peck, "Social-Class and Social-Mobility Factors Related to Marital Adjustment," *American Sociological Review,* 16:481.

55. James H. S. Bossard, "The Age Factor in Marriage," *American Journal of Sociology,* 38:538–47.

56. Karl Wallace, "Factors Hindering Mate Selection," *Sociology and Social Research*, 44:317–25.

57. Harvey J. Locke, *Predicting Adjustment in Marriage* (New York: Holt, Rinehart & Winston, Inc., 1951), p. 103.

58. Lewis M. Terman, *Psychological Factors in Marital Happiness* (New York: McGraw-Hill Book Company, Inc., 1938), p. 186.

59. The theory of complementary needs as a basis for mate selection has been presented by Robert Winch, *Mate Selection* (New York: Harper & Row, Publishers, 1958), and will receive a deservably more complete discussion in Chap. 6.

60. Burgess and Cottrell, *op. cit.*, p. 121.

61. Terman, *op. cit.*, p. 190.

62. Landis and Landis, *op. cit.*, Chap. 13.

63. Gilbert V. Hamilton, *A Research in Marriage* (New York: Albert and Charles Boni, 1929), p. 513.

64. Paul C. Glick and Hugh Carter, "Marriage Pattern and Educational Level," *American Sociological Review*, 23:294–300.

65. *NEA Journal* (November 1958), pp. 531–32.

66. W. A. Anderson, *Marriages and Families of University Graduates* (Ithaca, N.Y.: Cornell University Press, 1950), p. 15.

67. Ernest Havemann and Patricia Salter West, *They Went to College: The College Graduate in America Today* (New York: Harcourt, Brace & World, Inc., 1952), pp. 41, 78.

68. Paul C. Glick, *American Families* (New York: John Wiley & Sons, Inc., 1957), p. 154.

69. Robert O. Blood, *Anticipating Your Marriage* (New York: The Free Press of Glencoe, Inc., 1955), p. 51.

70. E. W. Burgess and Paul Wallin, "Monogamy in Personality Characteristics," *Journal of Abnormal and Social Psychology*, 39:475–81.

71. Thomas P. Monahan, "The Changing Nature and Instability of Remarriages," *Eugenics Quarterly*, 5 (1958): 73–85.

72. Research by Glick indicates that remarriage after divorce usually happens within the first five years or not at all. See Paul C. Glick, "First Marriages and Remarriage," *American Sociological Review*, 14:726–34. Divorced persons usually have a much shorter acquaintance and a shorter engagement or no engagement at all. All this suggests that some second marriages may well be marriage on the rebound. See August B. Hollingshead, "Marital Status and Wedding Behavior," *Marriage and Family Living*, 14:307–11.

73. Howard Becker and Reuben Hill (eds.), *Family, Marriage and Parenthood* (Boston: D. C. Heath and Company, 1955), p. 314.

74. Charles E. Bowerman, "Family Background and Parental Adjustment of Step-Children," *Research Studies of State College of Washington* (June 1956), pp. 181–82.

75. William J. Goode, *After Divorce* (New York: The Free Press of Glencoe, Inc., 1956), Chap. 22.

76. Thomas P. Monahan, "How Stable Are Remarriages?," *American Journal of Sociology*, 58:280–88.

77. U.S. Department of Health, Education, and Welfare, *Vital Statistics— Special Report*, Vol. 50 (November 1959), 40–45.

78. John Dewey, *Theory of Valuation, International Encyclopedia of Unified Science*, Vol. II, No. 4 (Chicago: University of Chicago Press, 1939), pp. 4–6.

79. Prenuptial agreement applications vary somewhat in form in different

sections of the United States. In essence, however, all contain about the same ideas as the forms shown here.

Questions for further thought

1. Is homogamous mate selection consistent or inconsistent with the American concept of democracy?
2. How is it that almost everyone knows of an instance of a mixed marriage which is highly successful?
3. Would the encouragement of various types of mixed marriages among those who are unprejudiced tend eventually to reduce hatred and intolerance among various groups?
4. Should an individual who is very devout, and somewhat aghast at the thought of an interfaith marriage, ever date persons of other faiths?
5. Why is it so often true that within Christian homes the wife assumes the role of religious leader?
6. Because all religions within the Judeo-Christian concept share the same fundamental code, what accounts for the many problems of interfaith marriage?
7. How best can a wife without a college education keep pace with a college-graduate husband?
8. If experience is such a good teacher, why is marriage to a divorced person a much greater risk?
9. In the light of trends, should more research on the various types of mixed marriages be focused on those that fail or on those that succeed?

Recommended film

One Love, Conflicting Faiths (Methodist Publishing House).

Suggested supplemental readings

BOOKS

Bach, Marcus. *Had You Been Born in Another Faith*. Englewood Cliffs, N.J.: Prentice-Hall, Inc., 1961.

The Basic Cana Manual. Chicago: Delaney Publication, 1963.

Bernard, Jessie. *Remarriage*. New York: The Dryden Press, 1956.

Berry, Brewton. *Almost White*. New York: The Macmillan Company, 1963.

Bossard, James H. S., and Eleanor S. Boll. *One Marriage, Two Faiths*. New York: The Ronald Press Company, 1957.

Bouyer, Louis. *The Spirit and Forms of Protestantism*. Cleveland: World Publishing Company, 1964.

Cahnman, Werner J. (ed.). *Intermarriage and Jewish Life in America*. New York: Herzel Press, 1963.

Cavan, Ruth Shonle. *The American Family*. New York: Thomas Y. Crowell Company, 1953. Chaps. 5–9.

Colacci, Mario. *Christian Marriage Today: A Comparison of Roman Catholic and Protestant Views*. Minneapolis: Augsburg Press, 1959.

Drake, St. Clare, and H. R. Cayton. *Black Metropolis*, rev. ed. New York: Harper & Row, Publishers, 1962. Vols. I and II.

Gordon, Albert I. *Intermarriage: Interfaith, Interracial, Interethnic*. Boston: Beacon Press, 1964.

Handlin, Oscar. *The Uprooted*. Boston: Little, Brown & Co., 1952.

Kelly, George Anthony. *Dating for Young Catholics.* Garden City, N.Y.: Double-day & Company, Inc., 1963.

Komarousky, Mirra. *Blue-Collar Marriage.* New York: Random House, 1965.

Lally, Francis J. *The Catholic Church in a Changing America.* Boston: Little, Brown & Co., 1962.

Lowell, C. Stanley. *Protestant-Catholic Marriage.* New York: Broadman Press, 1962.

Mayer, John E. *Jewish-Gentile Courtship.* New York: The Free Press of Glencoe, Inc., 1962.

McCloy, Shelby T. *The Negro in France.* Lexington, Ky.: University of Kentucky Press, 1961.

McKinley, Donald Gilbert. *Social Class and Family Life.* New York: The Free Press of Glencoe, Inc., 1965.

McManus, Eugene P. *Studies in Race Relations.* Baltimore: Josephite Press, 1961. Paperback.

Pelikan, Jaroslav. *The Riddle of Roman Catholicism.* Nashville: Abingdon Press, 1959.

Pike, James A. *If You Marry Outside Your Faith.* New York: Harper & Row, Publishers, 1954.

Queen, Stuart A., Robert W. Habenstein, and John B. Adams. *The Family in Various Cultures.* Philadelphia: J. B. Lippincott & Co., 1965.

Riker, Charles and Audry. *Understanding Marriage.* New York: Paulist Press, 1963.

Shoulson, Abraham B. (ed.). *Marriage and Family Life: A Jewish View.* New York: Twayne Publishers, 1959. Section IV.

Stuber, Stanley I. *Primer on Catholicism for Protestants.* New York: Association Press, 1953.

Thomas, John L. *The Catholic's Viewpoint on Marriage.* Garden City, N.Y.: Hanover House, 1958.

ARTICLES

Beigel, Hugo G. "Body Height in Mate Selection," *Journal of Social Psychology,* **39**:257–68.

Bell, Charles R., Jr. "Don't Sign with Your Fingers Crossed," *Christian Century,* **70**:446–48.

Benson, Purnell. "The Common Interests Myth in Marriage," *Social Problems,* **3**:27–34.

Besancewey, Paul H. "Unbroken Protestant-Catholic Marriages Among Whites in the Detroit Area," *American Catholic Sociological Review,* **23** (Spring 1962) : 3–20.

Biesanz, John. "Inter-American Marriage on the Isthmus of Panama," *Social Forces,* **29**:159–63.

Combs, Robert H. "A Value Theory of Mate Selection," *The Family Life Coordinator,* **10**:51–54.

———. "Reinforcement of Values in the Parental Home as a Factor for Mate Selection," *Marriage and Family Living,* **24**:155–57.

Connel, F. J. "Preparing for a Mixed Marriage," *American Ecclesiastical Review,* **122**:312.

———. "Sufficient Reason to Justify Dispensation from the Banns of Marriage," *American Ecclestiastical Review,* **122**:312.

Freeman, Linton. "Homogamy in Interethnic Mate Selection," *Sociology and Social Research,* **39**:369–77.

Glick, Paul C., and Hugh Carter. "Marriage Patterns and Educational Level," *American Sociological Review,* 23:294–300.

Golden, Joseph. "Social Control of Negro-White Intermarriage," *Social Forces,* 36:267–69.

———. "Pattern of Negro-White Intermarriage," *American Sociological Review,* 19:144–47.

———. "Facilitating Factors in Negro-White Intermarriage," *Phylon,* 20:273–81.

Hey, Richard. "Dissimilarity of Religious Background of Marital Partners as a Factor in Marital Conflict." Doctoral Study, Columbia University, New York, June 1963.

Heiss, Jerold S. "Interfaith Marriage and Marital Outcome," *Marriage and Family Living,* 23:228–33.

Hones, Lyle V., and Charles Morris. "Relations of Temperament to the Choice of Values," *Journal of Abnormal and Social Psychology,* 53:345–49.

McGinnis, Robert. "Campus Values in Mate Selection: A Repeat Study," *Social Forces,* 36:368–73.

Prince, Alfred J. "A Study of 194 Cross-Religion Marriages," *The Family Life Coordinator,* 11:3–7.

Slotkin, J. S. "Adjustment in Jewish-Gentile Intermarriages," *Social Forces,* 21: 226–30.

Thomas, John L. "Outgroup Marriage Patterns of Some Selected Ethnic Groups," *American Catholic Sociological Review,* 15 (March 1954): 9–18.

Traynor, Victor J. "Urban and Rural Mixed Marriages," *Social Order,* 6:154–58.

Veatch, Elsa Mae. "Problems of College Students from Interfaith or Interdenominational Marriages at West Virginia University, 1963." Master's Thesis, West Virginia University, Morgantown, West Virginia, May 1963.

"Would You Want Your Daughter to Marry a Negro?" *U.S. News & World Report,* 48 (May 9, 1960): 116–19.

Becoming

～ chapter *6* ～ marriageable

No one is a perfect mate; there are areas of conflict between even the most closely matched spouses. It is sound to select a partner whose background is similar to one's own, particularly as the complexities of living increase. In preparing for a successful marriage in a democratic society, however, the aim should be to widen the field of selection, not to restrict it. Therefore, the best way for young Americans to become more marriageable is to develop those personal qualities that will make them adaptable partners. Today, becoming as marriageable as possible is as important as selecting the right mate.

Homogamy of selection

Under the prevailing circumstances in our society, it is surprising that homogamy operates as much as it does. Apparently, when marriage is seriously considered, like tends to attract like. It is this factor that tends to stabilize marital selection even in a democratic society, where a Constitution guarantees freedom of choice based on equal rights for all its citizens.

ATTRACTION OF THE FAMILIAR. In a majority of his study cases, Strauss found that a remarkable resemblance existed between mates in background areas such as religion, social class, race, and so forth. In fact, many mates in his study closely resembled one another in a physical way.[1] Hollingshead reported similar findings, and suggested that a "consciousness of kind" appears to operate for many people, eliminating from their mate-selection possibilities those who are radically different in background.[2]

In spite of this truism, even the best "background matches" may have difficulty. Obviously, there is more to marital happiness than merely selecting a mate with the same background.

DESIRABLE PERSONALITY TRAITS. This attraction of similarity even in areas that seem different probably arises from stronger similarities of needs. Research indicates that couples with a reasonably happy marriage, and yet radically different backgrounds, have personality traits that are stronger and that fulfill the needs established by the respective backgrounds of the partners. The fulfillment of their basic desires thus counterbalance apparent differences of background. Several studies have been made on this principle. As a general rule, the students are asked to list the qualities they desire most in a mate. Hill's survey found the following characteristics most often checked: (1) dependability, (2) emotional stability, (3) pleasing disposition, (4) attractiveness, (5) good health, and (6) desire for home life and children.[3]

Christensen conducted a similar study with 1157 students[4]; his results were strikingly similar to Hill's. Neeley's study separated male and female responses, but there was very little difference in the first characteristics mentioned.[5]

All such studies can be of value in increasing marriageability and in the selection of a marriage partner. In fact, Strauss concluded that in 73.3 per cent of the cases the actual mate and the ideal were similar along all these lines.[6] There is danger, however, of assuming that checklists are perfect guides to marital bliss, or that unhappiness can be blamed on the partner's not measuring up to formal standards. This is usually not the case. There is a need to be realistic in choosing guidelines. Obviously, few individuals can meet all ideal qualifications at all times.

LIVING EASILY WITH OTHERS. Some people have a better-than-average chance of making a success out of almost any marriage they might enter; others might be expected to experience some difficulty no matter whom they marry. The difficult group has little ability to get along with anyone in or out of marriage. One rather crude but effective way for college students to judge their degree of marriageability is to consider how well they get along with their roommates. Certainly marriage is a much more intimate situation, but in any relationship pleasant people are easier to live with than grouchy ones. There are times in every relationship, of course, when the real task is to keep an equilibrium when the other individual has lost his temporarily. This task is much harder in marriage, because the pair is yoked permanently together, than in a roommate situation where there is the prospect of a change at the end of the school term. The extent to which one can control his moodiness, anxiety, insecurity, and suspiciousness—and particularly his ability to adjust to those reactions in someone else—is a workable index of his marriageability. Failure to build inner strength or to face adversity may indicate that there is no "right" mate because the individual is not the "right" kind of a person. Thus, marital success is strongly related to the capacity for becoming the type of person who can balance out the equation when the partner shows limitations.

Homogamy only establishes a field

Winch has long been contending that homogamy operates past the obvious mixtures to include some or all of the desirable attributes previously mentioned. He further contends that this only establishes a field of selection. From this field, however, the individuals who find the partners who fulfill conscious or subconscious needs usually have the happiest marriages. It may well be that individuals have at least two distinct kinds of needs: (1) parallel, or those which require some degree of similarity, and (2) complementary, or those which must be opposite in order to become compatible. Winch believes that in the most successful marriages the need patterns of each partner "complement" or fill in for the mate's weaknesses.[7] He believes that the tendency for individuals who are decidedly happy in marriage to select a mate unlike themselves in total emotional makeup far exceeds the tendency to select someone emotionally similar. Kerckhoff and Davis explain that there are various "filtering factors" which operate during the mate-selection process. The social attributes presumably operate at the earliest stages; values and parallel needs, in later stages; and complementary needs, still later.[8] Perhaps not all the so-called complementary needs are as yet identified, but a few examples of some of the known ones may serve to illustrate the theory.

ANXIETY. When a person is in a constant state of apprehension, he obviously lacks a sense of security. His opposite would be the optimistic, cheerful type of person. It is Winch's contention that, because their personalities complement one another, their opposite characteristics would prove attractive.

EMOTIONALITY. One individual might react to almost any situation with a great display of feelings. The most desirable trait for such a person's mate, according to Winch, would be a reassuring calmness that would stabilize the other's temperament.

Additional illustrations include the pairing of a domineering person with a submissive mate, or a serious type with a humorous personality.

Maslow lends support to the complementary-need theory in some of his writings.[9] Strauss, in studying 373 engaged or recently married couples in regard to the Winch premise, found a high percentage of similarity between wishes and actual fulfillment, but only 18 per cent of his subjects reported all their major desires were found in the relationship.[10] Strauss concluded that some people appear to have definite mate needs that are far removed from their expressed mate desires. This could be a reasonable explanation for the marital happiness that is sometimes found even though expressed desires remain unsatisfied. It must be noted, however, that the findings from some studies seriously question the validity of Winch's theory of complementary needs.[11]

Being the right mate

Most people have much deeper and more important basic needs than they are ever able to express verbally. Fortunately, many individuals can sense and meet those needs within one other. Perhaps, therefore, it is not as important to identify one's own needs as it is to identify those of other people and to be mature enough to meet these essential needs within a marriage. This adaptability varies with each individual and often accounts for marital happiness in circumstances which would seem most unfavorable. Studies by Locke support this contention.[12] In general, Locke's happily married subjects indicated a much higher rating in adaptability than did his unhappily married ones. Burgess and Wallin pay considerable recognition to this phenomenon, dividing it into three elements: (1) understanding, (2) knowledge of different kinds of responses appropriate to specific situations, and (3) ability to incorporate these responses into behavior.[13]

Much has been written about adaptability and the elements that constitute the quality. For the most part, there is general agreement on three elements: empathy, motivation, and flexibility.

EMPATHY. Recognition of the emotional needs of the partner is the prime requisite for marital adaptability. Empathy is a sensitive projection of the self into the other's condition; whereas sympathy might result in pity, empathy leads to understanding, which may then lead in adapting action to need. Research findings by Murstein suggest that a person's needs do change with age, and thus empathy is just as important to marital success in the later years as at the beginning.[14]

MOTIVATION. Most problems can be solved; yet some couples fail where others succeed in the same problem and circumstances. It is evident that adaptability includes an element of incentive or motivation or, as some call it, determination. This is an active element that varies with each individual. It is not enough to empathize with the spouse; there must also be a willingness to respond in a way that will bring out the best in the relationship.

FLEXIBILITY. In spite of other pleasing attributes, the individual who is too rigid in his behavior pattern can be difficult to live with at times. In today's society the individual must be able to bend without breaking. The extent to which each person can do this in marriage without threatening himself appears to be a definite part of adaptability. If it makes the individual uncomfortable to bring out the best in the mate, then he may not become adaptable—no matter how much empathy or motivation he may possess.

Conditioning factors

People become adaptable; they are not born that way. Certain experiences in life tend to condition a person toward greater or less adaptability. It would seem wise to examine some of the most influential factors in this connection.

FAMILY FACTORS.   Authorities are unanimous in their belief that most basic traits are formed early in life. This means that the family of orientation plays a vital role in the conditioning process toward or away from adaptability. Stokes, a prominent psychiatrist and marriage counselor, blames faulty family conditioning for much of today's neurosis.

> To tyrannize over children, to ignorantly fail to understand their natural and inescapable personality needs, to attempt to force upon them adult ideals and standards before they can be comprehended, to impose parent's will upon children by a show of overwhelming righteous anger and violence is more than the natural dignity and good feeling of a child can take. His fine qualities are destroyed and replaced by fear and hatred. Potential respect for law and order is undermined, and friendly, responsible social growth is turned into fearful dependence and suspicion. In brief, a neurotic character is created.[15]

There can be little doubt that a good start within the parental family is most important for adaptability. People tend to follow the parents' model in such things as how to settle an argument or how to influence others. Although most people do repeat their parents' behavior pattern, some are so disgusted by this pattern that they desperately reject it. Often this leaves a void of strained awkwardness in adaptability, for without the intimate knowledge of a better model the rejector has no pattern to follow. He may be worse off than the blind follower of a poor pattern.

Some parents unknowingly condition their children away from adaptability by an unawareness of the effects their actions are having and by an inability to change. This may be related either to their own early conditioning or to their being excessively engrossed in solving their own marital troubles. Terman's study supports both of these possibilities.

Terman's findings also indicated the number of siblings in a family to be of little importance, although they seemed to influence the wife's adaptability slightly more than the husband's. The factors most favorable in conditioning toward adaptability were listed by Terman as:

1. Superior happiness of parents in their marriage;
2. Childhood happiness;

3. Lack of conflict with mother;
4. Home discipline—firm but not harsh;
5. Strong attachment to mother;
6. Strong attachment to father;
7. Lack of conflict with father;
8. Parental frankness about matters of sex;
9. Infrequency and mildness of childhood punishment;
10. Premarital attitude free from disgust or aversion toward sex.[16]

Terman concluded that anyone with a background of these favorable factors would be a better-than-average marriage partner. The number one item in his findings was related to parental marital happiness. Other studies lend support to the fact that this single item is very significant to future marital happiness.

Table 6–1. **Relation of parents' marriage to own marital success**

	Childen's marriages were		
	Poor	Fair	Good
Where parents were—	Per cent		
Both very happy	12	13	75
Both happy	25	22	53
One very happy and other happy	30	25	45
One happy and other less than happy	27	33	40
One average, unhappy, or very unhappy and other likewise	38	34	28

Source: E. W. Burgess and Leonard Cottrell, *Predicting Success or Failure in Marriage* (Englewood Cliffs, N.J.: Prentice-Hall, Inc., 1939), p. 101. Copyright © 1939, by Prentice-Hall, Inc., Englewood Cliffs, N.J. Reprinted by permission of the publisher and authors.

Table 6–2. **Relation of grandparents' marriage to parents' marital success**

Marital status of grandparents	Per cent of children divorced
No divorces	14.6
One set divorced	23.7
Both sets divorced	38

Source: Judson T. Landis, "The Pattern of Divorce in Three Generations," *Social Forces,* 34:213–16. Copyright © 1956, by The Williams & Wilkins Co., Baltimore, Md. Reprinted by permission.

The reader must be cautioned at this point not to conclude that desirable character traits result only from happy family influences. As a matter of fact, recent research findings reported by Iowa State University showed no correlation between marital adjustment scores of parents and personality character traits of their fifth-grade children.[17] What studies have shown conclusively is that, as a group, people from homes where parents had happy marriages and where the relationships between parents and children were healthy had more successful marriages than did people from homes with unhappy marriages or where there was friction between parents and children. If marital success is not related to personality character traits, then it may well be related to the intangible talent of adaptability. Research by Carter supports this contention.[18]

This is not the same as saying that family influence is the only way to develop adaptability or that a happy home life will automatically lead to it. Certainly, people are conditioned by factors other than family life.

PEER AND INSTITUTIONAL CONDITIONING. The late Earl Koos suggested that each individual is conditioned by three worlds: (1) the family world, (2) the peer world, and (3) the institutional world. He further suggested that the individual is aided or abetted toward adaptability to the extent that these three worlds are integrated into a smoothly functioning whole. Koos felt that the most marriageable persons were those who had been conditioned favorably by all three factors, but that a strong favorable influence by any two could well offset an unfavorable influence by a third.[19] Cooley, many years ago, pointed out that the peer world was increasing as an influence on the nature of man. He suggested that it was approaching the family as an influence factor, and termed it *the looking-glass self*.[20] Other authorities have also given recognition to the increasing impact of the peer world as a conditioning agent.[21] The institutional world is also increasing as a focal point of influence. Scheinfeld points out that individuals are born male or female, but that it is institutions that teach people to be masculine or feminine.[22] Stoddard even suggests that the nature of institutional surroundings affects mental growth.[23]

There is no denying the fact that individuals now spend more time outside the home in the company of peers and under the influence of other institutions. Indeed, if the peer and institutional influences are healthy and strong, they may even offset the damaging influences of early home conditioning. Research by Robins and O'Neal, in a comparison of an adult group, who were former patients in a children's psychiatric clinic, with a control group, reported a much higher incidence of divorce in the experimental group, which had been in conflict with the social mores, than even among those in the control group who came from legally broken homes.[24] Thus, it should be emphasized that those reared in unhappy homes are not necessarily doomed to marital failure. Perhaps they should develop more insight and caution before approaching marriage, but they need not be the helpless victims of the past.

There is no excuse today for not advancing in adaptability, even if there were problems because of parents, peers, or institutions. It can be helpful first to understand the "how" of the condition; but to make an improvement, a will to change must be developed. If necessary, the individual can take advantage of all the professional help available in the modern era to carry out a change and become more adaptable. Overstreet believes that it is entirely possible in this day and age even for the most poorly adapted individuals to improve if they really want to do so.[25] It is not an easy task, and it usually takes considerable time; however, because such a change decidedly improves chances for marital happiness, it would seem well worth while. It has been demonstrated clinically that, regardless of previous conditioning, people can develop a greater degree of adaptability if they follow a few simple rules.[26]

Some people never marry

There are some people who may be unwilling or unable to make the necessary changes within themselves to become more marriageable. On the other hand, there are many willing and qualified persons who fail to marry. No study of marriageability would be complete without an examination of the factors involved in the circumstances of people who never marry.

SOME TRY TOO HARD. Some people show too much desire for marriage; they may even be overanxious for the experience. They get too serious about marriage too soon with everyone who might even be considered the least bit eligible. In short, they frighten others away. This appears especially true with women who were perhaps passed over at a younger age or who too lightly ignored earlier opportunities. Not wishing to allow the same thing to happen again, they may push forth every effort to "get the next man," but this pushing actually drives many men away. In the American culture, it is still considered the male prerogative to make the first overtures of an involvement that might lead to marriage.

DESIRE FOR A CAREER. Some people never marry because of a feeling that marriage and their chosen career would not mix. Winch states that a very strong career drive has been found to be a definite handicap to early marriage for both sexes, especially for women.[27] In the first place, preparation for a successful professional career takes several years of study. These are the years when people are ordinarily most likely to meet those most marriageable of the opposite sex. Thus, the strongly career-minded individual must pass up, ignore, or deliberately avoid relationships which give indications of seriousness. Later in life, there are fewer marital opportunities, and so a higher percentage of career-minded people may remain single. Today, in spite of advancement in education and the increasing opportunities for professional and vocational employment, most women prefer a happy marriage and family life. Where a choice is necessary, the primary goal for most women is still marriage. A recent survey on one college campus found that only 2 per cent of the women students had little or no interest in marrying in the future.[28] Some careers, however, may actually discourage or prohibit marriage. Not long ago, public school teachers had to be single women or older widows; nursing also imposed limitations on marriage opportunities. Liberalization of women's marital status as a job prerequisite in many fields began during World War II, out of a necessity for workers.

PARENTAL INFLUENCE. Failure to marry is sometimes related to family circumstances. Occasionally a parent is so disillusioned with marriage that his feelings spill over to the child. Such a child may grow up completely rejecting the possibility of marriage. This may be caused by things said or done by the parent both consciously and unconsciously. For example, one often hears expressions such as, "Stay single and enjoy life as long as you can. . . ." It may also be that the child independently decides never to marry, having seen so much quarreling and unhappiness associated with the parental marital relationship.

At the other extreme, some individuals are too devoted to their parents to consider an additional love. There are men who say the word *Mother* with such reverence that it is obvious why they have never married: no other woman could possibly hope to replace such mothers in the hearts of these men. Other men never reach a sufficient degree of independence to establish their own home units; without the reassuring security of their parents, they would be lost.

Some individuals fail to marry because of a strong feeling of financial responsibility toward parents or siblings. It is difficult for a man who is saddled with the burden of supporting aged parents to take on the added financial burden of a wife and future family. Many such men feel it would be entirely unfair to expect any woman to marry them under such conditions, and cease looking for a mate. Sometimes, it is not so much the financial responsibility for parents that interferes with marriage as it is the need to administer to their physical needs. Sometimes children miss the greatest opportunities for marriage before being free of family burdens. One study disclosed that children of a large family, especially the youngest girls, tend to remain single for this reason.[29]

Some people fail to marry because of parental interference or disapproval. When parents interfere, and try to delay and discourage marriage for their offspring, it is likely that their own marriages have been unsuccessful.[30] Some parents disapprove of the mate selected and force their children to choose between loyalties. Some young people are never quite able to find a mate who is pleasing to their parents, and consequently they never marry. But this is much less likely to happen nowadays than in former periods.

LACK OF OPPORTUNITY. In spite of the fact that about 93 per cent of Americans do marry, some persons fail to marry only because they have never had an opportunity to do so. This may be related to one of several differing conditions. In the case of women, one of the most obvious conditions is termed *the mating gradient*. It refers to the fact that men, as a group, tend to select mates who are no more than equal (and, usually, slightly beneath them) in socioeconomic status, and often in the areas of education and intelligence. Women, as a group, tend to do the reverse.[31] The special phenomenon of the mating gradient in American culture actually leaves an unmarried residue on the upper rungs of the female marriageability scale. This is an unfortunate tendency which humans are wise enough to prohibit, or at least to control, in domesticated animals.

Some individuals fail to meet the minimum requirements (physical or mental) of the state. Most of these are in custodial care of various institutions.

For other individuals, failure to marry is caused by a physical handicap. A deformity or generally poor health makes some people much less appealing as marriage partners. Sometimes it is not so much the lack of opportunity that stands in the way of marriage for people with handicaps as it is their own volition. A social consciousness concerning hereditary defects may cause some people to forego marriage. Having investigated the odds of reproducing offspring with similar or even more serious afflictions then their own, they voluntarily remain single "for the good of society."

Occupations may be directly related to marriage opportunities. In a complex society, night employment becomes increasingly necessary. For example, radio and television stations find their biggest audiences at night; so do theaters. Many manufacturers have found it more profitable to operate around the clock than to employ all their workers on daytime shifts. Other businesses (such as bakeries and wholesale transports), by the very nature of their products operate almost exclusively during the hours when other people sleep. With an increasingly interdependent and specialized society, this will probably always be necessary. Individuals who work at night usually have less chance to intermingle with the opposite sex, and consequently they find fewer opportunities for marriage.

Occupational limitations for marriage are sometimes connected with a specific vocational choice. Prime examples, especially for women, are such jobs as teaching, library work, and even social work. The number of eligible men whom women are likely to meet on such jobs is decidedly limited. There has been at least one extensive study of this situation for female school teachers. The findings suggest that the marriage rate for women teachers of ages twenty to twenty-nine is only one half to five eighths as high as for the general population of women in the same age category.[32]

High formal educational attainment sometimes reduces the opportunity for marriage. For the male population, this does not seem to be nearly as pronounced as it was formerly. Marriage while in training for the law, ministry, and especially medicine was once considered out of the question. As evidence of a change in this connection, the author recently found that in one medical school more than 75 per cent of the aspiring physicians were already married. Administrators of the school did not view this particular situation with as much concern as might have been expected a few years ago. In fact, some administrators regarded it as a healthy development and anticipated a future generation of more "humanized" professional men because of it. Still it is true that the high aspirations of a professional career force some men to postpone marriage. Unfortunately, by the time they are ready to marry there are fewer women available with the qualifications to correspond to their own professional status.

Educational limitations are more acute for the female, although there has been an improvement. In 1945 more than 95 per cent of the women aged thirty-five to forty-four who had not gone beyond the sixth grade were married, but only about 80 per cent of women who had attended college, and only 70 per cent of women college graduates of a similar age category were found to be married. An examination of the same situation five years later disclosed approximately 83 per cent of those with one or more years of college education were married.[33] A more recent study of identical-aged women with one or more years of college showed that an all-time high of 89.6 per cent were married.[34] Although the current corresponding figures for those with a four-year degree are not available, no doubt the percentage of those married has increased. Bell estimates it to be about 85 per cent.[35]

College-educated women, especially those with higher professional degrees, are usually in their middle or late twenties before they feel ready to consider marriage; by then many men who might have been interested in them have already married or are engaged. Furthermore, if the highly educated woman wishes to marry a man of at least equal professional status, she finds a large proportion of eligible males eliminated.[36] This selectivity results in a disproportionately higher percentage of professionally educated women who fail to marry even when they desire to do so.

Apart from education, age places some restrictions on the possibility of marriage. Census figures indicate that as age increases, a decreasing percentage of people marry. Although this figure may indicate personal preference, the fact remains the older the person the smaller the percentage of marriage possibilities, for the most suitable ones are usually already married. If the older person wishes to marry, his best chance to find a suitable mate may be from those widowed or divorced. If a woman is still single at thirty, the chances that she will ever marry are slightly less than 50 per cent, and the percentage decreases rather rapidly thereafter.

Table 6–3. **Women who will ever marry if not married by:**

Age	Per cent
20	93
30	48
45	9

Source: U.S. Bureau of the Census, Series P-20, No. 86.

In recent years failure to marry has often been ascribed to the changing sex ratio. It is true that events at various times in history have affected the sex ratio and this, in turn, has affected the opportunity for marriage. As Baber points out, the sex ratio of men to women in early American history was abnormally high. This was largely the result of mass immigration of men to this country; for example, in 1890 there were 107.6 men for every 100 women.[37] Since then, there has been less over-all immigration, but an increase in the proportion of women immigrants. In addition, the gap in longevity between the sexes has increased. As a result, the ratio between the sexes has gradually decreased until in 1964 there were only about 96.4 men for every 100 women.[38] These facts, however, do not present the total picture. To note the effect of this change on marriage, it is better to examine the ratio for adults of marriageable age only. The ratio of male to female births has increased in recent years so that the male-female ratio of fifteen-year-olds today is approximately the same as existed for infants in 1940. According to the last available statistics issued by the U.S. Department of Health, Education, and Welfare, there are approximately 105.3 males born to every 100 females, and in spite of a higher mortality rate for the male, men still predominate in numbers up to about the age of twenty-five.[39] Between the ages of forty-five and sixty-four, the ratio drops to 94.1 men to every 100 women, and is further reduced to 78.4 men to every 100 women at the ages of sixty-five and over.[40] Recent census data disclosed that there are still over 200,000 more single men than single women between the ages of fifteen and nineteen and 40,000 more single men than women between the ages of twenty and twenty-four.[41] Thus, in spite of change, the sexes have an almost 1:1 ratio in the most marriageable age groupings.

It should be pointed out, however, that there may now be less of a selection for women, particularly in certain regions. For example, urban living conditions appear to attract proportionately more of the female sex. In the major cities of the nation there are only 90.4 men of marriageable age available for every 100 females fifteen to twenty-nine years of age. This ratio changes to 101.8 to 100 in rural nonfarm regions, and still further to 111.4 men to every 100 women in the rural farm regions.[42] Even this is not the entire picture, for some cities have more of one sex than another. According to Baber, the three lowest male-female ratio cities are Atlanta with 82:100, Nashville with 82.3:100, and Richmond with 85:100; the three highest are Gary, Indiana, with 114.4:100; Detroit with 105.6:100, and San Francisco with 104.1:100.[43] There is also quite a wide variation by states. Washington, D.C., has the lowest ratio, 86:100, followed by Massachusetts with 90.2:100, Georgia with 92.3:100, and New York with 92.8:100. The highest ratios are found in Nevada with 117.1:100, Wyoming with 116.6:100, and Montana with 114:100.[44] There is also a great difference in the sex ratio in various regions and cities; among those people of the most marriageable age, there is an even greater variation of distribution by location.[45]

Even if all the foregoing were not true, the conditions of urban living would tend to lower the percentage married. An intensive and classic study of the impact of city life on marriage possibilities by Ogburn in the early 1930s concluded that urban living conditions of that time lowered the percentage married at any given moment by at least 10 per cent.[46] As Ogburn pointed out, there are so many more differing religions, occupations, and nationalities in the city that it becomes increasingly difficult for mates with similar backgrounds and tastes to meet. Unless they meet in school, they almost never do.

The continuing truth of Ogburn's findings is revealed by the personal columns of large metropolitan newspapers, which often include advertisements similar to the following:

> Wanted—by male professional engineer, age thirty-five, and never married, a chance to meet a charming white woman between the ages of twenty-four and twenty-nine. Object matrimony. Must have a college education and enjoy meeting people in highest social circles. Also must desire home life and children, and have a devotion toward fine morals. Phone _____, or write Box _____.

There is also an increasing number of "young adult" clubs being formed in cities. Many such clubs have membership restrictions on race, age, education, and other background factors; of course, they insist on a nonmarital status. Sometimes they advertise for membership by sponsoring activities such as dances, art shows, musical or drama presentations. Whatever the stipulation or activity, the arrangements are designed for young marriageable-age people to become better acquainted; perhaps sufficiently for marriage.

The lonely hearts clubs are a more direct method that has become highly developed in recent years. The purposes of many such clubs are most questionable, but others seem more honest. At one point in his graduate study the author compiled a list of such clubs advertising in pulp magazines. More than 200 were identified in the southeastern section of the United States alone. Vedder states that there is now a national organization of marriage brokers in America; they have more than 800 members and hold annual conferences.[47]

Wallace reported that, in seventy-five months of running a fictitious personal-acquaintance service, he received 59,417 inquiries in response, generally, to newspaper and magazine advertising.[48] At the time the service was disbanded, approximately one in every five members being enrolled was a college graduate and one fourth of those listed graduate education or degrees. The age range of applicants for his service was eighteen to eighty-four, and varied by sex in different age categories.

Table 6–4. **Age and sex ratio of applicants for personal-acquaintance service**

Age	Male-female sex ratio
18–26	5:1
27–32	4.5:1
33–38	3:1
39–44	2:1
51–56	1:1.5
57–65	1:2
Over 65	1:1

Source: Karl Miles Wallace, "An Experiment in Scientific Matchmaking," *Marriage and Family Living,* **21**:345. Copyright © 1959, by The National Council on Family Relations, Minneapolis, Minn. Reprinted by permission.

Wallace summarized his experience by saying: "Over the years it was observed that a great many of the members were in occupations and environments that afforded little normal contact or social life with eligible members of the opposite sex."[49] That this situation is not unique to American metropolitan areas is demonstrated by the fact that 777 matrimonial ads appeared in one month in Copenhagen's two largest daily newspapers. The advertisements were placed by private persons; 56 per cent of them were men; 44 per cent, women.[50]

INACCURATE IDEAS. Occasionally there is an individual who fails to marry because of an inadequate knowledge of what marriage involves; frequently this lack makes him feel inadequate for marriage. Some people may consider themselves inferior to others and unworthy for marriage. Some do not feel strong enough in health or character for the responsibilities of marriage, and so lead a life of celibacy. It is perfectly natural for people to have such feelings at times, so this in itself should not be a hindrance to marriage. College students indicated, in one study, that the majority felt inadequate at some time for marriage.[51] Current clinical observation does not indicate that this condition has changed.

Previous love affairs may also result in unhealthy attitudes toward marriage. Some individuals appear never to recover enough from a disappointing experience to consider marriage again. In some cases, the memory of a love affair is perpetuated long after it should have vanished, for the former lover is deceased or married to another. As time goes on, however, negative aspects of the former relationship are repressed and only the more pleasant and idealized memories remain. In fact, the memory may grow into sheer fantasy. The image of the former lover may become so distorted that should the person return, he would go unrecognized. With time the image is refined to perfection, so that no mortal could compete with it. The person who forms such an image has closed the door to any possibility of marriage.

Some people have unrealistic ideas as to what a mate should be. They are seeking the "perfect" mate, regardless of how imperfect they themselves may be. Such people simply have too selfish a set of requirements.

Guilt feelings for past actions may deter a person from marriage. Such feelings are best discussed with a competent counselor. Through a counselor's help and guidance, the heterosexual-involvement process might then be considered more objectively.

Some people fear marriage. Probably many of those who resist marriage because of a previous sad experience with love or because they set unrealistic standards, actually fear marriage. There may be fear of the sexual part of marriage, even dread of pain or unpleasantness. Some women may consider marriage to be a form of exploitation by men; others fear childbearing. These fears may be related to earlier conditioning such as unfortunate experiences, distorted information, or misinterpreted remarks made by some married person.

Others may fear the financial aspects of marriage. Perhaps they remember the difficult economic struggle of their own parents. Such people may hesitate to marry, fearing to give up their present economic security for the uncertainties within marriage.

Others fear that a loss of personal freedom may accompany marriage. Although it is true that certain freedoms are submerged within marriage, others are gained. For most people the gains far outweigh the losses, but for some the price is too great. Such people enjoy independence and prefer living alone and making their own decisions without the necessity of consultation as required in marriage.

Figure 6-1. Some people simply have too selfish a set of requirements ever to get married.

Still there are others who honestly, in all sincerity, state that they have failed to marry because of a lack of interest in the opposite sex. Marriage simply has no appeal to them—it is not particularly revolting, but "what is so wonderful about it?"

AN UNAWARENESS OF REAL REASONS. Often the real reasons for failure to marry may be unrelated to the reasons sincerely believed or given. This does not mean that the reasons given are pure invention, for they may well be in operation, but they are not the deeper underlying causes, which may be completely unknown even to the person himself.

PERSONALITY VARIATIONS. Perhaps one of the most basic reasons for failure to marry is related to some aspect of personality. A person must be attractive to the opposite sex. Neither a repulsive disposition nor an unattractive appearance improves the chances for marriage. A girl need not be a ravishing beauty nor a boy a "Mr. America" to attract the opposite sex, but most people could be more physically attractive if they would use what they have to better advantage. It is the wise woman who realizes that it is more important to be attractive than to be stylish. Some styles are just right for some women and all wrong for others. Even within each style there are variations that are best for each individual. Appearances are usually taken as a measure of personality. To illustrate this point, some researchers asked 140 men to examine photographs of twenty-four young women and to size up their personalities. There was a surprising amount of agreement (whether actually right or wrong is an unknown).[52]

A sharp deviation from the accepted norm in moral standards may decrease the chances of marriage. More important than many realize is that people are often eliminated from marriageability because of appearing too "prissy" when their convictions run counter to those of others. It is not that their own standards are ideal but that they always disapprove of others' behavior. It is little wonder that such people rarely get beyond one or two dates with anyone.

The inner self stands in the way of the marital chances for many who remain single. Klemer confined his doctoral study to the subject of why women fail to marry. His findings indicate that for the great majority, it is a deep inner-self deviation, usually unknown to the woman herself.[53] Another study requested 100 adults to describe bachelors over the age of thirty-five whom they knew well. Altogether, 185 bachelors were described. Of this number, 120 were classified as being of unmarriageable personality. They were either hopelessly in love with themselves, their mothers, or other men; sexually promiscuous; or alcoholics. Of the remaining sixty-five, a total of eight were considered "doubtful."[54] Wallace comments that the data collected on the members of his personal-acquaintance service suggest that the great majority were less sociable, more religious, more rigid and inflexible, more intolerant, more demanding, and harder to please than normal.[55] Baber reports a study of the campus of Pomona College where juniors and seniors were asked to list the disagreeable qualities of the opposite sex, from among those they had dated, that prevented them from seriously considering marriage to those people. The two things listed most frequently by 100 men about 358 women were: (1) shallowness, weakness, and (2) self-centeredness. The same two items were listed more frequently (but in reverse order) by 300 women about 1102 men.[56] This indicates that the element of adaptability within personality plays a larger role in marriageability than perhaps many people realize.

PROBLEMS OF SINGLENESS.   People who remain single have a few special problems to face and solve. One of these problems is combatting loneliness and finding adequate companionship. Sometimes they conclude that no one really cares about what happens to them, because as friends marry, they find themselves more and more left out of things or being the odd one at social affairs.

An additional problem of the single person is rigidity. Man is a creature of habit, and so it is only natural for a single person to create a pattern of living most suitable to himself. If he is not careful, he may place too much importance on satisfying personal needs without regard for others. Sometimes the unmarried person, seeking human companionship, interferes in the affairs of others. The single person also faces the embarrassment of being continually harrassed by the matchmaking efforts of friends and family members. Celibacy may be viewed with suspicion even today. Until democracy is truly personal, with no restrictions based on sexual bias, many will continue to believe that men remain single by their own choice and women by someone else's choice.

There are special problems for the single adult in the areas of giving and receiving love and affection. Love is a basic emotional need of everyone, but the most common methods of giving and receiving love for the adult, sexual coitus and raising children, are socially denied the unmarried. Such people must find suitable substitutes. Some utilize friends and relatives; others seek love through some cause such as welfare work; others shower animals with attention. Many women seem to find a love satisfaction through working with small children in various kinds of institutions.

The lack of an organized and regular sex life for the single adult is a most difficult problem, and one that society has done little to solve or to understand. The sex drive may be every bit as strong for many who remain single as for those who marry, but there are few socially acceptable ways in which it can be satisfied.

In a world organized and oriented around the couple, there are indeed many difficulties for those who fail to marry.

SOME SHOULD NOT MARRY. In spite of the difficulties of adult single life in the modern American culture, some people should not marry. Married life would probably incur more acute problems for them than to remain single. Anyone who is indifferent about marriage should not marry. The desire for married life should be strong, for marriage is a significant commitment to a way of life. In some cases, marriage might interfere with some people becoming the socially useful and creative persons they should be. Fortunately, many such persons realize the possibility of this type of conflict and choose not to marry.[57]

Another facet of the indifferent attitude relates to those who would choose marriage rather than endure their present situation, whatever it is. The wish to escape unpleasantness is a poor excuse to marry. A prime example of this is the desire to escape loneliness, but absence from loneliness is never guaranteed by marriage.

People should not let social pressure force them into marriage. To choose to remain single places the individual in a minority group, but to marry for social reasons may eventually bring about even less acceptance should the marriage fail.

Summary

Adequate courtship and careful mate-selection practices are important for marriage, but it is equally important to become as marriageable as possible by developing desirable personality traits. Some people are more marriageable than others because of a healthier conditioning in their family life, and in their peer and societal world. It is possible, however, for even the most unmarriageable person to improve if he really wants to do so.

Some people remain single by choice, and perhaps should not marry. Others, however, fail to marry because they have never discovered how to make themselves more marriageable. On the other hand, no one should ever marry merely to escape the criticism of being single.

Notes

1. Anselm Strauss, "The Ideal and the Chosen Mate," *American Journal of Sociology*, 52:204–208.

2. August B. Hollingshead, "Cultural Factors in the Selection of Marriage Mates," *American Sociological Review*, 15:619–27. See also table on expected homogamy versus actual for interfaith marriages in Paul C. Glick, "Intermarriage and Fertility Patterns Among Persons in Major Religious Groups," *Eugenics Quarterly*, 7:31–38.

3. Reuben Hill, "Campus Values in Mate Selection," *Journal of Home Economics*, 37:556.

4. Harold T. Christensen, "Student Views on Mate Selection," *Marriage and Family Living*, 9:85.

5. Wayne C. Neeley, "Family Attitudes of Denominational College and University Students," *American Sociological Review*, 5:517–19.

6. Strauss, *op. cit.*

7. See Robert F. Winch, "The Theory of Complementary Needs in Mate-Selection," *American Sociological Review*, 20:552–55; and *Mate Selection* (New York: Harper & Row, Publishers, 1958).

8. Alan C. Kerckhoff and Keith E. Davis, "Value Consensus and Need Complementarity in Mate Selection," *American Sociological Review*, 27:295–303.

9. A. H. Maslow, *Motivation And Personality* (New York: Harper & Row, Publishers, 1954), Chap. 5.

10. Anselm Strauss, Doctoral Study, University of Chicago, Chicago, Ill., 1945.

11. See, e.g., J. A. Schellonberg and L. S. Bee, "A Re-examination of the Theory of Complementary Needs in Mate Selection," *Marriage and Family Living*, 22:227.

12. Harvey J. Locke, *Predicting Adjustment in Marriage* (New York: Holt, Rinehart & Winston, Inc., 1951), p. 192.

13. E. W. Burgess and Paul Wallin, *Engagement and Marriage* (Philadelphia: J. B. Lippincott & Co., 1953), pp. 620–25.

14. Bernard I. Murstein, "The Complementary Need Hypothesis in Newlyweds and Middle-aged Married Couples," *Journal of Abnormal and Social Psychology*, 63:194–97.

15. Walter Stokes, *Modern Pattern for Marriage* (New York: Holt, Rinehart & Winston, Inc., 1948), pp. 90–91.

16. Lewis M. Terman, *Psychological Factors in Marital Happiness* (New York: McGraw-Hill Book Company, Inc., 1938), pp. 110–11.

17. Lee G. Burchinal, Glenn R. Hawkes, and Bruce Gardner, "Marriage Adjustment, Personality Characteristics of Parents and the Personality Adjustment of Their Children," *Marriage and Family Living,* 19:367–72.

18. Don C. Carter, "The Influence of Family Relations and Family Experiences on Personality," *Marriage and Family Living,* 16:212–15.

19. Taken from notes of lectures given by Koos while the author was a graduate student at Florida State University.

20. Charles H. Cooley, *Human Nature and the Social Order* (New York: Charles Scribner's Sons, 1922).

21. See, e.g., E. W. Burgess and Harvey J. Locke, *The Family: From Institution to Companionship* (New York: American Book Company, 1945), esp. p. 244.

22. Amram Scheinfeld, *Women and Men* (New York: Harcourt, Brace & World, Inc., 1944).

23. George Stoddard, *The Meaning of Intelligence* (New York: The Macmillan Company, 1943), pp. 347–92.

24. Lee N. Robins and Patricia O'Neal, "Marital History of Former Problem Children," *Social Problems* (Spring 1958), 347–58.

25. Bonaro W. Overstreet, "The Readiness to Like and Be Liked," *National Parent-Teacher,* 49:18.

26. See a classic treatment on methods for changing habits by Laurance F. Shaffer, B. V. H. Gilmer, and Max Schoon, *Psychology* (New York: Harper & Row, Publishers, 1940).

27. Robert F. Winch, "Courtship of College Women," *American Journal of Sociology,* 55:269–78.

28. Robert R. Bell, "Some Factors Related to Coed Marital Aspirations," *The Family Life Coordinator,* 11:91–94.

29. James H. S. Bossard and Eleanor S. Boll, *The Large Family System* (Philadelphia: University of Pennsylvania Press, 1950), p. 284.

30. Alan Bates, "Parental Roles in Courtship," *Social Forces,* 20:483–86.

31. For a more detailed discussion of the mating gradient phenomenon, see Joseph K. Folsom, *The Family and Democratic Society* (New York: John Wiley & Sons, Inc., 1943), pp. 490–91.

32. Harold H. Punke, "Marriage Rate Among Women Teachers," *American Sociological Review,* 5:505–11.

33. *Statistical Bulletins,* Metropolitan Life Insurance Company (August 1945), 4–6, (April 1951).

34. U.S. Bureau of the Census, Series P-20, No. 81.

35. Bell, *op. cit.*

36. Educated women do get proposals, but usually not so many from the caliber of man desired. For example, a survey of 186 well-educated single women disclosed an average of 3.29 possibilities of marriage. Paul Popenoe, "Where Are the Marriageable Men?," *Family Life,* 13: 6, 1.

37. Ray E. Baber, *Marriage and the Family* (New York: McGraw-Hill Book Company, Inc., 1953), p. 21.

38. U.S. Bureau of the Census, Series P-25, No. 293.

39. The ratio is even higher for whites. See U.S. Department of Health, Education, and Welfare, *Vital Statistics, Supplement,* 13, 6 (September 11, 1964).

40. *Ibid.*

41. *Ibid.*

42. U.S. Bureau of the Census, Series P-20, No. 81.

43. Baber, *op. cit.,* p. 22.

44. *Ibid.*

45. T. Lynn Smith, "A Comparative Study of the Age Distribution of the Population of Major Cities in the United States," *Social Forces,* 38:240–45.

46. William F. Ogburn, *Recent Social Trends in the United States* (New York: McGraw-Hill Book Company, Inc., 1933), p. 681.

47. Clyde B. Vedder, "Lonely Hearts Club Viewed Sociologically," *Social Forces,* 30:219–22.

48. Karl Miles Wallace, "An Experiment in Scientific Matchmaking," *Marriage and Family Living,* 21:342–48.

49. *Ibid.,* p. 347.

50. Helge Anderson, "An Analysis of 777 Matrimonial Want Ads in Two Copenhagen Newspapers," *Acta Sociologica* (Denmark) (1958), pp. 173–82.

51. Anne F. Fenlason and Helen R. Hertz, "The College Student and Feelings of Inferiority," *Mental Hygiene* (July 1938), p. 389.

52. Paul F. Secord and John E. Muthard, "Personalities in Faces," *Journal of Psychology,* 39:269–78.

53. Richard H. Klemer, Doctoral Study, Florida State University, Tallahassee, Fla., 1953.

54. Paul Popenoe, "The Old Bachelor," *Family Life,* 15:1.

55. Karl Miles Wallace, "An Experiment in Scientific Matchmaking," *Marriage and Family Living,* 21:348.

56. Baber, *op. cit.,* pp. 130–33.

57. Evelyn Ellis, "Social-Psychological Correlates of Upward Social Mobility Among Unmarried Career Women," *American Sociological Review,* 17:558–63. Ellis suggests that there is evidence to support the idea that women who drive hardest toward a career, and who become most ambitiously motivated along vocational lines, are not particularly marriageable persons.

Questions for further thought

1. In what ways is striving to become as marriageable a person as possible consistent with American democracy?
2. Is suggesting that one must compromise between the mate he would like to have, those who are available, and those he is likely to get, automatically mean a lowering of standards?
3. Does adjustment mean a condition where one person changes to suit the whims of the other?
4. What is the difference between flexibility of personality and flexibility of values?
5. Do children of divorced parents in the college-educated population suffer as many adverse effects on adaptability as children of divorced parents of lower education?
6. Should a girl who has lost out before by trying too hard reverse her procedure and play hard to get?
7. At about what age does a girl reach the point of diminishing returns? Should such a girl accept a doubtful proposal rather than risk losing her chance ever to marry?

Recommended film

Choosing for Happiness (McGraw-Hill Book Company, Inc.).

Suggested supplemental readings

BOOKS

Ellis, Albert. *The Intelligent Woman's Guide to Manhunting.* New York: Lyle Stuart, 1963.

Horney, Karen. *The Neurotic Personality of Our Time.* New York: W. W. Norton & Company, Inc., 1937.

Katz, Robert L. *Empathy.* New York: The Free Press of Glencoe, Inc., 1963.

Klemer, Richard H. *A Man for Every Woman.* New York: The Macmillan Company, 1959.

Maslow, A. H. *Motivation and Personality.* New York: Harper & Row, Publishers, 1954.

Nelson, Frederic. *Bachelors Are People, Too.* Washington, D.C.: Public Affairs Press, 1964.

Overstreet, Harry A. *The Mature Mind.* New York: W. W. Norton & Company, Inc., 1949.

Rosten, Leo C. *Hollywood.* New York: Harcourt, Brace & World, Inc., 1941.

Strecker, Edward A. and Vincent T. Lathberry. *Their Mothers' Daughters.* Philadelphia: J. B. Lippincott Co., 1956.

———. *Their Mothers' Sons,* rev. ed. Philadelphia: J. B. Lippincott Co., 1951.

Winch, Robert F. *Mate Selection.* New York: Harper & Row, Publishers, 1958.

ARTICLES

Benton, Margaret. "The Woman Who Wants to Marry," *Family Life,* 15:3–4.

Bowerman, Charles E., and John W. Kinch. "Changes in Family and Peer Orientation of Children Between the Fourth and Tenth Grades," *Social Forces,* 37:206–11.

Buerkle, Jack V. "Self Attitudes and Marital Adjustment," *Merrill-Palmer Quarterly,* 6:114–24.

Kernodle, Wayne. "Some Implications of the Homogamy-Complementary Needs Theories of Mate Selection for Sociological Research," *Social Forces,* 38:145–52.

Langhorne, M. C., and Paul F. Secord. "Variations in Marital Needs with Age, Sex, Marital Status, and Regional Location," *Journal of Social Psychology,* 41:19–37.

Magary, Louise. "Severe Disturbances in Young Women Reflecting Damaging Mother-Daughter Relationships," *Social Casework,* 40:202–207.

Wallin, Paul. "Marital Happiness of Parents and Their Children's Attitudes to Marriage," *American Sociological Review,* 19:20–23.

Wilson, Donald P. "The Woman Who Has Not Married," *Family Life,* 18:1–2.

Building
love enough
chapter 7   # for marriage

As the time for marriage approaches, the individual responds to those of the opposite sex with feelings, physical and emotional, that indicate an awakening of sexual desire. Romantic fantasies first intermingle with the physiological manifestations of puberty, "puppy love," and idolization. The love of self reaches out to include others at each stage of normal developmental love, and finally focuses on one special person. When do two people love each other enough for marriage, and how can they be sure? Indeed, is love the best assurance of a happy marriage? To answer these questions, it is necessary to examine the evolution of love as a social concept and as part of personal development.

A prerequisite for marriage

Being in love is probably the most important prerequisite for marriage in American society. Ask any American couple why they married, and the most usual reason given is: "Because we were in love." Burgess and Wallin report that only 12 per cent of the young men and 15 per cent of the young women whom they interviewed thought it acceptable for people in America to marry when not in love.[1]

In American society, love followed by marriage is glorified in poetry, fiction, songs, and movies, but in many other societies it is regarded as a sign of weakness, and the people who yield to it are generally ridiculed. It is not that other societies deny love, but rather they do not consider its presence or absence at the time of marriage very significant. Ralph Linton, an anthropologist, explains that many societies do not expect young couples to be in love at the time of marriage, but believe love will develop as the couple learn to live together in marriage.[2] This was also the belief in the predemocratic, Puritan era of America.[3] Apparently the concept of love in the United States emerged concurrently with the concepts of personal democracy and freedom of choice.

The attention Americans devote to love may appear slightly ridiculous to those nations whose conceptualization of democracy has gone little beyond the power to choose governmental leaders. It is not uncommon, therefore, to discover that when others write about America, their comments are rather caustic. De Sales wrote: "America appears to be the only country where love is a national problem."[4] It is undoubtedly true that in no other culture has love become so institutionalized. In another sense, however, De Sales' statement probably came closer to being a truth when written than now; actually, today there are signs in a few other societies of a tendency toward greater acceptance of love as a prerequisite for marriage. This is particularly apparent in those countries where newer concepts of democracy are emphasizing the importance of the individual.[5] In the Oriental world, however, the concept of marriage has changed but slightly since ancient times, and romantic sexual love is still considered a kind of human madness.[6] It is reported that in India love is of no significance in the choice of marital partners.[7]

Anthropological studies indicate little evolutionary basis for love as a prerequisite for marriage. This further supports the thesis that the present American cultural concept of love is closely related to the development of freedom of choice as a fundamental part of democracy. It is reported that among the Zuni, love for the mate is actually looked upon with shame by the relatives.[8] The few cases of romantic attraction occurring among Trobriand Islanders have been reported as usually ending in suicide.[9] It appears that love is both denied and forbidden in the culture of the Dobu.[10]

In the United States, it is natural, however, that love before marriage should be emphasized, for the American ideal rests upon the power of individual judgment in important decisions, whether in electing a president or choosing a spouse. Personal judgment is dependent upon healthy personalities, and it is a well-known fact that personality growth depends upon an adequate expression of love; consequently, it is essential that Americans marry for love.[11] As Blanton states it:

> Love's greatest glory lies in the fact that it alone provides the strength, protection, and encouragement without which full growth is impossible. We are all aware of this truth when it comes to the life of a helpless infant. Unfortunately, too many of us ignore its equal applicability to humanity as a whole.[12]

Love can be defined

The word *love* appears to engender confusion in every culture. In English, much of this confusion is caused by the multiple uses of the word for many different conditions.

A VARIETY OF MEANINGS. In the majority of languages there is a decided lack of expressive words denoting a strong preference or fondness for various objects, situations, or attitudes, or even animals and flowers. The word *love* has been forced to apply to all these attitudes and conditions. As a consequence, people speak of "loving" things, causes, activities, or such principles and ideals as God and country. Actually the American College Dictionary lists fourteen definitions of *love*. In this discussion, however, the word *love* is used in its primal sense, to mean deep affection and physical attraction between human beings.

A serious study of love is hampered by the fact that love is a topic about which those with the most experience have the least to say. Silence seems to come with wisdom in this area of life. The teen-ager may try to describe love, but older people are usually somewhat hesitant or simply add to the confusion by prefacing the word with all manner of nondescriptive adjectives such as *true, real, lasting,* or *unwavering.* Love is frequently considered an uncontrollable phenomenon; it has been characterized as impulsive and spontaneous and that to restrain it consciously is out of the question. Literary masterpieces such as *Romeo and Juliet* have strengthened these popular folk axioms that no one can fight love.[13] In truth, all manner of things are done in the name of love.

MORE DISCRIMINATION NEEDED. If marriage is to be based on love, it would be wise to use the word most discriminately. First of all, it must be restricted to describing an attraction between people. *Love* should not be used to describe a fondness for certain foods and such other things as sports or music, for there is no reciprocal response from the loved object to the lover. These are not even live relationships. The use of the word *love* should be further restricted to an attraction between two persons that can be reciprocated. Because a one-way relationship would not justify marriage for adults, the word *devotion* would better apply to the situation than *love*. Devotion has a definite place in developing the capacity to love enough for marriage, but devotion alone is not sufficient for marriage. Perhaps Piaget has defined it best when he said in effect: "What one loves in others is not so much the individual as the possibility of a bond of affection."[14] To build love enough to justify marriage, there must be a two-way exchange which can be continuously maintained.

LOVE CAN BE STUDIED. Some people doubt that love can be discussed in the first place. Is it possible to study love academically? The answer is in the affirmative: love can be studied. It is based partly on emotion, and emotions can be understood. In a democracy, marriages based on love make sense, but it is necessary to understand the meaning of love before it is possible to base marriage on it.

Love is a developmental task

Love in a democracy can be studied in terms of a developmental task. A developmental task is a growth responsibility which arises at or about a certain period in the life of an individual. The successful achievement of each task leads him toward happiness and toward success with later tasks, while failure almost always leads to unhappiness in the individual, disapproval of society, and difficulty with later tasks in life.[15] This does not mean that an accomplished task in human development is set or complete forever. A refining of each task goes on throughout life and is perhaps never entirely finished. Unless the individual is fairly successful with the first tasks he faces in life, however, he is quite likely to fail with future ones.

THE CONCEPT APPLIED TO LOVE. The capacity to love enough for marriage must be developed gradually through years of interaction with other people. There are no short cuts; each individual must begin at the beginning if he is to be successful. Love enough for marriage must be learned like any other lesson, whether it is to acquire good manners at the table, to talk properly, or to read quickly. All these tasks of socialization take practice and mastery of each step. Relationships based on love are not sudden diseases of adolescence; rather, they are life-long processes which begin to manifest themselves in the earliest days of life and persist as personal needs throughout life.

AN ACQUIRED ABILITY. The ability to love enough for marriage is not inborn in a person; it is acquired in the course of growing up. As a natural consequence, the capacity will vary from person to person, depending largely upon his degree of success with each previous step. If a person has not been able to pass successfully through all the stages of love as a developmental task, then he will not be ready for the stage of love most conducive to successful marriage. The problem in the American society is not love, but the fact that too many people marry before acquiring the capacity for love necessary for a personally democratic marriage.[16] To learn love as a developmental task, the individual must have some love relationships that do not end in marriage. Each experience will contribute something vital toward developing the capacity for love that will justify marriage.

The stage of self-centeredness

The development of a love strong enough for marriage starts at birth. The infant centers his interest on his own needs and pleasures; for him, this is an accomplishment. Unfortunately, some individuals never get much further in developing their capacity for love. Extremely egocentric adults who seldom do things for others, who are too demanding and perhaps too hard to please, are basically arrested at the self-centered stage because of failure in the self-love tasks of infancy.

SELF-LOVE.   The stage of self-centeredness begins with the infant who at first loves himself with no recognition of the identity of his love object. This *autoeroticism* is manifested as thumb-sucking, and playing with toes and genitals. Gradually, the infant begins to realize that he is playing with his own body. This love of self as a recognized entity is called *narcissism*. If these first love experiences are not interfered with by well-meaning adults, the infant begins to recognize that other people are for love also. This third stage is called *alloeroticism*. These three steps are necessary for the normal development of self-centered love.

There must be an ability to love oneself first before one can begin to love others. This was recognized in Biblical times by the commandant: "Thou shalt love thy neighbor as thyself."[17] The person who seeks much self-love as an adult has, in all likelihood, experienced considerable frustration in this task as an infant. To help people move on to the next stage it is necessary to accept and love them in spite of what they do. To show disgust or to punish a child by withholding love responses is believed by many authorities to be critical to both his capacity to learn to love, and to his later ability to learn the proper behavior expected by society.[18] If the child is frustrated in his first important relationships of learning to love, he more than likely will develop hostility later in life.[19] Thus, the ability to learn to love someone else begins with self-love or self-acceptance. If feelings of inadequacy, inferiority, guilt, or worthlessness are developed instead, the individual will probably become too wrapped up in himself ever to advance to the stage of loving people. He will still be trying to solve the first task. Some psychologists point out that to deny an infant the right to love, as a disciplinary measure, may produce a personality that is more susceptible to suicide.[20]

The stage of family love

Usually it is the mother who establishes the pattern for the second task of love. When she nurses or cuddles the infant, or soothes him with her loving calm voice or tender smile, his love begins to reach out to the family. Studies by Harlow suggest that at first this stage is most dependent upon warm, comforting, body-to-body contact.[21] These mother-and-child love experiences become "contagious" and begin to involve other members of the family.

THE ROLE OF THE FATHER.   There can be little doubt that the father plays an important role at this point in the child's development of love. His voice is deeper and gruffer and his touch is less gentle, but the

Figure 7-1. In this simple fashion, love begins to grow. (Courtesy of the P. H. Hanes Knitting Company.)

father's affectionate manner suggests to the child that there is more than mother's love to enjoy. This recognition prepares the child to accept other people and, because of this pleasant experience with father love, the child begins to feel that all adults are warm and friendly.

LOVE MIMICRY. As the child grows older he observes the expressions of love and affection other family members use toward one another. By these examples he learns to express his love in a like manner. At an early stage, many children begin to evidence a slight preference for the parent of the opposite sex. Through observation of parental love expressions, the child soon learns that there is a greater power of love between adults of the opposite sex. This awareness usually develops soon after recognition of gross anatomical and costume differences between sexes.

It is quite common to hear young children say that when they grow up they will marry Mommy or Daddy. It is a wise parent who understands this part of the child's love development, and provides experiences to help him move on toward the next stage. The individual who never solves this family stage of attraction to the parent of the opposite sex may develop an Oedipus or Electra complex. When this condition exists, the love of the parent of the opposite sex may become such a strong obsession that the individual is never able to substitute anyone else of the opposite sex. This is sometimes observed in the behavior of adults who feel an overwhelming obligation toward the parent of the opposite sex. Eckert points out that the relationship of a father to his daughter strongly affects her later attitudes toward men and her development of a capacity to love deeply enough for marriage. The father often becomes a symbol of all men to his daughter.[22] Ordinarily, the parents' encouragement of the child's interests to those outside will direct the child's love beyond the family.

The stage of expansion

The child changes as he grows, and so does the nature of his love. If he associates a sense of safety and well-being with family love, his interest will begin to include other people. With increasing ease he will accept new people, including pals and grownup friends such as postmen, milkmen, and other delivery men. He learns that love is associated with an interdependence of individuals, and so later on he will also include those who have authority in his life, such as teachers, ministers, doctors, and policemen. He will continually reach out to new people; he regards the world with trust, for he has experienced no reason for fear.[23] This does not mean that a poor experience with parents will prevent a person from developing the capacity to love deeply enough for marriage. Parents play an important part in this drama, but many a child who has been denied parental love has found the love which he needs from substitutes such as older siblings, grandparents, or sympathetic neighbors.

Soon the child shows an increased interest in those of similar sex and age. He identifies with his own sex and enjoys things of particular interest to that sex. This strong attraction toward members of the same sex is usually maintained until early adolescence.[24] It often includes a deep comradeship with one particular "best" friend. This adolescent habit of loyalty to one friend may condition his future capacity for fidelity to one mate.

From this strong friendship, the individual realizes that he has special value to another person. The termination of this stage occurs earlier with girls than with boys; that is, girls become interested in boys before boys become interested in them.[25] Naturally, there is also a considerable variation within each sex. If the experiences of loving someone of the same sex have been unsatisfactory, the individual may stay longer in that stage, attempting to solve this part of the task of love before advancing to the next. Even some adults are unable to transfer their affection to the other sex because the prior task remains unfinished.

It is probably safe to say that the child loves many times before he even begins to walk: himself, his parents, siblings, and then the other children in the immediate neighborhood. Then love extends to other adults besides his parents. If he successfully passes through all love-task experiences, the individual develops a healthy concept of love, and comes to understand its meanings for later marriage.

The stage of multiple loves

It has not yet been determined how much of the awakened interest in the opposite sex arises from physical-maturation processes and how much arises from social custom. No doubt, both are influential. Gradually, an interest in the opposite sex begins to take precedence over an interest in one's own sex. Instead of shying away from girls, boys begin to approach them. In this stage it is normal for the individual to show an interest in several people of the opposite sex at the same time, with much confusion over which one he prefers. A selective process should soon take place; if not, the individual may fail this task and remain somewhat confused as an adult, never able to concentrate on one person of the opposite sex long enough for marriage, or for sufficient satisfaction within marriage.

The irrational stage

The irrational stage of the development of love enough for marriage consists of two phases: the attractive phase and the imaginative. Some individuals experience both phases; others, only one.

ATTRACTION. In the attractive phase, the individual begins to recognize that certain people of the opposite sex please him more than others. He may feel repelled by some and attracted to others without understanding why. Common expressions of young adolescents in this phase include: "Don't ask me why, I just don't like her," or "I can't understand it, but I like her."

Often the preference depends upon a similarity between the love object and a parent, but the identification is usually subconscious. In a sense, the adolescent has found a parental substitute, but a substitute parent is not sufficient justification for marriage.

USE OF IMAGINATION. By the overuse of imagination, the young adolescent may experience feelings of attraction toward an older adult. It may be a teacher or a movie star. Sometimes young people have adventurous dreams of how glamorous and wonderful life with this idolized adult would be. Most adolescents soon realize the improbability of the fulfillment of this dream and so move on from the irrational to the romantic stage of love.

The romantic stage

The romantic stage of love usually begins with the unconscious realization of the limitations of irrational love. In the American society this tends to occur in the early teens. The individual finds a more available person of the opposite sex and tries to recreate that person into the unobtainable person of his irrational dreams. The person selected becomes the "right one," "the one and only." The youth finds it easier to attribute the idol characteristics to someone at hand than to discover the idol. Young couples in this stage may try to act out the kind of affairs they have read about in novels or magazines, heard about in songs, or have seen acted out in the movies or on television. After a short acquaintance, a dream-like courtship begins, and feelings of destiny abound. Adults have had a tendency to laugh at these affairs and to refer to them as "puppy love," but they would be wise to consider the consequences more seriously today. An adolescent may become virtually obsessed with the idea that the object of his adoration is a glamorous being and that they cannot live without each other. The obsession sometimes takes a violent and compulsive form, including a willingness to sacrifice honor, self-respect, duty, and perhaps even life. As Duvall and Hill have stated so well: "The only trouble with puppy love feelings is that if they are taken too seriously, they may lead to a dog's life."[26] The Romantic school of literature has popularized this stage of love as being "just," "right," and "pure" and justifying a defiance of all conventions, regardless of society's standards of morality. Such literature suggests that anything that stands in love's way can legitimately be disregarded.[27] The romantic stage is chiefly characterized by a desperate longing. Actually, the longing is for what one could not get in the preceding stage. So the person down the street becomes the glamorous and unobtainable idol.

DURATION. The romantic-love stage contains the seeds of its own destruction, for the idea that the mate is perfect is incompatible with marriage. People who wish to remain in the romantic stage should never get married, for marriage is too intimate a relationship to support romantic delusions. It is probably safe to say that if two individuals wish to keep their love at the romantic stage, the worst thing they could possibly do is to marry each other. Romance is more involved with feelings than with thinking, and consequently does not usually last long. It is difficult for both to retain the same degree of intensity, and as soon as one of them begins to know more about the other, the illusions fade and the romance soon ends.

ROMANCE IS NOT DENIED. It is true that there should be some romance in the love that precedes marriage, but it should be a relatively short interval in the total love relationship. As a stage in the developmental love process, romance is essential, but marriage based on this aspect of love will mean many heartaches for most individuals. Most people experience the romantic stage of love several times. Research indicates that most girls between the ages of twelve and eighteen have experienced the romantic stage at least half a dozen times.[28] Romance is a very worthy stage of love, but it is neither the only stage nor the last one before marriage. Its presence does not guarantee success, nor does its absence mean failure in marriage. It appears to be a more or less necessary stage in the democratic process of mate selection. Love enough for marriage, however, needs greater knowledge and appreciation of the partner's real nature than the romantic stage affords.[29]

A matter of degrees

Popular phrases would indicate that a person is either in or out of love, with no possibility of an intermediate state. It is more realistic, however, to consider love as a continuum, with little love at one end, warm love in the middle range, and deep love at the far end.

Figure 7-2. Romantic love appears to be a more or less necessary stage in the democratic process of mate selection. (Courtesy of the Kansas State University News Bureau.)

Within this scale a person is always in love, but the important factor that needs to be determined is the degree of the present love. In this continuum it is possible to love more than one person of the opposite sex at the same time, but to different degrees. If an individual does not know which of two individuals to marry, then perhaps neither love is of a degree to justify marriage. Such an individual simply has to wait for the fuller development of one of the relationships; or to drop one of the partners and work for the fuller development of the relationship with the one retained, fully realizing that the one dropped may be just as suitable as the other.

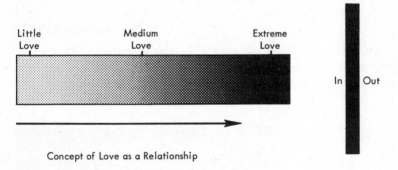

Concept of Love as a Relationship

Popular Concept of Love

Figure 7-3.

To fall in love suddenly and mutually is still not enough love for marriage. Love must be further developed over a longer period of time. It must be nourished for a time before it really begins to blossom. This does not mean that there is no such thing as love "at first sight." Indeed there often is an attraction between two individuals at first sight, but this degree of love is not sufficient for marriage. Sometimes, almost from the moment of their first meeting, two persons are aware of a compulsive pull toward each other. This may be because they have met at a moment when each is susceptible to the idea of love and marriage; it may be a chance meeting when each is confronted with a crisis in life or with the necessity for making a major decision. David Rioch, a psychiatrist, believes this to be the explanation for most cases of so-called love at first sight: "Love offers an out that is not publically disapproved; rather it is an out that society even approves and looks upon with sentimental frankness."[30] Rarely do such attractions carry over into a permanent marriage. People who are happily in a marriage that quickly follows their initial acquaintance are happy in spite of a brief courtship, not because of it. Love at first sight is possible, but a love relationship that can justify marriage is developed only as two people become better acquainted over a long period.

A GROWING THING. Love that justifies marriage usually emerges from a casual acquaintance. In the study by Burgess and Wallin, more than one third of the most successful couples were already somewhat acquainted, and an additional one fourth were already friends before serious interest began to develop between them.[31] A study of college couples found that more than two thirds of their most successful relationships started from indifference and then grew steadily in intensity.[32] The usual pattern begins with marked disinterest, moves slowly upward through attractive love, and then either reverts to indifference or advances to a degree of love strong enough to justify marriage. Ordinarily, two people are not simultaneously attracted at the same level.[33] Love runs an erratic course; it is up and down, never smooth, and often beset by doubts and jealousies.[34]

MIXED EMOTIONS. A relationship may involve affection, hostility, and hate. One authority states that hatred is only love "tortured by its own hunger and thirst."[35] Karl Menninger has described this ambivalence as a feeling of wanting to change another person. He explains that it springs from a desire to destroy that part of another believed to be dangerously inconsistent with one's own personality.[36]

Love strong enough for marriage

In determining whether love is strong enough for marriage, two important questions should be answered carefully: (1) Is the relationship a growing one? (2) To what degree of love has the relationship progressed? It is most important that the couple also understand why they are in love and how much they are in love.

HOW TO GAUGE THE DEGREE. There is no simple formula to determine the degree of existing love. Some idea of the degree of love may be estimated by thinking in terms of how marriage would affect the relationship. Some writers in the field of marriage education have made checklists for couples to use as a general gauge.[37] Bowman lists thirty-seven questions, and states: "A love that cannot stand the test of thirty-seven questions could never stand a test of thirty-seven years of marriage, or for that matter, even three years of marriage."[38] Marriage involves living with a person, not merely loving him. Whether the love will be preserved through marriage is of more concern to the couple than how deep or boundless it may seem during courtship.

THE "I" STAGE. Perhaps the simplest way to determine the varying degrees of love is by the pronoun measure. When most people begin to date, their first concern is usually "What's in it for me?"

People in the first degree of love are usually eager to rush into marriage because they are afraid the relationship may break up if prolonged. There is usually some glossing over or denial of disagreeable facts in order to prolong a relationship that is proving satisfactory to at least one of the partners at the moment. There may be a loss of ambition, loss of appetite, and a loss of interest in everyday affairs. In the "I" degree of love, little is known about the partner but that little is believed to be adequate for the needs of the "I," who is willing to assume the rest. This love intensity is popularly termed *infatuation*. Problems and barriers that are obvious to others are likely to be disregarded. It is usually a situation of many erotic vicissitudes that seemingly vary with the distance between the couple. Its two major components are physical attraction and emotional-need satisfactions.

Physical attraction occurs when the love object is physically pleasing. This is a natural part of the love process and not to be denied in any of the stages; however, in the "I" degree it is usually the strongest part, for little else is yet known about the love object. Physical attraction is also based on sex appeal. Sex is an integral part of the higher degrees of love, but it is an overwhelmingly large part of the "I" degree of love.

Certainly some of the power of love stems from sexual arousal, but there can be much confusion when love and sex are considered synonymous. The influence of Freud is at least partly responsible for this confusion, for he continuously referred to *the love object* when he really meant *the sex object*.[39] A strong sex attraction by itself is insufficient grounds for marriage. Men and women are so constituted biologically that sex desires, demanding though they may be, are quickly satisfied. A clue as to whether sex is the primary attraction for marriage is the frequency with which boredom looms when sexual excitement has been temporarily quieted.

Another index of the "I" measure is that needs are expressed in the peremptory manner of a dictator, who tolerates others only as long as he has a use for them. When these needs are not met, interest in the partner begins to die.

A couple should examine the reasons for their mutual attraction. If the relationship is most strongly oriented simply to the fulfillment of their basic needs, then it is quite possible that each partner is still most interested mainly in the personal pleasure he derives from the relationship. To base a marriage exclusively on the satisfaction of needs—whether they be emotional or physical—is to desire the possession of the person, not his affirmation. Overstreet states, in effect, that love enough for marriage means gladly granting another person the full right to his unique personality; that one does not truly love another when he seeks to enslave him by law or by bonds of dependence or possessiveness.[40]

It is wise to wait and permit other elements to develop within the relationship, if they will, rather than to assume that the satisfaction of needs constitutes justification for marriage. If the potential is there, the relationship will naturally grow easily into the consideration of the partner's interests, and the love relationship will progress into the "we" stage. Love enough for marriage must be an unconditional, spontaneous giving without regard to personal gain. There can be no bribery, no enticement, and no duress.

THE "YOU" STAGE. The second measure of love as a relationship is the pronoun *you*. In its extreme form, it is a state of personal sacrifice to the cause of the other individual: "You are the one that is more important"; "I want to please you." Although the "you" stage is perhaps better than the "I," it is still not enough to justify a lasting marriage in a democratic society. Certainly the wish to help the growth of the partner toward his greatest potential is altruistic, but sharing is a sounder foundation for a relationship than one-way giving. Marriage in a society that strives for equal rights for all demands that both partners benefit mutually from marriage. One partner cannot for long think more of the other than of himself. Unfortunately, many Americans have been led to believe this is possible, and the idea has been perpetuated by some authors.[41] Love that involves continuous sacrifice to the wishes of another, and even the denial of one's own emotional and intellectual existence, borders on masochism. Voluntary slavery is an unhealthy impulse; it is not a sound basis for marriage.

THE "WE" STAGE. In the "we" stage of love the couple are thinking and planning together in terms of what is best for their relationship. What is best for "us" becomes as important as what is best for "me" or for "you." The ancient Greeks better understood the importance of the "we" measure. They had two words for love: *eros* and *agape*. *Eros* was typified as similar to the measurement of "I," with emphasis on fulfilling the sexual appetite; it was possessive and demanding. *Agape*, in contrast, included overflowing joy and fellowship and a pleasure in being and giving. The "we" stage of love implies a full giving of oneself freely, but with no loss because mutual strength is gained. Along with a genuine concern for the partner and a joy in seeing the progress of his accomplishments, there is a desire in the "we" stage to foster circumstances through which both partners can achieve much more than either could alone.

When the couple begin to think as much of the relationship as they do of themselves, and can lose themselves in values common to both, then they are approaching the degree of love that will justify marriage. Magoun quotes one authority on love as saying that the kind of love that justifies marriage "does not consist of gazing at each other, but in looking outward together in the same direction."[42] It becomes a creative relationship that continues to grow with increased knowledge of the partner, his likes and dislikes, his virtues and his vices. This kind of relationship takes time to grow.

Physical attraction is present in the "we" stage, but it has more significance than a mere pleasurable experience; it is not used in an effort to create a relationship that is not feasible.[43] Perhaps love that justifies marriage is not composed of unique ingredients as much as it is a uniquely balanced combination of ingredients which are present in almost every relationship. In addition to erotic feelings, it arouses tenderness and joy with admiration and respect for another as individuals and for both as a pair.[44]

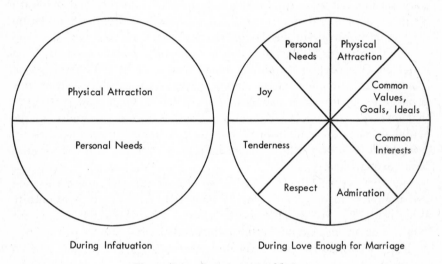

During Infatuation   During Love Enough for Marriage

Figure 7-4.   Components of love.

If these components are not fairly well balanced in the relationship, then the degree of love is not sufficient to justify marriage. If such is the case, the couple should slow down and not rush into marriage. Perhaps by taking more time and getting to know more about each other and the possibilities of what can be created together, the relationship can move into the "we" stage. If it does not, then it is better that the couple not marry.

> To make marriage itself—the union with the beloved—your only or your supreme aim is a great mistake. The reason for this is quite evident if you think about it. You make marriage your aim: you get married. What then? ... It is indeed certain that if you had no common purpose before, then so far from drawing nearer to one another you will draw further apart. If two people who have the same aim meet on the way and say to one another, "Let us go forward together," and go on hand in hand, then and only then will their marriage bring them happiness—but not if, being attracted to one another, they both turn away from their road.[45]

Comparison of low and high degrees of love as a relationship[46]

Low degree	High degree
1. Interest dies out quickly after a given involvement ends.	1. Interest slow to leave after a given involvement ends.
2. Interest develops at first sight, based on little actual knowledge; much is assumed.	2. Interest develops with time and with knowledge of the partner's strengths and weaknesses.
3. Little growth in the relationship with the passing of time; much vacillation.	3. Some vacillation, but an over-all growth with time.
4. Problems and barriers are often disregarded; there is defensiveness about them if they are pointed out by others.	4. Realistic recognition of some differences—faced objectively.
5. Pretense about disagreeable things.	5. Sincerity even about disagreeable things.
6. Pretended mutual interests when these actually do not exist.	6. Many sincere mutual interests.
7. Emotional insecurity; many hidden doubts, fears, suspicions, and jealousies.	7. Emotional security and trust; doubts honestly faced; feelings of contentment.
8. Loss of ambition, appetite, and interest in everything except the partner.	8. Courage to venture into new activities, and renewed interest in all mankind.
9. Search for self-satisfactions; extreme sensitivity to own feelings and needs.	9. Awareness of own feelings and needs, with sensitivity to the needs of the partner and the relationship.
10. Appraisal of other person's actions only in relation to own felt needs.	10. Awareness of other person's actions, but concentration on his intentions.
11. Greater part of interest based on physical attraction: beauty and sex appeal.	11. Physical attraction is balanced by other things: tenderness, joy, admiration, and respect.
12. Physical contact for the sake of pleasure, little emotional meaning; boredom in its absence.	12. Meaningful pleasure in physical contact, as a natural reaction to an already strong attachment.
13. Need to be thanked.	13. No sense of self-sacrifice.
14. Frequent intense feelings ("it's like walking on air").	14. Occasional feelings of light-headedness, but mostly calmness and assurance—clear-headedness.
15. Feelings that this time it is the right one (we are made for each other).	15. Realization that one can and does love many times at different levels.

Love after marriage

Much has been written about love before marriage, but very little about what happens to love after the wedding. If love is such an important prerequisite for marriage in a democracy, then it must also have some importance as a part of the relationship afterward.

Love is a dynamic process. As it grows, it reaches out beyond the mate to include other people. It contains a genuine growing concern for others, and a willingness to contribute one's share to the improvement of the world. This includes a strong support of institutions, feelings of obligation, and duty to others beyond the marriage. It radiates out in its values and concerns for the happiness and well-being of all mankind. It is motivating, and releases energy for work. It is creative, bringing an eagerness to learn about and to work for worthy purposes and ideals in life.

Love which is strong enough for marriage is also realistic: problems, including faults and weaknesses, are accepted with a focus toward improving and building a stronger relationship. It is truthful; it is a sharing of thoughts, feelings, attitudes, ambitions, hopes, and interests.

Through the security of marital love, the individual is free to scale new heights of ambition and to share his love with others. This is only possible, however, where there is truly love enough before marriage. Unfortunately, too many people are still getting married without this degree of love. When they do, they usually become trapped in their own little world rather than continuing to grow.

Summary

Love is the most important prerequisite for building a happy marriage in the democratic American society. As other societies accept democracy as encompassing individual freedom and personal happiness, the concept that love is essential for marriage becomes increasingly understood.

Love should be considered within the developmental-task concept. The various growth responsibilities of love as a developmental task are: self, family, expansion, multiple, irrational, romantic, and relationship consciousness. The refinement of each task-stage goes on throughout life, but success in the later stages depends upon experiencing some measure of satisfaction in all the earlier stages.

Love enough for marriage can be estimated by the pronoun measure; the extreme of each pronoun measure is a guide in determining whether love is sufficient to justify marriage. Furthermore, when love is strong enough for marriage, it continues to grow after marriage.

Notes

1. E. W. Burgess and Paul Wallin, *Engagement and Marriage* (Philadelphia: J. B. Lippincott & Co., 1953), pp. 393–95.

2. Ralph Linton, *The Study of Man* (New York: Appleton-Century-Crofts, Inc., 1936), Chap. 11.

3. Edmund S. Morgan, *The Puritan Family* (Boston: Trustees of the Public Library, 1944), pp. 12–15, 21–22.

4. Raoulde Rossy de Sales, "Love in America," *Atlantic Monthly* (May 1938).

5. See, e.g., T. Peter Omari, "Changing Attitudes of Students in West African Society Toward Marriage and Family Relations," *British Journal of Sociology,* 11:197–210.

6. Oswald Schwarz, in A. M. Krich (ed.), *Women: The Variety and Meaning of Their Sexual Experience* (New York: Dell Publications, 1954), p. 290.

7. S. Chandrasekhar, "The Family in India," *Marriage and Family Living,* 16:339.

8. Ruth Benedict, *Patterns of Culture* (Boston: Houghton Mifflin Company, 1934), p. 108.

9. Bronislaw Malinowski, *The Sexual Life of Savages in North Western Melanesia* (New York: Liveright Publishing Corp., 1929), pp. 117–18, 317.

10. R. F. Fortune, *Sorcerers of Dobu* (New York: E. P. Dutton & Co., Inc., 1932), p. 30.

11. For additional reading concerning the uniqueness of love as a prerequisite for marriage, see Linton G. Freeman, "Marriage Without Love: Mate Selection in Nonwestern Societies," in Robert F. Winch, Robert McGinnis, and Herbert R. Barringer (eds.), *Selected Studies in Marriage and the Family* (New York: Holt, Rinehart & Winston, Inc., 1962), pp. 439–55.

12. Smiley Blanton, *Love or Perish* (New York: Simon and Schuster, Inc., 1956), p. 21.

13. A study of the 1224 most popular songs in the United States over a sixty-year period revealed that almost two thirds of them dealt with love. The most frequent theme was the lonely or disappointed lover. The second most popular theme was the unfulfilled love or longing, with a strong suggestion that marriage was the logical and inevitable outcome. See Norman Charles, Doctoral study, University of Pennsylvania, Philadelphia, Pa., 1958.

14. J. Piaget, *The Moral Judgment of the Child* (London: Routledge & Kegan Paul, Ltd., 1932), p. 354.

15. Robert J. Havinhurst, *Human Development and Education,* New York: Longmans, Green & Co., Inc., 1953), p. 2.

16. For an excellent treatment of this subject, see Karen Horney, *The Neurotic Personality of Our Time* (New York: W. W. Norton & Company, Inc., 1937).

17. Leviticus 19:18; also Deuteronomy 6:5.

18. Ian D. Suttie, *The Origins of Love and Hate* (New York: The Julian Press, Inc., 1952).

19. Margaret A. Ribble, *The Rights of Infants* (New York: Columbia University Press, 1943); Daniel A. Prescott, "Love and the Child," *Child and Family,* 2:7–16.

20. See William McCord, *Origins of Crime* (New York: Columbia University Press, 1959); Andrew F. Henry and James F. Short, *Suicide and Homicide* (New York: The Free Press of Glencoe, Inc., 1954).

21. Harry F. Harlow, "The Nature of Love," *The American Psychologist,* 13:673–85.

22. Ralph Eckert, *Sex Attitudes in the Home* (New York: Association Press, 1956).

23. The need for other trusting adults in a child's life is well described in Dorothy W. Baruch, "Are Teaching Techniques Meant for Children?" *Journal of Consulting Psychology,* 8:111.

24. One recent research study suggests that attraction between members of the opposite sex now begins earlier than formerly. See Carlfred B. Broderick

and Stanley E. Fowler, "New Pattern of Relationships Between the Sexes Among Preadolescents," *Marriage and Family Living,* 23:27–30.

25. In spite of their earlier interest, however, the girls' sexual desire develops later than the boys. This is discussed in Chapter 8 in the section on maturation differentials as deterrents to premarital coitus.

26. Evelyn M. Duvall and Reuben Hill, *When You Marry* (New York: Association Press, 1953), p. 30.

27. The basis for this type of love won considerable support in nineteenth-century prose, poetry, and drama. It was not depicted as a rewarding association with another, but rather as an exultation of the self. See Hubert Becher, *Love and Marriage in Modern Literature* (Frankfort Am Main: Joseph Knecht Veriag, 1959).

28. Albert Ellis, "Questionnaire Versus Interview Methods in the Study of Human Love Relationship; II: Uncategorized Responses," *American Sociological Review,* 13:62–64.

29. For an expanded discussion of this point, see Hugo G. Beigel, "Romantic Love," in Winch, McGinnis, and Barringer (eds.), *op. cit.,* Chap: 7.

30. Gimble Lectures, Stanford Medical School, Stanford, Calif., April, 1957.

31. Burgess and Wallin, *op. cit.,* p. 160.

32. Clifford Kirkpatrick and Theodore Caplow, "Emotional Trends in the Courtship Experience of College Students as Expressed by Graphs with Some Observations on Methodological Implications," *American Sociological Review,* 10:619–26.

33. *Ibid.* See illustrated charts in reference above.

34. Clifford Kirkpatrick and Theodore Caplow, "Courtship in a Group of Minnesota Students," *American Journal of Sociology,* 50:114–25; and Burgess and Wallin, *op. cit.,* p. 180.

35. Suttie, *op. cit.*

36. Karl A. Menninger, *Love Against Hate* (New York: Harcourt, Brace & World, Inc., 1942).

37. See, e.g., Clifford R. Adams and Vance O. Packard, *How to Pick a Mate* (New York: E. P. Dutton & Co., Inc., 1946), pp. 52–54; Henry A. Bowman, *Marriage for Moderns,* 2nd ed. (New York: McGraw-Hill Book Company, Inc., 1954), pp. 40–49.

38. *Ibid.*

39. T. A. Reik, *A Psychologist Looks at Love* (New York: Farrar, Straus & Company, 1944), p. 7.

40. Harry A. Overstreet, *The Mature Mind* (New York: W. W. Norton & Company, Inc., 1949), p. 113.

41. See, e.g., Roy A. Burkhart, *From Friendship to Marriage* (New York: Harper & Row, Publishers, 1937), pp. 72–73; Harry S. Sullivan, *Conceptions of Modern Psychiatry* (Washington, D.C.: William A. White Psychiatric Foundation, 1947), p. 20.

42. Antoine de Sant Exupery, quoted in F. Alexander Magoun, *Love and Marriage* (New York: Harper & Row, Publishers, 1956), Chap. 1.

43. Holmes and Hatch have advanced the theory that the betterment of the race or species is achieved by the operation of sexual selection based on beauty. But what is beauty? In the Gay Nineties, for instance, the ideal woman was a fragile, delicate, somewhat sickly creature. S. J. Holmes and L. E. Hatch, "Personal Appearance as Related to Scholastic Records and Marriage Selection in College Women," *Human Biology,* 10:65–76; furthermore, research in Italy discloses that the fertility of the most beautiful women is less than that of other

women. See Corrado Gini, "Beauty, Marriage, and Fertility," *Human Biology,* 10:575–76.

44. For a fuller discussion of the elements of love enough for marriage, see Joseph K. Folsom, "Steps in Love and Courtship," in Howard Becker and Reuben Hill (eds.), *Family, Marriage and Parenthood* (Boston: D. C. Heath and Company, 1955).

45. The Tolstoy Home, *Diaries of Tatiana Tolstoy,* translated by Alex Brown (New York: Columbia University Press, 1951), pp. 90–91.

46. Only the individual by himself can make a proper judgment of just what degree of love he and his partner are experiencing.

Questions for further thought

1. In what ways is love the only basis for marriage consistent with the American concept of democracy?
2. Is a marriage based on factors other than love—such as money, security, or status—wrong?
3. Explain the findings of Terman (Lewis M. Terman. *Psychological Factors in Marital Happiness* [New York: McGraw-Hill Book Company, Inc., 1938], pp. 221–22) in terms of a stage of love?
4. Are people who appear willingly to suffer in order to please their mates fundamentally unselfish or selfish?
5. Could love ever become a tragedy?
6. Which personality needs are most satisfied by association with those whom one loves?
7. What generalizations in terms of love can be made about the plots of stories in "true-story" magazines?
8. Why is it as important to learn to be a gracious receiver as to be a generous giver?
9. What are some factors in modern society which sometimes make it difficult to distinguish between infatuation and a love strong enough for marriage?
10. What is the difference between knowing a person and loving him? Is there also a similarity?

Recommended films

This Charming Couple (McGraw-Hill Book Company, Inc.).
Is This Love (McGraw-Hill Book Company, Inc.).
How Do You Know It's Love (Coronet).

Suggested supplemental readings

BOOKS

Becher, Hubert. *Love and Marriage in Modern Literature.* Frankfurt Am Main, Germany: Joseph Knecht Veriag, 1959.
Bettelheim, Bruno. *Love Is Not Enough.* New York: The Free Press of Glencoe, Inc., 1950.
Blanton, Smiley. *Love or Perish.* New York: Simon and Schuster, Inc., 1955.
Cleckley, Hervey. *The Caricature of Love.* New York: The Ronald Press Company, 1957.
Ellis, Albert. *The Art and Science of Love.* New York: Lyle Stuart, 1960.
Fromm, Erich. *The Art of Loving.* New York: Harper & Row, Publishers, 1956.
Gorer, Geoffrey. *The American People: A Study in National Character.* New York: W. W. Norton & Company, Inc., 1948.

Maslow, A. H. "Love and Healthy People," in Ashley Montagu (ed.), *The Meaning of Love*. New York: The Julian Press, Inc., 1953.

Steiner, Lee R. *Romantic Marriage: The Twentieth Century Illusion*. Philadelphia: Chilton Company, 1963.

Suttie, Ian D. *The Origins of Love and Hate*. New York: The Julian Press, Inc., 1952.

Wallace, Karl Miles, and Eve O'Dell. *Love Is More Than Luck*. New York: Funk & Wagnalls, Inc., 1957.

West, Jessamyn. *Love Is Not What You Think*. New York: Curtis, 1959.

Wylie, William P. *The Pattern of Love*. New York: Longmans, Green & Co., Inc., 1958.

ARTICLES

Bolton, Charles D. "Mate Selection as the Development of a Relationship," *Marriage and Family Living,* 23:234–40.

Foote, Nelson. "Love," *Psychiatry,* 16:247.

Fromm, Erich. "Love and Its Distintegration," *Pastoral Psychology,* 7:37–44.

Goode, William J. "The Theoretical Importance of Love," *American Sociological Review,* 24:38–47.

Hobart, Charles W. "The Incidence of Romanticism During Courtship," *Social Forces,* 36:362–67.

Knight, Thomas S. "In Defense of Romance," *Marriage and Family Living,* 21:107–10.

LeBarre, Weston. "Wanted: A Pattern for Modern Man," *Mental Hygiene,* 33:2–8.

Saul, Leon J. "The Distinction Between Loving and Being Loved," *Psychoanalytic Quarterly,* 19:412–13.

Williams, Allen V. "What Is Adolescent Love?" *Child Study* (Fall 1950), 103–104, 121–22.

Winter, Gibson. "Love and Conflict," *Pastoral Psychology,* 9:33–40.

Appraising the
physical expression

chapter 8   of love

American society permits unchaperoned, private, and paired dating among young people at the age when the male sex drive is usually at its strongest stage of development. In addition, there seems to be a stronger sex drive and curiosity among young people of both sexes today than in any previous era. These sexual impulses are further aroused by a commercial environment designed to exploit sexual excitement. This can be observed in movies, in best-selling novels, and in the beat and lyrics of popular music. Much consumer advertising implies subtly or overtly that sex is a lot of fun and will be even more fun if the advertised product is purchased. Thus, there is little question that many of today's youths need help in perceiving and establishing norms of sexual behavior.

The naturalness of physical attraction

It is only natural for young people to express their affection for one another in a physical way. Most adults unconsciously do this to some degree in their daily social exchanges. For instance, total strangers may simply shake hands, but those who are better acquainted may not only grasp hands but also place their other hand on the friend's shoulder. Physical display of affection for a close friend is as natural as a verbal display. Thus, as a couple move from their first date toward a more intense relationship, physical contacts naturally increase, and so may sexual tensions. But this is nothing for which youth need be ashamed. Sexual desire is inborn; of itself, sex is not vulgar, but it may be used in a vulgar manner. Leuba suggests that sexual attractiveness is the art of arousing erotic reactions strong enough to be pleasant, but weak enough not to shock or violate ethical sensitivities. To use sex appeal as the only method of attracting a person is both crude and unfair, but to use sex appeal as one of several methods of attracting one of the opposite sex is both legitimate and necessary.[1]

Physical expressions of affection may stimulate a desire for complete sexual release. For some individuals, petting may awaken new sexual responses. Because sex desire may be more repressed by cultural conditioning in some people than in others, petting may awaken the previously inhibited response. The research findings of Kinsey show conclusively that the heavier the petting—and the more often it is engaged in—the more likelihood there is that intercourse will occur.[2]

Varieties of sexual release

There are many kinds of sexual release besides coitus. Some of these variations are considered more acceptable by some groups than by others, and some practices are more readily available to certain groups than to others.

NIGHT EMISSIONS.   A common sexual manifestation, especially of young adolescent boys, is nocturnal emission; this is frequently termed a *wet dream*. It is a condition in which accumulated semen is released during sleep. It is an involuntary act, often accompanied by erotic dreams and, although not confined to any one age group, it most commonly occurs between the ages of sixteen and twenty. In Kinsey's studies, 91 per cent of the men recalled having had the experience in their youth.[3]

MASTURBATION.   Sexual release or pleasure can be induced by masturbation, the practice of self-manipulation of the genitals. The superstitions that surrounded this practice in the past have gradually been dispelled. Most psychiatrists and psychoanalysts are of the opinion that masturbation is a harmless activity and that its effects have been greatly over-dramatized. Perhaps the worst hazard of masturbation is that, being a creature of habit, man might find the practice more convenient than marital sex. This would then lead to poor marital sex adjustment. Kinsey's research with women in this connection tends to throw doubt on this line of reasoning. Although orgasm may not be the only method of measuring marital sexual satisfaction, it is a relatively good index, and the majority of those who reported masturbation before marriage also reported a considerably higher orgasm rate in marital intercourse than those individuals who reported never masturbating. Approximately 90 per cent of men and 60 per cent of women in the most recent surveys conducted by the Institute for Sex Research (formerly commonly referred to as the Kinsey Institute) reported using masturbation as a sexual outlet with much less emotional disturbance about it than former generations experienced.[4]

HOMOSEXUALITY. Another form of sexual release is homosexuality, the sexual excitement aroused between members of the same sex. According to Kinsey, about 50 per cent of males still unmarried at age thirty-five have some overt homosexual experience, but only 4 per cent are exclusively homosexual. Many are heterosexual and report using homosexual activities only as a "second" sexual pursuit.[5]

PROSTITUTION. In spite of modern restrictions, prostitution still provides a means of sexual indulgence for some people. Kinsey's research suggests that the services of prostitutes are used more by unmarried males between the age of thirty-six and forty, who have not progressed beyond the grade-school level in education, than by any other group.[6]

PETTING TO CLIMAX. Petting, without actual genital contact, is also reported in use as a means of releasing sexual tension. Persons who indulge in this practice are frequently referred to as *technical virgins*, for—although they sometimes experience orgasm from the petting experience—there has been no direct genital contact.

Kinsey reported finding that at least 46 per cent of the men and 26 per cent of the women at the college level have experienced at least one sexual climax from petting. The typical median frequency for both sexes was five times yearly.[7] Many studies indicate that some college-age girls can seemingly pet to climax without actual penis penetration. Additional studies indicate that this is an impossibility for others, most particularly for high school age girls. Even among the college students, many report increasing difficulty in refraining from coitus during each episode of petting to climax.[8]

SUBLIMATION. According to Franz Alexander, subordination of the sexual impulse to activities other than sexual intercourse is possible:

> All sexual emotions have nonsexual equivalents. It is not their quality but the degree of tension involved and the mode of discharge which makes them sexual. Linguistic usage registers this fact by employing the same word for nonsexual and sexual love.[9]

The possibilities of sublimation for most individuals, however, are considered to be quite limited. Kinsey's findings indicate that such activities as vigorous exercise are especially noneffective.[10] Some people are able to control sex urges by creative work, but not every kind of work seems effective. It must be something that engulfs the entire imagination, and this seems to be difficult for many young adults.

Lessening of outside controls over premarital coitus

Many cultural forces, which in past generations strongly supported the taboo on complete freedom of sexual expression outside of marriage, appear nowadays to have slackened their influence. The most influential have always been religion and the law. The mores of the culture and the sex differential have also tended to favor such restrictions.

RELIGION.   One of the chief influences on sex behavior has been religion. The earliest Biblical writings decreed that coitus should be confined to marriage, and one of the Ten Commandments forbids adultery. Fundamentally, this edict was based on the principle that adultery would be a violation of property rights, for the wife of that era was considered the property of the husband. Thus coitus with another man's wife violated her husband's property rights. This property-rights concept also implied the prohibition of coitus with a woman even promised to another man. Thus, in effect, all premarital sexual copulation was prohibited.[11]

Although the words and teaching of Jesus on sex behavior were liberal, Paul gave a strict interpretation on this matter:

> ... To avoid fornication, let every man have his own wife and every woman have her own husband. ... I speak this by permission and not by commandment ... for I would that all men were even as I myself. ... I say therefore to the unmarried and widows, it is good for them if they abide even as I but if they cannot contain, let them marry, for it is better to marry than to burn.[12]

Chastity before marriage is still regarded by religion as an ideal, but there is much less mention made about it than in former times. Instead of appealing to fear as Paul did, most modern religions appeal to reason. The problem for young people who belong to such religious groups is to adhere to the values of their church without the presence of a constant religious authority reminding them of what those values are. Their major difficulty comes when they date, and perhaps begin to fall in love with, others who have different standards.[13]

THE MORES.   All behavior that affects society is, to a certain extent at least, subject to its control. Even eating is regulated by etiquette. Actually, a sex life completely free from the control of any progressive society has never been known or realized.[14]

The most common way in which past societies have placed controls around sex behavior has been through the establishment of the double standard. That is to say, one standard of behavior is acceptable for men, and a more restricted code of behavior is demanded of women. In order to establish a double standard and make it work, it was necessary to assume that women had no real sex feelings; therefore, those women who might feel sexually aroused could not admit it even to themselves. Copulation outside of marriage was thus made psychologically almost impossible for most females.

In consigning this responsibility to the woman, it was suggested that "nice" girls did not behave in a sexually promiscuous manner. Then, too, when a girl broke the code, she was almost certain to be found out, for in earlier times the possibility of pregnancy was very real. In that era pregnancy outside of marriage left the woman little else but to become a prostitute. Thus, the biological double standard of possible premarital pregnancy supported the cultural double standard.

The only acceptable sexual releases for women were (1) a deep subli- mation of sex in religion or (2) a deep involvement in marriage with a complete sublimation in the husband and family. Thus, through the perpetuation of the patriarchial family, the female was kept from "doing wrong." In past centuries, if a woman wished an affair with a lover, it was usually wiser to marry any man first and then to have the affair. If pregnancy resulted, and it nearly always did, the child might be passed off as legitimate.

The history of sexual morality has always been the history of male supremacy. Today, however, women are challenging the double standard. More and more lines are being crossed, and a "desexing" of certain behavior patterns has occurred. For example, kissing has traditionally been considered a strong expression of affection, but in today's society it is frequently used merely as a friendly greeting, for pleasure, or as a gesture; it may be given to the date as the girl's duty, taken as the boy's privilege, or considered as a symbol of conquest and an invitation to further sexual involvement. The influence of Freud and the American democratic ideal of equality have done much to change the concept of the double standard. American society recognizes that women have sex feelings, just as men do.

LEGAL RESTRICTIONS. The preservation of chastity before marriage has, in some periods, been assured by legal restrictions. The first legal code proscribing adultery and fornication, and providing penalties for offen- ders, was instituted in 2000 B.C. by Hammurabi of Babylonia. In many respects the code of that time was much more consistent than the modern code of the various states within the American society.

In the United States, the state laws on sex crimes are as varied as the laws of marriage and divorce. Sexual behavior permitted in some states is prohibited in others. Fornication, or sexual coitus before marriage, is specifically prohibited by law in thirty-eight states, while adultery is similarly prohibited in all but five.[15] The major inconsistency arises from differences in the definition of *fornication*. The statutes of many states indicate that a single or occasional act of sexual coitus outside of marriage does not violate the law. These states require proof of cohabitation over a period of time or a habitual sexual relationship between two persons before declaring fornication. In 1940, the State Supreme Court of Okla- homa made the decision that "voluntary" sexual copulation between unmarried men and women is not a statutory offense, but only a "mere- tricious transaction."[16] That interpretation is in sharp contrast to the law in Massachusetts, which has decreed that even a single act of sexual coitus between two unmarried people constitutes fornication, and as such is punishable by both fine and imprisonment.

In several states fornication is related to the age when females are no longer considered to be sexual minors. Coitus with a female minor, even though she agrees to the act, constitutes statutory rape, for such a woman is not considered to be old enough to understand fully what she is agreeing to do. For example, the New York courts have said that coitus with an unmarried woman above the age of sexual maturity is not unlawful, but perhaps is immoral. Here again, however, there is much variation between the states. In Georgia, the legally defined age of sexual maturity for an unmarried woman is fixed at fourteen; in Pennsylvania, at sixteen; in New York, at eighteen; and in Tennessee, at twenty-one. If, however, a male entices a female of any age to participate in coitus by a promise of future marriage and does not follow through, this is usually considered a more serious offense and is termed *seduction*.

Law officials appear much more hesitant to interfere with a couple today than formerly. The author's personal correspondence with several state attorney generals indicates that the most common practice today is simply to let the couples off with a warning. It was quite different in Colonial times, when public confessions were frequently required.

THE YOUTH IDEAL. Youth ideals have been reported in various surveys to indicate that petting has little or no relationship to popularity during dating. Fundamentally, however, there is great variation in the definition of the ideal behavior for different stages of the involvement process within a culture. What might be considered acceptable behavior with one partner might be thought unacceptable with another. If the boy and girl know each other only slightly, one pattern of conduct might be considered acceptable, whereas the level of acceptable behavior is usually different if the couple know each other well.[17] A detailed examination of various research studies discloses that definitions of ideal practice vary greatly from actual practice. In addition, in several major studies, when a category of "uncertain," (of what was ideal behavior) was included, as many as 28 per cent of the youths checked that response. When young people are asked whether a girl must pet to be popular, the majority usually answers in the negative, but the answers, again, are based on the ideal, not necessarily on the actual behavior. Youths are aware of social norms and generally conform to the expected answers on surveys. Perhaps this very awareness keeps some individuals "in line," but this appears much less certain today than formerly.

SEX DIFFERENTIALS. In the past, a somewhat pronounced sex-maturation differential seemed to exist between the sexes. This also tended to be a controlling factor in sex behavior. The Kinsey study indicated that men arrived at their peak of sex desire at about age fifteen. There appeared to be a steady increase in intensity of desire among young women

Table 8–1. **Report of 52 men and 28 women college students showing differences between ideal and actual sexual practices**

Condition	Sex	Light petting		Heavy petting		Coitus	
		Ideal	*Actual*	*Ideal*	*Actual*	*Ideal*	*Actual*
First few dates	M	1	6	1	12	0	10
	F	0	1	0	2	0	0
Frequent dates	M	11	5	3	8	1	20
	F	3	4	0	2	0	1
Going steady	M	16	5	8	12	5	23
	F	9	4	1	10	0	2
Engaged	M	10	2	14	6	16	9
	F	9	1	11	7	1	4

Source: Robert L. Karen, "Some Variables Affecting Sexual Attitudes, Behavior and Inconsistency," *Marriage and Family Living*, 21:235–39. Copyright © 1959, by The National Council on Family Relations, Minneapolis, Minn. Reprinted by permission.

in their teens, but the increase was not nearly as pronounced as for males.[18] It is not known how much of the maturation differential that does exist today is biological and how much arises from cultural conditioning. It would appear that both factors are operative, however, and most authorities are of the opinion that culture is the major influence. Thus, with the concept of increased freedom for women, the sex drive differential does not appear as pronounced as formerly. Nevertheless, the sex drive is usually more pronounced in the male, and the lesser drive of the female still tends to confine much of premarital sex expression to activities other than complete sexual union.

Motivations

Various motivational factors operate at different degrees of involvement. An examination of the relative influence of each factor is pertinent to this study.

UNJUSTIFIED MOTIVES. Many aspects of human behavior are at times related to rebellion, and sex behavior is no exception. Sometimes there is rebellion against parental wishes, particularly by individuals who are not getting along well with their parents. Such individuals may feel that any behavior that runs counter to parental dictates is a good way "to get even." Sometimes an individual of a minority group may rebel against society as a whole. Such rebellion leads to all kinds of disapproved behavior and might very well explain why there is relatively more premarital sexual experimentation among the nonwhite races in the American culture.

Material gain is also a motive for extramarital sex; this is the prime motivation of prostitutes. As Karpf points out, prostitutes seldom involve themselves emotionally with their customers.[19] There is another kind of prostitution emerging in modern society which is perhaps best termed *pseudo prostitution*. Pseudoprostitutes never consider themselves professional prostitutes, yet the desire for certain gifts and entertainment is sufficient motivation for them to maintain a sexual relationship.

An attempt to satisfy emotional needs, such as anxiety or a search for personal identity, may lead a person into considering premarital intercourse whether actually done or not. This is well depicted in J. D. Salinger's *The Catcher in the Rye*. Some individuals have a great fear of failure in the sexual area of marriage and wish to test their sexual capacity before marriage. They reason erroneously that failure outside of marriage would be less disastrous than failure in marriage.

Perhaps many motivations for coitus, both in and out of marriage, arise from social externals, such as the attempt to prove oneself "superior" or socially "acceptable," or even the desire to measure one's personal sexual appeal to others.

Curiosity is also a motivation for premarital coitus, particularly in today's society, with its commercial emphasis on sex. Hearing so much about sex may increase the desire to learn what it is all about. A deep longing for affection may motivate some individuals to participate fully in extramarital sex as a substitute for a truer affection. Sex for them is a way of feeling close to somebody, at least temporarily. It may become a means of holding a partner (this seems to be primarily a female motive). Sometimes the use of sex for this purpose is associated with abnormal attitudes toward the opposite sex and toward life itself.

Another motivation is fear of other, less "normal" sexual tendencies; persons so motivated may participate in premarital coitus in an attempt to keep themselves from getting involved in homosexual relationships.[20]

Thrill-seeking is an additional motivation. Sometimes the physical union is sought for its own sake, and there is little interest or personal regard for the partner.[21]

Some people participate in premarital coitus because of a fear that the habit of always "stopping short" might establish a pattern that would prevent their enjoyment of intercourse after marriage. This belief, which seems in accord with the theories of conditioned-response behavior, is not borne out by the Kinsey studies. His reports indicate that the habit of stopping short of coitus before marriage does not create a block and has no effect on sex adjustment after marriage.[22]

Another motivation is social pressure, or the "everybody-is-doing-it" idea. This is strongly evident in college dormitory "bull" sessions, which leave some individuals with the feeling that they are not fully matured if they have not experienced the sexual episodes discussed. Because status can usually be best achieved by accepting the group pattern, the prerequisite of sexual experimentation forces a number of individuals to comply who otherwise lack the desire for intercourse.

Some people rationalize that premarital coitus is good preparation for the sex act within marriage. They sense a need to learn something about it before marriage, and justify their actions by stating they would feel embarrassed entering marriage not knowing how to go about the sex act. They erroneously believe that premarital experience will provide training in the physical techniques needed for an adequate sexual relationship within marriage. A good sex adjustment, however, does not take place simply between any male and any female, but between a specific man and a specific woman, so sexual experimentation before marriage does not prepare one for marriage or for sex compatibility within marriage.

Some people feel that the sexual capacities of each partner should be tested before marriage, but this experience seldom gives an accurate picture of possible sex adjustment because the conditions before marriage differ so greatly from those afterward. Individuals rarely need to be concerned about their ability to perform the sex act with each other. Even the fact that both reached full physical satisfaction in the sex act prior to marriage would not assure that they would be suitable marriage partners, for marriage is much more than sex. Sexual compatibility can be developed only in harmony. Basic attitudes toward sex are not revealed by simply exploring some of its physical aspects before marriage. At best, such exploration proves only that the couple are physically fit for mating, and this can safely be assumed in most cases. (Serious doubts are best dispelled by medical consultation.) If the coital experience had proved unsatisfactory, the couple might conclude that they were not well matched; whereas, if they had waited for the more ideal conditions of marriage, the experience might have been mutually successful.

QUESTIONABLE MOTIVES. Some motives for nonmarital coitus—if not unjustifiable—are at least questionable, for they are based directly on utilitarian needs. Someone with awakened sex needs, for example, may find it very difficult to forego coitus after the termination of a marriage. According to recent surveys, physical exercise is no sure sex substitute for the sexually experienced. The older unmarried individual may also have pronounced sex desires. Kinsey's findings indicate that most older single men, and many older single women, have not waited for society's permission to indulge in sexual expression.[23] The social implications for the older unmarried individual are particularly serious. For the single woman especially, fear of discovery and feelings of guilt or possible despondency when the relationship ends must be considered as problems likely to arise when she accepts a nonmarital sexual commitment. Can she go the limit physically or emotionally without the security of a sound and permanent state such as marriage? In addition, the single woman must consider her decision in the light of social obligations; for example, can she do these things without inflicting harm to society (such as perhaps involving someone else's husband)?

There is a great need for further study on what might be done to help the dilemma of older unmarried individuals who have strong sex needs or desires. Perhaps society should either revise its professed sex conventions for these individuals or find and approve adequate substitutes. Some older individuals feel that society's rules regarding sex outside of marriage do not apply to them; they feel that they have as much right to sexual expression as those who marry.[24]

As an expression of love.   The natural wish to express deep affection in its strongest physical form is another coital motivation. One study found that an overwhelming majority of premaritally experienced women had given themselves in coitus for love and anticipation of marriage with the partner, but only 22 per cent of the men gave the same reason.[25]

> ... Most girls have only a couple of vague rules-of-thumb to go by, which they cling to beyond all sense and reason. And these, interestingly enough, contradict each other. One is that anything is all right if you're in love (romantic; from movies and certain fiction, the American dream of love) and the other is that a girl must be respected. Particularly by the man she wants to marry (ethical leftover from Grandma). Since these are extremely shaky and require a girl's knowing whether or not there is a chance of love in the relationship, sex to her requires constant corroborative discussion while she tries to plumb the depths of a man's intentions.[26]

When love and affection are motives for one partner, it does not necessarily follow that they are for the other. Ehrmann reported from his studies on the campus at the University of Florida that of those females who had experienced premarital coitus with anyone other than their future husbands, a high portion involved relationships within an engagement which was subsequently broken; only 8 per cent of the premarital coitus was with someone with whom they were not in love with at the time.[27]

Prince and Shipman discovered in their study that the average woman who had gone steady with the same person for fourteen months was much more likely to have experienced premarital coitus. After couples became engaged the average interval before coitus was seven and one half months for both sexes.[28] Another research study asked the question: "Have you ever felt you went too far and have you ever wished you had gone farther?" The results disclosed that a much smaller percentage of engaged couples than of other dating couples who had experienced coitus considered it as having gone too far.[29]

The research of Burgess and Wallin found little increase in the amount of premarital coitus by college couples who moved into the going-steady

Table 8–2. Degrees of intimacy felt suitable by men students

	Per cent approving for various levels of involvement			
Intimacy condition	First date	Infrequent dating	Going steady	Engaged
No intimacy	54.4	12.8	—	—
Good night kiss	36.3	52.7	2.7	1.6
Necking	7.3	30.6	41.3	22.6
Heavy petting	0.5	1.7	33.2	42.5
Sexual intercourse	1.5	2.2	12.8	33.3

Source: William Simenson and Gilbert Geis, "Courtship Patterns of Norwegian and American University Students," *Marriage and Family Living,* **18:**334–38; and personal correspondence with Gilbert Geis. Reprinted by permission of Gilbert Geis. An identical table appears in Ruth S. Cavan, *American Marriage: A Way of Life* (New York: Thomas Y. Crowell Company, 1959). Copyright © 1959, by Thomas Y. Crowell Company, New York.

Table 8–3. Degrees of intimacy felt suitable by women students

	Per cent approving for various levels of involvement			
Intimacy condition	First date	Infrequent dating	Going steady	Engaged
No intimacy	74	25	—	—
Good night kiss	23.2	66.2	7.4	6.2
Necking	1.4	7.3	60.3	21.5
Heavy petting	—	—	27.9	58.5
Sexual intercourse	1.4	1.5	4.4	13.8

Source: William Simenson and Gilbert Geis, "Courtship Patterns of Norwegian and American University Students," *Marriage and Family Living,* **18:**334–38; and personal correspondence with Gilbert Geis. Reprinted by permission of Gilbert Geis. An identical table appears in Ruth S. Cavan, *American Marriage: A Way of Life* (New York: Thomas Y. Crowell Company, 1959). Copyright © 1959, by Thomas Y. Crowell Company, New York.

stage of involvement. The going-steady period of their subjects ranged from thirteen to more than forty-one months. They also found that engagement made a difference. They concluded from their study that couples engaged longer than sixteen months were quite likely to have experienced coitus.[30] Kirkendall found that 80 per cent of college men engaged over a year have had intercourse with the partner.[31] Many other

Table 8–4. **Responses of 250 college women and 160 college men to question: "Have you ever felt you went 'too far'?" and "Have you ever wished you had gone farther?" classified by intimacy level for different stages of involvement**

| | Per cent answering | | | |
| | Went too far | | Wish had gone farther | |
Level	*Females*	*Males*	*Females*	*Males*
	During casual dating			
No intimacy	—	—	—	50
Kissing	13	—	20	100
Necking	14	50	34	73
Petting	54	25	30	72
Intercourse	65	44	33	75
	During going steady			
No intimacy	—	—	—	—
Kissing	—	20	41	20
Necking	7	8	22	53
Petting	37	32	31	55
Intercourse	61	44	26	56
	During engagement			
No intimacy	—	—	—	—
Kissing	50	—	—	—
Necking	25	—	33	67
Petting	26	31	20	31
Intercourse	41	41	—	18

Source: Robert R. Bell and Leonard Blumberg, "Courtship Stages and Intimacy Attitudes," *The Family Life Coordinator,* **8:**61. Copyright © 1959, by The E. C. Brown Trust, Portland, Ore. Reprinted by permission.

studies suggest that, as a group, college-educated women are more likely to approve of coitus in long engagements.[32]

Because love approves of those things which tend to build a relationship, premarital coitus might be acceptable for some couples under certain conditions, but each partner's motivations must be identical before this condition could exist. Outside of marriage, there is no way to be absolutely certain of this agreement. When any action between two individuals is not mutually acceptable, it has gone too far. Yet, even when the motives are identical, the engaged couple are wrong when they rationalize that they are "the same as if they were married." The engaged couple have not assumed legal responsibility for the act; neither do they have moral sanction nor an established financial or emotional inter-dependence for the consequences of the act.

The extent of premarital coitus

Many scholarly research studies of premarital coitus rates had been conducted in American society long before the Kinsey reports, but they did not receive as much publicity or so arouse the public interest. The earlier work included studies by Bromley and Britton, Davis, Hamilton, Ramsey, and Terman.[33] The study by Terman was probably the most extensive, covering a fifty-year span beginning in 1890. Terman's results indicated a marked and consistent increase in premarital coitus with each decade.

Table 8–5. **Extent of premarital coitus by date of birth—in per cent**

	Born before 1890	Born 1890–99	Born 1900–1909	Born 1910 and later
Men				
None	50.6	41.9	32.6	13.6
With spouse only	4.6	7.6	17.2	31.9
With others only	38.6	27.5	16.5	13.6
With spouse and others	9.2	23.0	33.7	40.9
Women				
None	86.5	74.4	51.2	31.7
With spouse only	8.7	17.7	32.7	45.0
With others only	1.9	2.5	2.1	3.1
With spouse and others	2.9	5.8	14.0	20.0

Source: Lewis M. Terman, *Psychological Factors in Marital Happiness* (New York: McGraw-Hill Book Company, Inc., 1938), p. 321. Copyright © 1938, by The McGraw-Hill Book Company, Inc., New York. Reprinted by permission.

After reviewing his findings, Terman suggested that for men born after 1930 and for women born after 1940, virginity at marriage would be exceedingly rare. He further predicted that premarital coitus with the future spouse would be almost universal by the middle 1950s.[34] After considerable analysis of their own findings and the reports of others, Burgess and Wallin concluded that Terman's predictions were too high. They agreed that premarital coitus steadily increased after the turn of the century, but fixed the present rate at about 50 per cent for women. Furthermore, they estimated that about two thirds or more of these episodes were restricted to the future spouse.[35]

The Kinsey data, in contrast to the Terman findings, indicated that the revolutionary change in sexual behavior patterns began not after 1890, but after World War I.

THE NONCOLLEGE GROUP. It is necessary to keep in mind that some of these studies were confined to college-educated people, others to non-college-educated people, and some, such as the Kinsey study, included a cross section of people.[36] Various studies show that the extent of pre-marital coitus is definitely related to educational level attained.[37]

The Kinsey findings indicate that about 90 per cent of men over twenty years of age who have not gone beyond grade school, have experienced premarital coitus. The rate falls to about 84 per cent for those who terminated their education with high school.[38] A study of 4164 World War II white selectees between the ages of twenty-one and twenty-seven disclosed that a higher percentage of the lesser educated than of the college-trained inductees had experienced premarital coitus.[39]

THE COLLEGE GROUP. Studies indicate that the principal sexual be-havior pattern at the college level is necking and petting. This does not contradict the fact that there is premarital sexual experimentation on campus, for there is a great difference between reality and the youth "ideal." Furthermore, Newcomb reports that a survey of attitude studies indicates an increasing tolerance of deviant sexual behavior even among the young people who hold strict standards for themselves.[40]

The studies among college students indicate that premarital sex rela-tions increase as students get older, and there is sharp increase for both sexes shortly after graduation. A study at the University of Florida, which extended over a four-year period, found that approximately 65 per cent of 567 men students and 13 per cent of 265 women students surveyed had experienced premarital coitus *while on campus.* This survey, as with so many others of its kind, did not touch upon the amount of coitus possibly experienced before coming to college. The large discrepancy between men and women in reported experience apparently arose from the fact that many men had sex relations with noncollege women, but most of the college women indicated that their experiences were strictly with college men.[41] The earlier survey by the Institute for Sex Research indi-cates that about 50 per cent of college men and from 17 to 19 per cent of college women have had premarital sex relations before graduation; the more recent survey places the rate today at 70 per cent for men and at 25–30 per cent for women. Between graduation and marriage, however, a much higher per cent of the college women have had intercourse, aver-aging ten or eleven times a year; and increasing to about sixteen times the year before marriage.[42]

Kinsey estimated that of the college-educated males remaining un-married until twenty-five, about 64 per cent experienced premarital coitus[43]; his figures for both men and women college graduates are surprisingly similar to those of Bromley and Britton's study fifteen years earlier.[44] The closer supervision of behavior on campus, (such as restricted hours for women students and regulations on having automobiles) may restrict sexual experimentation. Kinsey's findings seem to support this thesis by indicating that 50–75 per cent of premarital sexual episodes occur in the home.[45]

SEXUAL DIFFERENCE RATE. All studies show an appreciable sexual differential in the amount of coitus reported. In all studies, men report many more sex experiences than do women. One study found nineteen-year-old men reporting as much premarital sexual experience as older upper-division college men.[46] Part of the sexual differential rate may result from the possibility that men may be more likely to exaggerate their sexual experience, whereas women may be somewhat reluctant to report it.

Effects of premarital coitus

It has been suggested that intense physical intimacies often lead to complete coitus; but is there anything wrong with this? Why does the culture discourage it?

HARMFUL EFFECTS. The most common objection to premarital coitus is the possibility of pregnancy. If a young couple engage in coitus outside of marriage, and pregnancy occurs, is marriage feasible? If the couple are not well matched, would marriage be wise? They must remember that children need parents who love each other. If the couple feel forced to marry because of pregnancy, they are not likely to provide the love necessary for the child. Perhaps, in such cases, some action other than marriage would be wiser. Studies indicate that marriages forced by premarital pregnancy have double the divorce rate of ordinary marriages.[47] These same studies found that even when such marriages endure, the partners reported themselves less happy and more quarrelsome than partners in other marriages.[48]

The pregnancy itself, however, may not account for all the problems. A study of 368 Catholic marriages that followed pregnancy, and which resulted later in the couples' seeking permission to separate, pointed out the conditions common to each:

1. There was only a modest close relationship with parents before marriage, combined with an attempt at strict regulation of dating by the parents.
2. The parents had been very unfavorable toward the marriage, and there had followed much in-law trouble.
3. It was more likely to have been an interfaith marriage.
4. There were doubts about marriage in the first place.
5. There was a lenient attitude toward sex before marriage, and a higher-than-average rate of adultery afterward.

6. [There was] considerable immaturity of one or both partners.

7. [There was] much bickering and quarreling, as there was a lack of compatibility.

8. In all likelihood both were teen-agers [at the time of marriage].

9. [There was] a short acquaintance and a short or no engagement period prior to marriage.[49]

Premarital pregnancy is much less of a problem when marriage has already been planned by both partners. Under these circumstances, if pregnancy is suspected, the girl should first see a physician for a more positive diagnosis; then, if the pregnancy is confirmed, she should notify the boy. Both should then arrange for a conference with a trusted counselor to help them decide whether they should marry at this time. The less the couple talk to others at this crucial stage, the better. Only after counseling should the couple confide in their parents. If a couple intended to marry anyway, perhaps the pregnancy will merely hasten the event. When premarital pregnancy occurs under these conditions, most parents soon become realistic enough to support their children, even though they may quite frequently at first express disappointment in the couple's lack of control.

If marriage seems unwise, the best procedure is to have the baby and then place it for adoption. The most undesirable action of all is abortion carried out in an illegal manner. Such action not only violates the law,[50] but is also unreliable and dangerous. Illegal abortions are frequently performed under crude and unsanitary conditions that lead to serious infection and death. The possibility of sterility or decreased fertility as a direct result of such abortions is very great. It has been estimated that in the United States, illegal abortions result in sterility about 33 per cent of the time,[51] and they result in the deaths of 10,000 women every year.[52] In spite of these facts, studies by the Institute for Sex Research estimate that the usual results following premarital pregnancy are: (1) marriage, in 20 per cent of the cases where the female is under twenty years of age, and in only 6 per cent of the cases for women twenty-five and over; (2) an illegitimate child in 6 per cent and 3 per cent of the cases, respectively; (3) illegal abortion in 69 per cent and 86 per cent of the cases, respectively; and (4) "presumably" spontaneous abortion in 3 per cent and 5 per cent of the cases, respectively. Furthermore, 18 per cent of the illegal abortions later result in various postoperative physical complications; another 14 per cent result in extremes of negative emotional reactions; and 4 per cent result in social repercussions.[53]

The possibility of pregnancy needs to be reckoned with by all those who wish to indulge in coitus outside of marriage. It is possible that premarital pregnancy may not be as serious a problem now as it once was, and that its gravity will continue to decrease. Thus, the fear of pregnancy may no longer be a deterrent to premarital coitus. According to Levine and Pines:

When the new oral contraceptives become widely available, as they soon will be, pregnancy as retribution and as a deterrent will become even less significant. The major influence then, as now, will be what Kinsey classified as "moral considerations."[54]

An equally serious consideration for delaying coitus until marriage, however, is the possibility of contracting venereal disease. The "V.D. Fact Sheet" of the U.S. Public Health Service reported an over-all decrease in syphilis and gonorrhea through the use of "wonder drugs," such as penicillin, during the twenty-year period prior to 1950.[55] Since 1954, however, there has been an alarming increase in the incidence of both syphilis and gonorrhea, and new strains of both diseases, that are increasingly resistant to penicillin, have been discovered. Of course, some of the increase may be caused by improved methods of reporting, such as the public health-education programs that encourage more people to have checkups. In 1943, however, about 100,000 units of penicillin could effect a cure of gonorrhea, but now more than 2 million units may be injected without success. Japan reports that 30 per cent of its cases of gonorrhea have failed to respond even to massive doses of penicillin. In England and the United States, failures are reported to be increasingly frequent.[56] Brown, a U.S. Public Health physician, estimates that there are about 1.2 million persons in the United States currently in need of treatment for syphilis, but who have not reported their condition. Unless these people are discovered and treated, Brown forecasts that one in every 200 cases will become blind; one in every 50 will become insane; one in every twenty-five will become crippled; and one in every fifteen will die of syphilitic heart ailment.[57] In 1960 the United States spent $12 million to treat and maintain its syphilitic blind and $46 million for those rendered insane by the disease.[58]

This does not include the worst tragedy: the number of other people who become infected because of contact with the untreated cases. Since 1955 many metropolitan areas have shown a tremendous upsurge in venereal diseases. The 1960 rate in New Orleans was up 818 per cent over the 1955 figure; San Francisco showed an increase of 591 per cent; Houston, 378 per cent. For the United States as a whole, the rate increased by 72 per cent in 1960 over that of 1959.[59] According to Dr. Leona Baumgartner, Chairman of the U.S. Surgeon General's Task Force on Syphilis, the rate for teen-agers increased 50 per cent in 1961 over 1960, and 73 per cent for the age group twenty to twenty-four.[60]

Worst of all, according to Abramson, is that more than half of the new cases are in the age group fifteen to twenty-four.[61] Magoun states that between 3.8 and 4.2 per cent of male college seniors have contracted venereal disease.[62] More eighteen-year-old girls are being infected than women of any other age group.[63] Furthermore, the rates are much higher for the nonwhite races: about thirty-five times greater for the age group fifteen to nineteen, and about thirty times greater for the age group twenty to twenty-four.[64] Conditions are reported to be as bad in many other countries. At a recent World Health Organization Conference, fifteen countries reported a frightening resurgence of syphilis and gonorrhea.[65]

It is quite possible that in the not-too-distant future newer methods of prevention and treatment of venereal disease will come to light. Researchers at the University of Michigan, for example, are now experimenting with a protein vaccine to provide immunization to syphilis. Thus far they report only 50 per cent effectiveness with laboratory animals, but they are optimistic for the future.[66] Should such hopeful research results develop, the fear of venereal disease may no longer prove a strong reason for curbing sex desires outside of marriage.

Guilt feelings are a third serious factor that discourage premarital coitus. Such feelings may result from the knowledge that one has violated his personal standards or those of friends and family. Added to this is the fear of discovery and subsequent public disapproval. There is always the possibility of the partner's telling someone, for coitus outside of marriage is never completely private. To keep such actions secret requires deceit in dealing even with close friends and parents.

Even those people who might have no qualms about discovery may feel guilt because they have infringed upon moral law. Even when premarital coitus is not legally wrong, it is considered by many people to be ethically wrong. The effect of such feelings on character and personality may be enough to cause loss of self-respect. Increased tensions may develop from a sense of shame. Even when there are no guilt feelings at first they may develop later when the person is thinking of a future marriage. Sometimes, a couple who have engaged in coitus feel obligated to marry each other in order to find peace of mind.

The strongest reasons given by couples against sexual experimentation is their belief that it is not right and that it is better to wait for marriage. In various surveys, men have reported these reasons as a deterrent over three times as often, and women over four times as often, as any other factor.[67]

Once sex feelings have been awakened, it may be difficult to re-establish control. Thus, one of the advantages of remaining a virgin before marriage may well be in learning and establishing the habit of self-control, which is often so necessary in many respects within marriage itself. Marriage is not a Utopia where every time one partner expects relations he is graciously obliged by the other. There is often a denial of many things in marriage, including sex. Perhaps one of the best ways of being prepared for this self-denial is by learning discipline before marriage. One of the explanations advanced for there being less premarital coitus among the middle socioeconomic class than other classes is that people in the

Table 8–6. Reasons for not having intercourse before marriage

Reason	Per cent checking: 11 colleges 1952–1955		Number checking: University of Wisconsin, 1957	
	614 Men	*1735 Women*	*30 Men*	*100 Women*
Wish to wait until marriage	50	81	17	19
Family training	41	66	10	14
Religious beliefs	33	32	27	40
Fear of pregnancy	27	27	7	12
Fear interfere with marriage	19	21	—	—
Fear of losing self respect	—	—	7	10
Fear of losing partner's respect	—	—	7	12
Fear of hurting parents' feelings	—	—	7	9
Fear of social ostracism	12	17	—	—
Others	—	—	13	3

Source: Judson T. and Mary G. Landis, *Building a Successful Marriage* (Englewood Cliffs, N.J.: Prentice-Hall, Inc., 1958), p. 216. Copyright © 1958, by Prentice-Hall, Inc., Englewood Cliffs, N.J. Reprinted by permission. A. J. Prince and Gordon Shipman, "Attitudes of College Students Toward Premarital Sex Experience," *The Family Life Coordinator,* 6:57. Copyright © 1957, by E. C. Brown Trust, Portland, Ore. Reprinted by permission.

middle class are conditioned early in life toward a deferred-gratification pattern; that is, they can more easily than others deny themselves immediate pleasures for the sake of a greater future reward.[68]

Sometimes sex before marriage serves as a substitute for sex within marriage and may even encourage a further delay of marriage. Premarital relations are more likely to lead to more extramarital coitus, for after enjoying intercourse with many others, some people are never satisfied within a monogamous relationship, and their premarital irregularities become a habit. The Kinsey data confirmed the tendency of premarital coitus to lead to extramarital coitus. His findings disclosed that a significantly higher percentage of the premaritally experienced group had extramarital experiences; such women also continued promiscuous sex relations with other men even when their own marriages had failed.[69]

Premarital coitus may also lead to an overemphasis of the physical aspect of a relationship. An exaggeration of the sexual elements may obscure other important considerations between the couple. Indeed, a preoccupation with sex can retard the growth and development of the relationship. Two such individuals might marry in the belief that they were suitable for each other, when the only quality they had actually measured was the sexual. Such attraction may hold some courtships together, but is seldom strong enough to hold a marriage together for very long. Sexual factors are dangerous and misleading when they dominate the relationship. Necking, petting, or even premarital coitus may not intrinsically be destructive but if they prevent adequate exploration of other areas of interaction they constitute a real danger. When a person first finds a partner who arouses him sexually, it may be mistaken for love strong enough for marriage. When necking or petting arouses sexual feelings—especially when it has never happened before—the person may confuse the sensation for love or for sin; actually neither may be the case.

Various studies have been made of the effects of coitus on the relationship during the engagement period. Some couples report that they think it had no effect on their relationship; some feel it weakened it; and others seem to feel that it actually strengthened their relationship.

Table 8–7. **Effect of premarital coitus during engagement on the relationship as reported by various per cents of couples**

Effect	Per cent of men reporting	Per cent of women reporting
Strengthened the relationship	46	55
Weakened the relationship	7	19
Factor in subsequent breakup of relationship	7	13
Had no effect on relationship	40	13

Source: A. J. Prince and Gordon Shipman, "Attitudes of College Students Toward Premarital Sex Experience," *The Family Life Coordinator,* 6:57. Copyright © 1957, by the E. C. Brown Trust, Portland, Ore. Reprinted by permission.

Burgess and Wallin report that many engaged couples who had premarital coitus and later married felt that the experience had actually increased their feeling of closeness during the engagement period. In contrast, these same researchers found that engaged couples who had decided against coitus before marriage reported feeling that the very fact of deciding against it had made them closer.[70] It appears it is not the question of coitus that makes an engaged couple closer, but the frankness and trust of a mutual give-and-take agreement.

Research reveals, however, that there are more broken engagements after coitus than when there has been none. Of engaged couples without coitus, about 63 per cent later married; only 16 per cent of the couples who had coitus once or a few times married; and of those couples who often had coitus, only 21 per cent later married.[71] Apparently sometimes there is a loss of respect for the partner after coital intimacies, or perhaps the episodes proved unsatisfactory. Kirkendall believes that very few couples can experience coitus before marriage without damage to their relationship. He feels that when coitus takes place before marriage one partner is taking advantage of the trust or weakness of the other and that a loss of respect begins then. Often, when the girl agrees to coitus before marriage, the boy begins to have some doubts about her capacity for fidelity. He may wonder: "How can I be sure that someone else has not had relations with her, or will have in the future?" After the conquest, coitus is not as exciting. It is somewhat inconceivable that any individual could continue a high level of respect for another when he subjects that person to great risk without guaranteeing security through a public acceptance of responsibility.[72]

For some individuals, premarital coitus might develop into a traumatic experience. Some girls may find the experience revolting; others will find it at least somewhat disappointing. The harmful result of this reaction is that the individual may feel unfit for marriage when this may not be the case at all. It is almost impossible to test total sexual compatibility outside of marriage. Unpleasant or disappointing experiences may contribute to frigidity within a later marriage. The difficulty of rehabilitating girls who have experienced a poor conditioning pattern in sexual relations is very great. An improvement must be made, however, or sexual adjustment in marriage will be increasingly difficult.

THE EFFECTS ON MARITAL SEX ADJUSTMENT. It has been said that premarital coitus may have an adverse effect upon sex adjustment within some marriages, but the studies by Kinsey make it necessary to qualify the statement. He found that women who were virgins at marriage did not find as much satisfaction in coitus at the beginning of marriage as those who experienced coitus *and enjoyed* it before marriage. Almost half of the women who had experienced premarital coitus had not enjoyed it, and this group included the highest percentage of women who never enjoyed coitus in marriage even after fifteen years.[73] The studies by Burgess and Wallin, and Kanin and Howard, further suggest that

Table 8–8. **Sex enjoyment for women in marriage as related to experience**

	Per cent indicating enjoyable responses		
Extent of response	*No premarital experience*	*Premarital experience with husband only*	*Premarital experience with husband and others*
Orgasm never or only sometimes	29.3	25.0	17.6
Orgasm usually	50.3	51.4	47.1
Orgasm always	20.4	23.5	35.3

Source: E. W. Burgess and Paul Wallin, *Engagement and Marriage* (Philadelphia: J. B. Lippincott Co., 1953), p. 363. Copyright 1953, by J. B. Lippincott Co., Philadelphia, Pa. Reprinted by permission.

initial sex adjustment is usually somewhat better for women who have experienced coitus before marriage, and enjoyed it, than for premarital virgins who report satisfactory sexual responses after marriage.[74]

Further analysis indicates that this differential may be more closely related to the strength of the sex drive than to the sex experience itself. This possibility is indicated by the fact that the frequency of orgasm in marital coitus among women is directly related to the frequency of enjoyable coitus before marriage. Thus, all that can be safely concluded from these studies is that women with a relatively high sex drive apparently respond to coitus sooner and perhaps more frequently experience enjoyment than do those with a relatively low sex drive. The better postmarital orgastic responses of the one group can perhaps best be explained by factors other than that of having experienced premarital coitus.

Table 8–9. **Coitus ending in orgasm in marriage as related to number of enjoyable episodes of premarital coitus with spouse**

	Per cent		
Extent of orgasm experience in marriage	*Happened frequently*	*Happened occasionally*	*Happened rarely or once*
Never or only sometimes	18.8	21.7	29.9
Usually	51.2	51.3	49.2
Always	30.0	27.0	21.4

Source: E. W. Burgess and Paul Wallin, *Engagement and Marriage* (Philadelphia: J. B. Lippincott Co., 1953), p. 362. Copyright 1953, by J. B. Lippincott Co., Philadelphia, Pa. Reprinted by permission.

The ability to achieve orgasm in sex relations is not a complete test of the adequacy of the sex relationship. On total sex-adjustment scores, no relationship—favorable or unfavorable—was found between the marriage of a given couple and their experience of premarital coitus.[75] It may well be, as the research findings of Kanin and Howard suggest, that when orgasm is successfully experienced before marriage, wives may begin marriage with a higher rate of sexual satisfaction. It does not necessarily follow that they will continue to have greater satisfaction than the virgin wives throughout marriage. In many cases it appeared that the premarital virgins soon caught up.[76]

OVER-ALL MARITAL-ADJUSTMENT EFFECTS. Early studies emphasized that premarital coitus was not beneficial to the total marriage adjustment. The findings of one study led the researcher to suggest that marriages were the happiest where wives had not experienced even petting before marriage. The same study, which was confined to upper-class college women, estimated that premarital virgins had about six times the possibility of being totally happy in marriage than those who were not virgins.[77] Another early study of both sexes reported that 57 per cent of virginal men and only 46 per cent of nonvirginal men were decidedly happy after marriage. The percentages for women were 49 and 37 in favor of virginity.[78] More recent studies do not lead to such strong conclusions. Locke, for example, found a relation for men between nonvirginity at marriage and later divorce. One third of the happily married men and one tenth of the divorced men in his study were virgins at the time of marriage. With the women, however, Locke found very little relation between premarital virginity and divorce. Among the happily married group, 84.4 per cent were virgins at marriage, while 85.3 per cent of the divorced women reported virginity at the time of marriage.[79]

It is very difficult to isolate any one factor such as premarital coitus and then determine its exact effect on a total marriage adjustment. There are so many factors related to divorce and unhappiness in marriage that it becomes increasingly difficult to determine cause and effect. Coitus with prostitutes or casual dates might have one particular effect on future marriage. With couples who are deeply in love, coitus might have an entirely different effect on the marriage. Terman found a negligible relationship between premarital coitus and total marriage happiness when the intercourse was only with the future spouse,[80] but he concluded that premarital coitus with partners besides the spouse showed in his study a notable marital happiness differential: "One's chances of marital happiness are at present favored by the selection of a mate who has not had intercourse with any *other* person."[81] Burgess and Wallin concluded:

> The relatively small prediction rate warranted by our data on sex experience prior to marriage [confined to engaged couples] are in striking contrast with the importance attached by moralists to premarital chastity [for the sake of future marriage happiness].[82]

Table 8–10. **Total marital happiness score related to virginity**

Condition	Mean happiness score	Condition	Mean happiness score
Husband virginal	70.9	Wife virginal	72.5
Coitus only with wife	69.3	Coitus only with husband	69.7
Coitus only with others	67.1	Coitus only with others	66.7
Coitus with others and wife	64.2	Coitus with others and husband	65.6

Source: Lewis M. Terman, *Psychological Factors in Marital Happiness* (New York: McGraw-Hill Book Company, Inc., 1938), p. 324. Copyright © 1938, by McGraw-Hill Book Company, Inc., New York. Reprinted by permission.

Justifiable degrees of physical intimacy

What degree of sexual behavior is justified? There are several basic questions that must be answered before an honest decision can be made.

PERSONAL READINESS. Readiness for the consequences that might result from their personal behavior is essential to an intimate relationship. Both partners must determine the extent of their willingness to bear mutual responsibility for the consequences of their action, such as a greater personal attachment. Necking, for example, may lead to a stronger attachment for at least one partner. This can cause severe emotional difficulties if the other partner ends the relationship or finds someone else. Is the couple prepared for the guilt reactions that might arise, whatever the extent of the behavior? Guilt reactions are rare as long as the individual follows genuine convictions. Personal readiness depends upon the honest acceptance of the total responsibility of the couple for their actions. For those who consider a certain degree of physical intimacy to be wrong, no matter what that degree happens to be, it is probably good if they stop short of it. Violation of one's belief usually results in regret.

SOCIAL RESPONSIBILITY. The degree of justifiable physical intimacies also depends upon the degree of the couple's social responsibility. Even engaged couples are not legally responsible to society for their actions. Some people believe that the sex act itself is of no more concern to the community than any other physiological act. Some feel that when two confident people mutually and willingly enter into coitus, their action is of no concern to society and does not affect society in the least.[83] If the results should happen to include such things as an unhappy forced marriage, an unwanted and/or unloved child, sterility, lowered fertility or death from abortion, undiscovered venereal disease, or warped personality characteristics of one or both partners, is this not a valid concern of the democratic society?[84]

PAIRED READINESS. The third criterion of the justifiable degree of physical intimacy is the extent of readiness of the two individuals to operate as a pair. As Reik has stated: "All the world loves a lover, but not all the world loves a man because he wants to go to bed with a woman."[85] The behavior of prostitutes points up the distinction between sex as a service and as a mutual experience: their "business associations" mean nothing emotionally, but their sex relationships with their husbands or sweethearts undoubtedly have a different character; they may take part as persons rather than only as bodies.[86] Of course, if a man falls in love with a prostitute who is not in love with him, there may be exploitation. Cousins states that "where sex is merely a commodity . . . the faintest spark of personal affection grows to be worth a fortune."[87] The degree of sex behavior prior to marriage must satisfy the demands of both partners for a continuing, mutually satisfying, meaningful, and enriching experience, otherwise barriers are created and the relationship suffers.[88] At each stage of dating the question arises as to the degree of intimacy that will increase confidence and trust between the partners and not arouse fear, suspicion, or distrust. Will the action taken lead to deceit, or will it draw the couple together? Expressing affection by physical means should not be considered an act one person "does to" another, but rather as an intimate mutual experience that a man and a woman enter into together.

ONLY MARRIAGE OFFERS ASSURANCE. To assure all these deeper qualifications, it is best to marry before experiencing complete sexual relations. Although happiness is not guaranteed under these circumstances, the odds are in favor of it.

> I do not think the union of true lovers apart from marriage is impure. I believe that such lovers make a very serious mistake—[a] mistake that may turn out to have been cruel. I believe that society is utterly right in condemning such unions, and that those who really understand will always refuse to enter on them. But *impure* is not the word to apply to them. They are clear and beautiful compared to the bodily intimacies of those who marry without love.[89]

Sex, rightly used, is the most intimate expression of love between two individuals.

> When naked both, thou seemest not to be
> Contiguous, but continuous parts of me:
> And we in bodies are together brought
> So near, our souls may know each other's thoughts,
> Without a whisper.[90]

Summary

The various forms of sexual expression, apart from coitus, include nocturnal emission, masturbation, homosexuality, prostitution, petting to climax, and sublimation. Sublimation appears to be the least popular mode today, and traditional prostitution is decreasing, although pseudo-prostitution is definitely increasing. Masturbation is regarded as much less of a problem by psychiatrists than was formerly believed by society. Petting to climax seems to be a by-product of campus dating, though rarely practiced by other groups.

Although fornication and adultery are generally prohibited by law throughout the United States, the definition of such acts varies with each state.

The cultural belief that a woman must follow a stricter moral code than men (the double standard) probably evolved quite naturally from the superior strength of the male, his jealous possessiveness of the mating privilege, and his understandable desires to be nursed when wounded, and fed when hungry. He, in turn, provided the woman with a means of survival and protection she herself lacked in a rough and primitive world.

The effects of the double standard in the Western world led to the social denial of the sexual urge in women. The strongest deterrent to premarital coitus by the female was, of course, neither social nor moral but perhaps psychological—the fear of pregnancy. With few reliable means of conception control, it was likely the girl would become pregnant and be ostracized by society. Little was left for such girls but prostitution.

Religion and the law, as well as cultural mores, discourage premarital coitus, and the maturation differential between the sexes, in early youth particularly, also acts as a deterrent.

The extent of premarital coitus varies by sex, education level, and age. The harmful results include pregnancy and the resulting hazards of illegal abortion, venereal disease, serious guilt reactions, an ill-advised marriage, and the danger that premarital coitus will lead to extramarital irregularities.

In spite of these adverse effects, Kinsey concluded from his surveys that there were strong qualifications to the statement that premarital coitus affected marital sex adjustment adversely.

There are many motivations that may lead to premarital sexual relations, including several that are unjustifiable, such as rebellion against authority (parental or social), material profit, curiosity, possessiveness, and fear of homosexual inclinations.

Utilitarian motives may not be unjustifiable, but they are highly questionable as reasons for nonmarital coitus. Those whose sexual desires are awakened may seek partners for this purpose alone.

The degree of premarital physical intimacy that is justified depends upon the degree of personal readiness, social responsibility, and the mutual readiness of the couple.

Only marriage offers the assurance that these will be fulfilled. Although it cannot guarantee a favorable sexual relationship, marriage favors the continuity of such a partnership.

Premarital coitus does not inevitably lead to marriage failure. Individuals who have experienced it are not doomed, but coitus is not necessarily a part of the preparation for marriage, and some relationships are actually damaged by it. There is usually little gained through premarital coitus except immediate pleasure, and that only at a tremendous risk and possibly exorbitant cost. Even the pleasure cannot be fully enjoyed for it must be hidden. Perhaps complete sexual experience before marriage, in some cases, would not really be giving physical expression to love as much as it would be giving physical expression to sex impulses.

Notes

1. Clarence Leuba, *Ethics in Sex Conduct* (New York: Association Press, 1948), p. 43.

2. A. C. Kinsey, *et al., Sexual Behavior in the Human Female* (Philadelphia: W. B. Saunders Co., 1953), pp. 280–81, 399. Hereinafter referred to as Kinsey (1953).

3. A. C. Kinsey, *et al., Sexual Behavior in the Human Male* (Philadelphia: W. B. Saunders Co., 1948), p. 342. Hereinafter referred to as Kinsey (1948).

4. Reported by Paul Gebhard, Director of the Institute for Sex Research, Bloomington, Ind., in a paper at the Ohio Council on Family Relations annual meeting, Dayton, Ohio, April 26, 1964. The earlier studies fixed the rate for females at 25 per cent. See Kinsey (1953), *op. cit.,* p. 181.

5. Perhaps it should be noted that such activity seems to be surrounded by greater understanding today than formerly. In fact, one state (Illinois) has recently passed legislation specifying that homosexual conduct in private is no longer a crime.

6. Kinsey (1948), *op. cit.,* p. 342. For more recent studies, see Committee on Homosexual Offenses and Prostitution, *The Wolfenden Report,* Introduction by Karl Menninger (New York: Stein and Day, 1963).

7. Kinsey (1948), *op. cit.,* p. 346; and Kinsey (1953), *op. cit.,* p. 271. The Institute's more recent data (see Gebhard, *op. cit.*) show an increase for both sexes to a rate now of about 50 per cent each.

8. For a fuller discussion of this see W. R. Reevy, "Vestured Genital Apposition and Coitus," in *Advances in Sex Research* (New York: Hoeber-Harper, 1963).

9. F. Alexander, *Fundamentals of Psychoanalysis* (New York: W. W. Norton & Company, Inc., 1948), p. 48.

10. Kinsey (1948), *op. cit.,* pp. 205–13.

11. Exodus 22:6; also Deuteronomy 22:29, and Leviticus 19:20–21.

12. I Corinthians 7:1–9.

13. For a more detailed discussion of this point based on current research findings, see Jean Dedman, "Relationship Between Religious Attitude and Attitude Toward Premarital Sex Relations," *Marriage and Family Living,* 21:171–76.

14. Charles W. Margold, *Sex Freedom and Social Control* (Chicago: University of Chicago Press, 1926), p. 7.

15. Harriet F. Pilpel and Theodora Zavin, *Your Marriage and the Law* (New York: Holt, Rinehart & Winston, Inc., 1952).

16. *Rachel* vs *State of Oklahoma,* 1940, 107P (2nd), 813.

17. Lester A. Kirkendall, *Premarital Intercourse and Interpersonal Relations* (New York: The Julian Press, Inc., 1961). That sex behavior is related to cultural conditioning is well explained in Harold T. Christensen and Gladys R. Carpenter, "Value-Behavior Discrepancies Regarding Premarital Coitus in Three Western Cultures," *American Sociological Review,* 27:66–74.

18. Kinsey (1953), *op. cit.;* pp. 352–54.

19. Maurice J. Karpf, "The Effect of Prostitution on Marital Sex Adjustment," *Marriage and Family Living,* 15:65–71.

20. The author has encountered counseling cases of this nature. For a well-written discussion of this point, see David Riesman, "Permissiveness and Sex Roles," *Marriage and Family Living,* 21:211–17; H. H. Hart, "Fear of Homo-

sexuality in College Students," in B. M. Wedge (ed.), *Psychosocial Problems of College Men* (New Haven: Yale University Press, 1958), 200–13.

21. See Kirkendall, *op. cit.*

22. Kinsey (1953), *op. cit.*, pp. 407, 408.

23. *Ibid.*, p. 344; and Kinsey (1948), *op. cit.*, p. 365.

24. For interesting reading on this subject, see Helen Gurley Brown, *Sex and the Single Girl* (New York: Bernard Geis Associates, 1962), esp. Chap. 10.

25. A. J. Prince and Gordon Shipman, "Attitudes of College Students Toward Premarital Sex Experience," *The Family Life Coordinator,* 6:57.

26. Nora Johnson, "Sex and the College Girl," *The Atlantic Monthly* (November 1959).

27. Winston W. Ehrmann, *Premarital Dating Behavior* (New York: Holt, Rinehart & Winston, Inc., 1959), p. 179.

28. Prince and Shipman, *op. cit.,* p. 57.

29. Robert R. Bell and Leonard Blumberg, "Courtship Stages and Intimacy Attitudes," *The Family Life Coordinator,* 8:61.

30. E. W. Burgess and Paul Wallin, *Engagement and Marriage* (Philadelphia: J. B. Lippincott & Co., 1953), pp. 350–51.

31. Kirkendall, *op. cit.,* p. 258.

32. See, e.g., John R. Cuber and Betty Pell, "A Method for Studying Moral Judgments Relating to the Family," *American Journal of Sociology,* 47:21; A. H. Jones, "A Method for Studying Moral Judgments—Further Considerations," *American Journal of Sociology,* 48:496.

33. Dorothy Bromley and Florence Britten, *Youth and Sex* (New York: Harper & Row, Publishers, 1938) ; K. B. Davis, *Factors in the Sex Life of Twenty-Two Hundred Women* (New York: Harper & Row, Publishers, 1929); Gilbert V. Hamilton, *A Research in Marriage* (New York: Albert and Charles Boni, 1929); G. V. Ramsey, "The Sexual Development of Boys," *American Journal of Psychology* (April 1943), 217–34; and Lewis M. Terman, *Psychological Factors in Marital Happiness* (New York: McGraw-Hill Book Company, Inc., 1938), p. 323.

34. Terman, *op. cit.,* p. 323.

35. Burgess and Wallin, *op. cit.,* pp. 350–51.

36. Whether or not Kinsey's study was proportionately representative of the general population is subject to considerable scrutiny. Nonetheless, it was cross-sectional in that it included more than one segment of society. Few other studies have ever attempted anything so elaborate. Some researchers who criticize Kinsey's methods are also subject to criticism in that much of their research has mainly been confined to a small, select portion of society.

37. See, e.g., R. T. Ross, "Measure of the Sex Behavior of College Males Compared with Kinsey's Results," *Journal of Abnormal and Social Psychology,* 45:754.

38. Kinsey (1948), *op. cit,* pp. 349–51, 550.

39. Leslie B. Hohman and Bertram Schaffner, "The Sex Lives of Unmarried Men," *American Journal of Sociology,* 52:503.

40. Theodore M. Newcomb, "Recent Changes in Attitudes Toward Sex and Marriage," *American Sociological Review,* 2:659–67.

41. Winston Ehrmann, "Student Cooperation in a Study of Dating Behavior," *Marriage and Family Living,* 14:322–26.

42. Kinsey (1953), *op. cit.,* pp. 334–37, and Gebhard, *op. cit.*

43. Kinsey (1948), *op. cit.,* p. 348.

44. Bromley and Britten, *op. cit.*

45. Kinsey (1953), *op. cit.,* p. 311.

46. F. W. Finger, "Sex Beliefs and Practices Among Male College Students," *Journal of Abnormal and Social Psychology,* 42:57–67.

47. Harold T. Christensen and Hannah H. Meissner, "Studies in Child Spacing, III: Premarital Pregnancy as a Factor in Divorce," *American Sociological Review,* 18:641–45.

48. Harold T. Christensen and B. B. Rubenstein, "Premarital Pregnancy and Divorce: A Follow-up Study by the Interview Method," *Marriage and Family Living,* 18:114–23.

49. John L. Thomas, "The Problem of 'Forced' Marriages," *Social Order,* 4:99–104.

50. See Pilpel and Zavin, *op. cit.,* Chap. 12.

51. "Proceedings of the Conference Held Under the Auspices of the National Committee on Maternal Health, Inc., at the New York Academy of Medicine, June 19 and 20, 1942" (New York: Williams and Wilkins, 1944).

52. Margaret Banning, "The Case for Chastity," *Reader's Digest,* 31:4–5.

53. Paul H. Gebhard, *et al., Pregnancy, Birth, and Abortion* (New York: Hoeber-Harper, 1958), pp. 65, 205.

54. Milton I. Levine and Maya Pines, "Sex: The Problem Colleges Evade," *Harper's* (October 1961).

55. U.S. Public Health Service, "VD Fact Sheet" (December, 1951).

56. George Kent, "VD Strikes Anew," *Parents' Magazine,* 36:62.

57. William J. Brown, "Let's Stamp Out VD Now!" *This Week Magazine* (September 18, 1960), 20.

58. Kent, *op. cit.*

59. Martin Abramson, "VD—Return of an Old Scourge," *Today's Health* (December 1960), 50.

60. *Associated Press News Release* (January 1963).

61. Abramson, *op. cit.*

62. F. Alexander Magoun, *Love and Marriage* (New York: Harper & Row, Publishers, 1956), p. 158.

63. Kent, *op. cit.,* p. 130.

64. Report of the 1960 White House Conference on Children and Youth. See also latest "VD Fact Sheet," *op. cit.*

65. Kent, *op. cit.,* p. 130.

66. Abramson, *op. cit.,* p. 84.

67. See Burgess and Wallin, *op. cit.,* p. 351; Kinsey (1948), *op. cit.,* p. 364; and Kinsey (1953), *op. cit.,* p. 344.

68. Louis Schneider and Suerre Lysgaard, "The Deferred-Gratification Pattern," *American Sociological Review,* 18:142–49. This idea is reported to work especially for men who are upwardly mobile. See Frank Lindenfeld, "A Note on Social Mobility, Religiosity, and Students' Attitudes Toward Premarital Sexual Relations," *American Sociological Review,* 25:81–84.

69. Kinsey (1953), *op. cit.,* pp. 427–31.

70. Burgess and Wallin, *op. cit.,* pp. 357–62.

71. *Ibid.*

72. Kirkendall, *op. cit.*

73. Kinsey (1953), *op. cit.,* p. 406.

74. Burgess and Wallin, *op. cit.,* p. 362; Eugene J. Kanin and David H. Howard, "Postmarital Consequences of Premarital Sex Adjustment," *American Sociological Review,* 23:556–62.

75. Burgess and Wallin, *op. cit.* The research of Hamblin and Blood supports this also. See Robert L. Hamblin and Robert Blood, "Premarital Experience and the Wife's Sexual Adjustment," *Social Problems*, 4:122–30.

76. Kanin and Howard, *op. cit.*

77. Davis, *op. cit.*, pp. 42, 59.

78. G. V. Hamilton and Kenneth MacGowan, *What Is Wrong with Marriage?* (New York: Albert and Charles Boni, 1929).

79. Harvey J. Locke, *Predicting Adjustment in Marriage* (New York: Holt, Rinehart & Winston, Inc., 1951), pp. 92, 133.

80. Terman, *op. cit.*, p. 324.

81. *Ibid.*, p. 329.

82. Burgess and Wallin, *op. cit.*, p. 329.

83. See, e.g., Havelock Ellis, *Studies in the Psychology of Sex* (Philadelphia: Davis, 1910–1926), Vol. 6, p. 417.

84. For additional points of view, see Rene Guyon and David Mace, "Chastity and Virginity: The Case for and the Case Against," in A. Ellis and A. A. Barbanel (eds.), *The Encyclopedia of Sexual Behavior* (New York: Hawthorn Books, Inc., 1961), pp. 247–57.

85. Theodor Reik, *Psychology of Sex Relations* (New York: Farrar, Straus & Company, 1945), p. 5.

86. M. Sherif and H. Cantril, *The Psychology of Ego-Involvements* (New York: John Wiley & Sons, Inc., 1947), p. 388.

87. Sheila Cousins, *To Beg I Am Ashamed* (New York: Vanguard Press, 1938), p. 182.

88. Luther E. Woodward, "Viewpoint of the Mental Hygienist," in symposium on "Sexual Behavior: How Shall We Define and Motivate What Is Acceptable?" *Journal of Social Hygiene*, **36**:139.

89. Herbert A. Gray, *Men, Women, and God* (London: Student Christian Movement, 1923), p. 64.

90. Sir Francis Kynaston, "To Cynthia, On Her Embraces" (London: 1642). Can be found in George Ellis, *Specimens of Early English Poets* (London: W. Bulmer and Company, 1801), 3 vols.

Questions for further thought

1. What concepts relative to premarital intimacy are consistent with American democratic ideals?
2. If the practice of chaperonage in a former era was such an effective means of controlling premarital coitus, why has the practice all but been abandoned today?
3. To what degree should common practice triumph over tradition in the determination of standards of behavior?
4. Suppose a boy with several years of schooling ahead of him is confronted by a girl with the statement that he is the father of her expected child, and she demands that he marry her. If neither professes to love the other, what should the boy do?
5. What suggestions are appropriate for a couple who are deeply in love, and who feel increasingly a great deal of physical attraction for each other, but who do not want to go beyond the moral code of society?
6. Would shortening the engagement period affect the degree of intimate involvement before marriage for many couples?

7. What accounts for the fact that such a high percentage of recent best-selling novels has been based on the theme that virginity before marriage is an antiquated idea and that fidelity after marriage is only slightly less so?
8. Do reports such as those of Kinsey and his associates encourage or discourage greater sexual experimentation?
9. Does knowledge of sex aid in its control or stimulate more interest in it?

Recommended films

While the River Waits (Academy Pictures Corporation).
How Much Affection? (McGraw-Hill Book Company, Inc.).
Dance, Little Children (U.S. Public Health Service).

Suggested supplemental readings

BOOKS

Bailey, Sherwin. *Common Sense About Sexual Ethics: A Christian View.* New York: The Macmillan Company, 1962.
Benjamin, Harry, and R. E. L. Masters. *Prostitution and Morality.* New York: The Julian Press, Inc., 1964.
Bieber, Irving, *et al. Homosexuality: A Psychoanalytic Study of Male Homosexuals.* New York: Basic Books, Inc., 1962.
Brown, Helen Gurley. *Sex and the Single Girl.* New York: Bernard Geis Associates, 1962.
———. *Sex and the Office.* New York: Bernard Geis Associates, 1964.
Cory, Donald Webster, and John P. Leroy. *The Homosexual and His Society.* New York: The Citadel Press, 1963.
Deschin, Celia S. *Teen-Agers and Venereal Disease: A Sociological Study.* Washington, D.C.: U.S. Department of Health, Education, and Welfare, 1961.
Ehrmann, Winston. *Premarital Dating Behavior.* New York: Holt, Rinehart & Winston, Inc., 1959.
Ellis, Albert. *Sex and the Single Man.* New York: Lyle Stuart, 1963.
———. *The American Sexual Tragedy.* New York: Lyle Stuart, 1962.
———. *The Case for Sexual Liberty.* Tucson, Arizona: Seymour Press, 1965.
Feucht, Oscar E., *et al., Sex and the Church.* St. Louis: Concordia Publishing House, 1961.
Fry, Thomas A., Jr. *Get Off the Fence: Morals for Moderns.* Westwood, N.J.: Fleming H. Revell Company, 1963.
Hirsch, Arthur H. *Sexual Misbehavior of the Upper Cultured,* New York: Vantage Press, 1956.
Kilpatrick, James Jackson. *The Smut Peddlers.* Garden City, N.Y.: Doubleday & Company, Inc., 1960.
Kirkendall, Lester A. *Premarital Intercourse and Interpersonal Relations.* New York: The Julian Press, Inc., 1961.
Kronhausen, Phyllis and Eberhard. *Sex Histories of American College Men.* New York: Ballantine Books, 1960.
Lewinsohn, Richard. *A History of Sexual Customs.* New York: Harper & Row, Publishers, 1958.
Mueller, Gerhard. *Legal Regulation of Sexual Conduct.* New York: Oceana Publications, 1961.
Murtagh, John M., and Sara Harris. *Cast the First Stone.* New York: McGraw-Hill Book Company, Inc., 1957.

Nemecek, Ottokar. *Virginity Prenuptial Rites and Rituals.* New York: Philosophical Library, Inc., 1959.

Reiss, Ira L. *Premarital Sexual Standards in America.* New York: The Free Press of Glencoe, Inc., 1960.

Ruitenbeek, Hendrik M. (ed.). *The Problem of Homosexuality in Modern Society.* New York: E. P. Dutton & Co., Inc., 1963.

Schur, Edwin M. (ed.). *The Family and the Sexual Revolution.* Bloomington: Indiana University Press, 1964.

Sluvenko, Ralph. *Sexual Behavior and the Law.* Springfield, Ill.: Charles C Thomas, Publisher, 1965.

Sorokin, Pitirima. *The American Sex Revolution.* New York: Porter-Sargent, 1956.

Stiles, Henry R. *Bundling: Its Origin, Progress, And Decline in America* (1871). New York: Book Collectors' Association, 1928.

Vincent, Clark E. *Unmarried Mothers.* New York: The Free Press of Glencoe, Inc., 1961.

Whitman, Howard. *The Sex Age.* Garden City, N.Y.: Doubleday & Comany, Inc., 1962.

Young, Leontine. *Out of Wedlock,* rev. ed. New York: McGraw-Hill Book Company, Inc., 1964.

ARTICLES

Angelino, Henry, and Edmund V. Mech. "Some 'First' Sources of Sex Information as Reported by Sixty-Seven College Women," *Journal of Psychology,* 39:321–24.

Bell, R. R., and J. V. Buerkle. "Mother and Daughter Attitudes to Premarital Sexual Behavior," *Marriage and Family Living,* 23:390–92.

Breed, Warren. "Sex, Class, and Socialization in Dating," *Marriage and Family Living,* 18:137–44.

Christensen, Harold T., and Bette B. Rubinstein. "Premarital Pregnancy and Divorce," *Marriage and Family Living,* 18:114–23.

Duvall, Evelyn M. "Premarital Sex—The Counselor's Challenge," *Pastoral Psychology* (December 1959), 25–32.

Goode, William J. "Illegitimacy, Anomie, and Cultural Penetration," *American Sociological Review,* 26:910–25.

Hamblin, Robert L., and Robert Blood. "Premarital Experience and the Wife's Sexual Adjustment," *Social Problems,* 4:122–30.

Harper, Robert and Frances. "Are Educators Afraid of Sex?" *The Humanist,* 16:122–28.

Herzog, Elizabeth. "Unmarried Mothers: Some Questions to Be Answered and Some Answers to Be Questioned," *Child Welfare,* 41:199–350.

Johnson, Nora. "Sex and College Girls," *Atlantic Monthly* (November 1959), 112.

Kirkendall, Lester A. "Premarital Sex Relations: The Problems and Its Implications," *Pastoral Psychology,* 7:46–51.

Kirkpatrick, Clifford, and Eugene Kanin, "Male Sex Aggression on a University Campus," *American Sociological Review,* 22:52–55.

Murdock, George P. "Sexual Behavior: What Is Acceptable?" *Journal of Social Hygiene,* 36:1–31.

Ramsey, Glenn V. "The Sexual Development of Boys," *The American Journal of Psychology,* 56:217.

———. "The Sex Information of Younger Boys," *American Journal of Orthopsychiatry* (April, 1943), 349.

Reiss, Ira L. "The Double Standard in Premarital Sexual Intercourse: A Neglected Concept," *Social Forces*, 34:224–30.

————. "Letter to the Editor," *Marriage and Family Living*, 25:113–14.

Rowan, Matille, and Reuben Panner. "Work with Teen-Age Unwed Parents and Their Families," *Child Welfare*, 38:16–21.

Vincent, Clark E. "Unmarried Fathers and the Mores: 'Sexual Exploiter' as an Ex Post Facto Label," *American Sociological Review*, 25:40–46.

Timing

marriage

Biologically, the best age for child-bearing is the best time for marriage. Legally, chronological age is important, and each state has laws defining the minimum age necessary for obtaining a marriage license. As important as biological and legal readiness, however, is the individual's moral, emotional, social, and economical development. Maturity in all these respects is essential to marital success. Adequate dating experience, careful selection procedures, and personal adaptability can contribute to this maturity. Yet, in spite of both partners' better-than-average adaptability, some marriages fail on a circumstantial basis. Many of these circumstances might be avoided by giving proper consideration to the timing of the marriage.

Military obligations

There is little doubt that a permanent military-preparedness program will remain a part of American life for some time to come. This means that most young men must give some time to military service. Unfortunately, the most likely time they will be called upon to do this will coincide with their marriage age.[1] The logical question so often asked by young couples is whether to marry before, after, or during military service.

MILITARY MARRIAGES. Some marriages occur in spite of military service; other marriages are contracted because of the circumstances surrounding the conscription period. It would seem, therefore, that the question to ask before "When should I marry?" is "Should I marry at all?" If the answer is "No," there is no problem; if the answer is "Yes," then further exploration is necessary. Why marriage now? Why not later?

Starting marriage under the shadow of a pending military obligation is not ideal for building a good basic marital relationship. It is difficult to build anything worthwhile when surrounded by uncertainty. Marriage followed by military service raises many problems, such as what to do during the interval. Should the young bride follow her husband from camp to camp? Is she prepared to spend days and nights by herself (inductees have little free time)? If she chooses to stay home, then all the adjustment process must be postponed until he returns. During the interval there is no marital growth together, and consequently little feeling of really being married. If she stays home, he is unlikely to have enough free time to travel home to her. Married life will then entail a lonely existence for both of them.

Frequently, women fail to understand these problems; some even wish to become pregnant before their husbands go away. A woman may feel that if the worst should happen to her husband while he is in the service, she will have his child to remember him by. To consider a child as a souvenir of a dead love does not seem the healthiest attitude for rearing the child.

CHANGE IN NEEDS. Both partners will change in the interval of separation far more than either can visualize. It will be next to impossible to resume their marriage exactly where they left off, for each spouse will have experienced many events unshared by the other. Marriage contracted immediately before the husband leaves for military duty means that two strangers must come back together again and begin the most intimate of all human relationships as if they had never been apart. This can rarely be done successfully. There is always some degree of shock at the discovery of the new partner even when they have not yet married, but the shock of reunion is much more severe in the close relationship of marriage. Hill reports that reunions after military service often give rise to severe crisis situations.[2] In timing marriage, it would seem wise to postpone the event until after the military obligation has been fulfilled. Furthermore, when the man returns from military duty, it would seem advisable to have a reacquaintance period before marriage. Each partner should take the time to learn about the other, who is no longer the "girl left behind" or "the boy who went away."

Chronological development

It must be acknowledged that there are certain advantages in a marriage that takes place reasonably early in life. Sometimes postponing marriage leads young people into sexual experiences that lead to abortion, social condemnation, illegitimacy, and venereal disease. Earlier marriage may not eliminate all these problems, but it might materially reduce them.

More young marriages than others include the condition of premarital pregnancy. Burchinal reported that in a small study of teen-age brides in Iowa, almost 40 per cent were positively premaritally pregnant; where the groom was also a teenager, the pregnancy rate was 87 per cent.[3] Moss and Gingles conducted a similar survey in Nebraska with comparable results.[4] These facts, considered with the increasing number of births out of wedlock, indicate that much more sexual experimentation is going on now than formerly. The involvement process begins much earlier today and is accompanied by much more freedom. In many cases sexual involvement begins before a sense of responsibility has been developed.

It is possible that earlier marriage would alleviate part of the problem. A study of the nation as a whole discloses that the highest proportion of unmarried mothers in a given year are fifteen- to nineteen-years-old. Of course, this may be explained by the fact that the percentage of teenagers in the total population has increased in recent years. It may well be that the percentage of illegitimate births for the ages twenty to twenty-nine—in proportion to the total population twenty to twenty-nine—constitutes a much higher rate of illegitimacy than found in other age groupings, just as it always has in the past.

Table 9–1. **Illegitimacy rate distributed by race-age groups**

Unwed mother age	Per cent white illegitimate of total white births		Rate per 1000 live births	Per cent nonwhite illegitimate of total nonwhite births		Rate per 1000 live births
Under 15	1.6		46.7	2.6		80.9
15–19	38.1		6.9	37.9		42.6
(15–17)		(17.9)	11.4		(20.0)	50.0
(18–19)		(20.2)	5.2		(17.9)	33.9
20–24	32.3		2.2	28.7		20.2
25–29	13.8		1.1	15.5		14.3
30–34	8.1		1.0	9.4		13.3
35–39	4.7		1.2	4.7		13.0
40 and over	1.4		1.4	1.2		12.4
Total average rate	100.0		2.2	100.0		21.8

Source: U.S. Department of Health, Education, and Welfare, *Vital Statistics—Special Report, Illegitimate Births: Fact Sheet* (1963). Adapted by permission.

There is little doubt that early marriage often has some advantages when it comes to child care. Young people can take the demands and noise of children in stride quite easily, and the vitality so necessary for successful parenthood is theirs in abundance.

THE TREND TOWARD EARLIER MARRIAGE. Statistics show that the median age for both brides and grooms has been decreasing for several decades.

Table 9–2. Trend in median age bride and groom, first marriages

Year	Age	
	Bride	Groom
1890	22.0	26.1
1910	21.6	25.1
1930	21.3	24.3
1950	20.5	23.3
1955	20.2	23.1
1963	20.0	22.0

Sources: U.S. Department of Health, Education, and Welfare, *Vital Statistics, National Summaries,* **50,** 28 (November 1959); and U.S. Bureau of the Census, "Population Characteristics," *Current Population Reports,* Series P-20, 105, 3. Adapted by permission. It needs to be noted that until recently some states did not report such statistics. Furthermore, of those that did, some reported data on first marriages only; others grouped together ages at first and subsequent marriages; and some reported the mean rather than the median. By all methods, however, the trend has been downward.

Some people have attributed the increase in teen-age marriages to the fact that there are proportionately more teen-agers in the population today. The total population under twenty-one years of age in the United States increased from 61.2 million in 1955 to 79.2 million at the end of 1964.[5] A more accurate comparison made on a proportionate basis, however, suggests that there has been a percentage increase in young marriages beyond that which would normally be expected in relation to the population increase for that age group.

Table 9–3. Increase in youth marriages

Year	Per cent of twenty-year-olds already married	
	Men	Women
1910	8.6	36.2
1960	17.7	48.9
	Per cent of twenty-five-year-olds already married	
1910	45.5	65.7
1960	66.1	80.4

Source: U.S. Department of Health, Education, and Welfare, *Vital Statistics—Special Reports* (1961). Adapted by permission.

Table 9–4. **Per cent of each sex married who ever marry by age groups**

Age	1950 Men	1950 Women	1960 Men	1960 Women
Under 15	0.0	0.3	0.0	0.4
15–19	8.0	38.4	14.2	47.4
20–24	44.2	68.4	67.1	84.6
25–34	82.0	89.1	93.8	96.0
35–44	89.7	91.6	96.4	99.9

Source: U.S. Bureau of the Census (March 1950), Series P-20, No. 33; and *Vital Statistics: National Summaries,* Vol. 40, No. 28 (November 1959); and U.S. Department of Health, Education, and Welfare, *Special Reports* (1961). Adapted by permission.

In reality, the true marriage age may be much lower than the statistics show because falsification of age by teen-agers probably occurs rather frequently,[6] and the incident of age falsification may be increasing of late.[7]

AGE AT MARRIAGE IN OTHER CULTURES. The average ages for marriage in most countries are higher than in the United States. In England the average age at marriage stands at 29.5 for men and 26.5 years for women[8]; in Italy, it is twenty-nine for men and twenty-five for women.[9] According to Svalastoga, the mean age for males in Norway is twenty-nine and for females it is twenty-six; in Sweden it is 28.3 for males and 25.6 for females, and in Denmark the mean age is about twenty-seven and twenty-four, respectively.[10] The average age for marriage in France is reported as 26.7 years for men and 23.3 for women.[11]

People in the Arab world and in certain parts of India marry even younger than Americans do. The legal age in Egypt is eighteen for men, and sixteen for women, and the majority of their citizens are reported to marry close to the legal age.[12] According to the Child Marriage Restraint Act of 1929, males in India must be eighteen years old before marriage and females at least fourteen. In spite of this, the 1951 India census indicated that within the five- to fourteen-year-old group, there were 2.833 million married males, 6.18 million married females, 66,000 widowers, and 134,000 widows; but those marriages ordinarily do not include physical consummation until later in life.[13]

According to the latest United Nations Demographic Yearbook, the over-all age at first marriage throughout the world appears to be falling a little. The average age, however, is still higher than in the United States: twenty-seven for men, and twenty-four for women.

VARIATION BY SOCIAL CLASS. In all cultures, the average age for marriage differs sharply along occupational and social-class lines. Two of America's classic studies on social class, (shown in Table 9–5 below), found a differential on average marriage age in American social classes.

Table 9–5. Variations by social class in average age at marriage

Social class	In Yankee City	In Elmtown	
Upper-upper	27.9	Mid-twenties	
Lower-upper	26.6	„ „	
Upper-middle	26.1 -	„ „	
Lower-middle	25.1	Early twenties	
		Bride	*Groom*
Upper-lower	24.4	Late teens	Early twenties
Lower-lower	23.2	Mid-teens	Very early twenties

Source: (Yankee City) W. Lloyd Warner and Paul S. Lunt, *Social Life of a Modern Community* (New Haven: Yale University Press, 1941), p. 255. Copyright © 1941, by the Yale University Press, New Haven, Conn. Reprinted by permission; and (Elmtown) A. B. Hollingshead, "Selected Characteristics of Classes in a Middle Western Community," *American Sociological Review*, **12:**106, 116. Copyright © 1947, by the American Sociological Association, Washington, D.C. Reprinted by permission.

An examination of current census data indicates that American women married to unskilled workers or to farm laborers are, on the average, about three to five years younger at marriage than women married to professional men.

In an Iowa study of teen-age marriages, Burchinal used the occupational prestige of fathers (as defined by the North-Hatt Scale[14]) as a basis for social-class differentiation. His findings indicated quite conclusively that young marriage is more common for people of lower socioeconomic background.[15]

SECTIONAL VARIATIONS. Average age at marriage also varies by region and section within the same country. In the United States, the highest marriage ages are found in the Northeast, and the lowest marriage ages are found in the South. The brides and grooms of the Northeast are usually two years older than their Southern counterparts. According to the last available composite of state statistics, the youngest brides and grooms are found in Idaho.[16] There are age variations within other states, but the trend toward a decrease in marriage age is reported in all the states.

RACIAL VARIATIONS. As a general rule, the difference in marital ages according to race is not as pronounced today as formerly. At present in the United States, there is less than a two-year differential between the two groups broadly classified as whites and nonwhites, with the nonwhites being younger.[17]

CHANGING ATTITUDES TOWARD MARRIAGE AGE. Surveys among the general populace to determine attitudes toward early marriage indicate considerable indifference, but, there does seem to be a growing edge of opposition.

For more than a century, American leaders did everything possible to encourage early marriage. There was little need to delay marriage past puberty, for the simple cultural patterns and economic skills could be mastered at a relatively early age. In rural America, a boy of sixteen was almost as skillful as his father in the work necessary to maintain family life. Furthermore, families proved to be a decided asset on the early American frontier for they brought a certain stability to communities by supporting the development of other institutions such as schools and churches, and by encouraging the enforcement of law and order.

Young people, however, appeared reluctant to marry young in spite of the urging of their elders. Brigham Young, the pioneer leader, advised young men on the frontier to marry by eighteen. He exhorted them to build a cabin and then "get you a bird to put in your little cage."[18]

Special problems of early marriage

It would be unrealistic to select any arbitrary age as dividing those qualified for marriage from those unqualified. Any "ideal" age for marriage must be considered only as a median point in the average age range. Individual variation will naturally occur in both directions from any average figure. Such a figure represents a composite average for large numbers of people, and can never be applied to each individual case. There is little doubt, however, that growth and experience comes with age, improving one's marriageability.

CHANGING PHILOSOPHY.   As a group, people appear to experience their greatest change in life values somewhere between the ages of sixteen and twenty-two. It is in this period that tastes, ideals, standards, and goals usually undergo a complete overhauling before becoming an essential and integral part of the human being. It is evident that the closer an individual is to having a permanent philosophy of life at the time of his marriage, the greater the likelihood of his success in that relationship. In frontier American society, the philosophy of life was bolder but less complex. Because the individual was often fighting for sheer physical survival throughout his lifetime, his basic philosophy was much the same at sixty as it had been at sixteen. The choice of eighteen as a marriage age might be perfect if neither mate were to change afterward, but the probability of sharp changes in the ensuing years makes it uncertain that they still will be well matched by age twenty-two.

In today's marriages, love, intimate responses, and personal happiness have a high priority, but these are more difficult to achieve when the partners lack a common philosophy by which to direct their lives.

PERSONAL DEVELOPMENT.   Martinson suggests that early marriage tends to impede the development of personal and social adjustment, and then fosters confusion at that arrested level later on when attempts are made to redevelop a philosophy. He found that the shorter the interval between high school graduation and marriage, the greater the ego deficiency, particularly in males.[19]

Martinson's findings were based on tests of teen-agers matched by age, nationality, intelligence, father's occupation, community of residence, high school attended, and year of graduation. Then by use of the Bell Adjustment Inventory, Kuder Preference Records, grades in school, and extracurricular activities, a comparison was made between a control group of single teen-agers and those who had married within four years after graduation. Interestingly enough, the single boys of the control group were found to be not only better adjusted, but also slightly more masculine.[20]

This implies that not only are many teen-agers not fully enough developed in their basic philosophy for modern marriage, but when they do marry early there is considerably more interference with the development of these aspects.

The study by Moss and Gingles in Nebraska, using methods similar to Martinson's and the Mooney Problem Checklist and the Minnesota Personality Scale, was inconclusive in establishing statistically significant differences in philosophic growth between single girls and married control groups.[21]

The longitudinal investigations of Kelly, however, supported the conclusion that too early a marriage contributes to the deficient philosophic development of both partners. Kelly tested engaged couples averaging 26.7 years of age for the men and 24.7 years for the women. On retesting the same group twenty years later, he found little change in values, vocational interests, attitudes, personality, or in initial similarities between each couple.[22]

From these studies it seems safe to conclude that marriage below a certain age, particularly for boys, contributes to an ego deficiency or lack of a totally developed philosophy for the individual. More research is needed in this area if modern marriages are to be strengthened.

A HIGHER DIVORCE RATE. Perhaps one of the tragedies of the modern era is that the earlier the marriage, the higher the divorce rate. In a comparison of happily married couples and divorced couples, Locke reported a much lower percentage of divorce for women married after age eighteen and for men married after twenty-two. His over-all data showed that the happily married group averaged almost two years older at time of marriage than did the divorced group.[23]

A HIGHER UNHAPPINESS RATE. Even if divorce is not resorted to, a higher proportion of young marriages turn out unhappily. Inselberg found a positive correlation between high school marriages and the extent of in-law conflict, sexual maladjustment, and economic difficulties.[24] In a comparison study of men married before twenty-two years of age with

those married after that age, Burgess and Cottrell found a greater likelihood of poor marital adjustment in the younger group. Using eighteen
as the comparison age for women, they again found a greater chance of
poor marital adjustment in the younger group. In fact, good marital
adjustment was found in almost three times as many women who married
at about thirty than was found in women who had married at eighteen
or younger.

Table 9–6. Marital adjustment by age at marriage

| | Per cent of marriages | | | | | |
| | Poor | | Fair | | Good | |
Age at marriage	Wife	Husband	Wife	Husband	Wife	Husband
16–18	46.9	—	34.4	—	18.7	—
19–21	28.5	38.5	29.2	32.7	42.3	28.8
22–24	20.9	17.3	29.1	33.9	50.0	48.8
25–27	22.5	24.6	27.5	29.5	50.0	45.9
28 and over	17.7	—	24.2	—	58.1	—
28–30	—	18.8	—	20.3	—	60.9
Over 31	—	28.8	—	24.3	—	47.0

Source: E. W. Burgess and Leonard S. Cottrell, *Predicting Success or Failure in Marriage* (Englewood Cliffs, N.J.: Prentice-Hall, Inc., 1939), pp. 115–17. Copyright © 1939,
by Prentice-Hall, Inc., Englewood Cliffs, N.J. Reprinted by permission of publisher
and authors.

The results of many studies appear to invalidate an old popular idea
that marriage close to the age of thirty was likely to be unstable because
the individuals had become too set in their ways. If rigidity does set in
the single person after a certain age, it appears to be offset by other
factors.

THE CURRENT DILEMMA. At one time in American society, young people were socially ready for marriage before they felt a strong personal
desire for the venture. Today the reverse seems true. Contemporary youth
may be readier in a physical sense than any other group in history but,
relatively speaking, their sense of social responsibility is often much
weaker. Society has provided youngsters with intensive sex stimuli by
bombarding them with songs, stories, and movies linking the concepts of
love and sex as though the two were identical. Young people have been
freed from chaperonage and even encouraged in their desire for paired
privacy. They are conditioned toward a peer-dictated sex practice regardless of personal moral commitments. Yet society has done little to help
young people prepare for marriage; instead it continues to attribute a
wonderful state of ecstasy now and forever for all who enter marriage.[25]

Physical development

It is most important that the partners in marriage be sufficiently developed physically to meet the demands of an adult daily work load. In the American culture, it is still the primary responsibility of the male to earn a living for his family. This may incur less of a physical strain than formerly but it still entails long-term endurance. This applies equally to the traditional female responsibilities of childbearing, child-care duties, and household chores and management.

At any age, persons with physical disabilities should evaluate the adverse effects their handicap may possibly have on a marriage. If over-all stamina is enough and the handicap noncongenital, marriage and a family need not be precluded.

It has long been known that youth is the easiest time of life for childbirth. Although the safest age for childbearing was assumed to be in the early twenties, recent obstetrical evidence suggests that the best age for child birth may be before twenty. Meigs states that it is natural for women in the American culture to begin bearing children before they reach the age of twenty and that too long a delay after the twentieth birthday may even be harmful. He points out that research findings indicate that endometriosis is likely to result if the female menstrual period is not interrupted occasionally between the ages of fourteen and twenty-six.[26] The endometrium is the mucous membrane that lines the uterus. Unless an embryo is implanted, it is shed regularly with the menstrual flow. Apparently, if this shedding process is not interrupted occasionally, the endometrium is not as likely to remain intact.

The ability to bear or sire children usually coincides with the onset of puberty. Many studies indicate that puberty now starts a little earlier than was formerly the case.[27] Thus, it appears that both men and women are biologically capable of becoming parents long before they may be socially ready for marriage.[28] Byrd, an obstetrician, states emphatically that the safest age for childbirth now lies between the ages of seventeen and twenty-one.[29] Studies conducted during the 1930s on mothers under twenty years of age indicated a higher-than-average rate of premature births and a significantly higher infant mortality rate in that group. Recent studies by Dr. B. F. Poliaskoff of Georgia and Dr. John M. Nokes of Virginia have shown that the younger woman's labor tends to be shorter and relatively free from complications and that the birth weight of her child is close to average. She is not more likely to have a premature delivery, postpartum hemorrhage, puerperal morbidity, lacerations of birth canal, or palpresentations of the fetus. She has as many or more well-born infants who survive the first seven days of life. The incidence of stillbirths of unknown etiology is particularly low, in this age group, being about two or less per thousand live births (the incidence is as high as fifteen to twenty per thousand live births in the age group over thirty-five.[30]

Studies of a few years ago indicated the infant mortality rate was beginning to increase in the United States. The suggestion was made that this increase might be caused by the increase in teen-age mothers, who follow notoriously poor diets at times. Although infant mortality increased from 1955 to 1959, it has been decreasing since. In fact, the rate has hit a new record all-time low each year since 1961, and in 1964 stood 10 per cent below the 1955 rate and 50 per cent below the 1940 rate.[31] The temporary upsurge is now believed to have been caused by a nation-wide outbreak of infection caused by a strain of *staphylococcus* immune to modern hospital treatment, but this has been brought fairly well under control.

Economic development

To meet the responsibilities of marriage, self-discipline is needed in the handling of money and property. Some people are not adequately ready in this respect even at forty. When a person can forego the spending of most of his money on immediate pleasures for the more important long-range goals, he may be approaching economic maturity. The ability to make wise use of cash in the purchase of everyday essentials must be developed before marriage.

Another facet of economic development concerns the individual's training for his chosen vocation. In this era of specialization, actual vocational training is often not yet initiated in the teen years. The young person must think carefully before taking a permanent job with a low level of education. In such jobs he may reach a dead end early in his career.

Economic maturity in the modern sense includes not only the ability to earn enough money for current family expenses but also (1) the ability to provide for the future welfare of dependents, (2) the capacity to command a job with unlimited opportunities. Salary is no longer the single criterion of an individual's economic status. Considerations of professional prestige, financial independence, and the enrichment of family life through travel and recreation are today's marks of economic maturity.

Moral development

Moral development implies an adequate code of conduct that will strengthen and enhance the intimacies of marriage. A democratic society helps the young couple to observe a moral pattern by favoring certain attitudes that will benefit both their personal and family life. Children born of a marriage should be welcome, and the parents are expected to learn and practice good child-care principles.

The willingness to give up personal pleasures for the sake of the family is part of moral development. It even includes a cheerful willingness to stay up several nights when necessary to tend a sick child and yet still retain humor and patience on the job each day and with one's mate. Moral maturity also fosters a feeling of security and confidence for the transmittal of the cultural heritage to the offspring.

Moral scruples naturally demand an observance of marital fidelity, but moral maturity enriches the intimate relationship. It is generous, not merely dutiful, and offers fulfillment and release in a manner and time most satisfying to the desires of the partner. If each partner responds to the needs of his mate, his moral maturity is further developed, enabling him to sense and fulfill the needs of their children.

Social development

A readiness to accept the responsibility demanded of all adults toward the support and improvement of the community is an indication of an individual's social readiness for marriage. This includes contributing a proper share of financial, social, and intellectual support to civic improvement programs. The socially mature person views marriage not as an escape from personal problems but, rather, as a way of life that brings new challenges and opportunities.

As Park so appropriately illustrated years ago, it is only through group interaction and cultural exposure that the biological nature is changed into human nature, and thus the biological creature evolves into the social person.[32] Baber has aptly pointed out that the adult who never grows up, who continues to live in a state of "suspended adolescence," is usually a marriage liability "of the first order."[33]

Emotional development

Objectivity is the sign of a level of emotional development adequate for marriage. It includes the ability to discriminate between facts and feelings with the strength to act according to facts. Because, as MacMurray has said, "We are intellectually civilized and emotionally primitive,"[34] there are times when even the most self-controlled person succumbs to emotion. The degree to which the individual recognizes and then rightfully compensates for these mistakes is a measure of his emotional readiness for marriage. The extent to which a person is willing to admit that he is not perfect is an important index of his emotional development.

Everyone has problems with which he must learn to live, but an adaptability to the facts of life will ease many such stresses. Continuous, futile efforts to change the unchangeable must be abandoned if marriage is to be considered seriously. The emotionally mature person is not easily thrown into a state of confusion, discouragement, or disorganization by disappointments or frustrations. He does not usually regress to the "good old days" nor create a vacuum around himself while dreaming of what "might" be. Perhaps one of the best measures of emotional readiness for marriage is the extent to which the individual considers the best years of his life to be the present ones, no matter what they might be.

Emotional maturity culminates in the transference of attachments from the comforting shelter of the parental family to a wholehearted enjoyment of the heterosexual relationship of marriage.

Educational obligations

Until recently very few students dared to face the combined strong disapproval of parents and school authorities toward marriage. Before World War II it was not uncommon for colleges automatically to drop students who married. Nowadays expulsion because of marriage is rare, especially in nonsectarian colleges. Not only have the attitudes of college administrators toward married students changed, but the attitudes of the students themselves have changed.

Table 9–7. **Changing attitudes of students toward marriage while in college**

Year	Per cent favoring marriage for undergraduates	
	Boys	*Girls*
1952	20	50
1957	30	57
1963	45	68

Source: Judson T. and Mary G. Landis, *Building a Successful Marriage* (Englewood Cliffs, N.J.: Prentice-Hall, Inc., 1958), pp. 181–83. Copyright © 1958, by Prentice-Hall, Inc., Englewood Cliffs, N.J. Adapted by permission. Also, the author's own survey, Ohio University, Athens, Ohio, 1963.

HIGH SCHOOL MARRIAGES. Newspapers and magazines often present feature stories about the fantastic increase in high school marriages.[35] Objective studies, however, fail to support these claims. A survey covering more than one third of all the high school students in the state of California revealed 2.4 per cent of sophomore girls married, 4 per cent of juniors, and 5.7 per cent of senior girls. Married girls outnumbered married boys by more than nine to one.[36] Burchinal surveyed the high schools of Iowa and found that married students comprised only 1 per cent of sophomore girls and 0.1 per cent of sophomore boys; 1.8 per cent of junior girls and 0.3 per cent of junior boys; 2.1 per cent of senior girls and 0.8 per cent of senior boys. He did discover, however, that 55 per cent of the high schools in Iowa, regardless of size, had at least one married student.[37] A similar survey in Illinois found married students comprised 0.1 per cent of sophomore boys and 1.4 per cent of sophomore girls; 0.2 per cent of junior boys and 1.8 per cent of junior girls; 0.7 per cent of senior boys and 4.1 per cent of senior girls. Altogether, married girls outnumbered married boys by seven to one.[38] A survey of the secondary schools of New Mexico found there were over five married girls to one married boy.[39] De Lissovoy reports the following rates for Pennsylvania: sophomore boys, 0.03; sophomore girls, 0.63; junior boys, 0.20, junior girls, 1.18; seniors boys, 0.56, seniors girls, 1.68.[40] Perhaps it should be noted that Pennsylvania has always had a higher-than-average marriage age. Mudd and Hey report that over the United States as a whole, approximately 5.7 per cent of high school seniors are married each year; 4 per cent of juniors; and 2.4 per cent of sophomores.[41] High school marriages are more common today than formerly, but they do not form as high a percentage as some feature writers would lead their readers to believe.

All these studies show that when a high school boy marries, he tends to marry a high school girl, but most high school girls who marry choose a boy already out of school.

High school marriages have not been accepted by school administrators as realistically as they are now accepted on the college campus. High school marriages are viewed with special alarm if the students choose to stay in school. When questioned about the situation, many high school administrators express their fear that the married ones will discuss their intimate experiences with the unmarried students and that they will encourage them to marry also; married high school students are said to be irregular in attendance, often are (or soon become) pregnant, show less interest in school, and expect special privileges.[42]

Few high school administrators have done anything to help the married students, such as offering increased and improved counseling services or adding courses in marriage and family preparation. Instead, they encourage the married students to withdraw, and they assume that this withdrawal ends their responsibility in the matter. Some schools expel students who marry; others automatically expel or suspend students who become pregnant. Of eighty-four schools surveyed in Illinois, only twenty-nine allowed the married high school student to continue without some restrictions.[43]

COLLEGE MARRIAGES.   On many campuses in recent years, the graduate school has shown the largest percentage of increase in enrollment, and this accounts in part for the increased percentage of married college students. There has also been, however, a steady increase in the percentage of married undergraduates on some campuses. Glick and Carter report that census figures disclose that roughly one out of every six undergraduate college students is married. This, of course, includes noncoed schools as well as coeducational ones. When professional and graduate schools are included, the figure rises to one out of four.[44]

Table 9–8. **Married graduate and undergraduate students at Kansas State University, 1960–1961 school year**

	Per cent married	
Academic condition	*Men*	*Women*
Undergraduates	21.0	15.6
Graduates	61.0	56.2
All students	26.0	18.0

Source: Table compiled by author from figures released to the public by school administrators.

After making a survey of several state and private colleges, Christopherson states that college administrators appear to be accepting the presence of the married student. This is evidenced by the replacement of "veterans' villages"—temporary barracks-type housing units—with more permanent residential units.[45]

The trend toward marriage in college was started by the World War II veterans. Hundreds of thousands of GI's took advantage of the educational privileges accorded them after the war, and entered colleges throughout the nation. The veterans were older than the average undergraduate; many felt they had fallen behind schedule because of the war, and further education seemed the best way to catch up. The government subsidy made them economically independent of their parents. Furthermore, they were ready to settle down; they had a strong desire for a home and the emotional security attached to it. The girls they knew were older too, and many of them had already finished school. They, too, were ready to settle down and were often willing to work, if necessary, after marriage.

College marriages did not decrease drastically after the veterans finished their schooling. In fact, some college have as many or more married students today than they did immediately following World War II.

The success of the veteran in both marriage and college started a trend. Improved postwar economic conditions are also an encouraging factor, for the many part-time job opportunities help student marriages financially and are more easily fitted into the daily schedule. It seems quite clear, however, that there are two distinct types of college marriages on campus today. The great majority involve older students, many of whom are in graduate school. Their problems are not much different from those of young married couples who are not in college. The other type involves the young students who marry either just before, or soon after, their arrival on campus. Their problems are indeed different and need some special attention.

It seems quite common today for parents to continue to subsidize the young college student after marriage as they did before he married. Some students see nothing wrong with this procedure, saying, in effect: "If they were willing to support me in college unmarried, why not continue to supply the same amount after marriage?"

There are arguments both for and against this point. The great American tradition has always been that, when people marry, they should be self-supporting. The value of a college education, however, is so highly prized by parents today that apparently many are quite willing to break with tradition. Many of these parental subsidies, however, have strings attached: parents often believe this support gives them the right to advise and direct the young couple. Many couples appear quite willing to accept the money, but not the controls that accompany it.[46]

Generally speaking, the war veteran's academic record was good. There are many unpublished accounts by professors testifying to the fact that the veteran pushed his teachers to the maximum. Under the circumstances, this might have been expected, but the surprising development to some is that the present group of civilian married students also do well

Figure 9-1. Generally speaking, the war veteran's academic record was good. (Courtesy of the Kansas State University News Bureau.)

academically. A survey on one campus disclosed the grade-point average for all students to be 2.48, while for the married men it was 2.55, and for married women it was 3.02.[47] Further research indicates that, as a group, married students with children achieve even better grades than married students without children.[48]

Marriage alone, however, does not of itself promote a high grade performance. All of the studies on high school marriages, for instance, show

Figure 9-2. Full-time study plus a job may be too much of a burden. (Photograph courtesy of the A. H. Robins Company, Inc.)

the opposite result. Apparently, there are other factors contributing to high grades besides the fact of being married. Some authorities have suggested that the higher grades of the married college student resulted from (1) a difference in maturity level, and (2) the decided decrease after marriage in social activities requiring extensive time and energy.

Purely from clinical observation, and admittedly without any research to support the contention, the author is inclined to believe that much of the difference in performance lies in the factor of maturity. It is a well-known fact that the overwhelming majority of married students (of both sexes) are older than other college students. Indeed, in 1961, when Marie Pfeiffer (as part of her doctoral study at Ohio State University) proposed to interview only those married college students in cases where both partners were under the age of twenty-one, she found fewer than 100 qualified. This was rather amazing, for there were about 5000 married students enrolled at the university.

Census figures list as married only 1.8 per cent of college students between the ages of eighteen and nineteen; 10.8 per cent of those between twenty and twenty-one; 40.3 per cent of those between twenty-two and twenty-four; and 70.1 per cent of those between the ages of twenty-five and thirty-four.[49]

Recently two researchers compared the academic performance of a married group of students with that of a group of unmarried ones; the groups were matched by age, college entrance test scores, and other factors. The results indicated that marriage itself leads, not to higher grades, but to lower grades.[50] An additional study compared before- and after-marriage grades of a group of undergraduates who married while in college with those of a matched control group whose members had remained single. The results suggested that getting married while in college, by itself, did not significantly affect one's grades.[51]

SPECIAL PROBLEMS OF COLLEGE MARRIAGES. Married college students have not only the problems of all college students, but also the problems that are unique to married life.

Table 9–9. Average monthly cost of all Kansas State University undergraduate married couples for school year 1961–62

	Cost (dollars)
Rent and utilities	85.00
Food and drugs	85.00
Clothes (purchase)	5.00
(laundry and upkeep)	12.00
Life insurance	13.00
Household and school supplies	18.00
Medical, dental, and health insurance and expenses	16.00
Recreation	3.00
Automobile (includes taxes, license tag, upkeep)	30.00
Miscellaneous	15.00
TOTAL	282.00

Source: Survey made by students in marriage and family classes.

One of the acute problems is related to increasingly higher living costs. The veteran who had a $120 monthly federal subsidy, extremely cheap housing, and odd-job income managed fairly well. A 1948 survey at Michigan State University indicated that the average married college couple's monthly expenditures were slightly under $150.00.[52] Since 1948, however, there has been a steady increase in the cost of living for everyone.

The great majority of today's young married students do not receive a federal subsidy, nor do they have as much possibility of an educational "grant" from a former employer or sufficient cash saved (as perhaps some of the older present students do). The young married couple must earn, borrow, or beg it all. Part-time jobs are plentiful, but they do not bring in enough money to cover all expenses.[53] Therefore, in many cases, both partners must work. When it is necessary for one partner to take a full-time job, it is usually the wife who gives up her education to put her husband through college. Research on the campus of Kansas State University shows that the girl seldom finishes college if she marries while still a freshman; however, most girls who married in their senior year go on to graduate. The real tragedy is that sometimes a first-rate woman scholar sacrifices her education to put her second-rate scholar husband through college.

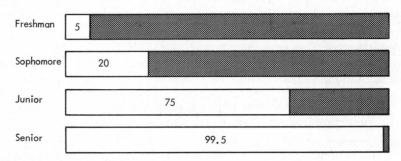

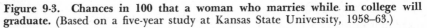

Figure 9-3. Chances in 100 that a woman who marries while in college will graduate. (Based on a five-year study at Kansas State University, 1958–63.)

Adequate housing is still an acute problem for many married students. Some college administrators at first considered the influx of married students to be a temporary condition, for most of the married students were war veterans. Thus the housing provided was often substandard; it usually consisted of old army barracks brought in from the nearest temporary World War II base. These dwellings were not so bad at first, but gradually the cost of repairs exceeded their actual worth. Even then, many college housing authorities did little about the problem except to demolish the unslightly barracks when the student families moved out. Because of this lack of foresight, many universities are far behind in meeting the needs of permanent housing for their married students.

Many campuses report a long waiting list for university-built apartments, so many married couples are forced to seek housing off-campus. Too often what they can find or can afford is not conducive to building a happy marriage. A recent survey of fifteen colleges with a total married student population numbering in the tens of thousands indicated less than 9000 permanent campus married housing units.[54]

Many young married couples begin college hoping to avoid pregnancy until after graduation, but sometimes it does not work out that way. Earlier studies found that only about 35 per cent of the young married students' children were planned. About half of the couples who had unplanned babies stated they had done everything they knew in an attempt to avoid pregnancy.[55] Of course, it must be realized that what these students "knew" (as revealed in the closer details of these studies) was not very much. The author's close work with present-day college students leads him to believe that today's young married students are much more sophisticated about birth-control methods. When an unplanned pregnancy does occur, however, it is usually viewed with much alarm.

Undergraduate married college couples are usually at their height of fertility; therefore, methods of conception control that might work for older, less fertile, couples apparently are not completely effective. If their plan had been for the wife to work, the unexpected pregnancy may mean postponing or terminating the husband's college education.

Even when the children are wanted and planned for, they still bring many special problems for the married student. One study made of this situation disclosed that most married students with children cited such problems as the absence of room for the children to play, higher rent (landlords usually charge more if there are children), and the difficulty in arranging for child care if the mother had to work or the parents wished to go out.[56] Furthermore, the noise and distraction make it difficult to study in cramped quarters. The added responsibility for their care places a strain on both parents. They must have energy for night duty during the child's infancy and in time of illness, and they must also find time to play with the children.[57]

Full-time study or work is a heavy enough burden for most people. Establishing and running a home add a tremendous strain to the schedule. Seldom can one person adequately carry a combination of any two of these responsibilities by himself for very long. In fact, sometimes it requires a superhuman effort from both partners even when the responsibilities are shared. When the wife is working or also in school, it is essential that the husband help with the chores at home. If he expects to be waited on hand and foot or considers it beneath his dignity to do the dishes, scrub floors, or change the baby's diapers, he is expecting too much. Both spouses must be willing to sacrifice a lot.

Indications are that some frustration arises for married students in the area of social life. They simply cannot afford to spend much money on recreation. Furthermore, many of the campus activities and interests are geared to dating couples, and exclude, by nature, married students, or at least make them feel unwelcome. Thorpe found that married students placed time for recreation very low on their priority list, far behind time for study and for sleeping. In fact they averaged about seven hours of sleep nightly,[58] which seems more than many single students average.

Marriage while in college takes a special kind of couple who are willing to devote years of their life to acquiring an education. No one is forcing them to remain in school; they are in school because they want to be. If the husband is willing to cooperate in the housework, if the wife does not place too much value on completing her own education, if conception control is fairly effective, and if the couple accept the challenge of hard work and personal sacrifice, they can probably be successful while they remain in school. Several studies of married veterans indicated that, in general, such marriages were quite successful. In a study at the University of Utah, 96 per cent of the married men and 94 per cent of the married women rated their college marriage as either happy or very happy.[59] Married veteran students at Purdue were asked: "Knowing what you know now, would you marry before finishing college if you were unmarried?" Seventy-five per cent of the couples answered in the affirmative, although some would have delayed the marriage until later in their college career. The remaining 25 per cent either answered "No" or were uncertain.[60]

Because the first few years of marriage are considered the most critical for most couples, it has been assumed that if the college marriage survives until graduation, then it will continue to be successful. This may not be the case at all; indeed, it appears that the first few years *after* graduation are the most critical for youthful student marriages.

Clinical observations by the author, supported by the observations made by several other family-life educators, confirm the possibility that the real strain on the young college marriage comes later than for most marriages. Often it seems that young students who married while in college have a focus on marriage that helps maintain it while on the campus. The focus, however, is not realistic for the working-world marriage. Frequently, in college marriages, there is too much sacrifice of the present for the future. Many unpleasant things are tolerated in the hope of a great change later. Many such couples are working so hard in school and on part-time jobs that there is little opportunity to establish a family pattern. Some are too rushed to take time to live with each other. If the first years of marriage are supposed to be devoted to the developmental tasks of establishing responses and habits for the later years of marriage, then many youthful college marriages have not yet really begun. Each partner is living in a kind of make-believe world, hoping and dreaming of how different the marriage will be later on. A kind of moratorium on

Table 9–10. **Marital happiness as related to 17,533 husbands in fifty-nine occupations**

		Per cent			Number of cases studied
Rank	Occupation	*Unhappy*	*Average*	*Happy*	
1	Chemical engineers	7.5	9.8	82.7	133
2	Ministers	11.2	9.3	79.5	174
3	College professors	9.8	13.8	76.4	450
4	Athletic coaches	14.9	9.7	75.4	134
5	*College students*	15.9	9.1	75.0	629
6	High school teachers	10.8	15.3	73.9	111
7	Engineers	11.5	15.8	72.7	304
8	Teachers	11.9	15.4	72.7	707
9	Electrical engineers	9.5	18.1	72.4	105
13	Accountants	13.9	16.3	69.7	294
16	Physicians	18.4	14.5	67.2	654
17	Bankers	17.5	15.4	67.1	292
25	Lawyers	18.8	17.1	64.1	771
31	Dentists	17.5	20.1	62.5	300
47	Farmers	21.1	25.6	53.3	1230
59	Traveling salesmen	35.9	24.3	39.9	198

Source: E. W. Burgess and Leonard S. Cottrell, *Predicting Success or Failure in Marriage* (Englewood Cliffs, N.J.: Prentice-Hall, Inc., 1939), pp. 399–400. Copyright © 1939, by Prentice-Hall, Inc., Englewood Cliffs, N.J. Adapted by permission of publisher and authors.

basic marital adustments is declared until after graduation, when each spouse will come forward with preconceived notions of what the marriage should actually be. By then, having tolerated so many irritations while waiting for this event, can each partner still give and take? The author knows of no published research in this connection, but his own unpublished surveys following the progress of student marriages suggest that youthful college marriages are less successful after graduation, when they have an undue proportion of breakups. Furthermore, a very high per cent of youthful college marriages fail to graduate, and from this drop-out group comes an even higher rate of eventual marriage failure.

If a student feels he must marry while still in college, he must be sure to take time for the development of the marital relationship, and never lose sight of the present while focusing on the future.

Paired readiness

A successful marital relationship depends upon more than maturity. The important timing factor is the readiness of the individuals for marriage with each other. This qualification is called *paired readiness*. It does not depend upon two faultless human beings finding each other, but upon the mutual adjustment of two less-than-perfect individuals who can interact for the greater benefit of their relationship.

The capacity of a couple to leave each other alone, even while together, and to respect the mystery of the other's uniqueness, is essential to their readiness as a pair. The essence of paired readiness is expressed in the lines of a letter reported to be written by the poet Rainer Marie Rilke, unencumbered by sociological jargon:

> But once the realization is accepted that even between the *closest* human beings infinite distances continue to exist, a wonderful living side by side can grow up, if they succeed in loving the distance between them which makes it possible for each to see the other whole and against a wide sky![61]

Summary

This discussion has stressed the importance of becoming as ready as possible for marriage. In timing marriage, it is necessary to explore the ramifications of military obligations, age, and physical, economic, moral, social, and emotional development, as well as educational aims and conditions.

Because reunions after separation are more likely to result in crises, and marital adjustments that should commence immediately would have to be postponed, it is strongly suggested that marriage be delayed until after the man has fulfilled his military obligations.

Age at marriage has been decreasing in the American society for several decades. It is unrealistic to select an arbitrary age as dividing those who are "too young" from those who are "old enough" for marriage. Marriages before the age of twenty, however, usually include several problems that arise primarily because of the age factor. One of these special problems is the greater risk of a change in values, which results in dissatisfaction with the mate who has not changed in a similar manner. Such unions result in higher rates of failure and unhappiness than do others.

Today's young people appear physically ready for marriage long before they are ready economically, morally, socially, or emotionally; yet, maturity in all these areas is particularly important in a society that increasingly emphasizes personality fulfillment within marriage.

The special problems of marriage while one or both partners are still in school are serious. Research studies suggest that there are two distinct types of college marriages. If the couple are older and have voluntarily re-entered educational life, there is not necessarily any cause of alarm although they may be faced with many problems. The marriages of young college students, however, often face innumerable difficulties. Many require a parental subsidy that usually incurs some parental direction.

Some young married students find it difficult to study. Increasing living costs may make it necessary for them to drop out of school. Once out of college, few students ever return to graduate. Adequate housing, fool-proof conception control, and the taxing care of children are additional problems. Many student marriages appear to be stable, when the truth is the couple have not really begun to adjust to each other maritally since their separate adjustments are primarily to the school situation. Removed from the academic routine, such unions face a postponed and more rigorous adjustment period.

There is another kind of readiness for marriage, more important probably than any individual criterion. This essential qualification is paired readiness.

No matter how well qualified the partners are individually and as a pair, however, there will be problems, and new ones will continue to threaten each marriage with every passing year. The presence of problems, however, does not mean that the pair is not ready for marriage. The individual's readiness for marriage is measured by the degree of ability he has to face and solve all the problems that do arise. Few, if any, people are fully mature along all the various lines examined. The individual, however, should be well along the way and still making progress toward improvement before he marries.

Sometimes marriages fail because of other obligations that place too much stress on the relationship. Had such unions been postponed until a time of less pressure or conflict, they might have succeeded.

Notes

1. According to conscription authorities, about 80 per cent of physically and mentally qualified young men experience military service before they are twenty-six years of age. See *United States News & World Report,* **48**:55.

2. Reuben Hill, *Families Under Stress* (New York: Harper & Row, Publishers, 1949).

3. Lee G. Burchinal, "Adolescent Role Deprivation and High School Age Marriage," *Marriage and Family Living,* **20**:381.

4. J. Joel Moss and Ruby Gingles, "The Relationship of Personality to the Incidence of Early Marriage," *Marriage and Family Living,* **21**:377.

5. *Statistical Bulletin,* Metropolitan Life Insurance Company (December 1964), 45.

6. See Harold T. Christensen, *et al.,* "Falsification of Age at Marriage," *Marriage and Family Living,* **15**:301–304; *Schoolgirl Brides* (Cleveland, Ohio: The Women's Protective Association, 1924).

7. Unpublished research by the author involving thirteen counties in southeastern Ohio for the years 1954–63 inclusive indicates a decided increase over the years in the falsification of their ages by teen-age couples in order to marry younger than permitted by law.

8. J. M. Mogey, "The Family in England," *Marriage and Family Living,* **16**:322.

9. Corrado Gini and Caranti Elio, "The Family in Italy," *Marriage and Family Living,* **16**:355.

10. Kaaro Svalastoga, "The Family in Scandinavia," *Marriage and Family Living,* 16:374.

11. Dominique Ceccaldi, "The Family in France," *Marriage and Family Living,* 16:326.

12. M. Kamel Nahas, "The Family in Egypt," *Marriage and Family Living,* 16:293–300.

13. S. Chandraseklar, "The Family in India," *Marriage and Family Living,* 16:337.

14. C. C. North and Paul K. Hatt, "Jobs and Occupations: A Popular Evaluation," *Opinion News,* 9:3–13.

15. Burchinal, *op. cit.,* p. 382.

16. U.S. Department of Health, Education, and Welfare, *Vital Statistics: National Summaries* (November 25, 1959), 42.

17. *Ibid.*

18. Brigham Young, *Journal of Discourses,* Vol. 12.

19. Floyd M. Martinson, "Ego Deficiency as a Factor in Marriage," *American Sociological Review,* 20:161–64.

20. Floyd M. Martinson, "Ego Deficiency as a Factor in Marriage—A Male Sample," *Marriage and Family Living,* 21:48–52.

21. Moss and Gingles, *op. cit.,* p. 373.

22. E. Lowell Kelly, "Consistency of the Adult Personality," *American Psychologist* (November 1955), 659–81.

23. Harvey J. Locke, *Predicting Adjustment in Marriage* (New York: Holt, Rinehart & Winston, Inc., 1951), pp. 101–102. A random sample of census data discloses almost identical results. See U.S. Bureau of the Census, Series P-20, No. 67.

24. Rachel M. Inselberg, "Social and Psychological Factors Associated with High School Marriages," *Journal of Home Economics,* 43:766–72.

25. A high percentage of young divorced women come from lower-socioeconomic-level homes. See, William J. Goode, *After Divorce* (New York: The Free Press of Glencoe, Inc., 1956).

26. Joe Vincent Meigs, M.D., "Plea for Younger Mothers," *Newsweek* (November 8, 1948) , 46.

27. The average American diet today provides for far better nutrition than in former years, and this probably accounts for much of this change. See Margaret S. Chaney, "The Role of Science in Today's Food," *Marriage and Family Living,* 19:142–49.

28. According to the Associated Press, the American Medical Association records indicate the world's youngest mother was Lina Medina of Lima, Peru, who had a baby boy by caesarean section at the age of five years seven months. *Associated Press Release* (March 1949).

29. Oliver E. Byrd, *Pregnancy and Childbirth* (Stanford, Calif.: Stanford University Press, 1956), p. 42.

30. Taken from the report of the Fact-Finding Committee of the Kansas group for the 1960 White House Conference on Children and Youth. This part of the report contributed by Evalyn Gendel, M.D., Assistant Director of the Division of Maternal and Child Health, Kansas State Board of Health, Topeka, Kansas; and William Roy, M.D., Obstetrician, Medical Arts Building, Topeka, Kansas (processed material, 1960).

31. *Statistical Bulletin,* Metropolitan Life Insurance Company (December 1964), 45.

32. Robert E. Park and E. W. Burgess, *Introduction to the Science of Sociology* (Chicago: University of Chicago Press, 1921), p. 76.

33. Ray E. Baber, *Marriage and the Family* (New York: McGraw-Hill Book Company, Inc., 1953), p. 194.

34. John MacMurray, *Freedom in the Modern World* (New York: Appleton-Century-Crofts, Inc., 1932), p. 47.

35. As an example, the *Child Family Digest,* 18:73, quotes the *Christian Parent Magazine* as stating that in 1959, Dallas, Texas had 480 married students in their public schools, including twelve in junior high school and nine even in grade school. The number sounds large, but actually is a very small percentage of the total student body in a city of over 700,000 people.

36. Judson T. Landis, "Attitudes and Policies Concerning Marriage Among High School Students," *Marriage and Family Living,* 18:128–36.

37. Lee G. Burchinal, "School Policies and School Age Marriages," *The Family Life Coordinator,* 8:45.

38. Ruth S. Cavan and Grace Beling, "A Study of High School Marriages," *Marriage and Family Living,* 20:293–95.

39. Wilson H. Ivins, *Student Marriages in New Mexico Secondary Schools* (Albuquerque, N.M.: University of New Mexico Press, 1954).

40. Vladimir De Lissovoy, "Student Marriage Rate Remains Low in Pennsylvania," *Pennsylvania School Journal* (April 1964).

41. *National Parent-Teacher,* 55:24–26; many statewide high school marriage studies have been compiled into a single table. This can be obtained from Dr. Mary Ellen Hitchcock of the University of Delaware.

42. Landis, *op. cit.,* p. 132; and Cavan and Beling, *op. cit.,* p. 294.

43. *Ibid.*

44. Paul C. Glick and Hugh Carter, "Marriage Pattern and Educational Level," *American Sociological Review,* 23:296.

45. Victor A. Christopherson, "College Marriage in Public and Private Institutions of High Education 1943–1958," *The Family Life Coordinator,* 8:49–52.

46. Clinical cases of the author and of others in the field indicate this as being the focal point of in-law problems for married students.

47. Arthur Glogau, "A Teaching Technique for a Course on Marriage and the Family," *The Family Life Coordinator,* 7:25–28.

48. Svend Riemer, "Married Students Are Good Students," *Marriage and Family Living,* 9:11–12.

49. U.S. Bureau of the Census, *Current Population Reports* (1964).

50. J. Anthony Samenfink and Robert L. Milliken, "Marital Status and Academic Success: A Reconsideration," *Marriage and Family Living,* 23:226–27.

51. David B. Cohen, F. J. King, and Willard H. Nelson, "Academic Achievement of College Students Before and After Marriage," *Marriage and Family Living,* 25:98–99.

52. Judson T. Landis, "On the Campus," *Survey Mid-Monthly,* 84:17–19.

53. Many more graduate students now receive either an assistantship or a fellowship. Many of these stipends are much higher than formerly. People considering graduate study should fully investigate this possibility.

54. Christopherson, *op. cit.,* p. 51.

55. Shirley Poffenberger, Thomas Poffenberger, and Judson T. Landis, "Intent Toward Conception and the Pregnancy Experience," *American Sociological Review,* 17:616–20. A similar survey on the campus of Purdue University disclosed almost identical findings. See Harold T. Christensen and Robert E. Phil-

brick, "Family Size as a Factor in the Marital Adjustment of College Students," *American Sociological Review,* **17**:309.

56. Theodore B. Johannis, "The Marital Adjustment of a Sample of Married College Students," *The Family Life Coordinator,* 4:29.

57. Christensen and Philbrick, *op. cit.,* p. 312.

58. Alice C. Thorpe, "How Married College Students Manage," *Marriage and Family Living,* 13:104–105, 130.

59. Rex A. Skidmore, Therese L. Smith, and Delbert L. Nye, "Characteristics of Married Veterans," *Marriage and Family Living,* 11:102–104.

60. Christensen and Philbrick, *op. cit.,* p. 310.

61. Izette de Forest, *The Leaven of Love: A Development of the Psychoanalytic Theory and Technique of Sandor Ferenezi* (New York: Harper & Row, Publishers, 1954), p. 108.

Questions for further thought

1. What factors for determining the time one is ready for marriage are most consistent with the American concept of democracy?
2. What conditions existed during and immediately after World War II which contributed most to the high divorce rate that followed?
3. What conditions encourage age at first marriage to be so much lower in the United States than in most of the rest of the world?
4. What kinds of maturity are considered the most essential for a successful modern marriage? Why? Which are the least important? Why?
5. Why must young people of today be more mature for marriage in many ways than was formerly necessary?
6. What most influenced college administrators to change their former attitude toward married students?
7. What special provision for the social life of married students should colleges make?
8. What are the arguments for and against parents subsidizing a college marriage?
9. What suggestions are in order for a couple contemplating marriage before finishing their education?

Recommended films

When Should I Marry? (McGraw-Hill Book Company, Inc.).
Are You Ready for Marriage? (Coronet).

Suggested supplemental readings

BOOKS

Becker, Howard S., *et al., Boys in White: Student Culture in Medical School.* Chicago: University of Chicago Press, 1961.

Frank, Lawrence R. "Housing For Married Students," in Ruth S. Cavan (ed.). *Marriage and Family in the Modern World.* New York: Thomas Y. Crowell Company, 1960. Pp. 275–82.

Land, Elizabeth, and Carrol V. Glines. *The Complete Guide for the Serviceman's Wife.* Boston: Houghton Mifflin Company, 1956.

Pagent, Norman W. *Facts About Teenage Marriages.* San Bernardino, Calif.: Family Service Agency, 1962.

Saul, Leon J. *Emotional Maturity*. Philadelphia: J. B. Lippincott Co., 1947.

Sakol, Jeanne. *What About Teen-Age Marriage?* New York: Julian Messner, Inc., 1961.

Too Young to Marry? Public Affairs Pamphlet 236.

ARTICLES

Aller, Florence D. "The Self-concept in Student Marital Adjustment," *The Family Life Coordinator*, 11:43–45.

Avery, E. Curtis. "Toward Understanding the Problems of Early Marriage," *The Family Life Coordinator*, 10:27–34.

Barkley, Margaret V., and Agnes A. Hartnell. "High School Marriages: What They Mean for Home Economists," *Journal of Home Economics*, 55:431–434.

Bowerman, Charles E. "Age Relationships at Marriage, by Marital Status and Age at Marriage," *Marriage and Family Living*, 18:231–33.

Burchinal, Lee G. "Do Restrictive Policies Curb Teen Marriages?" *Overview*, 1:72–73.

Cavan, Ruth S., and Grace Beling. "A Study of High School Marriages," *Marriage and Family Living*, 20:293.

Chambliss, Rollin. "Married Students at a State University," *Journal of Educational Sociology*, 34:409–16.

Christopherson, Victor A., Joseph S. Vandiver, and Marie N. Krueger, "The Married College Student, 1959," *Marriage and Family Living*, 22:122–28.

Clark, Alma Beth. "Economic Contributions Made by Families to Their Newly Married Children," *Dissertation Abstracts* (April 1962), 3636.

Foog, Lucy Van Ness. "Characteristics and Attitudes of Girls Withdrawing from an Ohio City School for Reasons of Pregnancy or Intention to Marry." Master's Thesis, Ohio State University, Columbus, Ohio, June 1963.

Green, Joseph. "High School Marriages," *Youth Leaders Digest*, 22:230–31.

Gerson, Walter. "Leisure and Marital Satisfaction of College Married Couples," *Marriage and Family Living*, 22:360–61.

Haveman, Ernest. "To Love, Honor—and Study," *Reader's Digest* (October 1955), 21–24.

Havighurst, Robert J. "Early Marriage and the Schools," *School Review*, 69:36–47.

Henton, W. June Marcum. "The Effects of Married High School Students on Their Unmarried Classmates," Master's Thesis, University of Nebraska, Lincoln, Neb., February 1963.

Hunter, Joyce Turner. "Scholastic Achievement of Married Women Students," *Marriage and Family Living*, 21:110.

Inselberg, Rachel M. "Marital Problems and Satisfactions in High School Marriages," *Marriage and Family Living*, 24:74–76.

Jensen, Vern H. and Monroe H. Clark. "Married and Unmarried College Students: Achievement Ability and Personality," *The Personnel and Guidance Journal*, 37:123–26.

Landis, Judson T. "Attitudes and Policies Concerning Marriages Among High School Students," *Marriage and Family Living*, 18:128–36.

Lee, Anne Marold. "A Study of Married Women College Students at Indiana State Teachers College," *Teachers College Journal*, 31:118–19.

Marchand, Jean, and Louise Langford. "Adjustment of Married Students," *Journal of Home Economics*, 44:113–14.

Pfeiffer, Marie Stoll. "Social and Psychological Variables Associated with Early College Marriages," *Dissertation Abstracts* (January 1962), 2381.

Sahinkaya, Rezan, and Kenneth Cannon, "Effect of War upon Early Marriage," *Journal of Home Economics,* **49**:203–207.

Schroder, Ralph. "Academic Achievement of the Male College Student," *Marriage and Family Living,* **25**:420–24.

Southard, H. F. "Early Marriages," *Child Study,* **32**:10–15.

Sussman, Marvin B., and Lee Burchinal. "Parental Aid to Married Children: Implications for Family Functioning," *Marriage and Family Living,* **24**:320–32.

Taylor, Arnold Gene. "Early Female Maturation as a Factor Related to Early Marriage," Master's Thesis, Utah State University, Logan, Utah, June 1963.

United Nations Economic and Social Council, "Consent to Marriage and Age of Marriage," E/C N. 6/317 (January 20, 1958), Annex, 1–6.

Vanscoyoc, Marthellen R. "Early Marriage: A Comparison of a Divorced and Married Group," Doctoral Thesis, Ohio State University, Columbus, Ohio, 1962.

Womble, Dale L. "Functional Marriage Course for the Already Married," *Marriage and Family Living,* **23**:278–83.

Planning ahead to
～ chapter 10 ～   married life

When planning ahead to married life, the couple must be fully aware that however deep the religious or cultural significance of the wedding may be to them, it is not a magical incantation. The wedding ritual itself cannot guarantee a lifetime of happiness or successful marital adjustment. The wedding only marks the beginning of their mutual efforts to attain marital happiness through love, knowledge, and—above all—intelligent planning.

Although the wedding itself is an important ceremony, the couple must not forget that it is only a prelude to the marriage. With this as their perspective, the couple can safely concentrate on the special details of the wedding.

The wedding

A newspaper account following the wedding gives public recognition of the couple's new status. The couple may feel that the newspaper announcement of their wedding serves little purpose, but its function actually serves deeper purposes that are essential to every marriage.

A PUBLIC ANNOUNCEMENT. A wedding is a public exchange of nuptial vows, attended by varying amounts of ritual and ceremony. It publicizes the fact that a man and a woman have contracted, vowed, and sealed an essentially social relationship. As Sumner and Keller have stated,

> It is vital to society that the entrance of its members into the status of wedlock shall be generally known, so that they and their offspring can thereafter be "placed" in their setting as husbands, wives, children, families,

with the result that their rights and duties toward each other within the relation, and toward others outside of it, can fall under the local system of composition and regulation.[1]

A wedding implies publicity. Secret marriages or elopements deprive a couple of a most important part of the ceremony: social recognition of the validity of the new relationship. A study of marriages of couples who had eloped revealed the deep significance of the public recognition factor in a marriage ceremony. Of 738 elopements, 46 per cent resulted from parental opposition. A smaller proportion of parentally opposed elopements continued happily than did those couples who eloped for other reasons; however, only 45 per cent of all the elopements studied turned out to be happy marriages.[2] An examination of the records of a thirteen-year period in one area of Philadelphia indicated that 16 per cent of the marriages were hasty or elopements; from that group came 21 per cent of the divorces in the same area.[3] Another study in Tennessee showed that the average announced marriage lasted about four times longer than a marriage by elopement.[4]

A RESPONSIBLE LEGAL PARTNERSHIP. A wedding also institutes a legal partnership. It creates a new status of responsibility, recognized, approved, and encouraged by others, including administrators of the law. This new civil status includes certain rights, opportunities, and obligations which had been heretofore denied.

SECONDARY EFFECT. The psychological effect of a wedding in bringing a couple a deeper sense of their commitment to one another is also vital. The ceremony should impress upon the couple the importance of their promises. A wedding can be of great help in reminding them of the seriousness of dedicating a lifetime to each other. Without ceremony or rituals, there is more likelihood that one or both partners will treat the relationship too casually.

A wedding schedule

After the couple have decided to marry, they should begin to plan a general schedule of the events leading up to the ceremony.

PARENTAL BLESSING. Probably the first, and foremost step, is securing parental approval. Various research studies show conclusively that parental approval is important to future marital success; conversely, parental disapproval is closely associated with marital failure or maladjustment.[5] Although parents sometimes place their stamp of approval on an ill-advised marriage, they more frequently advise against it. Parents are usually much more objective about the situation than the couple could be. Parental disapproval is often a strong indication that something is wrong with the relationship, at least at that time. Not only do parents basically operate from a more detached viewpoint, but, by virtue of having lived longer, they have a greater perspective for judgment of character, and a deeper knowledge of their offspring's strengths and weaknesses. Parental disapproval is not always justified; indeed, a few parents may look upon the marriage of a son or daughter as a bereavement. Although they are overjoyed at the happiness of their child, at the same time they feel a sense of loss. Nevertheless, parental approval is directly related to marital adjustment. One study reports that more women were willing to marry against parental opposition than if there were strong religious or educational differences.[6] Yet of these three factors, parental approval would probably prove to be the most important to later marital success.

CHOOSING A WEDDING DAY. After obtaining parental approval for the marriage, the wedding date should be chosen. A tentative date should be set first. This may be no more specific than an agreement on the season of the year for the wedding. Many couples prefer the summer months. The season of fewest marriages has always been the first quarter of the year, with the annual peak in June, and the secondary peak in August or September.[7]

The tentative date should be cleared with both immediate families. This will rule out the possibility of a conflict with other important family obligations. Of course, the date also depends on the groom's availability— i.e., his vacation, his graduation, or his military leave. It may also depend upon the availability of the facilities where the couple wish the wedding to take place.

From this point on, it is traditional for the bride to set the exact date; she must allow plenty of time to prepare her clothes and to make reservations for a reception. The bride will normally set the exact date in relation to her anticipated menstrual cycle. A word of caution needs to be stated in this connection. It is unwise to set the exact date too far in advance of the onset of menstruation, for the added strain and excitement of the last few weeks preceding the wedding may cause a temporary disruption of the cycle. David Mace, a noted marriage counselor, suggests that the date be set a week or so after the usual expected time for menstruation; thus there would be less likelihood of the inconvenience of menstruation on the honeymoon.[8] Such a choice, of course, increases the chance of conception occurring on the honeymoon if control measures are not employed.

SPECIFIC PLANS. Specific plans for the wedding often involve compromising dreams with realities, and part of these realities may be parental wishes. Sometimes it appears as though the bride's mother takes over completely. It has often been observed that many weddings appear to be, in effect, a "second" marriage for the bride's mother. It should be remembered, however, that weddings must conform in some degree to the social expectations of the friends and associates of the bride's parents. Such obligations may appear irrelevant and even selfish to many couples, yet, such feelings are real and important to many parents.

Because of differences in age and differences in degree of involvement, parents and children may clash over wedding plans. In such cases, each party must give a little. Perhaps the key to a peaceful solution is a reminder that this happy event is no occasion for a family squabble. Of course, if there is a drastic difference of opinion, the bride is entitled to express her preferences, but she should be ready to compromise on many details.

The type of wedding, and the specific plans, may also be related to whether either one or both of the parties have been married before. A study by Hollingshead indicates that premarital parties, the form and size of the wedding, its cost, and value of gifts received are related to whether or not it is the first marriage for both parties.

Table 10–1. **Wedding condition variations according to previous marital experience**

Condition	No other marriage	Woman married before	Man married before	Both married before
Per cent who had bachelor parties	33.7	31.1	13.8	4.6
Per cent who had showers	81.0	27.4	56.9	32.3
Number of showers	1.6	0.4	1.0	0.4
Per cent of formal weddings	69.7	4.8	29.3	6.2
Per cent of single-ring ceremonies	26.4	54.8	55.2	60.0
Number in bridal party	7.2	4.1	4.9	3.5
Number of wedding guests	172	34	77	30
Per cent of cases where bride's family paid for wedding	45.7	14.8	23.1	3.1
Per cent having a reception	87.7	51.6	79.3	44.6
Number of guests at reception	166	42	82	23
Cost of wedding	$948	$348	$571	$176
Value of cash gifts	$527	$168	$271	$ 70
Value of other gifts	$978	$336	$505	$182
Per cent taking a wedding trip	94.5	75.8	79.3	61.5
Number of days on trip	9	6	9	6
Cost of wedding trip	$320	$254	$371	$174

Source: August B. Hollingshead, "Marital Status and Wedding Behavior," *Marriage and Family Living,* 14:311. Copyright © 1952, by The National Council on Family Relations, Minneapolis, Minn. Reprinted by permission.

After setting the tentative wedding date, the wedding place should be selected. If there is not time to arrange for a church ceremony or the couple do not wish a church wedding, the college chapel or perhaps the home of the bride might be preferred.

Several things should be considered when choosing the place for the wedding. First of all, religious dictates must be considered. For instance, if it is a mixed religious marriage and one party is Catholic, the Catholic Church would require that the service be performed by a priest, and no one else. In that case, the wedding would have to take place on church premises. Sometimes Protestant ministers are willing to reaffirm such a marriage and give it their blessing. This must not be misconstrued as a second wedding service. Some members of the clergy refuse to perform the ceremony unless one or both spouses are members of a particular congregation. This attitude varies with the churches and with the clergyman. Under no circumstances can a Catholic church be used as a place for two non-Catholics to wed.

The geographical convenience of the place chosen for the wedding must also be considered. Can it be reached by the majority of relatives and friends who will be invited? If at all possible, the place selected should evoke pleasant memories and be of significance to at least one of the partners. The college chapel sometimes has special appeal for these reasons.

Specific wedding plans are also related to size and cost. The size of the wedding party and the expense should express the major social characteristics of the bride's parents in the community. The wedding, however, should not be used to create false status. As one writer has stated: "A wedding, like a garment, should fit. It should be appropriate to the standard of living and social position of the couple."[9] Frequently, weddings are too elaborate for the social level of the bride and her family. It is never wise to attempt to climb socially through an elaborate wedding, for the attempt seldom succeeds.

The cost of a wedding soars when many "fringes" are added, but in today's society it is difficult to resist ordering many of these extras. As soon as the engagement is formally announced, the bride's mail usually is flooded with all kinds of circulars, suggesting the addition of this or that for the wedding. Many of these suggestions have much romantic appeal, but to keep costs down, most of them should be ignored. Because the expense and size of a wedding are usually related to the number of guests, the bride and her family, in consultation with the groom and his family, must decide on the guest list.

In planning expenses, it is wise to consider the ability of all involved to pay their shares. The expenses should never become so high that they are a burden to the groom, the bride, or her parents. No one should ever go into debt for a wedding.[10]

Traditionally, wedding expenses are borne by the various parties concerned. As a rule, the groom and his family pay for the bride's bouquet, her mother's flowers, the bride's going-away corsage, the wedding trip, the wedding ring, the minister's fee, the marriage license, gifts for the bride, and gifts for the best man and the ushers. There is generally no set fee for the officiant, the amount being left up to the good judgment and financial ability of the groom. If the groom is well off financially, he should contribute more generously. The contribution may also be related to the helpfulness of the officiant. If he had given the couple premarital counseling, for example, then they should offer more than if he had only performed the ceremony. Generally, custom dictates that the bride and her family pay such expenses as the wedding gown, the bride's personal trousseau, the wedding reception and breakfast or dinner, the transportation of the bride and her guests to church and to the reception, the wedding decorations and music, the invitations and announcements, and gifts for the groom and the bride's attendants. Modern American wedding customs do not include a dowry, but historical accounts indicate that dowries once were given in American society. One such account describes an occasion when the father placed his newly married daughter on one side of a scale and balanced her weight with gold.[11] This was an exceptional event even in those days, however, for seldom did a couple receive more than a few cooking utensils and a spinningwheel or maybe a horse and a plow.[12] Dowry customs differ with the culture. In Italy the reception is usually held in the bride's home, and almost all Italian couples take a honeymoon trip. The bride usually brings a dowry, and the husband is in charge of it; nevertheless, it remains the wife's property. Furthermore, in the Italian culture of today, only 30 per cent of the new couples normally go to a new dwelling after marriage; about 40 per cent live in the husband's parental home, and another 30 per cent live in the bride's parental home.[13] In Scandinavia, the parents of the bride usually make all the arrangements for the wedding and pay all the expenses.[14] In Arab societies, a piece of jewelry sent to the girl by the man normally signifies an engagement; shortly thereafter the religious officiant of the community calls on the bride's family and the father of the bride announces approval of the marriage. A dowry (its amount previously agreed upon) is announced, registered, and paid by the groom to trustees of the bride. There is also a deferred dowry, a large sum which is deposited by the husband in the event of divorce or his death. Legal documents are signed by the groom, a trustee of the bride, and witnesses. The bride's family normally prepares the furniture for the newlyweds, which they take to their home. The furniture is always considered the property of the bride.[15]

It is probably safe to say that the character of weddings is basically feminine. Many a girl has her mind set on having a glamorous wedding. To deny her the experience may needlessly inflict a lifelong disappointment or frustration, for the wedding is usually the high point of a woman's life, unequalled, perhaps, except by the birth of her first child. Women are more likely to be sentimental about the wedding; thus, the bride's wishes, within reason, take precedence over those of the groom.

A wedding also has greater social significance for the woman than for the man because marriage represents a greater change in her life and status. Her name changes, and so usually does her place of residence. She may give up her vocation to assume the major responsibilities of home and motherhood. Thus, there is reason for the traditional belief that the bride's wishes have priority.

The social activities planned around the wedding are decided partly by the bride and groom, but chiefly by the bride, her parents, and her friends. There are other traditional wedding conventions and rituals that are better observed than ignored. Before making extensive plans, it is wise to consult those familiar with the marriage ritual and to read books on wedding etiquette.

The premarital consultation

Today's premarital consultation should include both a physical and a psychosocial examination.

THE PHYSICAL EXAMINATION. It is advisable that every couple consult a qualified medical doctor before marriage. He may provide them with basic information that will contribute to their physical and mental health. Any questions that either the man or the woman may have concerning physical functions, sexual drive, and physiological or emotional cycles should be brought to the physician for discussion. There is a direct relationship between good health and marital success, but only a thorough physical examination can assure both mates that each is in a state of general good health. If there should be a physical problem, it is best for both partners to understand it before marriage.

The reassurance of a thorough physical checkup can inspire confidence and reduce worries and fears for both partners. If requested, the woman's capacity for normal pregnancy and childbirth can be assessed by her physician and an evaluation of the man's potential for fatherhood can be made. Hereditary problems should also be discussed with the physician, and the extent of any possible pathology in either mate explained fully to both. If there is a possibility of congenital anomalies, the physician may recommend further consultations with a specialist in the field.[16]

If at all possible, it is best for both partners to be examined by the same physician or at the same clinic. This makes it easier to arrange medical appointments and to discuss many points of common interest.

The physical examination may reveal some minor deficiency of sexual anatomy in either the man or the woman, and this should be cleared up before the wedding if possible. One study of 650 prospective brides revealed that 3 per cent had tumors, cysts, or other abnormalities which required surgery. An additional 20 per cent were found to have a tilted uterus, which might, in some cases, interfere with coitus or childbirth.

About 35 per cent had some abnormality in the color or texture of the tissues covering the cervix, and slightly more than 20 per cent had a sufficient excess of moisture in the vagina to constitute a condition called *leukorrhea*, which can be cleared with treatment.[17] It is much better to discover such conditions before marriage rather than afterward.

Common checkpoints in a thorough physical examination are for tuberculosis, tumors, or heart murmurs as well as an examination of the major internal organs. In addition, there should be vaginal smears for gonorrhea, blood tests for venereal diseases, and, of course, a definition of the particular Rh factor involved.

There is usually an examination of the female hymen, the fold of membrane across the opening of the vagina. The hymen is not intact in every female virgin. If the membrane is thin and elastic, stretching easily, it will not interfere in any way with coitus. If it is rather thick and inelastic, a series of dilations may be recommended. Such treatment usually takes a few weeks, and thus it is wise to have the premarital examination fairly early. It is absolute folly for a bride with a strong, intact hymen to undergo a crude and possibly painful sexual initiation, which is usually traumatic for both partners. A gentle dilation can eliminate the possibility of pain or discomfort during intercourse. Dewees reports that only about 10 per cent of his patients had hymens elastic enough to make honeymoon intercourse comfortable without prior dilation.[18] This is also an opportune time for the bride to acquire knowledge of contraception. If she is to be responsible for using a contraceptive device, she should be measured, fitted, and instructed in its proper use.

It is often assumed that the male has more premarital sexual experience and knowledge than the female. Indeed, one physician reports that most grooms coming for consultation are more mature in their sexual experience and knowledge than brides.[19] There is a danger, however, in a man's thinking that he knows everything that he needs to know about sex. Actually this may not be the case at all.

Occasionally, there are men who worry about being undersexed or oversexed. The reassurance of a physician may be all that is necessary to help the couple overcome this anxiety. The physician may help both mates to consider that sex relations are normal, and to look forward to their sexual relationship with a natural but enlightened anticipation.

Regardless of the state legal requirements, it is advisable to have a comprehensive physical examination. In spite of differences of state laws, the American society has perhaps progressed further in premarital health regulations than other societies. Among the Arab nations, only Egypt is concerned about a premarital examination, but these are conducted only on a voluntary basis. The health centers there have neither the authority to prevent infected persons from marrying nor the power to enforce their treatment.[20]

Since 1942, French law has required a premarital examination for both partners, including chest x-rays and blood tests. The results, however, are merely recorded; they are never shown to anyone, and constitute no obstacle to marriage.[21]

THE PSYCHOSOCIAL EXAMINATION. An individual might feel ready for marriage and then become totally confused by the advice of relatives and friends. The prospective bride should not be surprised when her mother, grandmother, aunts, older sisters, and friends—some of whom are not even married—offer "helpful hints" on how to handle a man and how to meet the most intimate emergencies of marriage itself. Frequently the prospective groom is given equally free advice on such things as the temperament of women and their "common" responses. Much of this advice is often little more than a display of ignorance and bias, more nonsense than wisdom. Such ready recommendations may build up unwarranted suspicions and fears rather than confidence and anticipation. Reliable marital information is best obtained from professional counselors.

The trained marriage counselor, on the other hand, is guided by the results of research, clinical practice, and his wide experience in observing married couples' reactions to difficulty. The professional marriage counselor can present both the biological and psychosocial factors of a successful marriage. He neither moralizes nor preaches; his aim is to help the couple work out the best possible relationship for their pending marriage. He will point out the particular inhibitions and fears that might interfere with the marital harmony of that particular couple. It is a wise pair who, prior to marriage, place their confidence in the trained, experienced judgment of a professional counselor, and who avoid discussing intimate things with relatives and friends. The couple can gain valuable insight into the marriage relationship by discussing their questions with a counselor before the wedding. Even their physician may not be the most competent person for evaluating the readiness of the couple. He may be able to answer questions on the physical aspects of sex and yet be quite limited in psychosocial factors. Some medical doctors are simply not prepared either by nature or by training to offer the best counsel on human functions beyond the physiological approach. On the other hand, if the family physician is interested in this aspect of health, he may be very helpful. In some localities, there are clergymen, educators, and social workers who are qualified for marriage counseling. There are others in the same professions, however, who are limited in this area. One study reported that many clergymen confined their marital counseling to advising on how to act in marriage according to the precepts of the Bible. As a group, however, they did not have the necessary training or experience for counseling on the intimate relationships of marriage. Many of the clergymen reported they had difficulty in counseling even in financial matters. It was also reported that many of these ministers avoided even talking about sex because they believed that the couple would feel uneasy discussing it with a minister.[22]

Some communities today have planned-parenthood clinics, which are excellent places to go to for premarital examinations. Physicians working in these clinics have had special training in the psychosocial and physiological aspects of marriage. Private institutions for marriage counseling have also been established. The American Institute of Family Relations in Los Angeles, for example, has been operating since 1930 with a high degree of success. In addition to consulting with engaged couples on the emotional aspects of marriage, it employs physicians to examine and advise them on the physiological side of the marital relationship.

There is an increasing trend toward premarital counseling in today's society. One research study found that about four times as many women today seek professional premarital counseling from competent sources than did their mothers.[23] Most premarital consultation services also include marriage-prediction tests, which rate a couple's marriageability. Interested couples can examine some of these tests for themselves in various marriage texts,[24] and most marriage counselors have copies available upon request. The true value of marriage-prediction tests, perhaps, lies not in their capacity to forecast marital success or failure, but, rather, in their ability to indicate the areas in which the couple are likely to have difficulty or success. The questions brought up by these tests, however, often help a couple to face problems that they had previously sensed but had been unable to define.[25]

The American Institute of Family Relations at Los Angeles uses emotional-maturity tests quite extensively in premarital counseling. The former director of the Institute, Paul Popenoe, has claimed on many occasions that there has not been one divorce among couples who came to the Institute during its first eight years of operation. Another authority in the field states that, of those couples who came to him for premarital counseling and whose marriages were predicted successful from tests and personal analysis, not one had yet divorced or separated. Conversely, most of those couples who went ahead in spite of his prediction of marriage failure were already in serious trouble or divorced.[26] Studies have shown that premarital counseling, with or without predictive tests, is helpful to most couples. During a fifteen-year period, the Reverend Milton G. Gabrielson, Pastor of the Bay Shore Congregational Church in Long Beach, California, performed more than 500 weddings for couples who had received premarital counseling from him. Of this group, only fourteen marriages ended in divorce, and more than half of those divorces he had predicted during the counseling.[27] In Columbus, Ohio, the late Reverend Roy A. Burkhart would not consent to marry a couple unless they had first come for premarital counseling. During one thirteen-year period, he counseled more than 1100 couples; only nine of these marriages later ended in divorce.[28] Premarital counseling, however, is not a guarantee of a successful marriage; ordinarily, only those fairly well matched are willing to go to a marriage counselor in the first place. This can be a clue to the possible outcome of the future marriage. If the potential spouse is somewhat hesitant to submit to a paired-readiness

Figure 10-1. There is an increasing trend toward premarriage counseling in today's society. (Drawing by David Stone; courtesy of the Book-of-the-Month Club, Inc.)

examination, it might be a sign of problems not yet apparent. More caution than usual should be observed under such circumstances.

Civil or religious ceremony

Another decision facing the engaged couple is whether the ceremony will be a civil or a religious one.

HISTORICAL DEVELOPMENT. History indicates that the wedding ceremony was originally performed by the father of the bride in early Hebrew, Greek, and Roman times. The Christians included a blessing on the marriage, and this later became a most important part of the ritual. With the Protestant Reformation, marriage became a state civil contract (in defiance of the strong Catholic insistence that marriage could be performed only by the Catholic Church). The laws of many European countries today prescribe that a couple have two marriage ceremonies: the civil and the religious.

MODERN CULTURAL PRACTICES. An examination of marital laws in other cultures indicates that the separation of church and state marriage laws is still in effect. Brazilian law, for example, requires a civil wedding, yet most couples go immediately to a priest for a second marriage ceremony. The social sanction of the community for the marriage often depends more upon the religious than on the civil ceremony. In Brazil, the church does not recognize civil marriage; yet the state does not recognize the religious marriage unless it is sanctioned by a legal document which states that the ceremony will take place in a specific church and will be supervised by a particular priest.[29] In France, the civil ceremony must precede the religious ceremony.[30] Italy today has three forms of marriage services: (1) the civil; (2) the religious according to Catholic rites; and (3) the religious according to other church rites, subject to civil jurisdiction. Only 2.3 per cent of the weddings in Italy, however, are civilly performed.[31] Svalstoga reports that in the Scandinavian countries 82 per cent of weddings are church affairs, but that there is a wide variance between countries. For example, civil ceremonies comprise only 8 per cent of the weddings in Sweden and 14 per cent in Norway, but they constitute 34 per cent of the weddings in Denmark.[32] There are two legal classifications of weddings in England today: the Church of England ceremony and the civil ceremony. In the Church of England wedding, at least one of the parties must be a member of the particular parish in which the ceremony is performed. All religious ceremonies other than those of the Church of England are considered civil marriages and must follow the form prescribed by Parliament. All marriages must be preceded by published banns. These banns are published in the church (for those who are to wed in the Church of England) or in the registry office of the district (for those who are to be married in other churches or by civil authorities).[33]

EARLY AMERICAN CUSTOMS. America effected a unique and worthy solution to the problem of church and state jurisdiction: it simply delegated to all bona fide clergy the civil authority to perform marriages. Actually, by American law, the wedding ceremony must be a civil affair. By giving the clergy the civil authority to perform marriages, however, both the civil and religious sanction are inherent in one service; the official who performs the ceremony is then responsible for reporting it to the proper public office. This was not always true in American culture. Under early Virginia law, only the Church of England clergy could perform a marriage, and it was not until after 1780 that other clergymen were allowed to perform marriages in that state.[34] The right to perform wedding ceremonies is exclusively in the hands of the clergy in Maryland, West Virginia, and Delaware. There is one exception in Delaware: the Mayor of Wilmington is also allowed to perform a wedding ceremony.

THE CIVIL CEREMONY. The religious service, over and above the legal requirement, is a matter of individual preference. Except in the three states previously mentioned, a civil ceremony is recognized as valid in American courts. Many couples feel that the civil ceremony performed by a judge or justice of the peace lacks the dignity, beauty, and social or religious significance so important at the beginning of marriage. It is sometimes more abrupt and seemingly more mercenary, often offending the sensitivity and hopes of the couple. Even though this criticism might apply to some church weddings too, the disillusionment seems not as great. Koos quotes the anguished comments of a bride after a nonchurch wedding:

> I've never been made to feel so terrible in my life. It was like a business proposition, like borrowing money at the bank.... He called in two clerks as witnesses, and they grinned at us as though we were doing something that wasn't just the decent thing to do.... Harry kissed me, but not the way I had expected it at all. He was just as embarrassed as I was, and we got out of there as fast as we could.... The whole ceremony didn't take three minutes, and made us feel like three cents.[35]

THE RELIGIOUS CEREMONY. The religious ceremony, in contrast to the civil ceremony, reaffirms the couple's allegiance in their faith. It usually gives the couple the blessings of the church and the support and dignity of its beliefs concerning marriage. In the American culture, even many of those with only nominal religious connections prefer a church wedding and say they would not feel married if the ceremony had not taken place in a house of worship, or at least under the leadership of a clergyman.

The findings from various studies indicate a direct relationship between a religious wedding and the future success of the marriage. Although many civil marriages are also successful, it appears that a much higher percentage of church marriages turn out happily. It is probably not the fact of being married by a clergyman that makes the difference, however, but the fact that, generally, people who prefer a religious officiant have a more serious attitude toward the marriage vows. Such persons are likely to be more emotionally mature than those who must seek the services of a justice of the peace.

Apparently, the majority of Americans prefer that their marriages be performed by a member of the clergy. Census data indicate that about 80 per cent of all weddings are church affairs, and the figure rises to 84 per cent when it is a first marriage for one or both partners.[36]

Table 10–2. **Happily married and divorced who were married in a given place and by a given person**

	Per cent			
Person or place	Men remaining married	Men divorced	Women remaining married	Women divorced
At home	27.7	15.5	29.2	14.8
Church	12.7	9.3	11.1	8.2
By judge	1.2	2.6	1.2	0.5
At minister's home	38.7	39.1	40.4	46.5
By justice of the peace	13.3	29.2	11.7	27.3
Elsewhere	6.4	4.3	6.4	2.7

Source: Harvey J. Locke, *Predicting Adjustment in Marriage* (New York: Holt, Rinehart & Winston, Inc., 1951), p. 238. Copyright © 1951, by Henry Holt and Company, Inc., New York. Reprinted by permission of Holt, Rinehart & Winston, Inc., New York.

An interpretation of the marriage
VOWS

The specific form of the wedding ceremony causes no particular concern in any state within the American society. An informal service is as legal as the most ritualistic and formal ceremony.

COUPLES MARRY EACH OTHER.   The one element common and essential to every wedding ceremony is the expression of decision and intent on the part of the couple. A mutual pronouncement of their desire to marry each other must be indicated in the exchange of vows by the bride and the groom.

VARIATIONS OF CEREMONY.   Actual wedding ceremonies vary so much that no single ritual could be quoted *in toto* that might apply in all respects to any wedding. The ceremony varies not only between denominations, churches, and temples, but among officiants, regardless of affiliation. The ritual might be changed to conform to the couple's wishes. There have been occasions when couples have written their own convictions into the service. Certain elements, however, are common to most religious wedding ceremonies. These include:

1. An address to the couple and the congregation by the minister, priest, or rabbi on the religion's tenets on marriage.
2. The exchange of vows followed by prayer.[37]

The honeymoon

The historical basis behind the so-called honeymoon dates back to the pre-Christian era, when a man was exempt from military service for a year after marriage while he settled his home and started his family.[38]

SPECIFIC QUALIFICATIONS. The honeymoon itself has specific qualifications. In the first place, it cannot be postponed. A delayed honeymoon is little more than a vacation. It is possible to postpone the wedding journey, but the honeymoon itself cannot be postponed; it must take place immediately after the marriage.

Although most couples take a wedding trip, the journey is almost incidental to the honeymoon. The honeymoon itself is an interval of intimacy and privacy during which the pair may become psychically adjusted to their new state. If a couple are properly prepared through their courtship, a honeymoon may be unnecessary for their psychic adjustment. Most couples, however, will have many unsuspected adjustments to make.

The honeymoon might take place in the new apartment of the married couple. This is not inconceivable, provided that relatives and friends are thoughtful enough to stay away. The honeymoon should be free from the advice or suggestions of relatives and friends. To insure such privacy, however, a wedding trip is usually mandatory, and it is best to go where neither is known.

WEDDING JOURNEYS. In Johannis' study of 146 students' wives, only twenty-four reported not having had a wedding trip. Eight of the twenty-four no-wedding-trip wives stated that a couple should be sure to take a trip during the honeymoon period, indicating that they felt the first adjustments could be better achieved away from familiar surroundings or friends and relatives.[39] A survey of former students of a marriage course at Stephens College disclosed that about 79 per cent of the girls had experienced a wedding trip.[40] The results of an additional study suggested the greater likelihood of a wedding trip if it were the first marriage experience for either of the partners. In that study, 94.5 per cent of couples marrying for the first time actually took a wedding trip. Where the man had been previously married, only 79.3 per cent had a trip.[41]

A TRANSITIONAL STAGE. A honeymoon is a transitional stage between single and married life; it is couple-focused. The individuals are no longer single; neither are they yet settled down as a married couple. During this interval they must learn more about one another and how to live more easily with one another. The importance of the journey is that it enables the couple to make these first adjustments free from other considerations. To have a honeymoon the couple must be available and free to each other, with no other commitments. David Mace describes the necessity for a honeymoon as follows:

> From one point of view, getting married could be represented as a rather terrifying experience. For something like a third of their lifespan two people have lived independent of each other—probably without even knowing of each other's existence. They have formed their own personal habits and learned to live their own private lives. Now, after a comparatively short acquaintance, they come together in the closest human intimacy, living together, sleeping together, yielding themselves up to each other. At the time, they don't think of this as an invasion of their privacy. Their strong desire for each other draws them together and they make their surrender eagerly. But for all that, the mutual unveiling of their bodies and minds can sometimes have profoundly disturbing and quite unexpected consequences.... To make these early adjustments as easy as possible, we have wisely provided the institution of the honeymoon.[42]

The honeymoon itself should be full of excitement, thrills, and anticipation of a delightful intimacy. It is the advanced stage of the bliss characteristic of the engagement period. Two deep emotions intermingle in most marriages during the first weeks: the growing pleasure of the sex experiences, and fears of the undefined future. Adjustments to these strong realities can best be made when the two are free from any other obligations.

A BEGINNING. The honeymoon is the beginning of a new way of living, and early efforts are always marked by a degree of awkwardness. In one research study, forty out of fifty married women reported that their honeymoon had not been the happiest part of their married life.[43] Whether the honeymoon is easy or awkward, a marriage will probably be much better for the experience. Naturally, if the honeymoon is well planned and well executed, the marriage is off to a better start. The fifty women in Brav's study had been married on an average of 12.5 years, yet more than 90 per cent stated that the details of their honeymoon were still clear in their memories: 74 per cent described their honeymoon as a complete success; 64 per cent described it as "the achievement of all the premarital romantic desires"; 68 per cent felt the honeymoon was not really necessary to a happy marriage, but 30 per cent felt otherwise.[44] A honeymoon offers an opportunity for easing the strain of a sudden change from single life to marriage under the most favorable conditions.

AN OPPORTUNITY. An interlude of travel and independence gives a couple time to get over the self-consciousness of their new roles in society.

The central interest is the two people and their relationship, not anything else. They may continue conversations on points of agreement and disagreement as they did during their engagement, and possibly work through specific problems. They will also make new discoveries about each other, which are perhaps best made with no outside interference. Many new discoveries will be a cause of joy, and these should be expressed to each other.

Along with the natural desire to share everything on a honeymoon, there is also an impulse to tell the beloved everything as well as to promise almost anything. Sharing all is good, but telling all can be dangerous. The honeymoon is no time for a detailed confession of past transgressions nor a time for a critique of the partner's weaknesses. A full confession may produce shock effects. Each partner should be allowed the privilege of discovery; divulging a long list of personal details can deprive the partner of a sense of adventure. It might also prove boring, which is disastrous for any relationship.

The honeymoon is a time for the couple to get over any false modesty. Modesty may be natural, but false modesty simply becomes selfishness. The mate, not personal inhibitions, should be the center of all attention during the honeymoon. Thus, as the honeymoon progresses, the two grow closer together. This is the major and only purpose of a honeymoon.

The importance of planning for a honeymoon

To fulfill the major purpose of a honeymoon, detailed planning prior to the wedding is essential.

WHO DOES THE PLANNING? The most important rule is that the wedding trip should be planned by both mates. Only in this way is there a possibility of its being a successful marital experience for both. The Johannis study of honeymoons of married college students found that 77.5 per cent of the wedding trips were planned jointly; 17.5 per cent planned by the husband; 1.7 per cent by the wife; and in four cases by others. Of the four cases planned by others, the replies indicated that three were planned by the U.S. Army—that is, the husband was assigned to a different post, so the couple took their wedding trip in that particular direction. In one case it was planned by the bride's parents.[45]

Regardless of who plans the trip, there are certain things to avoid. Too many couples make their honeymoon a travel tour, crowding too much into a brief interval and spending too many hours with other people. The major purpose of the trip is defeated when this happens. The only important thing is that the couple be together, not where they go nor how much money they spend. The honeymoon should include some planned activities to prevent boredom. There should be time for relaxed meals, leisurely walks and talks, and hours of isolation for the new love-making experiences.

A wedding trip which is unrealistically planned can become a liability rather than an asset to a new marriage. Wiley, writing about wedding trips, describes them as one of the most strenuous of adjustment periods. He is not even certain that they are a good idea.[46]

Before going on the trip, the couple should leave word with some reliable person as to how and where they can be reached in case of an emergency. Reservations should be made far in advance, so the couple can concentrate entirely on each other immediately after the wedding and not on last-minute calls to hotel reservation clerks.

Today many couples prefer an automobile for the wedding trip rather than any public means of transportation. In Johannis' study, 90 per cent of the wedding trips were made by car, and only 6 per cent by train. Two couples traveled by bus, two by plane, and one couple had a thirty-day camping trip on horseback into the mountains.[47]

COMMON HAZARDS.   One of the most common hazards of a wedding trip is that each day's travel is likely to be too long. There should be no hurry. Hurry and long traveling days produce fatigue, and fatigue

Figure 10-2. Today, many couples prefer an automobile for the wedding trip. (Courtesy of the Bell Telephone System.)

is the worst enemy of all human relationships. It is best to avoid a tight schedule. The trip should be a time for rest. Couples start their honeymoon after the excitement of the wedding and reception, which often produce nervousness and emotional exhaustion. In one study, 21 per cent of new brides reported fatigue and exhaustion and an additional 20 per cent reported overstimulation and extreme tension after their wedding ceremonies.[48] An arduous travel schedule would then entirely defeat the purpose of a honeymoon.

Figure 10-3. Weddings can produce nervousness and emotional exhaustion. (Courtesy of the Bristol-Myers Company, makers of Bufferin.)

No two wedding journeys can ever be exactly alike. For that matter, no two trips of any kind can be exactly alike. What one couple might enjoy, another couple might not like at all. A camping trip into the mountains, for example, would certainly be no joy for two tenderfeet.

It is advisable to depart from the traditional spots, like Niagara Falls, in favor of places which characterize the individuality of the particular relationship. In the Johannis study 35 per cent of the couples reported visiting coastal resorts on their journey, while 27.5 per cent visited inland resorts or scenic areas, including eight camping couples who stayed in national parks; 28.3 per cent reported spending the time in large cities; 16 per cent just kept the car on the road, moving to a new job, military post, or to college; and two couples spent the time working as lookouts for the U.S. Forest Service. Actually, only 13.6 per cent of the couples studied by Johannis stayed at a single resort for the entire honeymoon period.

Another common honeymoon temptation is to crowd too many experiences into the trip. The couple's greatest source of satisfaction and happiness should come primarily from the hours of intimate companionship. For the bride particularly, the wooing and love play that precede sexual intercourse may be of greater importance than the sex act itself. Lack of privacy or time can crowd these vital periods of intimacy out of the day's program. The opportunity for wooing is lost in an atmosphere of hectic social activities. The couple must have enough private time together for each to become more realistic as a person to the other; the abstract idealization of bride and groom wears away only as each becomes better acquainted with the mundane daily habits of the other.

This is not to deny that some time should be spent with other individuals. A little time spent with others is important so that the couple can get an idea of how their neighbors will react to them as a married pair. This can be a valuable experience before returning to familiar surroundings and familiar people. Basically, however, the trip is a time of leisure, of loafing and sleeping.

THE FINANCIAL ASPECT. The trip should be scaled to the financial assets of the couple. Trying to do and see too much may precipitate a money crisis that can set the stage for many early and utterly senseless quarrels. In contrast to the traditional concept that the groom pays all the honeymoon expenses, the Johannis study found that in 35.3 per cent of the cases, the trip was jointly financed. However, in about one third of these cases, "jointly financed" meant supplementation by cash wedding gifts. Almost half (47.1 per cent) of the trips were financed by the husband alone, and an additional 5.9 per cent were financed by the husband aided by resources other than the wife. In five cases, cash wedding gifts helped finance the wedding trips: four were contributions mostly by the husband's parents, and one by the wife's parents. There were two cases of wedding trips financed on borrowed money.

POSITIVE SUGGESTIONS. A few positive suggestions from people who have experienced a wedding journey are perhaps in order. The first suggestion is to consider the cost. It was suggested by 28.4 per cent of wives polled that this is one of the first and foremost considerations. These wives cautioned that the couple spend no more than they can afford and keep some money in reserve for returning home. They suggested spending enough to make it a memorable occasion, but not so much as to make it a tremendous splurge. The second suggestion was to choose a place of mutual interest. Several wives suggested that in choosing the honeymoon location a couple should consider a place that is fairly new to both. They felt this would be better than choosing a place with which one partner was more familiar. The wives also suggested that a very carefully planned, jointly cooperative conception-control plan be decided upon before the wedding. It was felt that this would contribute greatly to sex adjustment during the early sexual experiences of the couple.[49]

A poll taken by the *Woman's Home Companion* discloses that women believe the most important thing on the honeymoon is the right man. This, they said, is more important than the place, the money spent, or even the clothes worn. Again, this points up the fact that too much time can be spent in planning the wedding and honeymoon and not enough time spent in planning the marriage. In addition, about 50 per cent encouraged modest expenses on the journey, suggesting that the money could probably better be spent in other ways.[50]

LENGTH. A wedding trip can be too long. It is possible for a couple to begin to see too much of each other and to become irritated with little personal idiosyncrasies. The trip should end while it is still enjoyable. The end should find the couple refreshed and relaxed. With the foundations of their adjustment set, they should be ready and eager to take up their work again. In the later days of the journey there should be some time spent in discussions of home-making plans. This stimulates an eagerness to get into the regular routine of marriage itself. In the Johannis study, the following suggestions were given by wives concerning the length of the journey.

1. Perhaps more important than anything else, the trip should be determined in relation to the husband's job.

2. It is important to return from the trip in time to set up housekeeping before getting into other regular routines. Housekeeping must be set up in an orderly fashion; otherwise, there will be a lot of confusion. It would be best to return from the journey a day or two before one or both must go back to work or into some other daily pattern. This would enable the couple to set the housekeeping routine rather than trying to do two jobs at once.

American middle-class couples take honeymoons averaging nine days.[51] In the Johannis study, 23.8 per cent spent seven days; 13.9 per cent, from eight to thirteen days; and 14.9 per cent, fourteen or more days, with the longest time being thirty days. The average length was seven days. In the American culture, the average indicated by most surveys appears to be somewhere between a week and ten days.

Sexual intimacies on the honeymoon

It seems appropriate that some consideration be given to the matter of sexual intimacies after marriage. Even if marriage does not mark the beginning of this experience for some couples, they might be reminded that too often the physical relationship is taken for granted with little mutual planning.

THE FIRST EXPERIENCE. A question often asked is: Should the couple have complete coitus on their first night together? It is only natural that most couples whose love is strong enough for marriage would desire

complete sexual union on the first honeymoon night. It was not uncommon, however, for earlier books in the field of marriage to suggest a
postponement of intercourse. Most people, however, consider these suggestions absurd. Unless there is a specific reason, such as some physical
indisposition or perhaps an extreme degree of fatigue, the couple most
certainly should have intercourse on their wedding night. The first
experiences together are unlikely to be idyllic, but to deny them is foolish.

THE BEST APPROACH.   To get the best from their first experiences together, the bride and groom should:

1. Approach sex relations on the wedding night with adequate factual
knowledge.
2. Understand that intercourse is not meant to be painful.
3. Have an adequate control of conception available, fully understood
and to be used if desired.

Much of the basis for early suggestions that intercourse be postponed
on the first night was related to the so-called trauma considered possible
with the initial sexual experiences. Modern research shows that this has
been greatly overemphasized in the American culture, and it very rarely
happens anymore. Most such traumas are found only in fiction. As one
writer has said:

The popular literature is full of the shocked "raped" bride or, at least,
the bride who is ignorant and unprepared for the first night of her marriage. But the ignorant bride and the insensitive, self-centered groom are
much less likely to be found in the college-educated segment of the population.[52]

If couples do not expect too much from the first sexual experiences,
they are less likely to be disappointed. Enjoyable sex response is a
matter of learning and grows with the years. Couples who achieve complete sexual satisfaction during the honeymoon are to be considered the
exception rather than the rule. After all, there is little else that one does
well at first. Mates will make as many mistakes in this area of life as they
do in others. After a while, with practice, most couples become more
proficient and relaxed about sex.

It is probably safe to say that the honeymoon represents the poorest
level of sexual adjustment that most couples will ever have. Inhibitions
take time to overcome. The bride may find the inhibitions of a lifetime
impossible to overcome in her earliest sexual experiences, but she should
not be unduly distressed by the fact. One research study of 190 wives of
university students disclosed that 17 per cent evaluated their sexual
experiences during the first two weeks of marriage as "unsatisfying" or
"very unsatisfying." Despite the sexual difficulties of the wedding night,

however, many reported some degree of sexual satisfaction on the honeymoon.[53] Brav found that almost 60 per cent of the women in his study failed to achieve complete sexual harmony during their honeymoon, but over half of those who failed still called the honeymoon a complete success. Actually, 74 per cent of Brav's subjects described the honeymoon as a "complete success."[54]

Sex relations on the honeymoon often establish a pattern of understanding, cooperation, and unselfish consideration that will influence all the relationships of the couple. This is more important than the complete sexual satisfaction of either partner. Actually, sexual harmony is most easily achieved when the major purpose of each mate is to please the partner. Because of the prevalence of this concept in the Arab world, it is reported that there is little sexual maladjustment, or concern about sex after marriage.[55]

A successful honeymoon

What, then, makes a honeymoon a success? It would seem that its success depends as much on expectations as accomplishments. If one does not expect perfection, he is more likely to consider his honeymoon successful. One can expect to make discoveries about the mate that will be joyous, and these should be accentuated; other discoveries may prove discouraging. It is the relation of what is accomplished to what is expected, however, that determines whether a honeymoon has been a success. Regardless of what has taken place, if a couple return to regular routines with an eager anticipation and are looking forward to their married life together, then there has been a measure of success.

Summary

Although it is necessary to plan for a wedding and honeymoon, couples should not become so absorbed in such details as to neglect the continued planning for their married life to follow.

The major purposes of a wedding should be kept in mind, and important steps should be followed leading up to it. Both the physical and the psychosocial aspects of the relationship need to be fully examined and understood with the help and guidance of competently trained professionals.

The religious ceremony, rather than the civil, is preferred by most couples. Certain procedures, phrases, and expressions are common to all religious ceremonies regardless of the setting, and there are also many variations even among similar sects and denominations. Couples sometimes include their own convictions in the wedding ceremony.

The purpose of a honeymoon is to help the couple make the easiest transition possible from single to married life. The honeymoon need not include a trip, but a trip usually makes it easier to carry out the purposes of a honeymoon, provided such a trip is well planned.

A well-planned wedding and honeymoon are an asset to any marriage. During the detailed activities leading to the wedding, however, the couple must continue to plan their mundane affairs for the months immediately following the wedding. Only by taking the long view can the couple fully attain the gradually increasing joys of married life together.

Notes

1. William G. Sumner and A. G. Keller, *The Science of Society* (New Haven: Yale University Press, 1927), p. 1696.

2. Paul Popenoe, *Modern Marriage* (New York: The Macmillan Company, 1940), pp. 222–27.

3. William G. Kephart and Ralph B. Strohm, "The Stability of Gretna Green Marriages," *Sociology and Social Research,* 36:291–96.

4. Arthur Hopson, "The Relationship of Migratory Marriages to Divorce in Tennessee," *Social Forces,* 30:449–55.

5. See, e.g. E. W. Burgess and Leonard S. Cottrell, *Predicting Success or Failure in Marriage* (Englewood Cliffs, N.J.: Prentice-Hall, Inc., 1939), p. 169; Harvey J. Locke, *Predicting Adjustment in Marriage* (New York: Holt, Rinehart & Winston, Inc., 1951), pp. 118–19.

6. Jessie Bernard, Helen E. Buchanan, and William M. Smith, *Dating, Mating, and Marriage* (Cleveland: Howard Allen, 1958), p. 145.

7. U.S. Department of Health, Education, and Welfare, *Vital Statistics: National Summaries* (1963), 39.

8. David Mace, *Marriage, The Art of Lasting Love* (Garden City, N.Y.: Doubleday & Company, Inc., 1952), pp. 47–53.

9. Henry Bowman, *Marriage for Moderns* (New York: McGraw-Hill Book Company, Inc., 1954), p. 275.

10. The average wedding today costs about $1000. See Alexandra S. Potts, "Brides: The Nation's Billion Dollar Babies," *Public Relation Board Newsletter,* 7, 9 (June 1961), 344; and Robert Wacker, Jr., "Our Wild Extravagance—The Great Big Wedding," *McCall's Magazine* (January 1960), 50–51, 117–18.

11. Anne H. Wharton, *Colonial Days and Dames* (Philadelphia: J. B. Lippincott Co., 1908), p. 75.

12. *Ibid.*

13. Corrado Gini and Caranti Elio, "The Family in Italy," *Marriage and Family Living,* 16:355.

14. Kaaro Svalastoga, "The Family in Scandinavia," *Marriage and Family Living,* 16:375.

15. M. Kamel Nahas, "The Family in Egypt," *Marriage and Family Living,* 16:295.

16. For a concise article on heredity, see Ray C. Anderson, "The Influence of Heredity on Family Health," *Marriage and Family Living,* 19:136–41.

17. Morris Fishbein and Ruby Jo Reeves Kennedy (eds.), *Modern Marriage and Family Living* (New York: Oxford University Press, Inc., 1957), pp. 170–71.

18. Lovett Dewees, "Premarital Physical Examination," in Morris Fishbein and E. W. Burgess (eds.), *Successful Marriage* (Garden City, N.Y.: Doubleday & Company, Inc., 1947), p. 59.

19. Nadina R. Kavinoky, M.D., "Premarital Medical Examination," *The Journal of the American Medical Association* (October 16, 1954), p. 693.

20. Nahas, *op. cit.,* p. 296.

21. Dominique Ceccaldi, "The Family in France," *Marriage and Family Living,* 16:328.

22. Bruce M. Brown, "Ministerial Marriage Counseling in a Lower-Class Setting," *The Family Life Coordinator,* 7:10–14.

23. Paul Landis, "Marriage Preparation in Two Generations," *Marriage and Family Living,* 13:155–56.

24. See, e.g., Locke, *op. cit.,* pp. 319–38; Burgess and Cottrell, *op. cit.,* pp. 420–29; E. W. Burgess and Paul Wallin, *Engagement and Marriage* (Philadelphia: J. B. Lippincott & Co., 1953), pp. 801–808; Lewis M. Terman, *Psychological Factors in Marital Happiness* (New York: McGraw-Hill Book Company, Inc., 1938), pp. 352–55; or Geolo McHugh, *A Courtship Analysis* (Durham, N.C.: Family Life Publications, Inc., 1961).

25. This statement is based on the author's own clinical experience.

26. Clifford R. Adams and Vance O. Packard, *How To Pick a Mate* (New York: E. P. Dutton and Company, Inc., 1946).

27. Wesley Neal, "He Builds Permanent Marriages," *Christian Advocate* (June 7, 1951), 8.

28. Hartzell Spence, "Look What the Church Is Doing Now!" *Saturday Evening Post* (February 5, 1949), 72.

29. Donald Pierson, "The Family in Brazil," *Marriage and Family Living,* 16:311.

30. Ceccaldi, *op. cit.,* p. 328.

31. Gini and Elio, *op. cit.,* p. 355.

32. Svalastoga, *op. cit.,* p. 375.

33. J. M. Mogey, "The Family in England," *Marriage and Family Living,* 16:320.

34. Willystine Goodsell, *A History of Marriage and the Family* (New York: The Macmillan Company, 1934), p. 387.

35. Earl L. Koos, *Marriage* (New York: Holt, Rinehart & Winston, Inc., 1957), p. 143.

36. U.S. Department of Health, Education, and Welfare, *Vital Statistics of the United States, 1960,* 3:1–18. To note that these figures have not changed much over the years see August B. Hollingshead, "Marital Status and Wedding Behavior," *Marriage and Family Living,* 14:308–11.

37. For a very typical wedding service in fuller detail, see *The Book of Common Prayer,* of the Protestant Episcopal Church in the United States of America (New York: Oxford University Press, Inc., 1938), pp. 300–304.

38. Deuteronomy, 24:5.

39. Theodore B. Johannis, "Married College Students and Their Honeymoon," *The Family Life Coordinator,* 8:39–40.

40. W. Clark Ellzey, "Marriage Questionnaire Report," *Marriage and Family Living,* 11:133.

41. Hollingshead, *op. cit.*

42. Mace, *op. cit.,* pp. 46–47.

43. Stanley R. Brav, "Notes on Honeymoons," *Marriage and Family Living,* 9:60, 65.

44. *Ibid.*

45. Johannis, *op. cit.,* p. 39.

46. Philip Wiley, "Honeymoons Are Hell," *Redbook* (November 1952).

47. Johannis, *op. cit.*, pp. 39–40.

48. Betty Hannah Hoffman, "Are Honeymoons Happy?" *Ladies Home Journal* (June 1961), 36–37, 104.

49. Johannis, *op. cit.*, pp. 39–40.

50. Sixty-fifth Companion Poll, "What Makes a Perfect Honeymoon?" *Woman's Home Companion Magazine* (May 1948), 13.

51. Hollingshead, *op. cit.*, p. 311.

52. Bernard Buchanan, and Smith, *op. cit.*

53. Eugene J. Kanin and David H. Howard, "Postmarital Consequences of Premarital Sex Adjustment," *American Sociological Review*, 23:556–62.

54. Brav, *op. cit.*

55. Nahas, *op. cit.*, p. 298.

Questions for further thought

1. In what ways is it consistent with American democratic principles to plan ahead for the wedding? Honeymoon? Marriage?
2. What is the basis for the publishing of the banns? Is this justifiable in a democracy?
3. Why does the state consider itself as having jurisdiction over weddings?
4. If having a complete premarital physical examination is so important for marriage, why don't more people have them?
5. Why aren't there any tests that can conclusively show whether or not two people should marry each other?
6. Should a couple wait until they are formally engaged to seek premarital counseling, or should they secure it earlier?
7. Is the preparation preceding the wedding, or the effort following it, more important to marital success?
8. What elements within a religious wedding ceremony specifically pertain to marital success?
9. What is the best procedure to assure the avoidance of excessive fatigue following the wedding and reception?
10. Are wedding journeys likely to go out of style? Are they essential to successful marriage?
11. What was the original purpose behind many of the customs which still surround a wedding, such as the bride's wearing "something old, something new, something borrowed, and something blue," the throwing of rice at the couple, and so forth?

Recommended films

Before They Say "I Do" (National Council of Churches).
I Do (National Council of Churches).

Suggested supplemental readings

BOOKS

Bentley, Marguerite. *Wedding Etiquette Complete*. Philadelphia: John C. Winston, 1956.

Eichler, Lillian. *The Customs of Mankind*. Garden City, N.Y.: Doubleday & Company, Inc., 1937.

Howard, George E. *A History of Matrimonial Institutions*. Chicago: University of Chicago Press, 1904.

James, E. O. *Marriage Customs Through the Ages.* New York: The Macmillan Company, 1965.

Kelly, George A. *The Catholic Marriage Manual.* New York: Random House, 1958.

Knox, Ronald. *Bridegroom and Bride.* New York: Sheed & Ward, 1957.

Mace, David. *Hebrew Marriage.* New York: Philosophical Library, Inc., 1953.

Morris, J. Kenneth. *Premarital Counseling: A Manual for Ministers.* Englewood Cliffs, N.J.: Prentice-Hall, Inc., 1960.

Patai, Raphael. *Sex and Family in the Bible.* Garden City, N.Y.: Doubleday & Company, Inc., 1959.

Plamer, B. *Manual of Church Services: With a Summary of State Laws Governing Marriage.* New York: Fleming H. Revell Co., 1950.

Scheinfeld, Amram. *The Basic Facts of Human Heredity.* New York: Washington Square Press, 1961.

———. *The Human Heredity Handbook.* Philadelphia: J. B. Lippincott Co., 1956.

Wylie, William R. *Human Nature and Christian Marriage.* New York: Association Press, 1961.

ARTICLES

Anderson, Ray C. "The Influence of Heredity on Family Health," *Marriage and Family Living,* 19:136–41.

Corsini, Raymond J. "Multiple Predictors of Marital Happiness," *Marriage and Family Living,* 18:240–42.

Dohen, Dorothy. "Religious Practice and Marital Patterns in Puerto Rico," *American Catholic Sociological Review,* 20:203–18.

Elia, Andrew D. "Teamwork in Premarital Counseling," *Pastoral Psychology,* 10:33–38.

Ellis, Albert. "The Value of Marriage Prediction Tests," *American Sociological Review,* 13:710–18.

Mahoney, E. J. "Civil Marriage Permissible Solely for the Civil Effects," *Clergy Review,* 37:37–38.

———. "Rites in a Marriage by Proxy," *Clergy Review,* 35:106–107.

———. "Validity of Civil Marriage," *Clergy Review,* 34:326–27.

Maxwell, Margaret. "Protestant Marriage in Eighteenth-Century France," *Social Science,* 30:89–93.

Wiley, Philip. "Honeymoons Are Hell," *Redbook* (November 1952).

Williams, Foster J. "A Community Program of Premarital Counseling," *Pastoral Psychology,* 10:39–44.

Wiser, Waller B. "Launching a Program of Premarital Counseling," *Pastoral Psychology,* 10:14–17.

Solving problems
for happiness

chapter 11

Marriage is not the answer to all life's problems. Although the wedding might resolve many problems of the single life, it poses a new set of variables that can be solved only by the patient and the mature. The transition from the independent decision-making of single life to the continuous consultations and considered judgments of marriage is not always easy. The sooner the reorganization is started, however, the better.

The case of Jim and Annabelle illustrates the futility of even the most conscientious efforts in problem-solving based on the individual approach:

Theirs was a whirlwind courtship. Jim had just been discharged from the service when he first began dating Annabelle. He had spoken many times of his intentions to attend college and become an electrical engineer. How romantic all this must have seemed to Annabelle, a cute little girl in her senior year of high school who had never been more than fifty miles from home. Soon they were husband and wife at State University. The only difficulty was that Jim did not yet have his degree; furthermore, his veteran's pay did not stretch far enough for two. He had to find a part-time job. Annabelle too looked for work, but she was unqualified for most available jobs. Study was not easy for Jim, and his young bride spent money as though he were already earning a professional income. Soon there was a child, and within another year another child. Annabelle had the responsibility for a family, a small budget on which to manage, and a husband who needed to study every spare moment. There was little time for fun. Still, they felt that since hundreds of other couples had survived under similar circumstances, they should not express their increasing disappointment to the other. Finally the money ran out. At about the same time Jim failed to make his grades, and Annabelle found herself pregnant once more. This proved to be too much for both of them. In trying to solve mutual problems as though each were still single, they never attained the power in attacking problems as a pair.[1]

Modern criteria of happiness

The extreme emphasis placed upon each partner's developing his potential through marriage makes marital conflict a more important consideration today than formerly. Years ago most married couples made adjustments on a minimum level within the problem areas. This was possible because expectations of personal welfare were lower. But many of today's couples are discontent because their marital problems are not being solved as quickly as they arise.

ROUTINES CONFINE ROMANCE. Marriage requires a certain routine to expedite the daily duties of the household, but often routine is allowed to rule the family and rule out romance. The case of Betty and Roger illustrates this possibility.

> After marriage, Betty continued to work in the office for the same company that employed Roger as a field representative. Of necessity, their courtship had been confined to weekends when Roger was in town. After their marriage, Roger complained that Betty was always busy weekends with household chores and responsibilities which could not be done during the week. He felt they had actually had more time together before marriage. Betty, on the other hand, felt that Roger behaved more like a weekend guest than a husband.[2]

Settling down to married life necessarily confines romance to specific times and shorter intervals. This curtailment may uncover or accentuate problems that were there all the time. In a sense, this is healthy. Waller and Hill maintain that the type of solidarity peculiar to the honeymoon and the early months of marriage must break down sooner or later. No couple can continue to live at such a high emotional pitch. Thus, when the breakdown finally does happen, conflict inevitably begins to appear.[3] This, however, is not as bad as it may seem to the young couple who are involved, for only after this takes place is it possible for a genuine paired relationship to begin.

The frequency and intensity of marital problems depend greatly on the thoroughness of problem-solving before a crisis arises. Important ideals are usually discussed by most couples prior to marriage, but it is even more important to discuss the way to implement and uphold these ideals. Even when implementation is attempted in courtship, much remains to be worked out in marriage.

WORKING FOR COMPATIBILITY. Few people can define emotional adjustment, but it is necessary for them to achieve it if their marriage is to be successful. Compatibility in marriage is not so much a condition as it is a job to be done. In this connection Harper defines marriage as "a dynamic process of adaption and readaption to the changing external and internal demands of the continuing companionship."[4]

Few couples ever come to a state of complete agreement or satisfaction in all areas of marriage; conversely, few who experience disappointment and frustration in marriage are in complete disagreement on everything. Locke found in his study that usually even divorced couples had some areas with a degree of agreement.[5] Although he found some couples with very high marital-adjustment scores, Terman failed to find a single perfect marriage.[6]

MARITAL ADJUSTMENT AND THE FAMILY-LIFE STAGE. According to the developmental-task concept, adjustments continue to be necessary in every area of marriage as the couple passes from stage to stage within the family-life cycle.

The first stage of the family-life cycle is the beginning of marriage, and it lasts (for college graduates) an average of about two and a half years. An additional four to five years are confined to the childbearing stage; this is followed by the child-rearing stage, which lasts about seventeen and a half years and a "child-launching" stage of about six and a half years. Altogether, there is an average of about twenty-eight years of married life with children in the home. After the last child leaves the home, there comes the empty-nest and old-age stage. This lasts on an

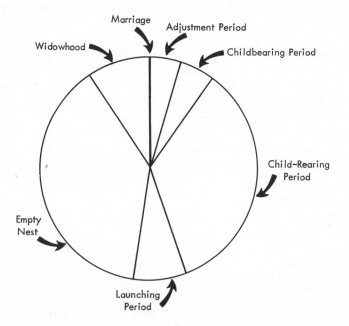

Figure 11-1.   Middle-class family life cycle.

average of from eighteen to twenty years, or until the death of one spouse. After this there is ordinarily about an eight- to ten-year interval before the death of the second spouse. This last stage is ordinarily classified as widowhood.[7] Lansing and Kish suggest that, for marital harmony, it is more important for a couple to know their stage in the family cycle than their age.[8]

There are adjustments to be made in many major areas within each of these stages. For example, there are problems of sex adjustment in the early years of marriage that are usually not found later; however, sex adjustment is still necessary in the last stage of marriage; only its aspects differ. Money problems exist throughout married life for most people, but seldom are identical aspects of this particular area faced in each family stage. At first the money problem may focus on control or priority of each mate's wants. Later the problem may be how to stretch the available money to cover all needs as the family expands in size. Still later, in the empty-nest stage, decisions on money may be focused on whether to give surplus funds to the children when they can use it in their young marriages, or to hold it for them as a future legacy. Marital adjustment is a series of adjustments, each relating to an area of marriage within a given stage.[9]

Working through problems

It is not the solution to any one problem but rather the ability to solve all problems that is important to marital success. There is seldom a "right" or "wrong" solution to any one problem, be it complicated or simple. If one approach works satisfactorily for a couple, it is obviously right for them, at least at that time.

For example, one couple known to the author solved their money-management problem in the area of food purchases simply by the husband's taking over the role of purchaser. This is certainly not the only solution to such a problem, but it was at that time a satisfactory arrangement for that couple. This solution made it necessary for the husband to devote much of his Saturday free time to shopping, but it was worth it to both of them because she was a compulsive buyer. Without his supervision, she could not resist loading up the grocery cart with all kinds of luxurious food items.

There can never be a list of rules to cover all possible situations in marriage. For one thing, people rarely know when differences will arise in their marital relationship. As a result, they are usually taken by surprise. However, by working through a problem-solving process early, a couple's relationship is much more likely to be maintained with integrity regardless of the weight or frequency of the problems encountered. As Winch has stated:

If a person knows what to expect of a situation and is prepared with a repertoire of responses appropriate to the situation, he is adjusted to that situation. American men reared in civilian life are not ready for combat; they do not know what to expect, nor do they have an appropriate set of responses. The purpose of basic military training is to teach them what to expect and to respond appropriately. . . . As they acquire these expectations and responses, they are in the process of becoming adjusted.[10]

LEARNING TO DISAGREE. Marriages are rarely doomed by rough problems, but marital happiness can fade if only faint measures are taken to remedy difficulties. Personalities are too different and marriage too intimate for harmony and love always to rule. Couples must learn to work and play together, but they must also learn how to disagree. If they do not, there will be difficulty regardless of how trivial the problems may seem to others. As Hart has said:

> When one person feels resentment against another, the other is likely to feel resentment in return. This intensifies the first resentment, and so the hatred grows. Someone has to break the vicious circle.[11]

In the process of coming to terms with the reality of marriage, sometimes the relationship appears to deteriorate or become disenchanted, at least on the surface. This mainly applies, however, to those who are unable to establish adequate processes for finding solutions to difficulties.[12]

The importance of early success

The truism "Nothing succeeds like success" certainly applies to marital adjustment. By working out little problems and developing an approach to problem-solving early in married life a couple may prevent big problems from ever arising.

When couples are first married they are more eager to be agreeable, and adjustments seem to come more naturally. Being younger, they will be more flexible and will not have set up poor response patterns to marital disagreements. It is, indeed, much easier to work through a problem-solving process before rigid habits are established. Retired people, looking back over their past, pick the busy years of family-rearing as the happiest time of their married lives rather than the so-called carefree years of youth.[13] This, in spite of the fact that they probably had more problems in that stage of marriage than at any other time in their lives. Having established a problem-solving process earlier in marriage, however, they found the problems of child-rearing could more easily be taken in stride.

Statistics disclose that divorce is much more probable in the early years of marriage than later. Because there are as many, if not more, problems in the later years of marriage, the duration of many marriages depends upon the promptness with which a process for solving problems is established. This, in turn, helps the couple to weather more serious crises later. According to Monahan, much time usually elapses after separation, before divorce occurs. Actually, many couples who divorce, separate during the first year or so of marriage. Thus, the "critical" time in marriage is the first few months.[14]

Table 11-1. Percentage distribution of divorces and annulments by duration of marriage in years

Duration of marriage		Per cent of total divorce
Under 1 year		6.1
1–4 years		34.1
1 year	9.8	
2 years	9.2	
3 years	8.0	
4 years	7.1	
5–9 years		24.6
5 years	6.1	
6 years	5.4	
7 years	4.7	
8 years	4.3	
9 years	4.1	
10–14 years		15.1
15–19 years		8.6
20–24 years		5.4
25–29 years		2.9
30–34 years		1.7
35–39 years		0.8
40 years and over		0.7
	Total	100.0

Source: U.S. Department of Health, Education, and Welfare, *Vital Statistics: National Summaries* (November 25, 1959), 49–58. Reprinted by permission.

Admission that problems exist

The first step after the couple recognize a problem is to admit that the problem exists. This sounds simple, but it is the major step in the problem-solving process. Couples need to recognize and be willing to admit that a problem exists. The worst response to a difficult problem is to act on the assumption that, if it is ignored, the situation will resolve itself. Some couples insist that they have never disagreed; anyone who has studied marriage relationships knows better. Magoun would like to ask such people: "Which one of you is sacrificing your integrity on the altar of the other's demands?"[15] It is doubtful that a one-sided effort can ever completely solve an inescapably two-sided situation, and every problem within marriage has two sides.

SILENCE IS NOT ALWAYS BEST.   There are some individuals who believe problems should be endured in silence. They may feel that it is a virtue to endure the unendurable, or they may simply be afraid of stirring up more trouble. They prefer to preserve peace at any cost, including their own mental health. Some people may find it difficult to express things verbally, but continued silence under oppression usually induces tensions in other areas of marriage.

In a successful marriage, there is no such thing as peace at any price. As Terman has said: "The greatest single danger to marital happiness is for one spouse to like, and the other dislike, to argue."[16]

BENEFITS OF MARITAL CONFLICTS.   The only dangerous argument in marriage is the one that leaves the problem unsolved. A violent discussion does far less harm than suffering silence, provided the conclusion satisfies both. Many people who feel that disagreement and argument are the worst things that can happen in a marriage never honestly face their differences of opinion.

It is true that, in trying to talk out their problems, some couples seem to get into deeper trouble without solving anything. Even so, marital success often depends more on the ability to resolve disagreements than on a capacity to avoid them. As Baber states:

> There are actually times when quarreling may clear the air better than calm discussion; it relieves both parties of pent-up emotions; second, it shows each how deeply the other feels on the point in question, opening the eyes to the necessity of reaching an acceptable agreement.[17]

However, Baber goes on to warn that quarrels need to be rationally planned and conducted or they may start by spontaneous combustion. "It takes more skill and will than most people have to turn heat thus generated to constructive, rather than destructive, purposes."[18]

Marriage is a deep emotional relationship that cannot be maintained by the superficial expedient of expressing only positive emotions and suppressing all negative reactions. Correctly handled and followed through, conflict can do little harm and may do a great deal of good. On the other hand, serious harm often results when married people bottle up disagreements or resentments and attempt to conceal their dissatisfactions from each other. If to bring about the discussion of a major problem means that a conflict will result, it is still much better than covering the truth by silence.

This does not mean that in marriage a couple should quarrel for no reason. There is a "proper" time and place for quarreling. For example, when either partner feels insecure about something else or overfatigued, quarreling should be avoided. Fatigue results in frayed nerves, and is probably the worst enemy of all positive human relationships. If a couple finds an argument brewing when one mate is tired, sleepy, hungry, or anxious, it is advisable to break off hostilities promptly and to postpone discussion of the matter until both are fresh and clear-headed. There used to be an old saying to the effect that one should settle all his troubles before going to sleep. Sometimes, however, it is better to go to sleep and leave the disagreement until later. Clear-headed and in the light of day, both may be much more objective about the problem.

POSITIVE AND NEGATIVE QUARRELING: There are two types of quarreling that may develop from domestic discord. One is negative quarreling, which is rarely of value. It is damaging to self-images as attention shifts away from the problem and focuses on injuring the partner. Its ultimate result is destructive: it bruises love, alienates affection, and seldom solves anything.[19] Such quarreling becomes an ever-widening, vicious circle. When the ego of one partner is injured, the natural reflex is to strike back. Thus, the ego of the first one is damaged even further, and the gap widens between the couple, possibly to a point beyond rebridging. There is a right way and a wrong way to handle the conflicts of married life. Too many couples take the wrong way simply because it never occurs to them that there is an alternative.

The kind of quarreling that can be termed *positive, constructive,* or *productive,* however, can help a marriage. People are better able to consider criticism that is directed toward their actions or their statements rather than toward themselves as characters or personalities. Positive quarreling keeps the focus on the problem or the issue involved and away from the ego threat to each personality. It is even possible that, by precipitating an argument, one partner may help the other to release pent-up hostilities that had been retarding the progress of the relationship. (This possible benefit from quarreling, however, is no excuse for deliberate malice or rudeness.) Positive quarreling focuses upon the issues under dispute. Such quarreling is positive because it releases tensions, improves understanding, redefines the situation, and leads to problem-solving or better adjustment.[20] If one partner senses a problem but feels that the relationship is not stable enough for positive quarreling, it is best first to find a healthy outlet for letting off steam. This would avoid risking negative quarreling when bringing up the problem; the problem, however, must be admitted before it can be solved.

CLUES TO HIDDEN PROBLEMS. There are several clues by which a person can recognize a problem that might be still below the surface. Terman suggests that a deeper problem exists when a mate resorts to considerable nagging or complaining.[21] This may be especially true when there is much nagging about trivial things or constant complaining about things over which the couple have little control. There may be continuous grumbling about such things as the lack of money for entertainment, or the wife's hatred for cooking, or the husband's dislike for his job. Chronic complaining about such things usually indicates a deeper problem in another area of the marriage. The partner who is sensitive to these clues can better anticipate the need to help the mate express the real problem.

It is always wise to work for a two-sided approach when expressing a problem. Personal attacks upon the partner, even when he is obviously to blame, should be avoided, for this will never settle the situation. It is never only one partner's problem; it is always "our" problem, for it affects the entire marital relationship.

Identification of the real problem

After recognizing and admitting that a problem does exist, the next step is to identify the real problem. This may sometimes prove more difficult than the subsequent solution of the problem.

OBSTACLES TO IDENTIFICATION.   There are many hindrances to identifying or defining the real problems of human relationships. One of the biggest obstacles is fear itself. Many people are afraid of problems of any kind; some may prefer to run away rather than face the real issues, as when a wife "goes back home to Mother." Fear may make some people suddenly turn uncooperative. After admitting a problem exists, some may refuse to identify it because they are afraid of facing trouble.

Embarrassment is another obstacle to an honest diagnosis. Some people find talking about problems in certain areas of living, such as sex, personally embarrassing.

Another thing that stands in the way of identifying real problems may be a confusion of secondary reactions—that is, what seems to be a problem may be only a symptom. It does little good to treat symptoms while ignoring causes. The "obvious" cause, or the cause first suggested by the individual himself, may not actually be the real cause at all.

This false identification may be related to a distorted perspective. It is easy to fall into the trap of focusing on the nearest thing and thus lose sight of the entire picture. As Mace has said, "If heat is rising from your living room floor when you know the furnace isn't on, you would be a fool not to go down into the basement and find out what's happening."[22] Yet this dismissal of primary clues is common. When perspective is lost, little problems may be allowed to grow to disastrous proportions.

Secondary reactions, which sometimes blur the identification of the real problems, may be caused by tensions originating outside the marriage. Compulsions and frustrations resulting from these extramarital tensions may provoke and stimulate discord within the marriage unless the couple can identify them adequately. As Hill has said,

In a society of rapid social change, problems outnumber solutions, and the resulting uncertainties are absorbed by the members of society, who are for the most part also members of families. Because the family is the bottleneck through which all troubles pass, no other association so reflects the strain and stress of life. With few exceptions persons in a workaday America return to rehearse their frustrations within the family, and hope to get the necessary understanding and resilience to return to the fray.[23]

An example of how outside tensions may cause marital discord was demonstrated by Burgess and Cottrell. They reported a distinct difference in marital happiness ratings when marriages were divided by certain occupations of the husbands.[34] Certainly some occupations incur special difficulties which directly affect the peace of the family.

It is necessary to develop some method of relieving outside tensions. If a couple are unable to quarrel constructively, they must find other tension-relieving devices. Some, for example, use games such as golf for this purpose; some paint pictures, some play a musical instrument, others fish or hunt or work on hobbies such as a garden or even model railroads.

Identifying the real problem within marriage involves recognizing conditions which may serve as blocks to understanding, such as fear and embarrassment, distorted perspective, extramarital tensions, or the absence of acceptable tension-relievers. Once the real problem is identified, it might of itself lead to a ready solution, which obviates a long, self-conscious re-examination of past marital details.

Choosing a solution

After recognition, admission, and definition of a problem, the next step is an exploration of various solutions that might be acceptable for the couple.

Kiss-and-make-up may work fine at first, but later often runs up against the law of diminishing returns. A far better rule is to kiss-and-*think-up*—think up ways of avoiding the clashes which would otherwise call for making up. That kind of imagination exercise helps us not only to safeguard our happiness, but also to build up our minds.[25]

LISTING SOLUTIONS. The exploration process for solutions may be divided into two basic stages. The first stage is the listing of all the possible solutions; the second is the evaluation of the solutions. If a couple does not at first list all the possible solutions, they may get bogged down in attempting to evaluate proposals before all the solutions are ever offered. Each individual usually has preconceived ideas of the best solution to any problem; many such quick solutions are quite unsuitable. It is better, therefore, to list all possible solutions before accepting or evaluating the answers offered by either mate.

STUDYING EACH PROPOSAL. The second stage of the exploration of solutions is the evaluation of all the proposals which have been made and the weighing of the pros and cons of each proposed solution. Couples may have to do some investigating before they can make a complete evaluation of every proposal. They may have to read or consult with experts in the particular field of the problem.

Sometimes after listing and evaluating all the possible solutions to a problem, the couple are at a loss to choose one of several possible and mutually acceptable solutions. Under these circumstances, it is usually best to experiment with different solutions for awhile. This can help determine which one seems to work out the best, not only for each individual but for the marriage as a whole.

THE MALE AND FEMALE VIEWPOINTS. The third step, acceptance, is sometimes made more difficult by the fact that men and women differ physiologically, socially, and so forth, and often view their problems differently. What might appear to be the most valuable or plausible solution to one sex may not be at all acceptable to the other.

Everyone's behavior is based upon cultural conditioning. Prior to marriage, husbands and wives did not live identical lives, and thus it is only natural for them to view many problems differently. Individuals are culturally conditioned in two basic ways: through a single experience that leaves an indelible impression, or through the continued repetition of a lesser experience until it becomes second nature to react a particular way to a given stimulus. Cultural conditioning thus accounts for most fears, tastes, and attitudes.

When individuals have been so conditioned that their responses are normally considered out of proportion to the stimulus, they are described as having a complex in that area. Most individuals have a few complexes, but men and women, as groups, have some different complexes because contrasting conditioning factors have either created or increased fundamental differences between the sexes.

Whether good or bad, complexes cannot be removed by argument or demand. A partner who is aware of his mate's complexes, however, can go a long way toward making a relationship more harmonious by setting off desirable stimuli instead of stimuli which might prompt undesirable responses. If a wife reacts to her husband as if he were another woman and he continues to react to her as if she were another man, their problems are compounded. With few exceptions, the sexes cannot completely view problems the same way. Indeed, no two people—even if they are of the same sex—have identical cultural conditioning. It is never possible to penetrate another person's world completely, and so it is probably next to impossible for one sex to look at life entirely through the other's eyes.

It is easy enough for either sex to justify his own point of view when choosing a solution, although it may not be any more valid than the mate's proposal. Once a mate recognizes that his partner's behavior may have a different basis of reality, it is easier to choose a mutually acceptable solution. No matter how irrational the partner's behavior may appear, it is usually logical to him in terms of his own interpretation.

THE ART OF COMPROMISE. Sometimes, in trying to solve a problem, each partner offers a valid plan which the other rejects. They must then choose between the two solutions to the problem. This means compromise. Compromise implies an agreed-upon decision in which both individuals feel more has been gained than lost. Although one mate may agree to go almost all the way on one part of the issue, the other mate must agree to go as far against his own inclination on another part of the same problem.

Sometimes, when a compromise on one problem seems out of the question, couples can resort to accommodation. In one form of accommodation, the couple may agree to disagree in a particular area. This requires the establishment of "keep-off" signs, which both agree to respect. In another type of accommodation, the couple agree to settle the problem in relation to which one appears the more involved. One partner agrees to do as much on another problem. This may be the only recourse in cases where it appears impossible to reach an agreement on the proposed solutions.

Figure 11-2. Accommodation may be the only solution for some problems.

Making a proposed solution work

After listing all the possible solutions, evaluating and exploring each, and choosing one, the next step is to put the solution into operation. It is necessary for both partners to put forth their best efforts to make that solution work for their marriage.

BEING REALISTIC.   The first thing to remember is to be realistic. This means, first of all, to keep the focus within marriage on a positive plane rather than on a negative one. A common mistake in marriage is for a couple to think and talk in terms of failure when working for success. This is like driving at ninety miles an hour with the emergency brake on; it is a wearing process. Continuous focusing upon negative possibilities arrests the forward drive of good intentions. This is not the same as saying that the couple should be naïve or overoptimistic when arriving at a solution; rather, they should be hopeful and realistic. It takes time to see exactly how a proposed solution is working out; a few failures should not cause abandonment of the proposal. Immediate and complete compliance with any new solution is impossible, for it takes time to learn new tasks and new patterns. This calls for considerable patience and tolerance. In learning any new pattern of behavior, everyone slips back to old habits occasionally. Eventually, by repetition, a new task can be learned. It takes time for an individual to change, whether it be through his own efforts or with the help of someone else. Seldom will discord in a marriage be resolved as quickly as it appears to have arisen. If the problem is related to personality differences, its resolution may require even more time.

Part of the time factor is based on each partner's taking a good look at himself and making a realistic reassessment of his attitudes. Once a solution has been agreed upon, there must be a sincere willingness to attempt to make it work. If either mate is unwilling to alter his habits, suitable agreements between spouses are very difficult to maintain. It is useless merely to tell someone that he *should* be different; a situation must be provided in which he *can* be different or whereby he can understand the need for change. There are some things about all individuals, however, that cannot be changed through their own efforts or even with the help of others. There are some things that simply must be accepted.

The direction in which a person is moving and the fact that he is moving are as important as the position he has presently reached. Thus, the success of any solution requires plenty of time to ascertain whether there is progress in the desired direction.

THE WORTH OF A SOLUTION.   Sometimes it is well to ask whether the problem is really worth all the effort of finding a solution. Many new discoveries are made about the mate early in marriage. Although it is true that, when couples learn to solve problems early, they may more safely disagree later on other matters, some things are not worth wasting energy on. Such things as leaving the cap off the toothpaste tube, strewing clothes around, leaving closet doors open, or leaving the lights on are really trivial. Although at times they can be very provoking, they may not be worth the effort of the problem-solving process. Egos can easily become involved in these inconsequential matters, causing spouses to continue to hold fast to their positions because of a sense of honor or pride. After such disputes, many of these slight irritations may become more serious than ever before. As Blood states it: "Sometimes the persistent recurrence of the offending behavior gradually piles up molehills of irritation into mountains of anger."[26]

When the problem falls in the category of what might be called a foolish or inconsequential situation, it may be best to take it humorously. Humor can often solve trivial concerns without running the risk of building them into irritations or spending excessive amounts of time and energy. Another unilateral effort which sometimes works is to develop an immunity in some of the bothersome areas. This implies accepting or ignoring the provoking behavior and developing a degree of tolerance for it. Frequently this means simply reducing expectations as to the spouse's behavior in some particular areas. In psychology this has been called *negative adaptation*. The classic example often given is the oyster's response to the irritation of a grain of sand: it smooths it over and makes a pearl.[27] If one mate has a few behavior traits that seem irksome, the other can safely assume that he has his own share.

BE OF GOOD FAITH. Each partner must do his best to make the agreed-upon solution work. When there is resentment or hostility, probably no solution will work. Locke found that the speed with which a person gets over anger is highly correlated with marital adjustment, and that slowness constitutes an obstacle in bringing about a solution to any problem.[28] Being of good faith requires cooperation. Mace states, in effect, that the acceptance of duties which have to be shared is part of cooperation. If one fails to assume his fair share, an unjust burden falls on the other partner.[29] Whenever exploitation crowds out cooperation, the marriage relationship is seriously impaired. Self-interests must yield to the welfare of the relationship. The common purposes or goals which are shared by a husband and wife give unity to the marriage, but it takes cooperation to accomplish them.

JUMPING TO CONCLUSIONS. Various research studies have disclosed that good communication is significantly related to marital adjustment.[30] Effective marital communication requires the creation of a permissive atmosphere in which each mate feels secure enough to look at the facts as they are rather than as he prefers, or assumes, them to be. Many communication weaknesses between spouses are caused by unwarranted assumptions. All too frequently one spouse assumes he knows what the other means or feels, but he never verifies the assumption by asking. There is a tendency to project one's own feelings into the spouse's reactions. Too many mates make assumptions without checking their reality. Before feeling hurt or angry, partners should ask each other what is meant, felt, or intended. The mate should explain and, if necessary, the doubtful partner should paraphrase the answer for verification. After repetition of this process, both are more likely to understand what the other really means. A husband may smile at his wife with the best of intentions, but if she feels he is laughing at her, there is misunderstanding. The short-circuiting of the communication process sometimes results from the difference between the intellectual and the emotional meaning of an act. Seldom is any act as important as its meaning. But the only way to discover its meaning is to ask.

Review of decisions

The last step in the problem-solving process is to review the decision in operation to see how it is actually working out. Even if it seems satisfactory or final as a solution, it is a good thing to review it once in a while. This gets partners into the habit of talking over and reviewing their entire marriage periodically and can promote better all-around communication.

Feelings need to be shared, and reviewing the solutions is an excellent method of doing it. Pleasant experiences can be heightened and unpleasant reactions dissipated in this manner.

In reviewing decisions, it helps to explore each other's desires and to be alert to the shifting needs of each partner. Although the changes may be gradual, needs do change. In time, basic needs may differ drastically from the original wants. The ability to adjust to new situations and needs is essential. Winch cites a classic example of how needs may change. At the time of marriage, one husband was a frustrated young man who needed considerable encouragement and sympathy. This his mate gave to him. Then he became famous and received much praise from others, so that he no longer needed reassurance from his wife. They were unable to understand this or to discover his new needs, and consequently each became very unhappy with the marriage.[31] Adjustment in marriage is based on the achievement of the expectations a couple have of their marriage. If they expect little but achieve that little completely, the marriage is successful for them. Marital expectations also change according to changing needs, thus it is necessary to review decisions in operation.

SEEKING HELP. In spite of the best problem-solving efforts, a couple may be unable to solve all their problems. This may be especially true when one partner shows neurotic or psychotic tendencies. Whenever serious discord prevails after a couple have sincerely attempted to follow a problem-solving process, they should not hesitate to seek professional help.

The most common problem areas

It is often helpful to know ahead of time those areas in which marriage problems are most likely to occur.

Table 11–2. Length of time required to achieve adjustment in marriage

Area of adjustment	Per cent				
	Satisfactory for both from the beginning	*Satisfactory for only one from the beginning*	*One to twelve months*	*One to twenty years*	*Never satisfactory*
Sex	52.7	12.3	12.5	10.0	12.5
Money	56.2	11.4	9.0	13.1	10.3
Social	67.1	9.5	4.3	5.3	13.8
In-Law	68.6	10.9	3.9	7.0	9.6
Religious	74.0	7.6	1.6	6.8	10.0
Mutual Friends	76.4	7.8	4.6	3.3	7.9

Source: Judson T. Landis, "Length of Time Required to Achieve Adjustment in Marriage," *American Sociological Review,* 11:666–77. Copyright © 1946, by The American Sociological Association, Washington, D.C. Reprinted by permission.

Table 11-3. Present stage of adjustment for couples married an average of twenty years

			Per cent replying					
Area of adjustment	Good for me, but not for spouse	OK for spouse, but not for me	OK for both (agreed)	Not agreed	Not OK for either, but working for betterment	At a standstill	Many quarrels	Never discussed anymore	Impossible
Sex	4.8	3.5	63.1	16.2	2.4	2.2	0.9	3.9	3.0
Social	3.0	3.2	72.1	9.8	3.4	2.4	0.7	2.1	3.3
Child training	2.4	3.4	70.7	13.1	5.8	0.5	2.8	0.7	0.6
Religion	3.4	2.6	75.8	8.3	2.6	2.5	0.2	3.2	1.4
Income	2.6	2.7	77.0	7.5	6.0	1.2	0.6	0.7	1.7
In-laws	3.0	2.6	76.5	8.4	1.9	0.7	0.2	3.0	3.7
Friends	1.5	1.6	82.1	7.1	3.0	0.9	0.6	2.0	1.2

Source: Judson T. Landis, "Length of Time Required to Achieve Adjustment in Marriage," *American Sociological Review,* 11:666-77. Copyright © 1946, by The American Sociological Association, Washington, D.C., Reprinted by permission.

ADJUSTMENT TAKES TIME. Perhaps the most extensive research in this connection has been done by Judson Landis. He inquired of many couples how much time it took them after marriage to achieve adjustment in different areas. Of the 409 couples in the original study, 99.2 per cent rated their marriages as "average," "happy," or "very happy," and only 0.8 per cent indicated that they were unhappy in any degree.[32] The six major areas identified by Landis from his study were: sex, money, social matters, in-laws, religion, and mutual friends. Landis includes a seventh area—the care and training of children—and indicated that several of these same couples, even after years of married life, were still working for a satisfactory adjustment in some of these areas.

ADJUSTMENT VARIATIONS. Landis' studies showed conclusively that adjustment is easier in some areas than in others. For example, it was fairly easy for most couples to find mutual friends, but not so easy to maintain a satisfactory financial adjustment. It is desirable for each couple to strive for agreement all along the line, but they should not despair over their inability ever to reach agreement in some areas. Most of the couples in Landis's original study were at least somewhat happy within their marriages, but there had rarely been complete agreement by many in all areas; even at the time of interview, satisfactory adjustments were lacking in certain areas.

A slightly higher percentage of those who considered the first six areas satisfactory from the beginning rated their marriages as "very happy" than of those who took from one to twelve months to reach adjustments in the same areas. When it took longer than a year to reach satisfactory adjustments, the percentage of "very happy" marriages was considerably lower. In marriages still unadjusted in three or more areas, no couple rated their marriage higher than average.[33]

No consistent relationship appeared between level of education and the length of time required to adjust in these areas. Social adjustment was somewhat more favorable among those who were highly educated, but problems of sex, money, and in-laws were more difficult for those with higher education. The extent of educational achievement seemed to make no particular difference to the length of time needed in solving problems of religion and mutual friends.[34]

Locke's study of happily married and divorced people included the checking of the most serious areas of marital adjustment, and his findings largely supported those of Landis.[35]

Summary

It usually takes much longer than the honeymoon period to reach a measure of satisfactory adjustment in most marital areas. It is necessary for couples to live together and to work together continuously in order to adjust their ideals, goals, and behavior patterns to one another. Complete satisfaction in all areas should not be expected immediately; however, it is vitally important to begin working through a problem-solving process as soon as possible. The sooner the problem-solving process is initiated in the marriage, the greater the opportunities for happiness in the years ahead.

Notes

1. A case in the author's files.
2. *Ibid.*
3. Willard Waller and Reuben Hill, *The Family: A Dynamic Interpretation* (New York: The Dryden Press, 1951), p. 253.
4. Robert A. Harper, *Marriage* (New York: Appleton-Century-Crofts, Inc., 1949), p. 8.
5. Harvey J. Locke, *Predicting Adjustment in Marriage* (New York: Holt, Rinehart & Winston, Inc., 1951), pp. 55–57.
6. Lewis M. Terman, *Psychological Factors in Marital Happiness* (New York: McGraw-Hill Book Company, Inc., 1938), p. 63.
7. Adapted from Paul C. Glick, *American Families* (New York: John Wiley & Sons, Inc., 1957) , with updatings from *Statistical Bulletin*, Metropolitan Life Insurance Company (August, 1964).
8. John B. Lansing and Leslie Kish, "Family-Life Cycle as an Independent Variable," *American Sociological Review*, 22:512–19.
9. See A. Joseph Brayshaw, "Middle-aged Marriage: Idealism, Realism, and the Search for Meaning," *Marriage and Family Living*, 24:358–64.
10. Robert Winch, *The Modern Family* (New York: Holt, Rinehart & Winston, Inc., 1952), p. 451.
11. Harnell Hart, "Detour Around Reno!" William F. Bigolow (ed.). *The Good Housekeeping Marriage Book* (Englewood Cliffs, N.J.: Prentice-Hall, Inc., 1938).
12. See Peter C. Pineo, "Disenchantment in the Later Years of Marriage," *Marriage and Family Living*, 23:3–11.
13. Judson T. Landis, "What Is the Happiest Period of Life?" *School and Society*, 55:643–45.
14. Thomas P. Monahan, "When Married Couples Part: Statistical Trends and Relationships in Divorce," *American Sociological Review*, 27:625–33.
15. F. Alexander Magoun, *Love and Marriage* (New York: Harper & Row, Publishers, 1956), p. 300.
16. Terman, *op. cit.*, p. 29.
17. Ray E. Baber, *Marriage and the Family* (New York: McGraw-Hill Book Company, Inc., 1953), p. 179.
18. *Ibid.*
19. Evelyn M. Duvall and Reuben Hill, *When You Marry* (New York: Association Press, 1953), pp. 188–90.
20. *Ibid.*
21. Terman, *op. cit.*, p. 99.
22. David Mace, *Marriage, The Art of Lasting Love* (Garden City, N.Y.: Doubleday and Company, Inc., 1952), p. 61.
23. Reuben Hill, *Families Under Stress*, New York: Harper & Row, Publishers, 1949), p. vii.

24. E. W. Burgess and Leonard S. Cottrell, *Predicting Success or Failure in Marriage* (Englewood Cliffs, N.J.: Prentice-Hall, Inc., 1939).

25. Alex F. Osborn, *Applied Imagination: Principles and Procedures of Creative Thinking* (New York: Charles Scribner's Sons, 1953), p. 45.

26. Robert O. Blood, *Anticipating Your Marriage* (New York: The Free Press of Glencoe, Inc., 1955), p. 222.

27. See almost any standard college text in the area of general psychology.

28. Locke, *op. cit.*, p. 204.

29. Mace, *op. cit.*, p. 63.

30. See, e.g., Charles W. Hobart and William J. Klausner, "Some Social Interactional Correlates of Marital Role Disagreement, and Marital Adjustment," *Marriage and Family Living*, 21:256–63.

31. Winch, *op. cit.*, p. 463.

32. Judson T. Landis, "Length of Time Required to Achieve Adjustment in Marriage," *American Sociological Review*, 11:666–77.

33. *Ibid.*

34. *Ibid.*

35. Locke, *op. cit.*, pp. 75–76.

Questions for further thought

1. What aspects of marital adjustment are the most consistent with the American democratic process?
2. How long should the settling-down phase of marriage take?
3. Which of the similarities and differences between the sexes make it easier for mates to get along together? Which make it more difficult? Are the sexes more different than they are alike?
4. In problem-solving is the primary step in determining ends or means?
5. When do good intentions excuse undesirable behavior? When do they not?
6. Should romance in marriage ever be sacrificed to such things as getting the dishes done or mowing the lawn?
7. For what areas of marriage might accommodation be the best solution?
8. Because no one really knows reality, how can anyone ever be certain of what another person means by verbal expressions? For example, how many meanings are there in the following: "I love you"; "I can't afford it"; "Our relationship is different"?
9. How much emphasis should married couples place upon remembering anniversaries, daily good-bye kisses, and other such demonstrations of affection?

Recommended films

Love Is for the Byrds (Brigham Young University).
Jealousy (McGraw-Hill Book Company, Inc.).
Resolving Family Conflicts (University of Michigan Television Center).
Have I Told You Lately That I Love You? (University of Southern California).

Suggested supplemental readings

BOOKS

Arnold, F. X. *Woman and Man: Their Nature and Mission.* New York: Herder and Herder, 1963.

Blood, Robert O., and Donald M. Wolfe. *Husbands and Wives: The Dynamics of Married Living.* New York: The Free Press of Glencoe, Inc., 1960.

Callwood, June, *Love, Hate, Fear, Anger and the Other Lively Emotions*. Garden City, N.Y.: Doubleday and Company, 1964.

Duvall, Evelyn M. *Family Development*, rev. ed. Philadelphia: J. B. Lippincott Co., 1962.

Eisenstein, Victor W. (ed.). *Neurotic Interaction in Marriage*. New York: Basic Books, Inc., 1956.

Ellis, Albert. *How To Live with a Neurotic*. New York: Crown Publishers, Inc., 1957.

Foote, Nelson, and Leonard S. Cottrell. *Identity and Interpersonal Competence*. Chicago: University of Chicago Press, 1955.

Henry, George W. *Masculinity and Femininity*. New York: Collier Books, 1964.

Karlsson, George. *Adaptability and Communication in Marriage*, rev. ed., Totowa, N.J.: The Bedminster Press, 1964.

Lignon, Ernest, and Leona Smith. *The Marriage Climate*. St. Louis: The Bethany Press, 1964.

Montague, Ashley. *The Natural Superiority of Women*. New York: The Macmillan Company, 1953.

Overstreet, Harry A. and Bonaro W. *The Mind Alive*. New York: W. W. Norton & Company, Inc., 1956.

Porterfield, Austin. *Marriage and Family Living*. Philadelphia: F. A. Davis Company, 1964.

Stewart, Maxwell S. *Problems of Family Life: And How to Meet Them*. New York: Harper & Row, Publishers, 1957.

Tashman, Harry F. *The Marriage Bed: An Analyst's Casebook*. New York: University Publishers, Inc., 1959.

Thurber, James, and Elliott Nugent. *The Male Animal*. New York: Random House, 1940.

ARTICLES

Bossard, James H. S., and Eleanor S. Boll. "Marital Unhappiness in the Life Cycle," *Marriage and Family Living*, 17:10–14.

Brownfield, E. D. "Communication—Key to Dynamics of Family Interaction," *Marriage and Family Living*, 15:316–19.

Collver, Andrew. "The Family Cycle in India and the United States," *American Sociological Review*, 28:86.

Folsom, Joseph K. "Value Analysis and the Resolution of Marital Conflicts," *Merrill-Palmer Quarterly*, 6:105–13.

Gravatt, Arthur E. "An Exploratory Study of Marital Adjustment in Later Maturity," *The Family Life Coordinator*, 6:23–25.

Hamilton, Eleanor. "Communication in Marriage: An Endless Challenge to the Loving," *Modern Bride* (Spring 1960), 78.

Harper, Robert A. "Communication Problems in Marriage and Marriage Counseling," *Marriage and Family Living*, 20:107–16.

Lansing, John B., and Leslie Kish. "Family-Life Cycle as an Independent Variable," *American Sociological Review*, 22:512–19.

Rutledge, Aaron L. "Missing Ingredient in Marriage—Nearness," *Social Science*, 36:53–58.

Developing sexual
∽ chapter 12 ∽   harmony

For some couples sexual harmony seems to come early in the marriage and with a minimum of conscious effort. For others, sexual adjustment requires weeks and even months of deliberation and trial. Some couples never obtain a satisfactory sexual relationship. This inadequacy may seriously handicap a marriage relationship that might otherwise be completely satisfying. The continued absence of sexual fulfillment may drive some couples to divorce or infidelity.

This is not to alarm couples if their first sexual experiences are not satisfactory, for actually 47 per cent of the couples in one study reported that their initial sexual relations were much less than mutually satisfying.[1] If the relations do not show improvement after a time, however, there is a greater risk that the sexual problems will adversely affect the rest of the marriage.

The power of sex in marriage

Sex within marriage is the elemental power that holds the total marital relationship in place. The power of the sexual force is often apparent only from the polarized pattern of interests, ideals, and goals expressed by the couple. Sex within marriage is seldom overt, yet it has far-reaching effects on the entire pattern of the marriage.

The complexities of sexual adjustment make it difficult to determine whether a poor sex relationship is the cause or the effect of an unhappy marriage. Such things as repressed hostility, suspicion, or selfishness may prevent one or the other partner from letting go sufficiently to create a good sex relationship. Often troubles elsewhere in the marriage cause difficulties to appear first within the sex relationship. Thus the way a husband and wife get along sexually may either affect or reflect their over-all marital adjustment.

A better sex relationship within marriage is often most easily achieved by first setting out to improve the other areas of marriage. Although men are usually more able to compartmentalize their sexual responses, sex for both mates is usually improved if the rest of the marriage is improved. Conversely, satisfaction with the sexual experience increases the sense of fulfillment in other areas of the marital relationship.

The importance of sex as an isolated act can be overemphasized. Drummond calls it "the thing which takes the least amount of time and causes the most amount of trouble."[2] Of the 10,080 minutes in a week, the average couple spends less than 1 per cent in specific sexual activities. Terman had concluded that "the data in fact indicate that all of the sex factors combined are far from being the one major determinant of success in marriage."[3]

The findings of most studies, however, suggest that couples who have achieved the highest degree of mutuality in their sex relations, are usually among the most happily married. Although studies may differ in their ratings of the importance of sex, the findings of all studies agree that sexual adjustment is definitely related to total marital adjustment. Davis concludes: "In married life the sex relationship, both its physical and emotional aspects, indisputably plays the major part."[4] In Thomason's study of Pennsylvania couples, those who considered their sexual adjustment perfect had over-all marital-adjustment scores of at least 190 on the Adams Marriage Audit. Husbands lacking sex adjustment scored only 115, and wives sexually unadjusted scored only 82 points.[5]

THE VALUES OF SEXUAL HARMONY. Although sex does not make up the whole marriage, a satisfactory sex life can enrich a total marriage relationship. In the sexual relationship, each partner can contribute to and gain from the marriage simultaneously. A good sex relationship can increase the ability of both partners to face difficulties within their personal and married life. Understanding and responsiveness in a mate are two characteristics that add to the delights of marriage. So, although some marriages can and do exist on the strength of bonds other than sex, the total relationship is usually enriched when the sex relationship is good.

Criteria of sexual harmony

It is difficult to determine the extent of sexual success within marriage, for it depends upon the criteria used in making the judgment. The two most obvious measures are: (1) adequacy or frequency of orgasm, and (2) frequency of coitus based on mutual agreement and strong sex drives.

FREQUENCY OF ORGASM. The frequency of orgasm as a criterion most usually applies to the wife, for it is a factor that varies more in the female than the male. The Kinsey data indicate that orgasm in coitus is experienced by almost 100 per cent of husbands but by only between 70 and 77 per cent of wives.[6] Stone's study of more than 8500 women indicated that 34 per cent usually experienced orgasm in the marriage sex relationship; 40 per cent, occasionally or rarely; and 20 per cent, never. He later checked these findings with an additional 3000 women and the results were much the same.[7]

Terman has suggested that the achievement of sexual climax by the wife affects not only the sexual adjustment but the entire marital relationship. Although he did not think it necessary for a wife to achieve orgasm every time, he believed the marriage had a better chance for happiness if she usually did. Terman reported average marital happiness scores of women based on orgasm frequency as: 58 for women who never achieved orgasm, 66 for those who sometimes did, 70 for those who usually did, and 75 for those wives who always reached climax.[8] Terman, however, went one step further and tested the happiness scores of husbands as related to the frequency of orgasm for their wives. The average results of the husband happiness scores were: 60, with wife who never achieved orgasm; 67 with wife who sometimes did; 69 with wife who usually did; and 73 with wife who always reached climax.[9] Hamilton concluded from his studies that the wife must achieve orgasm in at least 20 per cent of the copulations for the marriage to be successful.[10] These and other studies indicate that although not absolutely essential, sexual climax is usually associated with marital happiness. But again the question arises: Are these marriages happier because the wives were able to achieve orgasm a higher percentage of the time, or were the wives able to achieve a higher percentage of orgasm because the marriages were happier? Some couples had high happiness scores even though the wives never experienced orgasm, but the expectation today is toward greater satisfaction for both partners.[11] Just how detrimental failure to achieve orgasm is to a particular marriage, however, depends on the extent of importance the couple attach to it. If achieving orgasm is placed high in the hierarchy of values, difficulty is much more disappointing than for those who emphasize it less. Stokes writes of his experiences as a psychiatrist and marriage counselor:

> I find something deeply significant in the fact that, during all my practice as a counselor, I encountered only two instances in which a woman regularly achieving orgasm with her husband came to me contemplating divorce. . . . When divorce was finally decided upon, in each of these marriages the spouses wept bitterly and parted with reluctance.[12]

A review of current survey data indicates that repeated coitus leading most frequently to incomplete orgasm may leave an individual in a pitch of nervous excitement that ultimately builds resistance to, or final rejection of, the sex act. Such people may actually be worse off than those who never have experienced orgasm, for chronic frustration can lead to disturbed emotions, unnatural body fatigue, headaches, backaches, and neurotic behavior.

Conversely, every complete orgasm conditions both spouses for future coital satisfaction. Although brides may feel sexually inadequate early in marriage or upset later, sexual activity should continue. Time is on the side of sexual fulfillment. One third of the most responsive wives of one study reported that their first experiences of full sexual climax did not occur until three to six months after the wedding.[13] Studies have been made on the length of time after marriage before wives first experienced orgasm. Summaries of the studies by Terman (of wives married an average of eleven years), by Thomason (of wives married an average of four years), and by Landis (of wives married on an average of three years) revealed that the percentage who recalled experiencing orgasm at least once on the honeymoon or within four weeks afterward, were only 51.1, 50, and 53, respectively. The additional percentages recalling an occasional orgasm experience within from one month to one year after marriage were 25.7, 27, and 30, respectively. The percentages recalling orgasm not occurring for more than a year were 16, 7, and 6, respectively. The percentages reporting still no achievement of orgasm were 7.1, 7, and 11, respectively. It should be noted that 9 per cent of Thomason's group did not reply to this question.[14] Kinsey's data indicate that 49 per cent of wives experience orgasm on varying occasions within the first months of marriage; 75 per cent, within one year; 83 per cent, within the fifth year; 87 per cent, by the tenth year; and 90 per cent, by the fifteenth year of marriage. Kinsey's study goes beyond this to indicate that, of the wives who had experienced orgasm, it occurred within 63 per cent of the coital episodes attempted the first year of marriage; within 71 per cent of the coital episodes attempted by the fifth year; within 77 per cent of the coital episodes attempted by the tenth year; 81 per cent of the coital episodes attempted by the fifteenth year; and within 85 per cent of the coital episodes attempted by the twentieth year.[15]

AGREEMENT ON FREQUENCY OF SEXUAL RELATIONS. A second index of sexual success within marriage is the degree of mutual agreement on how often to have coitus. Some women have an increased desire for coitus shortly before or immediately after the menstrual period.[16] Other factors may affect the frequency of coitus, such as fantasies, thoughts, and daydreams. The various substitutes available to mates in place of sexual activities may also influence desire. People who work outside the home are more likely to come in contact with others of the opposite sex. Then, too, the pressure of commercial advertising is chiefly directed to stimulating suggestive sexual reaction. If there is a great difference between the sexual drives of mates to begin with, these environmental stimuli may cause serious problems. They may even arouse an unsatisfied mate to the point of attempting affairs with others. Kinsey's data suggests that this is much more likely in the first years of marriage to occur among those who are poorly educated.[17]

Although there were individual variations of sexual desire within each sex as great or greater than between the two sexes, Kinsey's data indicate that twice as many men as women are sexually aroused by simply observing the opposite sex, and that many times more men than women are strongly aroused by erotic stories. As a group, males enjoy talking about sex more than females do, and are more sexually stimulated by what they hear. The Kinsey data indicate that when the categories of "definite" and "frequent" are combined with "some response," there is a decided difference in the proportion of erotic responses between males and females, as groups, to many different stimuli.

Table 12–1. **Activities which bring on some degree of erotic response**

	Per cent indicating	
	Female	*Male*
Observing opposite sex in either clothes or nude	58	72
Observing own sex	12	16
Observing portrayals of nude figures	12	54
Observing genitalia of opposite sex	48	Almost all
Observing own genitalia	9	56
Observing commercial moving pictures	48	36
Observing burlesque and floor shows	14	62
Observing animals in coitus	16	32
Observing portrayals of sexual action	32	77
Experiencing phantasies concerning other sex	69	84
Reading literary material	60	59
Hearing erotic stories	14	47
Hearing sadomasochistic stories	12	22
Being bitten	55	50

Source: Alfred Kinsey, *et al., Sexual Behavior in the Human Female* (Philadelphia: W. B. Saunders Co., 1953), pp. 651–71. Copyright © 1953, by W. B. Saunders Co., Philadelphia. Adapted by permission of publisher and The Institute for Sex Research, Indiana University, Bloomington, Ind.

How often sex relations are desired within marriage is related to many motivational factors, including the different ways in which each mate regards sex. A husband should study the natural responses of his wife and, if possible, plan their sexual activities for the times she is more likely to participate fully. The wife, in turn, should study the particular needs of her husband and cooperate with him as fully as possible. The wife should be liberal in matching her husband's desires; she should not allow narrow mental attitudes to restrict her responses, physical or psychological, to his natural needs. She should also realize that men, more than women, seem to desire coitus when other things in their lives have gone wrong, the sexual activity apparently relieving other tensions also. Probably because of cultural conditioning, women (those of the upper classes particularly) seem to enjoy coitus as an expression of contentment with the rest of their lives. Consequently, after a trying day of discontent, women are less likely to be sexually aroused than their husbands. Because in the American culture husbands usually initiate coital activity, this may be one reason why even the most responsive of wives may fail to achieve orgasm every time. Perhaps if coitus were more often initiated by wives, a higher percentage of orgasm responses would follow.[18]

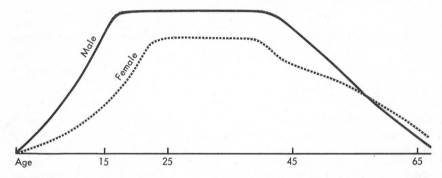

Figure 12-1. Author's conception of what research suggests about sex desire of average male and female.

Lack of response may simply indicate that a person has not yet been sexually awakened. It is difficult for a person to be aroused by what he does not know and for which he has no associated desires. It may well be that prior to experiencing the pleasures of sex, some people lack a conscious desire for coitus; this seems especially true for females. Part of this difference may be hormonal. As Kephart explains:

> The male has certain sex glands, such as the prostate, which manufacture sperm-carrying fluids. These fluids, in turn, act as internal sexual stimuli, and in most males the need for periodic physical release is a strong one. In contrast, the female has no prostate or corresponding type of gland, and hence no seminal fluids produced. Whatever her sexual needs therefore, they are different from those of the male—it is incorrect to equate the sexuality of men and women.[19]

Most of the difference, however, probably arises from cultural conditioning. Women are not necessarily slower to respond or less ardent once they have enjoyed full sexual satisfaction. A study by Ford and Beach indicates that often the fully aroused female is more than a match for the average male. Males, however, are aroused more easily and more frequently than females.[20] Wives, more than husbands, appear to enjoy caresses and fondling, often without any expectation of actual sexual consummation.[21] Even the wife's premenstrual peak in sex desire is reported to be more affectional than erotic.[22]

The fact that men will pay or keep the concubine, the harem, the prostitute, or the "other woman" indicates that the average man is more sexually inclined than women. This is further substantiated by Kinsey's reports that there is much less female practice of masturbation and homosexuality or participation in extramarital affairs.[23] Many studies report greater sexual desire on the part of husbands.[24] Kirkpatrick reports that one study revealed that about 25 per cent of husbands desired coitus more frequently than their wives did, and about 17 per cent of the wives were having intercourse far beyond their desires.[25] It is also interesting that males report intercourse in marriage less than their wives mention it.[26] There is, however, considerable individual variation within the sexes, and the range of variation is quite extensive. Furthermore, 14 per cent of the women in Kinsey's study reported having multiple orgasms during each sexual coitus, a thing unheard of for most males.[27] This figure closely matches the 13 per cent of wives reported in Terman's study as having two or more orgasms during a single act of intercourse.[28] The rate of sexual maturity of boys discloses a considerable variation in age when certain sex-connected activities begin.

Table 12–2. **Per cent of each age group of boys indicating when a certain sex-connected activity or condition first began**

Age (years)	Ejaculation	Voice change	Nocturnal emission	Pubic hair
10	1.8	0.3	0.3	0.3
11	6.9	5.6	3.7	8.4
12	14.1	20.5	5.3	27.1
13	33.6	40.0	17.4	36.1
14	30.9	26.0	12.9	23.8
15	7.8	5.5	13.9	3.3
16	4.9	2.0	16.0	1.0

Source: Glenn V. Ramsey, "The Sexual Development of Boys," *The American Journal of Psychology,* **56:**217. Copyright © 1943, by The American Journal of Psychology, Austin, Tex. Reprinted by permission.

There appears to be a wide variation in the habits of coital frequency. Some couples report indulging in coitus at least once a day. In Kinsey's study, the reported frequencies ranged from one coital experience in thirty years by a couple apparently in good health to at least thirty or more coital experiences per week throughout a thirty-year period of married life.[29] Many books in the field of marriage state that the average frequency of coitus in American marriage is once or twice weekly. Some couples, however, engage in coitus much more often than that even after years of marriage. Others apparently have excellent marital adjustments with only an occasional experience of actual coitus.

EFFECT OF AGE ON COITAL FREQUENCY. There are many factors that may influence the intensity and frequency of sexual desire within marriage. Age itself may be one factor. According to Kinsey's data, the frequency of coitus usually tapers off as the individual advances in age. The mean coitus frequency for married males ages sixteen to twenty was 3.75 times per week, and for males fifty-six to sixty, it was 0.83. Once every three weeks was the average for sixty-year-old men, with only 5 per cent no longer sexually active. Although 30 per cent of the men were inactive by seventy, several were still active when over eighty. The Kinsey statistics for women indicated an average of 1.8 episodes per week at fifty, tapering off to 0.9 a week by sixty.[30] Two physicians at the Duke University School of Medicine recently studied the sexual activity of people sixty to ninety-three years of age, according to age, race, and socioeconomic class. They found that 54 per cent of the married persons surveyed and 7 per cent of the divorced and widowed were still sexually active. There appeared to be an abrupt lessening of sexual activity after seventy-five, largely owing to illness. Negroes were found to be more sexually active than whites; males, more active than females; and those from the lower socioeconomic class, more active than other classes. Those with strong sexual urges in youth usually reported experiencing moderate urges in old age, while those with weak to moderate urges in youth usually reported lack of sexual feeling in old age.[31] An additional survey reports finding that 70 per cent of married males past the age of sixty-five were still sexually active. The other 30 per cent became impotent in the following order: 10 per cent between the ages of forty and fifty-nine; 38 per cent, between the ages of sixty and sixty-five; and 52 per cent, sometime after reaching age sixty-five.[32] It appears that neither total celibacy nor high frequency of orgasm endangers the physical health of either sex. The frequency of coitus appears to slow down with advancing age no more abruptly than the other physical functions.

After menopause, it is not unusual for a woman's sexual interest to be stronger than her husband's. Much of this increase may arise from elimination of the fear of pregnancy.

Kinsey reported further that the frequency of coitus decreases with an increase in religious participation, and it also diminishes as the degree of educational and professionalization increases.[33]

Other factors that influence the frequency of coitus are such extenuating circumstances as the length of time married, health conditions, hormone balance, occupation, mode of life, and opportunities for sexual participation.

The only practical standard for frequency of intercourse should be determined by whatever the couple mutually accept, and this may be quite changeable. Insofar as the development of sexual harmony is concerned, moods indeed are often better guides than a calendar. Thus compromise on both sides may often be necessary. The idea that only the wife should decide when to have coitus is as unwarranted as the assumption that intercourse is the husband's privilege but the wife's duty. Compromise is easier when the couple realize three important marital truths: (1) coitus is usually more important to husbands, and there seldom is complete mutuality; (2) the difference in sex drives between mates is usually greatest at the beginning of marriage and often disappears with time; (3) alternate acceptances of the other's desires is the practical solution to sexual adjustment when differences continue. Recent research shows that maritally satisfied husbands are much more likely than dissatisfied husbands to consider their wives' desire for frequency of coitus to be similar to their own. This was also found to be true for maritally satisfied wives in comparison to maritally dissatisfied wives, though not to the same extent.[34]

Table 12–3. **Number of times per month intercourse preferred by husbands and wives**

Times	Per cent indicating	
	Husbands	*Wives*
Four or less	17.6	25.0
Five to eight	35.8	38.4
Nine or more	46.5	35.7

Source: E. W. Burgess and Paul Wallin, *Engagement and Marriage* (Philadelphia: J. B. Lippincott Co., 1953), p. 633. Copyright © 1953, by J. B. Lippincott Co., Philadelphia. Reprinted by permission.

Obstacles to sexual adjustment

A good sex adjustment within marriage is dependent upon many variables. The more important factors include social restrictions, psychological conditioning, physiological changes, and education.

SOCIAL RESTRICTIONS. Some of the strongest sexual inhibitions are exerted by society itself. This may be related to the fact that many individuals are unprepared for meeting sexual problems in marraige; they believe that sexual adjustment is the one part of marriage that will come naturally. This may be true for the lower animals but it has little relation to human *married* sex life. Doing "what comes naturally" is simply mating and requires little or no regard for a partner's feelings. If mating were the only end for which marital intercourse was intended, there would be no problem of sexual adjustment. The fact that sex does not work every time, as the movies and storybooks suggest, sometimes results in a rude awakening for the couple to the realities of sex in marriage. Sex, however, is not the only function restricted by rules of society; natural elimination, eating, sleeping, and even bathing are so limited. Humans perform those functions in the manner most acceptable to society as a whole. Sexual indulgence too, is regulated and adapted to the time, place, and pattern that conform to the purposes of society and the civilized expectations of other individuals. Because a democratic society demands respect for the individual and his freedom of choice, it is necessary that the sexual drive be controlled, especially during the formative years of childhood. Thus, when old enough to marry, many people must unlearn former lessons. As Ruth Benedict, the anthropologist, has pointed out, boys are first taught to treat all girls as sisters. Later, the male peer group teaches that all women are objects for potential sexual exploitation. Then, after marriage, the man finds that neither of the first two lessons were right, for now he must be a great lover, and sex is supposed to be synonymous with love.[35] Since his earliest years, the male is conditioned to regard sex as something to be enjoyed, and this very eager anticipation may precipitate maladjustment in a bride who is not so eager. Thus, for marital sex adjustment, many men must re-evaluate much of what they thought they knew about love and women.

The female must also make many readjustments. The behavior that society had always indicated as terribly wrong for her is now suddenly terribly right, at least morally and legally. Instead of rejecting the male's advances, she is now expected to cast off all sexual inhibitions and give a passionate response. Acts which she perhaps had previously considered perverted are now expected of her as marital duties. According to Kinsey, this dichotomy is especially true in the middle and upper classes.[36] From a review of her anthropological studies, Margaret Mead suggests that in America the present feminine lag in accepting sex within marriage is almost entirely the result of social training.[37] Baber suggests that the female sex drive is as strong as the male's, but that social pressures retard and suppress it. He believes that "when society gets adjusted to the idea that woman is just as capable of great sex passion as is man, it is likely to prove a boon to marriage for the wife will feel free to abandon herself without shame to the fullest possible enjoyment of intercourse."[38]

A marriage ceremony, however, is not enough to transform an inhibited girl into a passionate woman. Conditioned responses that have been built up over a period of twenty or more years will not suddenly change, just because one wants them to change. Readjustment of values takes time. One medical study of more than 1000 marriages concluded that sexual difficulties were seldom organic in women; they were, rather, a variance of mental behavior, including attitudes and socially conditioned behavior patterns.[39]

The study by Kinsey indicates that many men have extremely erroneous ideas about sexual physiology and female responses.[40] Sex appears to be one subject about which many people know a little and then assume a lot. Individuals should enter marriage ready to learn and to work at reaching a good sex adjustment. Sex within marriage is not an isolated activity; it should be integrated into the whole intricate pattern of married living.

PSYCHOLOGICAL CONDITIONING FACTORS. Many family-life educators, as well as child psychologists, have often remarked about the fact that sex seems natural to a child until his attitude is distorted by the educational processes. Thus, it appears that childhood experience is a factor which may inhibit good marital sex adjustment. Although the adults may be unaware of it, the attitudes of children are continually forming as reflections of the attitudes of their elders. Even the adult's silence about sex is meaningful to the child. Instead of taking his mind off a subject, silence may foster a feeling of uneasiness and terror. Conclusive evidence from Hamilton's study pointed to a high correlation between sexual adequacy for the female and early childhood sex educational experiences. In his study, 84 per cent of the women who had learned by the age of six where babies came from reported sexual adequacy within marriage. Of those who had not learned before they were twelve, only 42 per cent reported being sexually adequate within marriage.[41] Terry made a detailed analysis of each of Hamilton's most poorly adjusted cases. She found that such psychological phenomena as frightening sexual experiences during childhood were held in common by many of those women. Those who were the least adjusted sexually reported evasive sex instruction during childhood, and they were much older before they learned the facts. They had often been distressed by thoughts of their parents having intercourse. In many cases there was an expressed wish that sex never existed, and several of these women did not want their husbands to see them undressed.[42] In both male and female, the belief that sex was sinful or dirty was shown by the research of Burgess and Cottrell to be closely correlated to sexual maladjustment.[43]

Karl Menninger suggests that psychological conditioning may produce unconscious factors that inhibit good sexual adjustment. For example, holding back in coitus may be the projection onto the mate of an unconscious hatred toward a parent. Poor sex adjustment might also be related to a subconscious love of someone other than the spouse.[44]

Within the American culture, sex is considered a private affair. Thus, crowded home living conditions may interfere with good sexual adjustment. Although not always true, the presence of children in the home and the emotional stress of managing them may for a time decrease a mother's responsiveness. After the children have grown up, many couples again begin to enjoy a more active sexual relationship. When there are young children about, there are always the hazards of intrusion and interruptions. In the American culture privacy seems conducive to satisfactory sex relations. When first married, a couple may focus primarily on the sex act itself, but with children, the primary focus is switched to their needs, and the marital sexual needs become secondary. When the children's needs always come first, it may be impossible for a couple to abandon themselves completely to each other within the sex act.

This problem was brought to the attention of the author by a couple seeking counsel because their sexual adjustment, which had been good, was steadily deteriorating. There was little evidence of anything beyond the sex act itself to account for this. During the counseling interviews, however, it was disclosed that the couple had a one-bedroom apartment and that their child shared the room with the couple. The wife reported that on occasions when they began to engage in the sex act, she was aware of the child's stirring. Acting on this clue, they decided to move the child into the livingroom before they engaged in love play; later they reported that the added sense of privacy had helped considerably in their recapture of former sexual joys. Sex, being a private affair, requires a complete freedom from fear of interruption. Ideally, there should be no chance of annoyances and no fear of detection or disturbances by others.

The fear of pregnancy may also be a conditioning factor which inhibits good marital sex adjustment. There is, however, some inconsistency among research studies in this connection. Terman did not find fear of pregnancy to be significantly associated with wives' sexual adjustment.[45] His findings, however, have been seriously questioned by many marriage counselors because of evidence to the contrary from their own clinical cases. King, in his study of Negro couples, found that fear of pregnancy did have an effect on enjoyable sex relations, affecting more than 36 per cent of the husbands and 39 per cent of the wives.[46]

At one time, the maternal death risk was undoubtedly a serious factor affecting sexual adjustment. At present there is little need for such concern, but in 1900 the maternal mortality rate was about nine per 1000 live births. The rate is now only about three per 10,000 live births,[47] so the fear of pregnancy should not be so inhibiting a factor. Certainly, any couple following the most modern practices of conception control should suffer no such sexual maladjustment. Some people dislike to take special contraceptive precautions if it necessitates an interruption of the lovemaking. Fortunately, there are preventatives today that cause no such inconvenience.[48] A talk with a well-informed medical doctor would be advisable before the couple decides which methods to employ. Some couples feel that taking precautions against conception kills the spontaneity of the sex relationship. They take a laissez-faire attitude, which has no connection with a positive religious conviction on the subject of birth control. After one or two pregnancies, however, the absence of proper conception-control measures may be more inhibiting for some couples than a temporary interruption.

Whether or not conception-control devices are used, the healthiest attitude for any young couple indulging in coitus is the knowledge that a pregnancy, whenever it occurs, will be perfectly acceptable to both partners. If this attitude is lacking, perhaps, there should be no coitus at all. Certainly, proper contraceptive measures can reduce the possibility of pregnancy, but there is always some possibility that pregnancy might occur. Couples who feel they can accept a pregnancy, should it occur, usually have better sex adjustment than those who feel that they cannot possibly "afford" a child.

Young couples should occasionally recheck the contraceptive techniques their physician has prescribed, especially after the birth of each child. Clinical evidence suggests that nothing restricts sexual freedom as much as a chronic fear of pregnancy, especially in the woman who does not feel ready for motherhood. Certainly a couple may admit that they do not desire pregnancy at a particular time, but there undoubtedly will be inhibitions in the sex relationship if they feel pregnancy absolutely must not happen.

Fear of pregnancy may also be related to the stage of the marriage itself. For example, a newly married couple dependent for income upon the wife's job are quite likely to find their sex responses affected by fear of conception. As a factor in sex adjustment, the fear of pregnancy is particularly evident when the wife already has had a number of pregnancies resulting in more children than the family can afford or more than she can handle. In this connection, Locke quotes one divorced woman as saying, "I was scared all the time I'd get pregnant. I didn't like to have intercourse because I was scared. I had a child every year."[49] Thus, the anxiety brought about by concern over too large a family or health problems associated with frequent pregnancy can have a serious effect on sexual attitudes; however, this need not be the problem it was in former times. Stokes suggests that "the complete enjoyment of sexual life is possible only when anxiety over conception control is absent."[50]

Psychological factors that inhibit good sex adjustment are usually acquired attitudes, and because they are acquired they can be changed. These attitudes are formed by previous experiences. By helping such people to understand the underlying causes, a skillful counselor can often effect a change in their attitudes that leads to better sexual relations within marriage. Butterfield, who is nationally recognized as a sound marriage counselor, has indicated that he can eliminate most of the psychological causes of poor sex attitudes.[51] This may be an enthusiastic overstatement of the virtues of marriage counseling, but it indicates the value of understanding the psychology of acquired attitudes.

In the process of changing or reconditioning distorted sexual attitudes, it is necessary that the person or couple be instilled with the understanding that sex pleasure is both normal and right. Recreation is as much a part of sex as procreation. Much re-education may be necessary before some couples can achieve a state of complete abandonment to the sex act itself. It is sometimes possible for the couple, directed by a counselor, to discover the source of their acquired attitudes and to work at reducing their interference. The counseling experience may help a wife learn to relax and to respond to her husband's desires and her own sexual urges. Often, it is only through information derived from counseling that a woman learns of the sensations to be experienced in the marital sex act. Counseling may encourage experimentation by a couple and improve their communication with one another while working out this most intimate relationship between man and woman.

Sometimes the inhibitions and fears that a woman associates with sex arise not from any direct experience of sex, but from her reaction to a situation which held poor sexual connotations in her mind. Mating with a man with a natural interest in sex does not remind her of a prior sexual encounter but may evoke within her a rejection of sexual emotion. Counseling may help such wives to focus their resentment against their own attitudes rather than upon their husbands. By encouraging positive attitudes toward sex in persons who have suffered negative psychological conditioning, it is possible to recondition individuals for a better sex adjustment within marriage.

Couples must learn by experimentation. Only then, by honestly expressing their reactions to each other, are they able to work toward achieving full sexual harmony. From his wife's sighs and words of appreciation the husband learns which parts of her body are most enkindled by his touch. Her responses can greatly speed his learning process within the marriage. It is also necessary for each mate to be alert to those conditions most conducive to sexual arousal in the other. Darkness, for example, is preferred by some, and dim illumination by others; sweet whispered endearments may be desired with caresses by some or absolute silence for total concentration and abandonment by others. Each partner should learn the times and seasons for the other's awakening and, in turn, should never hesitate to tell the other what seems particularly pleasing or delightful within the experience. Inability to do this because of false modesty, conceit, or ignorance is a great obstacle to sexual success.

PHYSIOLOGICAL FACTORS.   In some cases, physiological conditioning factors might inhibit marital sex adjustment. Because of the physical energy necessary for sexual satisfaction, sex adjustment is directly related to the general health of the couple. Organic disturbances such as structural malformations or hormonal imbalances may also affect sexual adjustment. Burgess and Cottrell found that sexual difficulties related to organic disturbances—such as structural malformations, diseases, and temporary illnesses—occurred in about 5 per cent of the couples studied.[52] In young married couples, the extremes of these malfunctions are rare, however, probably because persons with such severe problems avoid marriage altogether.

Occasionally cases of sexual maladjustment are ascribed to a lack of hormonal balance. Two different sources have reported that the administration of testosterone, which is a male hormone, can increase the vigor of the sexual drive.[53] In checking this possibility, the author recently consulted eighty-two physicians about the research data. The great majority felt there was some doubt about the efficacy of this hormonal treatment. All admitted that with an extreme case of hormone unbalance, testosterone might have some effect. A huge majority of the medical men, however, felt that the reported benefits probably resulted in great part, from psychological suggestion.[54] In other words, because the patient believed his sexual drive would be increased, he relaxed and became self-assured enough to effect an actual improvement.

Another physiological inhibition is premenstrual irritability. A number of women experience recurrent cycles of depression or irritability for a short time before their menstrual periods. Because of the decreased possibility of pregnancy at that time, this is the interval during which many couples would ordinarily plan their greatest sexual activity. By understanding the physiological origin of these conflicting drives, the couple should make a conscious effort to keep the wife's cyclic irritability from being an obstacle to their sexual enjoyment. By treating their wives more indulgently on some days each month, husbands might prevent such problems from becoming serious. Wives, however, should not take advantage of this situation to justify poor behavior. If both partners recognize that the wife's edginess is a physiological variation, then each can be more watchful of their tempers. Intervals of elation and of depression often follow a physiological cycle, in men as well as women, with surges of great activity alternating with spells of enervation. It is fortunate when these periods follow the same cycle in both partners.

Fatigue is another physiological factor that may be a deterrent to satisfactory sexual adjustment. The daily routine, especially for the woman today, may tax her strength so completely that she has little energy left for sexual activities. Based on his clinical experience, the author has found fatigue to be one of the great unsolved problems of today's marriages. Many gynecologists are concerned over the chronic depletion of strength caused in today's women by all the stresses and strains of working while rearing young children. This double duty not only undermines the quality of the sexual performance, but it also reduces the frequency and intensity of sexual desire. A young child requires constant care, hour after hour, day after day, and year after year. Multiply this task by several children, which is the modern trend among the middle class, add to it the care of the house and additional community obligations. The result is that the average woman is frequently too tired at the end of the day to achieve a satisfactory love experience.[55]

The proper timing of the sex act is often the best solution to the problem of fatigue. Couples might consider engaging in intercourse before the end of the day, because at night both may be weary from work and naturally tired at bedtime. A couple should engage in love play only when relaxed. Perhaps even an occasional trip away from the children would improve and maintain marital harmony.

EDUCATIONAL FACTORS.   It is surprising that even among college graduates there is tremendous ignorance concerning the fundamentals of both male and female anatomy. Many marriage educators believe that the great majority of individuals today know little more, if as much, about sexual anatomy than people knew one hundred years ago.[56] The author's own teaching experience, corroborated by that of many other marriage educators, indicates that there are few college girls or boys who can adequately describe the copulating organ of the opposite sex. It therefore seems pertinent to introduce here a review of genital anatomy, which might help to relieve inhibitions or awkwardness resulting from confusion or lack of objective information.

The male copulating organ is the penis. It is an elongated cylindrical organ, suspended from the lowermost part of the abdominal wall, and usually hangs limply from the body. Skin extends over the end to form the prepuce, or foreskin. In many males, the foreskin has been removed by circumcision; this prevents tightness that might interfere with erection, and facilitates cleanliness. The penis contains many large veins which, during sexual excitement, become engorged with blood, causing the penis to increase both in length and in circumference. It becomes firm and rises to an erect position, approximating a right angle but curving slightly toward the body. This position corresponds somewhat to the internal curve of the female organ. During erection, the penis is rigid enough to be inserted into the female vagina and, through a series of muscular contractions ending in ejaculation, the seminal fluid is deposited within the female. The total amount of this white, viscous fluid ejaculated in one sexual intercourse seldom exceeds a half-teaspoonful.

The most sexually sensitive part of the male penis is the ridge near the tip, the glans, which contains a cluster of nerves. Located inside the body of the penis at the base is Cowper's gland. Upon sexual excitement, this gland produces a clear, alkaline fluid which basically serves as a lubricant for the passage of semen through the male urinary duct during intercourse. It is not semen, as some individuals think.

The outer parts of the female copulating organ are collectively called the vulva. This consists of two sets of lips, the outer, and the inner, plus the clitoris. The outer, or larger lips, called *labia majora*, consist of two thick folds of tissue which extend from the fatty pubic area in front almost to the rectal opening behind. The *labia majora* are covered with hair; their main purpose is to cover and protect the inner genitalia.

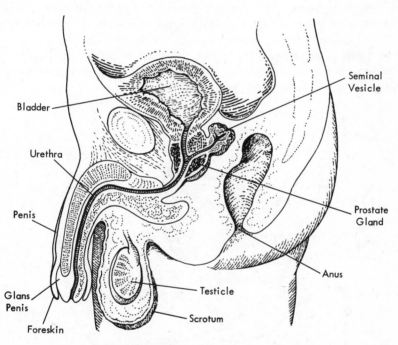

Figure 12-2. Cross section of male sexual anatomy.

Inside the large lips, with much the same structure, lie the smaller lips, *labia minora*. The small lips are joined at the top by the clitoris, a small body of tissue about a quarter-inch in length, corresponding to the glans of the penis. The clitoris is usually well covered by the upper folds of the outer lips, and contains many blood vessels which, upon sexual stimulation, dilate and fill up, causing an enlargement or small erection of the organ. It is tipped with a cluster of nerves, which are involved in the erectile process, and which stimulate the pleasurable sensations of intercourse.

Directly below the clitoris and on either side of the urinary duct, a colorless lubricating substance, similar to that from Cowper's gland in the male, is secreted during sexual excitement. As an additional lubricant, Bartholin's glands, a short distance from the vagina, produce a mucous secretion which prevents the friction of intercourse from irritating the tender membranes. Love play and petting stimulate these glands, thus preparing the female for intercourse. Ordinarily, the amount of secretion is a fair index of the erotic readiness for intercourse.[57] Beyond the vulva is the vagina, a hollow tube which extends backward and upward, containing many muscular folds capable of expanding to accommodate a large penis or of contracting to enfold a smaller one. Thus, the size of the male penis usually has little to do with good or bad sexual response. The vaginal opening enlarges with time and with intercourse experience; because the vagina is capable of great stretching after adequate secretory stimulation, there is little likelihood of pain from penis penetration. After penis penetration the couple should give a little time for the accommodation of one organ to the proportions of the other. Intercourse may then proceed.

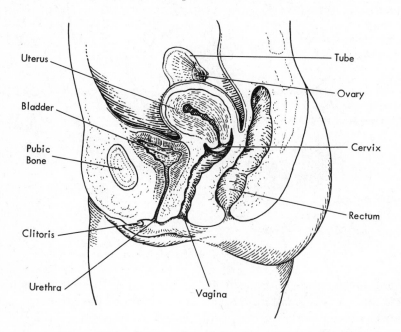

Uterus
Bladder
Pubic Bone
Clitoris
Urethra
Vagina
Tube
Ovary
Cervix
Rectum

Figure 12-3. Cross section of female sexual anatomy.

Sexual climax, or orgasm, is obvious in the male, for it induces ejaculation; the seman is ejected in a series of spasms, and shortly thereafter the penis begins to relax. In the female orgasm, the vaginal muscles contract, and there is a throbbing of the pelvic floor. Usually there is increased quickening of breath and perhaps an exquisite tingling sensation for a few moments. There may be spasmodic throbbing and even constriction in the genitalia area that gives the female intense pleasure. Some authorities believe that orgasm either from the clitoris or from deep vaginal stimulation is possible in the woman. Continued penile contact with the clitoral region, however, is considered the best way to induce the fullest female response.[58]

This fundamental knowledge of both male and female anatomy and response often provides a couple with a much stronger start toward a satisfactory sexual adjustment.

Lack of fundamental technical knowledge on the performance of the sex act can limit sexual adjustment for some couples. This does not mean that sexual maladjustment is often caused by faulty techniques. Although the technique may be somewhat clumsy and awkward at first, this is probably the least matter for concern with most couples. Partners should learn a technique together, because the particular technique of one couple is not necessarily the best for another. There are, however, a few basic practices that all couples should know.

First of all, extensive foreplay or preparation is needed, especially by the female. Husbands should be cautioned against rushing the sex act. Feelings of guilt or nastiness associated with sex sometimes drives the male to extreme haste, as though he were anxious to get it over with. Such undue haste deprives the wife of the sexual excitement and stimulation resulting from natural physical stimulation and psychological readiness. Indeed, expressions of love and special tenderness earlier in the evening prepare the wife to welcome later advances.

There is no rule of sexual behavior that can guarantee orgasm. Achieving climax is essentially an experience that each couple must learn together, but the proper preparation of the female for the sex act is essential. Terman's study found that only 8.7 per cent of happy wives reported that the husband did not prepare them long enough before coitus, while 41.7 per cent of the unhappy wives so reported.[59] In King's study, 12 per cent of the wives reported that their husbands did not pet long enough before actual intercourse. Furthermore, these wives felt that had there been more petting they would have experienced a higher degree of complete sexual satisfaction.[60] Thus, the cardinal principle, as fas as techniques of successful coitus are concerned, is for the husband to take plenty of time to prepare the wife, both physically and psychologically. This would include caresses, kindly words, appreciative remarks, expressions of devotion, all intermingled with physical love-making itself. The more modest or shy the wife is, the more likely she is to need and appreciate this preliminary courting. The sex act should be led to gradually as the culmination of a series of love expressions. It is a rare woman who would find pleasure in being surprised by her mate's hurrying through the sex act.

The studies of Kinsey indicate that women are not much slower than men at reaching a climax in intercourse if they have been adequately aroused.[61] A complaint often registered by wives, however, is that husbands are too eager to end the act after the climax. Afterplay should be as well considered as foreplay, and after intercourse there should be a time for peaceful relaxation together, which idealistically ends in refreshing sleep.

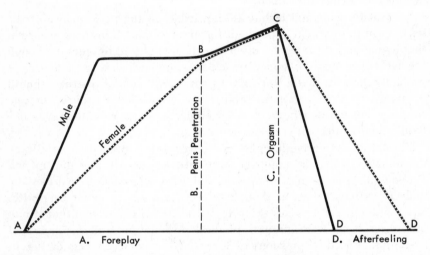

Figure 12-4. **Male and female response in the sex act.**

Another fundamental factor of technique is the attitude of each spouse to the "normal" method of performing the sex act. Actually, almost any method of performing coitus may be considered natural and normal if the couple mutually desires or accepts it. There is no precise way to perform the sex act. Kinsey's research indicates that about 50 per cent of married college graduates, with mutual acceptance, occasionally try something other than the method considered orthodox in their culture.[62] Burgess and Cottrell concluded from their research that there is a wide variation in sex behavior from couple to couple, and from time to time in the same couple. Furthermore, they believed that variations in the sexual act did not constitute a problem of adjustment unless they operated to produce chronic frustrations or reactions against sexual activity.[63] It is probably safe to say that, as long as husbands and wives find that whatever they do is mutually agreeable, the method enjoyed makes little difference. Consistent with physical well-being, no restrictions need be placed upon the method of expression, the frequency of expression, the intensity of expression, or the duration of expression throughout the couple's lifetime of sexual activity.

It is not true that only vulgar or degenerate people are pleased by sexual experimentation beyond that commonly considered "proper." In fact, anthropological studies show that several coital methods accepted as "moral" in the American culture are considered immoral by other groups. A variety of methods, depending upon the circumstances at the particular time, rather than repetitive routine, may actually be best for most couples. Modern couples seem to prefer the attitude that any method is good as long as both partners are happy with it. This includes various positions as well as other intimacies. Kinsey's studies suggest that more young couples are trying various methods today without any ill effects upon their sexual adjustment.[64]

Couples should be very cautious in applying suggestions given in books advocating a "standard" technique. Such standardized practices do not express an individual couple's sincere and natural feelings. Certainly, a knowledge of technical details in the art of love may be helpful, but their practice does not guarantee complete sexual adjustment. Indeed, research studies show only a slight correlation between sexual-satisfaction scores and the use of techniques advocated by most sexologists.[65] Anything in a standard technique book should be considered only as generally descriptive or as an *approximate* guide. Coital behavior should be subject to change according to the inclinations of the individual couple. There is no standard technique that is perfect for all couples. As Ellzey has stated so well: "Sex is not just a matter of anatomy. If it were we could prepare anyone for sex adjustment in marriage in about fifteen minutes."[66]

Meaning and purpose of sex

The meaning and purpose of sex may be at variance between partners. This is particularly true when the mates come from different social backgrounds. To some women a kiss is a prelude to more intimate relations leading to coitus, while for others kissing is no more significant than a social greeting.

PHYSICAL PLEASURE. Some people use sex as a means of personal gratification, enjoying it only as a pleasurable, physical sensation, but the limitations of sex are severe when it is used only in this way. If the goal of coitus is simply physical pleasure, then tensions are sure to increase when there are shortcomings. In his study, King discovered that the best sexual adjustment was found among wives who before marriage regarded sex with (1) interest and pleasant anticipation, or (2) indifference or even disgust, but not with an eager longing for physical ecstasy.[67]

It is probably safe to say that some of the disappointment in modern marital sex relations occurs because tremendous expectations of sexual pleasure, beyond the possibility of fulfillment, are built up for the couple. Many descriptions in the literature of the manifestations of orgasm are often more poetic than real. Rarely experienced physical sensations are made to seem almost inevitable in every experience. Then, too, the literature has often put too much emphasis upon both sexes reaching simultaneous orgasm; when not achieved, and most often it is not, the disappointment can lead to feelings of inadequacy and failure.

Too often tensions are built up as a couple attempts to reach the exotic physical reaction they have read about. The strain of trying to reach this legendary state and the fear of failure may then prevent even normal pleasures.[68] It is possible that self-conscious efforts to achieve completeness in sex relations may actually hinder marital adjustment. The false standard of expecting orgasm every time within the sex act may cause considerable frustration. Kavinoky, a physician, believes that the fear of inability to measure up to this American culture standard has contributed to frigidity, impotence, and many other marriage problems.[69] Yet there has been no clinical evidence proving that all women have the capacity for climax during intercourse.[70] Streker, a psychiatrist, believes that the physical rewards of the perfect sexual relationship have been too greatly emphasized by his own profession as well as in fiction and so-called scientific literature.[71]

EMOTIONAL GRATIFICATION. Besides the immediate sensual pleasures, sex may also serve deep emotional needs. It can be used as a means of expressing the devotion and belief of each spouse in the other. Many wives today are comparatively undisturbed by their failure to achieve orgasm every time. Even though she herself may not reach orgasm, a woman often finds satisfaction in knowing that her husband has, and in the realization that she has contributed to his pleasure.[72] There is a certain satisfaction in being directly responsible for giving pleasure to one's mate. People may engage in sex, not to become physically excited, but to express their love for their mates. This is especially true of many women.

Sex is sometimes indulged in as an impersonal adventure, with no deeper purpose than immediate pursuit and conquest. For some, this means an expression of sympathy and pity. It may be a way of seeking emotional self-assurance. It can be an expression of anxiety or the need for punishment. It can be a weapon to hurt someone, to withhold from somebody, to make someone jealous, or to avenge or defile another. Some women and some men think of marriage as little more than legalized prostitution, a license insuring protection, affection, or some other material value, and this affords them emotional assurance.

PROCREATION. The basic biological purpose of sex is the preservation of the species. The basic social purpose of marriage is the propagation of the culture and the society. The government of almost every nation reduces taxes for the family with the birth of each child. Because almost every government is aware that its people, its children, and its infants are its greatest natural resource, in times of emergency it conscripts single men first, married men later, and fathers of the largest families perhaps not at all. Although methods of planning for children may be in dispute throughout the world, the need for procreation has rarely been challenged.

Yet, if the purpose of sex were reproduction alone, then most couples would not engage in intimate relations very frequently during their lives. Obviously, procreation, though fundamental, is not the only element necessary for sexual harmony; rather, the couple's attitudes toward procreation should be in harmony for good sexual adjustment.

COMMUNICATION. Another purpose of sex within marriage is that of communication. The very definition of the word *intercourse* implies this. Simple physical release is copulation, but intercourse is possible only in associations representing an interchange and sharing of feelings; it is not an accidental occurrence but, rather, an achievement. Sexual contact with a prostitute is not the same sharing experience as is the relationship between a loving husband and wife. In the latter case there is an attitude of affectionate sharing and an earnest desire to communicate their feelings for one another, a consecration of their love. In true sexual intercourse there is a direct meeting of two human beings, expressing within the mutual act a complete giving—not only to each other but to the marital relationship as a whole. This sexual communication can be deeper than speech, containing secrets which verbal articulation can never capture. Intercourse is a language of complete self-surrender which cannot be fully expressed in any other way.[73] The Bible phrases sexual consummation as the husband and wife's coming to "know" each other, and this is truly what intercourse is.

In man, the sexual experience is not limited by the act itself or by a specific time. It offers multiple rewards, including direct sexual gratification and the emotional satisfaction of fulfilling the needs of the partner and the relationship. Sex within marriage goes far beyond procreation for it plays such a strong role in enriching happiness, personality development, and the couple's entire marital existence. It is a communicative effort as well as a procreative endeavor. Sex is unification, for it is a means of uniting two persons. Through intercourse, the two become one, both physically and spiritually. Sex, then, can be legitimately used not only to reproduce but also to intensify, beautify, and consecrate a love that two people have for each other. It is the most intimate expression of the interrelatedness of two persons. As Baber has stated: "To consider sex entirely physical is as crude as to define violin music as merely horsehair scraping on catgut; to make sex entirely psychic is to deny our animal origin."[74] Stokes writes:

> Much as I value the experience of good sex, all my life I have felt that the mutually trusting, affectionate relationship comes first and that without it sex is reduced to an unsatisfactory caricature.[75]

In American society today, emphasis on sexual purpose seems to be shifting away from procreation and closer toward a communicating, unifying endeavor, that ultimately should lead to creative achievements. Actually, the swing seems to have halted momentarily on a rather hedonistic emphasis on sex for sheer personal fun and physical pleasure or as a means of reassurance for the partner.

Americans are indeed in a stage of flux as the culture slowly moves toward the acceptance of more meaningful sex relationships based on the individual's personal needs as well as those of society. Couples may achieve this now if they make every effort to establish the proper attitudes in the beginning of their marriage.

MULTIPURPOSED ENDEAVOR.   Sex within modern marriage is actually a multipurposed endeavor; that is, it can serve different purposes at different times. It can provide pleasure or relief, the rejuvenation of a tired body or spirit, the means of expressing love, or the creation of a stronger relationship; it may even provide children. It may be used to achieve all these goals at the same time, or any one of them at chosen times, and still be right within a given marriage. Perhaps this variety is best described by Levy and Munroe:

> Sometimes the pair will be close and affectionate. Tenderness will pass into a rather solemn possession, a confirmation of their abiding love for each other. At other times their mood will be wholly frivolous. Intercourse then will be just a rattling good time without deeper implications. Or the husband will seek protection and cuddling at his wife's breast. Or he will lie like a girl while she takes possession of his body. At times he will vulgarize the act with smutty words or take a fine pleasure in hurting his wife and forcing her to his will. Or the couple may play at an illicit relationship, acting out a little seduction farce for their own benefit. They will try out odd positions and experiment with unusual parts of the body. Often, too, intercourse will be a routine satisfaction of bodily need about as romantic as orange juice, toast, and coffee for breakfast. Uninhibited married couples will take all of these variations and find them good.[76]

Summary

Sex provides an opportunity to make a good marriage even better. Couples are involved in the sex relationship constantly, for it is a recurring biological urge, requiring great cooperation.

To attain sexual harmony, each partner should accept the other as a human being entitled to a personal life as well as to sexual fulfillment.

It is also necessary to accept oneself as a man or a woman and to accept the privileges and responsibilities accorded that gender by nature and society. The sexual drive should be neither resented nor denied, especially because it is the sexual element that makes marriage different from all other enduring human relationships. Obviously, there would be little marriage without the sexual element which is the source of both the physical and the psychic attraction between men and women.

Sex fulfillment in marriage does not happen by accident; it is achieved through insight stemming from knowledge. It is neither sacred nor sinful, but can be affected by personal attitude. Sex is the elemental power that polarizes the entire marriage.

A good sex relationship within marriage is worth every effort. Now that sex has been raised to the plane of a creative achievement, it may be considered in terms of an art. Any art, however, requires time, patience, thoughtfulness, perseverance, and understanding for its fullest development.

If a couple feel they are not achieving sexual harmony within marriage, they should seek help. Some gain sufficient help from books on the subject; others need experienced counselors. To seek help with sexual adjustment is not something of which to be ashamed; it is a sign of intelligent recognition of a serious problem which merits attention and respect.

There are degrees of achievement in sex relations as there are in all other aspects of marriage. Human beings never reach perfection in anything, at best they merely approach the ideal. If a couple is successful in their sexual relations a good portion of the time, then they have attained a reasonable degree of sexual adjustment. It is important that at various times the couple find within their sexual experience together adventure, excitement, release from tension, contentment, unity and spiritual oneness, and even comfort or consolation in times of sorrow or trouble. Successful sexual intercourse should help promote the joy, solidarity, stability, and creativeness of the entire marriage.

Notes

1. Judson T. Landis, "Adjustment After Marriage," *Marriage and Family Living,* 9:33.

2. Isabell Drummond, *The Sex Paradox* (New York: G. P. Putnam's Sons, 1953), p. 319.

3. Lewis M. Terman, *Psychological Factors in Marital Happiness* (New York: McGraw-Hill Book Company, Inc., 1938), p. 373.

4. Katharine B. Davis, *Factors in the Sex Life of Twenty-Two Hundred Women* (New York: Harper & Row, Publishers, 1929), p. 38.

5. Bruce Thomason, "The Relationship of Certain Aspects of Marital Sexual Behavior to Total Marital Adjustment," The University of Florida, Gainesville, Fla. Mimeographed.

6. A. C. Kinsey, *et al., Sexual Behavior in the Human Female* (Philadelphia: W. B. Saunders Company, 1953), p. 393.

7. Abraham and Hanna Stone, *A Marriage Manual,* rev. ed. (New York: Simon and Schuster, Inc., 1952), p. 208.

8. Terman, *op. cit.,* pp. 300–309.

9. *Ibid.*

10. Gilbert V. Hamilton, *A Research in Marriage* (New York: Albert and Charles Boni, 1929), Chap. 22.

11. For a more recent study which suggests this see Paul Wallin, "A Study of Orgasm as a Condition of Women's Enjoyment of Intercourse," *Journal of Social Psychology*, 51:191–98.

12. Walter R. Stokes, "How Important Is the Wife's Orgasm?" *Sexology Magazine* (March 1965), 512–14.

13. Clifford Adams, "An Informal Preliminary Report on Some Factors Relating to Sexual Responsiveness of Certain College Wives" (University Park, Pa.: Pennsylvania State University, 1953).

14. Judson T. and Mary G. Landis, *Building a Successful Marriage,* 4th ed. (Englewood Cliffs, N.J.: Prentice-Hall, Inc., 1963), p. 389.

15. Kinsey (1953), *op. cit.,* p. 408.

16. O. L. Timklepaugh, "The Nature of Periods of Sex Desire in Women and Their Relation to Ovulation," *American Journal of Obstetrics and Gynecology,* 26:339.

17. A. C. Kinsey, *et al., Sexual Behavior in the Human Male* (Philadelphia: W. B. Saunders Company, 1948), p. 585.

18. Paul Gebard, Director of the Institute for Sex Research, Bloomington, Ind. (commonly called the Kinsey Institute), reported to the Ohio Council on Family Relations annual meeting in Dayton (April 24, 1964) that this is exactly what is taking place today. That is, the frequency of marital coitus is decreasing, being governed more by wives' initiation than formerly and as a result the percentage of episodes ending in orgasm for wives is increasing.

19. William M. Kephart, *The Family, Society and the Individual* (Boston: Houghton Mifflin Company, 1961), p. 9.

20. Clellan S. Ford and Frank A. Beach, *Patterns of Sexual Behavior* (New York: Harper & Row, Publishers, 1951), pp. 261–67.

21. Kinsey (1953), *op. cit.,* p. 392.

22. Timklepaugh, *op. cit.,* p. 335.

23. Kinsey (1953), *op. cit.,* Chap. 16; and for an interesting article relating to the biological differences in women and men, see Frank K. Shuttleworth, "A Biosocial and Developmental Theory of Male and Female Sexuality," *Marriage and Family Living,* 21:163–70.

24. See, e.g., Terman, *op. cit.,* Chaps. 11 and 12; and E. W. Burgess and Paul Wallin, *Engagement and Marriage* (Philadelphia: J. B. Lippincott & Co., 1953), Chap. 20.

25. Clifford Kirkpatrick, *The Family* (New York: The Ronald Press Company, 1955), p. 439.

26. See, e.g., Hamilton, *op. cit.*

27. Kinsey (1953), *op. cit.,* pp. 375–76.

28. Terman, *op. cit.,* p. 305.

29. Kinsey (1948), *op. cit.,* p. 195.

30. Kinsey (1948), *op. cit.,* pp. 231–35; and Kinsey (1953), *op. cit.,* p. 569.

31. Gustave Newman and Claude R. Nichols, "Sexual Activities and Attitudes in Older Persons," *Journal of the American Medical Association* (May 7, 1960), pp. 33–35.

32. Isadore Rubin, "Sex over 65," *Sexology,* 28:622–25.

33. Kinsey (1953), *op. cit.,* pp. 569–71.

34. Paul Wallin and Alexander Clark, "Marital Satisfaction and Husbands' and Wives' Perception of Similarity in Their Preferred Frequency of Coitus," *Journal of Abnormal and Social Psychology,* 57:370–73.

35. Ruth Benedict, "Continuities and Discontinuities in Cultural Conditioning," *Psychiatry* (May 1939), 161–67.

36. Kinsey (1948), *op. cit.,* pp. 573–82.

37. Margaret Mead, *Sex and Temperament in Three Primitive Societies* (New York: William Morrow & Co., Inc., 1935).

38. Ray E. Baber, *Marriage and the Family* (New York: McGraw-Hill Book Company, Inc., 1953), p. 245.

39. Robert L. Dickinson and Lura Beam, *A Thousand Marriages* (Baltimore: The Williams and Wilkins Co., 1931).

40. Kinsey (1953), *op. cit.,* Part III.

41. Hamilton, *op. cit.,* p. 298.

42. Gladys O. Terry, "A Study of Psychodynamic Patterns," *American Journal of Psychiatry,* 8:881–99.

43. E. W. Burgess and Leonard S. Cottrell, *Predicting Success or Failure in Marriage* (Englewood Cliffs, N.J.: Prentice-Hall, Inc., 1939), pp. 218–43.

44. Karl A. Menninger, "Impotence and Frigidity," *Bulletin, Menninger Clinic* (1937), 251–60.

45. Terman, *op. cit.,* p. 373.

46. Charles E. King, "The Sex Factor in Marital Adjustment," *Marriage and Family Living,* 16:237–38.

47. *Statistical Bulletin,* Metropolitan Life Insurance Company (January 1960), 5.

48. Dr. John Rock, M.D., in a Kennedy Lecture at Ohio University (January 12, 1965), reported there are over 4 million constant users of oral contraceptives in the United States today, many of whom have found a "new lease on sexuality" because of it. This is further substantiated by Monte J. Meldman, M.D., who states in effect that a by-product of birth-control pills is that some women have become more interested and willing to have intercourse. See Monte J. Meldman, M.D., in *Psychosomatics* (May–June 1964).

49. Harvey J. Locke, *Predicting Adjustment in Marriage* (New York: Holt, Rinehart & Winston, Inc., 1951), p. 144.

50. Walter Stokes, *Modern Pattern for Marriage* (New York: Holt, Rinehart & Winston, Inc., 1948), p. 22.

51. Oliver M. Butterfield, *Love Problems of Adolescents* (New York: Emerson Books, Inc., 1941), p. 45.

52. Burgess and Cottrell, *op. cit.,* p. 221.

53. Jacques Leclerzq, *Marriage and the Family, A Study in Social Philosophy,* translated by Thomas R. Hanley (New York: Pustet, 1942), p. 295; and G. A. Seward, *Sex and the Social Order* (New York: McGraw-Hill Book Company, Inc., 1946), p. 226.

54. Unpublished research of the author.

55. See, e.g., "Plight of the Young Mother" (February, 1956); or "My Fifteen-Hour Day" (April 1956), *The Ladies' Home Journal.*

56. See W. L. Stone, "Sex Ignorance of College Students," *Family Life,* 20:1–3.

57. For a more detailed discussion see William C. Young (ed.), *Sex and Internal Secretions,* 3rd ed. (Baltimore: The Williams & Wilkins Co., 1961), Vols. I and II.

58. See, e.g., G. Lombard Kelly, *Sex Manual* (Augusta, Georgia: Southern Medical Supply Company, 1953), p. 35.

59. Terman, *op. cit.,* p. 373.

60. King, *op. cit.,* p. 238.

61. Kinsey (1953), *op. cit.,* p. 626.

62. *Ibid.,* p. 361.

63. Burgess and Cottrell, *op. cit.,* Chap. 12.

64. Kinsey (1953), *op. cit.,* p. 400.

65. Terman, *op. cit.,* Appendix I.

66. W. Clark Ellzey, *How to Keep Romance in Your Marriage* (New York: Association Press, 1953).

67. King, *op. cit.,* p. 240.

68. Case studies by both Lehfeld and Ellis suggest that much of female frigidity is caused not from deep-seated feelings of guilt, shame, or hostility, but rather from the horror of making a mistake or of being incompetent. See Hans Lehfeld, M.D., and Albert Ellis, "Symposium on Aspects of Female Sexuality," *Quarterly Review of Surgery, Obstetrics and Gynecology* (October–December 1959), 217–63.

69. Nadina Kavinoky, "Premarital Examination," *Western Journal of Surgery, Obstetrics and Gynecology,* 51:315.

70. It needs to be noted, however, that the work of Dr. William H. Masters, in St. Louis, suggests that *practically all* women can experience orgasm, but that the experience is so mild in some that it may not be recognized for what it is. In regard to this, Davis goes so far as to suggest that today's wives have a duty to enjoy sex. See Maxine Davis, *Sexual Responsibility in Marriage* (New York: The Dial Press, Inc., 1964).

71. Edward A. Streker, "A Doctor Looks at Marital Infidelity," *This Week Magazine* (June 8, 1952), 22.

72. Kinsey (1953), *op. cit.,* p. 371.

73. Lester A. Kirkendall, "Semantics and Sexual Communication," *The Family Life Coordinator,* 7:63–65.

74. Baber, *op. cit.,* p. 240.

75. Stokes, Walter R., "How Important Is the Wife's Orgasm?" *Sexology Magazine* (March 1965), 512–14.

76. John Levy and Ruth Munroe, *The Happy Family* (New York: Alfred A. Knopf, Inc., 1938), p. 129.

Questions for further thought

1. Is the idea of sex within marriage as a creative activity consistent with the American democratic spirit?

2. In what ways might sexual satisfaction contribute as much to a "oneness" in marriage as it does to self-realization?

3. How is it possible for young people today to have so much misinformation about sexual activity?

4. Is talking to each other about their sexual relation likely to destroy some of its spiritual quality for a couple?

5. Suppose a young couple have been happily married and the sex adjustment has been quite satisfactory. Now all at once the wife notices the husband is reading books on various sex techniques and attempting to bring some of these new and somewhat startling practices into their life. What suggestions are in order?

6. What suggestions are in order for a young wife who loves her husband very much, but after three years of marriage has never experienced orgasm in their sexual relationship?

7. Do men experience something similar to menopause?

8. When older people lose most of their physical appeal, how can they continue to find one another sexually attractive or interesting?

9. Is unremedial sexual incompatibility justifiable grounds for divorce?
10. Is Balzac correct when he states: "A husband's interest and honor alike enjoin that he should never permit himself a sexual gratification which he has not made his wife desire as well"?

Suggested supplemental readings

BOOKS

Bailey, Derrick S. *Sexual Relations in Christian Thought.* New York: Harper & Row, Publishers, 1959.

Beigel, Hugo G. *Sex from A to Z.* New York: Stephen Daye Press, 1961.

Baruch, Dorothy W., and Hyman Miller. *Sex in Marriage.* New York: Hoeber, 1963.

Brown, Fred, and Rudolph T. Kempton. *Sex Questions and Answers,* rev. ed. New York: McGraw-Hill Book Company, Inc., 1960.

Butterfield, Oliver M. *Sexual Harmony in Marriage,* rev. ed. New York: Emerson, 1953.

Calderone, Mary Steichen and Phyllis, and Robert Goldman. *Release from Sexual Tensions.* New York: Random House, 1960.

Caprio, Frank S. *The Power of Sex.* New York: Citadel Press, 1962.

Chesser, Eustace. *Love Without Fear: How to Achieve Sex Happiness in Marriage.* New York: Signet Books, 1949.

Clark, Lemon, and Isadore Rubin (eds.). *150 Sex Questions and Answers.* New York: Health Publications, 1960.

Davis, Maxine. *The Sexual Responsibility of Woman.* New York: The Dial Press, Inc., 1956.

————. *Sexual Responsibility in Marriage.* New York: The Dial Press, Inc., 1964.

Eichenlaub, John E., M.D. *The Marriage Art.* New York: Lyle Stuart, 1961.

Freud, Sigmund. *Three Essays on the Theory of Sexuality,* translated and newly edited by James Strachey. New York: Basic Books, Inc., 1963.

Friedman, Leonard J. *Virgin Wives: A Study of Unconsummated Marriages.* Springfield, Ill.: Charles C Thomas, Publisher, 1962.

Henriques, Fernando. *Love in Action: The Sociology of Sex.* New York: E. P. Dutton & Co., Inc., 1960.

Kronhausen, Phyllis and Eberhard. *The Sexually Responsive Woman.* New York: Grove Press, 1964.

Levy, John, and Ruth Munroe. *The Happy Family.* New York: Alfred A. Knopf, Inc., 1938. Chap. 4.

Liswood, Rebeca. *A Marriage Doctor Speaks Her Mind About Sex.* New York: E. P. Dutton & Co., Inc., 1961.

Rainer, Jerome and Julia. *Sexual Pleasure in Marriage.* New York: Julian Messner, Inc., 1962.

Robinson, Marie N. *The Power of Sexual Surrender.* New York: The New American Library of World Literature, 1962.

Stokes, Walter R., M.D. *Married Love in Today's World.* New York: Citadel Press, 1962.

————. *Your Sex Life,* 2nd ed., New York: Sexology Corporation, 1961.

Stone, Hannah M. and Abraham. *A Marriage Manual.* New York: Simon and Schuster, Inc., 1953.

ARTICLES

Ard, Ben Neal, Jr. "Sexual Behavior and Attitudes for Marital Partners," *Dissertation Abstracts,* **23:**349.

Ellis, Albert. "Psychological Aspects of Discouraging Contraception," *Realist* (April 1959), 11–13.

Foot, Nelson. "Sex as Play," *Social Problems,* 4:159–63.

Kirkendall, Lester A. "Toward a Clarification of the Concept of Male Sex Drive," *Marriage and Family Living,* 20:368.

Landis, Judson T., and Thomas Poffenberger, "The Marital and Sexual Adjustment of 330 Couples Who Chose Vasectomy as a Form of Birth Control," *Marriage and the Family* (formerly titled *Marriage and Family Living*), 27:57–58.

"Plight of the Young Mother" (February 1956) or "My Fifteen-Hour Day" (April 1956), *The Ladies' Home Journal.*

Wallin, Paul, and Alexander Clark, "Cultural Norms and Husbands' and Wives' Reports of Their Marital Partner's Preferred Frequency of Coitus Relative to Their Own," *Sociometry,* 21:247–54.

Spending money

chapter 13

in marriage

In today's marriages money is either a factor for harmony or a focal point of conflict. Its proper use is probably more important than ever before in predicting happiness or unhappiness in marriage. As a matter of fact, there is some speculation, largely based on evidence of the increasing acceptance of newer concepts regarding sex, that, if not at present, certainly before long, money may become the major adjustment area within marriage.

An increasing dependency upon money

America as a society has become increasingly dependent upon money. It is not that Americans are incurably afflicted with materialistic greed but, rather that every member of the family needs money to live. In today's industrial society, the individual's survival depends almost entirely upon his acquisition of money. Indeed, if the citizen has no means of acquiring currency, it is necessary for the government to give it to him. Because of this financial necessity, money has become a chronic preoccupation of almost every adult. What Lynd said about the American family economy applies even more today: "Never before has so much of a living been bought."[1] Today, very few of the daily needs are produced at home. Winch illustrates the contrast between the present-day American family economy and that of a former era by a farmer's remarks in 1787:

> At this time my farm gave me and my whole family a good living on the produce of it, and left me one year with another 150 silver dollars, for I

283

never spent more than $10.00 a year, which was for salt, nails, and the like. Nothing to eat, drink, or wear was bought, as my farm produced all.[2]

Since 1930 the quantity of goods and services purchased for family consumption has increased about 60 per cent. When measured by the population increase since that time, it appears that some materials and services have increased far more. For example, expenditures for purchases of homes have increased more than 470 per cent; automobile purchase and operation expenses have increased 205 per cent, and commercial-type recreation has increased tremendously. In fact more than $6 billion is spent each year by American families for vacations.[3]

PRESSURES IN SOCIETY. In today's society, there are many pressures forcing individuals to spend money on things that were formerly unknown. For example, today there is much more employer concern over how the employee lives and on what he spends his money. When attaining a higher income bracket, the worker frequently acquires additional obligations, such as travel, subscriptions, contributions, memberships, and even social events. Major social organizations may be joined to promote business contacts.

CHANGES IN DEFINITION OF NECESSITIES. Many things that were once considered luxuries in a home are now considered necessities. At present, for example, six out of ten families are homeowners, with more than 50 per cent of the homes under heavy mortgage. Seventy-five per cent of today's American families own at least one automobile, and more than 10 per cent have at least two cars. More than 80 per cent own at least one television set, electric refrigerator, range, or automatic washing machine. Although it is estimated that about 7 per cent of earned income is put into savings or investments, this comes mainly from the top brackets. Installment debts are owed by more than 60 per cent of American family heads between the ages of twenty-five and thirty-four; 51 per cent of those between the ages of thirty-five and forty-four; and 42 per cent of those between the ages of fifty-five and sixty-four.[4] Because of these circumstances, many families are forced to borrow on their future, hoping to acquire additional income to pay for ever-increasing "necessities." If an unemployment crisis should arise (as in 1933 when 13 million men were unemployed), the impact on the entire American marriage and family system would be almost unimaginable. In the period between 1926 and 1936 more than 1.6 million homes went on the auction block.[5]

INCREASED GOVERNMENTAL PLANNING. Increased government economic planning also effects the family's money adjustments. Today's worker has two kinds of salary. One is earned pay; the other, cash take-home pay. Deductions are made from the gross earnings for federal income tax, social security, state income tax, retirement or pensions, various charitable contributions, and health- and disability-insurance programs.

Figure 13-1. Today's worker has two kinds of salary: earned salary, and take-home pay. (Courtesy of the New York Life Insurance Company.)

RISE IN LIVING COSTS. The present economic pattern is still spiraling upward, and each family works to gain enough income to keep up with rising living costs. Incomes have indeed increased along with costs. In fact, since the turn of the twentieth century, the average family income has risen from $651 to about $6500 per year.[6] The cost of living, however, has also increased since that time, and it actually takes much more money to live than it did before.

The Consumer Price Index (commonly called the CPI) measures the average changes in the price of specific goods and services bought by city families of wage earners and clerical workers. It is based on the prices of about 300 items, which are selected to represent all goods and services purchased by such families in forty-six cities. Detailed reports are issued monthly by the U.S. Bureau of Labor and are available upon request. For example, using 1935–39 as the 100 index years, the cost of living index by 1948–49 shows a rise to about 170. Using 1948–49 as 100, an additional increase of 40 per cent is derived for 1965.[7] The CPI, however, may be more advanced today than the figures indicate, for many new goods and services now represent noteworthy expenditures in the American economy. As an example, the medical-care component of the CPI increased three times more than the rest of the items in 1961.[8] The U.S. Department of Labor is at present undertaking a comprehensive survey of consumer spending habits as a prelude to re-evaluating and revising the list of items contained in the CPI.

A WIDE DEVIATION FROM THE MEAN. There seems to be wide differences in the distribution of family income; to speak of an average income per family in the United States does not give an accurate picture of the over-all situation. For example, although the average annual family income was listed in 1964 as $6500, the U.S. Bureau of the Census listed over 5 million American families with incomes of less than $2000; 16 million with incomes between $2000 and $6000; more than 22 million with incomes between $6000 and $15,000; and about 2.5 million with incomes of $15,000 or more.[9]

It is probably safe to say that money today has much less than half the purchasing power it had before World War II, although the actual dollars earned have not been completely absorbed by the rising cost of living.

Relation of income size to marital happiness

American families are at present greater consumers than producers, but what relationship does this economic fact have to marital happiness?

MODERATE INCOMES. Hamilton's study failed to show any relationship whatsoever between income and the degree of marital happiness or success.[10] The dividing point for comparisons in his study, however, was $5000, which probably accounts for the negative results. In 1929, the year his study was published, $5000 was too high a dividing point to show much significance in either direction. The studies by Burgess and Cottrell and by Terman also failed to find a consistent relationship between amount of income and marital happiness.[11] It must be stressed, however, that an overwhelming majority of the couples studied possessed moderate incomes. After reviewing their research findings, also based on a high economic status dividing line, Burgess and Wallin concluded: "The so-called economic factors in marital success can be almost entirely accounted for by other factors, such as personality, family background, and social participation."[12]

LOW INCOMES. Koos made a comparison of families with below-average incomes and families with above-average earnings. He discovered that families with below-average earnings had considerably more internal trouble and suffered more lastingly from such disturbances than did families with better-than-average income. Furthermore, the low-income families had long periods of worry over money matters which had decided negative effects on their marital happiness. When there is insufficient income to purchase essentials, accompanying feelings of insecurity often set up tensions. These, in turn, make the low-income couples irritable and quick-tempered, which results in considerable conflict.[13] Hollingshead made a comparison study of the various socioeconomic classes under public and private psychiatric treatment as compared with the total population. Burgess and Wallin suggest that much of the difficulty over money matters is simply related to personality, but it may be that the marked personality deviation patterns found by Hollingshead had their beginnings from worry over money matters.

Table 13–1. **Comparison of various socioeconomic classes—normal and psychiatric**

Socioeconomic class	Per cent of each class in the normal population	Per cent of each class in the psychiatric population
Upper	3.1	1.0
Upper-middle	8.1	6.7
Lower-middle	22.0	13.2
Upper-lower	46.0	38.6
Lower-lower	17.8	36.8
Unknown	3.0	3.7

Source: August B. Hollingshead and Frederick C. Redlich, "Social Stratification and Psychiatric Disorders," *American Sociological Review*, 18:163–69. Copyright © 1953, by The American Sociological Association, Washington, D.C. Reprinted by permission.

Lang analyzed the happiness ratings of 17,533 marriages, which included sixty different occupational groups. The happiness of these marriages was rated by their friends and acquaintances. The results show quite conclusively that a high proportion of families in low-income occupations had an undue high proportion of unhappy marriages.[14] From his study of divorced couples, Goode suggests that economic factors are significantly related to marital stability; furthermore, of all economic factors, stress from low income is a major consideration in marital failure.[15] Thus, it needs to be noted that, in cases of extremely low income, the lack of money for essentials contributes greatly to marital unhappiness. An additional factor noted by Burgess and Cottrell was that regular income contributes more to happiness than irregular income, regardless of how high the irregular income may be.[16]

EXPECTATIONS VERSUS POSSIBILITIES. The degree of discrepancy between expectations and actual realizations regarding money is an important factor for happiness within marriage. If little is expected, perhaps satisfaction is more easily achieved. If more is expected, satisfaction will be

more difficult to attain. Williamson's findings suggest that marital adjustment is directly related to the differential between the achieved and the
aspired standard of living.[17]

Many people become accustomed to spending more money when they
are single than they will be able to afford during the first years of married life. The level of their parents' standard of living is likely to have
been much higher. This difference should not discourage the young
couple, for they cannot expect to begin at their parents' economic status,
which was probably achieved only after years of hard work and careful
management. Thus, it is necessary for most couples to revise many spending habits after marriage. Usually a couple are willing to sacrifice at first
because of high hopes in the future. When such hopes do not materialize
as rapidly as expected, however, discouragement sets in, frustrations grow,
and marital maladjustments increase.

PROFESSIONALS BEGIN LOW.   Many professions at first offer only a low
income. If the couple can endure on those terms for a time, in all probability their financial condition will improve. The husband who is working toward a doctorate, for example, may be a graduate assistant for
some time. Such a job usually pays very little, and economic existence
is a struggle. This usually causes double difficulty because of the higher
aspirations of the couple and their family background levels of greater-
than-average expectation. Throughout this period there may be the added
apprehension that sacrifice and hardship are no guarantee that the husband will be awarded the degree. Then too, specialized professions demand further financial sacrifice even after degree attainment. Those who
are successful in training for the medical profession must then serve a
long internship with relatively low pay. Almost every young lawyer has
a low income until his reputation is established. It is probably safe to
say that, in relation to what most young college graduates regard as an
adequate standard of living, they will be at about a break-even point for
a long time after marriage. They may reasonably expect their income
to increase only slightly in the first few years, but to double or triple
after ten to fifteen years.

LIFE-CYCLE VARIATIONS.   There is usually less income at both the beginning and the end of a marriage. Yet frequently more income than
can be earned is needed at the beginning, as the couple try to establish a
home and raise their children, and at the end, when various crises are
likely to arise.

There is little doubt that spending patterns change soon after children
arrive, to provide for increases in such things as food, housing, utilities,
and clothing. Thus couples in the childbearing stage must re-evaluate the
importance of various expenditures. It is mothers with young children
who most often describe the lack of enough money as being a trouble.[18]
The cost of rearing a child has been estimated as three years of the family

Table 13–2. Median annual income for men by age and educational level

Educational level	Age group		
	under 25	*25 to 64*	*65 and over*
Elementary (8 years or less)	$3167	$5002	$2644
1–3 years of high school	3984	6219	3815
High school graduates	4643	6725	4390
College graduates	5054	9415	7287

Source: U.S. Bureau of the Census, Series P-60, *Supplementary Reports*; U.S. Department of Commerce, PC(51)-45 (March 31, 1964). Adapted by permission.

Table 13–3. Median annual income for United States families related to educational level and race of father

Educational level	Nonwhite	White
Less than 8 years	$2600	$3900
8 years	3800	5500
1–3 years of high school	3800	6200
High school graduate	4600	7000
1–3 years of college	5000	8000
College graduates	7200	9900

Source: U.S. Bureau of the Census, Series P-60, No. 43 (September 29, 1964), 1. Adapted by permission.

income, but this does not include a college education. It is presently estimated that, for the average middle-class family with a yearly income of $6200, rearing a child from birth through college costs $29,204 at present price levels.[19] Because children usually arrive ahead of the peak income years of the family, careful budgeting of available funds is essential. Furthermore, children are not cheaper by the dozen. Three children take roughly nine years' earning power of the lifetime budget. The maximum size of the family—that is, two or three children under eighteen—is usually reached when the father is between thirty-five and forty-five, but the maximum family income is not generally attained until the father is between forty-five and fifty-four years old.[20] A raise in pay, however, does not solve the problem if a couple then raise their standard of living accordingly. One research study reports finding a more consistent relationship between expenditures and income changes than between expenditures and income expectations.[21]

Figure 13-2. Rearing a child from birth through college costs $29,204 at present price levels. (Courtesy of The Savings and Loan Foundation, Washington, D.C.)

Table 13–4. Support dependence ratio at various ages

Age of husband		Per cent where dependents are		
	None	*One or more children*	*One or more children and one or more others*	*No children but one or more adults*
Under 25	43	48.1	5.4	3.5
25–29	31.1	56.7	9.0	2.2
30–34	22.1	62.1	12.6	3.2
35–44	17.3	53.1	23.9	5.7
45–54	20.3	25.2	35.0	19.5
55–64	33.2	11.0	24.6	31.2

Source: Paul C. Glick, "The Family Cycle," *American Sociological Review,* **12:**169. Copyright © 1947, by The American Sociological Association, Washington, D.C. Reprinted by permission.

Relation of money to values

Values involve judging the relative worth of things on the basis of the satisfaction or enjoyment they produce. Satisfaction, however, lies not in the purchase but in the purchaser. Marriage adds to the value problem because two persons should agree on every choice. The real problem in marital economics is not the money earned or spent, but the assessment of values the couple wish to attain through the use of money. If the values that each partner holds are not identified during the courtship, there may be great conflict as divergent values are revealed within the marriage. What causes value clashes between a husband and wife? Why would there be different priority ratings for the money available for extras? To understand the dynamics of finance within marriage, it is necessary first to understand the clashes of values.

THE NECESSITY FOR CHOICE. Money is first spent for basic needs; any that is left over is spent for those things desired but not absolutely essential. Seldom do couples have enough money to purchase all they desire, but as soon as a man's survival is assured even temporarily, his desires for goods beyond his actual needs begins to grow. Because basic needs are actually rather few (food, clothing, and shelter), the thousands of products and services desired will never be limited by logical need. Thus, no matter how much income a couple may have, they can always use more. When a few desired things (formerly termed *luxuries*) are acquired, additional possibilities are seen and almost immediately desired. Living necessitates making choices, balancing one value against another. Because there is seldom enough money to cover all the world's goods, successful marital adjustment can be achieved only by mutual agreement of the partners on elective expenditures.

An increase of middle or high average income does not necessarily reduce financial concerns. It usually merely increases the choice of material goods, which in turn can actually increase discord if the couple fail to agree on priority of choice. An increase in income may enable mates to fulfill two choices rather than forcing them to agree on one, but later other things will be strongly desired.

Some people attempt to avoid a mature choice by trying to purchase everything they like, hoping to pay for it in the future. Eventually, many such couples get deeper and deeper into debt, lose their credit rating, their friends, and often their marriage. Couples must decide between desires, for they cannot buy everything. Should they choose a short vacation, a concert series, books, hobby-craft additions, a piece of furniture, a suit for him, or a dress for her? There is no "right" way of spending money, but it should be used in the right direction, which is toward stronger marital harmony. Landis found that approximately one couple in five had never completely agreed on the priority of choices although they had been married on an average of twenty years.[22] Obviously, however, their spending habits did not disrupt their marriage.

SEXUAL DIFFERENCES. The basic differences between the sexes naturally cause some value clashes. The very fact that a man and a woman are making a judgment probably means a difference in value assessment.

These differences may not be great, but they are usually inevitable. Each sex naturally looks at things a little differently. Increases in this difference may be the result of cultural conditioning, but the fact still remains that men, as a group, appear more likely to think in terms of long-range money spending, while women appear more likely to think in terms of short-range money spending. More men seem to enjoy buying a few shares of stock whereas their female counterparts would rather buy something that could be used immediately around the house, such as china.[23]

Part of this difference in values may be explained by traditional role assumptions: man, the earner; woman, the spender. Husbands are largely production-oriented because they must earn the money, whereas wives are largely consumption-oriented because they run the household. Men are more likely to think in terms directly of making and saving money, while women are more likely to think in terms of saving by actually spending money wisely. The woman may think first in terms of her husband making more money and the man in terms of his wife spending more wisely when there are more things desired than funds or credit with which to acquire them.[24]

The extreme ignorance of each sex concerning those things the other considers necessities may also lead to conflict. What some consider elective pleasures, others may consider basic needs. Many young husbands and wives are rather shocked when first learning the cost of the mate's "needs." A husband may like to see his wife well-dressed but may not consider it a necessity in relation to other essentials. Some men have no real conception of what clothing and other womanly essentials actually cost. The wife may also be ignorant of the cost of such minor things as men's haircuts.

BACKGROUND DIFFERENCES. The priority patterns for spending money differ with every family. Thus, when partners come from families with pronounced differences in priority patterns, the likelihood of value clashes increases. Some families assign their most important priorities to such things as clothing, new automobiles, or entertainment. Others give a much higher priority to such things as education, investments for the future, or the purchase of a fine home. One family pattern may insist on saving, another on using; some purchase on credit with an eye toward the future, while others operate on a strict cash basis.

Different socioeconomic-class levels appear to have different priorities for spending. When couples marry across class lines, even standards of entertainment and dress may precipitate clashes. In middle-class society, money in the bank seems to create a peace of mind and a sense of security. Thus, a cross-class marriage may have priority differences not only on how money should be spent but also on whether it should be spent at all. Surveys disclose that family spending habits and patterns differ by social class even though the same income level is enjoyed.[25] Research by

Roth and Peck in this connection found considerable variation in marital-adjustment scores for couples of differing backgrounds.[26]

PERSONALITY DIFFERENCES. Psychiatrists have found that money attitudes are illuminating clues to personality. Some people are incapable of spending money without anxiety, for they find it difficult to let go of anything. At the other extreme is the individual who cannot seem to hold on to anything: if he has money, he must spend it. He has a compulsive urge to spend, which seems to result from a fear of missing something. Closeness with money is sometimes a manifestation of chronic irritability, as is the extreme opposite (spending before the money is earned). These compulsive patterns are symptomatic of deeper personality problems.[27]

DIFFERENCES IN ASPIRATIONS. Sometimes differing aspirations result in clashes even when the partners come from almost identical family backgrounds. In such cases the clashes may be the result of each wishing to have the marriage meet a different group ideal. Sometimes one mate is a social climber while the other has no inclinations at all in this direction. Conspicuous consumption chiefly characterizes those who think they must prove their social worth to others. They feel that fancy cars, memberships in country clubs, and cocktail parties will enable them to reach the upper levels of society. One mate may feel that everything done by the group must be done by the couple, even though the cost is prohibitive. This necessarily delegates other priorities to a lower rung on the ladder.

Some people may not aspire to higher social status but still wish for symbols that will give them a personal feeling of equality with all other individuals. Though they may be financially destitute, such symbols may be more important to them than even basic needs. A typical example is the purchase of a big automobile, which may give an insecure individual the illusion of being "equal" to everyone else.

Because money can buy almost anything, it gives some people the feeling of power over others. In the American culture one often hears the expression, "I wouldn't do that for love or money," implying that money may be equal to love as a power force.

CHANGES IN GOALS. Certain things may lose priority with the years; other values may gain in priority, or new ones may appear. Thus, money adjustment may never reach a plateau of stability.

The relation of happiness to the control of money

Money adjustment also depends upon which partner controls the spending of money. Mates with differing philosophies of control have many adjustments to make.

SOCIAL-CLASS INFLUENCE.   In the upper classes, spending is traditionally controlled by the hierarchy of elders. Their job is to see that money is spent wisely and stays within the family. This can prove frustrating to the younger generation, who prefer that their spending not be subjected to a "board of review."

In many lower socioeconomic families, the principal earner handles all the money and gives it out to the other family members as he sees fit. Most frequently the principal earner is the husband. The philosophy of this system is simply that who ever earns the money has the right to decide how to spend it.

PERSONALITY INFLUENCE.   Sometimes the urge to control money stems from an improverished childhood which fostered a deep sense of insecurity. For some who have developed neurotic tendencies, the control of money may become an unconscious symbol of their dignity. Even though the results may prove them incompetent to handle finances, their need to manage the money remains undiminished. To deny such a person this privilege would probably create more problems than it would solve. Such individuals need professional help in order to change. When this attitude results in irresponsible extravagance, vigorous controls may be the only temporary solution. Free access to savings or checking accounts should not be permitted, for it might lead to disastrous financial results for the family. If such a partner insists on writing checks, perhaps he can be persuaded to put an allowance in a separate account. If both mates are the type who just "burn" money, the envelope system may prove helpful. This means dividing the income into envelopes labeled for specified expenditures, such as groceries or rent; of course, this does not prevent one partner from "raiding" the envelopes. People who possess a reasonable degree of self-discipline would probably find a joint checking account best for them. Indeed, joint accounts are the democratic approach to money management in marriage.

DEMOCRATIC INFLUENCE.   It is ironic that even in American society there are husbands who do not consider the housewife an earner. Yet in a democracy it must be recognized that each partner earns part of the income; thus, each has a right to spend some of it as he chooses. A husband who thinks his wife does not earn money while running the home should be forced to hire a housekeeper for a while. Democratic family living implies that any income is a family affair. It is necessary to self-respect and personal dignity for each mate to have an equal share in the financial planning.

It makes very little difference who actually handles the money in marriage. Roper estimates that wives do about 60 per cent of the actual purchasing independently, but that a team approach to family purchasing is an increasing development among younger couples.[28] Some families solve the shopping dilemma by assigning responsibility for certain purchases to the partner who has more knowledge in that area. Wolgast states that this is especially true in the purchasing of such items as automobiles (the husband making the decision) and household goods (the wife making the decision).[29] Obviously, it would be best for the mate better qualified in a particular field to do the buying in it. Otherwise a division of labor between partners in such activities as buying groceries or paying the rent and utilities should be agreed upon for convenience. Decisions as to who does these things might also depend on available energy, time, and special buying abilities of the mates or of the children (when they are old enough to shop responsibly).

COMING TO TERMS WITH FINANCIAL REALITY. In today's society, it is as important to keep accurate accounts of expenditures as it is to purchase efficiently. This is especially true when it comes to making out income-tax returns. Many a wise purchaser keeps such inefficient books that most of the savings are wasted needlessly in extra taxes.

Another aspect of a realistic financial sense is for the principal earner to concentrate more on advancing in his profession than on reducing expenditures. It is indeed a mistake to use time which could be spent ordinarily earning more money to do tasks that save less than the potential earnings. Such activity actually results in a decreasing income.

The proper evaluation of long- and short-term goals is important to a realistic handling of money. George and Alice both worked and skimped for years to build toward a comfortable future. They completely forgot how to play. At last Alice thought they had enough money and could now begin to enjoy it. In the meantime, George had elevated his sights. Thus, a clash followed. Unfortunately, Alice had little talent left for enjoying life even if George had agreed; she had lost her imagination. Perhaps if she had made her plans for pleasure attractive enough, George might have been more interested and some of the trouble would have been avoided.[30]

PARENTAL INFLUENCE. Couples who are financially dependent on their parents frequently find strings attached to their spending of money. The parents are likely to feel a responsibility to suggest what the couple should buy; thus, adjustments over money are postponed for the couple until later. Such problems, however, must be worked out sometime.

INFLUENCE OF THE FAMILY-CYCLE STAGE. As children get older, they should be taken into the family money-management process through allowances and family councils. When children are taken into the family's confidence on money matters, it usually results in a surprising amount of understanding and self-restraint on the youngsters' part. This makes for a much better family relationship. By using the family-council system, children's wants become a matter of choice instead of denial. Of course, this makes it much more difficult for parents to ignore children's wants by simply saying, "We cannot afford it." When spending is made a cooperative venture, with each member's wishes taken into account, families with modest incomes are as likely to be happy as those who are wealthy. The essential factor for the avoidance of clashes over money is agreement on values. It is more important than the budgetary system followed or even the choice of who handles the money.

Making money stretch farther

Couples who do not have enough money to meet their fundamental needs or who have little left over for special choices, need to learn how to get more from their dollar. This may not solve all their money problems, but it will help the couple learn to cooperate with each other until they are better able to solve some of their financial problems.

HOME PRODUCTION AND CAREFUL MAINTENANCE. One way to make money stretch farther is by increased home production; in other words, to make and to do as many things around the home as possible. The wife might do the simple sewing and canning that will provide basic, if not luxurious, needs. The husband should try to do as many home repairs as possible; if he is not handy with tools, he should try to learn.

Careful use of the things already owned can stretch the dollar too. By keeping things from breaking or wearing out so quickly, replacements are kept to a minimum. The old saying, "A stitch in time saves nine," applies here.

BY-PRODUCTS. There are additional benefits from trying to stretch money through home production and maintenance. Although production of some things in the home saves money, the production of other things might prove more expensive. The fact that home production and repairs have been attempted as a joint cooperative enterprise often brings the couple closer together in other aspects of life. Thus, the by-product of home enterprise may be more important than the material savings. Through such joint efforts, there is frequently a secondary gain; that is, as each mate is assigned a personal responsibility in production or maintenance within the home, he assumes more responsibility in other areas also. Sometimes additional financial responsibility deters individuals from extravagance and the careless use of money.

CONSUMER INFORMATION SOURCES. Fortunately, there are many information sources today designed to help married couples with money problems. There are various educational aids, organizations, surveys, and information centers. There are many books on household finance, offering facts and hints on budgeting, insurance, and consumership. Many high schools and colleges also offer classes in these subjects.

Two leading organizations that have helped young couples in the wiser use of available income are Consumer's Research, and Consumer's Union. These independent organizations derive their income from the sale of books, reports, and reprints; they accept no money, nor do they accept any article for testing. Instead, they buy the products on the open market, then test their performance, and publish their findings monthly. Newly married couples should take advantage of these reports. This is not to say that the findings reported are infallible. For one thing, the number of products the organizations can test is limited by their small resources. Furthermore, because of liability laws, adverse reports must be restricted to statements that could be proved in court if necessary. Owing to the limited funds, it is possible that sometimes there may not be enough units tested to give the highest permutation of absolute accuracy in extrapolation of the specific results to the general rating. Nevertheless, these reports are a great help in making a wiser use of available income.

Surveys are reported of the practices of other couples which may prove of value to the newlyweds. At the very least, these surveys may be used as a rough guide to what others are doing in various areas of family finance.

Table 13–5. Percentage of family expenditures for selected categories of consumption by income levels

Annual income	Food	Hous-ing	Cloth-ing	House-hold opera-tion	Auto-mobile	Medi-cal	Recre-ation
Under $1000	40.0	23.2	7.2	6.4	5.0	4.0	1.0
$1000–1999	38.3	20.4	8.8	8.2	6.3	4.6	1.8
$2000–2999	36.2	18.3	10.2	7.8	6.4	4.3	2.7
$3000–3999	33.0	17.4	10.3	7.9	8.0	4.9	3.4
$4000–4999	30.8	17.5	11.4	7.8	9.4	4.5	3.5
$5000–5999	27.8	14.7	11.6	8.1	11.2	4.9	4.8
$6000–7499	28.0	14.3	13.1	7.0	10.5	4.2	5.1
$7500–9999	25.2	13.0	14.6	7.2	14.4	4.3	4.8
$10,000 and over	19.7	18.8	13.7	10.9	12.6	4.9	5.5

Source: Helen G. Canoyer and Roland S. Vaile, *Economics of Income and Consumption* (New York: The Ronald Press Company, 1951), p. 134. Copyright © 1951, by The Ronald Press Company, New York. Reprinted by permission.

Not to be overlooked as a source of practical consumer information is the experience of young friends who have been recently married. In discussing the items considered good investments or foolish expenditures, the neophytes may profit from their friends' good judgment and their errors.

Of course, there are limitations on all sources of second-hand information. In the first place, no two families will have exactly the same values, goals, and expectations in life, so there is no "proper" list of percentages to follow when allocating the expenditures of money. Even the best surveys should be considered only general guides from which the couple can work out choices, encompassing their own tastes and interests. Much trial and error will ensue before the couple can find their own ways to make money stretch farther.

BUDGETS. The most common method for managing the family income is to set up a budget. There is no need for alarm if it is different from the average spending plan, for a workable budget must fit individual tastes and interests. Family finance experts have worked out and published "practical" budgets since 1909. These were originally calculated for city families of four; since 1947, budgets for elderly couples have also been published.[31]

A budget is a guide to intelligent spending through a reconciliation of basic needs and personal desires; therefore, the final form cannot be laid out in advance. A workable budget must grow out of experience. Others may offer facts, information, and direction, but the final spending patterns must ultimately be set by the individual couple.

Beginning budget-planners, in spite of published guides, often overlook many items. Some of the discrepancies arise because many young people lack a realistic picture of the actual costs of various items. Most young couples have much to learn about the costs of running a household. There are certain expenses that are fixed and others that are variable. Common regular expenses include both, such as housing, utilities, food, barber and beauty supplies, clothing, medical care, laundry and dry-cleaning, newspapers, magazines, books, membership dues, church gifts, entertainment, vacations, insurance, and transportation or automobile operation. Couples should never feel defensive if they choose to spend their money differently from their friends or neighbors. If they are meeting their honest values, then their budget is practical.

A budget should never become a hard-and-fast list of predetermined expenditures. It must be flexible and allow for variation. One of the main values in the early years of marriage is the process of budgeting rather than its results. Working on a budget forces the couple to study and plan their spending together, and it encourages them to discuss their individual attitudes toward money.

The worst trap is to choose a budget that fits the income instead of the individual needs and desires. Two couples with identical incomes may have quite different living styles, and both ways of life should be respected. Ordinarily, there is only one item in most beginning budgets that recognizes the impulsive and irrational nature of human beings: the item is labeled *miscellaneous*. In a sense this item is the only one that honestly reflects the individuality that should be preserved within every marriage.

MONEY, CREDIT, AND DEBTS. Even with every effort to manage the family income wisely, young couples never seem to triumph completely over money problems. Pace reported that 35 per cent of the couples in his study found it difficult to stay out of debt, regardless of their purchasing methods.[32] In one study of married college students, 34 per cent of the wives and 48 per cent of the husbands ranked financial troubles as their most serious marital problem.[33] This did not necessarily refer to marital conflict, but rather to things that most concerned the couple. A study of former University of Minnesota students also found that money management ranked as the major marital concern.[34] Locke found that 80.6 per cent of happily married men rated their wives "very satisfactory" in managing money in the home, but only 35.1 per cent of divorced husbands said this was true of their former spouses.[35] A poll taken by the *Ladies' Home Journal* a few years ago disclosed that money management ranked as the most important of all sources of marital concern listed.[36] In Wilson's study, only parental relationships and sexual adjustment ranked higher than money management as areas of concern.[37] The average couple simply lack sufficient know-how to purchase wisely. Because women independently make at least 60 per cent of the purchases, Bowman suggests that women considering marriage should ask themselves: "Would I marry a man only as well prepared to earn money as I am to spend it?"[38]

Each couple should study some of the social fallacies about spending money. For example, one of the most commonly voiced ideals is that one should never go into debt. Actually, if this rule were rigorously followed, the American economy would collapse. Such things as houses, cars, and major appliances must be purchased on credit by most people; however, couples should watch the interest rates they pay for such credit. Unscrupulous companies actually may make more profit on their "carrying charges" (a form of interest which permits charges generally greater than that allowed by law) than they do from the items sold. There are almost as many different ways to figure simple interest (generally considered as the annual cost of a loan) as there are different people in the loan business. Even recent Senate investigative committees could not agree on the proper way to compute interest charges.[39] Couples should fully investigate all the loan possibilities before purchasing on credit. One of the simplest ways to differentiate between various interest rates is to add up the total cost each way.

Another prevailing misconception in domestic finances is that a couple can never buy too much life insurance.[40] Many couples buy the wrong kind of policy and commit themselves to excessive premium payments for life. The chief purpose of life insurance is protection, not investment. A young family head should not begin investing money until he has provided adequate financial protection for his family in the event of his death. One can get much more insurance through policies commonly called *term* than with any other kind. In term insurance the policy owner pays a fixed amount per year for a previously agreed upon number of years. The operation principle is identical to automobile, house, or hospitalization insurance. At the end of the designated number of years, the policy is ended, has no cash or loan value, and no dividends (profits) from what has been paid in to the insurance company. When one purchases other types of insurance—such as ordinary life insurance, twenty or thirty-year pay-life, or endowments—he stands to get back some money from the insurance company eventually. With term insurance, nothing is ever received, but the cost is much less or the total amount of insurance coverage is a great deal more. All insurance policies, other than term, are investment-type policies, for the policy owner will get something back someday. What he will eventually get back, however, is usually not nearly as much as he could have earned by purchasing term policies and

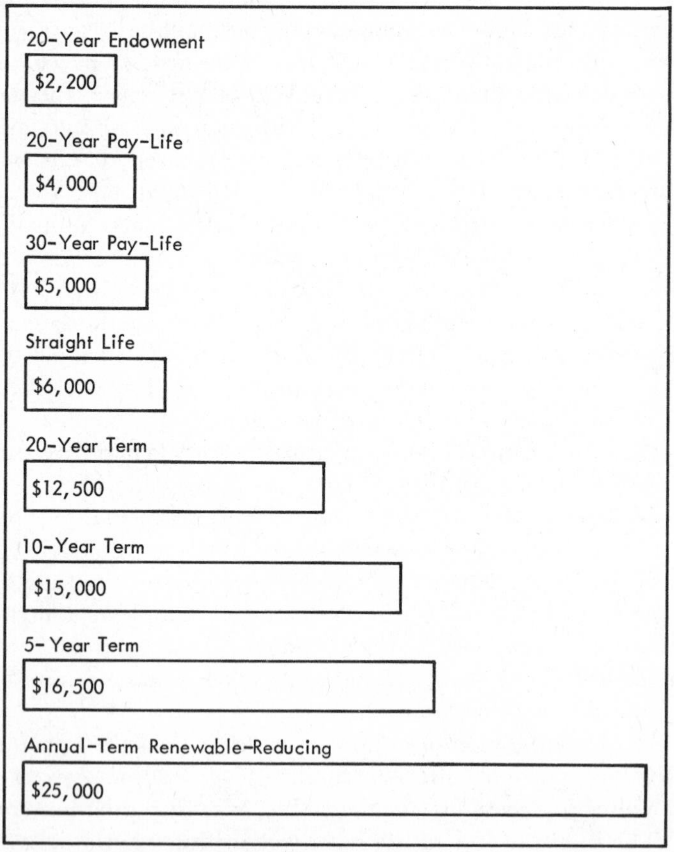

20-Year Endowment
$2,200

20-Year Pay-Life
$4,000

30-Year Pay-Life
$5,000

Straight Life
$6,000

20-Year Term
$12,500

10-Year Term
$15,000

5-Year Term
$16,500

Annual-Term Renewable-Reducing
$25,000

Figure 13-3. Average amount of life insurance that can be purchased for $100 per year by twenty-five-year-old males. (From three major companies.)

investing the difference in another way. All the insurance company does with the difference between the cost of term insurance and the higher rate charged on investment policies is invest it. Before signing any non-term insurance policy, the couple should compute the over-all costs of the premiums as compared to the returns the additional money might bring if it were invested in something else. At the end of a given period, they may actually have more available cash by having purchased stocks or even government bonds than if they had purchased even the best of all "endowments." As an example, one $18.75 United States Series E bond purchased each month for ten years has an immediate cash value of $2498.98. One hundred dollars a year will purchase the approximate following amounts of life insurance for a man, age twenty-two: (1) term (five-year renewable), $19,500; (2) term (ten-year nonrenewable), $19,300; (3) ordinary straight life, $7000; (4) life paid up at sixty-five, $6250; (5) endowment at sixty-five, $5400; twenty-year payment life, $4100; twenty-year endowment, $2200.[41]

When the wife also has an income, the couple may fall into the trap of thinking of the combined total as a permanent potential income. Unfortunately for these young couples, wives usually give up their salaried job when children begin to arrive. Those accustomed to living on two incomes may find it very difficult suddenly to have to live on one, especially when dependency expenses have increased. Young couples would be wise to live on one salary, saving the other salary or using it to purchase things that ordinarily might be postponed for years. They should not spend as though there will always be a double income.

Summary

The proper use of money is of great importance to marital happiness in today's industrial society. Goods and services for family living must now be purchased rather than produced within the home. In addition, there are more social pressures that force individuals into extended expenditures on products that were previously unknown. The definition of *living necessities* constantly changes. There is also more governmental influence over personal spending habits. For a number of years, America has been experiencing an upward-spiral in the economy, so it now takes more money for daily essentials.

Except in cases of extreme poverty, there are many considerations more important to marital happiness than level of income. These factors include regularity of income, reconciliation of expectations and reality, compromise on values, and consistent agreement on who is to control the spending.

Earnings may be stretched farther through home production, better maintenance of goods, consumer-information sources, a budget system, and wiser purchasing methods.

Most important, the couple must be aware of the underlying sociological and psychological problems involved in any decision dealing with money. Each family must decide in accordance with its own values the things for which it is willing to save, budget, or go into debt. Couples should consult counselors and books in the area of family finance for more detailed information.

Notes

1. Robert S. Lynd, "Family Members as Consumers," *Annals of the American Academy of Political and Social Science,* 150:86–93.

2. Robert Winch, *The Modern Family* (New York: Holt, Rinehart & Winston, Inc., 1952), p. 56.

3. "The New America the Census Shows," *United States News & World Report* (January 2, 1961), 72.

4. Federal Reserve Board, *Consumer Installment Credit,* Part I, Vol. I (Washington, D.C.: Government Printing Office), p. 111; and "The New America the Census Shows," *op. cit.*

5. Charles Abrams and John P. Dean, "Housing and the Family," in Ruth N. Anshen (ed.), *The Family: Its Functions and Destiny* (New York: Harper & Row, Publishers, 1949), p. 299.

6. Helen H. LaMale, "Bureau of Labor Statistics Studies Relating to Family Living," *Marriage and Family Living,* 20:255; and U.S. Bureau of the Census, Series P-60, No. 43.

7. U.S. Bureau of the Census, *op. cit.*

8. U.S. Department of Health, Education, and Welfare, *Bulletin* (January 1962), 29.

9. U.S. Bureau of the Census, *op. cit., Special Report* (September 29, 1964).

10. Gilbert V. Hamilton, *A Research in Marriage* (New York: Albert and Charles Boni, 1929), p. 97.

11. E. W. Burgess and Leonard S. Cottrell, *Predicting Success or Failure in Marriage* (Englewood Cliffs, N.J.. Prentice-Hall, Inc., 1939), p. 404; and Lewis M. Terman, *Psychological Factors in Marital Happiness* (New York: McGraw-Hill Book Company, Inc., 1938), pp. 169–71.

12. E. W. Burgess and Paul Wallin, *Engagement and Marriage* (Philadelphia: J. B. Lippincott & Co., 1953), p. 556.

13. Earl Koos, *Families in Trouble* (New York: Kings' Crown Press, 1948), p. 121.

14. Summarized in Burgess and Cottrell, *op. cit.,* pp. 139–43.

15. See William J. Goode, "Economic Factors and Marital Stability," *American Sociological Review,* 16:802–11; or William J. Goode, *After Divorce* (New York: The Free Press of Glencoe, Inc., 1956), Chaps. 4–5.

16. Burgess and Cottrell, *op. cit.,* pp. 398–401.

17. Robert C. Williamson, "Economic Factors in Marital Adjustment," *Marriage and Family Living,* 14:298–300.

18. Robert O. Blood and Donald M. Wolfe, *Husbands and Wives* (New York: The Free Press of Glencoe, Inc., 1960), p. 241.

19. "Cost $29,204 From Diapers Through College," *Associated Press Release* (April 4, 1960).

20. Paul C. Glick, "The Life Cycle of the Family," *Marriage and Family Living,* 17:3–9.

21. George Fisk, "Toward a Theory of Leisure—Spending Behavior," *Journal of Marketing* (October 1959), 51–57.

22. Judson T. Landis, "Length of Time Required to Achieve Adjustment in Marriage," *American Sociological Review,* 11:666–77.

23. Although it is true that the author is basing this specific example on observations in his clinical experience, nevertheless others have published studies which support this contention. See, e.g., Leona E. Tyler, *The Psychology of Human Differences* (New York: Appleton-Century-Crofts, Inc., 1956).

24. *Ibid.*

25. Pierre Martineau, "Social Classes and Spending Behavior," *Journal of Marketing* (October 1958), 121–30.

26. Julius Roth and Robert F. Peck, "Social-Class and Social-Mobility Factors Related to Marital Adjustment," *American Sociological Review,* 16:481.

27. Elise Boulding, "Orientation Toward Achievement or Security in Relation to Consumer Behavior," *Human Relations,* 13:365–83.

28. Elmo Roper, "Women's Buying Habits," *Social Order,* 7:47–61.

29. Elizabeth H. Wolgast, "Do Husbands or Wives Make the Purchasing Decisions?" *Journal of Marketing* (October 1958), 151–58.

30. From the author's files.

31. LaMale, *op. cit.*

32. Robert Pace, *They Went to College* (Minneapolis: University of Minnesota Press, 1941), p. 82.

33. Rex A. Skidmore, Therese L. Smith, and Delbert L. Nye, "Characteristics of Married Veterans," *Marriage and Family Living,* 11:103.

34. Pace, *op. cit.*

35. Harvey J. Locke, *Predicting Adjustment in Marriage* (New York: Holt, Rinehart & Winston, Inc., 1951), p. 282.

36. *Ladies' Home Journal* (January 1949), 26.

37. Pauline Park Wilson, *College Women Who Express Futility* (New York: Bureau of Publications, Teachers College, Columbia University, 1950), p. 54.

38. Henry A. Bowman, *Marriage for Moderns* (New York: McGraw-Hill Book Company, Inc., 1954), p. 403.

39. Reported to the author by his former teaching colleague, Dr. Richard L. D. Morse, while serving as president of Consumers Union on his testimony before Senate committees 1959–63.

40. Americans in 1961 owned two and one half times more life insurance than they did in 1951. See Metropolitan Life Insurance Company, *Statistical Bulletin* (November 1962), 3.

41. Jerome B. Cohen, *Decade of Decision* (New York: Institute of Life Insurance, 1961), p. 26.

Questions for further thought

1. What concepts of financial adjustment within marriage are most consistent with American democracy?
2. What effect does the fact that both mates have a college degree have on togetherness or differences in value priority of wants?
3. What is the minimum gross income on which one should be willing to marry? What would a complete family budget look like based on that figure?
4. What factors should be considered in determining whether the parents of

a girl, who has been used to a high standard of living, should be generous with their money to a young couple on a limited income?
5. Why does installment purchasing appeal so strongly to young couples? When is it justified?
6. What is a credit union and how does it operate?
7. Which of the following would be the least acceptable for credit buying: (a) gasoline on a long trip, (b) refrigerator, (c) automobile, (d) vacation in a fine resort hotel? Why?
8. Why is it so often true that young couples actually waste money instead of saving it by buying some things in large quantities?
9. What suggestions regarding life insurance are in order for a young couple with two small children (more wanted later) and a modest but promising income?

Recommended films

Family Economics (University of Michigan Television Center).
Installment Buying (Coronet).
Home Management: Why Budget? (Young America Films).
Your Family Budget (Coronet).

Suggested supplemental readings

BOOKS

Caplovitz, David. *The Poor Pay More: Consumer Practices of Low-Income Families.* New York: The Free Press of Glencoe, Inc., 1963.
Dublin, Louis I., and Alfred J. Lotke. *The Money Value of a Man.* New York: The Ronald Press Company, 1946.
Einzig, Paul. *How Money Is Managed.* New York: Penguin Books, 1954.
Feldman, Frances L. *The Family in a Money World.* New York: Family Service Association, 1957.
Fitzsimmon, Cleo. *Consumer Buying for Better Living.* New York: John Wiley & Sons, Inc., 1961.
Hanson, Arthur W., and Jerome B. Cohen. *Personal Finance—Principles and Case Problems.* Homewood, Ill.: Richard D. Irwin, Inc., 1958.
Lasser, J. K., and Sylvia F. Porter. *Managing Your Money,* rev. ed. New York: Holt, Rinehart & Winston, Inc., 1961.
Morgan, James N., *et al. Income and Welfare in the United States.* New York: McGraw-Hill Book Company, Inc., 1962.
Nickell, Paulena, Jean M. Dorsey, and Marie Budolfson. *Management in Family Living,* 3rd ed. New York: John Wiley & Sons, Inc., 1959.
Packard, Vance. *The Status-Seekers.* New York: David McKay Co., Inc., 1959.
———. *The Waste-Makers.* New York: David McKay & Co., Inc., 1960.
Ralph, Sally Anne (ed.). *Money Management for Young Moderns.* Chicago: Household Finance Corporation, 1963.
Troelstrup, Arch W. *Consumer Problems,* rev. ed. New York: McGraw-Hill Book Company, Inc., 1965.
Weeks, H. Ashley. *Family Spending Patterns and Health Care.* Cambridge, Mass.: Harvard University Press, 1961.
Whalen, William J. *Christian Family Finance.* Milwaukee: The Bruce Publishing Company, 1960.
Whyte, William H., Jr. *The Organization Man.* New York: Simon and Shuster, Inc., 1958.

ARTICLES

Feldman, Frances Lomas. "A New Look at the Family and Its Money," *Journal of Home Economics,* **49:**767–72.

Goode, William J. "Economic Factors and Marital Stability," *American Sociological Review,* **16:**802–11.

Jacobi, John A., and S. George Walters. "Social Status and Consumer Choice," *Social Forces,* **36:**209–14.

Martineau, Pierre. "Social Classes and Spending Behavior," *Journal of Marketing,* **22:**121–30.

Ross, Irwin. "When You Borrow, When You Buy—Watch Those Interest Rates," *Reader's Digest* (November 1963), 157–65.

Semon, Thomas T. "Family Income and Spending Capacity," *Journal of Marketing,* **26:**26–30.

Williamson, Robert C. "Economic Factors in Marital Adjustment," *Marriage and Family Living,* **14:**298–300.

Winthrop, Henry. "Some Psychological and Economic Assumptions Underlying Automation," *American Journal of Economic Sociology,* Part I (July 1958), 399–412; Part II (October 1958), 69–82.

Enriching married
living

chapter 14

Four areas of major concern in many modern marriages are (1) in-laws, (2) religion, (3) recreation, and (4) mutual friends. Although these areas may cause problems, they also offer great opportunities for enriching marriage.

In-law relationships

Because most people in the United States marry outside the ties of consanguinity, marriage usually unites not only two individuals but two different kinship groups.[1] The learning and sharing of the couple's familial mores constitute a most important function within a democratic society. This intermingling and joining of peoples of differing customs strengthen the beliefs and revitalize the practice of the constitutional freedoms. Nevertheless, the very forces that may contribute to enriching the couple's marriage may also be regarded with suspicion by the young couple. Indeed, in-laws are usually considered among life's mixed blessings.

Studies suggest the universality of in-laws as a concern in marriage. In fact both Duvall and Ullman report in-laws as a source of great complaint among married college students.[2] This was not as true of the veterans' marriages while in college, for then only 8 per cent of wives and 6 per cent of the husbands listed in-laws as being of serious concern.[3]

Ralph Linton, the anthropologist, indicates that in-law relationships have always been a source of difficulty in many societies of the world.[4] Lowie points out that parental in-law taboos are frequent in primitive people. As an example, he cites the Hukaghir in Siberia, where the daughter-in-law is forbidden even to look into the face of her father-in-law or eldest brother-in-law, and the son-in-law is forbidden to look directly into the face of either parent-in-law.[5]

RELATION TO MARITAL HAPPINESS. There is a definite relationship between in-law satisfactions and total marital-happiness scores.

Table 14–1. **Happiness ratings of recently married couples compared to degree of in-law satisfaction**

In-law relationship condition	Per cent		
	Very happy marriage	*Happy marriage*	*Average marriage*
Excellent	67	25	8
Good	44	40	16
Fair or Poor	18	45	37

Source: Judson T. and Mary G. Landis, *Building a Successful Marriage* (Englewood Cliffs, N.J.: Prentice-Hall, Inc., 1958), p. 407. Copyright © 1958, by Prentice-Hall, Inc., Englewood Cliffs, N.J. Reprinted by permission. The same pattern as above was found in Landis' study of 409 married older couples.

Landis found that, of those who did not find immediate satisfactory in-law adjustment, one third did later, but the first years were difficult. In an additional third of such cases, one mate eventually reported adjustment; the other, maladjustment. The remainder, even after twenty years or more of marriage, never became satisfactorily adjusted in the in-law relationship.[6]

Thomas conducted a five-year study in St. Louis, Missouri, of more than 7000 Catholic marriage failures. He found only 7 per cent of all the failures could be related directly to in-law trouble. In those marriages that had failed during the first year, however, in-law problems were named as the most common cause.[7] Thus, it appears that in-law relationships have a very important effect on total marital happiness and may possibly be directly related to early marital failures.

STEREOTYPES. Because fears of in-law interference are so prominent in all cultures, there has emerged an in-law stereotype. American cartoons constantly depict a man and his rancorous mother-in-law. Actually, such cartoons are somewhat erroneous sociologically, for it is more often the wife-mother-in-law relationship rather than the husband-mother-in-law relationship that causes marital troubles. It could well be that such cartoons have actually aided in-law adjustments by releasing the husband's hostilities through jokes. A counterpart of such humor between wives and mothers-in-law is lacking, and perhaps this is indicative of the too-serious sensitivities of the women over in-law problems. The phrase *mother-in-law* evokes a stereotype image; it has become an almost ominous word in the English language. Blood reported that in a free-association test, students typically gave such responses as *fight, bother, terrible, ugh, hatred,* and *hell,* to the word *mother-in-law.*[8] Because of the perpetuation of the stereotype in-law, many couples go into marriage expecting in-law trouble. Folklore has long perpetuated the idea that in-laws are usually difficult and are even potential enemies.

BEST FRIENDS. Actually, in-laws are often the newlyweds' best friends. Duvall found that more than one half of her study group had no in-law complaints, and many couples reported deep feelings of respect and gratitude toward their in-laws.[9] Many in-laws make a real contribution to the success of a young marriage and help the couple over rough spots in their adjustment. Unfortunately, the vivid and emotional descriptions of the difficult in-laws have increased the human tendency to generalize wantonly. In-laws are often an advantage to a young marriage in need of help. Sussman's study indicates that both sets of in-laws help newlyweds not only with advice but especially in times of economic crisis.[10] In-laws can be valuable assets to a young marriage, for they provide definite sources of psychic and physical assistance when needed.

The young couple should not go into marriage with a chip on their shoulders about their new family relationships. If they do, they will more than likely create trouble. If the couple are simply waiting for signs or clues of in-law interference, they will frequently misinterpret innocent things said by well-meaning in-laws. Both parents and children tend to lose their objectivity when misunderstanding develops.

A FEMININE PATTERN. In American marriage, in-law problems have a definite feminine pattern. Mothers, sisters, and wives often become much more entangled than fathers, brothers, and husbands. The Landis findings indicate that mothers are involved in more than 60 per cent of the in-law difficulty. In-law troubles can often be traced to the family member who guided the personality development of the child and bore the chief responsibility for passing on the culture. This probably is the reason in the American culture that in-law troubles involve mothers more often than fathers, and sisters more often than brothers. The studies by Malinowski support this thesis. He found that uncles in the society of Northwestern Melanesia provided much of the care of their sisters' children. In-law problems in that culture most often centered around uncles.[11]

In-law trouble is also somewhat related to the degree of attachment within the family structure. Many studies indicate that the mother is the preferred parent of both the husband and the wife. Winch suggests that the son is the preferred child, and the mother-son relationship is the strongest of all.[12] This would seem to explain why there is usually more in-law interference from the husband's mother. Duvall propounded

Table 14–2. **In-law with whom husbands and wives experienced friction**

In-law involved	Per cent of husbands reporting	Per cent of wives reporting
Mother-in-law	9	14.7
Sister-in-law	3.4	3.8
Father-in-law	3.2	3.2
Brother-in-law	0.6	1.8
Two or more of the above	5.1	5.9
	21.3	29.4

Source: Judson T. and Mary G. Landis, *Building a Successful Marriage* (Englewood Cliffs, N.J.: Prentice-Hall, Inc., 1958), p. 406. Copyright © 1958, by Prentice-Hall, Inc., Englewood Cliffs, N.J. Adapted by permission.

the interesting concept that as America becomes more of a two-income society, and the care of children consequently becomes more of a joint enterprise, perhaps neither sex will become as involved in offspring marital problems as mothers are today. Thus, the mother-in-law problem may decrease in the future.[13] Waller and Hill suggest that some in-law troubles may be based on mixed-up affectional relationships.

It may be that a number of subconscious factors are at work, especially in the relation between the man and his mother-in-law. The man's mother-in-law, perhaps cut short in her own emotional life, lives vicariously in her daughter, and tends, therefore, to fall in love with her daughter's husband. Her inhibitions lead her to resist any such attachment strongly, and accordingly she turns toward him the hostile side of her ambivalent emotions. On the side of the man, there is apt to be a strong transference upon the mother-in-law as a mother substitute, but ingrained inhibitions lead him to react strongly against this attitude. In addition, the mother-in-law arouses some interpersonality conflict because she resembles the wife in many respects but lacks her youthful charm, and this is a further source of hostility.[14]

The pattern, as revealed by most of research indicates that the wife, more often than the husband, thinks that in-laws are a problem, and her feelings are most often directed toward her husband's mother.[15]

THE FAMILY CYCLE. Specific in-law concerns are also related to the stages within the family cycle. For example, friction between in-laws is more likely to occur at the start of a marriage rather than later. The concern is usually more pronounced when the individual joins an unknown and possibly strange family. The sensitivities are compounded because each partner is trying to establish more independence from prior family ties while feeling still insecure in the new familial relationship. In-law problems later in marriage are usually concerned with the physical welfare of the aging parents. The efforts of government planning in recent times will no doubt lessen these anxieties. As one can see even today, social security and old-age-assistance programs have brought greater financial independence to many older citizens.

PREDISPOSING FACTORS. There are a number of predisposing factors in in-law attitudinal patterns. The age of the couple has a very strong influence on in-law attitudes. In-law trouble seems much more likely in youthful marriages than in older marriages, and it is also related to the educational attainments of the partners.

Table 14–3. **Relation of age at marriage to degree of in-law satisfaction**

	Per cent of in-law adjustment		
Age	*Excellent*	*Good*	*Fair or poor*
17–19	45	34	21
20–21	51	38	11
22–23	60	28	12
24 or older	63	30	7

Source: Judson T. and Mary G. Landis, *Building a Successful Marriage* (Englewood Cliffs, N.J.: Prentice-Hall, Inc., 1958), p. 413. Copyright © 1958, by Prentice-Hall, Inc., Englewood Cliffs, N.J. Reprinted by permission. The findings of Landis on the relationship of youthful marriage and increased in-law trouble are further supported by those of Ullman.[16]

Another major factor affecting in-law behavior is the degree of personal maturity of each spouse. If each gets along easily with his own parents, he will more than likely get along well with the spouse's parents. Unresolved parent-child tensions may sometimes be transferred to the same-sex parent of the spouse, and as a matter of fact, may be transferred equally to anyone who treats the person somewhat like a child. When a person has enjoyed a long-standing independence from his parents and has been more or less on his own for a while before marriage, there is less likely to be much in-law trouble. Conversely, when a long-standing interdependence, such as a mother-child relationship, has increasingly built up over many years, it cannot be destroyed overnight. Such mothers will probably continue to give helpful suggestions to their children, and their children are more than likely to continue to rely upon such advice and to consult their mothers even after marriage. This may again explain why in-law relationships have more of a feminine pattern. Rosen and d'Andrade state that the culture generally encourages more independence for men as a value in life.[17] Wallin found that wives at the time of marriage were more closely attached to their parental home and visited their parents more often after marriage than did their husbands.[18] Stryker's research found wives significantly more dependent upon their mothers than husbands were upon either parent.[19] Sometimes there is resentment of the closeness between the spouse and family. Unseemly dependence on the parents may seem like disloyalty to the spouse. Koos cites an illustration of this situation.

> I think we'd get along better if it wasn't for her family. But they don't want to let her get away from them, and she's always running home to them instead of coming to me. Why, they even knew she was with child before I did. Then she thinks I am unfair when I get mad about it. I think she should have gotten rid of them when she married me—I mean, she should have become part of our family, not stayed with her own.[20]

Many couples find it hard to discuss in-law feelings for fear of hurting the partner. This is especially difficult when each is uncertain of how the other feels about the situation. Often another factor conducive to feelings of insecurity is the realization by the mate of imperfection in his new role. The wife, for example, knows she is not yet the expert home manager that her mother-in-law is. This unfavorable comparison may cause her to become defensive about her shortcomings and touch off in-law trouble that would otherwise not exist.

Often the young couple may inadvertently exploit their in-laws, draining them of resources and overusing them for family services, and later show only ingratitude. When a young couple aspire to move upward in society, they may feel resentful because of a false belief that the parents are holding them back. Given time, many young couples attain a higher standard of living than their parents had, especially in terms of education or employment. Thus, even when there is no social-aspiration clash between the generations, artificial cultural barriers may be created.[21]

The extent of acquaintance between a couple and their parents-in-law before marriage is also related to the degree of in-law satisfaction. Marcus suggests that meeting and approving of the prospective partner's family before marriage is quite important to in-law adjustment; it is even more important to meet them before engagement. The extent of in-law pre-marital approval can be judged rather accurately by the degree of intimacy engendered in visits with them. The more intimate the terms of address that seem acceptable, the better the adjustment. Couples who are willing to address their parents-in-law as *Mother* and *Dad* appear much more likely to get along with them. The reactions of the two sets of parents to one another is also an index of future in-law adjustment. It is not essential that both sets of parents be acquainted before the marriage, but when they meet, in-law adjustment is naturally better if they like each other.[22] Conversely, parents who are dissatisfied with the other parents may feel that the potential spouse is not good enough for their child.

A mixed marriage may cause parental conflicts because of contrasting traditional customs. Thus, in-law troubles seem to be accentuated when either set of parents has had little acquaintance with the background, nationality, religion, or socioeconomic class of the others. Each may fear that their offspring will be forced to change the family patterns after the marriage. In-laws may particularly resent the outsider in a mixed cultural marriage. Marcus found much less in-law difficulty where the partners practiced the same religious and social patterns.[23]

The extent of liberalism and conservatism between the present generation and the parental generation is sometimes a factor for misunderstanding. Each generation has its own attitudes about many things, such as money, entertainment, and working wives. The more liberal views of the younger generation sometimes cause difficulties in the relationship with the older generation.[24]

The degree of education attained may also be a factor affecting in-law attitudes. Where the husband's education is equal to or better than the wife's, the in-law adjustment is usually better than when the reverse is true. Marcus also found that when the wife had taken a course on marriage, her adjustment with her in-laws was significantly better and it effected even greater adjustment for her husband with his in-laws.[25]

Place of residence is also an influential factor. In-law friction is accentuated when it is necessary to live with parents. In the American culture, a separate household for each couple helps to improve in-law adjustment. It is usually better for the young couple to live almost anywhere than with the parents. With the advent of a more mobile society, young people are more likely to live in other states. This factor might well contribute to a decrease of in-law problems in the future. Fortune reports that moving away is not possible among the Dobu, for there the newly-weds must spend six months of the year alternately with each set of parents; there is, needless to say, constant in-law friction.[26] The exception seems to be Swedish society, which is in direct contrast to the Dobu. In fact, in some cases there, living with in-laws has been shown to be an advantage.[27] The custom in Sweden is somewhat similar to the custom observed in the earlier history of the United States. That is, the elders still have a degree of power over younger individuals, who are conditioned to respect and obey elders. However, in the contemporary American culture it seems best for young people to live by themselves. As Winter has expressed it: "Any parent-in-law within the home will be to some extent a threat to the convenant of intimacy between the husband and wife."[28]

A contributing factor of more importance to in-law adjustment than formerly recognized is the level of parental maturity. Some parents fail to keep pace with the development of their children, refusing to recognize that their children are becoming independent. They continue to treat the adult offspring as though they were still children and unfortunately, treat daughters-in-law and sons-in-law in much the same manner. Admitting the maturity of offspring is sometimes a difficult task, and parents may revert to immature behavior themselves.

Some parents resent the transfer of a child's affection from themselves to another person. This is much more likely when parents have been overly protective and possessive, and lack outside interests. Such parents frequently meddle in the affairs of the young married couple, causing many heartaches and unnecessary emotional crises.

A few parents are emotionally ill. Dissatisfaction within their own marriages affect the in-law relationship within their children's marriage. Marcus found that, where parents are happily married, there is proportionately less in-law interference, and where children are happily married, they less frequently consult parents. Thus the chances of in-law interference are reduced.[29] Mothers sometimes feel an emptiness in their lives when a child marries and leaves home. They are often lonely and welcome a chance to be consulted or involved in the young couple's business. Thus, they sometimes step in when not invited. Another aspect of parental maturity is related to grandchildren. Grandparents like to advise on the raising and care of children, but this may become quite irritating to a young couple. The growing children commonly reflect their parent's feelings toward the grandparents.

The marriage of two people unites their two families as well as the couple. Sometimes both sets of parents place competing demands on the young couple, including conflicts on whom to visit on holidays.

A POSITIVE APPROACH. The best way to improve in-law relationships is to maintain a positive approach. This includes remembering that the success of the marriage must be the foremost consideration in all decisions. Once a man and a woman marry, they are faced with the challenge of identifying with each other. This means adopting new loyalties in which each comes first in the other's eyes. It means breaking away to some extent from both sets of parents. The success of the marriage must be placed above attachment to parents. Husbands and wives must come first.

A second important principle for a more positive approach is patience. It must be remembered that a child-in-law is a member of an "out-group." It takes time and readjustment for parents-in-law fully to accept the newcomer as a member of its family "in-group."

Another cardinal principle is to realize that, in a sense, each spouse marries an entire family. The vow "for better or for worse" includes accepting the close relatives on both sides. The idea that a person marries only an individual is a great fallacy. It is not possible completely to separate the spouse from his former family, and such a separation should not be attempted. Each couple must be mature enough to accept and enjoy the in-laws as an essential part of their family life.

It is important to learn to appreciate newly acquired family members for what they are and do. Arguments and criticism should be avoided whenever possible. There is probably nothing in life that parents want more for their children than happiness in marriage. Parents usually mean well. If young couples can remember this, it will be easier for them to be more appreciative. This sincere understanding will go a long way toward creating a better in-law relationship. In-laws are not always wrong. Often they are simply trying to save the young couple from mistakes they themselves made long ago.

Religion as an area of marital adjustment

Although the couples in Landis' earlier study had been married for an average of twenty years, 10 per cent indicated they had never made a satisfactory adjustment in the area of religion. Only 0.2 per cent, however, reported that they were then having many quarrels over religion. In fact, there were fewer quarrels in this area than in any other.[30]

CHURCH AFFILIATION. The studies by Landis, Weeks, and Bell, emcompassing more than 25,000 marriages, indicate that divorce rates are much higher where there is no church affiliation whatsoever than even among marriages with mixed religions.[31] Locke found about twice as many divorced couples as happily married pairs where neither partner had a religious affiliation.[32] Thus, church affiliation appears to be related to total marital adjustment.

CHURCH-ATTENDANCE PATTERN. Tensions may be produced between partners of the same religion if the church attendance of one differs greatly from that of the spouse. One study revealed that more than half of the engagements in which the girl attended church more regularly than the boy were finally broken, but few engagements were broken where the couple attended more equally.[33] Better marital adjustment also has been found where couples attended Sunday school beyond the age of eighteen.[34]

The Oklahoma City experiment on marital reconciliation through a family clinic found fewer than 2 per cent of the couples attending church when they went to the clinic. Reconciliation was reported to be much more of a possibility if the clinic could persuade these couples to become active in church.[35] It appears that continued church attendance after marriage is as important to many couples as attendance before marriage.

When there is at first a wide difference in partners' attendance patterns, it appears that the most successful marriages work out a com-

Table 14–4. **Relation of regularity of church attendance to marital happiness**

	Per cent		
Church attendance	*Very happy marriages*	*Happy marriages*	*Average marriages*
Regularly	54	34	12
Occasionally or never	43	36	21

Source: Judson T. Landis, "Marriages of Mixed and Nonmixed Religious Faiths," *American Sociological Review*, 14:401–407. Copyright © 1949, by The American Sociological Association, Washington, D.C. Reprinted by permission. In a more recent article Landis reports further study and concludes that similar church attendance patterns appear to be more closely correlated with marital happiness for both Protestant and Catholic families, but has little if any effect on Jewish families. See Judson T. Landis, "Religiousness, Family Relationships, and Family Values in Protestant, Catholic, and Jewish Families," *Marriage and Family Living*, 22:341–47.

promise. Locke's study found that after such people were married a while, wives began to attend church less frequently and husbands tended to increase their attendance, thus effecting a workable compromise.[36]

But it seldom improves a marriage for one partner to nag the mate into attending church more frequently. An effort to attend church more regularly when the spouse wishes it may improve a marriage relationship, but attendance by itself does not necessarily guarantee marital success. Most happily married couples either go to church together or stay away together.

INTERPRETATION PRACTICE. Religion may be institutionalized or individualized. In the institutionalized concept of religion, there is an organization that offers fellowship and stimulation within the group itself. Adherence to sectarian ritual habits without practice of religious beliefs is an empty exercise. Creeds are most important in terms of their effects upon actions.

Religious conviction cannot be judged merely by church attendance, the fidelity with which parents teach religious views to children, or by the forms of ceremonies that are observed. Bossard and Boll suggest that family rituals are changing from religious to secular affairs, but that the binding reasons may be just as strong.[37] There are signs of increasing secularization in other cultures as well. In Moslem practice, for example, the wearing of the veil over the face is almost a thing of the past, as is the harem and separate quarters for women.[38]

The extent of adjustment needed depends on whether differing religious creeds are important or disturbing to either partner. Members of zealous groups are likely to bring stress into their marriages to influence the nonparticipating member. Good religious attitudes can strengthen a marriage, and a difference of practices does not necessarily lead to conflict. It is true that the chances of success are greatly increased if the couple feels the same about the intensity, interpretation, and practice of religion. But if one's negligence in religious activities does not disturb the more devout spouse, the marriage is not necessarily disturbed. Serious family advisors do not suggest the absolute need for either a common church membership or attendance to insure marital success. To do so would imply a uniformity that is neither justified nor desired. When fanatical interpretation or differences of viewpoint consistently result in quarreling and conflict, religious affiliation becomes a disruptive rather than a uniting force. True religion inspires more faith than fear, for a frightened person often cannot be tolerant or understanding. As Terman has pointed out from his study: "The conclusions suggest, though by no means establish, that either very much or very little religious training is less favorable to marital happiness than a more moderate amount."[39] Peterson found the highest level of marital adjustment was attained by those who belonged to liberal religious groups, with non-church-going couples following closely behind. The lowest marital-adjustment scores were made by those belonging to institutionalized, authoritarian, strict churches that placed strong emphasis on fear.[40]

EXTERNAL FACTORS. There are several external factors relating to religion that affect marital adjustment. After the coming of children, for example, many couples show more interest in religion.[41] Through religious activities parents can exert a strong influence on the conditioning of their offspring for marriage. Catholic couples were found to have much more predictive possibilities of marital success if the following conditions were true within their homes:

1. No parental quarrels over religious or moral matters;
2. No premarital sex liberty;
3. No parental quarrels over religious education;
4. Reception of the sacraments at the established age;
5. Two or more years' membership in church organizations;
6. Religion made childhood happier;
7. First religious instructions were received in the home.[42]

RELIGION AND TOTAL MARITAL HAPPINESS. Certainly religion often contributes to total marital happiness. Most religions advocate shared family experiences and the rule of "forgive and forget." Religion can give courage to meet personal difficulties, and church attendance can provide fellowship and meaningful worship. Certainly these assets should encourage a stronger union between a man and a woman. As a group, those without religious affiliation are at greater risk in marriage than those with an acknowledged affiliation, but there are exceptions in both cases.

As John Dewey has pointed out: "Whatever introduces a genuine perspective is religious."[43]

There may be many elements in life that are basically religious and yet are not labeled as such. The real problem is to differentiate between those persons who simply profess religion from those who seriously practice it. Family failure is greatest among nonreligious people, but this also includes those who profess religion without practicing it.

A genuine faith stresses vitality and spirituality more than personal mannerisms or institutional conformity. As Groves has emphasized, religion at its best is not an addition to life but a transformation of life.[44] A true religion serves to support marriage, not to disrupt it. All religions have a concern for marriage and family life. Many church groups today have marriage-education programs and provide counseling aid when needed.

Faith serves as a characterizing force; it provides a code for living. As Randall has said: "All religions embrace a code for the guidance of living and a set of ideals toward which human ideals should be directed."[45] A faith provides man with a set of ethical patterns for his behavior. From such a code, the individual develops those traits most conducive to marital adjustment. Religion can and does motivate many people to conduct their lives more honorably. It is concerned with the ideal of human reciprocity; people who try to practice an ethical, humanistic philosophy will have little trouble in human relationships.

Faith also serves as a tolerating force. Those with faith try to place their primary emphasis on the individual as a person rather than on his material advantages or disadvantages. Because of this, religious persons are often better able to adjust one to the other. Most religions teach that perfection is not to be expected of others, and the truly religious person does not expect any more from others than he demands of himself. Indeed, he may be willing to forgive in others what he would not excuse in himself. Thus, he is better able to accept other people's imperfections and to appraise others in terms of their highest possibilities rather than in terms of their achievements. The basic principle of repentance and forgiveness can help to lift a couple above petty squabbles and give them the motivation to endure and forgive unkindnesses.

Religion can also serve as an equalizing force. Faith in a power higher than man himself may strengthen the acceptance of every other person as a brother under this power. Furthermore, family worship may induce a sense of humility, as all members pay tribute to a higher power, admitting their inadequacies and seeking strength, wisdom, and guidance together.

The sharing of the experiences of a faith may lead to mutual discussions on ideals and also to a spiritual growth, leading to solidification

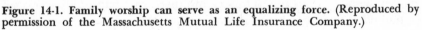

Figure 14-1. Family worship can serve as an equalizing force. (Reproduced by permission of the Massachusetts Mutual Life Insurance Company.)

of the home.[46] Thus, the truly religious couple is likely to have a more meaningful and richer marriage.

Recreation

The constructive use of leisure time is assuming increasing significance in American society. Many people have more time for recreational activities than was formerly the case, yet literature on the family shows little exploration of this part of life. Leisure activity has been a sadly neglected area of study.[47]

RELATION TO INDIVIDUAL HAPPINESS. Recreation is directly related to an individual's happiness. In the first place, it provides excellent opportunities for achieving self-discipline.

Recreation by means of games and sports is a valuable medium for lessons in gentlemanly and honorable sportsmanship. To win honestly, lose graciously, and to cooperate generously have made men out of selfish and cowardly individuals. Self-imposed discipline has moral value. Mastery over self fits a person to exert greater control over others and to meet critical situations more adequately.[48]

Recreation also contributes to the mental health of an individual. Through constructive recreation a sense of relaxation can be gained to ease the tensions incurred by the modern American industrial society. Unreleased aggression is a major cause of mental illness, and recreation makes it possible to channel off aggression. Play is one of the best antidotes for low morale and many other conditions that often lead to mental illness. Mental health is much keener when the individual has a chance to be creative, and constructive recreation is one of the best means known to satisfy creative desires.[49] Unfortunately, much of today's so-called recreation does none of these things. Instead of *re*creation, it is really *wreck*creation.[50]

MARITAL HAPPINESS. Although the Landis studies disclosed that 67.1 per cent of spouses agreed that the social-recreational activities area was satisfactory from the beginning, it should be noted that 13 per cent of the couples reported never making a completely satisfactory adjustment in this area.[51] That this area is important to future marital success and happiness is perhaps best shown by the results of various research studies. For instance, Burgess and Cottrell found that chances for marital happiness were fifteen times better when spouses shared and enjoyed all or most of their nonwork activities together than when they shared only a few.[52] Williamson found that agreement on recreation was one of the most significant differences between the well-adjusted and the poorly adjusted groups he studied.[53] In his comparison of happily married couples with divorced couples, Locke found that agreement on use of leisure time was more important than the specific activity engaged in, although both were contributing factors to marital happiness.

It is difficult to say, however, which is the cause and which is effect. Are couples better adjusted because they enjoy doing things together, or do they enjoy doing things together because they are better adjusted?

It is probably safe to say that mutually constructive recreation serves as a cohesive force, bringing the couple closer together. First, any activity spiced with laughter or zestful participation produces happy memories that cannot be completely erased no matter what follows within the relationship. Second, mutual leisure activities serve to counterbalance dullness. Too much habit and routine can threaten the happiness of any marriage relationship. Trouble spots are often viewed in a clearer perspective when mates have enjoyed play together. Constructive recreation may also build family pride into a marriage. Happy memories con-

Table 14–5. **Per cent of happily married and divorced reporting the mutual enjoyment of given activities**

	Men		Women	
Activity	*Happily married*	*Divorced*	*Happily married*	*Divorced*
Cards	39.5	39.1	38.3	51.3
Church	77.2	37.8	76.6	31.4
Dancing	26.9	37.8	24.0	39.1
Drinking	6.0	23.1	7.2	15.4
Gambling	1.2	3.2	2.4	1.9
Movies	65.9	69.2	69.5	74.4
Music	85.0	75.0	92.2	74.4
Politics	19.8	13.5	15.6	15.4
Radio	89.2	72.4	90.4	77.6
Reading	71.3	48.1	73.1	44.9
Sports	50.3	33.3	57.5	37.8

Source: Harvey J. Locke, *Predicting Adjustment in Marriage* (New York: Holt, Rinehart & Winston, Inc., 1951), p. 374. Copyright © 1951, by Henry Holt and Company, New York. Reprinted by permission of Holt, Rinehart & Winston, Inc., New York.

tribute to family integration by creating a warm feeling that this union has something separate, something over and above other marriages.[54]

CHANGES IN PATTERNS. Social pressure has had much to do with the various changing recreational patterns of modern living. Whyte points out that each "court" in suburban housing developments appears to produce a different pattern of nonwork action; that is, whether newcomers who move into a new section of suburbs will become civic leaders, bridge fans, or church-goers. The results are, to a large extent, influenced by the interests and unique concerns of that particular "court" or neighborhood within the suburb.[55]

Economic pressures, too, have an effect upon the leisure activities of couples after marriage. There are usually special business and professional expectations for the young couple. They must attend certain parties, be seen at certain functions, or occasionally entertain the boss at home for dinner. If the couple are not prepared for this situation, their recreational activities are more likely to be unsatisfactory.

Additional economic pressure is exerted by today's mobile living. The family that moves frequently is more dependent upon community recreational services.

It must also be noted that much of recreation has become individual-centered rather than family-centered. In a simple agrarian society, the total family served as the central unit for the recreation of its members.

The type of work done by individual family members today, however, differs considerably, and diversified work frequently demands diversified recreation. Husbands and wives are spending more time at separate activities within their own respective groups away from home. In one sense this is healthy, but in another sense it does not bring a marriage or a family closer together. The advent of television also serves as an obstacle to building effective communication within a family: it is actually taking, and not giving, attitudes. The report of a Senate committee, studying leisure-time activities, indicates that better than three fourths of families present total nonwork time is being spent passively watching others perform.[56] A study by McDonagh, which took place about the time television became widespread throughout the American culture, found that, in general, members of families with television sets were not talking as much or as effectively with one another as they had before. There can be little doubt but that such things as television do reduce the intimate, face-to-face communication which is so important in the formation of attitudes and friendships.

Table 14–6. **Amount of talking done by TV and nontelevision family members**

	Per cent	
Talking	*Television families*	*Nontelevision families*
More	8.4	13.8
Less	62.1	14.9
Same	29.5	71.3

Source: Edward C. McDonagh, "Television and the Family," *Sociology and Social Research,* **35:**120. Copyright © 1950, by The University of Southern California Press, Los Angeles, Calif. Reprinted by permission.

An additional aspect of the changing recreational pattern is its growing commercial quality. Public recreation has now become big business. The family runs a poor second in competition with commercial recreational agencies that cater to the individual needs of its members. All of this points up the need for the assumption of a new role in marriage; that of leisure-time manager. If some responsibility is not accepted by mates for this role, there will be increasingly fewer family activities.

Recreational patterns also differ by cultures. Within the various subcultures of America, leisure-time activity is found to be affected by climate. In the South, where the climate is warmer, there are more outdoor hours, and thus less time is spent in such activities as reading and television. Examination of many other cultures shows that recreation outside the home is now becoming a worldwide trend. Thamavit states this to be true of the family in Thailand.[57] Recreation in the home has become very limited in the Arab world, except on a few occasions (such as weddings). In this culture, men usually visit men, and women visit women. "Clubs and cafe houses take a good deal of the time for men. They often spend their evenings there, chatting or playing indoor games."[58] Mogey reports that except for some of the southern English urban families who "still remain an isolated nucleus unit of a married pair and children living in a house by themselves in the middle of a garden," recreation in England is becoming more diversified.[59]

Recreation is a universal human need, but only recently has it come to be considered a community responsibility. For example, in 1910 only 7.5 per cent of American cities with at least 2500 inhabitants, had public playgrounds; at present almost all such cities do.[60] There is also a growing use of public facilities for recreational purposes. Some recreational functions are being transferred to schools, churches, and community houses.

Currently, a new view on recreational activities is coming into focus. The advent of a so-called family night is part of the concept. The competition for the time of the family member has become so overwhelming that many families are setting aside one night a week as a meetingless night, reserved exclusively for the family. There is also a new slant on the use of vacations as part of family recreation. Many couples are able

Figure 14-2. Many families are setting aside one night a week as a meetingless night, reserved exclusively for family members. (Courtesy of the Hammond Organ Company.)

Figure 14-3. In playrooms, the family members—separately or as a unit—can play together.

to delay play together for a time, and then—through a vacation trip— again focus completely on playing together.[61] Frequently this results in family members becoming reunited and reacquainted with each other. In recent years, family camping has increased. Many families report that, once they have experienced this type of traveling, they would never again travel any other way. In addition to being an inexpensive way of travel- ing, family camping has been valuable in making the members happily dependent upon one another for communication and play.

Another new slant on recreation is the "new look" in the family home. There is a trend among the middle class to add a room to the house, which is usually called the *playroom*. Here the family, separately or as a unit, can play together. Today there is also much more equipment for play within the average backyard. In the modern home the backyard is quite often considered a part of the house itself. With charcoal burners and patios, informal outdoor entertainment of friends or family members has become more popular.

There is much positive good in all these new forces and changes within recreation. For example, several organizations sponsor activities for chil- dren. This actually strengthens the parent-child relationship by occa- sionally giving the parents greater freedom to pursue adult activities. A "breathing spell" for the mother and a chance for the spouses to become reacquainted while the children are well taken care of, can be a decided asset to modern marriage.

Today it is often necessary for mates to spend part of their leisure time apart. Activities enjoyed without the spouse may add versatility and balance to each personality, and thus lead to a more balanced marriage. In fact, any activity that refreshes and adds interest to living, without threatening the marriage relationship, is likely to add to the success of the marriage. Marriage has at times been too all-consuming as a relationship. Actually, each member has his own personality and his own needs; marriage should not be a relationship in which individual identity is lost or in which either partner becomes a slave to the other. It is natural for mates to continue to grow apart as well as together. Any activity that contributes to either aspect of this growth without adversely affecting the other is probably worthwhile. There can not only be too much freedom, but also too much togetherness.

> But let there be spaces in your togetherness,
> And let the winds of the heavens dance between you,
> Love one another, but make not a bond of love;
> Let it rather be a moving sea between the shores
>   of your souls,
> Fill each other's cup but drink not from one cup.
> Give one another of your bread but eat not from
>   the same loaf.
> Sing and dance together and be joyous,
> But let each one of you be alone,
> Even as the strings of a lute are alone
> Though they quiver with the same music.[62]

FAMILY CYCLE. Recreational needs change at different stages of the family cycle itself. First, there is a need for modification of many earlier practices. Actually, many of the recreational failures in marriage are caused by bad premarital recreational habits. Recreation plays a major role during courtship, but after marriage new responsibilities come first. Most premarital couples indulge in expensive types of recreation, and often young married couples are dissatisfied with the couple-centered activities that they can afford. Frequently, they are untrained to function in the activities more available to them.

There is also a shift in individual values toward leisure activities after marriage. Before marriage, men are likely to spend a good portion of their leisure time pursuing "thrills"; afterward, they are more likely to work in their gardens or wash their cars. The married man must curb his self-indulgences, interest, time, money, and pleasures for the sake of the whole family, and the rewards at first do not seem to warrant the sacrifice. Many colleges are at last becoming aware of the difference in recreational activities before and after marriage. Such things as student-union activities on campus are being made available to individuals and couples at low cost. Many of the activities now sponsored in student unions can be carried on after marriage as valuable couple-centered and individual-centered recreational activities, such as exhibits, instructions in various subjects, movies, concerts, hobby shows, coffee hours, sings, talent shows, and tournaments.

Further change in recreational activities within the family cycle occurs after the birth of the children. The number of activities engaged in by a family, as a family, depends upon its composition. In general, families with children under twelve years of age appear more likely to participate in recreation as a unit.[63]

Figure 14-4. Families with children under twelve years of age appear more likely to participate in recreation as a unit. (Courtesy of the Warner-Lambert Pharmaceutical Company.)

When the first pregnancy occurs, many activities are curtailed and several others eliminated entirely. This can cause deep frustration in some marriages. When the wife is pregnant, the couple must keep more to themselves, and after the children arrive, babysitters cost money. Furthermore, in today's society, children are not taken along to activities as perhaps they once would have been. When the child-rearing stage commences, the recreational pattern becomes almost entirely child-centered. This may lead to many unfair comparisons with how life used to be when each was single or how it still is with other couples. As parents, however, there are other opportunities open to the couple, in which they previously were probably uninterested, such as PTA, Scouts, and Little League.

Children may bring about economic pressures that curtail recreational activity. Many young fathers feel compelled to work overtime in order to get ahead, and thus they have less time for family play. When this happens, it is doubly important for wives to plan their schedules so that they can spend some leisure time with their husbands.

Although working hours are shorter in the present American culture, this is not true for all occupations. There are, for example, more demands outside regular working hours made on the white-collar workers for such things as luncheon clubs, civic groups, organized drives, church and social groups, PTA, political-action clubs, and hundreds more. The leadership role begins to assert itself as part of the new demands in the childbearing and child-rearing stages, and usually takes away from other forms of recreation. There is a danger that going too far in this direction will leave no time for the couple either alone or with other adults.

In the later years of the family cycle, the recreational pattern may change again. Older people generally have much more leisure time because many are no longer gainfully employed; however, they may no longer take part in activities in which they had previously participated. This is a problem that must be worked on in the American society. Stone found that 33 per cent of older people living with children average ten hours a day with nothing to do.[64] Many had never learned to play and now experience considerable frustration in not knowing how to use their leisure time.

Whatever is chosen as the major recreational interest ought to have the potential of lifelong enjoyment. No couple should attempt to find satisfaction in a sport or hobby simply because it is popular. They should follow their own inclinations, for no one needs to be an expert at an activity to derive enjoyment from it; in fact, a variety of activities rather than an obsession with one seems to stimulate daily pleasures that can be shared. Quiet pastimes should be alternated with more active games. By organizing the work schedule, a couple may then find more free time for family entertainment. Cooperative efforts such as nursery schools, babysitting "pools," and even vacations can help couples to get closer together again and to keep alive their spirit of play.

Mutual friends

In Landis' study, 76.4 per cent of the couples reported satisfactory agreement from the beginning in the choice of mutual friends, and only 7.9 per cent had never agreed in this area.[65] In spite of those figures, however, this area is increasing as a concern in contemporary marriages. In earlier days, most of a couple's friends were known to each partner. Today, several friends may be husband-centered; others, wife-centered; and a few, couple-centered. Sometimes engaged couples are critical of each other's friends. This certainly indicates possible marital trouble later. Burgess and Cottrell found that it was favorable to adjustment in marriage for both husband and wife to have many friends of both sexes.[66]

The geographical mobility of today's society increases the difficulty of making mutual friends. About four fifths of the persons who marry change their residence at the time of marriage or within a year or so.[67] The college-graduate family, particularly, changes residence often during the early years. Through the process of making new acquaintances frequently, however, they become more familiar with customs other than their own, and this experience favors the healthy maintenance of democratic family and social ideals. Friends of both sexes are indeed important to a happy marriage. In Locke's study, twice as many divorced as happily married couples were found to have "almost no" or "just a few" friends in common.[68]

EFFECTS OF SUBURBIA. Suburban living has its effect upon mutual-friend selection within marriage. Increasingly, more people select even their house location where they may have something in common with the neighbors who already live there. Coffee-breaks for suburban wives have replaced backyard fences as a means of ascertaining which neighbors have similar values. The ability to turn neighbors into friends also depends on where one lives. In a large-city apartment house, exclusiveness is both possible and expected, but in small towns or average-size cities, neighbors are more important as friends.

COMMON DENOMINATORS. There are various common denominators in the choice of mutual friends. Church groups, lodges, civic clubs, and other organizations are excellent places for couples in a new community to meet other people with similar interests, values, and beliefs. Church is frequently reported as "a point of entry" into a new community for families on the move.[69] The majority of happily adjusted couples tend to pick their friends according to the same principles that they used in choosing each other. Reporting on their extensive research on how successful couples pick their friends, Zimmerman and Cervantes state:

As a matter of fact the same analysis was repeated twenty times, including all kinds of groups from industrial workers to religious groups and located throughout the whole urban Northeast as far west as Chicago and south as Philadelphia. Everywhere we found the same result—families seeking the highest contribution to the future of our culture, as measured by intellectual training and motivation of any reasonable number of children, defined their domestic personal environment with the utmost care. By rigid selection of household friends, they try to rule out the divorced, delinquent, and anomic personalities. This family self-protection is as rigid or more rigid than the initial act of mating selection itself.[70]

The mutual friends of happily married couples were frequently like the family in religious faith, regional background, and economic class. The more intimate friends were usually more like the family than were other friends. Among friends of the more successful financial families, more than 70 per cent were of a similar economic class, but among the less financially successful families, only 58.5 per cent of friends were economically successful.[71] This suggests a greater liberality in the selection of friends among the middle-class families than the wealthier families.

Zimmerman and Cervantes also report that regional background, with its attitudes and tastes, is as significant a factor as religious affiliation in influencing the formation of family-friend groups.

Table 14–7. **Homogamy of best friends as contrasted with all friends by family income group**

Annual income group condition	Per cent of closest family friends in same group	Per cent of all family friends in same group	Per cent of this group considered best friends by other groups
Up to $2000	44	39.4	4.6
$2000–5000	66	59.4	23.7
$5000–10,000	64	56.9	29.3
More than $10,000	54	44.7	10.4

Source: Carle C. Zimmerman and Lucius F. Cervantes, *Marriage and the Family* (Chicago: Henry Regnery Corp., 1956), p. 105. Copyright © 1956, by Henry Regnery Corp., Chicago, Ill. Reprinted by permission.

THE LATER YEARS. A different criterion is used for the selection of friends as a couple grow older. Older people enjoy more informal social participation, often simply on a neighborhood basis. There is less restriction of friends by evaluation of income as people grow older.[72] Their selection of friends seems more equalitarian than that of many young couples. "Most said they had at least half a dozen [mutual] friends and about half said they had as many or more friends than they had before retirement."[73] Friendships in older years are in a state of constant flux or readjustment, often because of death or change of habits for improved health. Couples who are able to establish satisfactory patterns of choosing friends early in marriage, however, seem best able to find new ones when the need arises.

Table 14–8. Homogamy of friends in families by religious confession

Religion	Per cent of this group considered best friends by other groups	Per cent of family friends in that group for families not in that group	Per cent of best family friends in same group as family
Protestant	77.1	25.2	79.7
Catholic	37.6	12.0	37.4
Jewish	60.3	2.0	67.3
Other	63.3	7.9	63.0
None	27.8	6.1	38.6

Source: Carle C. Zimmerman and Lucius F. Cervantes, *Marriage and the Family* (Chicago: Henry Regnery Corp., 1956), p. 106. Copyright © 1956, by Henry Regnery Corp., Chicago, Ill. Reprinted by permission.

Table 14–9. Homogamy of family friend groups by region of origin

Region	Origin of family friends for families of this region	Origin of family friends for families not of this region
Pacific Coast	59.9	29.0
Rocky Mountains	29.8	6.5
Midwest	52.8	23.2
Southwest	34.1	7.9
South	32.4	6.1
East	42.5	14.6
Other countries	30.4	6.4

Source: Carle C. Zimmerman and Lucius F. Cervantes, *Marriage and the Family* (Chicago: Henry Regnery Corp., 1956), p. 107. Copyright © 1956, by Henry Regnery Corp., Chicago, Ill. Reprinted by permission.

Summary

This discussion has dealt with four areas of marital adjustment: in-laws, religion, recreation, and friendships. In-laws are a part of every cultural heritage and cause concern in almost all cultures. There is a definite relationship between emotional adjustment with in-laws and total marital happiness. Young couples are cautioned to remember that much in-law trouble comes from misinterpretation and a loss of objectivity. Furthermore, in-law difficulty usually has a feminine pattern, and this includes mothers-in-law more than any other relationship. If in-law difficulties are to occur, they usually do so in the first months of marriage. Various major factors affecting in-law attitudes include personality, maturity, age at marriage, the extent of premarital acquaintance, the extent of parental approval of the marriage, the social-activity pattern, the level of educational attainment, the place of residence, and the level of parental maturity. To avert problems, the couple should always place the marriage first, acquire patience, and remember that each must accept the other's family as his own.

Religious affiliation and attendance patterns are related to marital adjustment, but religious practice has even more influence. External factors that affect religion as an area of marital adjustment are the birth of children, premarital conditioning toward religion, and economic and educational status. Religious ideals can improve a marriage by serving as a supporting, characterizing, tolerating, and equalizing force.

Planned leisure time is an important but much neglected aspect of today's American society. Recreation may lead to individual happiness by developing self-discipline and contributing to mental health; it can also provide a cohesive force in marital adjustment. The changing recreation patterns in the American culture are brought about by social and economic pressures. There is much more individualism in recreation today, but too much leisure time is spent passively. Recreation changes during the family's childbearing and child-rearing years, and again as the couple get older.

The area of mutual friends becomes increasingly important in a highly mobile society. Suburban living itself affects the choice of mutual friends. Common denominators for the choice of friends are such factors as economics, religion, and region of origin.

By emphasizing the positive values within all these areas of marriage, the potential of greatly enriching their life together is unlimited for every couple.

Notes

1. The highest rates of inbreeding (first cousins and so forth) are found in Brazil, Japan, India, and Israel. Extreme low in-breeding rates exist in the United States and most of Western Europe. See Newton Freire-Maia, "In-breeding Levels in Different Countries," *Eugenics Quarterly* (September 1957), 127–38.

2. Evelyn M. Duvall, *In-Laws: Pro and Con* (New York: Association Press, 1954), pp. 224, 261; and Pauls S. Ullman, "A Sample of Married College Students and Aspects of Their In-Law Relationships," *The Family Life Coordinator*, 4:20.

3. Rex A. Skidmore, Therese L. Smith, and Delbert L. Nye, "Characteristics of Married Veterans," *Marriage and Family Living*, 11:103.

4. Ralph Linton, *The Study of Man* (New York: Appleton-Century-Crofts, Inc., 1936).

5. Robert H. Lowie, *Primitive Society* (New York: Liveright Publishing Corp., 1920), pp. 80–100.

6. Judson T. Landis, "Length of Time Required to Achieve Adjustment in Marriage," *American Sociological Review*, 11:666–77.

7. John L. Thomas, "Marital Failure and Duration," *Social Order*, 3:36.

8. Robert O. Blood, *Anticipating Your Marriage* (New York: The Free Press of Glencoe, Inc., 1955), p. 325.

9. Duvall, *op. cit.*

10. Marvin B. Sussman, "The Help Pattern in the Middle-Class Family," *American Sociological Review*, 18:22–28.

11. Bronislaw Malinowski, *The Sexual Life of Savages in North Western Melanesia* (New York: Liveright Publishing Corp., 1929).

12. Robert F. Winch, *The Modern Family* (New York: Holt, Rinehart & Winston, Inc., 1952), p. 299.

13. Duvall, *op. cit.*, Chap. 3.

14. Willard Waller and Reuben Hill, *The Family: A Dynamic Interpretation* (New York: The Dryden Press, 1951), p. 291.

15. In addition to all the studies previously cited, the reader is referred to the following: Sheldon Stryker, "The Adjustment of Married Offspring to Their Parents," *American Sociological Review*, 20:149–54; Paul Wallin, "Sex Differences in Attitudes to In-Laws: A Test of Theory," *The American Journal of Sociology*, 39:466–69; and Mirra Komarovsky, "Continuities in Family Research," *The American Journal of Sociology*, 62:42–47.

16. Ullman, *op. cit.*

17. Bernard C. Rosen and Roy d'Andrade, "The Psychosocial Origins of Achievement Motivation," *Sociometry*, 22:185–218.

18. Wallin, *op. cit.*

19. Stryker, *op. cit.*

20. Earl L. Koos, *Families in Trouble* (New York: King's Crown Press, 1948), p. 44.

21. See Ruth Cavan, "Family Tension Between the Old and the Middle-Aged," *Marriage and Family Living*, 18:324; or E. E. LeMasters, "Social-Class Mobility and Family Integration," *Marriage and Family Living*, 14:226.

22. Peggy Marcus, "In-Law Relationship Adjustment of Couples Married Between Two and Eleven Years," *Journal of Home Economics*, 43:35–37.

23. *Ibid.*, The research of Duvall, *op. cit.*, also supports this finding.

24. Robert M. Dinkel, "Parent-Child Conflict in Minnesota Families," *American Sociological Review*, 8:412.

25. Marcus, *op. cit.*

26. R. F. Fortune, *Sorcerers of Dobu* (New York: E. P. Dutton and Company, Inc., 1932).

27. George Karlson, *Adaptability and Communication in Marriage* (Aktiebolag: Uppsala, Almquist and Wiksells Boktrycker, 1951), p. 106.

28. Gibson Winter, *Love and Conflict* (Garden City, N.Y.: Doubleday & Company, Inc., 1958), p. 167.

29. Marcus, *op. cit.*

30. Landis, *op. cit.*

31. Judson T. Landis, "Marriages of Mixed and Nonmixed Religious Faith," *American Sociological Review*, 14:401–407.

32. Harvey J. Locke, *Predicting Adjustment in Marriage* (New York: Holt, Rinehart & Winston, Inc., 1951).

33. E. W. Burgess and Paul Wallin, *Engagement and Marriage* (Philadelphia: J. B. Lippincott & Co., 1953), pp. 290–91.

34. E. W. Burgess and Leonard S. Cottrell, *Predicting Success or Failure in Marriage* (Englewood Cliffs, N.J.: Prentice-Hall, Inc., 1939), pp. 122–26.

35. DeWitt Reddick, "They Give Marriage a Second Chance," *Child Family Digest* (February 1954), 43.

36. Locke, *op. cit.,* p. 241.

37. James H. S. Bossard and Eleanor S. Boll, *Ritual in Family Living* (Philadelphia: University of Pennsylvania Press, 1950), p. 22, *et passim.*

38. Dorothy Fahs Beck, "The Changing Moslem Family of the Middle East," *Marriage and Family Living,* 19:340–46.

39. Lewis M. Terman, *Psychological Factors in Marital Happiness* (New York: McGraw-Hill Book Company, Inc., 1938), p. 235.

40. James Peterson, Doctoral Study, University of Southern California, Los Angeles, Calif., 1951.

41. Gerhard E. Lenski, "Social Correlates of Religious Interest," *American Sociological Review,* 18:533–44. Active religious participation by parents reaches its peak when their children are small. See Sarah F. Anders, "Religious Behavior of Church Families," *Marriage and Family Living,* 17:54–57.

42. Gerald J. Schnepp and Mary Margaret Johnson, "Do Religious Background Factors Have Predictive Value?" *Marriage and Family Living,* 14:302.

43. John Dewey, *A Common Faith* (New Haven: Yale University Press, 1934), p. 24.

44. Ernest R. Groves, *Christianity and the Family* (New York: The Macmillan Company, 1943), p. 27.

45. John Herman Randall, *Preface to Philosophy* (New York: The Macmillan Company, 1945), Part IV: "The Meaning of Religion."

46. For example, grace before meals is reported at present to be a regular practice in over 70 per cent of Protestant families. See Roy W. Fairchild and John Charles Wynn, *Families in the Church: A Protestant Survey* (New York: Association Press, 1961), p. 184.

47. Kenneth R. Cunningham and Theodore B. Johannis, Jr., "Research on the Family and Leisure: A Review and Critique of Selected Studies," *The Family Life Coordinator,* 9:25–32.

48. Martin H. and Esther S. Neumeyer, *Leisure and Recreation,* 3rd ed. (New York: The Ronald Press Company, 1958), pp. 159–60.

49. William C. Menninger, "Recreation and Mental Health," *Recreation* (November 1948), 343.

50. Nash defines much of recreation in America as "the crazy things people do to keep from going crazy." Jay B. Nash, *Philosophy of Recreation and Leisure* (New York: Philosophical Library, Inc., 1953).

51. Landis, "Length of Time Required to Achieve Adjustment in Marriage," *op. cit.*

52. Burgess and Cottrell, *op. cit.,* p. 62.

53. Robert Williamson, Doctoral Study, University of Southern California, Los Angeles, Calif., 1952.

54. Bossard and Boll, *op. cit.,* p. 201.

55. William H. Whyte, Jr., *The Organization Man* (New York: Simon and Schuster, Inc., 1956), Part 7.

56. Congressional Record (1960).

57. Vibul Thamavit and Robert Golden, "The Family in Thailand," *Marriage and Family Living,* 16:388.

58. M. Kamel Nahas, "The Family in Egypt," *Marriage and Family Living,* 16:299.

59. J. M. Mogey, "The Family in England," *Marriage and Family Living,* 16:224.

60. *Recent Social Trends in the United States,* Report of the President's

Research Committee on Social Trends (New York: McGraw-Hill Book Company, Inc., 1933), 2 vols., p. 917.

61. The U.S. Bureau of Labor reports that paid vacations, once a coveted fringe-benefit of the executive, have now become common place even for factory workers. See *Report of the United States Bureau of Labor on Recreation* (1959), p. 197.

62. Reprinted from *The Prophet* by Kahlil Gibran, with permission of the publisher, Alfred A. Knopf, Inc., New York. Copyright © 1923, by Kahlil Gibran; renewal copyright © 1951, by Administrators C.T.A. of Kahlil Gibran Estate, and Mary G. Gibran.

63. John Frank Schmidt and Wayne C. Rohrer, "The Relationship of Family Type to Social Participation," *Marriage and Family Living,* 18:230.

64. Carol L. Stone, "Living Arrangements and Social Adjustment of the Aged," *The Family Life Coordinator,* 6:13.

65. Landis, "Length of Time Required to Achieve Adjustment in Marriage," *op. cit.*

66. Burgess and Cottrell, *op. cit.,* pp. 357–58.

67. Paul C. Glick, "The Life Cycle of the Family," *Marriage and Family Living,* 17:8.

68. Locke, *op. cit.,* p. 234.

69. Fairchild and Wynn, *op. cit.,* 199.

70. Zimmerman and Cervantes, *op. cit.,* p. 98.

71. *Ibid.,* p. 97.

72. Gordon J. Aldridge, "Informal Social Relationships in a Retirement Community," *Marriage and Family Living,* 21:70–72.

73. *Ibid.,* p. 71.

Questions for further thought

1. In what ways are religious ideals and American democratic ideals similar or different?
2. What basic function does religious affiliation perform in marriage that could not just as well be performed without it?
3. What are the main complaints against in-laws?
4. Is the in-law problem any greater today than it once was?
5. What suggestions are appropriate when a young couple find themselves economically dependent on parents, yet resent all the advice and attempted management of their affairs that accompany financial aid?
6. What are some similarities between the ways families choose friends, and the ways marriage partners choose each other?
7. Should a mate give up a friendship if it is interfering with his marriage?
8. Why is it so much more difficult nowadays for a recreational activity to create a genuine togetherness for all family members?
9. Why does the enthusiasm for family vacations appear to diminish as the children grow older?

Recommended films

The Family and Relatives (University of Michigan Television Center).
Music and the Family (University of Michigan Television Center).
Family Recreation (University of Michigan Television Center).
Religion and the Family (University of Michigan Television Center).

Suggested supplemental readings

BOOKS

Barbour, Harriot B. *Music for Family Fun.* New York: E. P. Dutton & Co., Inc., 1961.

Bowman, Henry A. *A Christian Interpretation of Marriage.* Philadelphia: Westminister Press, 1959.

Bracey, H. E. *Neighbours: Subdivision Life in England and the United States.* Baton Rouge, La.: Louisiana State University Press, 1964.

Cole, William Graham. *Sex and Love in the Bible.* New York: Association Press, 1959.

Dewey, John. *A Common Faith.* New Haven: Yale University Press, 1934.

Donahue, Wilma (ed.). *Free Time—Challenge to Later Maturity.* Ann Arbor, Mich.: University of Michigan Press, 1958.

Duvall, Evelyn M. *In-Laws: Pro and Con.* New York: Association Press, 1954.

Eisenberg, Hellen and Larry. *The Family Fun Book.* New York: Association Press, 1961.

Fairchild, Roy W., and John Charles Wynn. *Families in the Church: A Protestant Survey.* New York: Association Press, 1961.

Green, Arnold W. *Recreation, Leisure, and Politics.* New York: McGraw-Hill Book Company, Inc., 1964.

Kaplan, Max. *Leisure in America.* New York: John Wiley & Sons, Inc., 1960.

Lee, Robert. *Religion and Leisure in America: A Study in Four Dimensions.* Nashville, Tenn.: Abingdon Press, 1964.

Lenski, Gerhard. *The Religious Factor.* Garden City, N.Y.: Doubleday & Company, Inc., 1961.

Levi, Shonie B., and Sylvia R. Kaplan. *Across the Threshold.* New York: Farrar, Strauss & Company, 1959.

Miller, Norman P., and Duane M. Robinson. *The Leisure Age: Its Challenge to Recreation.* Belmont, Calif.: Wadsworth Publishing Company, 1963.

Neumeyer, Martin H. and Esther S. *Leisure and Recreation.* New York: The Ronald Press Company, 1958.

Paxman, Monroe and Shirley. *Family Night Fun.* Englewood Cliffs, N.J.: Prentice-Hall, Inc., 1950.

Porter, Blaine R. *Selected Readings in the Latter-Day Saint Family.* Dubuque, Iowa: William C. Brown Book Company, 1963.

Salisbury, W. Seward. *Religion in American Culture.* Homewood, Ill.: Dorsey Press, 1965.

Wilie, William P. *Human Nature and Christian Marriage.* New York: Association Press, 1961.

ARTICLES

Anders, Sarah R. "Religious Behavior of Church Families," *Marriage and Family Living,* 17:54–57.

Burchinal, Lee G. "Marital Satisfaction and Religious Behavior," *American Sociological Review,* 22:306–10.

Cavan, Ruth S. "Family Tensions Between the Old and the Middle Age," *Marriage and Family Living,* 18:324–27.

Glick, Paul C. "Marriage Instability: Variations by Size of Place and Religion," *The Milbank Memorial Fund Quarterly,* 41:43–45.

Jelden, Helmut. "Recreation—A Vital Problem of Our Time," *Soz. Welt* (1955), 110–16.

Marcus, Peggy. "In-Law Relationship Adjustment of Couples Married Between Two and Eleven Years," *Journal of Home Economics,* 43:35–37.

Wood, Leland F. "Religion as a Family Foundation," *Journal of Social Hygiene,* 36:181–86.

Wilensky, Harold L. "The Uneven Distribution of Leisure: The Impact of Economic Growth on 'Free Time'," *Social Problems,* 6:56–58.

Deciding on roles

chapter 15

Much of modern marital discord is related to discontentment or disagreement between mates over their respective roles. In a comparison of 100 happily married and 100 divorced couples on their role ideals, Jacobson found that divorced couples had experienced more conflict over views on roles within marriage.[1] Studies by Ort in this connection also revealed that role conflict is as likely to occur in the marriages of college graduates as in other marriages.[2]

Increasing role concern in America

It is only natural that there should be more concern over roles in American marriages than in many other marriage systems. As Kargman has said: "When two individuals upon marriage found their own family, they are at liberty (within the limits set by the political state) to set up their own system of self-government. It is this freedom which bears the seed of possible conflict."[3] Thus, the increasing emphasis upon the democratic system in America represents a constant challenge to older traditions in all areas, especially because young people no longer follow traditional role expectations. Today's couples must reject, ignore, or modify the older concepts, and it is partly because of this process of evaluation and decision that more concern is inevitable. Trouble often comes when one mate is pressured into assuming a role that he does not want or is not prepared to take.

PRESSURE FROM SOCIETY. Everyone acts and reacts in the complex network of relationships inherent in today's society. In the interaction between two or more persons, patterns of expectations emerge. These pat-

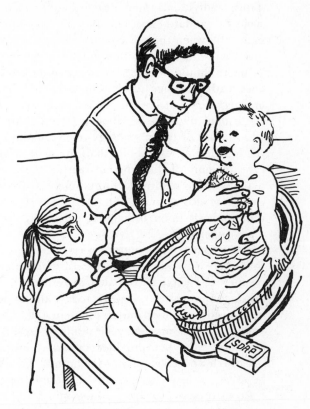

Figure 15-1. Increasingly, young people no longer follow traditional role expectations.

terns constitute the culture of the group. Culture is handed down by formal and informal educational devices. Patterns of culture enable man to engage in ordered and purposeful activities toward the solution of his needs. Much of his behavior is directed at other people, who are expected to respond in an appropriate fashion. Habits of reaction approved by the group serve as examples for the individual. This is also true of marital roles assigned to each sex by virtue of overt approval of their society. That is, the role of the husband in America contains general similarities of behavior for all men, and the role of wife contains general similarities of behavior for all women.[4] Pressures from society toward certain prescribed marital roles are still felt, even within higher educational circles. This is illustrated by much of the discussion in the 1960 White House Conference on Children and Youth:

Thus again, as constantly throughout the conference, the question reverted to the quality of parenthood and of family life. Mothers were called irresponsible for going to work outside the home. Fathers were blamed for not spending enough time with their children—or, conversely, for taking over the mother's role. . . .[5]

Thus, individuals may develop guilt feelings for their rejection of society's standard expectations. This rejection may lead to in-law troubles, especially when there is conflict between the role a wife wishes to assume and that which her mother-in-law thinks she should play.

There should be some systematized division of responsibility in accordance with marriage ideals. For efficient living, certain family functions are necessary outside the home; others, within the home. Much of the traditional division of labor was caused by sexual limitations. By the very nature of her physiology—menstruation, pregnancy, and lactation—the female was less mobile than the male; thus, it was sensible for her to care for more of the functions within the home. On the other hand, the male, with no sex-linked limitations was free for greater activity outside the home. Role division in the past was definitely related to necessity; the emphasis upon individual personality fulfillment was secondary to many other aspects of living.

RELATION TO INDIVIDUAL PERSONALITIES. Each mate must recognize that there is always some inconsistency between what is desired of a partner and what is conceded in return. Furthermore, in fulfilling role satisfactions within marriage today, the expectations of the individual are considered more important than the expectations of the culture. A young married man may be admired by his friends, enjoy prestige in his work, be a good provider, be moral, law-abiding, and even be active in church and civic affairs—yet he may be a failure in his wife's eyes if he does not meet her personal expectations of a husband's role.

CONDITIONING FACTORS. Many individual expectations stem from preconceived notions acquired from earlier family experience. Ingersoll states that children tend to absorb the authority patterns displayed by their own parents.[6] Generally, first learning experiences come from the home, thus, it is only natural that the first concepts of the marital roles develop from the basic family experience. Other patterns outside the family are also gathered along the way, both before and after marriage, and these too are important in motivating human behavior.

The influence of family experiences is nowhere more apparent than in the young couple's marital role relationships. This is illustrated by the research of Luckey. She took 594 former family-life students now married, and selected forty-one couples who reported high satisfaction with marriage, and forty other couples who reported significantly less satisfaction with marriage as measured by the Locke scale. Their responses were examined for likeness or identification with parents. The men who reported high satisfaction in marriage identified with their own fathers' roles significantly more than did men who reported dissatisfaction in marriage. There was no difference between satisfied and dissatisfied women in identification of themselves with their mothers' roles. The women who were more satisfied in their marriages, however, did perceive their husbands as being more similar to their own fathers to a much greater degree than did women who were unhappy in their marriages. In like manner, significantly more men who were satisfied in their marriages pictured their wives as similar to their own mothers, than did men who were dissatisfied in their marriages.[7] A husband, reared in a family where the father was authoritarian and the mother submissive will often unconsciously seek to perpetuate this pattern in his own marriage, even though he gives lip service to modern concepts of democracy.

Conscious, cultural sex influences are also conditioning factors. There are still many preconceived notions of what is "masculine" and "feminine." Dunn, who studied 436 high school seniors in northern Louisiana, found that the majority of both sexes gave adequate lip service to the idea that the wife and husband should share household tasks according to individual interest and ability rather than according to traditional concepts of "man's work" and "woman's work." On a specific test, however, both sexes responded more in accordance with the traditional division of duties than in any other way.[8]

Environmental circumstances also serve as conditioning factors to role concepts. In rural areas, for example, the traditional concept is still in operation, and the wife still performs as cook, mender, sewer, housekeeper, and child-rearer. In the urban business life, many wives must assume additional roles as companion, hostess, and representative of the family to the community.

Roles may also differ by ethnic groups. This is quite apparent in "foreign" sections in large cities.[9] Many ethnic groups still hold to the concept of the subordination of the wife to her husband. Frequently the father controls all the money earned by individual family members. Many such groups hold to the idea of unrestricted child-bearing, and even have some differing concepts as to husband-wife roles in relation to food habits, dress, table manners, and recreational preference for the sexes. The first and second generations of such groups may experience fewer marital-role conflicts than others within the American society.[10]

Social class also influences role expectations. The middle class puts more stress on upward mobility, and the wife's expected role is to support this upward movement.[11] Division of labor within the home seems more clear-cut in lower-class families. The men in the lower social classes seldom help with such household chores as washing or drying dishes, shopping for groceries, or cooking meals. Also, middle-class families tend to be more nearly equalitarian in their power-distribution patterns, while lower-class groups tend to reflect traditional patriarchal patterns.

The power structure

One of the newer role problems concerns the family power structure.

THE TRADITIONAL. Originally there was no role concern over power because the prescribed role for the husband was to serve as supreme head

of the family. This idea was supported in the Bible, and most people
in earlier societies accepted it:

> Wives, submit yourself unto your husbands, as unto the Lord. For the
> husband is the head of the wife even as Christ is head of the church; and
> He is the Savior of the body. Therefore, as the church is subject unto
> Christ, so let the wives be to their husbands in everything. Husbands, love
> your wives, even as Christ also loved the church, and gave Himself for it.[12]

Here was an honest reciprocal agreement, but the wife's power role
was subordinate to that of her husband's. This concept has been perpetuated in various circles by the basic belief that an absolute final
authority is necessary in all human relations. Joseph Smith, one of the
early leaders of the Mormon Church, is reported to have stated in this
connection: "There must be a presiding authority in the family. The
father is the head or president, or spokesman of the family."[13] The original concept of family power structure seems to have been that a husband
and wife were one person, but that the one person was the husband. To
carry out this concept successfully, it was necessary for the male to be
aggressive and masterful and for women and children to dedicate themselves to a submissive role.

Much of this concept came about from the idea that man was superior
to woman. Man was considered the thinker and doer; the woman, his
less gifted helpmate. Actually, all scientific studies in this connection
demonstrate that neither sex can be called "superior" or "inferior." The
evidence suggests that it is foolhardy to compare or measure the different
characteristics of each sex by identical standards. Each sex is complementary to the other; neither is superior nor inferior. Results of various
psychological tests indicate that the sexes think differently. Some of this
difference may arise from capacity; some of it from cultural conditioning.
This, however, does not necessarily mean that one sex is intellectually
superior to the other. Child-development studies at the Yale Clinic suggest that, at age six, girls are usually better in reading, writing, and
drawing than boys, but that boys are usually better in number work and
listening to stories.[14] There is much superficial evidence to support the
idea that man is superior to woman. Proportionately fewer women than
men have achieved greatness in many fields,[15] yet differences in motivation and opportunity were probably more important limiting factors
than sex. Until very recently women, were more or less second-class citizens: higher education was not open to them, and they were economically
dependent and had few legal rights. If a woman wanted to learn something, she should seek no greater authority than her husband, or so said
Paul in the New Testament: "If the woman would learn anything, let
her ask her husband at home."[16] Margaret Mead has stated that male ego

strength has depended upon man's assuming the position as the supporter of the family. Therefore, in order to guard and support male ego strength, culture has defined certain work roles as of first importance and denied them to women.[17] Perhaps this, in itself, has had much to do with the perpetuation of the concept that man is superior to woman.

There has also been a concept that woman is naturally submissive in nature, but this may be open to some serious questioning. Horney suggested some time ago that the idea of woman's greater dependency, the emphasis on woman's weakness and frailty, the idea that it is within a woman's "nature" to lean on someone, are myths mostly perpetuated by culture. Such characteristics are not necessarily inherent in the nature of woman.[18]

This is not to say that all role differences arise from the culture, for certainly some are caused by anatomy and physiology. Blind and deaf institutionalized children, who have no contact with a normal cultural influence, develop pronounced sex differences and activities. Boy's large muscles grow and develop at a much faster rate than those of girls, so it is natural for boys to feel a greater need for pushing, lifting, climbing, or anything that makes use of muscular strength. Girls' muscles are perhaps not as strong, but they appear to be more firmly coordinated. Thus, female finger dexterity is better, and girls enjoy such activities as dressing dolls and drawing more than boys do. Most girls learn to tie their shoes sooner than boys do. Obviously many concepts regarding power structure relate directly to inherent biological differences.[19] A study of primitive societies suggests, however, that culture is the greatest single influence upon the family power structure. Among such groups as the Mundugumor and the Tchambuli, Meade found that men tended to be more submissive, fearful, and nervous than in Western cultures, while women tended to be more virile, aggressive, and domineering. From childhood onward, each sex in that culture is more or less forced toward roles opposite to those assumed in Western cultures.[20]

Even a few family-textbook authors retreat to the traditional concept of power structure by implying that the male is boss outside the home and the wife is boss inside the home. This is sometimes rationalized as being "in keeping" with the spirit of democracy. The male is pictured as the primary representative of the family in the larger community; thus he must be invested with authority to speak for the marriage on outside matters. The female is pictured as the primary representative for socializing the children; thus she must be invested with the power to maintain discipline within the home. This, of course, brings up a question: Which one is the power should they disagree over something when both are present? Martinson even suggests that it is democratic for a wife to "defer" to her husband when he is home. Otherwise, he may come to be regarded by the children as a "junior partner" in the marriage.

"By a show of deference to his authority . . ., children may regard him as an equal to his wife."[21]

To the author this appears to be nothing more than a repetition of the traditional concept under a new disguise. It seems to repudiate the democratic goal of fulfilling each personality potential. In a true modern democratic marriage, there are no bosses; however, no studies have yet determined the efficacy of this equalitarian practice on the life adjustment of the children.

CHANGES IN THE OLD ORDER. Certainly there can be no denying that the old order changes. There is increased questioning of male judgment today, particularly within marriage. No longer are the husband's judgments on family behavior and welfare necessarily considered the last word. The widespread deletion from the wedding ceremony of the wife's promise to obey her husband is symptomatic of an increasingly equalitarian point of view. As Margaret Mead expresses it:

American women are better fed and better sheltered than almost any other women in the world. By and large their husbands seldom beat them. They are free to go almost anywhere in public life; they walk with faces uncovered, yet unexposed to disapproving comment or molestation. They can go to school just as their brothers can, and in fact often have a chance at a more modern education because it seems safer on the whole to do our experimenting on our daughters than on our sons. They can hold jobs, join unions, own businesses, sign checks, run for office, wear pants in public places. In most states their property is their own, and the worse limitations on their freedom are a few laws designed to protect their potential and actual maternity. If we were to go back and look over the issues raised by early generations of feminists, it would look as if a very large part of the battle they fought has been won.[22]

The concept of power-structure equality is spreading over the entire world as women increasingly become better educated. It has even been observed in the Arab world,[23] and Beck reports that there is a definite movement in this direction among Moslems.[24] Does this mean that the traditional concept of a single head of the home is all wrong? Not necessarily, for when both mates desire and believe in such a system it can operate smoothly and satisfactorily. A good example of this is found in the Mormon family pattern, although even here there is a change of intensity within the power structure. Basically, Mormons believe that patiarchal authority is a God-given endowment, and is necessary in their present lives and through eternity for a satisfactory system of family government. This is especially true in relation to religious controls.[25]

Elsewhere, a new concept is emerging, perhaps best termed *the compartmentalized system*. Under this system, each spouse has areas of absolute authority or major responsibility for decisions. Johannis found that mothers made most of the decisions on spending, except on large items (where fathers entered the power-structure picture).[26] This pattern seems to be an acceptable compromise for many modern families that do not subscribe to the older traditional concept of one absolute authority.

An even newer concept is that of shared responsibility in all areas. The power structure of the family is vested in the entire family itself, with nothing exclusive to either sex. There is a growing acceptance of this concept in the middle- and upper-class family structure. Johannis found that in about 63 per cent of the families in his survey, husbands and wives made all the decisions jointly. In another 11 per cent of the cases, even the children were brought into all decisions. The remaining 26 per cent followed the patriarchal, matriarchal, or compartmentalized system.[27] The working out of a satisfactory shared-responsibility plan has been shown to be associated with greater marital happiness. One researcher analyzed the engaged couples in the Burgess and Wallin study and divided them on the basis of a dominant scale into three groups: one in which the husband was dominant, one in which the wife was dominant, and one in which there was an equalitarian concept of power structure. The three groups were then analyzed on the basis of marital adjustment. The results indicated that the equalitarian concept was significantly associated with better marital adjustment for both mates.[28] This is not to suggest that every family or marriage is ready for this step. It is entirely conceivable that, when married couples are not ready for a shared-responsibility structure, it might, for a time at least, bring up more problems than it would solve. New concepts always take time to be put into effective practice. William Sumner wrote something about this many years ago, and it seems appropriate in many instances today: "The notion that a man's wife is the nearest person in the world to him is a relativeley modern notion, and one which is restricted to a comparatively small part of the human race."[29]

For many people, much learning and relearning will be necessary to achieve the responsible interaction necessary for democratic equality within marriage. Society itself must shift toward approval of this practice within the marital relationship. The necessity for this change is vividly demonstrated by the multiplicity of state laws regarding power over spending money earned by the wife outside the home. Only twelve states have community-property laws; that is, the earnings of both mates are under the control of both partners. In twenty-four states, whatever a wife earns is considered exclusively hers. In other states, the laws are less clear on this point, and in North Dakota and South Dakota, whatever a wife earns is still legally owned by her husband.

Many of today's marriages involve some sort of mixture between power extremes, with each couple struggling toward the equalitarian type. Furthermore, evidence suggests that either extreme, or any intermediate form, may be successful in a particular marriage at a particular time. For contemporary marital happiness, the crucial question is whether the couple can define and agree on a power-structure system.

Division of labor

The second major marital-role concern is in the division of labor. Certain work functions have historically been considered "male"; others, "female." The traditional division of labor implied that men worked outside the house and women worked inside the house. Originally, the male's tasks involved hard labor. When such work was finished, he needed to rest. In order for the man to fulfill his role as provider in an agrarian economy, he needed a wife who could make life comfortable when his day's work was done. Both roles contained well-defined rewards for adequate fulfillment. Ours, however, is no longer an agrarian society.

CONTRIBUTION TO HOUSEHOLD TASKS. One point of controversy over division of labor in modern marriages is exactly what household tasks should be assumed by which sex. This problem has been accentuated by recent emphasis upon companionship within the family. To be sure, there is a certain joy in doing things together, and this unity is important to every family. Much of the male's satisfaction in helping with household tasks, however, is dependent upon his attitude. It is not so much a question of how much he does but why he does it. Grandfathers formerly helped out in household work only in cases of emergency, and many males still resist housekeeping tasks or participate rather reluctantly. A decided asset to the needed attitudinal changes has been the advent of mechanical aids to housework. This has taken many household chores out of a strictly feminine category, and made them acceptable to many males.

It is probably safe to say that, from frequent participation in household tasks, husbands have contributed more toward improving the management of housekeeping methods than all the studies of management specialists ever have. Husbands have brought a fresher, more objective approach, and this has contributed greatly to the elimination of much drudgery in housekeeping.

Still, there are some men who resist helping with household tasks. They would prefer two outside jobs, and indeed their families might be financially and emotionally better off with such an arrangement. It should never be assumed that all families would thrive better if the husbands shared household tasks.

Even when two incomes are not necessary, there may still be problems over the division of household tasks. Research indicates that some husbands may be less tired in the evening than wives who have been laboring in the home all day. In fact, tests have proved that today's average housewife spends more energy in domestic tasks and child care than her husband does on his job.[30] There is some question, however, as to whether men are actually contributing more to household tasks or whether they are helping with new tasks within the home while the women are helping with more tasks outside the house.[31] With the advent of power tools, many wives now help with more outside chores, such as painting, mowing the lawn, repairing children's toys, and washing cars. Obviously then, the sharing of labor in the home is erasing the line between traditional roles. Johannis found many more couples sharing such tasks as care of the garden than was formerly true.[32] Blood and Wolfe conclude that little has actually changed over the years in regard to who assumes the *major* responsibility of various tasks although there is probably more sharing now.[33]

CARE OF CHILDREN. The trend toward a convergence in child-care roles appears unmistakable. One study reports that fathers are taking a much more active part in caring for, teaching, disciplining, and playing with their children. Furthermore, many fathers are reasonably content to do so, although sometimes pressed for time.[34]

Outside employment for women

Another area of social concern is the effect of employment on women. Whether or not a wife is to be gainfully employed outside the home depends largely upon the mutual considerations and goals of the couple. If the couple desire a higher standard of living, obviously the wife's contribution is invaluable. If their mutual goal is to attain the basic joys and comforts of home living, then the wife's employment is likely to mean a sacrifice.

An interesting reversal in mores is now in effect in many marriages. As White points out, some husbands, who a few years ago would have been ashamed to admit their wives worked, now boast about the economic contributions of their spouses.[35] Actually, the conflict faced by some young couples now arises because the wife is dissatisfied with work outside the home while the husband considers it her duty to be employed.

The percentage of married women employed outside the home has been increasing annually in American society.

The increase, however, is not general. One variable is geographic location. The U.S. Bureau of the Census figures show a higher percentage of double-income families in metropolitan areas than in the rural regions.[36] Outside employment for wives also varies with the number of years married. The majority of young wives are employed outside the home in the first year of marriage, but after five years of marriage the number is greatly reduced. Socioeconomic class also affects employment

Table 15–1. Full-time working women in the labor force

| Date | Number | | Per cent married working women | |
	Working women	Married working women	All married women	All working women
1890	3,704,000	515,260	4.6	13.9
1900	4,999,000	769,477	5.6	15.4
1910	7,602,000	1,890,661	10.7	24.7
1920	8,229,000	1,920,281	9.0	23.0
1930	10,396,000	3,071,302	11.7	28.9
1940	13,840,000	4,560,835	15.2	35.5
1950	18,063,000	9,273,000	24.8	52.1
1960	23,239,000	15,455,000	30.0	61.0

Source: U.S. Department of Labor, *Handbook on Women Workers,* Women's Bureau Bulletin No. 275 (1961); and James Mitchell, "Manpower, Challenge of the 1960s," U.S. Department of Labor (1960). Adapted by permission.

patterns. For example, middle-class mothers do not usually accept outside employment when their children are in the formative years; they normally wait until their children are in school before returning to the labor market. This condition seems to be changing. Bell reports that in 1940 only 7 per cent of mothers with preschool children were working outside the home, but by 1955 this had increased to 18.2 per cent.[37]

Between 1949 and 1958 the number of mothers with children under twelve increased 20 per cent; in this same period their number in the labor force jumped 80 per cent. A total of 15 million children under eighteen, and over 5 million children under the age of six, now have working mothers.[38] More than 40 per cent of lower-socioeconomic-class families, where husbands may frequently be unemployed, have other persons in the labor force; the great majority of these are wives.[39]

Age is another influential factor. The National Manpower Council, together with the Women's Bureau, sums it up in the following manner:

About 76 per cent of all women work before marriage; and of married women living with spouses about 60 per cent work before the coming of the first child. While 13 per cent between the ages of twenty and twenty-four with a preschool-age child continue to work, about 40 per cent between the ages thirty and forty with a school-age child work. About 37 per cent in the age bracket forty-five to fifty-four, where the children are more or less independent, work. About 25 per cent approaching retirement between the ages of fifty-five and sixty-four work, and about 7 per cent are still working past the age of sixty-five.[40]

Today's typical middle-class wife works or attends college while single and between the ages of eighteen and twenty-two. She continues to work after marriage for about two years, then drops out of the labor market until her children are all in school, after which she may return to work. The U.S. Department of Labor predicts that, during the 1960s, the number of women workers will increase by 31 per cent, or almost twice the expected rate of increase for men.[41]

Wives in the labor force are certainly a decided asset to the nation's economy. If they were all to withdraw from the labor force at once, the American economy would indeed suffer a severe blow. Their productive power is needed to maintain the national economy, just as their income is often needed to maintain a desired standard of living for the family. Altogether, about one out of every three workers today is a woman, and the total earning power of women today is about $51 billion.[42]

MOTIVATIONS FOR WIVES' EMPLOYMENT. A more detailed examination of the most common motives may reveal the deeper reasons for which so many wives are employed outside the home. The strongest motivation is the desire to increase income. This is sometimes a necessity, as when the husband is ill, incapacitated, unemployed, earns a low wage, or when the family has unusually heavy expenses.[43] Thus, the shift to outside employment was primarily motivated by the basic struggle for survival. Statistics show the proportion of employed wives to be higher as the husband's income level gets lower[44]; for many wives, work is definitely related to their husbands' earning ability. Statistically speaking, wives of husbands in lower-income levels and with small children are five times more likely to work as are wives of husbands in the middle-income groups.

Sometimes, wives attempt to raise the family's income level simply to raise its standard of living. If the husband's income is fixed and the family desires a higher standard of living, there are two choices possible: the husband may take on an extra job, or the wife may take a job outside the home. With the wife working, families find a way of attaining desired luxuries such as a nicer home, travel, new cars, or perhaps higher education for their children. Such women are not working for basic family survival but, rather, for a more desirable standard. As Buck has stated: "[Some] American women work to meet the cost of high living, not the high cost of living."[45]

Since World War II, innumerable employment opportunities have opened up for women. Because it is easier to get a job today, and the hours are shorter, the pay better, and conditions more attractive, work has more appeal for some wives.

Former obstacles to women's working have been eased or eliminated today—for example, the fewer children, the increased number of household appliances, prepared foods, readymade clothes, and certainly less public pressure to stay in the home.

It is also probable that some women work during the early years of marriage because homemaking without children does not constitute a full-time job.

More women are career-trained today, and many work to utilize their education and to develop their professional potential. In fact, some women may not be content to stay at home if they have special skills that are not being used. It is sometimes difficult for a highly trained woman to be content with dropping her career completely; she may need outside employment to feel fully useful. As the Commission on Education for Women of the American Counsel on Education has stated: "Many have not been convinced that in modern life only such a combination of efforts will give their lives full satisfaction although it is important for both young men and women to realize this."[46]

Some women work outside the home to make social contacts. Home confinement debilitates them, but they flourish with the stimulation of outside contacts. Work away from home makes them healthier and happier as persons.

The climate of the marriage relationship also influences some women to work outside the home. Sometimes such employment may help to hold a marriage together, or sometimes it is used to help break up a relationship. That is to say, some women enjoy work, and their elation contributes to their being better persons and wives; another woman may work with her husband in his business or profession and develop a very personal interest in it. In these cases, the fact of their working may actually improve the over-all marriage relationship. Other women work because they are dissatisfied with the marriage relationship. Their working outside of the home is simply part of their plan to sever the marriage. In other words, they are getting prepared for divorce. Many working wives who get divorces do not get divorces because they are working; rather, they go to work in order to get a divorce.

Some college-educated girls find only boredom in marriage. They have been educated and conditioned in a stimulating, intellectual environment which carried considerable prestige and ego-satisfaction; suddenly, they become homemakers. Coughland described the life of many young wives in the modern suburbs as *the suburban syndrome,* and suggests that for many such women it means a morbid existence with an emotional condition actually bordering on depression.[47] According to Lefferts, over 14 million prescriptions are filled each year for tranquilizers, over half of which go to middle-class housewives with no outside employment; and over 75 per cent of middle-class housewives under a physician's care are diagnosed as having psychosomatic complaints—largely related to their marital-role conceptionalization.[48]

Some women have not been trained for home management. It takes special skills to manage a home today, and too often these skills have been neglected in the girls' education. Much more planning and supervision are necessary in the home today than in former times. Even if a wife works and has a full-time housekeeper, or perhaps a nursemaid for her children, it is still necessary for her to assume the major responsibility of planning for and supervising the home. The homemaker-management role today must provide a favorable background against which the entire family can live and grow. Seldom is this possible unless the wife has proper knowledge of management.

A sense of personal worth is gained through accomplishment. Too often the emphasis in the American society has been on earning power, and too frequently people are evaluated only in relation to the amount of money they are able to earn. Thus, there has emerged a false value; that is, if one does not earn an income, he is not accomplishing anything and is not worth much. Traditionally, too, things masculine have been considered of more value than things feminine. Thus, perhaps some women work in an unconscious effort to be more like men. *Fortune Magazine* polls show quite conclusively that a much higher percentage of women wish to be men than vice-versa.

Table 15–2. **Answers to the question: "If you could be born over again would you rather be a man or a woman?"**

| | Per cent responding | | | |
Answers according to sex	*Prefer male role*	*Prefer female role*	*No preference*	*Undecided*
United States men	92	3	2	3
United States women	25	66	2	7
Canadian men	80	6	9	5
Canadian women	29	60	8	3

Source: Opinion News, **8,** National Opinion Research Center (Denver: University of Denver Press, 1947). Copyright © 1947, by National Opinion Research Center, Chicago. Reprinted by permission.

Some time ago Adler advanced the theory that much of the dissatisfaction in roles is brought about because women really wish to be men. He called this *masculine protest.*[49] Perhaps there has actually not been so much of a shift toward equality between the sexes in the American society as a shift toward women becoming more like men. For example, at one time most babies were dressed as girls, but now most of them are dressed as boys. There is other evidence to indicate that females are trying to become more like males. A few years ago, one cigarette company made its biggest pitch on the fact that their product was "a man's cigarette." Soon afterward, it was discovered that a much higher percentage of women began to smoke these cigarettes than ever before. But perhaps this is merely a sign that many women have awakened to the discrepancy of material value in those things manufactured for men, and the same type of article sold for women (the goods redesigned for women frequently are more expensive though often of cheaper quality), such as shoes, leather goods, electric shavers, suits, watches, and so forth.

Some women are actually unqualified for parenthood; thus they may work to escape the care of children. They simply cannot stand up emotionally to the task all day long every day. No matter how well prepared they may be educationally for child care, such women find children nerve-shattering. It is probably best for them to return to work, and allow someone else to care for the children.

Women may work more from force of habit than anything else. Some work before marriage and get so used to working outside the home that it simply never occurs to them to stay home afterward. This type of woman may get interested in community affairs, and, if so, usually finds even more satisfaction in those activities than in salaried employment.

A few women work to gain a sense of independence; they dislike the feeling of being "kept," which may arise from the assumption of the traditional female role within marriage. Work renders marriage optional for such women.

To some young brides, outside work offers a sense of future financial security. They feel that, if the husband should die or some other tragedy should happen, they will have some security. This, however, is probably more rationalization than anything else, for it would be just as logical for everyone to have two jobs. Then, if technological change eliminated one job, the other would still be there to fall back on. Statistically speaking, there is just as much chance of this happening as there is that a sudden tragedy might destroy a young marriage.[50] As Bowman has stated in this connection: "The possible problem of having to change from one pursuit to another at too late a period to make the change advantageously is one that challenges not only married women but everyone who devotes the better part of his life to occupation endeavor."[51] The husband, however, is not faced with as great a daily loss as is the wife who is approaching the stage when her children marry and leave home. For such women, returning to a former occupation may make sense.

It is probably safe to say that most women work today not for one particular reason, but for a number of reasons. For example, some women worked in wartime as a patriotic duty. After the war, inflation kept some wives on the job, while others continued working because they had discovered certain satisfactions they had not known in homemaking. Furthermore, some husbands found they preferred that their wives worked.[52] Many women work in order to keep up their appearance, realizing that they are much less likely to grow careless in dress if certain requirements are expected on the job. This seems rather unfortunate, for it means they are keeping up their appearance for the sake of a job and not for their own sake or that of their marriage.

INCREASING OPPORTUNITY. The fields of opportunity for women to work outside the home are constantly increasing. Harriet Martineau, a visitor to America in 1836, wrote that before that time only three respectable paying occupations were open to women in the American society: teaching, needlework, and keeping boarding houses or hotels. By 1836, women were being employed in mills and factories, printing offices, domestic service, and a few other occupations.[53] By 1951, of the 451 types of jobs listed by the U.S. Bureau of the Census, women had entered all but two: railroad engineer and fireman.[54]

THE TRUE PICTURE. The fact that certain fields of work are no longer closed to women does not necessarily represent the true picture of employment possibilities for women outside the home. Some occupations are open, but very few women are ever admitted into them.

Table 15–3. **Where women in America are employed**

Occupational field	Per cent total	Per cent nonwhite
Professional	13	6
Managers	5	2
Clerical	30	9
Sales workers	8	2
Service workers (non-home)	15	23
Factory	15	15
Domestic service	10	37
Trade, farm, and other	4	6

Source: U.S. Department of Labor, *Handbook on Women Workers,* Women's Bureau Bulletin No. 275 (1961). Adapted by permission.

There are about 450,000 domestic agricultural workers who migrate from state to state following the harvests, and women comprise about 30 per cent of these.[55] About 1 per cent of women workers are craftswomen, and only 5 per cent are managers, officials, or proprietors. Of those who are classified as professionals, more than 70 per cent are in two fields: school teaching and nursing. The remainder are primarily employed as medical and dental technicians, accountants, social workers, and librarians. The actual number of women physicians, lawyers, scientists, and engineers—although increasing—is still too small to measure on a percentage basis.[56] Women classified as service workers (not including sales personnel) are primarily employed as waitresses, beauty-parlor employees, laundry employees, and others who serve the public.[57] Thus, although many fields may not be closed to women, the real work many women find outside the home is likely to be routine in nature, in some cases even less stimulating than full-time homemaking.

EFFECTS ON MARITAL ADJUSTMENT.   Studies suggest that although there may be a greater feeling of equality when the wife works, it has little effect on the power structure, as evidenced by decision-making by nonworking wives. The husband's power on major decisions appears to decline when the wife works, but the extent is limited by other factors, such as education, age, and how much he earns.[58] Hoffman found that working mothers had even less control over children and minor decisions than nonworking mothers and that their husbands proportionately had more. If the husband's income was low and the mother worked, she was likely to have more power; however, if the husband's income was rather high, the power structure remained about the same.[59] Another study found that nonworking wives were more dominant in all areas, except purchase and living standards, than working wives.[60]

Household tasks for many working wives have simply been curtailed. Both mates appear to accept the fact that the wife cannot be expected to keep up both the home and an outside job. This has not meant necessarily that husbands contribute more but, rather, that the home is run on a reduced work schedule. It is not that the husband is able to do things that the wife formerly did, but that they both may be helping out with things in the home that one mate might have done alone. Dyer found that the most successful marriages of the two-income variety were those in which the spouses were able to share and help each other with various tasks within the home.[61] Blood and Hamblin estimate that working wives do 75 per cent of all the housework done by family members, and that nonworking wives do 85 per cent.[62] Hansen reports a typical response in interviews of working mothers about household tasks: "I've worked out so many short-cuts at home since getting my job, I wonder how I used to spend so much time doing my work."[63]

Much of the effect on the over-all marital adjustment has to do with the couple's attitudes about the wife's working. Research shows more conflict when husbands disapprove of their wives working,[64] but that would naturally be expected. Many of today's problems stem not so much from objections by the husband but from negative attitudes by the couple because she must work.

The effect upon the affectional relationship may develop in either direction. Clinical evidence gathered by the author and many others suggests that when both partners work, and their educational level is a

Figure 15-2. The junior executive's work frequently involves a nervous strain as tiring as physical labor. (Courtesy of The Clorox Company.)

college degree or higher, marital happiness appears to increase considerably. In his comparison of happily married and divorced couples,[65] Locke found no significant relationship between working wives and the adjustment of either spouse. Certainly a wife working after marriage may create affectional problems. If she continuously comes home fatigued and irritable, this may offset any economic benefits that her employment might yield. Her income may create additional money-management problems, for whose money is it? His? Hers? Theirs? How will it be used? For necessities? For Luxuries? For savings? The wife's income may constitute an ego threat to the husband, especially if it is larger than his. There may be additional affectional problems related to responsive integrity. Those who work are more likely to come in contact with many more people of the opposite sex, and sometimes vicious triangles are formed.

EFFECT ON CHILDREN.   The criteria for deciding whether wives should work may be entirely different from those for deciding whether mothers should work. For one thing, public opinion is still likely to condemn a working mother, no matter how intense her training in a career has been or how acute the needs of society for her particular profession.[66] Even friends are more likely to censure the working mother.[67] Because of this factor, working mothers may have mixed emotions—happy one moment that they are working, depressed the next because of guilt feelings.

There is no denying the importance of proper child care; it is a most essential function in society. When child care is neglected, the community and the entire society suffer, for neglected children mean more delinquency, more mental illness, and more general social disorganization. Fulfilling the biological requirements of parenthood, however, is no guarantee of the ability to fulfill the physical and emotional qualifications of parenthood. In fact, quite the opposite seems true for some people in modern society. Quite naturally, if both parents work, someone else must take care of the young children; unfortunately, under these circumstances, some young children are neglected. There is a definite need for legislation to assure that places where children are kept during the day are of adequate quality. At present many such places are nothing more than glorified babysitting institutions. It is impossible for one person adequately to care for twenty or perhaps thirty children at one time. The Women's Bureau, in cooperation with the U.S. Children's Bureau and the Child Welfare League of America, has completed a list of requirements for day-care centers, and federal grants are available to states for carrying out licensing programs. Much, however, remains to be done.

> ... At the present time, there are licensed day-care facilities for only 185,-000 children throughout the nation. There is little reason to doubt that some children for whom no adequate day-care services are available are being exposed to situations potentially dangerous to them.[68]

Already thirty-six states have established day-care licensing advisory committees. Perhaps soon such efforts will inspire positive legislation and a greater feeling of security when the mothers of young children go to work. Many newer concepts are emerging for the nursery school's role in supplementing the home to improve the physical, mental, and emotional development of young children; this purpose is beyond its former role of encouraging the social development of children with other children. From all these efforts, positive results may emerge similar to those of the current Swedish experiments. Sweden is probably a model country for social legislation in the area of providing care for small children of working mothers.[69] Contrary to general opinion, much research suggests that some women who work are actually better mothers than before they worked. Their outside employment is such a contrast to the constant strain of child care that, when the day's work is done, such women are able to return home refreshed by the joy of seeing their children and ready to give ungrudgingly of their ingenuity and patience. Many such mothers contribute more in the short time with their children than they could in the whole day before they went to work. Sometimes working mothers actually spend more time with their children than women who are home all day but send their children outside to play without supervision most of the time. A study in New York City reported that, as a group, mothers who worked devoted more time to their children than did nonworking mothers.[70] Much of recent research seems to challenge earlier theories about children being neglected when their mothers work. This is assuming, of course, that the children are not just left to their own resources. One researcher could find no difference in school grades between children with working mothers and those with nonworking mothers except on the basis of urban and rural residence.[71] A study of 23,050 high school students, Grades 9–12, in one area disclosed that the children of employed mothers were actually making better grades than were the children of unemployed mothers. Furthermore, the researcher could find little evidence in the adolescent youngsters to support earlier theories that the neglected, maladjusted child frequently develops from an employed-mother situation.[72] Similar results were found by Stanford University researchers, using five-year-old subjects.[73] Another study of children in Grades 4–8 reported identical results.[74] Another researcher in New York compared seventh-grade youngsters of working mothers with those of nonworking mothers by means of scores on the Stanford Achievement Tests. Those with employed mothers actually showed a higher level of achievement, although it was not statistically significant. When the IQ scores of the two groups were examined, however, it was discovered that those with nonworking mothers averaged 6.9 points higher. According to this, they should have been (although they were not) achieving more than the other group. The reason for this discrepancy is not known, but the suggestion is that children actually are aided toward higher scholastic achievement by the fact that their mothers work.[75]

Nye reports that insofar as intrafamily recreation is concerned, solidarity does not appear to be significantly affected by the wife-mother's employment. If the mother must give up something, she usually gives up neighborhood-visiting first.[76] The research by Hoffman is probably the most extensive in this area. Although the results of her studies suggest that maternal employment is sometimes favorable, she is the first to caution against such generalizations, warning that there are too many intervening variables to make valid comparisons on just the factors of work or nonwork: "The jump between maternal employment and child behavior is too broad to be covered in one leap."[77] As an example of these undetermined variables, Oettinger explains:

> We at the Children's Bureau are often asked, these days, what are the effects on children of maternal employment? To that question we have a single answer, loud and clear: "It depends." It depends on the kind of mother, the kind of child, the kind of family. It depends, among other things, on why the mother works, how much she works, what she does, and what her work does to or for her, how old her children are, what provisions she makes for them while she works, how they perceive the fact of her working.[78]

Eleanor Maccoby has this to say on the subject:

> It is not possible to close this discussion with a box score which will tell us whether maternal employment is, in sum, "good" or "bad" for children. It is clear that there is no single best way of organizing family life. Some mothers should work while others should not, and the outcome for the children depends upon many factors other than the employment itself.[79]

SUGGESTIONS FOR EMPLOYED WIVES. Some suggestions seem to be in order for women who plan to be employed outside the home after marriage. Probably of foremost importance is the choice of job. Each woman who plans to work should choose a job that is as challenging and interesting as possible. It contributes very little for a wife simply to go from one dull routine to another. A second suggestion is for careful consideration of the area of selectivity; that is, if the wife can select an area of work in which there is a scarcity of help, she is in a better position for bargaining as to hours and many other things pertinent to the family welfare. Many complications should be identified before the wife selects a job, and the selection should be made so as to eliminate as many of these as possible. For example, certain jobs mean more transportation problems, not only for the wife but for help hired at home. The wife should also choose a job in which the time off is coordinated with the free time of other family members. Before selecting or accepting any job, she should decide what is to come first in her life. If her first obligation is to her husband, her children, and her marriage, than the job should be selected with these things in mind. Perhaps part-time employment is the ideal solution for many wives and mothers. A study, conducted by Michigan State University with employed wives of students with children under five years of age, found that on the average 45 per cent of the wife's earnings went for "job-necessitated" expenses; that is, costs she had to pay just because she was employed. These included: income tax, social security, compulsory insurance, retirement, additional costs of food, clothing, transportation, child care, paid help, laundry services, clothing alterations, professional beauty care, personal grooming supplies, and miscellaneous things such as time- and labor-saving appliances. The study suggests that sometimes the working wife can actually come out ahead financially by working only part-time.[80]

Today's dilemma

Part of the dilemma facing married couples today is that neither sex is particularly satisfied with the traditional role assignments, yet each finds it difficult to break away from them completely. Society still considers that the demands of a husband's occupation take precedence over those of a wife's. His professional success is considered the most important consideration to the over-all welfare of the family. It is necessary for some women to accept the fact that their husbands' work outside the home still comes first.

Occupational hazards to marital adjustment. Certain occupational demands encroach more than others on marriage togetherness. Business executives and physicians, for example, must neglect their mates at times. After considerable study, Rosten suggests that this is frequently the crux of the difficulty within many marriages of theatrical people. He grants that the theatrical profession probably does attract an undue proportion of high-strung personalities, but he doubts that this explains the extent of the Hollywood movie colony's divorce rate. Caught up in such a personally demanding occupation, the performers simply have little time left for marriage.[81]

It is probably true that some men are "married" to their professions. A physician, for example, can successfully follow his profession only when he is permitted to be late for dinner or to leave in the middle of a bridge game. Women considering marriage to such professionals should ask themselves if they are willing to pay the price for marrying an extremely ambitious man. The author discovered a few years ago, while teaching in a well-known women's college, that many upper-middle and higher-socioeconomic-class students felt they were not ready to marry such a man. They had seen what life with an ambitious man would be from observing their own fathers, and they were not attracted by the demands.

Some professional people, however, allow no time for domestic life for the simple reason that they want it exactly that way. Sometimes, when their present jobs are not time-consuming, they look for new ones. A study of young business executives disclosed that many gave their first loyalty to their employers and were actually prepared to cut themselves off from any human ties that might hamper their advancement.[82]

Increasingly, corporations are defining the role of the wife as dependent upon the definition of the husband's occupation.[83] Some have even gone so far as to compile a list of responsibilities for the wife of the executive, a sample of which follows:

1. Personal—a good wife and mother, affectionate, well adjusted, adaptable, with a sense of humor and a desire to grow and mature with her husband.
2. Similar background to husband, with some business experience.
3. Knowledge of husband's business—its products and services.
4. An intelligent listener and sounding board when he shares his problems and experiences.
5. Understands that his work demands much of his time and attention. Never nags or demands too much of him in his career.
6. Never betrays a business confidence her husband has shared.
7. Except in an emergency—his office is a personal "no man's land" for her problems or presence.
8. Trusting when his work requires association with other women.
9. Builds a happy social life for her family—but never permits it to influence business or interfere with business.
10. A gracious, willing, and capable hostess—whether guests are expected or unexpected.
11. Encourages husband to take part in church and community affairs and does so herself.
12. Keeps the home attractive, neat, and inviting.
13. Keeps the home well organized, relaxing, and as problem-free as possible.
14. Subtly cautions husband when his pace is too rapid—makes sure he finds time for the relaxation he enjoys and benefits from most.
15. Entire family spends some time each day or weekend working together in a home project or sharing recreation.
16. Does her best to maintain a happy relationship with his family.
17. Sees to it that the family lives within his income.
18. When transferred—takes the lead in establishing her family in the new community.
19. Does not abdicate all responsibility for discipline to him.
20. Maintains a home and family in which he is a permanent chairman of the board.[84]

These are the concepts of modern business, and the pressures on the modern businessman for success appear to make the acceptance of some of the same concepts necessary within his marriage. Still it is estimated that about eight out of every ten college women would prefer such a marriage to a career of their own if they had to make a choice. Only about 8 per cent actually would prefer a career, and the remainder were uncertain.[85]

Increasingly, women are expressing dissatisfaction with their traditional role. A recent research analysis disclosed that only about 40 per cent of married women who work outside the home derive personal worth and dignity from work at home, and about 60 per cent of those who do not work outside the home felt the same.[86]

Any girl who decides on genuine home management (as contrasted with housekeeping) as her major career need have no feeling of inferiority. There is a great need today, however, for training programs that will bring women to appreciate and recognize values and satisfactions within the domestic role, and to find within it a challenge. Although many women complain that men do not give enough prestige to woman's role as a home manager, many women underrate their own importance. Buerkle and Badgley devised a scale which they call the Yale Marital Interaction Battery. With it, they tested thirty-six married couples who were having serious troubles. They compared the findings with those from 186 couples attending religiously affiliated couples' clubs in the New Haven area, whose marriages were not in trouble. The results showed a significant difference in the interaction pattern of the two groups, especially in situational tests calling for a high degree of role empathy. Although these researchers are the first to admit the need for further refinement of their scale, the results indicate that significantly more happy couples empathize with the partner's problems in the assigned traditional roles.[87]

THE ABSENCE OF A MODERN MAN.   The role concepts of modern husbands have changed less than those of modern wives. At least, men have not accepted as much change as have women. A law of physics states that for every force there must be an equal force in an opposite direction. Thus, if woman's role is changing, man's role must change also or there is likely to be considerable confusion. There is a necessity for males to do much re-evaluating if they are to profit from the capabilities and training of their mates. College men must recognize the fact that college women are their intellectual equals. Husbands should share their position as custodians of family wealth and power. They will have to recognize their wives' quality (and, often, superiority) as females become more educated and aggressive in community affairs.[88]

Rebecca Liswood, who is executive director of the Marriage Counseling Service of Greater New York, suggests that parents should teach boys respect for woman's judgment. A father should impress his son with the fact that, although men are strong and reliable, women have wonderful qualities too, including a thinking apparatus equal to any man's and the ability to perceive things that might elude a man.[89]

BIOLOGICAL LIMITATIONS.   Notwithstanding modern egalitarian ideals, there are biological differences that are frequently underrated by both sexes in assuming and defining roles within marriage. From the standpoint of marriage and the family, the male will remain essentially the provider, and the woman the childbearer. The child's physical connection with the mother before birth and his dependence upon her in the early months of his life are biological facts. For a good adjustment concerning roles within marriage, each individual must understand and accept these sexual characteristics. Modern couples should distinguish between laws that are purely discriminatory and those that have a basis in nature.

TRANSITIONS AND CONFUSION. At present, marital roles within the American culture are in a period of transition. In a traditional society, the rights and obligations connected with marital roles are clear and well defined. In such a society everyone knows what is expected of him and is equally clear about his obligations in return. In our society, however, there is little guidance from the past in defining marital roles. As Sumner has said: "It is very plain that what once was, or what anyone thinks ought to be, but slightly affects what, at any moment, is. The mores which once were, are a memory. Those which anyone thinks ought to be are a dream. The only thing with which we can deal are those which are."[90]

Today, mores are in a state of flux. Many of the insecurities of modern marriage arise from the loss of the assured responses of the old role expectations. In the rush of social change, new roles have not been clearly enough defined to take the place of the old. There are many inconsistencies. The roles of man and woman now overlap rather than being distinctly different and separate as they were in the past. Foote feels that nobody can agree exactly what today's marriage roles should be.[91] Many women wish their husbands to be strong when the test comes, and yet they themselves want to be independent. Kirkpatrick feels that women tend to want to have the privileges and rewards of several new roles, but are not as yet willing to accept the obligations that accompany them.[92] Perhaps there is no right or wrong way to assume roles in modern society beyond what each couple feel is workable. Courtship provides an opportunity for the identification of some of the expected roles within marriage. Those concepts may change within various stages of the family-life cycle but, if used correctly, the courtship period may lead to a better recognition of what kind of life the couple wishes to lead after marriage.

Summary

Increased concern over marital roles is normal and natural in a culture that increasingly emphasizes freedom for individuals. Pressures from society, however, often make today's mates feel guilty because of their personal rejection of the traditional patterns of behavior.

Many conditioning factors influence role expectations in marriage. These include early family experiences, cultural sex influences, environmental factors, and group factors such as ethnic and social-class background.

One major modern marital-role concern involves the family power structure. Originally, the male was supreme head of the family. His position has been supported by such influences as religion, law, a belief that

man was superior to woman and that woman was naturally more submissive, and even by some marriage textbooks.

All these influences are now under serious questioning. Consequently,
new family power structures are being created. One new form is the
compartmentalized system in which each mate has the major jurisdiction
for decisions in certain areas. An even newer concept is the shared system,
in which decisions are shared, even with the children, and there is no
"supreme" head of the family. This latter method works out best in a
democracy, provided that the partners are well prepared for it. Much
relearning is necessary, however, before most couples can operate effectively this way.

There is some role concern over the division of household tasks. Each
partner appears to be helping with more tasks today that formerly would
have been considered the exclusive responsibility of the other sex.

The trend toward more women working outside the home is unmistakable. This is even true for those families with young children. Many
factors contribute to this trend, but probably the most important reason
for which wives work is to increase the family income. There is certainly
an increased opportunity today for wives to work. A great many of the
jobs which women obtain, however, consist of dull, unchallenging routines. Except in two or three professions, women's employment opportunities are still quite limited.

Outside employment for wives has very little effect on the power structure within marriage. It usually means a reduced schedule within the
family for household tasks and little increase in role clash. It may change
the affectional relationship, but it is as likely to improve it. Although
more working wives than nonworking wives seek divorce, it is not necessarily the fact of working that causes the divorce: some seek work in
order to afford a divorce.

The wife's working sometimes means that the children are neglected.
This is unfortunate for all of society. Research studies suggest, however,
that in some cases the wife's working has no ill effects on the children;
in fact, sometimes it appears to have a good effect.

There are many frustrations for modern, well-educated wives who try
to conform to traditional marital roles. Some of these stem from the fact
that modern wives lack sufficient training or skills in homemaking, having sadly neglected this side of their education. There is a need to develop
a deeper appreciation for homemaking by both sexes.

In some cases, the professional career of the husband appears to dictate
the role of the wife. Often this role appears to be too low on the priority
list to suit a modern, ambitious girl. The time to consider the problem,
however, is before marriage, not afterward.

Modern couples cannot return to the traditional patterns of family
living and be happy. Instead, they must prepare themselves socially,

technically, and psychologically for today's life. Biological limitations will always mean that the roles of the sexes cannot be completely equal in all respects. In fact, absolute equality would, in reality, not be equal at all. American marital roles are in a transitional stage. When the newer concepts have become more equally accepted by both sexes, stronger marriages will emerge.

Notes

1. Alver H. Jacobson, "Conflict of Attitudes Toward the Roles of the Husband and Wife in Marriage," *American Sociological Review*, 17:146–50.
2. Robert S. Ort, "A Study of Role Conflicts as Related to Happiness in Marriage," *Journal of Abnormal and Social Psychology*, 45:691–99.
3. Marie W. Kargman, "A Sociolegal Analysis of Family Role Conflict," *Marriage and Family Living*, 21:278.
4. For a more detailed discussion of this, see Bernard Barber, *Social Stratification* (New York: Harcourt, Brace & World, Inc., 1957), Chap. 1.
5. Kathryne Close, "Impressions of the White House Conference," *Children*, 7:88.
6. Hazel L. Ingersoll, "A Study of the Transmission of Authority Patterns in the Family," *Genetic Psychology Monographs*, 38:225–302.
7. Eleanore B. Luckey, "Marital Satisfaction and Parent Concepts," *Journal of Consulting Psychology*, 24:195–204.
8. Marie S. Dunn, "Marriage-Role Expectation of Adolescents," *Marriage and Family Living*, 22:99–104.
9. See, e.g., Oscar Handlin, *The Uprooted* (Boston: Little, Brown & Co., 1951), Chap. 1.
10. See, e.g., Paul J. Campisi, "Ethnic Family Patterns: The Italian Family in the United States," *American Journal of Sociology*, 53:443–49.
11. Bernard C. Rosen, "The Achievement Syndrome: A Psychocultural Dimension of Social Stratification," *American Sociological Review*, 21:203–11.
12. Ephesians, 5:22–25.
13. Victor A. Christopherson, "An Investigation of Patriarchial Authority in the Mormon Family," *Marriage and Family Living*, 18:328.
14. Arnold Gesell and Frances L. Ilg, *The Child from Five to Ten* (New York: Harper & Row, Publishers, 1946), pp. 176–77.
15. Nine out of every ten doctorates presently granted in institutions of higher learning are conferred on men. See U.S. Department of Health, Education, and Welfare, *Special Report on Education* (February 1963).
16. I Corinthians, 14:35.
17. Margaret Mead, *Male and Female* (New York: William Morrow & Co., Inc., 1955).
18. Karen Horney, *New Ways in Psychoanalysis* (New York: W. W. Norton & Company, Inc., 1939), p. 113.
19. For a good discussion of this point, see Daniel G. Brown, "Masculinity-Femininity Development in Children," *Journal of Consulting Psychology*, 21: 197–202.
20. Margaret Mead, *Sex and Temperament in Three Primitive Societies* (New York: McGraw-Hall Book Company, Inc., 1935), p. 119.
21. Floyd M. Martinson, *Marriage and the American Ideal* (New York: Dodd, Mead & Co., 1960), p. 303.

22. Margaret Mead, "What Women Want," *Fortune Magazine* (December 1946), 173.

23. M. Kamel Nahas, "The Family in Egypt," *Marriage and Family Living,* 16:297.

24. Dorothy Fahs Beck, "The Changing Moslem Family of the Middle East," *Marriage and Family Living,* 19:340–46.

25. Christopherson, *op. cit.,* pp. 328–33.

26. Theodore B. Johannis, Jr., "Participation by Fathers, Mothers, and Teen-age Sons and Daughters in Selected Family Economic Activity," *The Family Life Coordinator,* 6:15–16.

27. Theodore B. Johannis, Jr., and James M. Rollins, "Teen-ager Perception of Family Decision-Making," *The Family Life Coordinator,* 7:7–74.

28. Yi Chuang Lu, "Marital Roles and Marital Adjustment," *Sociology and Social Research,* 36:365–68.

29. William G. Sumner, *Folkways* (New York: Ginn & Company, 1940), p. 364.

30. *Today's Health* (September 1960), 9.

31. The average family requires from twenty-two to thirty hours of work weekly in such tasks as plumbing, carpentry, yard work, gardening and lawn care, and working at special improvements. See Bruce Lee, "Who Works Longer —Husband or Wife?" *This Week Magazine* (April 29, 1956), 7, 21–22.

32. Theodore B. Johannis, Jr., "Participation by Fathers, Mothers, and Teen-age Sons and Daughters in Selected Household Tasks," *The Family Life Coordinator,* 4:61–62.

33. Robert O. Blood and Donald M. Wolfe, *Husbands and Wives* (New York: The Free Press of Glencoe, Inc., 1960), pp. 50–52.

34. R. J. Tasch, "The Role of the Father in the Family," *Journal of Experimental Education,* 20:319–62.

35. Lynn White, Jr., "The Changing Content of Women's Education," *Marriage and Family Living,* 17:293.

36. U.S. Bureau of the Census, Series P-60, Table 7; and various news releases since.

37. Daniel Bell, "The Great Back-to-Work Movement," *Fortune Magazine* (July 1956).

38. A fact presented to the annual conference of The Kansas Council on Children and Youth, October, 1962, Topeka, Kans., by Mrs. Catherine B. Oettinger, Chief of the Children's Bureau, Washington, D.C.

39. Special Labor Force Report No. 13, *Monthly Labor Review* (April 1961).

40. U.S. Department of Labor, *Handbook on Women Workers,* Women's Bureau Bulletin No. 275 (1961); and The National Manpower Council, *Woman Power* (New York: Columbia University Press, 1957), pp. 10, 68–69.

41. U.S. Department of Health, Education, and Welfare, *News Release* (May 24, 1963).

42. Estimated by Mrs. Esther Peterson, Assistant Secretary of Labor, in recent congressional hearing on a bill calling for equal pay for women. See *Congressional Record* (1963).

43. See an excellent discussion of this in M. S. Carroll, "Working Wife and Her Family's Economic Position," *Monthly Labor Review* (April 1962), 366–74.

44. Special Labor Force Report No. 13, *op. cit.,* Table 8.

45. Gilbert G. Buck, "You Can Only Estimate the Power of a Woman," *Fortune Magazine,* 54:92.

46. *The Span of a Woman's Life and Learning,* Commission on Education of

Women, of the American Council on Education, Washington, D.C. (April 1960), 2.

47. Robert Coughland, "The Changing Roles in Modern Marriage," *Life Magazine* (December 24, 1956).

48. George Lefferts, *The Trapped Housewife* (New York: Edward H. Weiss and Company, Inc., 1961), p. 5. Mimeographed television manuscript.

49. Heinz L. and Rowena R. Ansbacher, *Individual Psychology of Alfred Adler* (New York: Basic Books, Inc., 1956).

50. About half of widows under sixty-five find it necessary to work. *Statistical Bulletin,* Metropolitan Life Insurance Company (November 1962), 3.

51. Henry A. Bowman, *Marriage for Moderns* (New York: McGraw-Hill Book Company, Inc., 1954), p. 47.

52. For an eloquent defense of the working wife-mother, see David Yellin, "I'm Married to a Working Mother," *Harper's Magazine* (July 1956).

53. William F. Ogburn and Meyer Nimkoff, *Technology and the Changing Family* (Boston: Houghton Mifflin Co., 1955), p. 159.

54. *Ibid.*

55. Alice K. Leopold, "The Family Woman's Expanding Role," *Marriage and Family Living,* **20**:278–82.

56. U.S. Department of Labor, *op. cit.*

57. *Ibid.*

58. Robert O. Blood and Robert L. Hamblin, "The Effect of the Wife's Employment on the Family Power Structure," *Social Forces,* **36**:247–52; and Blood and Wolfe, *op. cit.,* p. 40.

59. Lois W. Hoffman, "Effects of the Employment of Mothers on Parental Power Relations and the Division of Household Tasks," *Marriage and Family Living,* **22**:27–35. This was also confirmed in a study by F. Ivan Nye, "Maternal Employment and Marital Interaction: Some Contingent Conditions," *Social Forces,* **40**:113–19.

60. Russell Middleton and Snell Putney, "Dominance in Decisions in the Family," *American Journal of Sociology,* **65**:605–609.

61. Everett D. Dyer, Doctoral Study, University of Wisconsin, Madison, Wis., 1955.

62. Blood and Hamblin, *op. cit.*

63. J. A. Hansen, "Should Mom Get a Job?" *Farm Journal* (September 1961), 80.

64. Artie Gianopulas and Howard E. Mitchell, "Marital Disagreement in Working-Wife Marriages as a Function of Husband's Attitude Toward Wife's Employment," *Marriage and Family Living,* **19**:373–78.

65. Harvey J. Locke and Muriel Mackeprang, "Marital Adjustment and the Employed Wife," *American Journal of Sociology,* **54**:536–38.

66. Hortense M. Glen, "Attitudes of Women Regarding Gainful Employment of Married Women," *Journal of Home Economics,* **51**:247–52.

67. Mirra Komarovsky, *Women in the Modern World* (Boston: Little, Brown & Co., 1953), p. 191.

68. U.S. Department of Health, Education, and Welfare, *News Release* (May 24, 1963).

69. See, e.g., *Social Sweden* (Stockholm: Social Welfare Board Annual Reports).

70. Mary Fisher Langmuir, "Wife Trouble? Get Her a Job," *American Magazine,* **36**:90–93.

71. Roy Prodipto, "Maternal Employment and Adolescent Roles: Rural-Urban Differentials," *Marriage and Family Living,* **23**:345–46.

72. F. Ivan Nye, "Employment Status of Mothers and Adjustment of Adolescent Children," *Marriage and Family Living*, 21:240–44.

73. *Today's Child* (December 1960), 4.

74. Horace B. Hand, "Working Mothers and Maladjusted Children," *Journal of Educational Sociology*, 30:245–46.

75. Durlyn E. Wade, "School Achievement and Parent Employment," *Journal of Educational Sociology*, 36:93–95.

76. F. Ivan Nye, "Employment Status and Recreational Behavior of Mothers," *Pacific Sociological Review* (Fall 1958), 69–72.

77. Lois W. Hoffman, "Effects of Maternal Employment on the Child," *Child Development*, 32:187–97. For an interesting research project, which also confirms Hoffman's finding, see Lawrence J. Sharp, "Employment Status of Mothers and Some Aspects of Mental Illness," *American Sociological Review*, 25:714–17.

78. National Manpower Council, *Work in the Lives of Married Women* (New York: Columbia University Press, 1958), p. 134.

79. *Ibid.*, p. 172.

80. "What Happens to Income of Employed Mothers," *Journal of Home Economics*, 54:857.

81. Leo C. Rosten, *Hollywood* (New York: Harcourt, Brace & World, Inc., 1941).

82. William E. Henry, "The Business Executive: A Study in the Psychodynamics of a Social Role," *American Journal of Sociology*, 54:286–91.

83. See, e.g., Edith Heal, *The Young Executive's Wife* (New York: Dodd, Mead & Co., 1958); or articles by William H. Whyte, Jr., "The Wives of Management," *Fortune Magazine*, 44:86; or "Corporation and the Wife," *Fortune Magazine*, 44:109.

84. *Dun's Review and Modern Industry* (New York: Dun & Bradstreet Publications Corporation, February 1957), pp. 73–75.

85. Lamar T. Empey, "Role Expectations of Young Women Regarding Marriage and a Career," *Marriage and Family Living*, 20:152–55.

86. Robert S. Weiss and Nancy Morse Samelson, "Social Roles of American Women: Their Contribution to a Sense of Usefulness and Importance," *Marriage and Family Living*, 20:358–66. Articles such as the one by Mary Bunting, "One Woman, Two Lives," *Time Magazine* (November 3, 1961), have added the weight of authority to the implication that marriage and a family for a woman are not doing something important or engrossing enough by themselves to make life worthwhile.

87. Jack V. Buerkle and Robin F. Badgley, "Couple Role-Taking: The Yale Marital Interaction Battery," *Marriage and Family Living*, 21:53–58.

88. The trend does seem to be toward more democratic, flexible roles. See Debi D. Lovejoy, "College Student Conceptions of the Roles of the Husband and Wife in Family Decision-Making," *The Family Life Coordinator*, 9:10.

89. Rebecca Liswood, "Raise Your Son to Be a Good Husband," *This Week Magazine* (October 2, 1960), p. 29.

90. Sumner, *op. cit.*, p. 78.

91. Nelson Foote, "Changes in American Marriage Patterns and the Role of Women," *Eugenics Quarterly*, 1:254–60.

92. Clifford Kirkpatrick, "Inconsistencies in Marriage Roles and Marriage Conflict," *The International Journal of Ethics*, 46:444–60.

Questions for further thought

1. In what ways are the traditional concepts of marital roles consistent or inconsistent with American democratic principles?

2. Does Christianity require that the husband be the head of the house?
3. What are some of the major sex inequalities that still exist in the home, community, organizations, and industry? What are some justifiable reasons for some of them? Are they all in favor of men?
4. If a group of people were seriously ill and there were two physicians of equal ability available, one a man and the other a woman, which one would most of the group prefer? Why?
5. What specific marks of male chivalry toward women should be preserved? Why?
6. How much sacrifice, if any, does a professional man have a right to ask of his family in order to be successful at his job?
7. Even though they may give adequate lip service to the idea, do young men really believe in complete equality? Do young women really desire complete equality?
8. Is the progress of society endangered by so strongly domesticating man that he will fail to push forward in his career?

Recommended films

Who's Right? (McGraw-Hill Book Company, Inc.).
Who's Boss? (McGraw-Hill Book Company, Inc.).

Suggested supplemental readings

BOOKS

Beard, Mary R. *Woman as Force in History.* New York: The Macmillan Company, 1946.

Burgess, Helen Steers. *How To Choose a Nursery School.* Public Affairs Pamphlet No. 310, 1961.

Cassara, Beverly Benner (ed.). *American Women: The Changing Image.* Boston: Beacon Press, 1962.

Cottrell, W. Fred. *The Railroader.* Stanford, Calif.: Stanford University Press, 1940.

Cussler, Margaret. *The Woman Executive.* New York: Harcourt, Brace & World, Inc., 1958.

deBeauvoir, Simone. *The Second Sex.* New York: Alfred A. Knopf, Inc., 1953.

Denton, Wallace. *The Role of the Minister's Wife.* Philadelphia: Westminister Press, 1962.

Donaldson, James. *Woman: Her Position and Influence in Ancient Greece and Rome, and Among the Early Christians.* London: Longmans, Green & Company, Ltd., 1907.

Farber, Seymour M., and Roger H. L. Wilson (eds.). *The Potential of Women.* New York: McGraw-Hill Book Company, Inc., 1963.

Friedan, Betty. *The Feminine Mystique.* New York: W. W. Norton & Company, Inc., 1963.

Havel, J. E. *La Condition de la femme.* Paris: Librairie Armand Colin, 1961.

Heal, Edith. *The Young Executive's Wife.* New York: Dodd, Mead & Co., 1958.

Helming, Ann. *A Woman's Place.* New York: Coward-McCann, Inc., 1962.

Hoffman, Lois W., and F. Ivan Nye. *The Employed Mother in America.* Skokie, Ill.: Rand McNally & Co., 1963.

Montagu, Ashley. *The Natural Superiority of Women.* New York: The Macmillan Company, 1953.

Rainwater, Lee, *et al. Workingman's Wife: Her Personality, World and Life Style.* New York: Oceana Publications, Inc., 1959.

Scott-Maxwell, Florida. *Women and Sometimes Men.* New York: Alfred A. Knopf, Inc., 1957.

Sherman, Helen, and Marjorie Coe. *The Challenge of Being a Woman.* New York: Harper & Row, Publishers, 1955.

Smuts, Robert W. *Women and Work in America.* New York: Columbia University Press, 1959.

Ward, Barbara E. (ed.), *Women in the New Asia.* New York: UNESCO Publication Center, 1963.

Whyte, William F. *Men at Work.* Homewood, Ill.: Dorsey Press, Inc., and Richard D. Irwin, Inc., 1961.

Wylie, Philip. *The Disappearance.* New York: Holt, Rinehart & Winston, Inc., 1951.

Weingarten, Violet. *The Mother Who Works Outside the Home.* New York: Child Study Association of America, 1961.

Zapoleon, Marguerite W. *Occupational Planning for Women.* New York: Harper & Row, Publishers, 1961.

ARTICLES

Anderson, Ella Smith, and Cleo Fitzsimmons. "Use of Time and Money by Employed Homemakers," *Journal of Home Economics,* **52:**452–55.

Babchuk, Nicholas. "The Privacy Relations of Middle-Class Couples: A Study in Male Dominance," *American Sociological Review,* **28:**377.

Bieri, James, and Robin Lobeck. "Acceptance of Authority and Parental Identification," *Journal of Personality,* **27:**74–87.

Christensen, Harold T., and Marilynn M. Swihart. "Postgraduation Role Preference of Senior Women in College," *Marriage and Family Living,* **18:**52–57.

Clover, Vernon T. "Net Income of Employed Wives with Husbands Present," *Studies in Economic Business,* Texas Technological College, Lubbock, Tex., 1962.

Couch, Herbert N. "Woman in Early Roman Law," *Harvard Law Review,* **8:**39–50.

Dache, Lilly. "Are Women Finished?" *Journal of Home Economics,* **50:**517–18.

Day, Lincoln H. "Status Implications of the Employment of Married Women in the United States," *American Economic Review* (July 1961), 391–97.

Deleeuw, Louise, *et al.* "Child-Rearing in Families of Working and Nonworking Mothers," *Sociometry,* **25:**122–38.

DeLuget, Jacqueline. "The Contribution of Home Economics Education to the Position of Women in the World Today," *Journal of Home Economics,* **50:** 625–28.

Duvall, Evelyn M. "Changing Roles in the Family Cycle," *Journal of Home Economics,* **42:**435–60.

Glen, Hortense M. "Attitudes of Women Regarding Gainful Employment of Married Women," *Journal of Home Economics,* **51:**247–52.

Hacker, Helen Mayer. "The New Burdens of Masculinity," *Marriage and Family Living,* **19:**227–33.

Hager, Wesley H. "Educating Woman for a Changing World," *Journal of Home Economics,* **49:**619–22.

Hale, Clara B. "Self-Expression for Marriage Partners," *Family Life,* **15:**1–4.

Harper's Staff. "A Special Supplement to Harpers on The American Female," *Harper's Magazine,* 225:117–18.

Hatch, Mary G., and David L. "Problems of Married Working Women as Presented by Three Popular Working Women's Magazines," *Social Forces,* 37:148–53.

Heer, David M. "Dominance and the Working Wife," *Social Forces,* 36:341–47.

Helfrich, Margaret L. "The Generalized Role of the Executive's Wife," *Marriage and Family Living,* 23:384–87.

Hurvitz, Nathan. "The Measurement of Marital Strain," *American Journal of Sociology,* 55:610–15.

Katz, Robert L. "The Role of the Father," *Mental Hygiene,* 21:517–24.

Kioll, Norman, and Bernice Friedman. "Cultural Lag and Housewifemanship: The Role of the Married Female College Graduate," *Journal of Educational Sociology,* 31:87–95.

Lepold, Alice K. "The Family Woman's Expanding Role," *Marriage and Family Living,* 20:278–82.

Lykos, Christine. "Attitudes of Husbands in Greek Orthodox Communities Toward the Gainful Employment of Their Wives," Master's Thesis, West Virginia University, Morgantown, W.Va., August 1963.

Marcus, Mildred R. "Women in the Labor Force," *Social Casework,* 41:298–302.

Mavity, Nancy Barr. "The Two-Income Family," *Harper's Magazine,* 203:57–63.

Montgomery, Charlotte. "Can Working Wives Make It Pay?" *Better Homes and Gardens* (November 1957), 68, 137–38.

Motz, Annabella Bender. "The Role of the Married Woman in Science," *Marriage and Family Living,* 23:374–76.

Peterson, Evan T. "The Impact of Maternal Employment on the Mother-Daughter Relationship," *Marriage and Family Living,* 23:355–61.

Reid, Margaret G. "The Economic Contribution of Homemakers," *Annals of the American Academy of Political and Social Science,* 251:61–69.

Saenger, Gerhart. "Male and Female Relations in the American Comic Strip," *Public Opinion Quarterly,* 19:194–205.

Sakanishi, Shio. "Women's Position and the Family System in Japan," *Annals of the American Academy of Political and Social Science,* 308:130–39.

Schaefer, Earl S., and Richard Bell. "Pattern of Attitudes Toward Child Rearing and the Family," *Journal of Abnormal and Social Psychology,* 54:391–95.

Siegal, Alberta E., *et al.* "Dependence and Independence in the Children of Working Mothers," *Child Development,* 30:533–46.

Slater, Carol. "Class Differences in Definition of Role and Membership in Voluntary Associations Among Urban Married Women," *American Journal of Sociology,* 55:616–19.

Stolz, Lois M. "Effects of Maternal Employment on Children: Evidence from Research," *Child Development,* 31:749–82.

Straus, Murray A. "Family-Role Differentiation and Technological Change in Farming," *Rural Sociology,* 25:219–28.

Tharp, Roland G. "Psychological Patterning in Marriage," *Psychological Bulletin,* 60:97–115.

Weil, Mildred W. "An Analysis of the Factors Influencing Married Women's Actual or Planned Work Participation," *American Sociological Review,* 26:91–96.

Weitzel, Kathryn. "The Working Wife—Her Present Dilemma," *Journal of Home Economics,* 49:689–93.

Whyte, William H., Jr. "The Corporation And the Wife," *Fortune Magazine* (November 1951).
————. "The Wives of Management," *Fortune Magazine* (October 1951).
Wolf, Anna. "Can Babies and Careers Be Combined?" *National Parent Teacher Magazine* (January 1959), 4–6.
"Woman, The Fourth Dimension," A Special Issue of the *Ladies Home Journal* (June 1964).

Beginning a
chapter 16   family

It is only within recent years that research scientists have initiated the systematized study of human reproduction. These studies have produced significant advances in knowledge of the biology, physiology, and psychology of the sex drive and procreation. Through the proper dissemination and application of this knowledge, family planning is today not only possible, but practical. Although a few cultural and religious groups may argue that birth control is immoral, there are as many dedicated churchmen, doctors, scientists, sociologists, and devout citizens who believe that it is immoral for mankind *not* to try to control a force of nature as powerful as reproduction. No one who believes in a democratic society can deny either group their constitutionally guaranteed freedom of choice in this matter. If one family or religious group chooses not to practice birth control, its freedom of choice should be defended by all citizens. If another person wishes to practice birth control, however, no one has the right to deny that citizen his freedom of choice or to prevent him from obtaining the necessary means to implement his personal belief and private choice.

To force the prohibition of planned parenthood on all citizens, in direct opposition to their religious and ethical beliefs, is not only immoral, it would seem in the United States to be a violation of the Constitutional Bill of Rights.

In any contemporary discussion of the democratic foundations of the family, therefore, the facts of family planning must be presented and viewed objectively. Indeed, it is only fitting and proper that each married couple consider seriously both the positive and the negative aspects of planning for their children.

Historical attitudes toward having children

Traditionally, the word *marriage* was usually followed by the three words *and a family*, because in most instances marriage led to a child within a year.

RELIGIOUS DICTATES. The Biblical decree, "Be fruitful and multiply," has been observed almost literally in the historical development of civilizations. In the early stages of civilization, large families were essential because of the high infant mortality rates. Indeed, merely to maintain the population status quo, it was necessary for every couple to have as many children as possible. It was with good reason that the Psalmist exhorted, "Lo! children are a heritage of Jehovah. . . . As arrows in the hand of a mighty man, so are the children of youth. . . . Happy is the man that has his quiver full of them."[1]

SOCIAL PRESSURES. The community expected almost every married couple to have children; in fact, it was considered their duty to have a family. Most of the Colonial marital laws specified that if no children issued from a marriage it was possible for that marriage to be dissolved. In some countries this is still true; indeed childlessness is legal grounds for divorce in Pennsylvania and Tennessee. In Colonial America there was sometimes even public criticism of a couple who had no children. Occasionally, to encourage procreation, subsidies and bounties were given to families with children and laws were passed against contraception. Furthermore, there was a glorification of motherhood by various forms of art. All of these social pressures tended to create a strong desire for children after marriage.[2] The songwriters and versifiers furthered the maternal cause by insinuating none too subtly that in producing a child the woman could rule the rest of the world, as in:

> They say that man is mighty,
> He governs land and sea,
> He wields a mighty scepter,
> On lesser powers that be.
> But a mightier power and stronger
> Man from his throne has hurled,
> For the hand that rocks the cradle
> Is the hand that rules the world.[3]

ECONOMIC PRESSURES. In an agrarian economy, large families were naturally highly valued. Children in an agricultural society were decided assets because a farmer with many sons was assured of manpower. Sons could help clear more land and increase production, thus assuring the family of greater economic success. Such sons indicated to the parents that they would be provided for in their old age. Nowadays, however, children seldom work for the parents and are rarely able to support them in times of need.

IGNORANCE. It must also be remembered that people in the past usually did not know how to control conception. Their attempts at artificial control were not only unreliable, but often dangerous and difficult to use.

Conception-control facts and myths

Because so many interpretations and biases surround the methods of conception control, an examination of some of the facts and myths on the subject is necessary before an objective view can be established.

The idea of conception control appears to have originated in ancient Greece. The teachings and writings of the early philosophers—Plutarch, Plato, and Aristotle—indicate a perception of the dangers of excessive reproduction. Many of their thoughts on the subject were later supported by the writings of Benjamin Franklin, as well as by the essays on the principles of population propounded by the Reverend T. R. Malthus in 1798. These early writers, however, were unable to offer any helpful methods to counteract excessive reproduction. Today, on the other hand, contraceptives can be prescribed for individual needs by competent physicians.

HARMFUL EFFECTS. The possibility of harmful effects developing from the use of birth-control devices has often been given as a reason for their avoidance. It has been charged that the use of contraceptives would encourage promiscuity. As pointed out in Chapter Eight, however, contraceptive devices seldom make people more sexually promiscuous than they were. According to most sociologists, the main reason people abstain from promiscuity is their sense of ethics and morals rather than their fear of pregnancy.

A second erroneous belief concerning birth control is that it is likely to cause physical injury. Although unapproved mechanical and chemical methods might lead to injury, clinically approved methods do not. A clinical study of more than 12,500 cases revealed not a single case of injury in any way from the use of contraceptive devices recommended by competent and trained physicians.[4]

There is sometimes apprehension that a couple's ability to conceive will be impaired even when they no longer practice birth control. In the Indianapolis study that compared young couples who had never used contraceptives with those who gave up control methods in order to have a child, it was found that both groups conceived in substantially the same average length of time.[5] The misapprehension is probably perpetuated by couples who were relatively infertile before they started using an artificial method of control. The use of medically approved contraceptives does not render a couple or individual sterile; it merely prevents conception during its use.

Another false deterrent to the use of contraceptive devices is based on the idea that they interfere with sexual pleasure. Studies on this possibility show the opposite to be true: the employment of contraceptive devices usually increases, rather than decreases sexual enjoyment by relaxing the couple, who might otherwise be tense and nervous because of their fears of pregnancy. Indeed, the use of contraceptives has greatly reduced many women's fears of pregnancy.[6] It is true, however, that certain methods do seem to interfere with the complete enjoyment of the sex act for one or the other partner. In this respect, each couple must try out several methods to discover the one that seems best suited to them. Psychologically, the use of contraceptives might adversely affect sexual adjustment for some couples if it gives rise to a sense of guilt. Probably such couples should make a serious study of the recommended rhythm method.

RELATIVE ACCURACY OF METHODS.   There is a vast amount of literature today on the relative merits and accuracy of various conception-control methods. The two chief methods are (1) the natural, or rhythm method; and (2) a mechanical or chemical method using some form of artificial device.

The natural method is based on the fact that there are some days within the menstrual cycle when conception is least likely to occur and other days when conception is most likely to occur. Thus, a couple wishing to avoid pregnancy would confine their sex relations to those intervals of the least possibility of conception. This is known as negative control. Conversely, couples wishing to conceive would concentrate their sexual activities to the interval in which conception would be most likely. This is known as positive control. In this connection, Stone has said:

> In general, the last ten days of the month, the ten days prior to the onset of the next menstrual period, can be considered to be fairly safe from the likelihood of conception. It is assumed that the first nine days of the cycle are also sterile, but this is much less certain because we do not know with certainty how long the sperm cells of the male can remain alive within the genital tract of the woman.[7]

There are many variables inherent in the natural method, whether it is used positively for conception or negatively for prevention. One of the difficulties is determining the time of ovulation. If ovulation time were accurately known, then the rhythm method might be used with some accuracy because fertilization can occur only within a relatively short time (usually two or three days) after ovulation. Determining the period of ovulation, however, is rather difficult. The daily temperature check was used as a means of ascertaining ovulation for some time. A characteristic sharp rise in temperature was at first believed to indicate ovulation, but it proved to be merely an indication that ovulation had already occurred.[8] Actually, the use of the temperature chart may be of help to couples wanting to conceive. For couples seeking to avoid pregnancy, however, the temperature check is of little value, for temperature may fluctuate for other reasons. Because a rise in temperature may not indicate ovulation in the individual woman, its use as a means of birth control is unreliable.[9]

The work of the Wistar Institute of Anatomy and Biology has revealed great variations in the intervals of fertility even among women having the same menstrual cycle. The Wistar findings indicate that, for most women, an eight-day interval of greatest fertility can be calculated within a given cycle, but that there is a wide variation within those eight days.[10] Dr. Farris of the Wistar Institute published the results of a ten-year study on human ovulation, which led to the development of the rat hyperemia test. In this test a sample of urine is taken from the woman on each of the days when ovulation is most likely to occur and the sample is injected into young female rats. The reaction of the rat's ovaries indicates whether or not the woman is ovulating. Although this is not very helpful for couples who wish to prevent conception, it could help those who want to conceive. Farris' research also indicated that sometimes ova are released on various days within the same cycle. This would seem to preclude any possibility of reliable conception prevention by the rhythm methods as now practiced.[11] Because menstruation follows ovulation, and not vice-versa, it is not possible to predict ovulation accurately (although in many cases the time of menstruation could be predicted accurately if the exact time of ovulation were known). Although the estrogen released by the corpus luteum appears to precipitate menstruation in most females rather regularly in from twelve to sixteen days after ovulation (fourteen days is the most common interval), the interval between menstruation and the *next* ovulation may be upset by unusual physical and emotional experiences. Thus, the menstruation cycle is never a completely reliable method of negative conception control. Furthermore, recent tests by researchers at the Boston University School of Medicine combined recorded changes in vaginal electro-potential measurements with analysis of urine specimens for 600 patients having difficulty conceiving. The results showed tremendous individualistic variations and indicated that the release of an egg cell for some women apparently occurs only about eight to ten days ahead of menstruation.[12]

The indeterminancy of the life expectancy of male sperm and female ova is another variable factor in the rhythm method. No one knows precisely how long spermatozoa may live after deposition within the female, nor how long after rupturing from the graafian follicle the ova may remain effective for fertilization. Research indicates a considerable variation: the spermatozoa of some males apparently thrive longer than those of others; the chemistry of some females appears to keep spermatozoa alive longer than does that of other females.

With complete reliance upon the rhythm method, there were from eighty-six to 105 pregnancies per one hundred woman-years of exposure to intercourse, according to the studies reviewed by Folsom. The use of contraceptives reduced the pregnancy rate to between twenty-seven and forty. These were studies made on an average clinical population. College

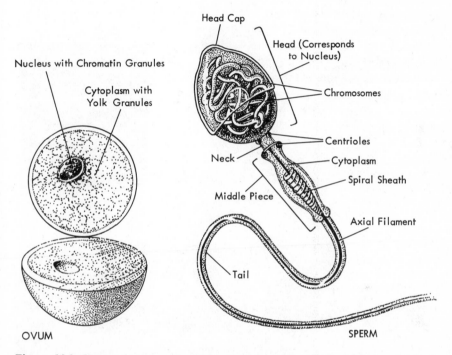

Figure 16-1. Human ovum and sperm. (Adapted from "The Miracle of Life," *Today's Health,* 38:35 [November, 1960]. Copyright 1960 by The American Medical Association. Reproduced by permission.)

women, with an average rate of thirty-one pregnancies per one hundred woman-years of exposure to intercourse, after instruction in the proper use of contraceptives, were able to reduce this figure to six. Furthermore, of those in this same group who later decided to have another baby, 50 per cent became pregnant within one month, and 75 per cent within three months, after discontinuing the use of contraceptives.[13] The results of these research studies suggest that the effective use of contraceptives for negative control depends on education and the full understanding of their proper use. College couples were able to use them much more

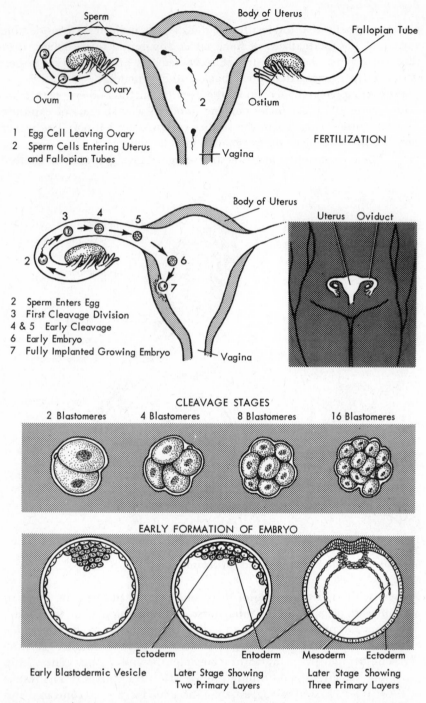

FERTILIZATION

Sperm

Body of Uterus

Fallopian Tube

Ovum   1

Ovary

Ostium

2

1   Egg Cell Leaving Ovary
2   Sperm Cells Entering Uterus
and Fallopian Tubes

Vagina

Body of Uterus

3   4   5

2

6

7

Uterus   Oviduct

2   Sperm Enters Egg
3   First Cleavage Division
4 & 5   Early Cleavage
6   Early Embryo
7   Fully Implanted Growing Embryo

Vagina

CLEAVAGE STAGES

2 Blastomeres   4 Blastomeres   8 Blastomeres   16 Blastomeres

EARLY FORMATION OF EMBRYO

Ectoderm   Entoderm   Mesoderm   Ectoderm

Early Blastodermic Vesicle   Later Stage Showing   Later Stage Showing
Two Primary Layers   Three Primary Layers

Figure 16-2. Human fertilization process. (Adapted from "The Miracle of Life," *Today's Health,* **38**:36 [November, 1960]. Copyright 1960 by The American Medical Association. Reproduced by permission.)

effectively than noncollege couples. A study of the opinions of physicians leaves little doubt about the relative merits of the two birth-control methods. The great majority of all the physicians interviewed felt that artificial contraceptives were much more effective than the rhythm method. Furthermore, 47 per cent of the physicians of the Catholic faith wholeheartedly agreed; an additional 23 per cent declined to give an opinion.[14]

Those who advocate the rhythm method as equal or better for negative control than medically approved contraceptive devices assume that more is known about determining the occurrence of ovulation and many other physiological factors than is actually the case at present. It is quite possible, however, that some promising developments may be coming soon. For example, there is a new drug that does not inhibit ovulation but seems merely to act as a regularizer of the menstrual period; it could become a reliable component of the rhythm system of conception control, provided it has no harmful side affects.[15]

To use the rhythm method with reasonable safety, a margin of extra days before and after the calculated interval of ovulation would be necessary. This would eliminate the possibility of spermatozoa still being potent at ovulation and the possibility of the ovum being fertilized after its release. Such a safety margin would necessitate avoiding intercourse about half of the days in the average female cycle. This is a longer period of sexual abstinence than most young couples are prepared to accept. For this reason the rhythm method is not always practical, even with women who have regular menstrual cycles.[16]

Those who are limited by church decree to the rhythm method of birth control, and who feel they have all the children they can now manage, must develop and accept a more rigid sex perspective than the average couple. Their sex life may be regulated more by restriction than by sexual desire. Better family planning is still possible within this limitation if the couple keep careful records and discuss their problem with a competent physician. Marital harmony for such couples may be further strengthened by frequent discussions and consultations with a spiritual director in sympathy with the dilemma facing young parents in a world of strong materialism and weak faith. Certainly it is possible for those of deep religious conviction to accrue benefits from self-denial and self-discipline based on love of God.

Alternatively, the couple may simply ignore the directives of the church authorities and follow their own inclinations in the matter, often believing that the directives imposed by those living a rule of celibacy are too unrealistic and stringent for the laity. It would seem that the latter choice is becoming more prevalent in many modern marriages. For example, several studies indicate that many Catholic women are clients of the contraceptive clinics maintained in large cities by the Planned

Parenthood League.[17] Middle- and upper-class Catholic women are even more likely to redefine the role of conception practice within marriage. One study of 3500 middle- and upper-class women revealed that 43 per cent of the Catholics in the sample were using one or more contraceptive devices not sanctioned by the Church.[18] Casey's summaries of more than six recent studies by Catholic family scholars disclose that a large percentage of Catholics now use Church-forbidden forms of birth control. This was especially true of those married ten years or more.[19] Kanin explains that middle- and upper-socioeconomic-class Catholics are torn between the Church ideals and the economic materialism and individualism prevailing in their social groups. This causes much inner conflict, but often such individuals rationalize the use of contraceptive devices, feeling that the Church is old-fashioned on this point and that outside of this area they can still be good Catholics.[20]

An artificial method of conception control, in contrast to the "natural" or rhythm method, employs some mechanical and/or chemical means to prevent the spermatozoa from reaching the ova. There are many artificial methods used in the American culture; many other methods unknown to most Americans are practiced in other cultures, but their range of effectiveness is wide and often somewhat speculative. Several studies have indicated that certain techniques are almost 100 per cent effective. It must be remembered that many of those studies have been conducted by laboratories with vested interests, such as the pharmaceutical companies manufacturing the particular devices being tested. Part of the variability in effectiveness of some contraceptives is probably related to the variability among couples. Far too many couples erroneously rely upon devices recommended by friends, drugstore clerks, or advertisements—as scientific a method as purchasing shoes out of a mail-order catalog or eyeglasses from a dime store. New methods are constantly being explored, including a technique for exploiting the olfactory sense, and one applying heat.[21]

There are several reasons why artificial methods of conception control are not utilized more generally. One of the least considered but most important drawbacks is cost. Any method that is expensive is less likely to be effective, for it leads inevitably to short-cuts that reduce the safety margin. Indeed, the frequency of the sexual urge in marriage makes the consideration of cost more important than might at first be anticipated. The procedure involved in using a particular method may also contribute to the frequency of its use. In other words, if the device must be inserted in the middle of sexual love play, no doubt there will be times when the couple will forego the interruption. Under these circumstances, it is not that the device is ineffectual but that its use is inconvenient. Many methods may be considered too inconvenient for the couple to practice consistently.

Another problem of artificial birth-control methods is that a supply of the contraceptive must be always readily available. Some couples report they stopped using contraceptives because of the nuisance created by the need constantly to replenish the supply.

The effectiveness of any contraceptive is a function of the proven fertility of the couple. The avoidance of pregnancy is no criterion of conception-control effectiveness if the couple have not discovered whether they can reproduce without contraceptives. Even when the method is effective, however, failure to use the product as directed probably accounts for a certain percentage of pregnancies. For best results, the use of all conception-control methods requires intelligence, maturity, and considerable control of the sexual impulses. The method may be fairly efficient, but if the couple using it are careless, negative control cannot be guaranteed.

Several researchers have concluded that the conditions leading to effective family planning are analogous to those leading to effective planning in any field.[22] That is to say, if a couple usually plan and organize other phases of their lives, they are more likely to plan and organize for children. After an extensive educational campaign and research survey in Puerto Rico, it was concluded that several factors were important to effective conception control. Among these were (1) the acceptance of a modern value system concerning the size of family and the spacing of children; (2) a definite view favoring small families; (3) sufficient information on conception-control methods; and (4) effective organization—that is, the ability to plan other phases of life as well. All these factors affected the reliability of whatever method was under consideration. The researchers therefore concluded that birth-control propaganda campaigns were ineffective unless they were preceded by marriage- and family-life education that created a motivation for organization of all phases of marriage and family life.[23] The lack of orientation might contribute significantly to the higher fertility rates of various groups. Rainwater also suggests that high fertility today may arise not so much from ignorance as from motivational factors.[24]

POSITIVE BENEFITS. Planned-parenthood clinics actually do as much work in positive conception control as in negative control, but the former is less publicized by their detractors. Such clinics have been very helpful to many couples who wanted to conceive. Twenty-eight states now have planned-parenthood centers which are affiliated with the Planned-Parenthood Federation of America. In addition, five other states provide child-spacing services, for those who cannot afford a private physician, through state or county maternal-health clinics.[25]

Perhaps one of the greatest benefits of family planning is that an intelligent choice is much more possible. As the Planned-Parenthood Federation of America has stated:

Planned parenthood which represents deliberate choice has but one alternative—chance, irresponsible chance. Children should be wished *by* their parents and not *on* their parents. Children should not only be well borne, but well-come. It is nothing short of immoral to leave birth to chance.[26]

Lawrence Frank said:

Planned parenthood is an affirmation—made deliberately and jointly by a man and a woman, who see in child-bearing a way of affirming their personal and social values, signifying the importance of love, and courageously projecting those beliefs into the future.[27]

Dr. John Rock advances the concept that *to reproduce* is quite different from *to beget*. The latter implies a simple biological process; the former means to bring children up in one's best image. This can hardly be expected to occur when one spreads himself too thinly as is necessary with lots of children in the family.[28]

Factors contributing to involuntary childlessness

Some couples desire children but are unable to have them. Others desire more children but seem unable to conceive again, regardless of the method of positive conception control used.

The first World Congress on Human Infertility representing 1300 physicians from fifty-three nations met in New York City in May 1953. One of the conclusions drawn was that 10 to 15 per cent of marriages throughout the world remain childless.[29] Census figures of 1964 indicated that 11.7 per cent of American married women, aged thirty-five to forty-four, have borne no children.[30] Studies by Whelpton, Thompson, and Dewees suggest that between one half and two thirds of childless marriages are involuntarily so.[31] Dewees describes involuntary childlessness as caused by multiple factors, such as injury, infection, surgical operations, unusual anatomy, growth defects, and glandular imbalances.[32] Probably about one half of today's childless couples might conceive, with proper help. Unfortunately, there are no reliable statistics to reveal how many marriages are childless because the couple are achieving 100 per cent effectiveness by negative conception-control practices; among college students recently surveyed, however, only 2 per cent of men and 1 per cent of women stated they definitely did not desire any children.[33]

If a couple have been unable to conceive after about a year of trying, they should seek competent medical help and possible treatment. There are several factors that can contribute to childlessness.

CHANCE. One factor may be chance itself. Even at best, the effective potency of sperm and ova is brief. If a couple engage in intercourse infrequently, it is possible that they are missing the intervals most favorable for conception.

INCOMPATIBILITY. It may well be that there are certain factors in operation between potentially fertile mates that render them sterile with one another. Childless couples who had been divorced and then remarried, had children with the second spouse; yet, upon remarrying each other, they again failed to conceive. James Peterson suggests that there is considerable evidence of a relationship in some marriages between infertility and poor sex adjustment. He reports that medical specialists, in treating infertility problems, are increasingly turning to marriage counselors for collaborative aid.[34]

MALE PHYSIOLOGY. The infertility of a couple may be caused by a defect in only one of the mates. For example, the male may produce too few spermatozoa to fertilize an ovum; when there are fewer than 20 to 30 million sperm per cubic centimeter of seminal fluid, relative infertility usually results.[35] Ova are surrounded by tiny cells. In order for one sperm to meet and fertilize an egg, many must first dissolve the surrounding cells.[36] It has been calculated that only about 2000 of the normal 400 million sperm cells ejaculated at the time of intercourse ever reach the "trysting" site.[37]

Frequency of intercourse may also affect the sperm count. After intercourse it normally takes a few days for the male to restore his sperm count to its highest level.

In addition to sperm count, there may be a high ratio of defective sperm, and this too will have its effect upon relative male fertility. If the secretions from the seminal vesicles and the prostate gland are not sufficient to prepare sperm for the possibility of fertilization, the fertility rate will be lower. It is these secretions that stimulate spermatozoa activity and effectively buffer the sperm in the acidic environs of the female vagina. Sperm are relatively dormant prior to glandular stimulations; thus, if these glands are not functioning normally, the sperm—even though plentiful—may be defective and incapable of fertilization.

FEMALE PHYSIOLOGY. It is estimated that about 20 per cent of the ova of normally fertile women are deficient, and thus incapable of fertilization. The range varies from nearly zero in some women to more than 50 per cent in others. In addition, some women do not produce an ovum in every cycle.[38]

The acidity within the female genital tract may also contribute to relative infertility because some spermatozoa are quite susceptible to hyperacidity. This is especially true if the sperm are not overly vigorous, or if there is not enough secretion from the prostate gland to neutralize the acidity.

AGE. Age may also contribute to childlessness. The older the male, the fewer and more defective are his spermatozoa. The older the female, the more defective are her ova and the stronger the acidity within her genital tract. It has been estimated that only about 4 per cent of couples in their early twenties are completely sterile, but that fifteen years later the fertility is reduced almost to the point of sterility in 25 per cent of the same couples.[39] It seems that the younger a girl starts her menses, the older she starts her menopause. Fertility usually terminates before the age of sixty, the median age being forty-nine. Some women, however, experience menopause as early as thirty-three, but about 50 per cent of women are beginning menopause by the age of forty-six.[40]

Table 16–1. **Age at which menopause completed**

Age	Percentage with menopause completed
40 or Under	1
42	4
44	7
46	19
48	31
50	51
52	73
54	88
56	97
58	99
60	100

Source: Alfred Kinsey, *et al.*, *Sexual Behavior in the Human Female* (Philadelphia: W. B. Saunders Co., 1953), p. 719. Copyright © 1953, by W. B. Saunders Co., Philadelphia. Adapted by permission of publisher and Institute for Sex Research, Indiana University, Bloomington, Ind. Table corrected for errors in original publication as suggested in correspondence with The Institute for Sex Research.

Organic factors sometimes contribute to relative infertility. A tightly closed cervix (the small opening from the vagina into the uterus), which does not allow passage of many spermatozoa, lessens the chances of fertilization. Excessive secretion of cervical mucus may also prevent sperm from entering.

The position of the cervical end of the uterus may also affect fertility. The uterus normally slopes forward at about a 45° angle, but if the tip is bent forward or backward, it is extremely difficult for a fetus to develop to full-term.

Some women have closed fallopian tubes, which prevent the meeting of ova and sperm. The fallopian tubes are the small oviducts which serve as passageways for the ova from the ovaries to the uterus.[41] Rubin's test may be used by physicians to determine whether or not these tubes are, in fact, closed. In this test, carbon dioxide gas is introduced into the uterus, and a gauge registers the pressure. If one of the tubes is closed, the carbon dioxide pressure increases, if both tubes are open, the gas passes into the body cavity where it is absorbed, and no increase of pressure is registered. (Sometimes the pressure of the carbon dioxide will reopen a collapsed tube.) Other tests use liquids rather than gas; by means of x-ray, the doctor can see how far along the tubes the liquids have passed.

Sometimes tumors interfere with conception by obstructing the passages, thus preventing the meeting of sperm and egg. Uterine tumors may prevent the implantation of the fertilized ovum or disturb its growth, thus causing spontaneous abortion. A thyroid imbalance, particularly in females, may also interfere with conception.

Certain diseases, such as gonorrhea, are also contributing factors to sterility. Occasionally, a severe case of mumps in the adult male may render him less fertile.

The Rh factor must also be considered in an evaluation of a couple's fertility. It was in 1937 that this factor was identified in the red blood cells of the Rhesus monkey by Landsteiner and Wiener. Although there are many Rh types, persons with the most common type are classified as Rh+. Rh— blood (no Rh factor) reacts against Rh+ blood by producing antibodies that tend to break down the Rh+ red blood cells. The only combination of blood types that causes problems in pregnancy is an Rh+ father and an Rh— mother conceiving an Rh+ child. If there is any leakage or exchange of blood between mother and child during pregnancy, the mother's Rh— blood begins to produce antibodies against the Rh+ fetal blood. In the first pregnancy there are usually too few antibodies produced to affect the fetus. The antibodies, however, usually remain in the mother's bloodstream, and upon subsequent pregnancy there is a slight possibility that this condition may affect the fetus, resulting in *erythroblastosis*. There are, however, fewer spontaneous abortions from this condition than was once believed. Fortunately, most modern hospitals in the United States are set up for immediate treatment of both the Rh— mother and the Rh+ newborn. Fern states: "Fewer than one marriage in eight is between an Rh— woman and an Rh+ man, and even in these marriages only one couple in twenty ever runs into any trouble.[42]

Sometimes couples are unable to conceive because of poor over-all health. Lowered vitality, shock, change of mode of life, defective nutrition, overfatigue, intoxication, infection, vitamin deficiency, and defective metabolism may all contribute to infertility. The relationship between anxiety and the inability to conceive, is demonstrated with couples who, believing themselves sterile, adopt children and then conceive one of their own. After the adoption of a baby, many couples settle down to a more relaxed way of living and, with reduction of anxieties and frustrations, the optimum conditions for conception are achieved. There

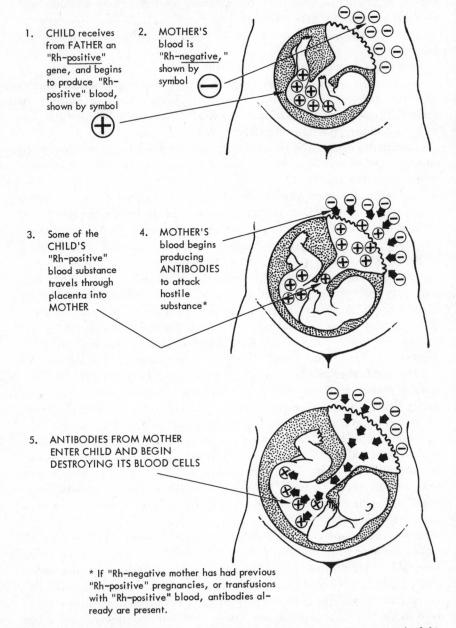

1. CHILD receives from FATHER an "Rh-positive" gene, and begins to produce "Rh-positive" blood, shown by symbol ⊕

2. MOTHER'S blood is "Rh-negative," shown by symbol ⊖

3. Some of the CHILD'S "Rh-positive" blood substance travels through placenta into MOTHER

4. MOTHER'S blood begins producing ANTIBODIES to attack hostile substance*

5. ANTIBODIES FROM MOTHER ENTER CHILD AND BEGIN DESTROYING ITS BLOOD CELLS

* If "Rh-negative mother has had previous "Rh-positive" pregnancies, or transfusions with "Rh-positive" blood, antibodies already are present.

Figure 16-3. (Adapted from Louise Zabriskie, *Obstetrics for Nurses*, revised by Elise Fitzpatrick and Nicholson Eastman [Philadelphia: J. B. Lippincott Co., 1960]. Reproduced by permission.)

seems to be some confusion as to the true possibilities of adoptive parents (considered sterile) to conceive naturally after the adoption. A study of 273 cases of adoption found that 200 women who had never before been pregnant conceived a child within approximately thirty-nine months after adoption and within ten years after their wedding.[43] The recently completed research of Weinstein, however, covering a wide sample of thousands of cases, indicates that—contrary to the popular belief—natural pregnancy follows adoption in only 14 per cent of the cases.[44]

Progress versus tradition

Historically, progress in every form has usually met opposition. Family planning is no exception. Honest opposition is healthy, for without it people become apathetic. Initially, even smallpox vaccination was opposed by many, and their arguments often sounded logical by conservative medical standards. In 1721 when smallpox vaccination was being introduced to America, Dr. Boylston inoculated his own son to show his confidence in the vaccine. Instead of winning admiration and advocates, however, he was mobbed by angry crowds. Many clergymen preached against vaccination, indicting it as an attempt by man to alter the course of nature.[45] Many projects designed for the progress of man have been labeled "interference" with nature. Pasteurization of milk, surgery, irrigation, artificial light, and even shaving have been condemned in the past as interference with nature, and, indeed, they are.

ADDED RESPONSIBILITY. If couples wish to control conception, it is absolutely necessary for them to agree on the method to be used. Birth control places the decision whether and when to have a baby directly upon the parents themselves. This is a different kind of responsibility than that of simply letting a pregnancy "happen." Indeed, it may be too much of a burden for some couples who find it difficult to agree even on trivial things.

Conception control may also increase psychological problems if it is at odds with the religious doctrines of the couple. It may even create an antireligious feeling among couples who disagree with their church's announced views. The young couple must judge for themselves whether it is worth their while to substitute a weak birth-regulation method for a strong security in their religion. The greatest dilemmas seem to face those couples with weak resolution in either direction; the fewest problems are encountered by those with the courage of their convictions.

The necessity of family planning

The values of family planning in modern society are not contingent upon a population explosion. There are several serious factors within the industrial civilization that makes intelligent and unselfish family planning essential.

A LONGER ADJUSTMENT PERIOD.   Family planning is essential in today's society because of the need for a longer marital-adjustment period. Today's couples need much more time together, because the average young married couple know much less about each other at the beginning of marriage than couples in an earlier American era did. Seldom are young couples today ready for children in the first year of marriage. Most must mature as husband and wife before they can attain the basic prerequisites of parenthood. This usually proves to be job enough for the first year or so of marriage. Time, unimpeded by adolescent anxieties about pregnancy, is needed to make the transition from courtship to marriage. The coming of children into the relationship during that time may forever arrest the maturation levels of both husband and wife.

The time required for working out initial marital adjustments varies with each couple, so that it is impossible to generalize. There is much evidence, however, that having a child during the first year of marriage sharply curtails the over-all happiness of many couples.[46] Bossard and Boll report that early pregnancy is related to an adverse effect upon developing family rituals:

> In families in which there was a period of adjustment of three years or more before a child arrived, there seemed to be a willingness and an established technique for ritual readjustment which lead to more satisfactory results during this period.... The arrival of children did not cause husband-and-wife conflict over rituals as it did in the case of the youthful marriages immediately disturbed by child-bearing.[47]

On the other hand, it is important that couples not wait too long before having children. If too comfortable and rigid a routine is established, there is a danger that the couple will not want to disrupt their isolated, adult serenity with a baby. Such couples might be worse off in the long run than those who have children very soon after marriage. An additional hazard incurred by waiting too long to start a family relates to the variables of fertility. If couples with a low fertility potential postpone their first pregnancy, they may find it difficult or impossible to conceive later. Thus, good family planning would favor having a baby before the third or fourth year of marriage.[48]

ECONOMIC CONSIDERATIONS.   Family planning is also warranted by economic considerations today. Most people now need more education than their forebears had, not only because technology requires greater skills but because marriage itself demands a higher standard of living. Furthermore, a college-educated wife should work for a while after graduation to apply her education pragmatically before being housebound with children.

In addition, couples need money in order to have children. The most expensive year for parents is the child's first year, which—for the average American family—costs about $1400; the least expensive year is the second, which costs about $912.[49]

Finances may be a limiting factor in family planning, but they should not be an eliminating factor. Financial difficulties for many couples in the United States are less often real than fancied. In one sense, who can ever afford to have children? For example, is it valid for a couple to say they cannot afford a child because they need a new car? Standards of living change. Thus, couples who rationalize that they cannot now afford to have children may find that their standard of living increases every year. After a few years they may still contend that they are not able to afford children. In postponing children for financial reasons, there is a great danger that the period of postponement may never end.

STATE OF HEALTH. Health considerations are most important in raising children. It is almost an axiom that the best parents are the healthiest parents. Most family-research studies show that people with the poorest health seem to do the least family planning, while those with the best health seem to do the most.[50] A survey of 15,000 physicians indicated that 97.8 per cent favored birth-control measures for reasons of health in family planning.[51]

When the wife is in good health, there is no physiological reason for postponing pregnancy. As Guttmacher, a leading authority in the field of obstetrics and gynecology, has stated: "I have seen no ill effects in the normal woman from a new pregnancy starting ten or twelve weeks after the completion of her last."[52] The collective opinion of more than 3000 physicians is that the average desirable minimum interval from the termination of one pregnancy to the beginning of the next is fourteen months, or twenty-three months between the actual births.[53] This usually gives enough time for the elimination of minor malfunctions between pregnancies. Guttmacher states that pregnancies should be delayed, however, when the following conditions exist: (1) malignancy, particularly of the breast; indeed, pregnancy is not advised for five years after a breast operation; (2) heart disease, if it is more than slight; (3) active or recently active tuberculosis; (4) persistent high blood pressure, and (5) a psychiatric disturbance caused by the preceding pregnancy.[54]

The majority of medical authorities agree that pregnancy is extremely hazardous if the mother suffers from chronic nephritis, organic heart disease, or tuberculosis. Recent experiments headed by Alexander Grendon, State Coordinator of Atomic-Energy Development and Radiation Protection for California, indicate that conception soon after x-ray examination (especially of the midsection) increases the infant's risk of mental and physical deformities and his susceptibility to leukemia and infection. These beliefs are also supported by Dr. Herman J. Miller, an authority on the genetic effects of radiation.[55]

According to Guttmacher, cesarean section, diabetes, pre-eclampsia, and eclampsia need not affect the interval between pregnancies.[56] The older woman who wishes to have a second child is advised to try to conceive sooner rather than later. Having the second child as soon as possible is recommended by some authorities if there are uterine tumors that might later interfere with pregnancy.[57]

Other health considerations are related to mental well-being. Too many pregnancies too close together can be a tremendous strain on a woman's emotional equilibrium. In fact, the woman's over-all mental and emotional state is often a more important consideration than her physical health. Pregnancy following a number of undesired children frequently results in induced abortions. Dr. Jerome Kummer, of the University of California at Los Angeles, has made an extensive study of this situation. He estimates that almost one million abortions are induced annually in the United States, usually by married women who feel they already have more children than they can manage.[58]

The age of the last child is an important consideration to marital happiness and itself justifies family planning. Older children need preparation for the coming of a new baby. It is therefore essential to family adjustment that the second child be planned for the most opportune stage in the first child's physical and emotional growth.

PREPARATION FOR PARENTHOOD. By planning their family, the couple can better prepare themselves for the responsibilities of parenthood. Contrary to what many people think, parenthood is not something that comes naturally. Most young people are unrealistically confident of their own ability to rear children properly. Only 4 per cent of the young people in Baber's study felt doubtful of their ability to rear children properly; 28 per cent felt positively certain of their ability.[59] This assurance is amazing in the face of their absolute lack of experience or training in child care. Too many young people learn too late that they should not have avoided courses in child development and child psychology that might have better prepared them for understanding and training their own children. LeMasters reported from his survey of 421 senior college women that less than 15 per cent had received any formal training for parenthood. Except for a few students who majored in home economics and education, these young people were not receiving what most authorities consider adequate preparation for parenthood.[60] Furthermore, except for those few couples who have been adequately prepared, parenthood is one of the most serious crises of young married life.[61] The haphazard experience in child care that some young people get within their own families is of questionable value. The oldest child in a large group is frequently given some responsibility for the care of younger ones; however, this experience seldom gives insight into proper child-care methods. In fact, adults who have had this experience frequently appear worse off than if they had had no experience at all. Duvall reports that 17,000 representative high school students from all sections of the United States, replying to the Purdue Opinion Poll of January 1959, averaged only about 60 per cent correct replies to important questions on child management.[62] Such findings certainly indicate that a preparation for parenthood is needed before most young couples start a family.

LITTLE INTEREST IN CHILDREN. Some people have little desire for children of their own. For them, parenthood would result probably only in despair and frustration.[63] Such people should probably avoid having any children, for a marriage with no children may be better adjusted than a marriage with unwanted children.

Certainly there is a definite need in society for adults with an objective or detached viewpoint. Such people should not feel defensive about their preference for childlessness in today's world. It should be observed that forcing couples to reproduce or not to reproduce because of social pressures is the symptom of tyranny, not a sign of a healthy democracy.

Interest in children and the desire to have additional offspring seem to diminish as the family increases. Numerous studies indicate that after the first two or three children are born, parents wish for fewer than they had first estimated as their ideal family size.

Thus, in a democratic society, the means for conception control should be openly available to those who want to plan their family size and to those who want no family at all. The result is better adjusted citizens.

The Catholic viewpoint on family planning

There is a wide variety of opinion on what the Catholic viewpoint concerning conception control actually is. Some writers have gone so far as to imply that the Catholic Church is unalterably opposed to all methods of birth control. This is not so. The Catholic Church was actually the first Christian denomination to sanction birth control and to call notice to the need for birth-control practices. The Catholic Church does not believe that a couple should have as large a family as possible. This idea does not appear in any of the official writings of Catholics; it has been perpetuated by others.

The basis of Catholic thought on conception control is related primarily to method.[64] The Catholic Church is opposed specifically to the use of artificial means of contraception. The current controversy within the Church on oral contraceptives may well result in a more liberal interpretation. With this scientific discovery by the Catholic, Dr. Rock, the Church's ban on pills and its approval of arbitrary abstinence may seem more like casuistry than good counsel.

It must be emphasized, however, that no religious group in America favors unrestricted reproduction. The Catholic viewpoint is best explained by this statement:

> The Catholic Church does not hold that married couple are under the obligation (1) to bring into the world the maximum number of children; (2) to exercise no prudence and common sense; (3) to bear offspring up to the so-called physiological limit; (4) to work unthinkingly for the maximum increase in population; or (5) to bring on an ever-increasing bumper crop of babies. It does not condone imprudence or intemperance.[65]

Thomas explains that "Catholic spouses will have the number of children they feel they can reasonably support and rear. Ultimately, the decision governing the number of children must rest on a mutual consent of the spouses."[66] Gerald Kelly offers the opinion that it is the societal obligation of each couple to base its decision on number of children on population needs, but no Catholic couple is compelled to exceed that particular need. "It [the duty to procreate] would bind each couple to make an ordinary, or an average, contribution in terms of the population needs." Kelly goes on to say that, under present conditions, the population need is about four or five children per couple, but that this would vary in society at different times.[67] It should be pointed out, however, that Kelly's view on population "needs" is not shared by all Catholic leaders. The official words of Pope Pius XII on this subject are:

> From the obligation of making this positive contribution, it is possible to be exempt, for a long time and even for the whole duration of married life, if there are serious reasons, such as those often provided in the so-called indications of the medical, eugenical, economic and social order. It therefore follows that the observance of the infertile period may be licit from the moral point of view; and under the conditions mentioned, it is so in fact.[68]

Modern couples desire children

This discussion must not be misinterpreted as suggesting that today's married couples do not desire children, for surveys disclose otherwise. In their studies of engaged couples, Burgess and Wallin reported that only 2.2 per cent of the men and 1.1 per cent of the woman absolutely did not want children after marriage, and only about 10 per cent of both sexes indicated no great desire to have children.[69] Burgess and Cottrell point out that the desire for children is still a strong motive for marriage.[70] Today's young couples want children as much or more than ever, but they want them at the time and in the number that seems best for total family happiness.

Bowerman's extensive study of American birth rates since the 1950s indicated a continuing decrease in the number of families with more than five children, a significant decrease in the percentage of childless families, and a sharp decline in the number of families with only one child.[71] The research conducted by Kiser also suggests that the trend is toward the moderate-size family.[72]

A factor sometimes overlooked in regard to family-size trends is the sex of the first children. Most couples desire to have children of both sexes. Thus, whether couples with two, three, or four children expect to have, or do have, an additional child is sometimes related to whether the first ones are all of the same sex. The importance of this factor is reported to increase in relation to the number of children born of identical sex.[73]

In the past, information on effective methods of conception control has not been generally available among the lower classes. Ronald Freedman, of the University of Michigan Research Center, reports that the higher-status parents today are having more children, and that the lower-income and less educated groups are beginning to exercise more effective negative conception control.[74] It appears that upper- and middle-class couples are having more children today than formerly, but when they want them. Such

Figure 16-4. The trend in the middle class is toward the middle-size family. (Courtesy of Glenbrook Laboratories.)

couples have now achieved positive control.[75] Bowerman states that the
birth-rate differential between rural and urban areas and among socioeconomic classes is being reduced, and there is now the possibility that
the wealthier and better educated couples will have more than their
proportion of births in the future.[76] In support of this, school authorities
are predicting that enrollments at the elementary level will probably not
increase substantially after about 1980.[77] According to the *Statistical
Bulletin* of the Metropolitan Life Insurance Company, there has been a
downward trend in births for the United States since 1955, and fewer
babies were born in 1964 than in any other year since 1953.[78]

It is no longer a question of whether married people should be permitted to practice conception control; they are practicing it. The problem
is to improve the use of such controls and to eliminate abuses. The
necessity for some form of effective control on family size and spacing
is recognized by all groups, including the clergy, physicians, almost all
responsible political leaders, and particularly by almost all wives.

The Indianapolis study on fertility indicates a slight increase in the
interval (now slightly more than one year) between the wedding and
the birth of the first child. About 95 per cent of Protestant middle-class
couples use contraceptive measures to delay pregnancy in the early stages
of marriage, and the percentage increases with the birth of successive
children.[79] A study of Cornell University graduates suggests that the
period between marriage and the birth of the first child is considerably
longer for college graduates than for noncollege graduates. Only 20 per
cent of those studied had experienced the birth of a child in less than one
year after marriage. In fact, nearly 30 per cent of the graduates surveyed
had waited until three years had passed before having their first child.[80]

Effect of children on marital happiness

Many people think that a bad marriage can be saved by a good child.
Unfortunately, research discloses that if a couple are not happy within
their marriage, they will seldom become more adjusted simply by having
children. If they cannot work out techniques of marital adjustment during the relatively simple childless period, there is little likelihood that
they will be able to make the complicated family adjustments after children are born.

Sometimes one mate might deliberately try to force conception as a
means of keeping the partner. The use of conception to trick a mate into
marriage or to pose an obstacle to possible divorce is unmercifully cruel
to the child.

DIVORCE AS A MEASURE. The erroneous belief that children can "save" a
marriage is probably based on the misinterpretation of the fact that more
divorces occur between childless mates than between those with children.

It is true that studies have shown that divorce is more frequent among childless couples, but only during the first years of marriage.[81] The differential in divorce rate between couples with children and those without is not uniform throughout married life: the rates tend to equalize as the marriages progress.[82] Although it may be true that more divorced couples had no children, it does not necessarily follow that divorce would have been averted had they had children. The truth is that happy couples have children and unhappy couples have divorces. Some couples avoid having children because they foresee the failure of their marriage. Recently the differential has been decreasing, as more couples with children seek divorce.[83] Thus, children are no insurance for better marital adjustment.

ADJUSTMENT AS A MEASURE. Another way of measuring the effect of children on marriage is by marriage-adjustment scores. Studies of such tests have found little difference between the happiness scores of childless couples and couples with children. Among couples who had been married a number of years, Terman found no correlation whatsoever between children and happiness in marriage.[84] Christensen found that, in general, happiness tends to decrease with an increase in the size of the married-college-student family, but that there was a correlation between the couple's happiness and their ability to control the family size according to their desires.[85] The Indianapolis studies on child spacing indicate that the better adjusted marriage had fewer children, while the worst adjusted marriages had the most children.[86] Landis concludes from his own study of 409 couples that those without children tended toward the extremes in adjustment, being either very happy or very unhappy, while those with children approached an average in happiness.[87] Burgess and Cottrell found that happiness in marriage was associated with a desire for children regardless of whether or not the couple had any children at

Table 16-2. **Marital happiness related to desire for children**

	Marital adjustment		
Condition	*Per cent poor*	*Per cent fair*	*Per cent good*
None, but desired	10	25	65
One or more, desired	20	35	45
None, not desired by one spouse or both	45	25	30
One or more, not desired by one spouse or both	65	23	12

Source: E. W. Burgess and Leonard S. Cottrell, *Predicting Success or Failure in Marriage* (Englewood Cliffs, N.J.: Prentice-Hall, Inc., 1939), p. 260. Copyright © 1939, by Prentice-Hall, Inc., Englewood Cliffs, N.J. Reprinted by permission of publisher and authors.

the time of the study. The poorest marital adjustment was found among couples with children they had not wanted rather than with couples who had no children and wanted none. It is probably safe to say that, if an unhappy couple have undesired children, marital-adjustment problems will only increase.

Summary

All the evidence points to the conclusion that only those couples who want children should plan to have them. Furthermore, the couples should be properly prepared for family life, and their marital relationship well adjusted before the first child arrives.

It is immoral and contrary to the basic tenets of freedom of choice guaranteed in the Constitutional Bill of Rights to deny any citizen the right to practice conception control; it is equally wrong to force conception control on any couple. Modern means of conception control, however, should not be denied to those who, by religion and ethics, believe family planning is essential for a better life, a stronger society, and a more intelligent and better educated citizenry. Conception control, by natural or artificial means, is merely a method for regulating the number and the timing of births for the better over-all development of the family.

Planning the size of the family is the responsibility of each married couple. Government and private programs may suggest, advise, or facilitate family planning, but the decision to plan, how to plan, and how long to plan must be made by the individual couple.

Freedom of choice in controlling conception is essential to a companionable, democratic marriage, and a prerequisite to maximum happiness in such a marriage.

The gradual shift from a family-oriented society to a culture increasingly oriented toward the individual, his physical and material welfare, and his opportunities for personal happiness within the marriage relationship, is the chief cause of the decline in birth rates of various socioeconomic groups. The recent increase in births in the professional class shows conclusively that the dissemination of contraceptive knowledge does not permanently lower the birth rate. Instead, it liberates the family from uncertainty and happenstance, offering the couple the opportunity to have the number of children they want at the most opportune time for the best over-all family adjustment.

Notes

1. Psalms, 127:3–5.

2. L. A. Hollingsworth, "Social Devices for Impelling Women to Bear and Rear Children," *American Journal of Sociology*, 22:19–29.

3. William Ross Wallace, *The Battle of Tippecanoe, Triumphs of Science, and Other Poems* (Cincinnati: McFarlin Company, 1838), p. 103.

4. Rachell Yarros, *Modern Women and Sex* (New York: Vanguard Press, 1953), p. 147.

5. Charles T. Westoff, Lee F. Herrera, and P. K. Whelpton, *The Use, Effectiveness, and Acceptability of Methods of Fertility Control* (New York: Milbank Memorial Fund, 1953), p. 900.

6. Alan F. Guttmacher and Joan Gould, "New Facts About Birth Control," Public Affairs Pamphlet, 136B, 2.

7. Abraham Stone, "The Prevention of Conception," in Morris Fishbein and Ernest W. Burgess (eds.), *Successful Marriage* (Garden City, N.Y.: Doubleday & Company, Inc., p. 285.

8. Emil Novak (ed.), *Obstetrical and Gynecological Survey*, 12:408.

9. E. L. Buxton and E. T. Engle, "Time of Ovulation," *American Journal of Obstetrics and Gynecology*, 60:539–51.

10. Edmond J. Farris, *Human Ovulation and Fertility* (Philadelphia: J. B. Lippincott Co., 1956).

11. *Ibid.*

12. See *Today's Health* (December 1962), 9; and "Rhythm Method Change Seen in New Concept," *Science News Letter* (October 6, 1962), 224.

13. Joseph K. Folsom, *The Family and Democratic Society* (New York: John Wiley & Sons, Inc., 1943), p. 259.

14. Gerald S. Schnepp and Joseph Mundi, "What Doctors Think of the Rhythm Method," *American Ecclesiastical Review*, 123:111–16.

15. See literature of the Philips Roxine Company, Inc., Columbus, Ohio.

16. Some Protestant groups contend that it is just as morally wrong for a couple to forego intercourse for so long a period as it is for them to use contraceptives. See John C. Bennett, "Protestant Ethics and Population Control," *Daedalus* (Summer 1959), 454–59.

17. David Loth, "Planned Parenthood," *Annals of the American Academy of Political and Social Science*, 272:95–101.

18. John W. Riley and Matilda White, "The Use of Various Methods of Contraception," *American Sociological Review*, 5:890–903.

19. Thomas J. Casey, "Catholics and Family Planning," *American Catholic Sociological Review*, 21:125–35.

20. Eugene J. Kanin, "Value Conflicts in Catholic Device-Contraceptive Usage," *Social Forces*, 35:238–43.

21. See essay by John Rock, M.D., in Roy O. Greep (ed.), *Human Fertility and Population Problems* (Cambridge, Mass.: Schenkman Publishing Company, 1964).

22. Kurt W. Back, Reuben Hill, and J. Mayone Stycos, "The Dynamics of Family Planning," *Marriage and Family Living*, 18:195.

23. *Ibid.*, p. 199.

24. Lee Rainwater, *And the Poor Get Children* (Chicago: Quadrangle Books, 1960).

25. Alan F. Guttmacher, *The Complete Book of Birth Control* (New York: Ballantine Books, 1961).

26. Planned-Parenthood Federation of America, *Religion Looks at Planned Parenthood* (1952), 3.

27. Janet Fowler Nelson, "Preparing for a Baby," in Morris Fishbein and Ruby Jo Kennedy (eds.), *Modern Marriage and Family Living* (New York: Oxford University Press, Inc., 1957), p. 369.

28. John Rock, M.D., in Kennedy Lecture, Ohio University, Athens, Ohio, January 12, 1965.

29. Abraham Stone, "World Conference on Human Infertility," *Marriage and Family Living*, 15:231–33.

30. U.S. Bureau of the Census, Series P-23, No. 12 (July 31, 1964).

31. P. K. Whelpton, "Reproduction Rate Adjusted for Age Parity, Fecundity, and Marriage," *Journal of the American Statistical Association*, 41:501–16; Warren S. Thompson, *Population Problems* (New York: McGraw-Hill Book Company, Inc., 1953), pp. 212–15; and Lovett Dewees, "Premarital Physical Examination," in Morris Fishbein and E. W. Burgess (eds.), *Successful Marriage* (Garden City, N.Y.: Doubleday and Company, Inc., 1947), p. 55.

32. *Ibid.*

33. Rose K. Goldsen, *et al.*, *What College Students Think* (Princeton, N.J.: D. Van Nostrand Co., Inc., 1960), p. 218.

34. Reported in a paper at annual meeting of The National Council on Family Relations, Salt Lake City, Utah, August 1961.

35. J. P. Greenhill (ed.), *The 1952 Year Book of Obstetrics and Gynecology* (Chicago: The Year Book Publishers, 1952), pp. 340–43.

36. Charles H. Birnberg, *Female Sex Endocrinology* (Philadelphia: J. B. Lippincott Co., 1949), p. 100, *et passim.*

37. Guttmacher and Gould, *op. cit.*, p. 18.

38. Edmond J. Farris, *Human Fertility and the Problem of the Male* (White Plains, N.Y.: The Authors Press, 1950), p. 191.

39. Guttmacher and Gould, *op. cit.*, p. 6.

40. A. C. Kinsey, *et al.*, *Sexual Behavior in the Human Female* (Philadelphia: W. B. Saunders Company, 1953). It needs to be noted in this connection some have speculated that the extensive use of oral contraceptives may eventually create a generation of women who will still be fertile past the age of sixty. See, e.g., *Today's Health* (January 1963), 10. This is just speculation, however, and some authorities, such as Dr. John Rock, discount it completely.

41. For a detailed discussion of this possibility, as well as others previously mentioned, see Alan F. Guttmacher, *Pregnancy and Birth* (New York: The Viking Press, Inc., 1957).

42. Burton H. Fern, "If Your Blood Is Rh Negative," *Parents Magazine* (November 1960), 46. For a more detailed discussion, see Fred H. Allen, Jr., and Louis K. Diamond, *Erythroblatosis Fetalis* (Boston: Little, Brown & Co., 1957).

43. Lee and Evelyn C. Brooks, *Adventuring in Adoption* (Chapel Hill, N.C.: University of North Caroline Press, 1939), quoting H. F. Perkins, "Adoption and Fertility," *Eugenical News*, 21:95–101.

44. Eugene A. Weinstein, "Adoption and Infertility," *American Sociological Review*, 27:408–12.

45. Howard Haggard, *Devils, Drugs, and Doctors* (New York: Harper & Row, Publishers, 1929), p. 224.

46. Harold T. Christensen, "Rural-Urban Differences in the Spacing of First Births From Marriage: A Repeat Study," *Rural Sociology*, 18:60.

47. James H. S. Bossard and Eleanor S. Boll, *Ritual in Family Living* (Philadelphia: University of Pennsylvania Press, 1950), p. 142.

48. David Mace, *Marriage, The Art of Lasting Love* (Garden City, N.Y.: Doubleday and Company, Inc., 1952), Chaps. 5 and 6.

49. *Today's Child* (May 1960), 1.

50. Lee F. Herrera and Clyde V. Kiser, "Fertility in Relation to Fertility

Planning and Health of Wife, Husband, and Children," *The Milbank Memorial Fund Quarterly*, **29**:342.

51. Alan F. Guttmacher, "Conception Control and the Medical Profession," *Human Fertility*, **12**:1–10.

52. Guttmacher, *Pregnancy and Birth, op. cit.*, p. 281.

53. Nelson, *op. cit.*, pp. 373–74.

54. Guttmacher, *Pregnancy and Birth, op. cit.*, p. 282.

55. *Today's Child* (January 1961), 6.

56. Guttmacher, *Pregnancy and Birth, op. cit.*, p. 281.

57. Guttmacher and Gould, *op. cit.*, p. 9.

58. "Illegal Abortion," *Today's Health* (September 1960), 10.

59. Ray E. Baber, *Marriage and the Family* (New York: McGraw-Hill Book Company, Inc., 1953), p. 295.

60. E. E. LeMasters, *Modern Courtship and Marriage* (New York: The Macmillan Company, 1957), p. 538.

61. E. E. LeMasters, "Parenthood as Crisis," *Marriage and Family Living*, **19**:355.

62. Evelyn Millis Duvall, "Research Finds," *Marriage and Family Living*, **22**:265.

63. At least 90 per cent of voluntarily childless couples are reported to have no interest in children. See Lois Pratt and P. K. Whelpton, "Social and Psychological Factors Affecting Fertility," *The Milbank Memorial Fund Quarterly*, **33**:1243.

64. See, e.g., John L. Thomas, "The Catholic Position on Population Control," *Daedalus* (Summer 1959), 446–53.

65. Clement S. Mihanovich, Gerald J. Schnepp, and John L. Thomas, *A Guide to Catholic Marriage* (Milwaukee: The Bruce Publishing Company, 1955), p. 256.

66. John L. Thomas, *The American Catholic Family* (Englewood Cliffs, N.J.: Prentice-Hall, Inc., 1956), pp. 72–73.

67. Gerald Kelly, "Official Statement on Rhythm," *Linacre Quarterly*, **19**:43.

68. George A. Kelly, *The Catholic Marriage Manual* (New York: Random House, 1958), p. 56.

69. E. W. Burgess and Paul Wallin, *Engagement and Marriage* (Philadelphia: J. B. Lippincott & Co., 1953), p. 705.

70. E. W. Burgess and Leonard S. Cottrell, *Predicting Success or Failure in Marriage* (Englewood Cliffs, N.J.: Prentice-Hall, Inc., 1939), p. 260.

71. Charles E. Bowerman, "How Many Children Do Young People Want?" in Ruth S. Cavan (ed.), *Marriage and Family in the Modern World* (New York: Thomas Y. Crowell Company, 1960), p. 472.

72. Clyde V. Kiser, "Is the Large Family Coming Back?" *Child Study* (Fall 1959), 23–25.

73. Deborah S. Freedman, Ronald Freedman, and Pascal K. Whelpton, "Size of Family and Preference for Children of Each Sex," *American Journal of Sociology*, **66**:141–46.

74. Quoted in *Today's Child*, **7**:6.

75. Census data show fewer childless couples now than formerly, and the educated population having more children than formerly. See Helen Hammons, "Eugenic Trends At Mid-Century," *Eugenics Quarterly* (December 1957), 219–21.

76. Bowerman, *op. cit.*, p. 472.

77. *Today's Child* (January 1963), 1.

78. *Statistical Bulletin*, Metropolitan Life Insurance Company (December

1964). The average number of children per family now stands at 2.62; the range is from 2.37 for the upper-class group to 3.97 for the lower-class group. See U.S. Bureau of the Census, Series P-23, No. 12 (July 31, 1964), 5.

79. *Thirty Years of Research in Human Fertility* (New York: Milbank Memorial Fund, 1959).

80. W. A. Anderson, "Spacing of Birth in Graduates' Families," *American Journal of Sociology,* 53:23–33.

81. "Divorce and Size of Family," *Statistical Bulletin,* Metropolitan Life Insurance Company, 31:2.

82. Paul H. Jacobson, "Differentials in Divorce by Duration of Marriage and Size of Family," *American Sociological Review,* 15:235–44.

83. *Ibid.*

84. Lewis M. Terman, *Psychological Factors in Marital Happiness* (New York: McGraw-Hill Book Company, Inc., 1938), pp. 171–73.

85. Harold T. Christensen and Robert E. Philbrick, "Family Size as a Factor in the Marital Adjustment of College Students," *American Sociological Review,* 17:309.

86. Robert Reed, "The Interrelationship of Marital Adjustment, Fertility Control, and Size of Family," *Milbank Memorial Fund Quarterly* (October 1947), 392.

87. Judson T. and Mary G. Landis, *Building a Successful Marriage* (Englewood Cliffs, N.J.: Prentice-Hall, Inc., 1963), p. 561.

Questions for further thought

1. In what ways is family planning consistent or inconsistent with American democratic practices?
2. In what ways are some couples possibly even more romantic about parenthood than they are about marriage?
3. What major factors should a couple consider in choosing the time to have their first baby? Or later ones?
4. Do very young couples "grow up" with their children?
5. What are the advantages or disadvantages of having one's children close together? A few years apart?
6. What is the ideal-size family?
7. Is the family allowance system (income tax deductions and so forth) a good thing for families economically? For the country? Does it have any effect on conception-control practices?
8. In the light of world birth-rate trends what should be the official position of the United States government on the subject of conception control? Of American families?
9. Do many college-educated wives have a baby just for the experience?

Recommended film

A Planned Parenthood Story (Mayo-Video).

Suggested supplemental readings

BOOKS

Bossard, James H. S., and Eleanor S. Boll. *The Large Family System.* Philadelphia: University of Pennsylvania Press, 1956.
Calderone, Mary S. (ed.), *Manual of Contraceptive Practice.* Baltimore: The Williams and Wilkins Co., 1964.

Dolan, Albert H. *All the Answers About Marriage and Birth Control.* Chicago: Carmelite Press, 1963 (Catholic Pamphlet).

Donner, James. *Women in Trouble.* Derby, Conn.: Monarch Books, 1959.

Fagley, Richard M. *The Population Explosion and Christian Responsibility.* New York: Oxford University Press, Inc., 1960.

Fletcher, Joseph. *Morals and Medicine.* Boston: Beacon Press, 1960.

Ford, Clellan S. *Field Guide to the Study of Human Reproduction.* Behavior Science Field Guides, Vol. 2. New Haven, Conn.: Human Relations Files Press, 1964.

Freedman, Ronald, Pascal K. Whelpton, and Arthur A. Campbell. *Family Planning: Sterility and Population Growth.* New York: McGraw-Hill Book Company, Inc., 1959.

Georg, I. E. *The Truth About Rhythm.* Milwaukee: P. J. Kenedy and Sons, 1962.

Grabill, Wilson H., Clyde V. Kiser, and Pascal K. Whelpton. *The Fertility of American Women.* New York: John Wiley & Sons, Inc., 1958.

Guttmacher, Alan F. *Babies by Choice or by Chance.* Garden City, N.Y.: Doubleday & Company, Inc., 1959.

———. *The Complete Book of Birth Control.* New York: Ballantine Books, 1961.

———. *The Consumer Union Report on Family Planning.* New York: Consumers Union, 1962.

Guttmacher, Alan F., Winfield Best, and Frederick S. Jaffe, *Planning Your Family: The Complete Guide to Contraception and Fertility.* New York: The Macmillan Company, 1964.

Kiser, Clyde V. *Research on Family Planning.* Princeton, N.J.: Princeton University Press, 1962.

Malthus, Thomas R., Julian Huxley, and Frederick Osborn. *On Population: Three Essays.* New York: The New American Library of World Literature, 1960.

Mann, David, Luther E. Woodward, and Nathan Joseph. *Educating Expectant Parents.* New York: Visiting Nurse Service of New York: 1961.

Meier, Richard L. *Modern Science and the Human Fertility Problems.* New York: John Wiley & Sons, Inc., 1959.

Moore, Edward Robert. *The Case Against Birth Control.* New York: Appleton-Century-Crofts, Inc., 1931.

Noonan, John T., Jr. *Contraception: A History of Its Treatment by the Catholic Theologians and Canonists.* Cambridge, Mass.: Belknap Press of Harvard University Press, 1965.

Rainwater, Lee. *And the Poor Get Children.* Chicago: Quadrangle Books, 1960.

———. *Family Design.* Chicago: Aldine Publishing Company, 1964.

Thomas, John L. *Marriage and Rhythm.* Westminster: The Newman Press, 1957.

Welton, T. S. *Rhythm Birth Control.* New York: Grosset & Dunlap, Inc., 1960.

Westoff, Charles F., Robert G. Potter, and Philip C. Sagi. *The Third Child: A Study in the Prediction of Fertility.* Princeton, N.J.: Princeton University Press, 1963.

ARTICLES

Adams, James Ray. "Attitudinal Ambivalence and Choice of Contraceptive Method," *Dissertation Abstracts,* 22 (February 1962), 2894.

Buxton, C. L., and E. T. Engle. "Time of Ovulation," *American Journal of Obstetrics and Gynecology,* 60:539–51.

Davis, Kingsley, and Judith Blake. "Birth Control and Public Policy," *Commentary*, 29:115–21.

(Editorial), "Rapid Falls in Fertility in Recent Years: Some Facts," *The Eugenic Review*, 55:127.

"Family Planning in Modernizing Societies," *Marriage and Family Living*, 25 (entire issue).

Fern, Burton H. "If Your Blood Is Rh Negative," *Parents' Magazine* (November 1960), 46.

Freeman, T. "Pregnancy as a Precipitant of Mental Illness in Men," *British Journal of Medical Psychology*, 25:49–54.

Gibbons, William J. "Fertility Control in the Light of Some Recent Catholic Statements," *Eugenics Quarterly*, 3:9–15, (Part I); and 3:82–87, (Part II).

Gokhale, V. V. "Vasectomy Camps in Ahmednagar District," *The Journal of Family Welfare*, 7:9–11.

Hanson, F. M., and J. Rock. "The Effect of Adoption on Fertility and Other Reproduction Functions," *American Journal of Obstetrics and Gynecology*, 59:311.

Kiser, Clyde V., and P. K. Whelpton. "Social and Psychological Factors Affecting Fertility," *Milbank Memorial Fund Quarterly*, 36:282–329.

Koya, Yoshio, *et al.*, "Seven Years of a Family-Planning Program in Three Typical Japanese Villages," *Milbank Memorial Fund Quarterly*, 36:363–72.

LeMasters, E. E. "Parenthood As Crisis," *Marriage and Family Living*, 19:353.

Loth, David. "Planned Parenthood and the Modern Inquisition," *Journal of Sex Education*, 3:52–55.

Monahan, Thomas P. "Is Childlessness Related to Family Stability?" *American Sociological Review*, 20:446–56.

————. "Marriage Fertility by Ages of Couples," *Human Biology*, 22:281.

Muramatsu, M. "Family Planning Practice Among the Japanese," *Eugenics Quarterly*, 7:23–30.

Nelson, Warren O. "The Physiology of Reproduction and Its Relation to the Regulation of Fertility," *Marriage and Family Living*, 25:74–80.

O'Gara, James. "Birth Control and Foreign Aid: A Catholic View," *Commentary*, 29:258–60.

Pincus, Gregory, *et al.* "Effectiveness of an Oral Contraceptive," *Science* (July 1959), 81–83.

Potter, Robert G., Jr., Philip C. Sagi, and Charles F. Westoff. "Improvement of Contraception During the Course of Marriage," *Population Studies*, 16 (November 1962), 160–74.

Pyke, Margaret. "Family Planning: An Assessment," *The Eugenics Review*, 55:71–79.

Quay, Paul M. "Contraception and Conjugal Love," *Theological Studies*, 22:18–40.

Rock, John, M.D. "We Can End the Battle over Birth Control," *Good Housekeeping* (July 1961), 44–45, 107–10.

Sanger, Margaret. "The Humanity of Family Planning," *The International Conference on Planned Parenthood* (1952).

Teare, R. D. "The Medico-Legal Significance of Death Following Abortion," *Medico-Legal Journal*, 19:81–88.

Thomas, John L. "The Catholic Position on Population Control," *Daedalus* (Summer 1959), 446–53.

Yeracars, Constance A. "Differentials in the Relationship Between Values and Practices in Fertility," *Social Forces*, 38:153–58.

Experiencing
pregnancy
and birth

Though having a baby is a normal event, it is one that suddenly gives rise to innumerable questions when it actually happens. Research surveys have pointed out that most Americans of every educational level need factual details about the biological process of birth and pregnancy. Such factual information should help to dispel any false anxieties about having a baby and also prepare the couple for more intelligent cooperation with their obstetrician and more sensible adjustments to their new parental state.

Signs of pregnancy

There are many varied but definite signs that alert the couple to the possibility of pregnancy; these first physical clues are called *presumptive signs*. The later and more definite clues are called *positive signs*. The same presumptive signs may not be evident in every case and indeed may be symptoms of a condition other than pregnancy. Thus, a woman may manifest presumptive signs without being pregnant. However, a combination of presumptive signs may be considered fairly conclusive evidence of pregnancy.

COMMON PRESUMPTIVE SIGNS. One of the earliest presumptive signs is the skipping of a menstrual period. Such things as nervous tension, worry, climatic changes, severe anemia, tuberculosis, untreated diabetes, thyroid disturbances, malnutrition, a cold, or an infection may also delay menstruation, but a woman who has been fairly regular may consider a delay of ten or more days rather strong evidence of pregnancy.[1] Even after pregnancy, some women may continue to menstruate for a time or two; the flow, however, is usually shorter and scantier than normal.

Morning sickness—nausea or vomiting, or both—is another presumptive sign of pregnancy. Morning sickness in early pregnancy is largely caused by metabolic changes brought about by temporary glandular imbalances which occur after conception. Better diet, improved health, and changed attitudes toward conception and labor are factors that have apparently reduced the incidence of morning sickness in recent years. Guttmacher points out that twenty or so years ago most pregnant women appeared to suffer from morning sickness, but that now only about one third have nausea and only one third experience both nausea and vomiting.[2] Morn-

Figure 17-1. Morning sickness is a presumptive sign of pregnancy. (Courtesy of the Bristol-Myers Company, makers of Bufferin.)

ing sickness is much less likely to occur if the woman eats the right foods in small amounts, has sufficient rest and exercise, and does not easily become emotionally upset.

Noticeable breast changes are a third presumptive sign of pregnancy. Along with increase in size, there may be an increase in tenderness. There may also be an appearance of strained blood vessels surrounding the breasts as the supply of blood to the mammary glands increases. During the latter part of the first month, there may be a tingling sensation and a feeling of extra weight in the breasts.

Increased frequency of urination is another presumptive sign of pregnancy. Pressure of the enlarged uterus upon the bladder gives the feeling that the bladder is always full, producing the sensation of needing to urinate more often.

An increase in the size of the abdomen is another sign of the possibility of pregnancy. Late in the third month or early in the fourth there is a slight bulge in the lower portion of the abdomen as the uterus expands.

Any one of these signs does not necessarily constitute sufficient evidence for pregnancy, because it may arise from other causes. If more than one presumptive sign persists, however, an appointment should be made with a physician for a professional diagnosis.

One of the first things the physician does in examining for pregnancy is to look for skin changes, particularly around the breasts. At about the eighth week of pregnancy, the tiny glands in the pigmented area around the nipples appear as little protuberances. Additionally, the colored circle of skin surrounding the nipples, especially in brunettes, becomes darker. The physician will also examine the vagina for discoloration, as very early after pregnancy the lining of the vagina becomes darkened.[3] He will also probably examine the patient for changes in the size, shape, and consistency of the uterus, for soon after pregnancy the tip of the uterus, and the uterus itself, begin to enlarge and soften. Tumors of the uterus and other pelvic disturbances, however, have at times confused even the most competent physicians.[4]

POSITIVE SIGNS. Positive signs of pregnancy are basically manifested by the baby rather than by the mother.

Many of these signs are apparent to the eye. For example, when the mother's abdomen begins to protrude noticeably, it is considered a positive sign that she is with child. Usually at about the fifth month a physician can, either by touch or observation, outline the fetus and a few of its parts.[5] A very dramatic positive sign is when the mother begins to feel life or movements within her. These, too, begin at about the fifth month.

The fetal heartbeat is another positive sign; it can normally be felt during the eighteenth week of pregnancy. Through a stethoscope, the fetal heartbeat sounds much like a watch ticking at the rate of about 160 beats per minute; later in the pregnancy, it slows down somewhat.[6]

Various laboratory tests are also used to determine pregnancy. A short time after conception, a special hormone is secreted by the pregnant female in sufficient quantity to be detectable in the urine. When the urine sample is injected into virgin female mice, it stimulates ovulation in the animal. The Aschheim-Zondek method, commonly called the AZ test, has been used since 1928 and has proved to be about 97 per cent accurate. About half a dozen mice are injected with the woman's urine at six intervals during a forty-eight-hour period. If the mice begin to ovulate, it indicates that a pregnancy hormone was present in the urine tested. Usually such a test can be run after about five weeks of pregnancy.

The Friedman method, commonly called the rabbit test, is similar to the AZ test. Usually it can be used sooner than the mice test, with results that are almost 100 per cent accurate. More recently, instead of rabbits, the South African clawed frog, *Xenopus laeuis*, has been used for the test. When the urine from a pregnant woman is injected into this frog, it automatically expels eggs in a matter of a few hours, thus providing almost conclusive evidence of pregnancy. This may have some advantages over the use of other animals. For one thing, the waiting period for results from mice and rabbits is ordinarily four days. Furthermore, the frog tests are less expensive for the same frog can be used for testing later, but the mice and rabbits must be killed after injection because the effects can be observed only by dissection.[7]

The hormone progesterone is used in another test for pregnancy. This hormone is taken in tablet form for three days. Dr. Harold A. Schwartz, a nationally recognized obstetrician and gynecologist in Chattanooga, Tennessee, believes that the use of the hormone tablets has advantages over the other methods. If the woman is pregnant, the progesterone helps to implant the egg even more solidly in the uterus, thus warding off possible abortion. But if the woman is not pregnant, the hormone dosage often helps to bring on a delayed menstruation.[8]

Selecting a physician

When a couple suspects pregnancy, they should first carefully select a physician for diagnosis and care. The choice is usually easier if the couple live within their home community, for they probably already know who is best qualified or they have a family doctor who will make a referral.

IN A NEW COMMUNITY. In today's society it is quite probable that many couples after marriage move away from their home communities.[9] The following suggestions are given to help a couple in a new community choose a doctor to care for the prospective mother and child. A referral from the respected home town doctor would, of course, solve the problem. Couples without such a recommendation might inquire at hospitals for a list of physicians who have the most obstetrical cases. Although hospitals usually do not recommend one specific physician, they would probably furnish a list of those obstetricians who supervise the most deliveries.

The couple might also consult their local public library. Most public libraries contain a directory of medical specialists. Included will be a list of specialists in obstetrics and gynecology certified by the American Board of Obstetrics and Gynecology. It might be advisable in some instances to compile a list of physicians and consult several before making a final choice.

CRITERIA. It is essential that a couple choose a physician who is competent to handle the entire course of pregnancy as well as any complications that might arise. This might turn out to be a needless precaution, but when a couple have a specialist, there are fewer causes for worry or doubt.

Hospitals may have established rules concerning methods of delivery, rooming-in policies, and whether husbands may be present at delivery; therefore, the physician's hospital affiliations should be ascertained. Delivery procedures and the extent of the physician's responsibility should be clearly defined before the couple make a final decision. The physician's personality is also important, for the couple must have complete confidence in him over the course of several months.

An additional consideration in selecting the doctor is the matter of fees. A specialist in obstetrics usually charges about twice as much as a general practitioner for a delivery. But because the wife will be seeing her obstetrician many times during the course of the pregnancy and after the birth of the child, the fee may be less, on a time basis, than that paid many general practitioners for the treatment of common illnesses not connected with pregnancy.

FOLLOW DIRECTIONS. Once the obstetrician has been selected, the couple should follow his directions. The physician has reasons for everything he suggests; he is building the entire case for delivery upon certain known conditions. If a couple do not approve of the way the doctor is handling the case, they should find another doctor.

The importance of special care during pregnancy and delivery

If birth is such a natural process, why do people in modern society insist upon special care during pregnancy and delivery? One has only to compare the records of past generations with the present to understand the importance of prenatal care. The concept of adequate prenatal care is actually a relatively recent medical innovation. Until about thirty years ago, it was customary for the patient or her family to see a physician perhaps only once during the pregnancy, and this merely to arrange for him to attend the delivery. A federal survey in 1933 of maternal deaths revealed that more than half of the pregnant women of that year had not received a prenatal examination by a physician, and of those who went to a doctor, 50 per cent had received poor prenatal care. Actually, in only 1 per cent of the cases was the prenatal care up to what would now be considered proper standards.[10] Philip Williams, a Philadelphia obstetrician, speaking at a meeting of the American Medical Association on maternal and child care in 1960, reported that 300,000 American babies would celebrate their first birthday that year who, had they been born forty years earlier, would have died in infancy. Williams also stated that the maternal and infant mortality rates could be further reduced if mothers would only begin proper prenatal care without delay at the first signs of pregnancy.[11]

THE PHYSICIAN'S ROLE.   In addition to the importance of proper care, the physician provides emotional support during pregnancy and birth. A competent physician inspires and radiates confidence. He may do this not only by demonstrations of his skill but also by helping the potential mother to understand what is happening during the pregnancy period. In this connection, it is a good thing for couples to write down their questions before each visit with a physician, so they will be sure to get them answered. Competent medical supervision during the prenatal period is the best insurance for a sound baby, a safe delivery, and a healthy future for the entire family.

THE PHYSICAL EXAMINATION.   The doctor first gives the expectant mother a thorough physical examination. This includes a consideration of her general health in relation to organs and body structure. Then there is an evaluation of obstetrical soundness, which includes a checkup of the reproductive organs, the stage of pregnancy, and an evaluation of

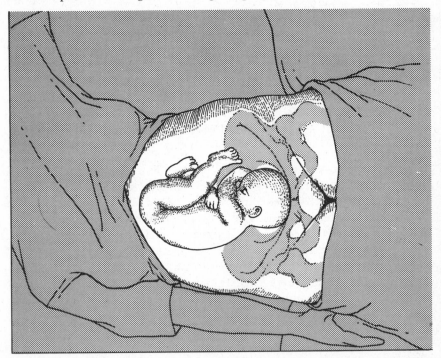

Figure 17-2. This is a full-term pregnancy, with the baby in normal position— its head toward the pelvic girdle, through which it must pass. (Adapted from Sol DeLee, *Safeguarding Motherhood* [Philadelphia: J. B. Lippincott Co., 1953]. Copyright © 1953, by J. B. Lippincott Co., Philadelphia. Reproduced by permission.)

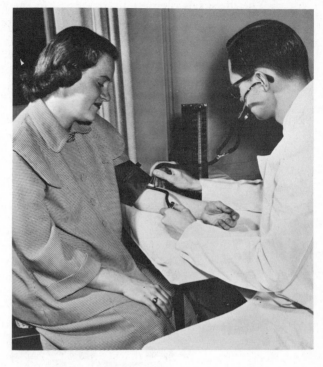

Figure 17-3. It is considered very important for the doctor to measure a pregnant patient's blood pressure during each of her visits. (From Louise Zabriskie, *Obstetrics For Nurses,* revised by Elise Fitzpatrick and Nicholson Eastman [Philadelphia: J. B. Lippincott Co., 1960]. Reproduced by permission.)

the type of pelvis and soft tissue through which the baby will pass. He usually will take the pelvic measurements at the first examination and record them. Periodic measurements of the baby's growth are made on subsequent visits. If it appears that the baby will be too large to pass through the pelvic girdle, then the doctor will make arrangements to deliver the baby by another method, such as cesarean section. The pelvic girdle is a ring of bone; it will not give or stretch as the baby passes through in a natural delivery.

In addition, there will probably be blood tests for anemia, syphilis, and the Rh factor. The physician will also take the health history of the woman and of her family. If the woman has a background of a disease such as tuberculosis or heart disorders, he can make special provisions to avert complications that might otherwise arise. The health history also includes all surgery previous to pregnancy, and the menstrual history.

SUBSEQUENT VISITS. The modern physician insists upon followup visits after the first examination so that he may keep a close check on all conditions and developments of the pregnancy. Most specialists insist upon seeing the patient about every three weeks during the first seven months of pregnancy, every two weeks during the eighth month, and once a week during the last month.

The physician is especially interested in the weight gain of the patient and will probably continue to take blood pressure measurements and urine specimens at each visit.

If the nonpregnant weight is normal for height and build, a gain of about twenty pounds during pregnancy would be considered ideal. "She should not gain less; at the most she may gain five pounds more."[12] There is usually little gain in the first trimester of pregnancy, perhaps altogether less than four pounds. During the second trimester the gain increases to about two pounds a month; ideally during the last trimester

Figure 17-4. (From Louise Zabriskie, *Mother and Baby Care in Pictures* [Philadelphia: J. B. Lippincott Co., 1953]. Reproduced by permission.)

the gain should be less than one pound per week. Too great a weight gain may bring about an added strain on the heart and cause added difficulty in breathing and in physical movement. With too much extra weight, the expectant mother is more clumsy and risks stumbling and injurying herself. Excess weight gain is also closely correlated with high-blood-pressure complications. A condition of toxemia is a much greater possibility if the weight gain goes close to thirty pounds during the pregnancy.[13] Toxemia rarely occurs if the mother follows a high protein diet and has frequent checks by her doctor.[14]

SELF-CARE. The doctor can only urge the mother to take better care of herself; the follow-through of his orders is up to her. A good diet is tremendously important for the pregnant woman and may itself prevent many difficulties. Proper diet will provide materials for building tissue in the baby's body and for replacing the worn-out cells of the mother. The diet must include a sufficient supply of vitamins, proteins, and minerals for both mother and child.

Proper exercise is also important during pregnancy. The best exercise seems to be walking, when the weather permits. The husband can often help his wife by taking walks with her in the evening; his companionship will relax and reassure her. Pregnancy for a woman is like the conditioning of an athlete for a big contest: living up to the training rules is the best assurance of doing well in the final event.

THE HOSPITAL. The best place for the baby to be born is a modern hospital. In case of complications, such as a possible Rh problem, the well-organized hospital can give immediate treatment to both mother and child. This factor of safety has contributed to the greatly reduced mortality rates for the newborn as well as the mothers.

Table 17–1. **Births in hospitals in the United States**

Date	Per cent	Date	Per cent
1935	37	1945	79
1936	41	1946	80
1937	45	1947	84
1938	48	1948	86
1940	56	1949	87
1941	62	1950	88
1942	67	1955	92
1943	73	1961	97
1944	76	1964	97.4

Source: Statistical Bulletins, Metropolitan Life Insurance Company (December 1947; July 1951; February 1954; August 1955); and U.S. Department of Health, Education, and Welfare, "Natatity-Level Area Statistics," *Vital Statistics,* Vol. 1, Sec. B (1962), and Vol. 13, No. 6, *Supplement* (September 11, 1964). Adapted by permission.

Predictions of time of birth

One of the first questions that most young couples ask as soon as pregnancy is known is: "When will the baby be born?" This is a natural question, but is not always easily answered.

NINE CALENDAR MONTHS. Almost everyone has heard that a baby is born about nine months after conception. Because no one knows exactly when conception takes place, physicians usually do not attempt to figure from the possible time of conception, but rather from the beginning of the last menstruation. Because this is usually about two weeks before the next ovulation, physicians ordinarily add 280 days to the beginning of the last menstrual period and designate that projected date as the most likely date of birth. This too is only an approximation. In a study of 17,000 cases, it was found that the chances of delivery being exactly 280 days from the beginning of the last menstruation were only four out of a hundred.[15]

Table 17–2. Approximate chance of baby being born each week after the twenty-seventh week, counting from first day of last menstrual period

Week	Days	Chance
28	189–196	1 in 625
29	197–203	1 in 625
30	203–210	1 in 525
31	211–217	1 in 240
32	218–224	1 in 240
33	225–231	1 in 135
34	232–238	1 in 115
35	239–245	1 in 58
36	246–252	1 in 39
37	253–259	1 in 22
38	260–266	1 in 11
39	267–273	1 in 5
40	274–280	1 in $3\frac{1}{2}$
41	281–287	1 in $5\frac{2}{3}$
42	288–294	1 in 12
43	295–301	1 in 34
44	302–308	1 in 74
45	309–315	1 in 140
46 and over	316 and over	1 in 140

Source: Alan F. Guttmacher, *Pregnancy and Birth* (New York: The Viking Press, Inc., 1956), pp. 44–45. Copyright © 1956, by Alan F. Guttmacher. Published by The Viking Press, Inc., New York. Reprinted by permission.

Sometimes women continue to menstruate for a time or two after conception. This makes it almost impossible to predict the date of birth by the method mentioned above. Under these conditions a physician may

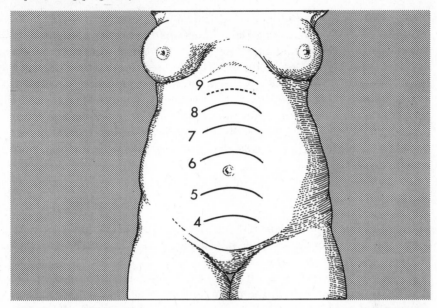

Figure 17-5. Changes in the level of the uterus during pregnancy. The broken line indicates the height of the uterus near term when lightening occurs. (Adapted from Sol DeLee, *Safeguarding Motherhood* [Philadelphia: J. B. Lippincott Co., 1953]. Copyright © 1953, by J. B. Lippincott Co., Philadelphia. Reproduced by permission.)

predict the date by checking the size of the uterus. The difference in the level of the top of the uterus in relation to the woman's navel and lower rib margin indicates to the skilled obstetrician the month to which pregnancy has advanced.[16]

VARIABLES. There are several variables to consider in predicting the time of birth. If the menstrual period is regular, there appears to be a better chance that the birth will occur very close to the 280th day from the beginning of the last menstrual period. Short periods of twenty-five days or less are frequently associated with earlier delivery. Longer menstrual cycles that go at least thirty-two or thirty-three days are more frequently associated with births beyond the 280th day.[17]

Multiple births also seem to affect the length of gestation. Twins ordinarily shorten the pregnancy period by about three weeks, and triplets and quadruplets are usually born even earlier than this. According to Dr. Richard L. Masland, Director of the National Institute of Neurological Diseases, U.S. Public Health Service, smoking may cause a premature birth. The more the pregnant woman smokes, the greater the chance of a shortened gestation period.[18]

UNRELATED VARIABLES. Such factors as race, size of the mother, and previous number of children seem unrelated to the length of pregnancy. There is even some doubt that age of the mother affects the length of pregnancy.[19]

DAYLIGHT OR DARKNESS. One myth surrounding birth is that far more children are born during the dark hours than otherwise. Research in this connection shows that there are about as many babies born in the day as in the night. One study of 134,335 cases showed that during a twenty-two-year period 25.85 per cent of the births occurred between 6:00 A.M. and noon; 22.39 per cent, between noon and 6:00 P.M.; 24.05 per cent, between 6:00 P.M. and midnight; and 27.51 per cent between midnight and 6:00 A.M.[20] The probable reason for believing most babies are born at night is that births that do occur then are more vividly remembered.

Prediction of sex

As soon as the approximate date of delivery has been calculated, the couple begin to wonder whether it will be a boy or a girl. Friends and relatives like to prognosticate too.

WHEN SEX IS DETERMINED. The sex of a child is determined at the time the sperm unites with the ovum, and nothing that happens thereafter will change it. This is commonly referred to as the X and Y chromosome theory. Although all ova are apparently the same, there are two types of sperm cells, those with an X chromosome and those without the X, commonly designated as Y. If a male X chromosome cell unites with the always-constant X chromosome cell of the female ova, the child will be a girl. When the Y chromosome cell unites with the ovum, the child will be a boy. Although it appears a matter of chance whether an X or a Y chromosome sperm will fertilize the ova, there is a fairly definite sex ratio of boys to girls born. At present, the ratio is approximately 105.3 boys born to every 100 girls born. The ratio of boys to girls at conception, however, is even greater. Various estimates place the ratio at from 120 to 150 male babies conceived to every 100 female babies conceived. Almost all spontaneous abortions are confined to male babies.

Little is known as to why more males are conceived than females. Various theories have been advanced, but as yet they remain unproved. One theory is that Y chromosome spermatozoa move faster than X's, and are thus more likely to reach the ova first. Another theory is that the acidity of the female genital tract is more favorable to Y spermatozoa; perhaps following ovulation, the acidity increases, which would assure the birth of more male children.

It is commonly accepted nowadays that the father's genetic characteristics determine the sex of a child. This, of course, is in relation to the X and Y chromosome theory. This may not be altogether true, however, because there are case histories of couples who have produced several children all of one sex, then upon divorce and marriage to other spouses, they produced children of both sexes. Later, upon remarriage to each

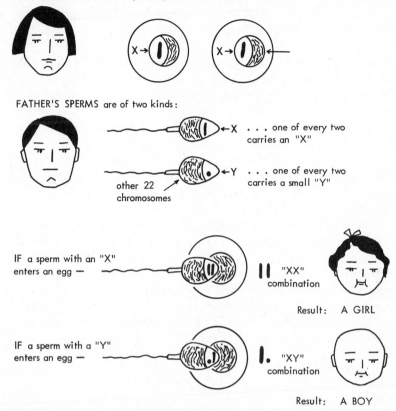

MOTHER'S EGGS all carry a large sex chromosome — the "X"

FATHER'S SPERMS are of two kinds:

←X . . . one of every two carries an "X"

other 22 chromosomes

←Y . . . one of every two carries a small "Y"

IF a sperm with an "X" enters an egg —

"XX" combination

Result: A GIRL

IF a sperm with a "Y" enters an egg —

"XY" combination

Result: A BOY

Figure 17-6. How a baby's sex is determined. (Adapted from Amram Scheinfeld, *The Human Heredity Handbook* [Philadelphia: J. B. Lippincott Co., 1956], p. 25. Copyright © 1956, by Amram Scheinfeld. Reproduced, and corrected according to latest research, by permission.)

other, they again produced children of only one sex, the same as at first. It may well be that the spermatozoa produced by some males are more susceptible to certain female conditions than others, but this has yet to be determined.

PARENTAL PREFERENCE. It seems that most parents prefer their first child to be a boy. In a study of 380 university students, 92 per cent of the men and 66 per cent of the women wanted their first child to be a male. When asked which sex they preferred first if they could have several children, 62 per cent of the men and 59 per cent of the women still wanted their first child to be a boy. Only 4 per cent of the men and 6 per cent of the women indicated a preference for the first child to be a girl; the remainder were indifferent.[21]

NO ABSOLUTE PREDICTIONS. There is no accurate way today of determining the sex of the unborn child. Some people believe that physicians are able to tell. Many doctors have perpetuated this myth as a sort of joke within the profession. In other words, they make predictions on the sex of the baby with as much certainty as an average citizen can predict an election outcome.

Some people believe that the sex can be ascertained by measuring the unborn infant's heart beat. Tests on thousands of cases, however, have shown predictions based on heart beat rate to be right only 50 per cent of the time. There are variations in heart beat rate for both sexes, and even within particular days in one fetus. Thus, this method is of no value in predicting the sex of an unborn child.

WHY KNOW? All manner of various actions might take place if couples knew the sex of their babies ahead of time. Certainly not all of these actions would be most appropriate. The author is wholeheartedly in agreement with Guttmacher, who states in this connection: "Actually, as an obstetrician of much experience, I secretly hope that no simple, practical method of diagnosing the sex before birth will be found. If this happens it will rob the birth act of much of its excitement and drama."[22] Although not generally known, considerable research in recent years has been devoted toward separating the potential male-carrying spermatozoa from the potential female-carrying ones. If such efforts are successful, it could be possible, by the use of artificial insemination, to predetermine the sex of one's children.[23]

Factors determining the size of the child

Another common question of married couples who are going to have a child is: "Will the baby be small, large, or normal in size?" The size of a child depends upon several variables.

SEX. Boy babies are usually a few ounces heavier than girl babies. Of course, there is much variation within each sex, but this is the general picture when large groups have been studied.

RACE. The size of the child is also related to race. White children are normally one pound heavier than Oriental babies, and half a pound heavier than Negro babies.[24]

MATERNAL AGE. Size is also related to the age of the mother and to the previous number of births. Younger women usually have smaller children than older women. Older women who have had several other children usually have bigger babies subsequently.[25]

SOCIOECONOMIC CLASS. The size of children has also been shown to be related to socioeconomic class. Babies of the economically privileged average about half a pound heavier than others. This may be due to several factors. One factor is that the economically privileged have fewer premature births than other groups, and of course, premature births are almost always smaller than those that have gone full term.

HEREDITY. The size of the child is also related to heredity. If the mother is descended from large people, she is much more likely to have large infants.[26]

ILLNESS. Maternal illness may also affect the child's weight at birth. Some diseases almost always seem to result in smaller babies, whereas others seems to result in larger babies. For example, there seems to be a correlation between maternal diabetes and babies of excessive size, and it does not seem to be related to the severity of the case or to the degree of control of the disease.[27]

NUTRITION. The mother's nutritional balance during pregnancy seems to have very little to do with affecting the size of the baby, but it might affect the size of the mother after pregnancy. A study of 23,500 consecutive deliveries at Johns Hopkins Hospital found only 251 babies who weighed over ten pounds. Of these, only thirty-five weighed more than eleven pounds; eight, over twelve; and only two infants weighed over thirteen pounds (one, thirteen pounds and seven ounces, the other fourteen pounds and four ounces).[28] According to medical literature, no baby has ever been born alive weighing more than fifteen and one half pounds. Although some infants have been larger, they were not born alive. The median weight of all registered births in the United States in 1964 was 3290 grams (approximately seven pounds, three ounces); 8 per cent weighed less than 2500 grams (five pounds, eight ounces) and thus were classified "immature"; 1.6 per cent of the new born weighed over 4500 grams (9.9 pounds), and only 0.2 per cent weighed over 5001 grams (eleven pounds). Nonwhite births averaged 180 grams less than whites.[29]

Pregnancy: an event

Pregnancy is not merely a biological event. In the human sense it is much more, for it involves many things beyond the actual carrying and bearing of a child.

A TRANSITION. In the first place, pregnancy is an interval of many transitions. When pregnancy is known to be a reality, both husband and wife must get used to the idea that it has finally happened. No matter how much the couple want a child, it will take them a little while to accept the fact of pregnancy and adjust to it.

Sometimes pregnancy occurs before marriage. In these cases marriage comes after conception is discovered, and to save social embarrassment the birth is often described as "premature." The period of transition also gives friends, relatives, and acquaintances a chance to get used to the idea that the couple will soon be parents. New attitudes to the couple can normally be expected from friends and acquaintances after pregnancy becomes known. Frequently these include a new understanding and perhaps more sympathy, surrounding the couple with good will and a spirit of helpfulness. In fact, close friends and relatives are often too free with well-meaning advice for the expectant couple. This may even pose a problem for the couple when they try to separate friendly suggestions from the most up-to-date knowledge in the field.

EMOTIONAL ADJUSTMENTS. Emotional adjustments must be made by the couple after pregnancy is known. Each mate naturally enough will first view the possible effects the pregnancy will have on his individual life and reality. The wife is likely to think first of how she will manage under the present conditions, while the husband will probably think first about how he must manage financially in the future.

The change of status of both husband and wife into parenthood begins as soon as the pregnancy is known. The husband usually accepts the role as supporter of the wife's feelings, but he also knows he must assume a more important role as breadwinner.

It is perfectly normal for expectant mothers, even among planned pregnancies, to wonder at times whether they really want a baby. Prospective parents should talk about this with each other, or with someone close, who understands these emotions and can help the wife to accept her own feelings. Sometimes the physician can help; however, this is mainly the husband's role. Perhaps his greatest task during the pregnancy is to reinforce his wife's desire to have the child. If he is successful at this, usually everything else will work out satisfactorily. It is especially necessary for the husband to have a strong conviction of faith at this time. He cannot afford to parade his own doubts before his wife. His attitude must express conviction that they can and will meet this situation successfully. At times it will appear that he must compromise and sacrifice his own desires to placate his irrational mate during pregnancy. Most husbands do more of this than their wives ever realize. The entire marital relationship can be helped considerably if the wife tries to see and appreciate the efforts that her husband makes in this connection.

A wife's moods change considerably during pregnancy. Depression, irritability, hypersensitivity, and possible impaired judgment are often characteristic of the pregnancy period. The best of wives are sometimes unable to control these various mood changes, but their husbands may help by remembering what Genné wrote:

> The husband is the most important single influence on his wife. The quality of this emotional relationship is of vital importance to all that is happening. In a very real sense, husbands are pregnant too.[30]

The husband can perhaps best help the mother-to-be by (1) showing that he is pleased and enthusiastic about the pregnancy; (2) reassuring his wife of his love (she usually needs more love than ever at this time); (3) helping with work at home as the wife becomes more fatigued as the pregnancy advances; (4) spending more time with his wife in planning for the future; and (5) taking an active interest in all the details of becoming a parent, such as the doctor's report and his wife's daily condition.

Both mates need to be careful or there may be an increased number of arguments. Clinical observation discloses the fact that in these particular disagreements the pregnant wife is usually wrong. Because her emotions are affected by the pregnancy, she is much more likely to be erratic in reasoning and logic. Although she may usually be wrong, however, it is perhaps best for her husband not to come out directly and say so. It is much better if the wife herself can understand her hypersensitivity and attempt to guard against it. Even some of the most stable wives will find themselves distraught at times by unexplained irritations that are apparently brought about by nothing. Trivial things that ordinarily would never get a second thought become monumental and may seriously upset the entire relationship.

For no significant reason, the wife may begin to cry during pregnancy. Frank discussions with an understanding physician about these various moods can frequently aid the entire marital adjustment during this time. For the wife to keep busy at something during the waiting period is also

Figure 17-7. During pregnancy, the wife may begin to cry for no significant reason. (Copyright © 1962, by Curtis Publishing Company.)

a good idea. This can help keep her from imagining problems that may never happen.

Although there is no direct nerve connection between mother and child during pregnancy, emotional upsets can increase blood pressure, and may cause oversecretion of various glands that might possibly affect the child indirectly. Some authorities discount such effects, but some studies appear to support the contention. For example, emotional stress and fatigue may disturb functions of the liver and the kidneys, and though the fetus may not be affected directly by this, it would certainly put a strain upon the mother herself.[31] During periods of stress such as fear, rage, and anxiety, chemicals such as acetylcholine and epinephrine are released into the blood stream and affect parts of the central nervous system. Mothers who undergo a considerable amount of emotional stress find that the fetal activity increases several hundred per cent. Babies born under these conditions are found to have increased symptoms of hyperactivity, irritability, squirming, crying, and feeding problems caused by increased gastrointestinal disturbances.[32] Thus, during the pregnancy period there is no better tonic than cheerfulness, and nothing so harmful as worry, anxiety, fear, and quarreling.[33]

Many wives discover during pregnancy that their own outlook on things becomes much improved if they are careful not to overplay the role of mother in advance. As always, good marriage relationships demand reciprocity. It is highly unlikely that a husband can continue to play the supporting roles that many pregnant wives demand when he finds himself displaced by an unborn child. Thus, the emotional adjustments after pregnancy are, to a large degree, dependent upon the maturity of the husband and wife. Pregnancy can be a period of joyful anticipation or a period of much conflict, depending upon the maturity of the couple.

PHYSICAL ADJUSTMENTS. There are various physical adjustments that must be made after pregnancy. In the first place, pregnancy is not an illness. In fact, many wives report improved physical health early in pregnancy. This may be owing to better care than they ever had prior to pregnancy. Pregnancy is a family affair, and the role of the husband-father now includes learning what is the proper care of his wife, and encouraging her to follow it. Landis and Landis found that more than 50 per cent of the wives they studied had noticed no change in their health during pregnancy. Of those who did notice a change, only one tenth thought that their health was poorer during the pregnancy.[34] Many women report better complexions during pregnancy; this may arise from a better balance of hormones than at any other time of the woman's life. Only occasionally is a wife an invalid during pregnancy. Most women can expect to live normally and happily during the pregnancy period. Rosengren reported finding that wives who are unhappy or insecure in other respects are the ones who are the most likely to assume a "sick" role during pregnancy.[35] Thus, it might be well to remember that part of the preparation for pregnancy begins long before conception, being related to the extent husbands and wives establish a workable problem-solving method at the start of the marriage.

An additional aspect of physical adjustment is that although the wife may feel well, she is much more easily fatigued during pregnancy. There is more strain upon her body than she realizes, and she sometimes does too much. She will need much more sleep. The husband should allow her to sleep as much as possible during pregnancy, for she will have many a sleepless night after the arrival of the child. During the last months especially, the woman may tire even more quickly. To offset this fatigue, there is a greater need for control of work and social life.

ECONOMIC ADJUSTMENTS. There are also many economic adjustments to be made after the pregnancy period begins. If she works, the wife will soon have to give up her job. This means not only additional adjustments but also important decisions. For example, does she plan to return to work after the birth? Her employer will probably want to know about this as early as possible. The couple must evaluate the wife's psychic needs for a career. If she enjoys her work, the long days at home before the coming of the baby may make her quite lonely.

Furthermore, if the wife has been working, family income will be cut sharply when she gives up her job. Expenses in the meantime will have risen. Thus, there is a greater need for careful spending when pregnancy is known. In the middle-class culture, after the first child, the mother will probably find herself in the home for at least the next ten years. During that period the financial burden will rest squarely on the shoulders of the husband. This may necessitate a sudden and severe adjustment for the expectant father. He must now firmly establish himself in his vocation. The wife should help the husband with these adjustments and be alert to signs of financial worry; she should perhaps exercise more restraint than ever in the purchases she makes.

GROUP-LIVING ADJUSTMENTS. There are other adjustments that must also be made after pregnancy. For one thing, it is necessary to learn about child-care practices, including a review of the latest literature on the subject. No matter what they think they already know about child care, the husband and wife should do some reading about infant and child care together. This assures them of knowing the same things and having a common base of understanding on the subject. It may also help to bring them closer in their thinking about this big event and how it will affect their marriage. The U.S. Children's Bureau has many excellent publications for helping the young couple prepare for their baby. The information is kept up-to-date and is compiled by noted authorities.

Adjustment for group living is important in preparing for the coming of the baby. It affects not only the husband and wife, but any other children they may already have, and their relatives and friends as well. It is a time to take other children into confidence, to prepare them for the new arrival, and to continue to share love with all the family members. The husband and wife should talk over ways of doing this and assuring that this is continued after the baby is born.

It is essential that the husband and wife keep in close communication during the pregnancy. Talks about the effects of a child on their routine are quite in order, and they should work out a plan for time alone together so that the baby will not divide them. Together, they should plan such things as where the baby will sleep and where his clothes will be kept. An important thing to remember in this connection is not to overdo for the child. Most couples provide too much; the baby can get along without many things that new parents believe are necessary.

SOCIAL ADJUSTMENTS. As pregnancy progresses, the recreation and social life of the couple must be adapted to the realities of the situation. Some activities must stop altogether and others should be greatly restricted. During the last stages of pregnancy, some things that the husband and wife did as a pair will no longer be practical. Such strenuous sports as bowling, or even home activities such as the repair of various rooms, should be curtailed. It is quite probable that because of these restrictions some wives will feel frustrated and restless. It is perfectly normal at times for a wife to feel resentment toward the husband as he continues his nights out with the boys or participates in various recreational and vocational projects she can no longer enjoy. If a wife is not careful, this resentment can result in a bitterness that will affect the entire marital relationship. The mature alternative is to face the responsibilities of a married woman as she looks forward to motherhood.

There is a need for a careful analysis of this entire situation by both mates. Husbands must understand how wives feel about these various physical and social restrictions. Through careful planning together, the couple can work out a mutually acceptable social life to allow each some freedom and both some time together.

SEXUAL ADJUSTMENTS. Some couples report a decrease in desire for coitus after pregnancy is known. In one study, 50 per cent of the wives and 75 per cent of the husbands reported no change in sexual desire during the first three months of pregnancy, but the desire decreased rapidly for both sexes throughout the last six-month period. More than 25 per cent of the wives noted a marked decrease in sex desire after pregnancy, but 20 per cent noted an increase in sex desire from the beginning of pregnancy.[36] Sometimes the wife's sudden loss of interest in sex is a shock to the couple. Although desire may decrease for some couples, total sex adjustment is reported by many couples to be better after pregnancy, particularly when the adjustment had been poor before.[37]

Most physicians recommend that intercourse be avoided in the last six to eight weeks of pregnancy. It is usually wise to consult the doctor in each case, as he is the only one who can tell if everything is normal. The idea behind the recommendation is to reduce the risk of introducing infectious bacteria into the vagina. Immediately after birth the uterus is more susceptible to infection.

Table 17–3. The effects of first pregnancy upon the sexual adjustment of 212 couples

Effect	Per cent of husbands reporting	Per cent of wives reporting
No effect	58	58
Unfavorable	23	25
Favorable	19	17

Source: Judson T. Landis and Thomas and Shirley Poffenberger, "The Effects of First Pregnancy upon the Sexual Adjustment of 212 Couples," *American Sociological Review,* 15:767–72. Copyright © 1950, by The American Sociological Association, Washington, D.C. Reprinted by permission.

Table 17–4. Reasons for cessation of intercourse during pregnancy

Reason given	Per cent of wives reporting	Per cent of husbands reporting
Doctor ordered it	38	29.9
Painful for wife	16.5	18.3
Fear of hurting baby	15.6	18.8
I didn't enjoy it	14.6	3.2
Fear of miscarriage	5.4	9.9
Nauseated wife	4.4	2.6
It didn't seem right	3.3	6.8
Spouse didn't enjoy it	2.2	10.5

Source: Judson T. Landis and Thomas and Shirley Poffenberger, "The Effects of First Pregnancy upon the Sexual Adjustment of 212 Couples," *American Sociological Review,* 15:767–72. Copyright © 1950, by The American Sociological Association, Washington, D.C. Reprinted by permission.

Within six to eight weeks after the delivery, sex desire usually returns to about the same degree as before pregnancy. A few decades ago, sex adjustment after birth was not as good, probably because obstetric practices were very poor. As Kavinoky has said:

Lacerations which were unrepaired from one pregnancy to another resulted in cystoceles, prolapse, and relaxed vaginal canals. Intercourse was painful when the tears were left to heal spontaneously. The profuse leucorrheal discharges from lacerated or infected cervices overlubricated the vaginal canal. In many, repeated deliveries occurring so rapidly that the patient hadn't recovered from one before the next pregnancy was started, resulted in very flabby, large vaginal canals. All these factors prevented many husbands and wives from enjoying intercourse after the first pregnancy. In addition to the poor approximation of the sex organs, the wife lacked desire for coitus. She was either pregnant, nursing, or in pain.[38]

FROM VANITY TO MATURITY.   Some women feel that they are less attractive during pregnancy than at other times. Some are bitter over the loss of their figure and may even blame their husbands for the loss of self-esteem. Research has actually shown that the majority of husbands rate their wives as more attractive during pregnancy; they report that their wives have a certain radiance that is not there before pregnancy.[39] The possible loss of attractiveness during pregnancy is of no concern to the mature woman. She will not only accept the changes, but will plan a carefully chosen hairdo, makeup, and clothing to retain her charm and attractive appearance.

The pregnant woman may be confronted with the complete facts of physiology for the first time in her life. Once pregnancy has commenced, there is a need for complete acceptance of life as it is. "It compels even the most fastidious woman to accept . . . [these facts] which now present themselves to her inescapably and in their crudest form but nevertheless in a way that reflects credit upon her."[40] Pregnancy is for adults. If a wife needs to grow up, this is the time for her to do it; if the husband must learn to accept responsibility, he had better do it now. Certainly every child deserves a pair of mature parents.

The first stage of birth

The biological process of birth itself starts when the longitudinal muscles of the uterus begin the contractions that will ultimately force the baby downward and out. The cervix is surrounded by a band of circular, rather elastic muscles, which had helped keep the baby inside the uterus. Now these muscles must reverse their usual functions, and relax to open the cervix. The contractions of the longitudinal muscles against the tight cervix sphincter muscles cause the so-called birth pains. At first, the action of the muscles on the baby and the mother is somewhat like an irresistible force against an immovable object, but the cervix sphincter muscles will eventually reverse their normal process and open. This change is called *dilation* and continues until the cervix is completely open. Only then will the baby's head pass into the vaginal canal. These contractions are somewhat similar to the cramping sensations of menstruation.

If the mother can relax as each contraction begins, she will experience less pain. As she relaxes, the cervical muscles are more likely to relax also. With time, the muscular contractions increase in strength and in duration, until they occur every few minutes and last for a half-minute or so. These continue until the cervical opening has increased from its normal one-eighth inch diameter to a width of about three inches. A woman who understands this and acts on the suggestions given may appreciably aid the birth of her child.

THE ROLE OF THE HUSBAND. In most hospitals husbands are allowed to be with wives during the first stage of birth. A husband can help by encouraging his wife to relax with each contraction. Few hospitals allow husbands to remain with the wife during the delivery. Some physicians are very supportive of this idea, however, thinking that it helps create a greater feeling that the birth is a family affair. The group, as a whole, are not so encouraging. Husbands have a very low priority rate if they should need medical attention during the delivery.

The second stage of birth

The second stage of birth begins when the cervix has dilated sufficiently to allow the baby to pass through the uterus and down the birth canal for delivery. Before the actual birth, the contractions occur every minute or so and last from thirty to forty seconds each. The baby then passes through the vagina, and on out into the world.

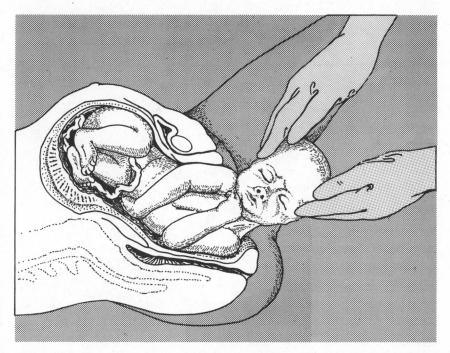

Figure 17-8. Near the end of second stage of labor. (Adapted from Sol DeLee, *Safeguarding Motherhood* [Philadelphia: J. B. Lippincott Co., 1953]. Copyright © 1953, by J. B. Lippincott Co., Philadelphia. Reproduced by permission.)

As soon as the baby is born, the attention centers for a while on taking care of him and the mother is encouraged to relax. When the physician cuts the umbilical cord, neither the mother nor baby feel it because there are no nerves in the cord. A newborn infant is very flexible, so the various pressures on his body during the birth process do not harm him.

EPISIOTOMY. To avoid undue laceration of the vagina during birth, the doctor sometimes makes a small incision in the vaginal opening, which prevents it from being torn as the baby passes through. Episiotomies are not always necessary on first births, and are quite rare for later ones. The vagina will usually stretch sufficiently for subsequent deliveries without need of surgery. Many women who undergo the training for educated childbirth have little need for such a procedure. After the cut has been made and the baby born, the doctor simply stitches the cut closed. It usually heals in less than a week, and certainly much faster and better than where it is torn by the birth process.

The third stage of birth

A few minutes after the baby is delivered, the placenta is expelled from the uterus. This is commonly called the *afterbirth*, and is accomplished

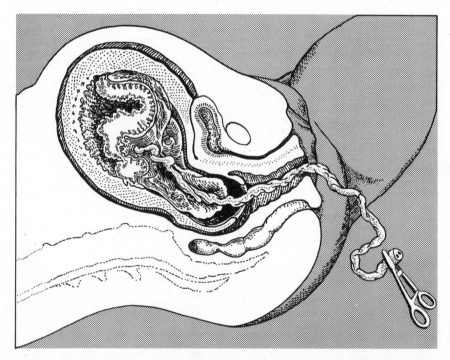

Figure 17-9. Beginning of the third stage of labor. (Adapted from Sol DeLee, *Safeguarding Motherhood* [Philadelphia: J. B. Lippincott Co., 1953]. Copyright © 1953, by J. B. Lippincott Co., Philadelphia. Reproduced by permission.)

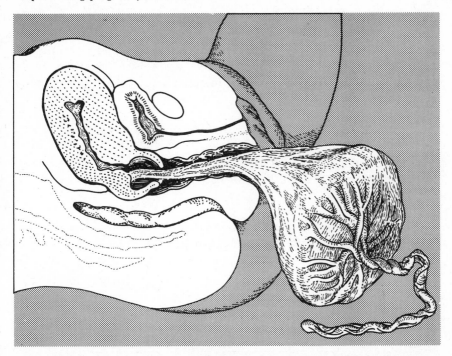

Figure 17-10. Near the end of third stage of labor. (Adapted from Sol DeLee, *Safeguarding Motherhood* [Philadelphia: J. B. Lippincott Co., 1953]. Copyright © 1953, by J. B. Lippincott Co., Philadelphia. Reproduced by permission.)

when the placenta separates itself from the uterine wall, and is ejected by one or two contractions from the mother.

The puerperium period

The puerperium period is usually defined as that time marked by the completion of the third stage of birth until six or eight weeks thereafter. The obstetrician's care does not end with the emptying of the uterus; it covers this entire period and includes an examination at the end of the period to ascertain that everything is in order.

PHYSIOLOGICAL CHANGES. Many changes begin to take place during this period in metabolism, blood pressure, and weight. There is often a loss of weight in the early postpartum period. The pulse is usually very slow because of changes in blood volume and the lowering of the blood pressure. These usually return to normal in about ten days.

Some women experience what are called *after-pains*. As soon as the birth process is over, all tissues begin to return to their former state. The uterus goes through a series of contractions and gradually returns to its original size and shape in about six weeks. This shrinking process, called *involution,* may be felt from day to day, but within about ten days it is no longer felt through the abdomen. Involution is brought about by a diminution in the size of the individual muscle cell and is controlled partly by endocrine glands.[41] Lochia, which is the discharge of the uterus and vagina after labor, gradually diminishes and ceases at the end of about three weeks.

Total length of labor

The length of labor varies with individual women and with various births for the same woman. Records indicate that labor is usually longer for the first child.

Table 17–5. **Time for 10,000 cases at Johns Hopkins from onset of first contractions till the end of the third stage of labor**

	Number of hours		
Condition	*Mean*	*Median*	*Mode*
First baby	13.04	10.59	7
Subsequent births	8.15	6.21	4

Source: **Alan F. Guttmacher,** *Pregnancy and Birth* (New York: The Viking Press, Inc., 1956), p. 166. Copyright © 1956, by Alan F. Guttmacher. Published by The Viking Press, Inc., New York. Reprinted by permission.

The length of total labor has been shown to be related to the extent of childbirth training. A study of 1000 women having their first baby, with 500 participating in a training program and 500 not participating, revealed that the average length of labor for the trained group was six hours shorter than for the nontrained group. Furthermore, the trained group had a much higher percentage of normal deliveries than did the other group.[42] The program for childbirth training consisted of lectures, exercise, and visits to the hospital labor and delivery rooms. Here prospective mothers met the hospital staff and saw the equipment used during delivery. The most important factor in the training program was the building up of confidence through becoming physically and emotionally ready for the birth experience. By increasing confidence, muscle control can best result in a reduction of labor and concommitant difficulties.[43]

The pains of birth

There are as many opinions about the pains of childbirth as there are mothers. Some women report that the sensations are little different from what they normally experience in menstruation. Some women beg for anesthetics almost from the onset of labor and feel severe pain. Obviously the pains of labor differ with each individual. Nevertheless, a good attitude, knowledge, and physical training seem to lessen the discomfort. The Clara Elizabeth Foundation for Maternal Health in Flint, Michigan, was originally sponsored by the General Motors Corporation for the purpose of training and educating women for better and easier child-bearing. Tens of thousands of cases have been handled by this organization. David Treat, who served a long term as director of this organization, believes that there are considerable individual differences among women in regard to the pains of childbirth:

> There are some women who have a low pain threshold for whom child-birth can be nothing but hard labor. There are some for whom the child-birth experience is one of great emotional elation. Many writers have been guilty of making it seem that all women could experience this lack of pain and high elation. It just does not work that way for many women. To set an expectation of no pain and great emotional elation for all women is neither realistic nor honest.[44]

Treat estimates that realistically no more than 30 or 40 per cent of women can, with a minimum of discomfort, deliver children without anesthetic. For the remainder, childbirth is painful and there is "no need to lie about it."[45] The knowledge that the pains are helping the woman to bring forth her own baby helps her to bear the suffering. Fortunately, the memory of physical pain fades quickly for most people.

QUALIFICATIONS FOR EDUCATED CHILDBIRTH. The term *natural child-birth* has been misused in the American culture. Semantically, it is actually a misnomer, for it implies that any other method is unnatural. Better terms would be *prepared* or *educated childbirth*. Natural child-birth does not mean delivery without anesthetic, only a reduction in the need for it. All childbirth is natural, but all childbirth is not painless. It is unfortunate that a misconception has dominated the minds of so many men and women since Grantly Dick Reed's famous book, *Child-birth Without Fear*, was published.[46]

Bearing children by the so-called natural method, which actually means the prepared and educated method, depends upon technique, but it is only one technique for bearing children. In the first place it depends on the woman's being highly motivated. Intelligent, well-prepared patients may find that it is a splendid birth technique; others may find it a terrible method. Its success is also greatly enhanced by the doctor's enthusiasm for it. Some women prefer the use of drugs during the birth process. At present there is no drug or combination of drugs that can eliminate all the pains of labor with complete safety in all cases.[47]

It is always best to follow the doctor's suggestions in the delivery room.

If he thinks the mother should have an anesthetic, she should follow his advice. He has had much more experience in bringing children safely into the world and is the best judge of her actual condition under such circumstances. Although some doctors may perhaps be too free in the use of anesthetics during labor, an anesthetic at least during the last moments of delivery is usually advised by most.

AN OVEREMPHASIS ON PAIN.   The emphasis in the past on possible pain and risk during childbirth has been much too exaggerated. Mothers have sometimes sought to inspire gratitude in their children by reference to the sacrifice and suffering they went through to bring them into the world. Instead of gratitude, however, only fear of the birth process is instilled into the offspring. Those who educate women for childbirth are all of the opinion that much of the difficulty and pain in giving birth arises from fears built up in the minds of the women. If the woman is afraid during labor, the cervical muscles will not relax and the other muscles will have to contract even harder. This then increases the pain and prolongs the birth.

The tremendous emphasis on pain has led to serious problems in the opposite direction. It has caused some women to anticipate such pain and discomfort that they failed to recognize the real thing when it began. The husband should urge his wife to take the approved exercises for childbirth. The woman should prepare both her body and her mind for this life-giving event.

The concept that birth is a terrible time is still reflected in modern society, for fear is difficult to eliminate. Kavinoky believes that much of this apprehension springs from the fact that many mothers have conditioned their daughters to fear birth because they themselves actually did have a terrible time: "The morbidity which results from the poor obstetrics of years ago was very real. There was reason enough for fear."[48]

The use of anesthetics was once looked upon as immoral and irreligious. Even an attendant physician was not considered important. Indeed, in an earlier era physicians were discouraged from being in attendance because they were males, and it was considered indecent for a wife to be attended by a male. Goodrich reports that in the sixteenth century a Doctor Wertt of Hamburg was burned to death for disguising himself as a woman in order to attend a delivery.[49] This mistaken morality has probably extended by centuries the sufferings of women in labor.

THE USE OF HYPNOSIS.   In recent years there has been much controversy over the use of hypnosis in childbirth. There was also much debate about the value of anesthetics when they first became available. In 1853 Queen Victoria was given anesthetics for the birth of one of her children, and thereafter they became more widely accepted.[50] Hypnosis may be described as an altered state of consciousness. It is usually achieved by concentration on one monotonous or rhythmic stimulus. When practiced by trained professionals, hypnosis has been demonstrated to be of some assistance to women in childbirth; however, it is not universally effective. Dr. Milton Abramson and Dr. W. T. Heron, early pioneers in obstetrical hypnosis, estimate that only about 20 per cent of pregnant women can respond fully to hypnosis and go through delivery without chemical anesthetics; another 75 to 78 per cent of women respond to a lesser degree, but probably derive some benefit from it; about 2 to 5 per cent of women are totally unresponsive to it.[51] The use of hypnosis in medical practice is not new. It is reported that physicians in ancient Egypt and Greece had made use of hypnosis, and the medicine men of some primitive tribes still do.[52] A team of Minnesota doctors compared the length of labor of 100 women under successful hypnosis with another group using standard anesthetics. The hypnotized group averaged two hours less in the first stage of birth.[53] It is not known whether either group had been educated for childbirth.

The feeding question

One of the first decisions to be made following the birth of the baby is whether he will be breast-fed or bottle-fed. Years ago there was no such problem: the baby had to be breast-fed. If the mother was not able to provide milk from her own breasts, a wet-nurse was called in to nurse the baby.

The first secretion from the mother's breast is called *colostrum*. It is not really milk, but it is easily digested by the baby and serves somewhat as a laxative. Colostrum has little food value, but for a day or so after birth, the baby lives mostly upon water and does not need much other food. Real milk usually begins to flow about the third day. The breasts grow hard, full, and heavy, quite tender and tense. Relief comes by nursing. The discomfort usually lasts about forty-eight hours, and then the breasts become softer.

COMPARATIVE ADVANTAGES OF BREAST- AND BOTTLE-FEEDING. Nursing at the breast is simple and perhaps the most inexpensive way to feed a baby. It eliminates worry about milk bacteria and spoilage, fuss over formulas and sterilizing of bottles and nipples. Breast milk is always fresh, clean, and warm. It contains more iron than cow's milk, in a much more easily assimilated form, and is usually much easier for the baby to digest.

Some women have unwarranted fears about nursing. It will not cause a mother to become fat nor her breasts to become flabby. In spite of psychiatrists' support of breast-feeding as an emotional boost for mothers and babies, statistics reveal that greater numbers of American infants are bottle-fed. A recent survey of more than 1900 hospital nurseries found 63 per cent of the newborn bottle-fed, as compared to 30 per cent in 1950. More of the college-educated group were found to be breast-feeding than others. There is less breast-feeding in the United States than in any other country.[54]

Some women cannot breast-feed a child because they do not have the necessary quantity or quality of milk. They should not feel depressed when this happens. The most important thing is that the baby be given tenderness and love during the feeding process. If there are other small children in the family, there is less chance to breast-feed, for there will be more demands upon the mother's time. Because the physiological process of producing milk is affected by fatigue and nerves, the emotional state of the mother can adversely affect the quality of her milk, which, in turn, can cause severe stomach upsets in the baby. The quantity of the milk might also be reduced by the mother's tensions. If the mother is in ill health, nursing may not be advisable because the ingested drugs might appear in the milk.

When the baby is bottle-fed, the husband can help feed the baby, especially at night, or he may take the early-morning feeding and allow the mother to sleep late as he goes off to work. When babies are bottle-fed, the husband may feel more a part of the total birth process, for he is able to offer physical help. It appears that when babies are bottle-fed, the husband-wife interaction process is more quickly re-established; then too, other people besides the husband can help, including babysitters, and the couple may return more quickly to a normal social life.

FEEDING SCHEDULES. Another aspect of feeding is that of scheduling. Hospitals usually feed babies on a four-hour schedule unless the babies are small or weak. It is necessary for hospitals to run on routines such as this; at home, however, the demand-schedule theory seems best. When the child cries, something is wanted. If the parents will listen attentively, they will soon learn that the baby's cries differ for different wants, so there is little danger of an alert couple overfeeding the baby.

Length of hospital stay

After they learn that the baby is doing well, the couple next want to know how long the mother must stay in the hospital. Ordinarily the mother today is walking about much sooner than in former times. Not too long ago, mothers were not allowed even to get up for seven or eight days after delivery, but nowadays, they are usually up within a few hours; almost immediately they go to the bathroom by themselves, and perhaps walk a little, depending upon their strength.[55]

Some hospitals have a rooming-in practice—the baby is kept in the room with the mother. Mothers of several children, however, may not desire this arrangement because they would rather rest. It may possibly be the only chance they will have to relax in a long time. Rooming-in, however, may be a good *first* experience.

The mother should stay in the hospital long enough to gather her strength, for after she leaves the hospital she will probably be on her own. If the hospital is not crowded, she should stay at least a week, and possibly ten days. She should gain as much of her strength back as possible before going home to a full schedule of work.

Multiple births

Multiple births are of two types: identical and fraternal. Multiple off-spring of the same sex with similar traits are called identical. It is believed that identical twins (or triplets, or more) result from the fertilization of a single ovum, the cells of which split apart, forming distinct but separate individuals. If the split is only partial in the ovum, two individuals evolve but are joined physically to one another; these are Siamese twins.

Fraternal multiple births may be of different sexes. Fraternal twins result from the fertilization of two ova by two different spermatozoa at about the same time. In some women, two or more ova are released at the time of ovulation and two or all may be fertilized. Triplets, quadruplets, and quintuplets may be identical, fraternal, or a combination of the two. Statistically speaking, twins occur about once every ninety-two births; triplets, about once in every 9000; and quadruplets, perhaps once in every 500,000 births.[56]

HEREDITARY FACTORS.   Hereditary factors seem to be involved in mul-tiple births. There seems to be a hereditary relationship involved in the tendency to release more than one ovum at each ovulation. Fraternal multiple births apparently result from a particular condition of the mother, for they are always produced from more than one ovum. Identical multiple births, however, might arise from a condition of either father or mother, which causes the ovum cells to divide completely. Much remains to be learned about this.

Multiple births have been shown to be related to race. Nonwhite mothers have more multiple births than white mothers, averaging a 15 per cent higher rate of twins, a 74 per cent higher incidence of triplets, and a 600 per cent higher incidence of quadruplets.[57]

AGE FACTORS.   Multiple births also appear to be related to the mother's age at conception. It is reported that the chances are seventeen in 1000 that a pregnant woman in her late thirties will have a plural birth, but only six in 1000 for pregnant teen-age women. Actually, the chances of multiple births increase progressively up to the ages of thirty-five to thirty-nine, and then begin to drop off again.[58]

Complications of birth

An examination of hospital records discloses that, with the development of the science of obstetrics, the chances of complications resulting from birth are very slim. In fact, about 85 per cent of all pregnancies are a

IDENTICAL TWINS	FRATERNAL TWINS
— result from the same single egg and single sperm.	— result from two different eggs, fertilized by two different sperms.

 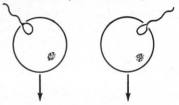

| After the egg begins to grow, it divides into equal halves with duplicated chromosomes. | The two different fertilized eggs develop separately into two different embryos. |

| The halves go on to become two babies, with exactly the same hereditary factors. | The two embryos grow into two babies with different hereditary factors. |

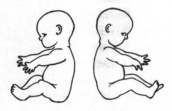 

| IDENTICAL twins are always the same sex (either two boys or two girls). They usually look much alike. They have exactly the same eye color, hair color, hair form, blood types, and all other hereditary traits. | FRATERNAL twins may be either of the same sex (two boys or two girls), or different in sex (a boy and a girl). They may be different in looks, coloring, hair form, blood types, and other hereditary traits. |

Figure 17-11. How twins are produced. (Adapted from Amram Scheinfeld, *The Human Heredity Handbook* [Philadelphia: J. B. Lippincott Co., 1956], p. 33. Copyright © 1956, by Amram Scheinfeld. Reproduced by permission.)

matter of no concern whatsoever; 10 or 11 per cent may have slight complications, but only 4 or 5 per cent result in serious complications. Many of the serious complications could be curtailed if a qualified specialist were called in.

Most women during pregnancy experience some discomfort, especially as the time for birth approaches, but this usually has no connection whatever with the possibility of complications. Pain in the back and in the legs may be brought about by pressure from the weight of the child, which has settled lower during the last trimester. Suitable clothing and shoes can eliminate much of this discomfort for most women. Especially helpful are low-heeled shoes that are large enough, for the feet occasionally swell. Resting at times with the feet up is also conducive to greater comfort.

MISCARRIAGE. Although miscarriage is not as frequent as many women have been lead to believe, it is one complication of birth that needs to be considered and discussed with the physician. Probably less than 10 per cent of all pregnancies end in miscarriage.[59] Miscarriages are seldom if ever caused by the activities of the mother. Hall states: "If any normal function such as intercourse, douching, or riding in a car seem to have precipitated a miscarriage, then such a pregnancy was certainly doomed from the start and miscarriage would have occurred anyway."[60] Dr. James P. Youngblood, of the University of Michigan Medical Center, explains that most miscarriages are really a blessing in disguise. Basically they are nature's method of preventing the birth of a permanently helpless infant. In about half the cases, there was either a faulty ova or a defective sperm. The remainder are most commonly caused by abnormalities of the uterus, hormone deficiencies, emotional factors, and various chronic illnesses.[61]

STILLBIRTH. Today fewer babies are still born than ever before. According to William Gaffey, Professor of Biostatistics at the University of California School of Public Health, the number of stillborn babies produced by white mothers has decreased by 50 per cent in less than thirty years. The rate has decreased from about thirty per 1000 births to less than fifteen, with the greatest improvement in rates of the first-born.[62]

BREECH BIRTH. When a baby is born other than head first, it is sometimes called a *breech birth*. Physicians today, however, check the position of the baby during the first stage of birth. If they find it is not descending head-first and if labor has not progressed too far, they are able to turn the baby while within the mother so that the head may appear first. DeLee estimates that the chances of breech birth are only about three in 100.[63] In modern hospitals, there is little need of concern over this condition.

CESAREAN BIRTH. Occasionally, it is better for the mother to have the child taken from her through an incision of the walls of the abdomen and uterus. This operation is called a *cesarean section* because of the belief that Julius Caesar was delivered in this manner. This manner of taking the child is sometimes necessary when it is known that the largest part of the baby is bigger than the mother's pelvic girdle. Actually, there are very few babies that grow larger than the pelvic opening, and also fewer deformed female pelvises today than formerly because in youth diet is better. The need for cesarean sections today is much less than formerly.[64]

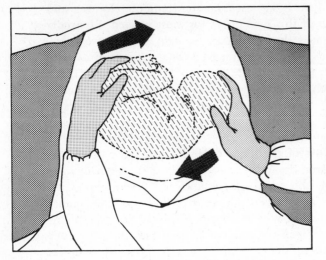

Figure 17-12. Turning a breech presentation. (Adapted from J. P. Greenhill, *Obstetrics in General Practice* [Chicago: Year Book Publishers, Inc., 1940], p. 247, Fig. 74C. Reproduced by permission.)

BLEMISHES. Baby blemishes are very rare; indeed, hospital records show that only one baby in 200 is born with any kind of marking, including all of those of minor significance.[65] Thus, there is little need for concern in this area.

Common misinformation

It is probably safe to say that no subject has inspired more misinformation and absurd folk tales than pregnancy and birth. Many of these are apparently the result of cultural lag. Birth itself was considered so secretive and mysterious a procedure that many myths were easily accepted and perpetuated. Frazier reports that among some preliterates, a woman in childbirth is considered unclean and is quarantined.[66] An enormous amount of magic is practiced in connection with birth in some societies. Furthermore, in modern society there is a widespread myth that childbirth is easier for preliterate women and that these women simply lie down, give birth, and then get up. Research in this connection shows there is little truth to this belief.[67]

Sometimes, even people who should know better may be influenced by superstition passed on by their less informed friends. Many well-meaning people implant ignorant ideas in the pregnant woman, which leads to needless upsets and fears. The results of studies in relation to what Americans really know and think about sex and human reproduction are quite shocking to many educators in modern American society. The evidence shows conclusively that even many well-educated Americans are still tangled in a web of taboos, superstitions, and misinformation.[68] The experiences of educators such as Perkins support these conclusions:

Experience as an instructor in biological science, and as a counselor for students, enabled the author to recognize that college students were inadequately informed and expressed attitudes about reproduction not based on facts, and behaved as if the natural biological and psychological functions of sex and reproduction were in the realm of mystery. The students didn't know and, to make the teaching situation more difficult, the students didn't know that they didn't know.[69]

A LACK OF EDUCATION. It is not that education has failed in the United States but that there has been a lack of adequate education in the pragmatic facts of sex and reproduction. This is a pathetic situation for over 90 per cent of the population normally marries, and of this group, more than 80 per cent have children. Thus, the task of parenthood faces the great majority of people, no matter what their occupation, religion, or politics. One college graduate, writing of her educational experiences, stated: "I could chatter about the minor English poets of the sixteenth century. I knew all about the love life of the earthworm . . . , but pregnancy amazed me."[70]

SPECIAL CLASSES. To offset some of this ignorance and superstition, many of today's physicians are conducting classes in the birth process for their own patients. In some communities, doctors get together and "pool" their patients who are in the last trimester of pregnancy for such education. Because most doctors are pressed for time, many have found this to be a valuable method of educating the prospective parents. Most physicians who have conducted classes with groups of expectant mothers consider the classes and the experience valuable beyond description. Realizing that the doctors' time is precious, organizations such as the Red Cross are also holding such classes in some communities. Well-trained people conduct the classes, thus freeing the physicians to continue their professional work. One organization has prepared a series of films showing normal labor and childbirth. These are often used by training centers or by individual doctors at the conclusion of their training program for childbirth.[71] Usually such films may be rented from the state board of health for a nominal fee.

The mortality rate

The chances of death resulting for either mother or child are exceedingly rare in the United States today. Although the possibility of childbirth risk is something like four times greater in nonwhites and in lower-socioeconomic-level groups, this is probably not caused by race or class genetics but by the sad economic fact that such groups are less able to afford specialists, the best hospitals, or good prenatal care. The risk, however, is being reduced in all races and in all classes. There is a slight increase of mortality rate with age. Guttmacher explains, however, that the increase is so slight that there is no need for concern if there has been proper care during the prenatal period:

> In all the studies on elderly primiparas, the maternal and fetal risk were slightly higher than in an average age group, but the increase was so insignificant that no woman is justified in being deterred from motherhood by it. Any woman, even though she is thirty-five or over when undertaking her first pregnancy, can confidently anticipate a very happy outcome if she receives the proper type of obstetrical care.[72]

In 1920, about sixty-two mothers died for each 10,000 live births. By 1930 this rate had been reduced to fifty-nine; by 1940, to thirty-four; by 1945, to twenty; by 1950, to eight; by 1955, to six; and the rate now stands at less than three maternal deaths to every 10,000 live births.[73] The infant mortality rate now stands at less than one half the 1940 rate.[74] Even this rate could be reduced another 5 per cent by better prenatal care.[75]

Table 17–6. **Infant mortality rate for the United States**

Year	Per 1000 live births
1959	26.4
1960	25.6
1962	25.2
1964	24.2

Source: Statistical Bulletins, Metropolitan Life Insurance Company (January 1961, and December 1964). Adapted by permission.

The future looks even more promising with the discovery of new drugs to fight infection, and new methods of delivery. For example, a new live-virus vaccine against measles developed by the Harvard Medical School has, so far, proved 100 per cent effective.[76] Not too far in the future, there will probably be very little or no risk involved in pregnancy and childbirth.

Summary

Birth is an exciting event in the life of every couple, but there are many questions that should be answered for the young husband and wife if they are to understand the effects it produces on their immediate activities as well as on their future.

The various presumptive signs of pregnancy are often inconclusive within themselves. When several of these signs persist, however, it is probable that pregnancy has occurred. The positive signs of pregnancy are usually manifested by the baby itself and give indisputable evidence that pregnancy is a reality. Choice of physician is important. Whenever possible, a specialist in obstetrics should be chosen as the wife's physician during pregnancy.

Some of the most common questions asked by couples after the discovery of pregnancy pertain to the time of birth and the sex and the size of the baby.

Pregnancy is a transitional period which gives the couple an opportunity to prepare for parenthood. During this interval, plans and adaptations in several areas must be made. Emotional adjustments, as well as physical, economic, group-living, and social adjustments must be made by the couple.

Highlights of the birth process have been outlined, including an identification of the various stages of birth and the usual procedures connected with each.

The latest research findings have been presented on the length of labor, the pains of birth, the choice of breast- or bottle-feeding, the length of the hospital stay, the possibility of multiple births, and possible complications.

Pregnancy and birth are a family affair, and the husband and wife must consider not only themselves during this creative interval but their friends, relatives, and particularly, their other children if they have any. The couple should anticipate this event with a sense of mutual fulfillment. A factual knowledge of the process will also help them to prepare for their child with greater assurance and comfort.

Notes

1. Sol DeLee, *Safeguarding Motherhood,* 3rd ed. (Philadelphia: J. B. Lippincott Co., 1953), p. 5.

2. Alan F. Guttmacher, *Pregnancy and Birth* (New York: The Viking Press, Inc., 1957), p. 26.

3. DeLee, *op. cit.,* p. 7.

4. *Ibid.,* p. 4.

5. *Ibid.,* p. 7.

6. *Ibid.,* p. 8.

7. J. P. Greenhill, *Obstetrics in General Practice,* 4th ed. (Chicago: Year Book Publishers, 1948), p. 457.

8. *Today's Health* (December, 1959), 11.

9. According to Paul C. Glick, "The Life Cycle of the Family," *Marriage and Family Living,* 17:8, about 80 per cent of those who marry change residences at the time of marriage or within the ensuing year.

10. Ernest R. Groves, Gladys Hoagland Groves, and Catherine Groves, *Sex Fulfillment in Marriage,* rev. ed. (New York: Emerson Books, 1961).

11. *Today's Child* (May 1960), 8:2.

12. Guttmacher, *op. cit.,* p. 107.

13. DeLee, *op. cit.,* p. 45.

14. Nicholson J. Eastman, *Expectant Motherhood* (Boston: Little, Brown & Co., 1957), p. 112.

15. Guttmacher, *op. cit.,* p. 44.

16. *Ibid.,* p. 48.

17. *Ibid.,* p. 45.

18. Stated in *Today's Child* (October 1962), p. 7.

19. Guttmacher, *op. cit.,* p. 45.

20. *Ibid.,* p. 162.

21. Simon Dinitz, Russel R. Dynez, and Alfred C. Clarke, "Preference for Male or Female Children: Traditional or Affectional?" *Marriage and Family Living,* 16:128–30.

22. Guttmacher, *op. cit.,* p. 66.

23. For some of the progress in this connection, see Robert Demarest, "Sperm Shape and Sex of Offspring," *What's New* (Chicago: Abbot Laboratories Publication No. 225, August–September 1961), pp. 2–3; or J. H. Tjio, and T. T. Puck, "The Sematic Chromosomes of Man," *Proceedings of the National Academy of Science* (December 1958), 1229.

24. Guttmacher, *op. cit.,* p. 60.

25. *Ibid.*

26. *Ibid.,* p. 61.

27. *Ibid.*

28. *Ibid.*

29. U.S. Department of Health, Education, and Welfare, *Vital Statistics of the United States,* Vol. 13, No. 6 (September 11, 1964).

30. William H. Genné, *Husbands and Pregnancy* (New York: Association Press, 1950).

31. Margaret A. Ribble, *The Rights of Infants* (New York: Columbia University Press, 1943), p. 106, *et passim.*

32. Lester Warren Sontag, "War and the Fetal-Maternal Relationship," in Robert F. Winch and R. McGinnis, *Selected Studies in Marriage and the Family* (New York: Holt, Rinehart & Winston, Inc., 1953).

33. The importance of the prospective mother keeping happy and unfatigued is discussed in M. F. Ashley Montagu, *Prenatal Influences* (Springfield, Ill.: Charles C Thomas, Publishers, 1962).

34. Judson T. and Mary G. Landis, *Building a Successful Marriage* (Englewood Cliffs, N.J.: Prentice-Hall, Inc., 1963), p. 524.

35. William R. Rosengren, "Social Sources of Pregnancy as Illness or Normality," *Social Forces,* 39:260–67.

36. Landis and Landis, *op. cit.,* pp. 522–23.

37. Judson T. Landis and Thomas and Shirley Poffenberger, "The Effects of First Pregnancy Upon the Sexual Adjustment of 212 Couples," *American Sociological Review,* 15:767–72.

38. Nadina R. Kavinoky, "Marital Adjustments During Pregnancy and the Year After," *Medical Woman's Journal* (October 1949), 1–2.

39. Leland Stott, Research paper on pregnancy study at Merrill-Palmer Institute, delivered at annual conference of The National Council on Family Relations, Rutgers University, New Brunswick, N.J., 1952.

40. Willard Waller and Reuben Hill, *The Family: A Dynamic Interpretation* (New York: The Dryden Press, 1951), p. 383.

41. DeLee, *op. cit.,* p. 93.

42. Herbert Thoms, *Training for Childbirth* (New York: McGraw-Hill Book Company, Inc., 1950), p. 76.

43. Herbert Thoms and Robert H. Wyatt, "One Thousand Consecutive Deliveries Under a Training for Childbirth Program," *American Journal of Obstetrics and Gynecology*, 61:205–209.

44. David B. Treat, "A Generation of Prepared Parents," *The Family Life Coordinator*, 7:8.

45. *Ibid.*

46. Grantly Dick Reed, *Childbirth Without Fear* (London: William Heinemann, Limited, 1947).

47. Dr. Max Sadove, of the University of Illinois Research and Education Hospitals, Chicago, reports that with the use of a fine piece of plastic tubing, he was able to transmit intermittent doses of a local anesthetic to the cervix region during the first stage, and to the pudendal nerve region during the second stage, of birth. It was used on 200 women patients, and the majority reported no pain at all. See Lawrence Galton, "News in Medicine," *Family Circle* (May 1963), 14. Swedish obstetricians Per Bergman and Tage Malmstrom have recently confirmed Sadove's findings in over 5,000 deliveries. See, *Parade* (February 21, 1965). However, Dr. Robert A. Kimbrough, Medical Director of the American College of Obstetricians and Gynecologists, blames 10 per cent of all deaths of mothers during childbirth on the use of anesthesia in the delivery room. Kimbrough states that the less used, the better for both mother and child, and that anything that completely eliminates pain is dangerous to the baby. See *Today's Child* (April 1963), 6. Some experiments are presently being conducted using pressurized suits, much like spacemen wear. No results of such experiments have been released at the time of this writing.

48. Kavinoky, *op. cit.*, pp. 1–2.

49. F. W. Goodrich, *Natural Childbirth* (Englewood Cliffs, N.J.: Prentice-Hall, Inc., 1952), p. 1.

50. Herbert Thoms, *Understanding Natural Childbirth* (New York: McGraw-Hill Book Company, Inc., 1950), p. 11.

51. M. Abramson and W. T. Heron, "An Objective Evaluation of Hypnosis in Obstetrics," *American Journal of Obstetrics and Gynecology*, 59:1069. For additional viewpoints about using hypnosis in childbirth, see the following: R. V. August, "Obstetric Hypoanesthesia," *American Journal of Obstetrics and Gynecology*, 78:1131–38; A. A. Earn, "Mental Concentration—A New and Effective Psychological Tool for the Abolition of Suffering in Childbirth," *American Journal of Obstetrics and Gynecology*, 83:29–36; "Self-Hypnosis Helps In Delivery of Babies," *Science Digest*, 50 (July 1961), 17; Jacqueline Juhl, "I Had This Baby Under Hypnosis," *Better Homes and Gardens*, 37:152–55.

52. *Ibid.*

53. See Ruth and Edward Brecker, "Childbirth Under Hypnosis," *Reader's Digest*, 71:55–58.

54. *Today's Child* (October 1961), 3.

55. DeLee, *op. cit.*, p. 103.

55. *Statistical Bulletin*, Metropolitan Life Insurance Company, 27:9.

57. *Ibid.*, p. 10; and U.S. Department of Health, Education and Welfare, *op. cit.*

58. *Statistical Bulletin*, Metropolitan Life Insurance Company, 31:6.

59. Alan F. Guttmacher, "Abortions," in Morris Fishbein and Ruby Jo Reeves Kennedy (eds.), *Modern Marriage and Family Living* (New York: Oxford University Press, Inc., 1957), pp. 207–209.

60. Robert E. Hall, *Nine Month's Reading* (Garden City, N.Y.: Doubleday & Company, Inc., 1960), p. 73.

61. *Today's Health* (January 1963), 10.

62. *Today's Child*, **8:3**.

63. DeLee, *op. cit.,* p. 90.

64. Newer methods contributing to the elimination of cesarean section are such as the vacuum extractor developed by the Swedish doctor, Tage Malm-strom. See *Today's Child,* **8:3**.

65. Eastman, *op. cit.,* p. 107.

66. J. G. Frazer, *The Golden Bough* (New York: The Macmillan Company, 1926).

67. *Ibid.,* pp. 294–95.

68. Gelolo McHugh, "What Americans Need to Learn About Sex," *Colliers Magazine,* **138**:36–40; or H. F. Kilander, "A Survey of the Public's Knowledge of Certain Aspects of Human Reproduction," *Journal of School Health,* **29**: 211–15.

69. Edward Vernon Perkins, "Reproduction Education in a College General Biology Course," *Marriage and Family Living,* **21**:41.

70. Marion Walker Alcaro, "Colleges Don't Make Sense," *Woman's Day* (May 1946), 64.

71. One such group of highly recommended films is produced by Medical Art Productions, Inc., P.O. Box 4042, Stockton, Calif.

72. Guttmacher, *op. cit.,* p. 167.

73. *Statistical Bulletins,* Metropolitan Life Insurance Company (June 1947; July 1951; February 1961; December 1964).

74. *Statistical Bulletin,* Metropolitan Life Insurance Company (December 1964).

75. Quoting Dr. James D. Ebert, Director of the Department of Embryology of the Carnegie Institute of Washington, *Today's Child* (October 1962), 2.

76. *Today's Child* (October 1961), 1.

Questions for further thought

1. In what manner is pregnancy a unique experience in the American democratic society?

2. How soon after a suspected pregnancy should the woman visit her physician?

3. How may a husband sublimate his sex drive during the last few weeks or months of his wife's pregnancy?

4. At what stage of development does the unborn baby become a human being?

5. How might one go about securing community support for organized classes on pregnancy and childbirth training?

6. What suggestions are in order for a young wife who is severely frightened about the possibilities of pain during childbirth?

7. To what extent should a pregnant woman continue to smoke or use other stimulants?

8. Is there anything a couple can do to increase their chances of having twins?

9. Should a couple marry when it is discovered that the woman is Rh— and the man Rh+?

10. Why is there such a wide difference in infant and maternal mortality rates in different regions of the United States?

11. What is the origin of some of the following old wives' tales: (a) a mother can dream a terrible dream and thus mark a baby; (b) a baby's cord might get knotted if the mother stretches her arms above her head; (c) if the bag

of water breaks early in labor, it will mean a more difficult birth; (d) a seven-month baby is stronger than an eight-month baby; (e) a mother cannot get pregnant as long as she is still nursing the last baby.

Recommended films

Biography of the Unborn (Encyclopaedia Britannica Films).
Prenatal Care (Medical Films).
Labor and Childbirth (Medical Films).
Childbirth: Normal Delivery (Medical Films).
Postnatal Care (Medical Films).

Suggested supplemental readings

BOOKS

Frohse, F., Max Brodel, and Leon Schlossberg. *Atlas of Human Anatomy*. New York: Barnes & Noble, 1959.
Genné, William H., *Husbands and Pregnancy*. New York: Association Press, 1956.
Guttmacher, Alan F. *Pregnancy and Birth*. New York: The Viking Press, Inc., 1957.
Hall, Robert E. *Nine Month's Reading, A Medical Guide for Pregnant Women*, rev. ed. Garden City, N.Y.: Doubleday & Company, Inc., 1963.
Harkavy, Myron B. *True Accounts of Unusual Experiences in Childbirth*. New York: Ace Books, 1962.
Karmel, Marjorie. *Thank You, Dr. Lamaze*. Philadelphia: J. B. Lippincott Co., 1960.
Lewis, Abigail. *An Interesting Condition: The Diary of a Pregnant Woman*. Garden City, N.Y.: Doubleday & Company, Inc., 1950.
Newton, Miles. *Maternal Emotions*. Philadelphia: Paul Hoeber, 1955.
Painter, Charlotte. *Who Made the Lamb?* New York: McGraw-Hill Book Company, Inc., 1965.
Phillips, Marion. *More Than Pregnancy*. New York: Coward-McCann, Inc., 1955.
Thoms, Herbert. *Childbirth with Understanding*. Springfield, Ill.: Charles C Thomas, Publishers, 1962.
———. *Training for Childbirth*. New York: McGraw-Hill Book Company, Inc., 1950.
Vellay, Pierre. *Childbirth Without Pain*. New York: E. P. Dutton & Co., Inc., 1960.

ARTICLES

Abramson, M., and W. T. Heron. "An Objective Evaluation of Hypnosis in Obstetrics," *American Journal of Obstetrics and Gynecology, 59*:1069.
Brown, O'Donnell. "A Summary of 100 Vaginal Deliveries in the Rotunda Hospital Following Previous Cesarean Section," *Journal of Obstetrics and Gynecology of the British Empire, 58*:555–57.
Buxton, L. "An Evaluation of a Prepared Childbirth Program," *New York State Journal of Medicine* (September 1956).
Ferreira, Antonio J. "The Pregnant Woman's Emotional Attitude and Its Reflection on the Newborn," *American Journal of Orthopsychiatry, 30*:553–61.
Freedman, L. Z., and H. Thoms. "Observations on Training for Childbirth," *Journal of the American Medical Women's Association* (February 1958), 13.
Freeman, T. "Pregnancy as a Precipitant of Mental Illness in Men," *British Journal of Medical Psychology, 24*:49–54.

Guttmacher, Alan F. "Don't Believe Those Old Wives' Tales About Having a Baby," *Parents,* **36**:82–83.

Jensen, F. E. "Having a Baby Is a Family Matter," *American Journal of Nursing,* **50**:674–75.

Mongeau, Beatrice, Harvey L. Smith, and Ann C. Maney, "The 'Granny' Midwife: Changing Roles and Functions of a Folk Practitioner," *American Journal of Sociology,* **66**:497–505.

Pollack, Joan S. "Why All These Myths About Pregnancy?" *Today's Health* (August 1959), 26–28.

Steer, Charles M. "Effect of Type of Delivery on Future Childbearing," *American Journal of Obstetrics and Gynecology,* **60**:395–402.

Thoms, Herbert, and Robert H. Wyatt. "One Thousand Consecutive Deliveries Under a Training for Childbirth Program," *American Journal of Obstetrics and Gynecology,* **61**:205–209.

Turner, John A. "Hypnosis in Medical Practice and Research," *Bulletin of The Menninger Clinic,* **24**:18–25.

Rearing children

chapter 18

Parenthood represents the last frontier in American society, for the great majority of young people approach parenthood with as little formal training and knowledge of the conditions involved as the early pioneers had when they first chopped their way through the wilderness of North America. Unfortunately, many of today's young couples have not been as well steeped in the practicalities of everyday living as were their early forebears. Furthermore, there has been little chance for formal preparation for parenthood in the modern educational system. Even where excellent classes are offered, too few people take advantage of them.

> Parents represent the last stand of the amateur. Every other trade and profession has developed standards, has required study and practice and licensing before releasing the student into his work. Only one profession remains untutored and untrained—the bearing and rearing of our children.[1]

The positive benefits of parenthood

Parenthood brings many joys and positive benefits. Not the least of these is the greater feeling of union within the marriage. This is largely brought about by the fact that children are entirely a creation of the couple together.

EMOTIONAL SATISFACTIONS. Many emotional satisfactions are enjoyed in parenthood which could not be possible in any other way. Not only do children represent a continuation of life into the future, but they enrich the present in a way that nothing else can. It is even possible for the parent to relive part of his own youth and vicariously satisfy some of the yearnings that had gone unsatisfied in the years past. Parents, however, should not take this too literally, for it is not possible to live entirely through the children nor is it wise to try. No one can live the life of another, and no parent should try to live the life of his own child.

Another emotional satisfaction of parenthood is the complete dependence of the child upon the mother and father. Everyone, in a sense, likes to feel that he is needed, and certainly it is the privilege of parents to enjoy taking care of their children, who need them so much.

Children may also provide a source of companionship, especially in the later years of life. They should not be considered an investment in old-age insurance, but there is much joy in seeing the accomplishments of grown sons and daughters.

FRESH EXPERIENCES. There is little doubt that rearing children is a continuously new experience in life. No two children are exactly alike. In fact, no two situations with the same child are exactly alike. Children present their parents with a constantly changing series of challenges every day. Managing these spontaneous situations will keep the parents alert and prevent their falling into rigid patterns of habit.

NEW MEANING TO LIFE. Children give new meaning to the life of an adult. The first child normally marks a turning point in a couple's life; before, the husband and wife were relatively free, but now they are responsible for a third person. New values are essential for the new family, new focal points of reference and a new perspective on life.

In a broad sense, children also deepen values that were already present. Normally, after having children, the parents' interest in the future of the nation and the world assumes more personal proportions. Such things as the national economy and the international situation cause more family-centered concern than was possible previously. Now the parent feels that he is contributing more directly and has a definite stake in the future, even in life after himself.

The problems of parenthood

To say that parenthood is all happiness, and that children represent nothing but joy, would be a gross misrepresentation of the facts. Studies indicate that the care of children is a major adjustment area within most marriages. The study by Landis of couples who had been married an average of twenty years revealed that the care and discipline of the children ranked next to sex among those problems upon which couples had failed to reach a mutually satisfactory adjustment.[2] In a more recent study of younger married couples, Landis discovered that disagreements over child-training ranked next to troubles with in-laws and economic difficulties as focal points of friction.[3] Problems of child care have always been important to mothers. More than thirty years ago Linquist asked 306 mothers to indicate the chief causes of fatigue, worry, and friction in their lives. The majority put at the top of the list, in each of the three categories, not housework, not marriage problems, not even financial concerns, but child-rearing.[4] Today's problems of child care seem to be causing increasingly serious concern to young mothers; more so, indeed, than in any former era. Kamarovsky stated: "...mothers of young children with little or no domestic help seem to be a particularly problem-ridden group. Overwork, tired muscles, constant and almost exclusive association with young children are among the most frequently mentioned grievances."[5]

SUDDEN CHANGE IN ROUTINE. Some of the problems of modern parenthood are related to the sudden changes in routine that take place after children arrive. A new orientation is necessary when the child comes into the home, for the arrival of the child upsets the status quo. Once again, as when they were first married, couples must work out a satisfactory arrangement. The entire process of adjustment in most major areas must be re-examined.

Because the infant is completely helpless, the lives of the others within the family must be reoriented around him and his habits. Babies must come first in a family; the mother's preoccupation with the child's care must take precedence over activities which the couple previously enjoyed together. The couple's schedule must be revamped to fit the baby's schedule. An infant requires attention for such things as feeding and changing, regardless of the hour. The sudden routine changes naturally place a strain upon each family member, and upon the marital relationship. As Levy and Munroe have stated,

> No matter how going a concern a marriage may be, the advent of children causes severe strain between parents. Newborn babies cannot be taken in their stride; they have none. Their very physical disorganization sets the pace for their influence on marriage ties. Children are as disturbing to marriage as their own physical eccentricities. Any orderly, smooth, satisfactory relationship carefully worked out between husband and wife is broken the very first night the child is home from the hospital. The inability of a child to do anything for itself means that demands are made on parents which create a new relationship between husband and wife. Their time and energy are no longer their own for companionship or intimacy. The little tyrant need only raise his voice a tiny bit to break up the parents' closest embrace. The warmth of the adult relationship is forever being disturbed by the child's demands for physical attention. At any hour of the night the newborn youngster can separate husband and wife without repaying them for their loss with even a friendly smile. The child's physical requirements have the right-of-way over their feelings toward each other and toward the child. No matter how much one or both of them may resent this intrusion, their only choice is to obey the child's call and sacrifice their own need for each other. Babies are tyrants.[6]

Because the child can communicate only by crying, parents must assume that he needs something when he cries. The prolonged wail of an infant in the dead of night, however, can mystify, frustrate, or even anger the most loving parent. Children mean episodes of trouble, danger, and illness, which invariably bring on anxiety and strain for parents. Little children may be unconventional, impulsive, unyielding, noisy, unappreciative, and—above all—difficult to understand. Of course, some of this conflict is related to the fact that adults often try to treat children as though they were little adults.

Not only do children block many adult desires in general, but they often block attempts to direct and control their childish behavior. This, in turn, may increase the adult's own sense of inadequacy and personal frustration.

Almost overnight children affect adults' freedom in such a way that even going to a movie involves plans, babysitters, and often feelings of apprehension and guilt. As children get older, the parents must focus much of their social planning on such things as cooperative nursery schools, Sunday school, or PTA. Whether or not the couple are free to attend activities of their own may also depend on the children's state of health. Thus, children's needs and interests compete for attention with those of the couple. Furthermore, as more children arrive, each partner's slice of attention gets thinner and thinner.

CONFLICT OF IDEAS. Frequently there is a conflict of ideas between the father and the mother on how to rear children. Both parents go into marriage with many preconceived ideas on the "right" and "wrong" methods of rearing children. Usually these differences do not become evident until after the first child is born. Davis reports that many of these differences are quite deeply entrenched, coming mainly from the parental background of each partner. Furthermore, when each represents a different social-class background, there are usually even more differences in child-rearing philosophy and techniques.[7] Attitudes about child care and discipline are shaped considerably by the parents' own childhood experiences. Normally, each individual tends to repeat with his own children the pattern from which he himself grew. On the other hand, if the pattern was one with which the individual wholeheartedly disagreed, he may go to the other extreme, completely rejecting it and going in an opposite direction.

Landis reported that one of the chief complaints of fathers about child-rearing practices was that their wives were too easy with the children, giving in too much, often pampering and spoiling the children. Wives complained that their husbands were too strict and harsh in their relations with the children. Because of the intensity with which they felt that the spouse was wrong, many parents countermanded one another's orders in the care and discipline of children.[8] This can prove most irritating, usually leading to further trouble between mates, not to mention increased rebellion on the children's part.

To enrich a marriage, it is important for parents to present a united front in the discipline of their children. Differences of ideas may cause not only failure with the children, but also tensions between the spouses. To be effective, discipline must be agreed upon by both parents. In fact, this may be more important than the particular kind of discipline actually used. This is not the same as saying that parents should never disagree over the discipline of their children. In fact, almost all parents will find some disagreements in this area at some time or other. Successful parents, however, will discuss these differences and reach a compromise when the children are not present.

There seems to be more conflict in ideas concerning child-rearing methods in families today than at any other time in history. Perhaps much of this is brought about by the evolution of the "new father." In some families, a shorter work week means the father is often home and more personally aware of family behavior than ever before; however, there is likely to be conflict when his ideas of discipline differ from those of the mother.

Fathers of a former era mainly dealt out punishment after the mothers had reported who deserved it. Now, however, the father is often asked to decide whether there shall be punishment at all. More problems are thus created, for the father is more involved in the entire area of child care than ever before. Many young fathers are willing to share in the responsibility of caring for the children, but become discouraged when they discover that marital tensions are sometimes increased rather than decreased. One study revealed that a group of young fathers continued displaying positive interest in babies up to about six weeks after birth, playing with them, feeding them, dressing them, and being generally helpful. Shortly after that time there was a noticeable drop in the level of participation of some of the fathers. Much of this decrease was caused by the father's change of attitude, but some of it was caused by the mother's expectations that the father continue to do more or better, when the fathers felt they were already doing more than their share.[9] None of this is to suggest that young fathers should not share in the responsibility of child care. The fact remains, however, that unless the couple have agreed upon methods of child care and discipline before the arrival of the baby, the father's participation in this new role sometimes creates more problems than it solves. Surveys of nursery schools in which mothers participate personally to improve their managing of children, indicate that this experience created greater disharmony in the home because the gap between the parents' points of view was found to be greater than before.[10]

NEW BURDENS. Another problem of parenthood is that new burdens must be assumed by both parents after children arrive. For the husband, the new problems may even include such things as competition at home for his wife's attention.

Clinical observations by the author lead him to believe that most husbands anticipate this situation and are quite willing to share their wives with their children without much protest. They are not willing, however, for the wife to spend all her time with the children. Furthermore, in middle-class families, many husbands seem to understand this particular situation better than their young wives. That is to say, in many cases it appears easier for the husband to accept the wife's increased work schedule, for it is the mother who protests that the children take up so much of her time that she has no opportunity to be with her spouse.

The husband may have to revise his schedule after the arrival of a child. Many things he did as a matter of routine may now have to be curtailed to meet the new demands. There is also an increased economic responsibility because the family's living costs will go up after the arrival of a baby. Most couples cut down on many other expenses if the family cannot earn more money.

As a father, a man must play many more roles than he did as a husband. The new roles include those of teacher, nurse, part-time housekeeper, and hero. How much the father enjoys these new roles is directly related to how well he performs them. In large measure, the child's ability to love and be loved, to enjoy life, and to develop a creative personality is a direct reflection of his father's capabilities. Nye reports that, in a modern society, the relationship of the father to the child appears to be fully as crucial as that of the mother to the child. The affectional bonds between girls and their fathers, especially during adolescence, appear as vitally important (if not more so) as that between fathers and their sons.[11]

The father must also serve as the model of his sex because his own behavior will help his children to understand the male role in today's world. Perhaps this is even truer today than in former times. When society was basically agrarian, it was a simple matter for small children to observe what their father did both inside the home and out, for the father worked in the fields close by. Today, however, a father's work may be many miles from home. It is difficult for children, or even for their mother, to know much about the nature of his work or to learn a masculine-activity pattern. The father must therefore plan for time to be active with his children so that they may grow up with an understanding of the male role. Ordinarily, the father is the closest contact growing children have with the male sex. Most of the child's other contacts are with females; his teachers in nursery school, kindergarten, grade school, and Sunday school are usually women. Even Cub Scouts have den mothers. Thus the child has little chance of understanding the male role unless

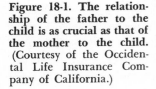

Figure 18-1. The relationship of the father to the child is as crucial as that of the mother to the child. (Courtesy of the Occidental Life Insurance Company of California.)

the father shows an early interest in him. It is probably safe to say that most children develop their earliest and most decisive ideas about masculinity from their fathers. Strong men particularly enjoy this responsibility, but it may prove burdensome to a weaker one.

An additional challenge to the father in modern society is to establish his influence as a person with his children. He does not need to be a worldwide expert to influence the minds of his children, but his careful consideration of questions or problems can evoke their respect and help them to think with honesty.

Fathers may not be "the best" in all areas of life but by displaying the courage of their convictions, they can give the child as much a sense of familial security as the most autocratic father at old-fashioned breakfast tables. Paternal dignity should not suffer comparison in the child's mind with television clowns playing cartoon husbands. The parents must distinguish for the growing child the difference between farcical entertainment and the values of human dignity in daily life.

The responsibilities of child-rearing are not easy, but the couple will be less discouraged if they know what to expect. Interviews with fathers within a year after the birth of their first child disclosed the following difficulties: housing, the burden of a heavy schedule, increased financial problems, disturbed sleep, lack of quiet or privacy, growing irritability at the wife's complaints of being left alone so much, insufficient recreation because of lack of funds or time, and difficulty in finding baby-sitters. Many called the early weeks of the baby's life at home a "nightmare" with the baby's constant crying, increased tenseness for the parents, fatigue, and discouragement.[12]

There are also many new burdens for the wife after the coming of children. One of the early problems arises on her return from the hospital when she realizes, perhaps all too suddenly, that the responsibility for the infant is now basically hers. She must make sure that he is fed properly, gets plenty of rest, and has his daily bath. Bathing the baby involves many nervous fumbles the first few times. Changing of diapers involves considerable laundry. Diaper laundry services are well worth the cost, particularly if the mother has not yet regained all her strength. When the baby cries for no apparent reason, younger mothers may wonder if they are doing all they should. It is probably safe to say that any discouragement upon returning from the hospital is only that of any neophyte faced with a new task and no experience. Time will provide the mother with experiences, and love will develop her maternal skills.

After returning from the hospital, it is only natural for a mother to be tired. Many wives report not having had a full night's sleep for several

Figure 18-2. Today's father must help his children to understand what it is to be a man. (Courtesy of the Metropolitan Life Insurance Company.)

months after a baby arrived. If the husband helps after his day's work, the strain of double duty for both parents may contribute to frayed nerves. It is best for each to alternate weekend tasks occasionally to allow the other a period of rest and change of activity.

> Therapeutic separation of parent and child at intervals with an adequate substitute is often good—not bad for a child.[13]

Today there is also the problem of getting help. Many young couples do not live near their in-laws and, if help is needed in the home, the couple will probably have to pay for it. Money for such help is well spent, even if it must be borrowed. The future health of both parents—and, indeed, the happiness of their marriage—is more important than the few dollars which they may find necessary to spend for hired help in the home after the first child arrives.

There is a definite need for an occasional spree after the coming of children. This includes a chance to get away from it all sometimes and relax. It is possible for some women to forget the pressures, to let the housework slide for a while, and to become relaxed again. Others are not able to do this, so some other safety valve is needed. Perhaps occasional help at home would make it possible for the young mother to get away from all their cares and responsibilities for a little while. It is probably advisable in some cases for wives to return to part-time outside employment after bearing children. Without a safety valve, hostility may develop between mother and child or between husband and wife. As Cyrus has said:

> Actually the intense, mutually exhausting emotional and physical relationship which develops between mothers and preschool children in the typical urban family lead inevitably to that worst of all maternal sins, overmothering and undercurrents of hostility, and that most fatal of all child responses: overdependence with undercurrents of resentment.[14]

Sometimes, the wife may take out her resentment on her husband, which can seriously damage their entire marital relationship. Some husbands are able to take this better than others, but most husbands are not adequately prepared for this role and perhaps are incapable of ever accepting it. Even though the mother has every reason for impatience at the end of the day, it is important that she avoid the tendency of taking such feelings out on the children or the mate.

There are additional burdens on the family upon the arrival of a new baby when there are already children in the home. Invariably there arises, to some extent, sibling rivalry. This is a natural phenomenon, for the second child is considered somewhat of an intruder by the first child. After all, the first one has had the parents all to himself up to this point. It is impossible for a small child to share his rights, privileges, and attentions completely with another child without some emotional upset. It is probable that the deep emotional reactions of the first child to the coming of the second child is similar to the reaction a wife might have if her husband brought home a second wife to live under the same roof.

Sibling rivalry is an ancient problem. It is known to have existed to some extent since earliest times. For example, the bitter jealousies between Cain and Abel were basically a manifestation of this phenomenon, as was that between Joseph and his brothers. Further illustrations of sibling rivalry are often found in fairy tales, such as the story of Cinderella. Perhaps it is not possible to eliminate sibling rivalry, but it can be kept to a minimum by conditioning the first child to welcome the new arrival as a playmate. Parents may begin long before the termination of pregnancy to create an anticipation within the first child for the coming of the second. Sometimes this is best done by helping the first child to realize that the baby belongs, not to the mother or to the father but to the family. If the child asks questions concerning the origin of the baby, it is also a good time to begin simple sex education. It can certainly be the beginning for the conditioning of positive attitudes toward sex. Simple answers must be given to all the child's questions. One need not go into detailed accounts with a small child; when he is ready for more information, he will come back with more questions.

Much can be done to alleviate the problem of sibling rivalry when the mother returns from the hospital. In the first place, older children

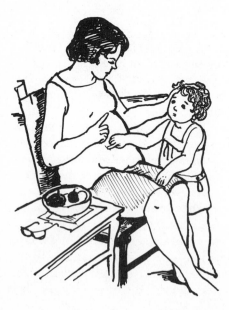

Figure 18-3. A second pregnancy is a wonderful opportunity to begin the sex education of the first child.

need considerable attention when the mother returns, for they may have been lonely and missed her during her absence. It is necessary to guard against making too much fuss over a new baby when well-meaning friends come to visit. Parents should make sure that the older children are not slighted on these occasions. By focusing on some recent achievements of the older children, a better balance of attention can be established.

The most common symptoms indicating potential sibling rivalry include such actions as (1) an attempt to injure the new baby, (2) a request to have a bottle, too, (3) attempts to stay up late at night and rise earlier in the morning, (4) temper tantrums and whining or bad humor, (5) reversion to pants-wetting, and (6) upon occasion, more illness than usual. The author was once acquainted with a family where the first child even began to go blind after the coming of the second, and it was later discovered that the condition was a psychosomatic protest at the coming of the new baby.

Even with the best preparation, some sibling rivalry is likely to arise. Whatever parents do, there will probably be times when older children will resent the younger. Perhaps even in later years of life, they may continue to harbor feelings of ambivalence toward a younger brother or sister. It is necessary for parents to understand this and not to be too harsh with older children who reveal such reactions. Only when parents show an empathic understanding is it possible for older children to begin making a healthy adjustment. After studying the literature on sibling rivalry, Bernard concludes:

> If standing on a crowded street corner, we could see all the adults about us in terms of their sibling relationships, we would see not the seemingly independent, self-resourceful individuals who pass us, but rebellious little sisters fighting against parental discrimination, resentful little brothers hating older sisters whose superiority in age and maturity frustrated their male egos, jealous older sisters resenting the attention bestowed on little sisters, sisters of all ages envying the privileges of brothers of all ages.[15]

The continually changing interaction process within the family may lead to other difficulties. As each child matures or other children are born, new problems arise, for the family is never in a static condition. One of the drawbacks to much of the child-development literature is that it has been focused on the one-child family. To be most helpful, more studies should center on the various interactions in larger families.[16] The trend in the modern middle class is to have several children, and this means many more family interactions. To relate child-development theory and practice to the interactions of a father, mother, and one child is to limit the study. Bossard gives the formula for determining the number of relationships in the family as

$$x = \frac{y^2 - y}{2}$$

where *y* represents the number of persons in the family, and *x* represents the number of relationships.[17] With this formula, it can readily be seen that the number of interaction relationships increases in geometric proportions to the number of people in the family.

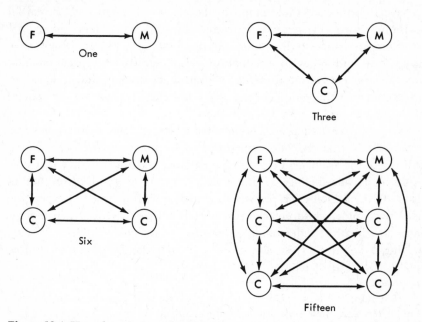

Figure 18-4. How the number of family interactions increases as number of family members increases.

A confusion of theories

Utter chaos appears to prevail in modern society regarding theories on child-rearing. Inconsistency prevails not only between theories but also in the parental practice of even one method of handling children.

THE ADULT-CENTERED WORLD.   As a general rule, the emphasis in society has been on an adult world. Consequently, child-rearing practices and theories were regarded as of little importance. In Colonial times, the basic social attitude was intolerance, and little personal indulgence was permitted children. As Stendler described it: "The early Colonial idea was to treat them rough."[18] Children were considered miniature adults who needed constant direction, supervision, and harsh discipline to make them conform to acceptable standards. Goodsell reports that less than three hundred years ago an unruly child in Massachusetts could be legally punished by death.[19] Another example of the prevalence of this concept is given by Earle: "Stern old grandfathers whipped their children at home for being whipped at school."[20] Couples were cautioned not to be too lenient with their children. Overindulgence was considered bad for children, bad for marriages, and bad for society. One couple that lost two children by drowning interpreted the tragedy as God's retribution for their having been too indulgent with them.[21]

Not everyone felt that way. In 1633 the Slavic educator, Comenius, published a book entitled *The School of Infancy*. This book was written and published for the purpose of aiding parents in the guidance of their children. Comenius' basic philosophy suggested that children were mentally different from adults, and consequently should not be treated as adults. By and large, however, such philosophies were smothered by the weight of support for adult discipline. This is typically represented by the advice of Watson, an accepted authority of some years ago: "Let your behavior always be objective and kindly firm. Never hug and kiss them, never let them sit on your lap. If you must, kiss them once on the forehead when they say goodnight. Shake hands with them in the morning."[22]

CONFLICTS AMONG VIEWS. As time progressed, conflicting views of child-rearing practices developed. Thus, the children in one generation were reared by one method; those in the next, by an opposite method. One investigation of 640 articles written between 1890 and 1949 on the subject of child care (related to discipline) revealed that most of the articles written in the late nineteenth century suggested that the mother follow a loose schedule; most of those written in the 1920s advocated a tight schedule and let the child "cry it out"; while most of those written in 1949 urged that she permit the child to regulate himself.[23]

A MANDATE FOR CONSISTENCY. These conflicting opinions on proper methods of rearing children have often led to gross frustration in both parents and children. This is not to deny that much of what has been written about child-rearing problems has been of value, but it has also produced many bewildered parents and irresponsible children. It becomes a pathetic farce for American parents to attempt to keep up with the latest philosophies of self-appointed guidance "experts." As Sussman has said:

> With each passing year new findings from research on child-raising are offered to parents, child-rearing practices seem to change as do fashions in women's clothes. Each method of rearing—breast- or bottle-feeding, self-demand or scheduled feeding, self- or forced toilet-training—is claimed to have special psychological significance in the development and growth of stable personalities. How are parents to act in the face of so many conflicting data and opinions on bringing up children?[24]

This plethora of "right" methods often brings today's young parents in conflict with parents-in-law because of different attitudes toward child-rearing. These attitudes differ not only between generations but among the latest feature articles in newspapers or magazines. The healthiest method to pursue would be for the parents to accept, rear, and enjoy their children with a natural but responsible casualness. Consistency of parental attitudes and behavior toward the children is of paramount importance. Discipline or lack of discipline by parental whim will confuse a child. Rewards or punishments should be meted out in regard to the conditioned expectations of the child, or else learning a behavior pattern is made impossible for him.

A CHILD-CENTERED WORLD.   Perhaps the most marked difference between Colonial concepts of child-rearing and modern theories is the shift from an adult-centered world to a child-centered world. This has been a long-term trend, for parental authority has been declining for many generations.[25] Parents were once privileged autocrats. Children were to be seen and not heard. They were expected to conform to adult wishes, to work hard, and to refrain from bothering their busy parents.

> When we were brought up there was one extreme—we were kept in the attic, while our parents lived in the best room; now it's just the other way—the parents are in the washhouse, while the children are in the best room. Parents now are not expected to live at all, but to exist for their children.[26]

As so often happens, the historical pendulum swung from one extreme to the other. Many children brought up under stern authoritarian rule became quite rebellious and resolved to do "better" by their children. Sensitive "experts" brought up in the same era defended the "rights of infants." Thus, there has been a jockeying back and forth from generation to generation, first to one extreme and then the other, but always leading to greater child-centeredness. Many early research studies pointed to the fact that most problem children, delinquents, and prepsychotics came from authoritarian families. Manic depression and schizophrenia were traced to oversevere parents.[27] Thus, the concept gathered momentum that the parents' chief value in life was simply to make a contribution to their children. To illustrate how far the pendulum moved in this direction, Folsom states that one clergyman proposed rewriting the Fourth Commandment to read: "Honor thy sons and thy daughters and all the children of men, that their days may be blest by what thou are able to accomplish for them and for those who shall come after them."[28]

A RETURN TO BALANCE.   There is a need for balance among child-rearing practices, and there are encouraging signs that this may be coming about. Parents must consider fulfilling their mature needs as much as their children's. Parents are not slaves who must devote their lives to the rearing of children, who in their turn, devote their lives to the rearing of their children, and on into infinity. Parents have a right to gratify their own impulses in addition as well as the duty to insure the proper development of their children's personalities. There is as much delinquency and as many problems where parents abandon their own adult interests and responsibilities to cater to the never-ending demands of their children as when they give no attention at all. Society cannot progress simply by substituting one evil for another. The substitution of tyrannical children for authoritative parents damages marriage, the family, and the very foundations of an intelligent democracy. Parents should continue to live for one another; children should not annihilate the marital relationship. This indeed would be a house divided against itself.

THREE APPROACHES.   There are three basic approaches to child-rearing. At one extreme is the authoritarian method; at the other is the extreme *laissez faire* method which leads to a child-dominated society. Between these two extremes lies the democratic method. Although few would advocate a return to the complete parent-dominated home, neither should anyone insist that parents become completely subjugated to their children's wishes. Cluttered livingrooms, damaged furniture, and constant noise and confusion can only add to the emotional tensions of all family members. There is certainly much confusion in today's democracy within the family. Many terms and phrases have been coined, some of which only add to the confusion. Some of these are such terms as *traditional, developmental, permissive,* and *restrictive.* The American family must eventually practice the democratic method or destroy itself.

The need for knowledge

Too little is really known about child care and development to justify some of the rash statements frequently made by status-seeking "experts." No single method is always *the* way. Various methods are effective with different parents, different children, and under different circumstances. Methods must and should be individualized. What works well with one set of parents will not necessarily work as well with another. Reviews of research and literature dealing with the effects of specific infant-training practices on personality formation have revealed no significant results associated with any particular practice.[29] Several of the theories are probably sound, but so far simply lack proof. As the well-known psychologist, Harry Harlow, has stated: "Although people have been observing children for a very considerable period of time, there are few psychological areas of greater intellectual gloom than the area relating to the effects of early experience [upon personality development]."[30]

Some parents would be better off if they had never attended a mental health lecture or read an article on child-rearing.... Many have become intimidated by the "experts."[31]

Basic principles

There are a few basic principles which are well established in the area of child-rearing. One of the most important rules for all parents to remember is that discipline, to be effective, should be fairly consistent. Parents should attempt to express discipline in terms of the act, not in terms of their own moods.

CONSISTENCY. There should also be consistency between the parents themselves in the matter of discipline. Parents should, as much as possible, present a united front. There should also be consistency between words and actions; parents should mean what they say, or not say it in the first place. Discipline should be guidance in personality growth. In other words, the child should learn something from it or it is not discipline. Punishment may be a part of discipline, but it is not discipline by itself. To spank or not to spank? is an irrelevant question. Terman suggests that discipline should be firm, not harsh, and accompanied by close relationships, for this is related to the future marital success of children.[32] After investigating seventy-two problem children and their relationship to their parents, Pearson suggests that "parental attitudes exert a more important influence on the formation of the child's personality than the actual events."[33]

Parents should not get discouraged when faced with child-rearing problems that arise even where they've gone "by the book." It is never possible to predict individual behavior or to prepare for every circumstance that will arise in the rearing of children. Study and experience are useful assets, but they cannot guarantee flawless child-rearing. Ordinarily, serious maladjustment does not occur unless a child is subjected to a chronologically extended and circumstantially extensive distorted pattern of development. Parents should not be too upset when they occasionally make mistakes. Serious maladjustment in children is rarely produced when isolated parental mistakes occur occasionally in a healthy pattern of parent-child relationships. Furthermore, parents are not the only ones who are influencing their children; there are many cultural influences that are beyond the control of the average ordinary parent. A child is influenced by a multiplicity of agents and agencies, and the older he becomes, the greater the number of these external forces. To be sure, parents can and do control the selection of many cultural agencies and may modify their influence on children. The extent to which they are able to do this, however, has a limit. Perhaps the best that parents can do is to provide opportunities for growth, and then stay out of the way of natural development. It will help a lot if they will keep the communication doors open at all times on all topics in the home. Just as a body has a built-in mechanism which continually directs its changes toward physical health, so personality has an "internal push" toward normal development. As Pollack has suggested, parents should realize they do not carry the total and exclusive responsibility for the child's development. There are other factors—including cultural, environmental, and peer standards—which are strong influences in spite of, or because of, everything that parents themselves do.[34]

FLEXIBILITY. More important than specific rules for the satisfactory rearing of children is the early development of healthy attitudes.

One valuable parental attitude is flexibility. Children's needs change. Thus, parents must be ready to meet the changing needs of the growing members of the family.[35]

UNIVERSAL EMOTIONAL NEEDS. There are emotional needs as important for young children as for adults. These needs include a sense of achievement, for everyone has a desire for recognition. Parents can help their children in this respect, and by so doing will contribute to their positive growth.

Furthermore, in order to grow, everyone must feel challenged occasionally. Otherwise, life becomes rather dull. New experiences provide a zest for living.

There is a need for a certain measure of independence, even in the very young. Through independence, children learn how to accept responsibility for later actions. No one becomes a responsible adult if he has not been allowed to assume responsibility as a child. Thus, parents can make a valuable contribution to their children by gradually increasing their experiences of independence.

There is also a certain need for security as children grow. If security is given to the child by the parents, he is much more likely to feel secure in other situations later on. Security includes the need for self-preservation of the ego. Parental trust has been described as the strongest ally in coping with the difficult problems of growing up. Without this trust, many children feel threatened and their confidence is undermined.

An additional part of child security is a sense of belonging. Recent research studies show how necessary this feeling is even for the very young infant. Salk, a psychologist at Elmhurst General Hospital in New York, tape-recorded the sound of a mother's heart beat and played it continuously for four days in a hospital nursery. Infants who were exposed to the sound tended to gain more weight, to cry less, and to suffer fewer stomach upsets than others.[36] The sound apparently has a soothing and beneficial effect in producing security for newborn infants; it is something with which they are familiar and it reassures them that they have not been completely abandoned after the possibly traumatic experience of birth. Lack of security in the home may show up later: children may refuse to confide in their parents, develop more active feelings of rebellion, and grow to believe they are being treated unfairly. Studies of a group of high school students showed that a positive relationship in the area of security was a contributing force toward their favorable regard of themselves.[37]

Family rituals can help bring the entire family together, especially on such occasions as holidays. Even certain bedtime rituals can help produce security in the very young. Bossard and Boll suggest that having a few family rituals brings about a feeling of happy memories and contributes a warm sense of family pride and security for each member.[38]

The most common universal emotional need is for love. Children need to love and to be loved; they need to grow in love and concern for others. Sewell suggests that the beginnings of love have much to do with the attitudes that parents give children.[39] Two authorities in the field of child-rearing state quite positively that there is no absolutely right or wrong way to handle children as long as there is love; they base their conclusions upon extensive scientific research in this connection.[40] The research of Spitz leaves little doubt that love by a mother or mother substitute is important to the physical and emotional health of children. Infants in an understaffed orphanage failed to develop socially and had an abnormally high mortality rate as compared with other infants raised with parental or parental-substitute love.[41] Kardiner, an anthropologist, reports that in primitive societies parents are affectionate when they themselves were loved as children, and indifferent when they were unloved in childhood.[42] This would seem to suggest that a prerequisite for rearing children is the development of the capacity to love. If children receive an ample supply of demonstrated love, they will develop a sense of worth or value that will assist them in constructing a satisfying image of themselves. Apparently, parents play a key role in this process.

Another universal emotional need is for individualism. Each person should be allowed to be what he *has* to be, not what parents or others *want* him to be. Some parents state proudly that they treat all their children alike. The very attempt to treat all alike means that there is an inequity, for no two children desire, demand, or need the same amount of demonstrated affection, privileges, responsibilities, or even material things, such as toys. To treat all "equally" is to superimpose a uniformity that may not afford each child his greatest opportunities for personality development. The attempt to treat all children alike might mean demanding the same behavior of a three-year-old as would be demanded of a six-year-old. As Pollack has said: "In evaluating the child's behavior and setting standards for him, parents should keep in mind the concept of age-adequate maturity."[43]

SOCIAL ACCEPTANCE. Each child should be considered a socially acceptable person within his own ability. It is entirely unfair to compare the achievements of one child with those of another. Because one child does not achieve as much in school as another does not necessarily mean that he is inferior. Such a judgment can be applied only to the realm of school achievement. Each child must be accepted for what he is, and complimented on what he does best.

A DECENT EXAMPLE. Another basic attitudinal principle is that parents should set a decent example. This may do more to influence the child's behavior, standards, and values, as well as his concepts of the world about him than any spoken words, advice, warnings, scoldings, or threats. The concept of "do as I do" is much more valuable than that of "do as I say."[44]

A FAMILY-CENTERED IDEAL. Parents should continually remind themselves that they, too, are persons with feelings, needs, emotions, and a conscience. Any family decision should be made in terms of what is best for the entire family, including the parents as well as the children. It is not democratic to satisfy the wishes and needs of one member to the detriment of those of the others.[45]

ENCOURAGEMENT OF COMMUNICATION. Wholesome family living is closely related to effective communication. According to Beasley, a family-centered democratic home meets four requirements: (1) it attempts to fulfill the basic human physical, social, and emotional needs of each member; (2) it attempts to create a permissive atmosphere within the authority pattern (parents are leaders, not bosses), encourages respect for all family members as persons, and takes into account the wishes and welfare of the total family rather than those of any one member; (3) it attempts to create the feeling among members that they belong together, that they are a group; and (4) it uses the family-council approach to problems, talking over ideas before any actions are taken.[46]

Group discussion trains children in problem-solving methods which they can then put into practice when they are older. This is good training for practicing democracy in their present and future families. Decisions which are made after everyone has had an opportunity to present his point of view are not only wiser, but also are more enthusiastically supported by family members and contribute to the family's "we" feeling.[47] Through the use of democratic decision-making within the family, a sense of fairness is developed, which encourages personal growth and the mutual affection of each family member for all others.

The desires of all family members can rarely be satisfied fully in any family. In building the democratic foundations of the family, compromises are necessary. Each family member is equally important. This is not the same as saying that each has equal ability or equal authority. Everyone's needs and wishes, however, deserve to be taken into consideration. To accomplish this, the family-council plan should not be too formalized. In fact, Beasley frowns on too many formalities, such as constitutions and by-laws.[48] According to Jones, the most successful family councils include the following elements: (1) in the beginning, meetings are planned to discuss simple things, such as something that pertains to pleasure and in which all can have a part; (2) a time is picked when the family is naturally together for the first family council meeting; (3) each is given a chance to express his ideas, and in the beginning perhaps the younger members are given only part of a larger plan to work on while the parents do the rest; (4) the ideas of each are considered without criticism, and then choices are made that are fair to each; (5) all the facts are gathered before any decisions are made; (6) the final decision is based on what brings about the most happiness to all the family members; (7) even parents must learn to make compromises where there is no endangering of health, education, or of other real values; (8) there is an encouragement for trial solutions when the group is unable to make a definite decision; and (9) a discussion should follow actions that seem to have been mistakes, instead of a simple "laying down" of the law. By encouraging these conditions, Jones believes, parents will be able to sit back objectively and observe the growth in responsibility and cooperation of all family members.[49]

Obstacles to perfect parenthood

Just as no marriage is perfect, neither is any family perfect. There are many obstacles to perfect parenthood.

SOME PARENTS KNOW BETTER. It is probably safe to say that many parents know more basic principles of child-rearing than they actually practice. Some find that they are unable to live up to what they know. What many parents really need is not more knowledge of child-rearing but more practical help from the specialists in implementing what they already know. This is often where the theorists have failed. Too often, the theorists themselves become lost in actual practice.

BABIES ARE NOT REASONABLE. Part of parental frustrations arises from the fact that babies are not reasonable. By the time they become parents, most people have forgotten what babies are really like. Thus, instead of becoming bundles of joy, the babies may become a source of anguish, frustration, and heartache. A frustrated person rarely performs as well as he otherwise might. There are some practical suggestions that have evolved from child-development studies in this connection. One is that parents with young children would do well to consider "child-proofing" their home to help ease irritations. Wall-to-wall carpeting, for example, often proves to be very foolish in a house with young children. Any paints that children use should be water-soluble. It is probably wise to have washable slipcovers for upholstered furniture when there are very young children in the family. Foam-rubber cushions are much more practical than spring cushions, while white draperies and fancy lace curtains only cause extra trouble.

There are many time-saving and energy-saving short-cuts that young couples could use for the benefit of the entire family. It would save much needless exhaustion if parents resigned themselves to the fact that lower standards of housekeeping efficiency are necessary when the family is young. Dust-free houses are a luxury which a family with young children cannot afford.

IMPOSSIBLE STANDARDS. Some frustrations of parenthood are related to impossible child-rearing standards. Such expressions as, "Never lose your temper with your children," are of little value for most humans. "Always be consistent" is actually inconsistent with human behavior. In many cases high standards lead to a feeling of failure even when parents may be doing a good job. There is a margin for error in child-rearing. Parents do not need to be perfect, and children are not nearly as fragile as some people would lead one to believe.

PERSONAL MALADJUSTMENT. Sometimes stress from outside sources prevents one or both parents from living up to their full potential within parenthood.

> Kenneth's mother and father, like most parents, tried to do their best for their child, and yet their own personal problems deprived the little boy of the most vital ingredients of growth and happiness—love and understanding. The story of his therapy ... of necessity included the re-education of his parents.[50]

Sometimes the inadequate parent appears to be oversevere, demanding perfection from a child to compensate for his inability to accept his own imperfections. Sometimes parents are seeking revenge on their own parents by releasing against their offspring the consequences of what they themselves suffered as children.

MARITAL CONFLICT. The greatest obstacle to perfect parenthood is marital conflict. At any given moment, 20 to 30 per cent of all parents are having marital difficulties. How could anyone be a good parent under these conditions? As every marriage counselor knows, marital adjustment is a strong influence on the character of children. Studies of children raised under the Israeli kibbutz system support this contention.[51] Stokes was one of the first psychiatrists to state directly that unhappy marriages constitute the chief cause of child and adult disturbances.[52] Dr. Murray Bass, at a New York Academy of Medicine symposium, said that "the best mirror in the house is the child"; that is, the alert pediatrician often can see an unstable marriage reflected in the youngster even before the parents themselves are aware of it.[53]

A strong correlation has been observed between a child's achievement in school and the emotional environment of the family. Recent tests suggest a relationship between a child's reading ability and his family climate.[54]

> Last winter when I was visiting in a first grade room, I saw a little girl struggling with all her might to learn how to read, but she wasn't getting anywhere. The teacher, the principal, and the school social worker checked into her case and found her to be a frightened child. Her parents fought night after night and she was afraid she wasn't going to have a home much longer. She was so churned up inside she couldn't think intelligently.[55]

Lauretta Bender, a child psychiatrist, points out that all surveys of problem boys show that more than 50 per cent are total nonreaders, regardless of intelligence or socioeconomic level.[56]

Probably the greatest factor contributing to delinquency in America at this time is the broken but still undivorced home.[57] Judge Philip B. Gilliam of the Juvenile Court of Denver, Colorado, in testifying before a Senate subcommittee, stated: "Most of the children I deal with come from broken homes . . . but the worst type of broken homes is where the parents are still living together. . . . Broken homes come from people and not from courts, and courts just sign the burial certificate of a dead situation."[58]

Judge C. E. Birney of the Thirty-Eighth District Court of Kansas reported that almost 35 per cent of delinquent boys and girls in the reformatories of that state represented legally broken homes; in addition, he estimated an almost equal number come from homes broken without legal sanction.[59] The Glueck tables, which are largely based on family information, are reported to have correctly identified forty-six out of fifty delinquent boys and fifty out of fifty delinquent girls in one setting.[60] Nye found a higher frequency of delinquent behavior among high school students where there was (1) unfair, strict, inconsistent, irrational, and/or unexplained punishment; (2) lack of parental love; and (3) quarrelsome parents.[61] Of 211 male neurotic patients at Northington General Hospital, seventy-eight represented an unstable but still "legally" intact parental marriage.[62] This is too high a percentage to be mere coincidence. It is estimated by New York health authorities that about 10 per cent of all fatal car accidents and 15 per cent of all home accidents involving young people are actually suicide attempts. In New York there are fifty attempts at child suicide for every completed act. Most of these, according to Dr. Harry Bakwin, a pediatrician-psychiatrist, are from unhappy and/or legally broken homes.[63] School children who tend to have accidents more than others are found to have emotional problems, and to have parents who are anxious, insecure, and nonassertive.[64] The research findings of Nye and of Landis lead both researchers to conclude that the experience of living in an unhappy home is just as traumatic for children as that of living in a divorced home.[65]

The tragic by-products of broken homes and divorce is an incalculable loss to our state . . ., it being estimated that 75 per cent of the young people in juvenile halls are the products of broken homes; over half of the inmates of our prisons have similar backgrounds. . . .[66]

Lee Kamier suggests that the three major causes of delinquency are (1) pathological brain structure; (2) social dislocation; and (3) pathological relationships within the family unit.[67] The U.S. Attorney General estimates that delinquency costs taxpayers more than $20 billion annually, and concludes that "the best guarantee against delinquency is kindly but firm parents who get along with each other and with their sons and daughters."[68]

Some time ago Taylor reported the opinions of high school students that "the first duty of parents to their children is to live happily themselves."[69] Since then, Taylor has gone even further in this connection:

The emotional tone of the husband-wife relationship is the climate in which the child thrives or starves. Therefore husband and wife should continue to cherish and cultivate their own love relationship, both as the best source of fulfilling their primary need for love, and, equally important, as the essential strand determining the quality of all other family ties.[70]

Dr. J. Louise Despert, a leading child psychiatrist, sums it up in this manner:

It is not divorce, but the emotional situation in the home, with or without divorce, that is the determining factor in a child's adjustment. A child is very disturbed when the relationship between parents is very disturbed.[71]

If the husband-wife relationship is poor, it serves as a block to all other relationships. Differences of opinion between the parents need not destroy the sense of security in a home, especially if the mates are able to discuss them. As Terman has concluded: "It seems clear that the first and probably the most important advantage that can be given to children is a background of happily married parents."[72] When the marriage is secure, parents need have little concern about the particular type of family pattern established or the type of child-training practiced. A happy marriage will almost always create the attitudinal climate most appropriate for the development of healthy personalities within children.

Summary

There are many benefits in parenthood. These include the emotional satisfactions that evolve from the expectation of linear descendents, the feeling of being needed, and companionship. Parenthood fulfills the need for fresh experiences, and usually gives greater purpose to the adult's life, but it is not without its obligations, and problems. The coming of a child into a home means sudden changes of routine; sometimes marital discord arises when parents do not agree on how to rear their offspring. Parenthood brings new responsibilities for both husband and wife.

Some parents become increasingly confused about how to rear children, because of the many conflicts between theories. Also, the priority level of these theories appears to change every few years. At one time, ours was an adult-centered society; now it appears to be too much of a child-centered world. The three basic approaches to family life are strict authoritarian rule, *laissez-faire* (or complete child freedom), and the democratic approach—the middle way of moderation which includes participation by all family members and freedom commensurate with the child's sense of responsibility.

Although much is yet to be learned about many phases of child development, several basic principles have been established. Each child has an "internal push" toward normal development, so if parents will only attempt to be as consistent as possible in their treatment of the child, his personality should develop in a well-adjusted fashion.

If their basic emotional needs are fulfilled by their parents, children usually develop their full potential as human beings.

Some parents know how to do a better job than they are actually doing, but certain obstacles appear to prevent their doing better, such as too high a set of standards, personality problems, and (especially) marital conflict. If parents can learn to be happy with each other, their children will undoubtedly be happier with the world in general and thus more easily achieve their full potential in life.

Notes

1. Evelyn M. Duvall, "Growing Edges in Family Life Education," *Marriage and Family Living,* 6:22.

2. Judson T. and Mary G. Landis, *Building a Successful Marriage* (Englewood Cliffs, N.J.: Prentice-Hall, Inc., 1963), p. 590.

3. *Ibid.*

4. Ruth Linquist, *The Family in the Present Social Order* (Chapel Hill, N.C.: University of North Carolina Press, 1931), p. 35.

5. Mirra Komarovsky, *Women in the Modern World* (Boston: Little, Brown & Co., 1953), p. 107. A Michigan State University study found that a statistically significant percentage of mothers of young children felt more tired than mothers of older children. See Elizabeth Wiegand and Irma H. Gross, *Fatigue of Homemakers with Young Children,* Agricultural Experiment Station Technical Bulletin No. 265 (March 1958), Michigan State University, East Lansing, Mich.

6. John Levy and Ruth Munroe, *The Happy Family* (New York: Alfred A. Knopf, Inc., 1938), p. 243.

7. W. Allison Davis, "Child-Rearing in the Class Structure of American Society," in *The Family in a Democratic Society,* Anniversary Papers of The Community Service Society of New York (New York: Columbia University Press, 1949).

8. Landis and Landis, *op. cit.,* pp. 590–92.

9. Rose Bernstein and Florence E. Cyr, "A Study of Interviews with Husbands in a Prenatal and Child-Health Program," in Ruth S. Cavan (ed.), *Marriage and Family in the Modern World* (New York: Thomas Y. Crowell Company, 1960), p. 507.

10. *Today's Child* (October 1961), 5.

11. F. Ivan Nye, "Some Family Attitudes and Psychosomatic Illness in Adolescents," *The Family Life Coordinator,* **6**:26–30.

12. Bernstein and Cyr, *op. cit.,* p. 510.

13. Quoting Dr. J. G. Howells of England in *Today's Child* (October 1962), 4.

14. Della Cyrus, "What's Wrong with the Family?" *Atlantic Monthly,* **178**:67–73.

15. Jessie Bernard, *American Family Behavior* (New York: Harper & Row, Publishers, 1942), p. 312.

16. It needs to be noted that this is changing in recent child-development studies; see, e.g., Robert R. Sears, Eleanor E. Maccoby, and Harry Levin, *Patterns of Child-Rearing* (Evanston, Ill.: Row, Peterson & Company, 1957).

17. James H. S. Bossard, "The Law of Family Interaction," *American Journal of Sociology,* **50**:292–94.

18. Celia Stendler, "Sixty Years of Child-Training Practices," *Journal of Pediatrics,* **36**:122–34.

19. Willystine Goodsell, *A History of Marriage and the Family* (New York: The Macmillan Company, 1934), p. 367.

20. Alice M. Earle, *Child Life in Colonial Days* (New York: The Macmillan Company, 1892), p. 197.

21. John Winthrop, *The History of New England from 1630 to 1649* (Boston: Little, Brown & Co., 1853), Vol. II, p. 411.

22. John B. Watson, *Psychological Care of Infant and Child* (New York: W. W. Norton & Company, Inc., 1928), pp. 81–82.

23. Clark E. Vincent, "Trends in Infant-Care Ideas," *Child Development,* **22**:199–209.

24. Marvin B. Sussman, *Sourcebook in Marriage and the Family* (Boston: Houghton Mifflin Company, 1955), p. 167.

25. J. M. Mogey, "A Century of Declining Paternal Authority," *Marriage and Family Living,* **19**:234–39.

26. Natalie to Kitty, in Tolstoy's *Anna Karenia,* as quoted in *Marriage and Family Living,* **21**:69.

27. Helen Witmer, "The Influence of Parental Attitudes on the Social Adjustment of the Individual," *American Sociological Review,* **2**:763.

28. *The New York Times,* March 7, 1932, p. 15, as quoted in Joseph Kirk Folsom, *The Family and Democratic Society* (New York: John Wiley & Sons, Inc., 1943), p. 357.

29. See Harold Orlansky, "Infant Care and Personality," *Psychological Bulletin,* **46**:1–48; and Alfred Lindesmith and Anselm Strauss, "Critique of Culture-Personality Writing," *American Sociological Review,* **15**:587–600.

30. Harry F. Harlow, "Current and Future Advances in Physiological and Comparative Psychology," *American Psychologist,* **11**:274.

31. Quoting Dr. Maurice Linden, Director of the Philadelphia Department of Health, Division of Mental Health, in *Today's Child* (October 1963), 1.

32. Lewis M. Terman, *Psychological Factors in Marital Happiness* (New York: McGraw-Hill Book Company, Inc., 1938), pp. 228–31.

33. G. Pearson, "Some Factors in the Formation of Personality," *American Journal of Orthopsychiatry*, 1:291.

34. Gertrude K. Pollak, "Some Principles of Positive Parent-Child Relationships," in Cavan, *op. cit.*, p. 494.

35. *Ibid.*

36. Alton L. Blakeslee, "Today's Health News," *Today's Health* (November 1960), 9.

37. Don C. Carter, "The Influence of Family Relations and Family Experiences on Personality," *Marriage and Family Living*, 16:212–15.

38. James H. S. Bossard and Eleanor S. Boll, *Ritual in Family Living* (Philadelphia: University of Pennsylvania Press, 1950), p. 201.

39. William H. Sewell, "Infant Training and the Personality of the Child," *American Journal of Sociology*, 58:150–59.

40. Irving Stout and Grace Langdon, "A Study of the Home Life of Well-Adjusted Children," *The Journal of Educational Sociology*, 23:442–60.

41. See Rene A. Spitz, "Hospitalism—An Inquiry into the Genesis of Psychiatric Conditions in Early Childhood," in *The Psychoanalytic Study of the Child*, I (New York: International Universities Press, 1945); or Rene A. Spitz, "The Role of Ecological Factors in Emotional Development in Infancy," *Child Development*, 20:147–51.

42. Abram Kardiner, *The Psychological Frontiers of Society* (New York: Columbia University Press, 1945).

43. Pollak, *op. cit.*, 493.

44. *Ibid.*, p. 493.

45. *Ibid.*, p. 494.

46. Christine Beasley, "How Can the Family Breed Democracy?" *Marriage and Family Living*, 15:201–207.

47. James H. S. Bossard, Eleanor S. Boll, and Winogene Sanger, "Some Neglected Areas in Family Life Study," *Annals of the American Academy of Political and Social Science*, 272:68–76.

48. Christine Beasley, *Democracy in the Home* (New York: Association Press, 1954), p. 76.

49. Alma H. Jones, "How to Hold a Family Council," in Cavan, *op. cit.*, 523–25.

50. Dorothy Baruch, *One Little Boy* (New York: The Julian Press, Inc., 1952), Jacket p. i.

51. Albert I. Rabin, "Kibbutz Children—Research Findings to Date," *Children* (September–October 1958), 179–85.

52. Walter Stokes, *Modern Pattern for Marriage* (New York: Holt, Rinehart & Winston, Inc., 1948).

53. *Today's Child* (May 1960), 6.

54. See, e.g., Norman Young and E. L. Gaier, "Implications in Emotionally Caused Reading Retardation," *Elementary English*, 28:271–75; Norman Chansky, "Reading Retardation Redefined and Reconceptualized," *Progressive Education* (September 1955), 134–38; or Elliott McCleary, "Rescuing the 'Child Failures,'" *Today's Health* (October 1960), 48–50, 71–75.

55. Earl H. Hanson (Superintendent of Schools, Rock Island, Ill., and participant in the James B. Conant Conference on Reading), "There's No Magic Formula for Learning to Read," *Parents' Magazine* (February 1963), 133.

56. Benjamin Karpman (ed.), *Symposia on Child and Juvenile Delinquency* (Washington, D.C.: Archives of Criminal Psychodynamics, Psychodynamics Monograph Series, 1959).

57. See, e.g., Anthony Weaver, *They Steal for Love* (New York: International Universities Press, 1959); Herbert A. Bloch and Frank T. Flynn, *Delinquency* (New York: Random House, 1956); or Sheldon and Eleanor Glueck, *Predicting Delinquency and Crime* (Cambridge, Mass.: Harvard University Press, 1959).

58. C. E. Birney, "Supervision of Children in Divorce Cases," *Journal of the Bar Association of Kansas* (November 1958), 177–85.

59. *Ibid.*

60. Richard E. Thompson, "Further Validation of the Glueck Social Prediction Table for Identifying Potential Delinquents," *Journal of Criminal Law, Criminology and Police Science* (July–August 1957), 175–84.

61. F. Ivan Nye, *Family Relationships and Delinquent Behavior* (New York: John Wiley & Sons, Inc., 1958).

62. L. Madow and S. E. Hardy, "Incidence and Analysis of the Broken Family in the Background of Neurosis," *American Journal of Orthopyschiatry* (July 1947), 523.

63. *Today's Child* (May 1961), 8.

64. Irwin Marcus, *et al., An Interdisciplinary Approach to Accident Patterns in Children,* Society for Research in Child Development, Monograph No. 76, Vol. 25, No. 2 (1960), 53–54.

65. F. Ivan Nye, "Child Adjustment in Broken and in Unhappy Unbroken Homes," *Marriage and Family Living,* **19:**358; and Judson T. Landis, "A Comparison of Children from Divorced and Nondivorced Unhappy Marriages," *The Family Life Coordinator,* 11:61–65.

66. Bethune Jones, *From the State Capitals* (June 1, 1963), quoting Assemblyman Don Mulford of Alameda County, Calif.

67. Karpman, *op. cit.*

68. Kenyon Scudden and Kenneth Beam, *The Twenty Billion Dollar Challenge* (New York: G. P. Putnam's Sons, 1961), p. 36.

69. Katherine Whiteside Taylor, *Do Adolescents Need Parents?* (New York: Appleton-Century-Crofts, Inc., 1937), p. 53.

70. Katherine Whiteside Taylor, "The Opportunities of Parenthood," in Howard Becker and Reuben Hill (eds.), *Family, Marriage and Parenthood* (Boston: D. C. Heath and Company, 1955), p. 461.

71. J. Louise Despert, *Children of Divorce* (Garden City, N.Y.: Doubleday & Company, Inc., 1953), p. 10.

72. Terman, *op. cit.,* pp. 142–66.

Questions for further thought

1. Why should the proper rearing of children be so important and unique an undertaking in a democracy?
2. How can one be sure that he is qualified for parenthood?
3. How is it possible for mates to take the job of rearing children too seriously?
4. Does happiness in marriage tend to fade after the coming of children?
5. One hears much about differences in child-rearing practices among the various social classes. What similarities are also in existence?
6. How can children in the same family vary so much in interests, attitudes, and even in moral behavior?
7. How far should parents allow the teen-age peer norm to influence their control over desired standards for their children?
8. What are the dangers of attempting to sponsor, in the home, a type of discipline in which one does not sincerely believe?

9. Should parents continue to show affection toward their children by such signs as kissing, for example, when the children grow older?
10. What are some of the most serious mistakes that parents can make in child-rearing?
11. Are there any topics which children should not discuss with their parents?

Recommended films

Roots of Happiness (International Film Bureau).
Communication and Interaction in Three Families (Kinesis).
Meeting Emotional Needs in Childhood (New York University Film Library).
The Family Council (University of Michigan Television Center).
Sharing Family Duties (University of Michigan Television Center).

Suggested supplemental readings

BOOKS

Atkinson, Butler. *What Dr. Spock Didn't Tell Us.* New York: Simon and Schuster, Inc., 1960.
Baruch, Dorothy. *New Ways in Discipline.* New York: Whittlesey House, 1949.
Caplan, Gerald (ed.). *Prevention of Mental Disorders in Children.* New York: Basic Books, Inc., 1961.
Cavan, Ruth S. (ed.), *Marriage and Family in the Modern World.* New York: Thomas Y. Crowell Company, 1960. Chaps. 22, 23.
Daniel, James P. *Child of Fury.* New York: Exposition Press, 1961.
English, O. Spurgeon, and Constance Foster. *Fathers Are Parents Too.* New York: G. P. Putnam's Sons, 1951.
Erikson, Erik H. (ed.). *The Challenge of Youth.* Garden City, N.Y.: Doubleday & Company, Inc., 1965.
Gallagher, J. Roswell, and Herbert I. Harris. *Emotional Problems of Adolescents.* New York: Oxford University Press, Inc., 1958.
Gilbreth, Frank B., Jr., *How To Be a Father.* New York: Thomas Y. Crowell Company, 1958.
Glidewell, John C., (ed.). *Parental Attitudes and Child Behavior.* Springfield, Ill.: Charles C Thomas, Publishers, 1961.
Glueck, Sheldon and Eleanor. *Family Environment and Delinquency.* Boston: Houghton Mifflin Company, 1962.
Grams, Armin. *Children and Their Parents.* Minneapolis: T. S. Denison & Co., Inc., 1964.
Gruenberg, Sidonie M. (ed.). *The Encyclopedia of Child Care and Guidance,* rev. ed. Garden City, N.Y.: Doubleday & Company, Inc., 1963.
Jackson, Shirley. *Live Among the Savages.* New York: Farrar, Strauss & Company, 1953.
Jones, Eve. *Natural Child-Rearing.* New York: The Free Press of Glencoe, Inc., 1959.
Kawin, Ethel. *Basic Concepts for Parents,* 2nd ed. New York: The Macmillan Company, 1963.
———. *Early Middle Childhood,* 2nd ed. New York: The Macmillan Company, 1963.
———. *Later Childhood and Adolescence,* 2nd ed. New York: The Macmillan Company, 1963.
Langdon, Grace, and Irving W. Stout. *Bringing Up Children.* New York: The John Day Company, Inc., 1960.

Lappin, Ben. *The Redeemed Children*. Toronto: University of Toronto Press, 1963.

Miller, Daniel R., and Guy E. Swanson. *The Changing American Parent*. New York: John Wiley & Sons, Inc., 1958.

Minturn, Leigh, and William W. Lambert. *Mothers of Six Cultures: Antecedents of Childrearing*. New York: John Wiley & Sons, Inc., 1964.

Neill, A. S. *Summerhill: A Radical Approach to Child-Rearing*. New York: Hart Publishing Company, 1961.

Nye, F. Ivan. *Family Relationships and Delinquent Behavior*. New York: John Wiley & Sons, Inc., 1958.

Roucek, Joseph S. (ed.). *The Difficult Child*. New York: Philosophical Library, 1964.

Schramm, Wilbur, Jack Lyle, and Edwin B. Parker. *Television in the Lives of Our Children*. Stanford, Calif.: Stanford University Press, 1961.

Whiting, Beatrice B. (ed.), *Six Cultures: Studies of Child Rearing*. New York: John Wiley & Sons, Inc., 1963.

ARTICLES

Blood, Robert O. "Consequences of Permissiveness for Parents of Young Children," *Marriage and Family Living*, 15:209–12.

Brim, Oriville G., Jr. "Changes and Trends in Child-Rearing Advice," *Child Study*, 36:23–27.

Christoph, Father Van F. "The Changing Role of the Father," *The Family Life Coordinator*, 5:24–28.

Clifford, Edward. "Discipline in the Home: A Controlled Observational Study of Parental Practices," *The Journal of Genetic Psychology*, 95:45–82.

Despert, J. Louise. "Child of Emotional Divorce," *The New York Times Magazine*, November 27, 1960, p. 102.

Dreikurs, Rudulf. "Raising Children in a Democracy," *The Humanist*, 18:77–83.

Gitlin, Irving. "Television and Children—A Look at the Research," *Child Study*, 37:33–36.

Kohn, Melvin L. "Social Class and Parental Values," *The American Journal of Sociology*, 44:337–51.

———. "Social Class and the Exercise of Parental Authority," *American Sociological Review*, 24:352–66.

Maccoby, E. E., and P. K. Gibbs. "Social-Class Differences in Child-Rearing," *American Psychologist*, 8:395.

McKinney, Mrs. F. "A Parent Protests Against the Experts," *Journal of Social Hygiene*, 39:386–89.

Monahan, Thomas P. "Family Status and the Delinquent Child: A Reappraisal of Some New Findings," *Social Forces*, 35:250–58.

Nye, F. Ivan. "The Rejected Parent and Delinquency," *Marriage and Family Living*, 18:291–99.

Porter, Blaine M. "The Relationship Between Marital Adjustment and Parental Acceptance of Children," *Journal of Home Economics*, 47:157–64.

Schindler, John A., M.D. "Family Relations: Greatest Cause of Illness," *The Progressive*, 28:9–13.

Smith, Philip M. "Broken Homes and Juvenile Delinquency," *Sociology and Social Research*, 39:307–11.

Taylor, Harold. "The Understood Child," *Saturday Review* (May 20, 1961), 47–49, 66.

Taylor, Katherine W. "Cooperative Nursery Schools, *Marriage and Family Living,* 17:302.

Templeton, Joe A. "The Influence of Family Size on Some Aspects of Teenagers' Attitudes, Perceptions, and Behavior of Home Life," *The Family Life Coordinator* (July 1962), 51–57.

White, Martha Sturn. "Social Class, Child-Rearing Practices, and Child Behavior," *American Sociological Review,* 22:704–12.

Facing crises

Any situation that appears to be insurmountable can be regarded as a crisis. Sooner or later every marriage faces such a situation.

Operational definition of a crisis

A crisis may be operationally defined as an unexpected or undesired turn of events in which the persons most involved feel either extremely hard-pressed or incapable of solving the problems alone. Old patterns of behavior cease to be rewarding and new ones are needed immediately. The seriousness of any crisis is a relative matter. Some events are intrinsically more hazardous than others; however, there are events that constitute a crisis only for certain individuals. In other words, the seriousness of a crisis depends upon the number of solutions possible for the persons involved.

PERSONAL RESOURCES. The individual who has inner resources at his command is less likely to encounter serious crisis situations. Because the seriousness of any situation depends somewhat upon the person's ability to adapt to quick change, flexible habits and an elastic daily routine will help the individual to adjust to difficult events.

FAMILY-PATTERN VARIATIONS. The elements that lead to a crisis seem strongly influenced by family patterns. The same event that might be regarded as a tragedy by one family might be considered trivial by another. This difference appears to be related to the cultural and social heritage of a family. Koos reported that middle-class families have a greater sensitivity to crisis than do lower- or upper-class families. More things seem to disturb middle-class families and they react more strongly to crises than do lower-class families. Middle-class families recover their earlier interaction pattern more readily, however, and are more likely than lower-class families to emerge with some positive benefit from a crisis. A crisis situation seldom appears to strengthen lower-class persons, probably because they have been poorly prepared both personally and collectively.[1]

OUTSIDE AID. Throughout history, certain sets of circumstances have seemed to lead to crisis situations. These patterns have been observed and noted for centuries, but it is only recently that governments and social groups have established agencies, staffed by specialists, to help individuals and families faced with crises they are unable to resolve. Not all people, however, readily accept outside aid. Some people feel it an added weakness to ask help; others may be afraid to admit failure. Furthermore, some people do not accept professional help as readily as they do that offered by questionable sources. Koos reported that the lower classes ordinarily seek more outside help in a crisis than do the middle classes, but that the sources are not the best available: "Most are non-professional, many are truly commercial, some are downright unethical."[2]

PRESCRIBED RITUALS. Many crisis situations have behavior precedents that are commonly known to everyone; others have none. Prescribed procedures not only make many crises easier to bear, but the ritual makes it much easier for the individual thereafter to readjust to life. Eliot states:

> When a crisis is one of a kind for which there is ample precedent in the social heritage of the group, the group culture usually includes a special set of morals, rituals, and attitudes which are supposed to deal with such crises satisfactorily if gone through by those most concerned.[3]

Temporary separation

One situation that often develops into a serious crisis, for young couples especially, is separation. Usually the separation is involuntary, such as that brought about by war. With husbands and fathers away for months or years, family morale is lowered; established values are questioned, and sexual morality is weakened. Death, disability, hunger, and loneliness are the dominant and damaging forces that influence personal behavior.

DIFFICULTY OF REUNIONS. The real crisis brought about by temporary separation ordinarily comes during the reunions that follow, rather than during the separation itself. While separated, each partner tends to build up an idealized picture of the other and of their relationship. While separated, couples also invariably grow apart, for instead of thinking as a pair they have been thinking and acting as two independent and isolated individuals. Separation makes it easier to forget the spouse's annoying habits and mannerisms, which then seem the more pronounced after reunion.

War is not the only cause of involuntary separation: illness may compel hospitalization for a period; many jobs require travel away from home occasionally. The U.S. Bureau of the Census reports that at least 800,000 husbands are temporarily away from home for reasons other than military service or desertion.[4]

IMPORTANCE OF COMMUNICATION. To guard against the possibility that a reunion will develop into a crisis, it is necessary for mates to make full use of communication media while separated. Each should keep the other posted not only on personal happenings but also on his reactions to general events. It is not enough to write letters about the day's events or occasionally to telephone; everything that might contribute toward a common meeting ground should be shared. This includes discussions of work, the children, the neighbors, plays or movies seen, books read, and the loneliness each feels for the other. This sharing also includes making decisions jointly, even though this might take more time, and the free exchange of new ideas and values, especially when these may conflict with former ideals and goals. Although it is not easy, marital adjustment must continue even when husband and wife are apart. In fact, spouses who pretend not to be disturbed by separation will probably have a more difficult time when reunited than those who honestly face up to the facts and continue to communicate in spite of the emotional hardship.

Offspring with differences

The arrival of a physically or mentally abnormal child usually constitutes a family crisis. It was estimated in 1960 that there were about 5 million children and adults in the American society who were mentally retarded.[5]

FAMILY REACTIONS. The usual first reaction of parents is to disbelieve the diagnosis. Some parents totally reject the facts of the child's true condition and continue to search for help far beyond reason. Sometimes this compulsive search turns into an aimless wandering from one specialist or clinic to another.

There is a subtle dividing line between a rational quest for help and pointless wandering. The necessity of deciding when to stop puts a severe strain on the emotional balance of any parents faced with this situation. The capacity to maintain psychic equilibrium is severely tested, and functions as well as relationships within the family are subjected to great strain.

DISAPPOINTMENT. Many parents are disappointed in themselves when deviations appear in their children. They feel a sense of loss, a sense of inadequacy, and a sense of failure.

FEAR OF COMMUNITY REACTIONS. Some parents are afraid of being ridiculed or rejected by the community should they decide to keep such a child at home. Others fear they will be criticized should they decide to send the child away.

Parental fears of social reaction are not entirely unfounded. It is only in modern times that society in general has developed compassion for defective children. The early Spartans, for example, took such children to the mountains and left them there to die.

Even today, when the child's handicap is severe, parents are justified in questioning his ability to adjust to the community. The possibility of maintaining the child within a protective institution should not be dismissed. This problem should be decided in consultation with competent social workers who have special skills in this field. They are well qualified, by training and experience, to guide parents toward a proper decision.

Childlessness

Another situation considered a crisis by some couples is their inability to have a child. This may be caused by low fertility rather than absolute sterility. Such couples may be able to conceive a child with medical assistance.

ARTIFICIAL INSEMINATION. When it is the husband who has a low fertility level, artificial insemination can sometimes be successfully employed. This procedure may also be effective in cases where conception has not occurred because of a physical defect in the wife that inhibits the natural union of sperm and ova. It is estimated that between 1000 and 1200 of the new born each year in the United States were conceived by artificial insemination.[6]

One research study reported that, among college youths, there was a much greater acceptance of the idea of using artificial insemination if the husband were the donor than if the donor were unknown. Still, artificial insemination does not seem to meet with much acceptance by society as a whole.[7]

ALTERNATIVES. In some cultures, when the husband is sterile, there is a sanctioned period during which the wife's mating with others is more or less taken for granted in order that the marriage not remain childless. Such episodes appear to be accepted as part of the annual ceremony called the *Karneval* in the Rhineland near the Bavarian region. It is reported that the spouse who would attempt to sue the mate because of infidelity during the Bavarian Karneval time would be laughed out of court.[8]

Adoption

For the couple who want a family, the most usual alternative to involuntary childlessness is adoption. Adoption is nothing new; reference to it is found in the Bible. Moses, for example, was adopted by Pharaoh's daughter. Adoption, however, has become much more common a practice only in recent years. (Fink gives the New York Children's Aid Society credit for being the first social adoption agency in the United States.[9]) In earlier times, there were many more orphans than eager adoptive parents. There were not even enough orphanages to care for all the parentless children, who were simply herded together into one place where they received a minimum of care until they were old enough to be released. Adoption was very rare and was considered an act of philanthropy. Little good was expected of adopted children, and they were generally regarded as hired help rather than as family members and legitimate heirs. Today, however, adoption is no longer considered an act of charity; instead, it is deemed a privilege both for the parents and for the child. Adoption is now so approved a method of acquiring children that there is great demand for such babies in America today. Vincent reports that, in California, the adoption rate between World War II and 1957 increased almost 600 per cent.[10] The number of adoption petitions filed in 1958 was close to 100,000, or practically double that of fifteen years before.[11] The number of children who were adopted in 1961 represented a 6 per cent increase over those adopted in 1960. Still, agencies in some sections of the United States are presently reporting a decline in adoption applications. It is believed that recent developments in methods of treatment for infertility have given new hope to some couples. Thus, some are not as eager to adopt children today as they might have been just a few years ago.[12]

A question frequently asked is: What is the source of the "baby supply?" Unwed mothers supply at least half of the adopted children[13]; the rest come from remarriages (where the second husband adopts the first husband's children); from relatives; and from dependent and/or neglected children of parents who perhaps are on relief.[14]

THE USUAL ADOPTION PROCEDURE. In the usual adoption procedure, the agency first collects all available facts about the child's background. These facts are usually not revealed to the prospective parents; nor is the identity of the new parents revealed to the natural parents. When the background facts are collected, a matching process begins. This process of matching prospective parents and children is so carefully conducted by some modern adoption agencies that often the child will physically resemble one of the new parents. Not only is the child carefully selected but the prospective home and parents are screened as well. The parents' social and economic position and potential—as well as their race, religion, intelligence, nationality, and moral and cultural background—are thoroughly investigated. A steady income and a demonstrated ability in managing money are prerequisites for adoption. Health is also considered: people who are relatively healthy have a better chance of adopting children than those who have chronic ailments. Age is also important:

couples who may be considering adoption should not hesitate too long before deciding one way or the other, for unless there is a surplus of available children in a region it is seldom possible for couples over forty years old to adopt children.

THE WAITING PERIOD. There is almost always a waiting period for the couple between filing an application and receiving word about the possibility of their adopting a child. The waiting period may often depend upon the child's age requested by the applicants. There are usually more older children than young babies readily available for adoption. If the couple insist on an infant, their waiting period will probably be much longer. There are certain advantages, however, to adopting an older child. For one thing, the child's intelligence and personality traits are evident, whereas the infant's are unknown. Then, too, a beautiful baby may not necessarily grow into a good-looking child. If physical appearance is important to the couple, they should select a child more or less well developed. Then, too, a health history is available for the older child but not for the infant.

The waiting period should be considered an opportunity rather than a burden. It may be likened to the period of pregnancy, providing the couple an opportunity to learn all they can about the habits and growth patterns of children as well as their physical care, modern training methods, and health standards.

A PROBATIONARY PERIOD. Ordinarily, there is a probationary period before an adoption becomes final. The couple are allowed to take the baby for a few months or a year, to see whether they really want the child. It speaks well for the matching procedures of the agencies that few babies are ever returned.

EXAMINE MOTIVES. Before placing an application for adoption the couple should examine their motives thoroughly.

SELF-INVENTORY FOR PROSPECTIVE CHILD ADOPTERS

Is our desire to adopt a child but an impulse, or is it rooted in earnest purpose? Will the result be mere ego-satisfaction or continuous purposeful investment? Do we have a genuine interest in children and youth as humanity's richest heritage? Is our love for each other so sure that a child will bind us even closer without jealousy? Are we willing to undertake twenty years or more of responsibility with many of our former interests displaced by or tributary to the child's welfare? For better or for worse—since adoptions, like other family relationships, carry no guarantee of perfection—will we stand by our adopted child in all circumstances as though he had been our physical offspring? Have we the ability to love the child for himself, whatever his background; to guard ourselves resolutely against the project of our ambition on to him; and to guide rather than to mold him—thus encouraging his growth power? Can we grow with him, and share our best with him, without expecting gratitude? Are we developing tolerance, habitual patience, emotional maturity, and the mental flexibility that insures against rut-bound middle age? When our adopted child grows beyond the early need for dependence, will we be ready to let him go, confident that our family life has given him the security indispensable to independence?[15]

BEWARE OF BLACK AND GRAY MARKETS.   Some people wish to bypass the long wait entailed in legal adoption procedures. They want a child when they want him. Needless to say, there are enterprising and unscrupulous persons who, for a price, will cater to such a demand. The temptation to patronize some of these sources is very great, especially for those who grow impatient with the prolonged processing of recognized agencies. Babies "found" through a friend or a well-meaning doctor, however, may involve great risk. For instance, the child may be unhealthy or defective. (No known defective child is ever offered for adoption by a recognized social agency without the prospective couple's being told the full details.) There are, of course, some couples who seek to adopt handicapped children; often they believe that such children would otherwise receive little love and personal care from the world. They assess the child's needs as greater than most, and are willing to provide the extra love and attention necessary.

No matter what their preference in children, however, couples seeking adoption should use only the services of agencies set up legally under the auspices of public, private, social, sectarian, or religious welfare organizations and granted an operating license by the state department of social welfare. A new law in Kentucky makes it possible both to levy a fine on and imprison anyone adopting a child through gray or black markets.[16] Perhaps more states will soon see the wisdom of passing similar laws. Ernest Miller, an adoption specialist and former Assistant District Attorney for the State of New York, states that there is a tremendous illicit traffic in babies, bringing prices as high as $6000 or $7000 a child. Much of this fraud is under international operation; frequently couples who pay the money never even get the child.[17] America averages 2500 legal foreign adoptions per year.[18]

RESTRICTIVE POLICIES.   Many legitimate agencies, because of their very purpose, have policies that prevent the accommodation of every prospective couple. For example, a non-Catholic couple should not seek a child through a Catholic adoption agency, for the Catholic Church does not permit children born of Catholic parents to be placed in non-Catholic homes. Many other religious agencies have similar restrictions. As a general rule, couples who are considering adoption should inquire first at their state department of social welfare or at their local council of social agencies. They will then learn the sources available to them and whether there are any particular restrictions that might disqualify them completely. If they are unable to find this information by themselves, many physicians, lawyers, and clergymen within the community would be happy to direct them.

WHEN TO TELL THE CHILD.   It is advisable to be honest with the adopted child. He should be told of his adoption while he is still young, but the parents should not continually stress the fact. They should state matter-of-factly that he was adopted and let it go at that. They need not go into a long story about how he was chosen (although at one time this approach was considered helpful). Adoptions are relatively common today, so it would be inappropriate to overdramatize the event to the child.

SOME CANNOT ADOPT.   Some people do not believe in adopting children. Frequently such people rationalize their attitudes on a religious basis, saying in effect that if God had intended for them to be parents he would have made it biologically possible. Some sincerely believe in a divine plan, so adoption is genuinely out of the question for them. Of course, some couples may use this story only as a social convenience, and may actually be quite content with their childless marriage.

Those who dearly love children but are unable to meet the required standards might go into community or church work and make a most valuable contribution to society. In a sense such couples really do become parents—not biologically or legally, but socially. In today's society there is a great need for such couples as leaders for all kinds of youth group organizations. Indeed, many couples find that such work is a fruitful substitute for children of their own.

Illness

More than 60,000 people are admitted into hospitals every day. In fact, over a twelve-month period, more than 0.5 million families are hit with medical expenses that equal or exceed their annual incomes.[19] Ill health can bring almost any family to despair and bankruptcy. Rusk reports that chronic illness is almost always fraught with both emotional and financial stresses.[20] It not only decreases social life, it also increases home-management costs. It makes planning for the future almost impossible and it changes the patterns of recreation and child care. As the patient's ability to function decreases, his interests diminish. In contrast, the duties of the spouse increase and he becomes overburdened. The healthy spouse often must learn many new skills for survival under these conditions.

TYPES OF ILLNESS.   There are various types of disability and illness not only chronic, but acute (such as automobile or industrial accidents), that might permanently injure a person. Unpredictable mental disorders may suddenly develop from the stresses and strains of family life or from the pressures of war, ill health, or financial difficulties. These are crises that may arise in any family.

Alcoholism is another type of illness that can affect family life. Many out-patient clinics are now trying to help the wives of alcoholic husbands to re-evaluate their own roles in this particular situation. The husband's recovery may present a real challenge to the wife. Kalashian states that "work with the wife is considered very important for the progress of the alcoholic married man."[21] Alcoholics are no longer limited to bleary-eyed old men on Skid Row. Today, thousands of people, both men and women, are addicted. The use of alcohol as a method of coping with life's problems is widespread in the American culture. The stresses imposed by its misuse have focused increasing attention on ways of dealing with the problem. New studies are constantly being undertaken to find out more about alcohol addiction. Many of these studies are in the psychosocial area as well as in the fields of physiology and biochemistry. The findings from some of these studies strongly suggest that the alcoholic individual has experienced a variety of frustrations prior to becoming addicted. The case histories of most alcoholics may include neurological disorders and a high degree of conflict within their family life.[22]

IMPORTANCE OF HEALTH AND HOSPITAL INSURANCE. Today's American family cannot afford to be without some type of health and hospitalization insurance. Such insurance can help to ease the increased financial burden brought on by a prolonged or serious illness. Even when families never collect a penny from the policy, they should consider the premium money well spent. There is a special kind of personal security in the knowledge that one has adequate health insurance.

AGENCY SERVICES. Today there are many more agency services available to help with family rehabilitation problems following accidents and prolonged or acute illness. Many communities now sponsor mental-health clinics or family-service associations. When there is doubt as to where to turn for help, inquiries may be made through the clergy, the local council of social agencies, or through the state board of health. No family today need stand completely alone in time of serious illness. But it is important to make use of the sources of help available and to cooperate with the trained specialists provided. Society today realizes the importance of keeping each person as healthy and as useful a citizen as possible.

Sexual infidelity

Some marriages experience a serious crisis when there is sexual infidelity; in others it apparently does not cause nearly as much alarm. It is difficult to determine whether there is actually more or less infidelity today as compared with former times. It seems clear, however, that if there is as much it may not be as disturbing anymore. Jacobson points out that adultery was the second leading cause for divorce in the United States about a hundred years ago, accounting for over 25 per cent of all divorces. This figure reduced to around 11 per cent after World War I, and now stands at less than 3 per cent of divorce grounds.[23] According to Kinsey, infidelity is much more common for lower-class men in the early years of marriage and does not necessarily develop into a crisis as often, wives in the lower class apparently being more accepting of such behavior than husbands.[24] Whyte's studies support this contention: ". . . the wife is expected to be completely faithful, and even the slightest flirtations are seriously regarded, . . . [but] the field of sexual adventure is not barred to him. . . ."[25]

Some readers may well wonder at this apparent sharp demarcation of acceptable behavior between the sexes in the lower classes. Perhaps Rodman explains it best:

> Members of the lower class face many deprivations which often make it impossible for them to live up to the middle-class values, so that a lesser degree of achievement also becomes desirable. They do not abandon the conventional values; rather, they lower their degree of commitment to these values. At the same time they develop alternative values that are more in keeping with the realities of lower-class life. . . . Words like *promiscuity* . . . are not part of the lower-class vocabulary, and . . . it is inaccurate to describe lower-class behavior in this way. These words have middle-class meanings and imply middle-class judgments, and it is precisely because of this that we ought not to use them to describe lower-class behavior.[26]

There is a common assumption that the upper classes in most cosmopolitan societies accept infidelity on the part of either spouse almost with indifference. Research studies to date, however, do not support this. The assumption has probably come about because, as Folsom explains, in the upper class "a sharp moral line is drawn between complete intercourse and petting, the latter being tolerated in greater degree, . . . even if extramarital."[27] Paul Gebhard, Director of the Institute for Sex Research, reported that among today's middle class there appears to be an increasing amount of petting and flirtation (extramarital), as at cocktail parties, but that it is conducted on a superficial level: if either party should get serious, the other would probably be offended.[28] The exact extent of infidelity in any group is not really known. Dearborn reports that about 20 per cent of married couples who come for counseling report infidelity on the part of one or both partners; usually it is the husband who is accused of unfaithfulness.[29] This does not mean, however, that infidelity occurs in 20 per cent of all marriages.

TYPES OF INFIDELITY. Sexual unfaithfulness may be characterized by frequency: it may have happened only once; it may have happened a long time ago, but has only now been discovered; or it may be chronic. Dearborn suggests that the husband's infidelity can usually be attributed to one of three things: (1) the wife's failure to achieve orgasm has made intercourse with her uninteresting; (2) the husband has an interest in some deviant method of sex expression which the wife is not willing to accept or condone; or (3) the husband has a greater sex capacity than the wife, and rationalizes that it would be unfair to her if he did not fulfill his greater sex need outside the marriage.[30] When wives are unfaithful, Dearborn reports that counseling reveals at least one of the following four conditions: (1) there has been a neglect of her sexual needs on the part of the husband; (2) the husband has proved to be a poor lover; (3) there has been a failure to achieve orgasm, and the husband has not helped her; or (4) there has been a wish for stronger or more aggressive action on the part of the mate, but he has failed to comply.[31]

SUPERFICIAL REASONS. The author doubts that any of these explanations are the underlying causes of infidelity. They appear to be surface phenomena, a part of a *post hoc, ergo propter hoc* fallacy. This is not to deny that several of these conditions may be in operation when there is sexual unfaithfulness. Sexual unfaithfulness, however, is more likely the result of a crisis rather than its initial cause. The "innocent" partner should try to identify the underlying precipitating causes. Sometimes individuals can do this by themselves, but usually professional help is necessary. This is not to suggest that adultery be condoned, but it must be acknowledged that infidelity may be indicative of more serious complications. Seldom is there a genuinely "innocent" partner when there is sexual unfaithfulness.

Change in income level

A sharp change in income level may also constitute a marital crisis. This is not always effected by a decrease in income; sometimes a sudden upturn in economic status may be as disruptive as economic loss or even social disgrace. Ordinarily, however, one thinks of economic disruptions in terms of economic depression. Depressions arise from conditions beyond the control of the individual couple, and thus may cause unmeasurable hardship and grief in family life. Economic change and growth sometimes force people out of work. It is probably safe to say that, with the advent of more automation in the future, many people may be faced with occasional periods of unemployment.

The usual results of depressions are that fathers may have to leave the home to seek work while the children are cared for by more affluent relatives. Standards of living drop and the home becomes disorganized as the struggle for subsistence continues.

Unemployment

Sometimes there is unemployment even without a depression. Each year in this country millions of workers and their families experience, or are threatened by, involuntary unemployment. At present, about 80 per cent of salaried employees retired or approaching retirement are covered by unemployment insurance.[32] For several years now, about 3 per cent of all family supporters have been unemployed at any given time. Unemployment leads to worry, discouragement, and despondency if there has been inadequate preparation for such a contingency.

FAMILY REACTIONS TO UNEMPLOYMENT. When unemployment occurs, it is usual to try to conceal the predicament from the neighbors. The family's first reactions are based on the hope that the situation is only temporary. The husband is inclined to speak of it as "a short vacation" which he deserves anyway. If unemployment continues, the husband then tries to find other work. If he finds none within his own special field, he applies for less-specialized and lower-paid positions. If he is still unsuccessful, he solicits almost any job, including odd jobs at odd moments. Before accepting odd jobs, however, an intermediate step is usually taken: other family members start to look for work.

If none of the family members is successful, the family continues to dip into available resources, such as savings. If their savings are small, they will be consumed in a short time. Credit-buying is attempted and various kinds of loans are then applied for, using as collateral whatever the family may own. Odds and ends may be auctioned, and then more valuable things are sold. Finally, families begin cashing in insurance policies. One outstanding feature of an unemployment crisis is that, for as long as possible, the average family continues to live almost on the same level as before. When all else fails, then they begin to think of cutting expenses. One of the first items sacrificed in the home is the telephone. In fact, telephone companies today feel that one of the best indications of the economic condition of any community is the volume of home telephone service.[33] Families also drop such items as club memberships and subscriptions. They may also move to a less expensive house or go to live with relatives.

If these steps do not lead out of the crisis, then the family applies for relief. This is considered one of the last resorts, and is often regarded as a personal disgrace.

Adaptation to the new level begins only when the unemployed family stops comparing the meager present with the more comfortable past and accepts the lowered status. Then a full round of family activities can begin, although of a different type than formerly.

INCOME REDUCTION. About 80 per cent of American families carry life insurance, with an average of a few thousand dollars per family. Such policies are not enough to maintain an income on the level the family had been accustomed to before the death of the breadwinner. Under these conditions, a young widow may be forced to give up her home and to seek employment. If the wife dies, the young husband may have to pay for a housekeeper as well as for someone to care for the children. These added expenses may sharply reduce his living standard.

PUBLIC ASSISTANCE. Many widows have no alternative but to appeal for public assistance. The Aid to Dependent Children Act provides a permanent public-assistance program for such emergencies. At present, more than 16 million people are receiving public financial assistance. Of these recipients, about 3.5 million are children under eighteen.[34] Public assistance is also provided for various forms of disability; for example, more than 100,000 blind people receive financial aid every year.[35] Another form of public assistance is old-age and survivors' insurance. Federal, state, and local administrations annually pay out almost $16 billion in public assistance.[36] Martz states: "Under the old-age and survivors' insurance program, about nine out of ten persons in the working population today will be eligible to receive benefits when they retire."[37]

VETERANS' BENEFITS. Another form of financial assistance is awarded to veterans. It has always been an American philosophy that the public is obligated to the families of war veterans, especially if the soldier was killed in action. Cumming states: "As early as 1626 the colony of Plymouth, after the war with the Pequot Indians, provided that any soldier disabled in the defense of the colony was to be maintained competently during his life."[38] Some veterans' benefits are available through insurance programs. There are many kinds of such programs, and it is reported that they now cover almost 24 million policies.[39] In addition, the Veterans' Administration has 173 hospitals, ninety-seven out-patient clinics, and seventeen domiciliary homes.[40] It has also provided funds toward the education of millions. Such training has enabled many veterans to improve their skills and to qualify for better occupations. Under Public Law 346, 7.8 million veterans have received free education, and 612,716 disabled veterans pursued further education under Public Law 16.[41]

Veterans' benefits have also included many noncontributary forms of aid, such as compensation for service-connected disabilities as well as pensions for nonservice-connected disabilities where there is a limited income. There are permanent pension plans based on age or disability for veterans of Indian wars, the Civil War, the Spanish-American War, and World War I. Congress has appropriated funds for vocational rehabilitation grants for veterans of World War II and the Korean conflict. In addition, there is the War Orphans' Act, and guaranteed loans for homes, farms, and businesses. There are certain housing grants for specified service-connected conditions. There are even grants for conveyance appliances, such as special automobiles for certain types of service-connected disabilities. There are also compensation or pension plans for dependents in case of death, and burial benefits.

Even though the husband is a veteran, many families are unaware of the possibilities of aid through the Veterans' Administration. Many are entitled to benefits of which they are completely unaware. In most communities, organizations such as the Veterans of Foreign Wars and the

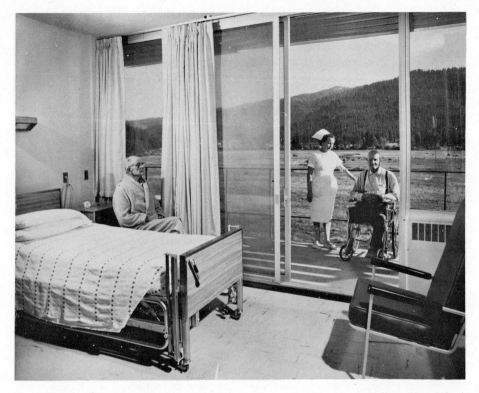

Figure 19-1. The Veterans' Administration maintains many well-equipped hospitals and domiciliary homes. (Photo courtesy of the Libbey-Owens-Ford Glass Company.)

American Legion maintain a service officer whose duties include helping veterans' families collect the benefits due them. Anyone who thinks he may be entitled to such benefits should look into this matter.

Old age

The coming of old age may constitute a crisis in many marriages. Koos states: "Old age is, of course, a relative matter. It is not unusual for the well-preserved father in his early forties to have a son or daughter ask about conditions in 'olden times,' nor are there many things more aggravating."[42] Sometimes it is a shock to people advancing into the launching or empty-nest stages of the family cycle to discover that in certain respects society considers them old. Every culture has a fixed point beyond which one is considered to be old, whether or not he agrees.

In American society, sixty-six is usually the point at which retirement occurs, thus it is customarily considered to be the point at which old age begins. "Some say a man is as old as he acts, others say a man is as old

as he feels. Thus, old age is many diverse things wrapped in one phrase."[43]
With advancing age, however, specific problems must be faced.

SHARPLY LOWERED INCOME. There is usually a sharply lowered income
after retirement. Many people count on their savings to carry them
through, but with the rising inflation of the past few decades, what might
have once been considered a respectable savings account is now insufficient. A recent survey in Wichita, Kansas, found that the average annual
income of a family where one or both mates were sixty-five or over, was
$2270. Actual household expenditures were approximately $2113, of
which only $5.14 per month was spent on entertainment.[44]

HEALTH PROBLEMS. An additional problem of old age is health. With
age, special problems of physical and mental upkeep arise, and medical
expenses may be high.

Contrary to popular belief, professional men usually live longer and
are healthier than other men. Recent research by insurance companies
indicates that the so-called early burn-out of the top executives and their
frequent heart attacks are simply a bugaboo, generally spread by executives themselves.[45] Work seems to be one of the best ways to keep healthy,
and the closer a man comes to the full development of his potential the
better his health is likely to be. The Wichita survey reported that 79 per
cent of old people voluntarily retired because of poor health and that
most retirement is voluntary rather than compulsory.[46]

CONFUSION OF RELATIONSHIPS. With advancing age, there may be much
confusion within various relationships. The position of a couple in old
age is rather nebulous in contemporary American society. As Koos explains it: "The couple in their later years reach back for the life they
have known, but find themselves pushed on toward a place in life . . . ill
defined."[47] Sumner explains that two different sets of mores regarding old
people have been in effect. Under one set of mores, everyone is taught
respect for the aged, who are valued for their wisdom and counsel or out
of affection and sympathy. Under the other set of mores, however, the
aged are regarded as burdens sapping the strength of a society inadequate
for its own tasks. In such cultures, the old are forced to die either by
their own hands or by those of their relatives.[48] Even in a beneficent
society, however, the older couple cannot, upon retirement, simply renew
those activities they enjoyed early in marriage. Increasingly, they may
lose contact with their offspring, and many old friends may have died.
Such couples, however, must increase their own areas of interaction.
Gravatt reports that most couples do this very well, and those persons
who had worked at white-collar jobs seem to make the best adjustment.[49]
Retirement is also an opportunity for closer associations with new-found
friends, who are in much the same predicament. People who have reached
the point of retirement can contribute greatly toward community improvement. Nelson Foote, of the General Electric Corporation, reported

at the Groves Family Life Conference in April 1961 that it has been
found that many older people, even without much technical training,
make excellent workers in social agencies.

A PURPOSE IS NEEDED.   With advancing age, it is necessary for people
to re-establish a purpose and direction for life. Healthy people retire *to*
work, not from work. Those who have enjoyed learning new things and
reaffirming basic philosophies find even more opportunity for these
activities after retirement. Mental health and emotional peace are the rewards for services well done. Especially through service to the community,
people in retirement find they can contribute greatly to the enjoyment
and welfare of others, which, in turn, adds zest to their own lives.

It is best for all people to keep their imaginations alive, for human
imagination can find creative outlets in nature, the arts, community and
church activities, and all kinds of hobbies. Those who have developed a
variety of interests usually find old age one of their most enjoyable life
experiences. It is important, however, to cultivate interests that can be
continued after the more strenuous activities must be abandoned.

> The attitudes, hobbies, talents, and skills you develop during your mid-
> dle years, your savings program, the diet you follow, the care you give your
> health, your philosophy of life—all will greatly determine your well-being
> after retirement. Retirement should not be a complete break with the past.
> It should be merely an extension of your plans for better living.[50]

Retirement is indeed a healthy state to anticipate. It is a time to develop
and utilize to the fullest those things always dreamed of but seldom
accomplished during the years when the hours nine-to-five were dedicated
to employers or to clients.

Death

Death is the one major crisis common to every marriage of every social
class. Death is inevitable; it may be postponed, but it can never be prevented. Every culture meets death in a way most fitting to its own
nature.[51] Life is a cycle of relationships which must face change. The individual begins life by having relationships imposed upon him. As he
matures, he participates in creating and establishing other relationships.
In marriage, he assumes an established status. As a parent, he must
impose relationships upon his own children. As more relationships grow,
others will dissolve. In the United States every year, about .75 million
marriages are broken by the death of a spouse.[52] Nimkoff once estimated
that approximately 25 per cent of all marriages were in a widowed state
at any given moment.[53] The normal death rate bereaves two American
families every minute—and this in time of peace. A problem which so
profoundly involves so many persons at all times deserves attention, however reluctant and however ignorant and helpless one may feel.

WOMEN OUTLIVE MEN. In the average marriage, there is a greater possibility that the wife will become a widow than that the husband will become a widower: the chances of widowhood are two thirds greater for the wife than for the husband.[54] Three fourths of the women widowed at age forty-five live another twenty-five years; more than half of those widowed at age sixty-five live another fifteen years, and more than half of those who are widowed at seventy live another ten years. More wives are outliving their husbands longer. In the 1920s, women averaged about 2.6 years' survival after the death of their spouse; at present they average almost five years. The ratio of widows to widowers is four to one; fifty years ago it was two to one.[55]

Table 19–1. **Mate survival possibility**

If husband is:	His chances of surviving his wife are:
5 years younger	50–50
Same age	40–60
5 years older	30–70
10 years older	22–78
15 years older	18–82
20 years older	10–90
25 years older	7–93

Source: Statistical Bulletin, Metropolitan Life Insurance Company (September 1957). Reprinted by permission.

EARLY BEREAVEMENT. Couples average eighteen years together after their last child leaves the home. In contrast, sixty years ago, one mate usually died an average of two years before the last child left the home. Still, there are some couples whose marriages will be broken early by death.

Table 19–2. **Annual number of newly widowed women in the American society, in relation to husband's age**

Husband's age	Number
Under 25	4,000
25–34	17,000
35–44	35,000
45–54	73,000
55–64	116,000
65 and over	204,000

Source: Statistical Bulletin, Metropolitan Life Insurance Company (September 1957). Adapted by permission.

Table 19–3. Chances in 1000 of joint survival for ten, twenty-five, or fifty years

Husband's age	Wife four years younger			Wife same age			Wife two years older		
	10 yrs.	25 yrs.	50 yrs.	10 yrs.	25 yrs.	50 yrs.	10 yrs.	25 yrs.	50 yrs.
17	978	932	539	977	927	501	977	923	476
21	977	914	419	976	906	375	976	901	350
25	976	886	296	975	875	254	973	867	228
29	971	843	181	968	827	142	966	817	120
33	961	783	88	956	762	61	953	749	47
37	943	704	32	937	678	18	933	660	12
39	932	658	17	924	627	9	919	607	6

Source: Statistical Bulletin, Metropolitan Life Insurance Company (November 1957). Adapted by permission.

Young children are often involved when there is an early death of a spouse. About two thirds of widows in their twenties have children under five years of age.[56] The death of a young bride or groom soon after marriage is extremely sad, but the tragedy is probably even greater for those who have been married for a while, for such a death removes the person about whom has been centered a lifetime of habits, attitudes, and mutual dependencies.

Bereavement has not been well studied. Much of this lack can be attributed to the inertia, taboos, and inherent methodological difficulties that surround studies of this nature. Society, in general, is against investigating this most universal of crises.

SHOCK. Like other crises, bereavement is believed to be characterized by a sequence of reactions. Perhaps the immediate reaction is that of shock—physical, mental, or emotional. Physical shock often produces symptoms of numbness, after which mental shock may set in, frequently characterized by a denial of the facts. The intellectual realization that death is both inevitable and universal does not seem to dull the initial shock of the loss. The bereaved spouse goes on living, but part of his personality is lost. Often he requires medical care, as if there had been an illness or an accident. Tranquillizers are prescribed extensively by many physicians for patients suffering a personal loss.

PROTEST. After the mate's death, there may be a manifestation of protest such as "it's only a bad dream." This is usually followed by a wishful hope to wake up soon. Incidents and ceremonies define the loved person as dead, yet the fact is difficult to accept. Sometimes the protest takes the form of violent crying, moaning, or weeping, and the continually repeated "Why did it have to happen?" There is sometimes a tendency to blame oneself, or others, or fate, or God.

RELIEF. Sometimes the immediate reaction to death is one of relief. This may be especially true where the deceased had some incurable affliction. There may be relief that it is all over, that the suffering is finally ended.

Sometimes the immediate reaction may be a wish to die with the deceased, or to have died instead of him. This wish may arise from a fear of separation, the desire to save the spouse, or the attempt to escape unbearable grief. It may have a guilt component or an element of faith in a future reunion.

HELPLESSNESS AND DETACHMENT. Secondary reactions to death may be feelings of helplessness. If the bereaved had been often consoled by the deceased, then he is usually more helpless.

When the reaction is expressed in detachment, there is usually little weeping. In this state, the bereaved ordinarily takes no acute or active role in the necessary arrangements, or else will go about the task in a daze and with a lack of direction. This reaction may take the observable form of despondency or depression, rather than active mourning. It is usually accompanied by a wish to be alone, loss of energy, decrease in participation, and loss of appetite and sleep. Such people may go through the adjustments in a mechanical way, often without full emotional realization of what has happened. It is usually necessary in such instances for a wide group of relatives and friends to carry such persons through the crisis.

THE VALUE OF RITUAL.   In the American culture, a stiff, unyielding ritual appears to help considerably. Thus, a mourning process begins after bereavement and before the funeral. There are certain things that need immediate attention, and this helps most people to accept reality. The funeral may be an ordeal for the family, yet it serves social and psychological values and functions. Death seems easier to accept after it has been publicly recognized.

TRIAL AND ERROR.   There are many trial-and-error events in the period immediately following bereavement. After the funeral, many people find themselves in a restless mood, overstimulated, overtalkative, and urged to constant activity. Selective memory processes nearly always come into operation, and memories of the dead person come back in flashes. During this period, one comes to think of the dead person, not as he was or as he would have wished to be, but as the bereaved would have wished him to be.

Many possible courses of action are attempted while the bereaved is struggling toward recovery and stabilization. First, there is usually a transfer of attachments from the deceased to some other person, either a family member or a friend. Second, there is an understanding that one must continue to participate in activities and causes. Third, there may be the wish to fulfill the wishes of the deceased, carrying on his life ambitions or living up to his expectations. There may be a wish to glorify his life. Some of these adaptive efforts should be encouraged, otherwise the bereaved might withdraw completely from real life into chronic depression and seclusion.

Signs of recovery

The last stage of bereavement is that of relative recovery, always a slow process. Anyone faced with bereavement should be cautioned not to get too busy, for an interval for meditation and reminiscence frequently is necessary for readjustment. Recovery depends on making the deceased part of a welcome memory and realizing that life is meant to be lived in the active present. The process of recalling past occasions with the deceased is a necessary part of the recovery. Once a specific memory has been recalled and reacted to, it becomes associated with a psychic pain which ordinarily inhibits its further recall. As more time passes, additional occasions are recalled, emotionally reacted to, and dealt with in a similar manner until at length the process is complete.

> When one's life has been interwoven at every point with the life of another, the death of that other leaves him with so vast a multitude of adjustments to make that he cannot possibly become aware of all of them at the same time; therefore the process of readjustment has to take place piecemeal.[57]

DREAMS. Sometimes the recollection takes the form of dreams. The "bereavement dream" has been described as an unconscious attempt to reconcile the true facts. When one dreams of the spouse, he is dead and yet alive. This indicates that complete reconciliation has not yet been achieved. In the dreams, the deceased is seen as if he were still alive, yet the dreamer knows better. Sometimes the anguish of the whole predicament is so great that the dreamer sobs aloud in his sleep and awakens with a sense of having again lived through the death of the spouse.[58]

Memories of the deceased will recur until all the significant events in the relationship have been recalled. As soon as they are all out, tension is reduced and the individual is ready for the next step of recovery.

A RENEWAL OF ROUTINES. The bereaved begins a renewal of many routines, but with new focus and interest. Responsibilities are assumed, and decisions made in the new emotional, social, economic, and physical setting. Close family contacts and guidance are most important at this point to help keep the individual from straying too far out on a tangent.

COMPLICATIONS TO RECOVERY. The road to recovery is not always as simple as it sounds, for it contains many stumbling blocks that may add complications.

One obstacle to recovery is the idealization of the deceased. Some people have the tendency to enshrine the departed as a paragon of everything wholesome and worthwhile.[59]

Another complicating factor is the social pressure to conform to a new role rather than to personal inclinations. Many activities formerly engaged in as a married pair are denied the survivor, who finds himself being excused from some former community duties. In large measure, the activities of the bereaved spouse are prescribed by the culture. In a discussion series at the Guidance Center of New Rochelle, New York, there was general agreement among the widowed that they were frequently considered fair game for sexual approaches after their husbands died.

> They felt that men expected favors, and often assumed they would be granted, just because of these women's lack of socially approved sources of sexual gratification. This occurred among husbands of their good friends as often as with other men. Wives were wary, and this was embarrassing.[60]

The survivor is expected to assume a different role even within group activities. Waller and Hill suggest that the cultural expectations of role assumptions for the survivor are so strong that, when he does not completely conform, he frequently senses that he may be acting disloyally toward the departed.[61]

An additional barrier is the problem of new role assignments and relationships with the rest of the family. A regrouping must be formed after the pair relationship is lost. Generally the first reaction of the family survivors is to close ranks and carry on as before; however, the departed member can never be completely replaced and so a new alignment is necessary. Thus, the strength of the family organization helps determine the widowed spouse's new relationships to other family members.

CONSIDERATION OF REMARRIAGE. The serious consideration of remarriage is a sign that recovery is almost complete. Here again it is necessary to work through and redefine relationships with the community and the family. Apparently this is an easier task for men than for women, for they are more likely to remarry.[62]

RECOVERY IS RELATIVE. Complete and total recovery may never be reached. Perhaps it is too much to expect. As Eliot suggests, recovery is by and large a matter of degree:

> The nearest I can come to an objective definition of such success is a condition in which there is acceptable evidence that the unpleasant tensions have been relaxed and reorganized into some tolerable or more satisfactory pattern.[63]

DEGREES OF RECOVERY

A. Total failure to readjust
  1. Suicide
  2. Early death
  3. Insanity
  4. Moral disintegration
  5. Obsession
B. Partial failure
  1. Eccentricities
  2. Physical illness or prostration
  3. Abulia, purposelessness
  4. Isolation
  5. Embitterment, misanthropy, cynicism
  6. Reversion to or recurrence of griefs
  7. Self-blame or personal hates
  8. Fears
  9. Loneliness
C. Partial success
  1. Resignation, "God's will," and so on
  2. Stoicism

3. Stereotyped formulas of immortality, misery escaped, and so on
4. Sentimental memorials
5. Effective repression of memories
6. Intensification of affections
7. Extension of affections
8. Deliberate absorption in distractions or duties
9. New or fantasied love objects

D. Conspicuous success
1. New love object
2. Thoroughgoing religious rationalization
3. Spontaneous forgetting, relaxation of tensions
4. Devotion to life work
5. Identification with role of deceased
6. Creation of constructive memorials
7. Transmutation of the experience into a productive reintegration of the personality[64]

Adjustment to crisis

No one knows exactly when he may be faced with a crisis. In fact, in the American culture there is a tendency to display disbelief that such things can happen.

ACCEPTANCE OF THE FACTS. The first basic factor for adjusting to crises is development of a realistic attitude that admits such things can and do happen. Learning to modify personal behavior by occasionally doing things differently helps to increase personal adaptability. Rigid routine is a liability to adjustment in the face of a crisis.

In accepting facts, it is necessary to realize that emotional upset in any crisis is normal and should be fully expressed.

ACCEPTANCE OF HELP. The function of outside help in any crisis is to ease the stress and strain of the situation. Agencies and organizations have been established to assist in these emergencies. No one should hesitate to accept the supportive aid from outside groups in a crisis. These services exist for his benefit and should be used without shame.

PREPARATION FOR THE UNEXPECTED. Adaptability to crises is related to how well the individual, the couple, and the family are prepared for the unexpected. The individual who loses himself completely in a marriage and gives up his personal identity may be unable to act independently of his spouse in any situation. Yet, in a crisis, independent thinking and action—as well as paired thinking and action—are needed. For the sake of the marriage and the family, no one should become too dependent on his spouse.

It is possible to learn something of value from every experience, including a crisis. Success in one crisis situation is likely to lead to success in handling other serious situations.

A crisis need not break up a marriage, but it is frequently used as an excuse for breaking up a marriage that was already failing. Perhaps one of the best preparations for crisis adjustment is the establishment of a satisfactory marital relationship as early as possible.

The family structure often determines a crisis pattern. In fact, the family climate can lead a family away from a crisis or force it into one. Bonds of unity within a family—such as common interests, affection, interdependence, and individual respect—can often help the family members to ward off a crisis before it occurs. The family that is integrated to function for the greatest benefit of all is least likely to disintegrate when faced with a crisis.[65]

Interrelatedness of crises

One crisis can cause many changes in many areas of family living. It is not enough therefore, to focus on the single crisis; rather, it is necessary to readjust in many areas touched by the event. The greater the crisis, the more the areas in the living pattern likely to be disturbed. Hill cites that involuntary separation in wartime is usually accompanied by other situations such as a sharp change in income level, housing inadequacies, new and increased role responsibilities, a need for new methods of discipline, and so forth.[66]

New areas of crisis

Because no one can accurately predict what tomorrow will bring, it is not possible to forecast exactly what new situations will be considered as crises for the American family of the future. New problems arise with each generation, but old problems sometimes fade away, never to reappear. Some of today's more common crisis situations will also disappear. Eventually, the combined efforts of individuals and society will work out effective means to cope with many crises. New crises emerge, however, as the world changes. The desperate need to provide a college education for the offspring and the financial difficulties thereby incurred loom on the horizon of many a modern family as a possible major crisis of the future.

Crises are an inevitable part of life, but they need not destroy a marriage if preparations are made in advance. Of course, the unexpectedness of the situation prevents immediate adjustment when the occasion arises. By preparing oneself and one's marriage, and by creating a strong family structure now, the chances of recovery from crises are greatly improved. One of the best ways to prepare to live with tomorrow's adversities is to learn how to live effectively and meaningfully with those of today.

THE MUSTARD SEED

A young woman, having lost her first-born, was so beset with grief that she wandered through the streets, pleading for some magic medicine to restore life to her child. Some turned away from her in pity; some mocked her and called her mad; none could find words to console her. But a wise man, noting her despair, said: "There is only one in all the world who can perform this miracle. He is the Perfect One, and resides at the top of the mountain. Go to him, and ask."

The young woman went up the mountain, and stood before the Perfect One and beseeched: "O Buddha, give life back to my child."

And Buddha said: "Go down into the city, from house to house, and bring to me a mustard seed from a house in which no one has ever died."

The young woman's heart was high as she hastened down the mountain and into the city. At the first house, she said: "The Buddha bids me fetch a mustard seed from a house which has never known death."

"In this house many have died," they told her. So she went to the next house, and asked again. "It is impossible to count the number who have died here," they replied.

She went to a third house and a fourth and a fifth, on and on through the city, and could not find a single house which death had not at some time visited.

So the young woman returned to the top of the mountain.

"Have you brought the mustard seed?" the Buddha asked.

"No," she said, "nor do I seek it any more. My grief had made me blind. I thought that only I had suffered at the hands of the death."

"Then why have you returned?" the Perfect One inquired. "To ask you to teach me the truth," she said.

And this is what the Buddha told her: "In all the world of man, and all the world of Gods, this alone is The Law: All things are impermanent."[67]

Summary

Sooner or later every marriage faces a situation which seems insurmountable. The extent of recovery depends upon personal preparation through the establishment of habits, customs, and routines. What is considered a crisis depends on family patterns. Through the years, society has come to recognize that some crises are inevitable, and it has established agencies and rituals to help carry people through the most trying parts.

Common crises in today's marriages include such things as temporary separation, defective offspring, involuntary childlessness, illness, sexual infidelity, change of income level, old age, and death of a mate.

Factors conducive to crisis adjustment include an acceptance of the facts, an acceptance of help, and a preparation for the unexpected. One crisis situation is usually accompanied by others, and new areas are constantly being created as the world becomes more complex.

Notes

1. Earl L. Koos, "Class Differences in Family Reactions to Crises," *Marriage and Family Living,* 12:77–79.

2. *Ibid.*

3. Thomas D. Eliot, "The Bereaved Family," *The Annals of the American Academy of Political and Social Science,* 160:184–90.

4. U.S. Bureau of the Census, Series P-20 No. 72, Table 1.

5. *We Speak for Them,* National Association for Retarded Children, Inc., 99 University Place, New York. Quoted in *Marriage and Family Living,* 21:47.

6. *Today's Health* (March 1963), 8.

7. Glenn M. Vernon and Jack A. Broadway, "Attitudes Toward Artificial Insemination and Some Variables Associated Therewith," *Marriage and Family Living,* 21:45–47.

8. *Time Magazine* (February 27, 1956), 35.

9. W. Fink, *The Field of Social Work* (New York: Holt, Rinehart & Winston, Inc., 1959), p. 211.

10. Clark E. Vincent, "The Adoption Market and the Unwed Mother's Baby," *Marriage and Family Living,* 18:124.

11. U.S. Bureau of the Census, *Statistical Abstract of the United States* (1958), p. 293.

12. *Today's Child* (September 1962), 1.

13. Federal Security Agency, Children's Bureau, *Adoption of Children,* Statistical Series No. 14, 7.

14. Jeffery C. Ray, "Social Class and Adoption Petitioners," *Social Problems,* 9:354–58.

15. Lee M. Brooks and Evelyn C. Brooks, "Adoption: Some Legal and Social Procedures," in Morris Fishbein and Ruby Jo Reeves Kennedy (eds.), *Modern Marriage and Family Living* (New York: Oxford University Press, Inc., 1957), p. 445.

16. Reported in *Children,* 9 (November–December 1962), 245.

17. *Today's Child,* 8:1.

18. "Intercountry Adoption," *International Child Welfare Review,* 15, 1 (1961), 3.

19. *Today's Health* (October 1960), 69.

20. Howard A. Rusk, "The Impact of Chronic Illness on Families," *Marriage and Family Living,* 19:193–97.

21. Marion M. Kalashian, "Working with the Wives of Alcoholics in an Out-Patient Clinic Setting," *Marriage and Family Living,* 21:130–33.

22. W. and I. McCord, *Origin of Alcoholism* (Stanford, Calif.: Stanford University Press, 1961).

23. Paul H. Jacobson, *American Marriage and Divorce* (New York: Holt, Rinehart & Winston, Inc., 1959).

24. A. C. Kinsey, *et al., Sexual Behavior of the Human Male* (Philadelphia: W. B. Saunders Company, 1948), p. 348; A. C. Kinsey, *et al., Sexual Behavior of the Human Female* (Philadelphia: W. B. Saunders Company, 1953), pp. 312–13.

25. F. Whyte, "A Slum Sex Code," *American Journal of Sociology,* 49:24–31.

26. Hyman Rodman, "On Understanding Lower-Class Behavior," in Marvin Sussman, *Sourcebook in Marriage and the Family,* 2nd ed. (Boston: Houghton Mifflin Company, 1962), pp. 186–89.

27. Joseph Kirk Folsom, *The Family and Democratic Society* (New York: John Wiley & Sons, Inc., 1943), p. 14.

28. Paper read at annual conference of the Ohio Council on Family Relations, Dayton, Ohio, April 24, 1964.

29. Lester W. Dearborn, "Extramarital Relations," in Fishbein and Kennedy, *op. cit.,* p. 316.

30. *Ibid.,* p. 317.

31. *Ibid.,* p. 318.

32. Saul J. Blaustein, "Income Maintenance During Unemployment," *Marriage and Family Living,* 20:221.

33. Personal communication with American Telephone & Telegraph Company officials.

34. U.S. Department of Health, Education and Welfare, *Bulletin* (January 1962), viii.

35. Helen E. Martz, "The Contributions of Public Assistance to Family Life in the United States," *Marriage and Family Living,* 20:213.

36. *Programs for Older People,* Report to the President, Federal Council on Aging, Washington, D.C. (1960), 67.

37. Martz, *op. cit.*

38. Roger Cummings, "Social Services: The Veterans' Administration and the Family," *Marriage and Family Living,* 20:241.

39. *Ibid.*

40. *Ibid.*

41. *Ibid.*

42. Earl L. Koos, *Marriage,* rev. ed. (New York: Holt, Rinehart & Winston, Inc., 1957), p. 314.

43. Milton L. Barron, *The Aging American* (New York: Thomas Y. Crowell Company, 1961), p. 115.

44. D. O. Cowgill, *Our Senior Citizens* (Wichita, Kans.: Community Planning Council, 1960), p. 25.

45. Gerald Walker, "Good News for Go-Getters!" *This Week Magazine* (June 12, 1960), 405.

46. Cowgill, *op. cit.,* pp. 33–34.

47. Koos, *Marriage, op. cit.,* p. 315.

48. William G. Sumner, *Folkways* (New York: Ginn & Company, 1940), p. 321.

49. Arthur E. Gravatt, "An Exploratory Study of Marital Adjustment in Later Maturity," *The Family Life Coordinator,* 6:23–25.

50. Joseph C. Buckley, *The Retirement Handbook,* rev. ed. (New York: Harper & Row, Publishers, 1956), p. 319.

51. See, e.g., Ruth Benedict, "Configurations of Culture in North America," *American Anthropologist,* 34:1–27.

52. *Statistical Bulletin,* Metropolitan Life Insurance Company (January 1961).

53. Meyer F. Nimkoff, *Marriage and the Family* (Boston: Houghton Mifflin Company, 1947), pp. 613–18.

54. *Statistical Bulletin,* Metropolitan Life Insurance Company (April 1960).

55. *Statistical Bulletin,* Metropolitan Life Insurance Company (June 1960, November 1962, August 1964).

56. *Statistical Bulletin,* Metropolitan Life Insurance Company (April 1960).

57. Willard Waller and Reuben Hill, *The Family: A Dynamic Interpretation* (New York: The Dryden Press, 1951), p. 465.

58. *Ibid.,* pp. 476–80.

59. *Ibid.,* pp. 496–97.

60. Marjorie P. Ilgenfritz, "Mothers on Their Own—Widows and Divorcées," *Marriage and Family Living,* 23:39.

61. Waller and Hill, *op. cit.,* pp. 494–95.

62. Paul C. Glick, *American Families* (New York: John Wiley & Sons, Inc., 1957), pp. 113–14.

63. Eliot, *op. cit.,* p. 291.

64. Eliot, *op. cit.,* pp. 184–90. Copyright © 1932, by The American Academy of Political and Social Science, New York. Reprinted by permission.

65. Notes from lectures given by the late Earl Koos while the author was a graduate student.

66. Reuben Hill, *Families Under Stress* (New York: Harper & Row, Publishers, 1949), Chap. 4.

67. *Buddhaghosha's Parables,* translated by T. Rogers, London, 1870, pp. 98ff.

Questions for further thought

1. In what way are social agencies justifiable under the concept of American democracy?
2. What suggestions are in order for a couple who appear to be mutually over-dependent on one another? Why?
3. Inasmuch as the divorce rate is lower during depressions than at other times, is depression a strengthening influence upon marriage?
4. What advice is in order for a distraught wife whose husband, at a party, appears enraptured by the charms of an attractive young widow? What accounts for the conduct of all these people?
5. Is there any justification for the adoption of a child by means other than through a recognized reputable agency?
6. In what ways do relationships between spouses during the child-rearing years affect their relationship in the empty-nest stage?
7. Should an elderly or ailing parent live with his children?

Recommended films

Palmour Street (Health Publication Institute).
Families Without Fathers (University of Michigan Television Center).
The Proud Years (Columbia University Educational Films).
The Steps of Age (International Film Bureau).
The Yellow Leaf (McGraw-Hill Book Company, Inc.).
A Baby Named X (Health and Welfare Maternity Center).
A Broken Dream (Michigan State Department of Health).

Suggested supplemental readings

BOOKS

Bassett, William T. *Counseling the Childless Couple.* Englewood Cliffs, N.J.: Prentice-Hall, Inc., 1963.

Bauman, Harold. *Grief's Slow Work.* Scottdale, Pa.: Herald Press, 1960.

Barron, Milton L. *The Aging American.* New York: Thomas Y. Crowell Company, 1961.

Cady, Ernest and Frances. *How to Adopt a Child.* New York: William Morrow & Co., Inc., 1956.

Caprio, Frank S. *Unfaithful.* New York: Fawcett Publications, Inc., 1961.

Delliquadri, Fred (ed.). *Helping the Family in Urban Society.* New York: Columbia University Press, 1963.

Doss, Carl and Helen. *If You Adopt a Child.* New York: Holt, Rinehart & Winston, Inc., 1957.

Egleson, Jim and Janet. *Parents Without Partners*. New York: E. P. Dutton & Co., Inc., 1961.

Farber, Bernard. *Family Organization and Crisis*. New York: Society for Research in Child Development, 1960.

Farber, Bernard, William C. Jenne, and Romolo Toigo. *Family Crisis and the Retarded Child*. Research Monograph Series A, No. 1, The Council for Exceptional Children, 1201 Sixteenth Street, N.W., Washington, D.C., 1960.

Feifel, Herman (ed.). *The Meaning of Death*. New York: McGraw-Hill Book Company, Inc., 1960.

Finegold, Wilfred J. *Artificial Insemination*. Springfield, Ill., Charles C Thomas, Publisher, 1964.

Katz, Alfred H. *Parents of the Handicapped*. Springfield, Ill.: Charles C Thomas, Publisher, 1961.

Kirk, H. David. *Shared Fate*. New York: The Free Press of Glencoe, Inc., 1963.

Kleemeier, Robert W. *Aging and Leisure*. New York: Oxford University Press, Inc., 1961.

Langer, Marion. *Learning to Live as a Widow*. New York: Julian Messner, Inc., 1957.

Lucas, Carol. *Recreation in Gerontology*. Springfield, Ill.: Charles C Thomas, Publisher, 1964.

Raymond, Louise. *Adoption and After*. New York: Harper & Row, Publishers, 1955.

Slaughter, Stella Stillson. *The Mentally Retarded Child and His Parent*. New York: Harper & Row, Publishers, 1960.

Smith, I. Evelyn (ed.). *Readings in Adoption*. New York: Philosophical Library, Inc., 1963.

Wenger, J. C. *A Death in the Family*. Scottdale, Pa.: Herald Press, 1964.

ARTICLES

Babcock, Charlotte G. "The Contribution of the Family Agency In Meeting Community Problems," *The Social Service Review*, 32:223–33.

Bailey, M. B. "Alcoholism and Marriage: A Review of Research and Professional Literature," *Quarterly Journal of Studies on Alcohol*, 22:81–97.

Bartholomew, G. W. "The Development and Use of Artificial Insemination," *Eugenics Quarterly*, 49:187–96.

Benson, Purnell H., Arlo Brown, and Sister Loretta Maria Sheehy. "Survey of Family Difficulties in a Metropolitan Suburb," *Marriage and Family Living*, 18:249–53.

Birbeck, Herbert E. "Parental Attitudes in Families Where Cerebral Palsy Is Present," *Dissertation Abstracts*, 21:1840.

Blackwell, James E. "The Effects of Involuntary Separation on Selected Families of Men Committed to Prison From Spokane County, Washington," *Dissertation Abstracts*, 20:1088–89.

Brieland, Donald. "Adoption Research," *Child Welfare*, 38:1–5.

Bullough, Vern L. "The Banal and Costly Funeral," *The Humanist*, 4:213–18.

Cohn, Pauline C. "The Impact of the Handicapped Child on the Family," *Social Casework* (March 1962), 137–42.

Deutsch, Cynthia P., and Judith A. Goldston. "Family Factors in Home Adjustment of the Severely Disabled," *Marriage and Family Living*, 22:312–16.

Gallagher, Ursula M. "Interprofessional Teamwork to Safeguard Adoption," *Children*, 6:101–104.

Gurselin, Orville, Raymond G. Hunt, and Jack L. Roach. "Social Class, Mental Hygiene, and Psychiatric Practice," *Social Service Review,* 33:237–44.

Hanson, F. M., and J. Rock. "The Effect of Adoption on Fertility and Other Reproductive Functions," *American Journal of Obstetrics and Gynecology,* 59:311.

Jacobs, L. "The Jewish Attitude Toward Artificial Insemination," *Journal of Sex Education,* 2:177.

Koos, Earl L. "Private Social Agencies and Family Stability," *Annals of the American Academy of Political and Social Science,* 272:110–16.

Levine, Jacob. "The Sexual Adjustment of Alcoholics," *Quarterly Journal of the Study of Alcohol,* 16:675–80.

MacDonald, Donald E. "Mental Disorders in Wives of Alcoholics," *Quarterly Journal of Studies on Alcohol,* 172:282–87.

Mandelbaum, Arthur, and Mary E. Wheeler. "The Meaning of a Defective Child to Parents," *Social Casework,* 41:360–67.

Mauk, Fern. "Helping the Unemployed Father," *Social Casework,* 43:422–27.

Neubeck, Gerhard, and Vera M. Schletzer. "A Study of Extramarital Relations," *Marriage and Family Living,* 24:279–81.

Rienow, Robert, and Leona Train. "The Desperate World of the Senior Citizen," *Saturday Review* (January 28, 1961), 11–13, 55–56.

Rusk, Howard A. "The Impact of Chronic Illness on Families," *Marriage and Family Living,* 19:193–97.

Sandgrund, Gertrude. "Group Counseling with Adoptive Families After Legal Adoption," *Child Welfare,* 41:248–52, 278.

Strauss, Robert. "Excessive Drinking and Its Relationship to Marriage," *Marriage and Family Living,* 12:79–82, 94.

Vincent, Clark E. "The Adoption Market and the Unwed Mother's Baby," *Marriage and Family Living,* 18:124–27.

Wark, Henry. "Adoption May Trigger Psychiatric Problems," *Science News Letter,* 82:358.

Warner, Marie Pichel, M.D. "Should You Adopt a Child?" *Today's Health* (June 1962), 28–30, 70–72.

Understanding marriage counseling

chapter 20

It is not unusual, on occasion, even in the best marriage for one or both mates to feel justified in seriously questioning the feasibility of continuing the relationship. A study of fifty-four couples, married on an average of only three years, indicated that about a third of the mates had already seriously considered separation at least once.[1] Undoubtedly, with time and an increased number of differences, the proportion increases.

The logic of marriage counseling

If more people availed themselves of adequate marital education, there would be less need for marriage counseling. Those who select a mate wisely and are prepared to face the realities of marriage are not likely to experience complete marital failure. Such individuals are much better prepared to meet and solve almost all marital problems by themselves.

EXPERT HELP MAKES SENSE. There may be times even in educated marriages, however, when home remedies for domestic problems appear to be failing. The best marriage may at times seem beyond salvaging to the couple, who feel they have exhausted their own resources. Although still possessing the will to succeed, the partners have no further ideas on the next proper step to take to improve the relationship. It makes as good sense to turn to a professional for help in such a disaster as it does in cases of serious injury or illness. The marriage counselor may make pertinent suggestions or reorient the focus of the couple to enable them to find their own way out of chaos.

THE SOONER THE BETTER. Marital failure is a long-term process. The relationship usually begins to deteriorate before the couple realize it and long before either spouse seriously considers giving up. Some couples go through the motions of solving their differences without even touching on the real problems—which, in time, become what seem to be insurmountable obstacles. There is usually time enough for preventing marital difficulties from developing into marital disasters if most couples could but recognize the symptoms earlier. If the couple recognize their problems but are confused as to what to do, they should seek out proper marriage counseling. It may not always work, but it is always worth the effort. Just as a physician can do more when patients visit him soon after symptoms appear, a marriage counselor can do more to help when his clients go to him soon after their fatal signs appear. Yet, physicians have saved many patients who delayed their visits; so, too, many marriages have greater safety margins than some couples realize.

Table 20–1. **Interval between consideration of serious trouble and possible divorce to actual decree**

Months	Per cent of couples getting divorces
0–5	6
6–11	15
12–23	30
24–35	23
36–47	17
Not Known	9

Source: William J. Goode, *After Divorce* (New York: The Free Press of Glencoe, Inc., 1956), p. 137. Copyright © 1956, by The Free Press, Glencoe, Ill. Reprinted by permission.

SELDOM AN INNOCENT PARTY. Because of the fact that there is time to seek help even after trouble has developed, neither partner should feel blameless for a broken marriage; there is seldom a genuinely innocent party to marital failure. This concept is more a legal fiction than a social reality. The fact that 85 per cent of American divorces are uncontested[2] indicates a willingness by the other partner to lose the marriage by default.

The historical development of marriage counseling

Marriage counseling is not a modern concept; however, there are many more philosophies, forms, and techniques used today than ever before. Early Hindu writings showed concern about family relationships and suggested the usefulness of marital counseling for distressed families.[3]

In addition, Napheys described a type of enforced marriage counseling that supposedly was in effect in one civilization in the pre-Christian era.

> It is said that in Zürich, in the olden times, when a quarrelsome couple applied for a divorce, the magistrate refused to listen to them at first. He ordered that they should be shut up together in one room for three days, with one bed, one table, one plate, and one cup. Their food was passed in by attendants who neither saw nor spoke to them. On the expiration of these three days, it was usual to find that neither of them would want a separation.[4]

Today, there are many more sophisticated techniques of marriage counseling, but few could claim greater success than that credited to the Zürich magistrate.

In the modern era. Most authorities credit the origin of modern marriage counseling to European societies. According to Popenoe, the European experiments with marriage counseling began in 1922 in Austria.[5] Bridgeman reports that by 1932 there were 200 marriage advice clinics in Germany alone. The earliest ones gave some information on sex adjustment, but their primary purpose was to control venereal disease.[6] The London Marriage Guidance Center was established in 1943; in April 1947, the National Marriage Guidance Council was established to function as a coordinating group for all local marriage-counseling organizations in the British Empire.[7] Mace states that, outside the United States, marriage-counseling services have undoubtedly progressed further in Britain than anywhere else. Today these British services include about eighty local marriage-guidance councils in England and Wales, and six in Scotland.[8] There is virtually no private practice of marriage counseling in Britain as there is in the United States. Financial support for the British services comes from donations by clients, from individual and organizational contributions, and from modest governmental and municipal grants.[9] Marriage counseling in the British Commonwealth is also conducted by the Catholic Marriage Advisory Council and by social-casework agencies. The counselors in almost all British agencies are volunteer workers who are screened and trained for a team approach and who receive no pay for their services.[10] Marriage counseling that encompasses much more than the control of venereal diseases is being practiced in many other places; for example, in 1950 eight cities in Finland had modern marriage-counseling clinics.[11]

In the united states. There were many pioneers in the early development of American marriage counseling. Among the first was the late Abraham Stone, who founded the Marriage Consultation Center of New York City in 1929.[12] In 1930, Paul Popenoe organized the American Institute of Family Relations, which is now probably the largest marriage-consultation center of its kind. In 1932, Emily Mudd organized the

Marriage Counsel of Philadelphia, now a part of the Division of Psychiatry in the School of Medicine at the University of Pennsylvania. A few universities have established training centers in the area of marriage counseling. Groves initiated the training programs for professional marriage counseling through an interdisciplinary approach at the University of North Carolina and Duke University; the disciplines included sociology, clinical psychology, ministry, and the law.[13]

Other universities offer marriage-counseling training through an internship program in psychology. There are also nonuniversity training centers, such as the Merrill-Palmer Institute in Detroit, Michigan, and the Menninger Foundation in Topeka, Kansas. Several universities today accredit training from these centers toward advanced degrees in various fields related to marriage and the family.

Varieties of marriage-counseling approaches

Today there are many sources and approaches to marriage counseling available to people who need help. Though not every couple may need to use these resources, all should be aware of their availability: "Where no counsel is, the people fall: but in the multitude of counselors there is safety."[14]

THE BY-PRODUCT APPROACH. Much of the marriage counseling practiced in the United States is a result of the by-product approach. In other words, it is an extra professional duty assumed by people whose major interest is in some other field, such as physicians, clergymen, psychologists, home economists, attorneys, and social workers. Marriage counseling is also offered to students by an increasing number of universities as a part of other counseling and guidance programs. Yale University initiated such a service as a part of its mental-hygiene program in 1925. In 1927, the University of Utah formed its Bureau of Student Counsel and included counseling on marital problems. A marriage-counseling service was made a part of the established counseling services at Pennsylvania State University in 1940. In addition, much marriage counseling is offered students as a by-product of college marriage courses by the respective professors. As a natural part of their own specializations, many professionals frequently must cope with marriage and family problems. In fact, the bulk of marriage counseling is still conducted by professionals who regard it as a secondary interest. A nationwide sample revealed that only one in every seven couples had ever sought outside help for any matter. Of those who had, however, about half had sought help with a marriage problem. Of those seeking help with a marriage problem, 44 per cent had gone to a clergyman; 23 per cent, to a physician; 12 per cent, to a psychiatrist; 6 per cent, to an attorney; 7 per cent, to various agencies; and only 8 per cent, to a professional marriage counselor.[15] These specialists in allied fields make a positive contribution to family welfare through their by-product marital-counseling efforts. Needless to say, any approach to marital counseling is only one of many methods possible today. Any service that helps to relieve tensions created by (1) a hostile environment, (2) lowered physical health and efficiency, (3) unconscious personality conflicts, or (4) a false understanding of oneself and one's values may be correctly considered as related to marriage counseling.[16]

Figure 20-1. A considerable amount of college student marriage counseling is conducted informally, as a by-product of college marriage courses, by the professors of such courses. (Courtesy of the Kansas State University News Bureau.)

CLINICS. Marriage counseling is also available today through public consultation centers. One of the advantages of such clinics is the small fee, for many are supported by taxes and contributions. The fees usually vary with the couples' ability to pay; in fact, some training-center clinics may charge no fee at all. The counseling center is used for internship training, and counseling cases are needed for practice. Occasionally, clinics of this nature are sponsored by industry. Many years ago, Western Electric, for example, introduced counseling services so that employees might unburden their troubles, domestic and otherwise.[17] Other industries are presently following this example.

Probably the most professionally significant counseling clinics are those sponsored by universities, churches, and social agencies. Many clinics specialize in a specific problem area, such as child guidance, which includes working with families in which there are children with personality problems. The first specific child-guidance center was established in 1909 by Dr. William Healy, who worked with delinquent children in Chicago.[18]

Clinics specializing as welfare societies are sometimes involved in family counseling. These agencies were first organized for the material relief of destitute families. Many operate with volunteer funds or are subsidized by tax revenues. Recently, there has been a trend for the tax-supported welfare agencies to handle the bulk of clients seeking economic relief and for other welfare agencies to concentrate almost entirely on helping families needing aid for personality and interaction problems. Sometimes marital conflict has been found to be the basic cause for the family's financial difficulties. These agencies hope that, once the marital problem has been solved, the family will be able to maintain itself without further financial aid. Most welfare societies are now giving a great part of their time to family guidance and closely related functions.

A newer movement in some areas is represented by mental-health clinics, which may be community-sponsored. These are mainly equipped to deal with childhood, adolescent, and marital problems. Many of these clinics offer guidance that is not specifically directed toward marriage counseling. As Carl Rogers, of the Counseling Center at the University of Chicago, has said: "We see between 800 and 1000 new clients a year and a good many of those do have marital problems, although we do not think of them as a special category."[19] A 1965 law in Michigan allows counties of that state to pass special assessments for the specific purpose of establishing marriage-counseling clinics.

COURTS. Marriage counseling is also conducted by the law courts. Although in 1910 in Buffalo and New York City there were family courts dealing with desertion and nonsupport cases, the first bonafide court of domestic relations was established in Cincinnati in 1914[20] under the leadership of The Honorable Charles W. Hoffman.[21] Earlier courts employed a few trained social workers, but the first major effort toward establishing a model domestic-relations court to rehabilitate broken families was started in 1924 in Lucas County, Toledo, Ohio.[22] The Court of Domestic Relations there is headed by Judge Paul W. Alexander, who began the project by appointing one of the women probation officers to serve as a marriage counselor attached to the court.[23] As Judge Alexander has stated: "The outstanding objective of the family court is to protect the family and restore it to society as a healthy law-abiding unit. The basic unit of our society."[24] The philosophy behind the establishment of family courts is that the state has as much responsibility to treat mal-adjusted marriages as it has to treat maladjusted juveniles. Alexander further explains: "The court has the function of playing peacemaker to the embattled spouses, administering to sick marriages, as well as merely issuing certificates for burial of the legal remains of a wholly defunct marriage by entering a divorce decree."[25] In keeping with this philosophy, the court is staffed with legal aids, social caseworkers, probation officers, marriage and family counselors, and physicians. In his justification for the family courts as a form of marriage counseling, Alexander explains:

> People in domestic discord seem, for the most part, never to have heard of the family service agencies or of pastoral or marriage-counseling services. Or if they have heard of them, their ideas about them are distorted or dim or downright hostile. Even if they had a perfect understanding of the services available, a large per cent of them would bypass even the best of agencies, even the friendliest and wisest of pastors, for a number of reasons. The principal reason is that they are hurt, threatened, frightened, angry, vindictive, confused, ashamed; their pride is wounded. In their overwrought emotional state, they want only one thing. They do not want to learn how to make a go of their marriage, how to save their family ... how to live with their ... spouses. They do not even want to learn how to live with them-selves. . . . They have recourse to the only regress they know: the law; and the law offers them the only remedy it knows; divorce.[26]

The work at Toledo has been relatively successful in dealing with mari-tal problems. As Alexander says:

> It is often argued by learned lawyers and sociologists that, by the time a distintegrating marriage gets into the divorce courts, it is so far gone it is too late to do anything about it except give it a legal burial. While this is very frequently true, it is not always true. Obviously, the longer the sore is allowed to fester, the harder it is to cure. But even old sores do not always require an amputation. . . . The experience of the family courts has shown that sometimes even the most stubborn-seeming spouses prove tractable.[27]

Even where there is no marriage counseling available in a divorce court, it is estimated that 20 to 40 per cent of all divorce suits filed are later dismissed or dropped. The parties become reconciled and get back together; in a large percentage of the cases, however, the reconciliation does not last, and divorce eventually follows.[28] One study found that one third of divorce cases in which children were involved (and consequently referred to the reconciliation court) were reconciled; of that one third, 75 to 85 per cent remained reconciled. Prior to the employment of a trained marriage counselor, only about 65 per cent of the reconciled cases remained reconciled, and not so many reached that stage.[29] Marriage counseling is obviously helpful even to those couples who have brought their cases to the divorce courts. Alice Ralls, an attorney, thinks that at least half of the people who start suits do not really want a divorce, but would prefer to straighten out the difficulties. She reports the experience of the King County Family Court where, of the cases reconciled through marriage counseling, 85 per cent have so far continued successfully.[30] Interviews by expert social workers or trained marriage consultants prior to a court hearing often reveal the motives and attitudes which led to the divorce petition. Sometimes the proceedings are halted at this stage. Frequently, the desires of neither partner would be fulfilled by a divorce decree. Many times there are resources within the relationship that can be used to reconstruct a tolerable family life. Indeed, various reports indicate that family courts have a very definite part to play in the total marriage-counseling picture and contribute much to the success of many marriages.[31]

FULL-TIME PROFESSIONAL MARRIAGE COUNSELING. Although marriage counseling has long been conducted as an informal activity, it has only recently come to be practiced as a full-time profession.[32] This trend has grown from the needs of couples throughout the country for services that would enable them to achieve greater satisfaction within their marriages. A full-time professional marriage counselor receives special training to qualify him for evaluating and handling the great variety of problems that may arise in marriage. People trained in this new profession develop skills and knowledge which are recognizably more effective than the trial-and-error approaches of the well-meaning relatives or laymen who handled many of the marriage problems of yesterday. Marriage counseling is now emerging as a profession that demands the full time of hundreds of specialists.

MISCELLANEOUS APPROACHES. A form of marriage counseling is sometimes offered through newspaper columns, and on radio and television. It is inconceivable that anyone could reasonably expect a complex marital problem to be solved by a paragraph or so in a newspaper or by a snap judgment on a television program, yet there are several syndicated columns that are apparently read by millions. Theoretically, these columns give advice on questions submitted by the readers. From the standpoint of effectiveness, marriage counseling conducted in this manner seems an impossibility. The first newspaper column on advice to the lovelorn was written in 1898 by Marie Manning, under the name Beatrice Fairfax.[33]

Marriage counseling is sometimes attempted by persons with unhealthy motivations, such as a desire for prestige, a morbid curiosity, or a need to direct and manipulate other people. Of course, not all laymen who attempt to be counselors have unhealthy motives; some may be well-meaning but uninformed, or they may be trying to work out their own problems by counseling others in trouble.[34] Many of these people are willing and eager to help, but are simply not qualified; sometimes they only make matters worse. Too many people consider themselves to be experts on life and love, but counseling—as a profession—is much more.

Then, of course, as in any profession, there are the charlatans. Perhaps there is no field today with more practicing charlatans than marriage counseling. These are people who recognize a quick way to make money. These persons, unqualified and unscrupulous, work in the guise of fortune-tellers, advice-givers, or "psychologists." A 1953 survey revealed that at least 25,000 charlatans were engaged in personal counseling in the United States and taking in more than $375 million annually.[35] Since 1953, over twenty states have passed laws designed to control the practice of psychology. Thus it is conceivable that marriage-counseling charlatans have increased since then, for many of the quack psychologists have simply taken down their "Psychologist" signs and substituted "Marriage Counselor" signs instead.[36] Such people may be making more money than ever. It is amazing how many people seem willing to be taken in by a quack in the counseling field.[37] Recently an inspection team, sponsored by The American Association of Marriage Counselors, made a sample survey (in one section of the United States) of the qualifications of those advertising to do marriage counseling. Davidson writes the following of their experience:

> We came across self-labeled marriage counselors who had been taxi-drivers, plumbers, or bartenders, with barely a high school education. Among the quacks there are phony clergymen, misguided idealists, gypsy fortune-tellers, unqualified ex-physicians, hypnotists, spiritualists, "psycho-analysts" with "degrees" from nonexistent or unrecognized universities.... They all have one thing in common: they are profiteering fishermen in the waters of human misery.[38]

The qualifications of a marriage counselor may be checked through the facilities of the American Association of Marriage Counselors, which was organized in 1948.[39] People who are in need of a highly skilled professional marriage counselor may consult this organization for the names and addresses of the nearest members. David Mace, Executive Director of the American Association of Marriage Counselors, reported at the annual conference of the National Council on Family Relations at the University of Connecticut in August 1962 that there were 500 fully qualified clinical members of the Association. The membership mainly represents many professions doing by-product marriage counseling, but most of these counselors have fairly high standards in training, experience, and interest. It is an interprofessional organization, founded on the belief that no single presently established profession is necessarily the best source of marriage counseling, but that the individual counselor's qualifications are the important prerequisites to good counseling.

Other associations may be of help in the field of marriage. One is the

National Association for Mental Health. The National Committee of Mental Hygiene was established in 1909; in 1950 it was combined with other groups to form the National Association for Mental Health. This organization favors marriage counseling and keeps a list of those members who are best qualified in this field. In 1911 the Family Welfare Association of America was established; in 1946 it changed its name to the Family Service Association of America. Upon request, this association will provide leads to possible marriage counseling help. In 1914 the American Social Hygiene Association was founded; its initial concern was to help eliminate venereal disease. When counseling and education for marriage and family life became its main functions, it was renamed (in 1960) the American Social Health Association. In 1888, the Child Study Association of America was established, and in 1928 branched into family-counseling services.

There are other ways to check on the qualifications of a marriage counselor. A clinical marriage counselor does not advertise widely; he relies on satisfied clients, agencies, and professionals for his referrals. He has been awarded degrees from reputable training centers. He often does not attempt to solve the couple's entire problem by himself; he may call in other trained specialists to aid in the counseling process. His fees are nominal and are discussed frankly with the couple. He keeps all information confidential. He does not diagnose a particular case, and in fact announces no particular analysis until he has made a careful study. He does not promise quick results; he is intellectually mature and emotionally stable. Because he must trace maladjustments to their sources, he needs training primarily in the area of human development and personal interrelationships (including those of a psychosexual nature). A marriage counselor should have a wide background in many fields, including sex anatomy, physiology, and genetics. He should have enough training in sociology to recognize the significance of social class as an influence on marriage patterns and the influence of culture, socialization processes, and intergroup relations; he needs a clear concept of the different philosophies of marriage of the various religious, racial, social, and economic groups. He should have some training in the field of medicine or psychiatry, including a knowledge of embryology and endocrinology. In addition to a basic knowledge of the legal aspects of marriage and the family, the marriage counselor must develop the particular counseling skills, such as the techniques of interviewing.[40]

The uniqueness of marriage counseling

The principal factor that distinguishes marriage counseling from other forms of counseling is its focus on the relationship between two individuals rather than on their personalities. It is possible that personalities might be improved, but that would be only incidental to the major purpose, which is to improve the relationship between a man and a woman. The methods by which this relationship improvement is effected varies considerably, depending largely on the background and training of the counselor. Because marriage is a relationship between two persons, problems often arise which are not attributable to one partner or the other, but actually reflect on the relationship between them. Many of the couples who consult a marriage counselor are in good physical and mental health; nevertheless, their marriage is suffering and needs professional help. Thus, the major task of a marriage counselor is to work with people who may be functioning reasonably well as individuals, but who are having difficulty getting along with each other. It is not a matter of one partner's getting "justice." This idea must be replaced by a desire to find the greatest strength possible in the relationship. Any relationship is damaged when justice is put first in a conflict situation, for no one can absolutely define the intangible limits of justice. Mudd defines marriage counseling as

> ... the process through which a professionally trained counselor assists two persons (the engaged or marriage partners) to develop abilities in resolving, to some workable degree, the problems that trouble them in their interpersonal relationship as they move into marriage, live with it, or (in a small number of instances) move out of it. The focus of the counselor's approach is a relationship between the two people in the marriage rather than, as in psychiatric therapy, the reorganization of the personality structure of the individual.[41]

DIFFERENCES FROM FAMILY COUNSELING. Marriage counseling differs from family counseling in that the latter may involve broader relations between any two or more family members or within the total family group. Marriage counseling may deal with the family group but only within the framework of the marriage relationship.

A LONG PROCESS. Effective marriage counseling is a time-consuming endeavor; it will not solve basic problems immediately. A series of meetings may be necessary before any progress is noted. Interviews usually last about an hour and are held about once a week. The author's own experience indicates that, when a genuine marriage problem is involved (rather than a desire for information or a more complicated personality problem which must be referred to other specialists) at least a dozen interviews are usually necessary to reach a satisfactory solution.

COUNSELING ONE PARTNER ONLY. It is usually advisable for both partners to be present. Sometimes, however, counseling with one partner works out satisfactorily for both. The biggest problem in seeing only one client is that the process may tend to take on the attributes of the more psychologically oriented personality counseling. Some counselors use the joint-conference technique, bringing the discordant couple into the office together, and conducting the interview as an impartial hearing of both sides. This approach, however, is based upon the false assumption that each partner hears and then replies to everything said about him. More often, this kind of confrontation becomes not a revelation of truth but a bitter renewal of the conflict, further intensified by the shame of exposure before a third person. Current counseling policy tends to favor separate interviews, with the counselor showing a sympathetic, nonmoralizing, noncoercive attitude toward each party. When communication has disintegrated into perpetual warfare, a cease-fire must first be called. Then each partner separately can discuss the problems with the counselor. Mudd states that several agencies are opposed to joint sessions. Most prefer a flexible policy with the same counselor handling both partners, unless their mutual suspicions and hostility are too great. Joint sessions are held when the counselor feels the couple is ready for them.[42] He would see each partner separately at first, permitting each partner to free himself of emotional tensions and to criticize the mate freely in private; later the two would be brought together for joint counseling. The willingness of both spouses to come for counseling is important. Counselors are generally agreed that little can be done for a client who comes under pressure from his spouse. A person must want counseling to be able to benefit from it.

It is interesting to note, however, that the partner who has refused counseling frequently becomes so impressed by the changes in the mate's behavior that he decides counseling is worth investigating. Even when only one partner is seeking help, and the other needs it more, the marriage relationship may be improved. This benefit results from the first mate's ability to discuss the problems with a sense of integrity, which helps to relieve his tensions. Better understanding and greater acceptance of the problems will also enable that partner to continue the marriage more realistically. Through the changes that the one partner makes, and the resultant improvement in the relationship, corresponding changes may be made by the other partner without his realizing it. Thus, the total relationship is improved even further.

THE COUNSELING PROCESS.   The counselor helps each client to bring the real problems to the surface so they can be examined. In this connection, Rutledge says marriage counseling is a process

> ... whereby professional skills and experience, within the context of an understanding and accepting face-to-face relationship, are brought to the assistance of spouses as they explore, evaluate, and clarify feelings and issues; as they seek to communicate verbally and emotionally; and as they learn to choose courses of action which will lead to some resolution of their problems.[43]

By bringing the real problems to the surface for examination, counselors help clients to relieve emotional pressures and to see the positive values of the relationship. The counseling procedure must allow the partners first to express their resentment, anger, and aggression without fear of condemnation or manipulation.[44] After the client's personal feelings have been somewhat clarified, the marriage counselor can help him to consider means of improving his total marital relationship.

Exploration of alternative courses of actions is essential; it should be kept in mind, however, that final decisions are made by the clients; the marriage counselor only assists them in exploring the probable results of possible actions. As Stoltenberg has pointed out, it is impossible for a marriage counselor to tell a couple exactly what they should do:

> Marriage counselors must necessarily work in a complex field where, although there are many knowns, there are also many unknowns. Difficult as is the physical world to capture and explain, this human one is infinitely more complicated. The person sitting in front of the counselor seeking help is vastly more than a machine or a simple animal; he is a human being with all of the wonder and mystery these words imply. How can a marriage counselor approach his work with anything less than reverence, openness, and humility as he works daily with living, plastic, sensitive human beings for whose destiny he is about to become partly responsible?[45]

Seldom does a counselor write a complete prescription for a marriage. Instead, his function is to help the couple clarify their own intentions in the light of their feelings, desires, and values. Before they make a decision, however, the marriage counselor must make certain that the clients have explored all possible avenues of action.

Sometimes a couple need only additional information to solve a particular problem. The marriage counselor gives practical information when it is needed, but he does not pose as an expert in all the various specialities.

A VARIETY OF TECHNIQUES. A variety of techniques is used by marriage counselors. Tests such as marital-adjustment scores are sometimes used to confirm whether or not a couple are having serious problems and to identify areas where the real trouble possibly lies. If the marriage counselor helps the couple unwind and talk about the problems sooner, rapport is more quickly established. There are various marital-adjustment tests. Locke and Wallace reported selecting the most fundamental items from several marital-adjustment tests and constructing a short test, which subsequently has proved to be very reliable.[46] Tests often used in this area are those devised by Burgess and Cottrell, Locke, Terman, and Burgess and Wallin.[47] An interesting method of evaluating alternative actions, if not carried too far, is the mathematical formula, based on game-and-decision theory, which some counselors now use.[48]

Criteria for success in marriage counseling

Counseling is not a cure-all; it may not work in every case. It does, however, offer an objective approach for the couple who have reached an emotional deadlock. The test of good marriage counseling is not that it eliminates all family troubles, but that it helps the couple improve their ability to solve problems as they occur.

CASE LEVELS. The extent of counseling success naturally depends upon the complexity of the problems, or the "case level." Sometimes all that is needed is the correction of misinformation or prejudice, or the suggestion of new values. This may be sufficient to alter attitudes in a particular case. When the partners have already examined the situation from all sides, trying many of the resources a counselor would suggest, and still find themselves at an impasse, the case is obviously much more difficult. Another case level concerns (1) couples who made a tragic mistake in marrying in the first place and whose relationship has perhaps been more or less hopeless from the start; or (2) couples whose ideals, values, and standards, have changed so much that, try as they may, they cannot restore the relationship to its former level. In many such cases change is not only possible, but desirable. The relationship may never be exactly what it used to be, but perhaps a new and even better plane can be reached on a more mature and realistic basis than was envisioned earlier.

DEFINITION OF SUCCESS. To establish a reliable criterion of success in marital counseling, it is necessary to define a standard. It is one thing to judge the success of marriage counseling on the number of marriages it can save or restore to their former romantic heights; it is another thing to judge its success on the degree of improvement it is able to effect in a relationship. Although the purpose of marriage counseling may be to save marriages, it would be surprising if all marriages succeeded simply through counseling: the pattern of most human endeavors and characteristics describes a curve of variability rather than a straight line. Thus, in spite of all efforts, some marriages will fail, some will be mediocre, and some will be outstanding.

The primary objective of modern marriage counseling is not to salvage a marriage but to enrich a relationship. In this connection, to bring a couple to the consideration of separation or divorce may, under some conditions, be a sign of progress. In other words, termination of the marital contract may, in some cases, be the most proper solution of the problems.

It may come as a surprise to many that divorce is an essential component of a democracy. Yet if a society offers its members freedom of choice in civil action, it cannot with justice deny them the freedom to refute the action if their choice leads to disastrous consequences. Just as a religion that professes freedom of will finds it necessary to offer forgiveness of sins, so a democracy professing freedom of choice must offer a means of rectifying errors of judgment.

Some couples today seem to be faced with a choice between preserving a miserable marriage or preserving a deep friendship. From the standpoint of today's goals, complete marital success is, in some cases, impossible. The interests of society at large and of the family itself may sometimes best be served by the separation of the marriage partners. The children, too, may be much better off living peacefully with one parent than being used by both as pawns in a perpetual domestic conflict. (The Catholic Church acknowledges this fact by making provisions for legal separation.) If, under such conditions, counseling contributes to separation, it should be credited with success rather than with failure.

The real controversy over divorce arises from the fact that too often the privilege is abused. All human freedoms are subject to irresponsible misuse, and divorce is no exception. When used by the irresponsible, separation and divorce can be cruel, exploitive, and tragic; when used by the responsible, they can be humane, kind, and liberating. In other words, although divorce itself can make sense, the divorce situation in American society makes very little sense.[49] According to the developmental-task concept, it would seem that no one should be allowed to remarry after a divorce at least until he has re-examined the entire situation and recognized the part he played in the failure of his first attempt. Competent professional counselors should then be consulted to prepare the divorced person for success in a second marriage.

IN OTHER CULTURES. The American society is not the only society with a high divorce rate. Fortune's study of the Dobu revealed that almost all their first marriages failed.[50] Murdock reported that marital failure is recognized in primitive societies and that some have a marital-failure rate much higher than that of the United States.[51] In a culture dedicated to individual freedom of choice, whether to marry, whom to marry, when to marry, and what constitutes marital success, are questions that may well lead to errors of decision.

Until adequate educational preparation for marriage is available and utilized by more people, innumerable marital mistakes will be made. There will be cases where the best solution is to sever the marriage. The divorce statistics of other cultures that are achieving individual freedom show even higher percentage increases than those of the American society.[52] If divorce is an evil, than it is sometimes a necessary evil in the metamorphosis of a people experiencing new freedoms before developing the maturity necessary to accept new responsibilities.

This is not to suggest that the chief aim of marriage counseling is to help couples obtain separations or divorces. Many marriages are strengthened and enriched by counseling; many are saved by such guidance.

All marriage counseling should be evaluated through its over-all effects on the marriage relationship, including increased communication between the partners, an increase in the number of their common goals, an increase in each partner's acceptance of the other for what he really is, and an increase in effectiveness of the marital relationship as a determining factor in the lives of the partners.

Summary

Even though the educated approach is most effective in the prevention of marital problems, a sizable number of marriages occasionally need help. Too many couples do not recognize their marital problems early enough, or cannot solve them without help.

Although marriage counseling is not a modern concept, the techniques introduced through the American approach are new. Marriage counseling is practiced in a number of ways: as a by-product of other professional services, as a clinical service, as a court function, and as a full-time profession. A couple seeking help should ascertain that the counselor is qualified. There are many organizations that will provide the necessary information.

Marriage counseling is unique in that its primary aim is to improve the relationship between two people rather than the personality of either. This often means that the counselor must refer the client to one or several specialists during the counseling process.

The effectiveness of marriage counseling depends upon the basic definition of counseling success. Today, the primary purpose of marriage counseling seems to be to improve the relationship rather than to save the marriage, but it often helps a couple to rebuild a marriage out of what might appear to them to be a hopeless shambles. Marriage guidance is the American democratic method of helping marriages in trouble. No couple should hesitate to seek such help when marital trouble arises. The earlier a trouble spot is identified, the better the chances of saving and improving the marital relationship. Perhaps the time will come when periodic tests will alert the couple to weaknesses developing within the relationship. Then, with proper follow-up counseling, serious differences may be circumvented and marital harmony maintained.

Notes

1. Theodore B. Johannis, Jr., "The Marital Adjustment of a Sample of Married College Students," *The Family Life Coordinator*, 4:25.
2. Harriet F. Pipel and Theodora Zavin, *Your Marriage and the Law* (New York: Holt, Rinehart & Winston, Inc., 1952), p. 276.
3. Ernest R. Groves, "A Decade of Marriage Counseling," *Annals of the American Academy of Political and Social Science*, **168**:72.

4. George H. Napheys, *The Physical Side of Women* (Philadelphia: H. C. Watts, 1882), p. 93.

5. Paul Popenoe, "The Marriage Clinic," *Parents' Magazine* (April 1932), 15.

6. Ralph P. Bridgeman, "Guidance for Marriage and Family Life," *Annals of The American Academy of Political and Social Science,* **160:**144.

7. *Marriage Guidance in a Local Community* (London: National Marriage Guidance Council, 1948), p. 4.

8. David R. Mace, "Marriage Counseling in Britain Today," *Marriage and Family Living,* **20:**379–83.

9. *Ibid.*

10. *Ibid.*

11. Reported in *Marriage and Family Living,* **12:**68.

12. Abraham Stone, "Marriage Education and Marriage Counseling in the United States," *Marriage and Family Living,* **11:**38–39.

13. Ernest R. Groves, "Professional Training for Marriage and Family Counseling," *Social Forces,* **23:**447–51.

14. Proverbs, 11:14.

15. Gerald Gurin, Joseph Veroff, and Sheila Feld, *Americans View Their Mental Health* (New York: Basic Books, Inc., 1960), pp. 305–309.

16. For a fuller discussion, see David R. Mace, "What Is a Marriage Counselor?" *Marriage and Family Living,* **15:**136.

17. F. J. Roethlisberger and W. J. Dickson, *Management and the Worker* (Cambridge, Mass.: Harvard University Press, 1939), pp. 593–604.

18. Joseph K. Folsom, *The Family in Democratic Society* (New York: John Wiley & Sons, Inc., 1943), p. 643.

19. Carl R. Rogers, "A Personal Formulation of Client-Centered Therapy," *Marriage and Family Living,* **14:**341.

20. Emily H. Mudd, *The Practice of Marriage Counseling* (New York: Association Press, 1951), p. 274.

21. Paul W. Alexander, "Legal Science and the Social Sciences: The Family Court," *Marriage and Family Living,* **20:**138.

22. Mudd, *op. cit.,* p. 274.

23. *Ibid.,* pp. 274–75.

24. Alexander, *op. cit.,* p. 138.

25. Paul W. Alexander, "Family Cases Are Different—Why Not Family Courts?" *Kansas Law Review* (1954), 27–28.

26. Paul W. Alexander, "Legal Science and the Social Sciences: The Family Court," *Marriage and Family Living,* **20:**138.

27. *Ibid.,* p. 139.

28. Quintin Johnstone, "Divorce Dismissals: A Field Study," *Kansas Law Review* (May 1953), 252.

29. Louis H. Burke, "Report of the Children's Court of Conciliation, a Department of the Superior Court of the State of California, In and For the County of Los Angeles," *Dicta* (December 1954), 443–50.

30. Alice O'Leary Ralls, "The King County Family Court," *Washington Law Review* (1953), 22–28.

31. See Paul W. Alexander, "The Follies of Divorce: A Therapeutic Approach to the Problem," *American Bar Association Journal,* **34:**106; and Paul W. Alexander, "The Family Court of the Future," *Journal of the American Judicature Society* (August 1952), 44–45. Wisconsin has adopted counseling as a preliminary procedure in all divorce actions, and Massachusetts law requires a ninety-day "cooling-off" period after the filing of a suit for divorce. Pending current

legislation in Montana and Massachusetts would make it mandatory for both spouses to submit to marriage counseling by court-appointed counselors during the ninety-day period. Pending laws in both Maine and Delaware would establish statewide systems of family courts.

32. Mace, "What Is A Marriage Counselor?" *op. cit.*, p. 142.

33. Lee R. Steiner, *Where Do People Take Their Troubles?* (Boston: Houghton Mifflin Company, 1945).

34. Aaron L. Rutledge, "The Future of Marriage Counseling," *The Merrill Palmer Quarterly* (Summer 1955), 142.

35. Lee R. Steiner, "Figures on Charlatanism," *The American Psychologist* (November 1953), 708.

36. As of March 1965, only California had legislation required a license to practice marriage counseling, with established standards for qualification. A similar law is pending in Missouri.

37. For a fuller discussion of this, see Steiner, *Where Do People Take Their Troubles? op. cit.*

38. Bill Davidson, "Quack Marriage Counselors," *Saturday Evening Post* (January 5–12, 1963), 18–24.

39. The address is 27 Woodcliff Drive, Madison, N.J.

40. General qualifications required for clinical membership in the American Association of Marriage Counselors, Inc., as of July 1964.

41. Emily H. Mudd, "Psychiatry and Marital Problems: Mental Health Implications," *Eugenics Quarterly*, 2:111.

42. Emily H. Mudd, "Can One Partner Be Successfully Counseled Without the Other?" *Marriage and Family Living*, 15:62–63.

43. Aaron L. Rutledge, "Marriage Counseling Today and Tomorrow," *Marriage and Family Living*, 19:386–90.

44. Emily H. Mudd, "Counseling: A Philosophy and Method," *Cyclopedia Of Medicine, Surgery, And Specialties* (Philadelphia: F. A. Davis, 1945).

45. Louise Stoltenberg, "A Philosophy of Sex in Relation to Counseling," *Marriage and Family Living*, 22:119–22.

46. Harvey J. Locke and Karl M. Wallace, "Short Marital-Adjustment and Prediction Tests: Their Reliability and Validity," *Marriage and Family Living*, 21:251–55.

47. E. W. Burgess and Leonard S. Cottrell, *Predicting Success or Failure in Marriage* (Englewood Cliffs, N.J.: Prentice-Hall, Inc., 1939), pp. 64–65; Harvey J. Locke, *Predicting Adjustment in Marriage* (New York: Holt, Rinehart & Winston, Inc., 1951), pp. 48–52; Lewis M. Terman, *Psychological Factors in Marital Happiness* (New York: McGraw-Hill Book Company, Inc., 1938), p. 50; or E. W. Burgess and Paul Wallin, *Engagement and Marriage* (Philadelphia: J. B. Lippincott Co., 1953), pp. 485–502.

48. Jessie Bernard, "Counseling Techniques for Arriving at Optimum Compromises: Game-and-Decision Theory," *Marriage and Family Living*, 21:264–74.

49. Manford Blake, *The Road to Reno* (New York: The Macmillan Company, 1961).

50. R. F. Fortune, *Sorcerers of Dobu* (New York: E. P. Dutton and Company, Inc., 1932).

51. George P. Murdock, "Family Stability in Non-European Cultures," *Annals of The American Academy of Political and Social Science*, 272:195–201.

52. See Kingsley Davis, "Statistical Perspective On Marriage and Divorce," *Annals of The American Academy of Political and Social Science*, 272:9–21; or William J. Goode, *After Divorce* (New York: The Free Press of Glencoe, Inc.,

1956), p. 11; or the latest *United Nations Demographic Yearbook,* New York: Columbia University Press.

Questions for further thought

1. What position should an outsider take when a friend's marriage is going on the rocks?
2. How can a couple go about finding the best available marriage counselor in their community?
3. What course of action would probably be best today for a small community lacking any competent marriage counselors?
4. How much does marriage counseling cost per interview?
5. What can be done when one mate refuses to cooperate in marriage counseling?
6. Do newspaper advice-to-the-lovelorn columns have any value?
7. Some people believe that divorce is really harder—emotionally, financially, and so forth—on the man than on the woman. Support or reject this contention, and give your reasons.
8. What suggestions are in order for a couple who married after a brief acquaintance, and obviously made a mistake?
9. Is an individual judge ever justified in denying a divorce to an unhappy couple?
10. Which philosophy best fits the American democratic concept: (1) "I believe in marriage, and I shall always do my best to make mine a successful happy one. If my best effort is not enough, however, I shall not let false pride interfere with securing a divorce." (2) "I shall never consider divorce under any circumstances." Why?
11. What does Henry A. Bowman (*Marriage for Moderns* [New York: McGraw-Hill Book Company, Inc., 1954], p. 282) mean when he states: "If we assume that every hasty, ill-advised marriage represents a couple joined together by God, we assume both that words are magic and can automatically enlist God's unaltered approval, and also that God is a party of many a tragic mistake"?

Recommended film

In Time of Trouble (McGraw-Hill Book Company, Inc.).

Suggested supplemental readings

BOOKS

Ackerman, Nathan W., Frances L. Beatman, and Sanford N. Sherman (eds.). *Exploring the Base for Family Therapy.* New York: Family Service Association of America, 1961.

Bergler, Edmund. *Divorce Won't Help.* New York: Harper & Row, Publishers, 1948.

Bridgeman, Ralph. *Marital Discord, Divorce, and the Family Court.* Toledo, Ohio: Lucas County Family Court Center, 1955.

Haussamen, Florence, and Mary Annie Guitar. *The Divorce Handbook.* New York: G. P. Putnam's Sons, 1960.

Herbert, W. L., and F. V. Jarvis. *The Art of Marriage Counseling: A Modern Approach.* New York: Emerson Books, Inc., 1960.

Hiltner, Seward, and Lowell G. Colston, *The Context of Pastoral Counseling.* New York: Abingdon Press, 1961.

Hudson, R. Lefton. *Marital Counseling,* Englewood Cliffs, N.J.: Prentice-Hall, Inc., 1963.

Johnson, Dean. *Marriage Counseling: Theory and Practice.* Englewood Cliffs, N.J.: Prentice-Hall, Inc., 1961.

Kling, S. G. *The Complete Guide to Divorce.* New York: Random House, 1963.

O'Gorman, Hubert J. *Lawyers and Matrimonial Cases.* New York: The Free Press of Glencoe, 1965.

Popenoe, Paul, and Dorothy Cameron Disney. *Can This Marriage Be Saved?* New York: The Macmillan Company, 1960.

Putney, Snell and Gail J. *Normal Neurosis: The Adjusted American.* New York: Harper & Row, Publishers, 1964.

Slade, Frances. *Divorce If You Must.* New York: Coward-McCann, Inc., 1960.

Spellman, Howard H. *Successful Management of Matrimonial Cases.* Englewood Cliffs, N.J.: Prentice-Hall, Inc., 1954.

ARTICLES

Alexander, P. W. "The Follies of Divorce: A Therapeutic Approach to the Problem," *American Bar Association Journal,* 36:105–108.

Bonnell, John S. "Why Parishioners Should Bring Their Problems to Their Pastor," *Pastoral Psychology,* 7:52–54.

Buck, Gertrude J. "Confession and the Courts," *American Ecclesiastical Review,* 142:77–86.

Chikes, Tibor, *et al.* "An Experiment in Marriage Counseling by Three New Jersey Churches," *Pastoral Psychology,* 12:29–34.

Foster, Robert G. "How a Marriage Counselor Handles a Case," *Marriage and Family Living,* 16:139–42.

Fulcomer, David, *et al.* "Interdisciplinary Marriage Counseling in a University Counseling Service," *Marriage and Family Living,* 23:273–75.

Geist, Joanne, and Norman M. Gerber. "Joint Interviewing: A Treatment Technique with Marital Partners," *Social Casework,* 41:76–83.

Kerckhoff, Richard K. "Interest Group Reactions to the Profession of Marriage Counseling," *Sociology and Social Research,* 39:179–83.

Levine, Lena, and Irving Brodsky. "Taking Stock of Marriage: An Illustration in Group Counseling," *Marriage and Family Living,* 18:162–67.

Mace, David. "Newspaper Columns," *Marriage and Family Living,* 12:100.

———. "What Is a Marriage Counselor?" *Marriage and Family Living,* 16:136.

Mogey, John. "Marriage Counseling and Family Life Education in England," *Marriage and Family Living,* 23:146–54.

Rutledge, Aaron L. "Should the Marriage Counselor Ever Recommend Divorce?" *Marriage and Family Living,* 25:319–25.

Whitlock, Glenn E. "The Use of Dreams in Premarital Counseling," *Marriage and Family Living,* 23:258–60.

Preparing
for marriage

chapter 21   ## tomorrow

No one can be completely prepared for marriage tomorrow simply by studying marriage today. Some of the most frustrated marriages today have resulted from couples' attempts to live by outmoded standards. The direction in which various things will change need not remain a complete unknown. Therefore, it behooves each individual to become aware of tomorrow's possibilities as well as today's realities. In the words of Margaret Mead:

> The most vivid truth of our age is that no one will live all his life in the world into which he was born, and no one will die in the world in which he worked in his maturity.[1]

The inevitability of changes

It is probably safe to say that family life in America has never been exactly like family life anywhere else. America was not settled predominantly by any one people; it is a mixture of peoples from many places.

A UNIQUE BEGINNING. This mixture of nations has made American family life unique in many ways. The vanguard of these various groups came to America to escape and to improve their circumstances. As they broke with tradition, their family life was altered. Then, too, in America it was next to impossible to keep old cultures completely intact. Ideas, theories, and rituals, although not freely exchanged, were influenced by those of neighbors from other countries. This interchange was made easier by the fact that each group usually welcomed change as a sign of independence from the ties of the "old country." A third factor contributing to an unprecedented family pattern was that the early settlers were basically a friendly people. There were many doubts, suspicions, and prejudices, but no one pattern of family life was forced upon any group. There was neither conqueror nor vanquished; no single group was accepted as superior to others. Exogamy increasingly became the rule through free association in social activities and in work. It seems that when the wishes, rituals, customs, and ideas of one group are not forced upon another, each group more quickly assimilates part of the other's pattern. The result is closer identification and harmony of all groups. Most important, America was a virgin land, and changes in every family pattern were necessary for sheer survival. Even if the other conditions had been lacking, the precariousness of life in a new land would have necessitated an acceptance of new ways.

INFLUENCES OF OTHER CHANGES. Family life has continued to change long after the original causes of change disappeared. Even within the memories of each reader, change has occurred. Because the conditions of environment are constantly changing, the family, too, is forced to change in order to retain its identity. Urban industrialization, social opportunities, political guarantees, and constitutional enforcements sharply affect the patterns of family life.

THE NEED FOR CHANGE. The pattern of life a hundred years ago, transposed intact to modern times, could not contribute much to survival in the present world; it would probably result in utter chaos. Family life must be judged by the extent to which it helps its members adapt to new conditions. Rigidity means destruction; only flexibility can lead to strength and progress. The "good old days" are best left in the past.

The difficulty is that change is logarithmic and the full significance of this fact is only now dawning upon society. One change brings about two; two bring about four; four mean eight, and by the tenth step, 1024 changes have resulted from the original single change. Man went along for centuries with very few changes. Sixty years ago life was little different from life a hundred years earlier; and life at the beginning of the nineteenth century was not too far removed from life in the first century.

Bernard Karsh cites an illustration (first given by the noted historian, J. Lewis Powell) of the enormity of accelerated change in today's society. If the entire history of man were condensed into an imaginary fifty-year period, it would read as follows: Ten years ago man left his cave, and five years ago he began to write. Two years ago Christianity began, and fifteen months ago Gutenberg invented the printing press. Electricity was discovered only ten days ago; the airplane, yesterday morning; the radio last night; the television, this morning; and the jet airplane, less than a minute ago.[2]

As a further illustration of the compression of events, McCain has pointed out that about half of everything known has been found out since

1900, and half of that since 1950.³ Obviously then, other momentous breakthroughs are about to occur, and it is essential that man be prepared to interpret them to his advantage.

Today's families are living in a time of change so radical and disruptive that much of the world is reeling from it. From 6 per cent machine-generated energy in 1860, the United States now receives 96 per cent of its energy by mechanical means and only 4 per cent from muscle. In assembling data for the 1960 census, fifty persons, more efficiently and more accurately, did the work previously done by 4100 persons just ten years earlier during the 1950 census.

To try to resist change is as futile as to try to command time to stand still. Change is a condition of life, and accelerated change is aggravated by cultural lags. To survive in a constantly changing society, it is necessary to examine carefully at frequent intervals the purposes and direction of action. When a need for change is necessary, he who hesitates is lost. The postponement of difficult decisions will only make them more difficult later.

EVOLUTION, NOT REVOLUTION. It would be as tragic to change the family too rapidly as not to change it at all. The family must change only in the same degree as other factors do. The world has experienced undue pressures from those who would "save the family" through radical change. The proposals of some of these false prophets always have appeal for certain dissatisfied elements, such as the followers of Karl Marx, with his warped views of capitalism, of Adolph Hitler and his "superrace," of Judge Ben Lindsey and his concept of "trial" marriage, or of Bertrand Russell and his philosophy of "free love." There is no magic formula for the problems of human life. But when change is inevitable, adaptability is essential.

INTERDEPENDENCY OF FAMILIES. The day of the self-sufficient family is long past; no family today can be an end unto itself. Families need society and the proper relationships to it to survive and grow. Even the few remaining strictly agricultural groups cannot endure without some contact with outside resources. What is sometimes overlooked is that interdependence of actions involves interdependence of responsibility.⁴ This does not mean a shifting of responsibility, but a sharing of responsibility. Parents cannot be held wholly responsible for their children's behavior because children are educated outside the home and are continuously exposed to the temptations of an irresponsible adult world. Society may legitimately blame the family for the ignorance and misdeeds of children only if society is willing to redefine itself as part of the family. Whether people like it or not, each individual is responsible, to a degree, for every other person.

The family expands in proportion to its sharing power with others; the "family" of today should be the community; but the "family" of tomorrow *must* be the world. A world state in some form or other is necessary, and therefore possible. Society consists of an increasingly tangled network of social interactions, the least common denominator of which is the family of orientation. Life is not a thing set apart; it is a process, and an increasing part of that process involves expanding associations beyond parental influence or supervision.[5] Research has found that 87 per cent of a fourth-grader's life is family-oriented, but only 50 per cent of an eighth-grader's life and only 37 per cent of a tenth-grader's life is so oriented.[6]

A BETTER LIFE. Because children, once considered assets, became liabilities, a reduction in family size was in order to secure today's essentials, or yesterday's luxuries. Americans have raised their standard of living: they have better food, more comforts and leisure, better education, and more travel. Yet the true effects of abundance have not been experienced. Automation increases productivity, which, in turn, should lead to an even higher standard of living and equality for the many.[7] Now "optimization" promises to exceed the effects of automation. The total 1950 sales of electric energy in America amounted to 286 billion

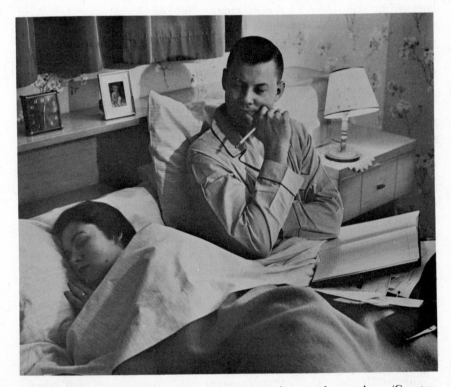

Figure 21-1. Today's white-collar worker must often work overtime. (Courtesy of the New York Life Insurance Company.)

kilowatt-hours. At that time it was forecast that electric power sales would total about 525 billion kilowatt-hours by 1960, yet the actual figure was almost 700 billion. It is now forecast that the figure will reach 1350 billion by 1970, and at least 2700 billion by 1980.[8]

PROBLEMS OF THE WHITE-COLLAR CLASS. Too often today's young white-collar worker has only two choices: one is to bring "paper-work" home at night, and work his way to success through overtime; the other is to keep regular working hours and become a failure. There is seldom a third alternative. Even when he does a satisfactory job and wins promotions, the white-collar worker is only burdened with additional work and responsibility. The concepts of family life for such people must change or go down to defeat.

A challenge to codes of living

It is not the intention of the author to debate the merits of all trends. It is common knowledge that some are disastrous, but all too often it has been assumed that all trends are bad when, in reality, many of them are not. Some changes are only necessary stop-gap measures; they do not represent the true picture, but only the transition between major changes.

MORE FREEDOM FOR WOMEN. The American crusade for women's rights began in 1848 in a made-over saloon on a side street in Seneca Falls, New York. Wide banners proclaimed the revolution—"WOMEN'S RIGHTS CONVENTION"—and the movement for the equality of woman gained force. Women's right to vote was guaranteed by the Nineteenth Amendment and almost all the individual states came to recognize women's equal rights in property and education. Other effects of these freedom movements are even more apparent within the family.

The mother of today—wearing slacks, shorts, or blue jeans around the house, pursuing a full- or part-time career outside the home, or standing up fearlessly for what she believes is right in various civic organizations—has come a long way from her grandmother. Her own granddaughters will be even farther ahead, with dust-free houses, filtered air, sonar-wave cleaning devices, instant foods, disposable clothing, and less time needed for housekeeping drudgery and "kitchen-mindedness." More time will be spent in home management to improve family living by stressing diet and budgeting instead of cooking and canning, and child-training instead of "child-supervising." All this necessitates keeping up with the entire family—intellectually, socially, and emotionally. It is no longer possible, nor would it be desirable, to marry a girl "just like the girl that married dear old Dad." Since World War II, two American women have won Nobel Prizes; the National Academy of Science has elected five women to membership; newspaper women have won five Pulitzer Prizes, and women authors of biography, poetry, history, drama, and fiction have

Figure 21-2. From an early beginning, the movement for the equality of women is now approaching reality. (Courtesy of Culver Pictures, Inc.)

won thirty-eight more.[9] Women now have the opportunity of being physically, mentally, and emotionally attractive all the time. This opportunity also can improve family living.

Today's woman is also freer to exercise her citizenship and leadership duties. She can now have an educational background equal to her husband's and, often, more leisure to study and keep abreast of issues of the day.

The modern woman will not give blind obedience to her husband, nor continually play second fiddle in the home; neither does she feel guilty for not doing so. Most modern religions interpret woman's role in society in a new light. Actually, it is not to be found anywhere in the teachings of Jesus or Peter that woman should always assume a secondary status; this concept stemmed from Paul, who had a rather negative attitude toward women and marriage.

THE PLANNING OF CHILDREN. Research shows quite conclusively that unwanted children are more likely to be rejected children in today's society. A wider use of conception-control measures and information has resulted in an increasing amount of family planning. This, in turn, tends to separate the sex act from the act of childbearing and makes the main purpose of marriage something other than procreation.

Cornell University scientists are now working on a process that involves collecting fertilized ova from outstanding cows and implanting them in less valuable cows, where they continue to develop normally. It is hoped that, through this process, it will become possible for cattlemen to obtain more calves from high-quality animals. The Cornell scientists have not stopped there, for they are also experimenting with the fertilization of eggs in a test tube. The "test tube" is actually a small culture flask that contains special nutrients in addition to the sperm and ova. They speculate that this may eventually lead to a process whereby ova from outstanding cows can be collected, fertilized in the laboratory, frozen, and stored until needed.[10] If this process can be perfected, it may be possible to apply it to humans. It may well be that sometime in the future (and keep in mind that the technological "future" is closer every decade) couples will be able to have all their children conceived in the same year. Thus, a woman would be free to continue a career or to become a wife and mother whenever she wished. She might be able to have children after the death of her spouse. According to Nimkoff, Dr. R. G. Bune, of the University Hospital, University of Iowa, has successfully stored human spermatozoa for a long period, and later used it for insemination purposes with no apparent genetic defects or health problems.[11]

SEX BEHAVIOR. Sex is currently being studied more objectively by more scientists. When it is honestly declared a positive value in its own right, sex may no longer be legally confined to marriage, for this is purely a matter of convention.

THE MARRIAGE BOND. Marriage has strong ecclesiastical support as a sacred and holy state. It has frequently been described as a divine permanent relationship; however, because no other relationship is held to be permanent, loopholes were left in this one, too.

In the Council of Trent, the Catholic Church proclaimed marriage to be a sacrament, but prescribed two conditions upon with divorce was acceptable: (1) *divortium a mensa et thoro* (divorce from bed and board), for a just cause, such as infidelity, the partners might go their separate ways but neither could remarry as long as the other lived; and (2) *divortium a vinculo matrimonii* (divorce from the bond of marriage), which stipulated that, whenever a marriage was proven not to be "truly a marriage," the partners might separate and be free to remarry. In the latter case, for legal purposes, the term *annulment* is used. Actually, the main difference between divorce and annulment lies in the fact that civil courts granting divorce are simply more liberal than ecclesiastical courts in their interpretation of what constitutes a "true" marriage. Such is the confusion in present society regarding this matter that, according to Pilpel and Zavin, it is not uncommon to find that what constitutes grounds for divorce in one state is considered grounds for annulment in others.[12] Furthermore, the grounds for divorce and annulment are so similar in some states (Georgia, for instance) that the courts in those states rarely grant an annulment. Thus, if children should later result from the brief union, there is never any question of their legitimacy. Grounds for annulment are inversely proportional to the "liberality" of the divorce laws in each state.[13]

Marriage may be ordained by God, and may represent the spiritual union of two people, but it has to be lived by man. A particular marriage may not be a true marriage at all because it was never founded as such, or has since been destroyed. In such a case, the legal severance of the marriage bond would seem acceptable. In 1867 the U.S. Bureau of the Census reported a total of 9937 divorces, or a rate of 0.3 per 1000 population. In 1946 there were 610,000 divorces (the highest annual number on record) or a rate of 4.3 per 1000 population. Since that time, the divorce rate has slowly dropped until at present it amounts to about 380,000 annually, or a rate of 2.2 per 1000 population. Altogether, there are now about 2.8 million living divorced persons. The trend is unmistakable. America is once more experiencing a higher proportion of successful marriages, probably as a result of better marriage education in the schools. Although the actual number of divorces per year increased by about 25,000 from 1958 to 1960, the increase largely results from more accurate reporting in more states. In fact, when the reports from new states are eliminated, and the present reports equated with those of the past, divorce rates declined 0.6 per cent in those two years, and an additional 3 per cent by 1964.[14] Of course, the rate will probably never be as low as it once was. If the goals of marriage had been the same than as now, there would have been much more divorce at that time. It is true that today's divorce privilege is sometimes abused, but it frequently serves an important purpose, and it is a necessary part of a modern democratic system. To abolish divorce completely would be far more tragic. When the purposes and goals for entering marriage change, than it seems logical that the definition of *true marriage* must change also. From the basic needs to control mating, to pass on the culture, and to assure economic survival, marriage goals have come to include the needs of complementary happiness through the fulfillment of personality. If a couple, as individuals, are not prepared for the inevitable complexities of modern married life, it is doubtful that they can have a true marriage when measured by today's goals. Family stability and monogamous marriage will rest more and more on companionship features rather than on institutional ones, or monogamy will not remain the pattern at all. Tomorrow's couples must stay together because they want to, not because the church, society, or the law commands it.

As a result of the changing goals of marriage, many of today's individuals are forced to re-examine the means by which they might obtain the highest fulfillment of their personalities. It may well be that America has or is about to reach its peak in percentages of individuals who marry. Public pressure to marry, and censure if one does not, is not nearly as intense today. Ever since the time of Pope Siricius in 385 A.D., when celibacy was first decreed for the clergy, there has been a constant controversy as to whether man was morally obligated to marry. The issue was not permanently decided for the Catholic clergy until the Lateran Council of 1215; however, it takes time for such concepts to be interpreted and applied universally.

The jealousy, suspicion, and prejudices that have constantly surrounded the single adult in American culture seem to be disappearing. It is undoubtedly true that many of today's citizens marry because it is expected of them; perhaps some would be much happier as individuals, as well as happier in their relationships with their present spouses, were they not married. It may well be easier to remain single in the future.

MORE MIXED MARRIAGE. Peoples of various ethnic groups are intermarrying in larger percentages; also, in any given year, mixed Protestant-Catholic marriages, sanctioned or unsanctioned by the Catholic Church, are increasing. Mixed nationality and racial marriages are increasing, but at a much lower rate. Increasingly these intermarriages are contracted for reasons similar to those of ordinary marriages rather than for the "mystery" of someone "different," as was the case in the past. It is possible that this newer kind of mixture will eventually do more to erase persecution and prejudice between groups than the combined efforts of all the so-called human-relations committees.

Trends in family functions

The family has often been described as possessing certain basic functions,[15] but this never meant that all such functions belonged exclusively to the family, or in the same degree. It is probably safe to say that at least a portion of all the basic functions will remain part of the responsibility of the family of orientation. There continue to be noticeable trends and shifts in the role responsibilities for certain of these functions.

PROCREATION. It appears that the function of repopulating the earth remains largely a family responsibility, reports of rising illegitimacy rates notwithstanding. Sex is normal, but the confining of childbirth to the family also appears normal. Although family size has decreased and illegitimacy has increased, about 95 per cent of all American births still occur in marriage. There has been a noticeable shift in attitudes toward illegitimacy and toward unwed mothers, for although they may still be condemned, it is now also realized that they need adequate attention and care during pregnancy. Thus, there has been a strong movement to establish institutions for this purpose. The removal of the illegitimate stamp from the issued birth certificate is also gaining greater endorsement.

Time was when the usual behavior toward the unwed mother was either to cast her out of the community, completely helpless, or to seek out the responsible male and demand that he protect her honor with his name. It has taken society a long while to realize that forced marriages are not the ideal basis for modern marriage goals. Such unions are seldom satisfactory either for the parents or for the child, to say nothing of society. The increased desire of childless couples for adoption has also eased some of the problems. In fact, sociologically speaking, some of today's illegitimacy appears to serve a very worthy purpose in other marriages.

PHYSICAL PROTECTION.   Even the protective functions of the family are shared and supplemented by outside agencies. Long-range weather forecasts are a permanent feature of today's society to protect the family from disasters. Special agencies such as the military-preparedness program, not to mention police and fire departments, also protect the family. In addition, many schools are now offering drivers' education as part of the family protective function. Nearly 6 million teen-agers now drive cars, or about one out of every fourteen of the nation's 80 million licensed drivers. One out of every ten fatal auto accidents presently involves a teen-ager.[16]

ECONOMIC WELFARE.   The tendency of the typical American to identify himself more easily with the grasshopper instead of the ant has made it necessary for society to legislate for the citizen's economic welfare. Social security does for many what they seem unable or unwilling to do for themselves. As when a part of any family function is first taken out of the exclusive control of the individual, social security met resistance for a time. Now not only is it generally accepted, but its coverage is extending to more individuals.

SOCIALIZATION.   There is no advanced society known, or ever known, where the major responsibility for the early socialization of the child has not rested in the hands of the parents. In American culture the major portion of this responsibility is still with the primary family, and is likely to remain there. With all the complexities of modern life, however, socialization responsibility has been assumed by outside groups. There are not enough of these groups as yet, so that juvenile delinquency continues to be a serious problem. Communities such as Pinnellas County, Florida, are the exception. There, juvenile delinquency has actually been kept at a constant rate since 1948 in spite of a tremendous influx of young families.[17] Additional responsibility is needed for the proper control of mass communication for today's youth. "Television is changing American children from irresistible forces into immovable objects."[18] A recent analysis of one entire week's television offerings revealed an appalling number of crime programs.

Table 21-1. **Number and nature of crimes on one week's television programs**

Number	Nature
161	Murders
192	Attempted murders
83	Robberies
15	Kidnapings
44	Conspiracies for murder
21	Jailbreaks
7	Attempted lynchings
6	Dynamitings
11	Extortions
2	Cases of arson
2	Cases of physical torture

Source: Today's Child (September 1958), 7. Copyright © 1958, by 2-to-5 World, Inc., New York. Reprinted by permission.

EDUCATION. At one time, most of the formal learning necessary for life could be transferred from parent to child. This was especially true where the child was likely to follow in his father's or mother's vocation. Now, however, vocational training and even the requirement for ordinary living skills are increasingly beyond the capacity of most parents. It is necessary for America to take greater advantage of the intellectual power of its citizenry. Society must see to it that everybody is educated to the limit of his capacity, and that he continues his education throughout his life. At last count, in one state only 16.7 per cent of the elementary school teachers held a four-year college degree; in another, only 17.6 per cent; and three others were all below the 40 per cent mark.[19] If America is one nation, then it is necessary to admit that the education of all is important to each citizen. The federal government is the only government of all the citizens, and it is the logical unit to undertake the abolition of ignorance. America cannot endure as a world leader when almost half its youth drop out of high school before graduation.[20] Education is no longer considered a right of every citizen, it is now considered his duty. From 1953 to 1963, the total enrollment of public elementary and secondary schools increased 44.6 per cent.[21] Between 1950 and 1960 the number of high school students increased by 48.7 per cent; the number of college students, by 53.6 per cent; the number of high school graduates, by 38.1 per cent; and the number of college graduates, by 39.8 per cent.[22] It is estimated that over 25 million students will be in college by the turn of the century.[23] Moreover, there is a growing realization that no one ever arrives at the pinnacle of all he needs to learn. Formal adult education today is one of the fastest-expanding areas of all schooling. Still, much remains to be done, for Paul Woodring reports that in this Atomic Age, when man is reaching for the stars, 400,000 American children are still attending one-room schools in which a single instructor teaches all subjects in six, seven, or eight different grades. At last count, there were 23,696 such schools still in operation.[24]

RECREATION. At one time, the family played together or did not play at all. Today's stress on individual growth and development—each according to his own interests, needs, and rate—makes diversified interests outside the home a necessity. All too often the leadership and censorship of recreation, especially the commercial variety, is far below par. The recreation trend is here to stay. The responsibility for its effects must be recognized and assumed.

AFFECTION. The family function of exchanging affection appears to be more pronounced than ever. The shift of some responsibilities away from the home has given more time for affection. There is a greater need for affection today because of the greater tensions of facing the world away from the home. The primary family unit must be secure from all threats. Such is often the case, but perhaps still not enough to offset the brutality of the external world. In one sense at least, this lack explains the strong influence of the teen-age peer group, the "going-steady" craze, and many of the other phenomena so startling to the modern parent. Teen-agers who are secure in home love have less need to seek affection prematurely away from home. Once the least significant of all family functions, the affection aspect now supersedes all others in importance to the primary family group. In this regard, Parsons states:

> We think the trend of the evidence points to the beginning of the relative stabilization of a *new* type of family structure in a new relation to a general social structure, one in which the family is more specialized then before, but not in any general sense less important, because the society is dependent *more* exclusively on it for the performance of *certain* of its vital functions.[25]

Trends in relationships

Undoubtedly today's homes are much more democratic in practice than those of a few decades ago. Many older-generation families were held together forcefully, although today's elders may describe the situation as one of "playing and working together." This description may be the result of convenient memory processes. There was not much play, and the games that were played were parent-directed with the object of achieving peace rather than assuring constructive growth. Understanding is rapidly replacing ordering and ruling, and many parents are attempting to become genuine guidance resources to their children.

FAMILY-CENTERED SOCIETY. The pendulum of orientation, steeped in Freudian psychoanalytic theory, swung to an extreme and resulted in parents who were neurotic, frustrated, and full of guilt feelings. But there appears to be a movement toward a better balance, as adults keep in mind the importance of personality development, but apply the principle equally to all family members.

THE FAMILY COUNCIL. In this process, all family members are given a measure of freedom in keeping with their degree of responsibility for the results of that freedom. Family members are learning to communicate with one another, and also to appreciate and understand differing points of view. Parents and teen-agers can get together and settle their differences. Several interesting experiences have proved this to be so.[26]

The family-council plan, started early and rigorously followed, appears to be the best answer yet to parent-teen-age misunderstandings. That this is important to successful marriages—and, indeed, to world peace—is well illustrated by the research findings of Harold and Gladys Anderson of Michigan State University. These researchers have recently completed a ten-year study of over 10,000 children in ten countries. They found that American children rank higher in frankness, honesty, responsibility, and sense of fair play than youngsters in other countries.[27]

Increase in family-welfare agencies

More agencies are increasing their activities for and with the family. This is, in part, caused by the nonisolated position of most families of today. When families kept to themselves, there were few agencies in operation, and fewer were needed. As family living becomes more complex, agencies for relationship control are increasingly necessary. In addition, the advent of industrialization has made it necessary for some parents to work at odd hours. Many industries work around the clock, and for some families this results in the absence of at least one parent when the children are home. Thus, it is necessary for agencies to supplement what once were exclusive family functions. As Yinger states: "Powerful forces create the kind of family system to be found in a particular setting. If the identity of these forces can be discovered, a family agency can work to maintain or secure the desirable elements."[28]

IMPROVED HEALTH. One of the obvious needs for today's family is to stay healthy. Agencies have had to aid the family in this connection. Examples include such things as laws designed to guard the purity of foods and drugs, and especially the major contributions of home economics studies in nutrition.

Average life expectancy is constantly increasing. Earlier gains reflected primarily the rapid strides in controlling infectious diseases. By contrast, the more recent gains are associated with new methods of dealing with the chronic and degeneration diseases of the middle and older ages that have come to dominate the mortality pattern.[29] Blakeslee states: "Today's fifth-grade student may well reach the age of ninety or one hundred—so may most of his classmates."[30]

Life expectancy of 120 years may be common in America by the end of this century, and some persons may live to be 140. Even longer life expectancies will not be improbable in the twenty-first century, if scientific advances [especially in nutrition] continue.[31]

Table 21-2. **Life expectancy at birth**

Date	Average life expectancy in years
1879–94	34.0
1909	46.3
1919–20	51.1
1929	55.8
1939	62.5
1949	67.7
1959	70.5
1964	81.0

Source: Statistical Bulletins, Metropolitan Life Insurance Company (February 1960; August 1964). Adapted by permission.

PERSONALITY GUIDANCE. There is a trend today for specialists in child study, mental hygiene, and psychology—working through such agencies as child-guidance centers, clinics, and from nursery school on through college—to aid the family in shaping the beginnings of a better adjusted personality for each individual. Increasingly, psychiatrists are emphasizing that the personality characteristics developed in early childhood are not necessarily established until the latter part of adolescence. Thus, there is a definite need for increased support of guidance agencies and programs to help all people to understand, tolerate, and positively approach their relationships with others. More is being learned about mental illness, and it is altogether possible that, in the not-too-distant future, through proper clinical help, nearly all people may be able to change their personalities in selected directions. Horn predicts that it will not be long before it will be possible to change human genes, control heredity, and thus alter the evolution of the human race.[32] For several years now, owing to more permanent releases, the number of mental patients in American hospitals has been reduced. The reduction in 1961 over 1960 amounted to a startling 1.7 per cent.[33] In addition, for the first time since 1947, there has been, each year since 1960, a reduction (proportionate to the increased juvenile population) in juvenile delinquency cases.[34]

PUBLIC HOUSING. Because of rapid changes in today's economy, more industries are finding it to their advantage to relocate (geographically) more often than ever before. Because of this industrial relocation, more areas than previously are suddenly finding themselves overcrowded. Local builders cannot afford to invest in such boom areas until the permanency of the change has been thoroughly assessed. In the meantime, crowded conditions make for much unpleasantness and family unrest. At least 2 million new houses are needed each year, yet not more than half that number are started; furthermore, not more than 30 per cent of the population can afford a conventionally styled new house at the minimum price charged by private builders. A massive public and private effort is needed to supply decent low-cost shelter for citizens, and the movement has already started.

PREVENTION, NOT CURES. Too many agencies have stressed cures at the expense of prevention. Koos found that families of extremely low income face the same troubles as other families, but the majority do not voluntarily go to agencies for help. Furthermore, he discovered that few agencies exist for the particular problems often encountered by low-income families, and those few are beyond their means educationally, economically, or "sophisticationally."[35] Unfortunately, some agencies have not changed enough since the time of Koos' study. "A young man in a work group said he knew about community neglect, because he lived in a housing project. The agencies seem to move like satellites around the project without ever touching the needs of the people there. But they don't seem to know this."[36] One study recently revealed that many parents with problems still go first to physicians, and then to friends and relatives. When the researchers inquired why they did not go to some of the established agencies, some agreed that they should. Many gave the impression, however, that they did not think much of psychologists, psychiatrists, and social workers.[37] Promotion of the general welfare means more than helping people; it also means preventing problems from arising.

NEED FOR COORDINATED EFFORTS. In the type of multibureaucratic society into which America is moving, it will be increasingly necessary for the functions of the various agencies not to overlap. Equally important, gaps must be bridged where additional services are needed but not provided. This can be accomplished only by a strong, coordinated effort and the careful supervision of the activities of each agency. Some progress along these lines has already been made in some communities. A sample of the outstanding coordinated efforts includes those undertaken in Toledo, Ohio; Flint and Highland Park, Michigan; Asheville, and Charlotte, North Carolina; and Seattle, Washington. The next step may well be the establishment of agencies that will provide social and emotional examinations, as well as physical examinations, for marriage.[38]

The trend toward better communities

Wherever and whenever a group of interested families can establish a common ground for communication, there exists the basic potential of a "good" community. With common needs and goals, a small group—meeting regularly and as frequently as possible and without losing sight of the main purposes—will grow until it has sufficient civic following. There must be understanding and support of the idea that institutions are a means to help people, not an end in themselves. This must be accompanied by a spirit of "belonging"—a feeling that it does not really matter who gets the credit just as long as the job gets done. Interested citizens can begin by supporting community projects for the improvement of culture and mental health, and by being as ready to praise their schools for a job well done as they now are to criticize. Happy families seldom remain happy in a disorganized community. At present, the United States has 147,733 more saloons, bars, cocktail lounges, and liquor stores than it has churches.[39]

FORMAL SUPPORT IS WAITING. A community that feels ready to act will be amazed to learn of all the trained leadership that is available for such efforts. Since 1892, the National Education Association has held formal discussions on ways of improving family life. As early as 1909, church groups were expressing their inadequacy to cope with the problem and urging others to participate toward the improvement of communities and family life. The National Council on Family Relations became a living organization in 1938, and at present has over thirty affiliated state groups. These are only a few of the many sources of help for citizens trying to get their community off to a good start.

LAY LEADERS ARE NEEDED. Typically, Americans today often wait for experts to tell them how to act, but the real power to act lies within themselves. Individuals are becoming increasingly aware of what needs to be done. Paid leadership is fine for some tasks, but the major load must be carried by citizen volunteers. Everyone has a leadership potential. Society particularly needs more feminine leadership, but good leadership must be shared to remain effective. It is tragic when a few well-meaning people spread themselves too thin in community projects. Such individuals might well be termed *do-gooders* not *good-doers*, and their families suffer as a consequence.

A NUCLEUS HAS FORMED. Many more institutes and conferences on family life are being held each year. Almost every state, and many a metropolitan area, has its own family-life council. Television courses on marriage preparation and adjustment are becoming more common.

A trend toward family research

With a greater awareness by industry of its stake in the family's future, increasing numbers of research grants are being awarded by private firms and corporations. From such basic works as Goodsell's history of the European family, Calhoun's history of the early American Colonial family, and Frazier's studies on the American Negro family, scholars have expanded into the study of interpersonal relationships within the family. Each year a growing body of knowledge is added to the relationship concept of family and personality development. In fact, such research has recently been described as being the largest in the entire sociological field.[40] As yet, only a limited amount of this qualified research is being disseminated to the public through books, magazines, pamphlets, lectures, and films. Much more research is needed, and plans are underway to accomplish it.[41] Such research will no doubt soon be able to ask why things happen (as do other sciences) rather than being confined to ascertaining whether they do happen and whether they are good or bad. With this new research power in human relations will come startling breakthroughs that may even lead to permanent world peace.

Predictions

Current evidence and the opinions of some of the best scholars indicate that the family of tomorrow will probably be different from that of today because of many predicted changes in the world itself.

ECONOMIC. Changes in the economic sphere will lead to fewer, larger, and more impersonal corporations. The day of the small business enterprise is coming to an end. Even profitable farming is now a big business. In addition, increased automation will mean that fewer jobs will be "reserved" for one or the other sex. With increased automation, goods should be available in great abundance. For example, American industrial automation can already turn out seven tons of tin-plate steel in three minutes, a process which took eight hours just a few short years ago.[42] Freight hauled by the "iron horse" may soon become only a legend. Instead, various supplies may be continuously transported through pneumatic pipelines to their prearranged and electronically computed destinations. Harvey describes the approaching era as one of computors and memory machines, and points out that 250,000 people already work with or on computors designed to record, analyze, plan, and map the future. He predicts that computors soon will be used by physicians, attorneys, stockbrokers, and for the selection of steaks and the breeding of horses. In addition, Harvey predicts that soon there will be an abundance of atomic reactors for cheaper electric power, and that the use of micro-electronics will be adding smaller and smaller things to the world by their miniature fuel cells. Even food preservation will be made easier by the use of atomic radiation.[43]

These changes will lead to more two-income families. The time will soon be at hand when the wife who does not work outside the home will have to explain why she does not. A positive contribution to the national economy is a responsibility of all citizens, regardless of sex. It has even been suggested that, in the future, a husband should not be held responsible for the financial support of his divorced wife if she is capable of looking after herself. Increasingly, situations may arise where it will be better for a husband to change jobs so that his wife can keep hers, rather than the other way around.[44] A survey of fifteen nations shows an increasing trend for women everywhere (but especially in the English-speaking countries) to work for pay.[45]

These economic changes will also lead to shorter working hours. From the sixty-hour work week of only a few decades ago, labor now commonly enjoys a forty-hour work week, and—in some places or industries—much less. Thus there will be more leisure time. This can be good if couples use it to their advantage, especially for the promotion of better relationships. It is quite probable that one of the fastest-growing fields in the future will be that of professional recreational guidance. All these changes will also tend to increase geographical mobility. Industries will move and continue to move in the future to be closer to their resources and/or markets. At one time the most important resource was power, then raw materials, and then the source of transportation to markets. According to Dr. Jack Dunlap, industrial psychologist and President of Dunlap and Associates, the most important commodity now is intelligence for extended research, so industry is closer to universities than ever before.[46]

POLITICAL. In the political sphere, there will be more government programs for the control of diseases. There were only 886 paralytic polio cases in all the United States in 1962, a decrease of 35 per cent from 1961. This represents the lowest number since 1920 and is about 7.5 times less than that in 1958. Polio actually accounted for less than half as many deaths in 1962 as did measles. The incidence rate will be even lower, for the great majority of people are now being vaccinated.[47] The common cold and other respiratory infections may soon be things of the past. Through the development of *hypothermia*, (the cooling of the body or parts of the body to temperatures close to $0°$ F.), both painless and bloodless surgery is within the realm of possibility today. More than 10.5 million operations are performed annually in United States hospitals. This is double the number performed just a few years ago, yet the risk has actually declined. The surgical death rate per year is 43 per cent lower at present than it was just twenty years ago.[48] Harvey predicts that medicine will soon offer many types of transplants, artificial organs, as well as Nylon and Dacron blood vessels.[89]

These advances are helping to increase life expectancy, which may result in a preponderance of political conservatives unless the older citizens can be persuaded to keep abreast of the times. There are five times as many people of sixty-five years of age and over as there were in 1900; there will be double that number by the year 2000. In fact, the number of those seventy-five and over will be greater in the year 2000 than the number of those sixty-five and over today.[50] Over $40 million and more than 6000 new research projects annually are now being directed toward extending human life.[51] There will also be more government planning and a more controlled economy, with few (if any) depressions.

There will be new emphasis upon planning for a useful retirement, and extended coverage of family health functions.

There will also be a renewed emphasis on the search for world peace through a common acceptance of responsibility to the entire family of man. At present, America, with less than 7 per cent of the world's population, consumes more than half of the world's raw materials.[52] Communications satellites for various purposes such as weather forecasting or medical consultation and representing many nationalities will perpetually circle the earth. Global television and global telephonic systems may then lead to a greater understanding among all persons.

A deeper concern over education will result in a rise in the status of teachers. Formal education for marriage and family life from "womb to tomb" will be required. From an original emphasis largely restricted to the developing of skills in cooking and sewing, high school home economics has evolved to a concern with the physical, economic, social, psychic, and artistic aspects of life. In 1959, more than 95 per cent of all high schools in the United States offered some courses in home economics, and almost 2.5 million girls, and over 60,000 boys were taking them. Many of the present 25,050 high school home economics teachers are emphasizing a family-centered approach in all such courses.[53] According to Bricker, this trend does not represent a radical departure for home economics but a return to its original intentions. In support of this, Ellen H. Richards is said to have described home economics as "constantly reinforcing the relationships between the elements of man's physical environment and his nature as a social being."[54] The 1960 White House Conference on Children and Youth voted overwhelmingly in favor of making education for family living a part of every school curriculum at all levels.[55] Pending legislation in Montana will make the course, "Family Responsibility," compulsory at the high school level. In the mad dash to place a man on the moon, society temporarily forgot about human relationships, but it is now returning to sanity. At the same cost of a successful manned moon shot, the United States could do any one of the following: (1) give $150 million to each of over 200 small colleges; (2) finance seven-year fellowships (average length of time necessary for a doctorate) at $4000 per person per year for over a million students; (3)

endow, at $200 million each, 150 medical schools; (4) build and permanently endow two new universities for each of the latest fifty-nine member nations of the United Nations: or (5) create sixty more permanent Rockefeller Foundations.[56] In the words of LeRoy Collins, former Governor of Florida and presently Director of the United States Human Relations Committee:

> We need to educate Americans at all ages to cope with each succeeding day of the world in which they live. We must not fail to specialize in the most important speciality of all—the art of living a responsible and meaningful life.[57]

Alvin Eurich describes the goal of education at present as no longer to produce a person crammed full of knowledge, but to put new emphasis on "developing wisdom, on leading our young people to higher levels of maturity in dealing with the ideas that have made a difference in the progress of civilization."[58]

SOCIAL.   In the social sphere, there will be a continued general acceleration in the pace of living. There will also be an increase in knowledge of mental and emotional disturbances, and the processes of growth, learning, and maturation. Nobel Prize-winner Dr. Herman J. Muller suggests that, through increased knowledge of genetics, man will soon be able to attain to modes of thought and capabilities which, by comparison with those of today, will seem inconceivably God-like.

There will be a shift away from a "Freudian" society toward one concentrated on improving relationships. A survey of over 2500 students in twenty-four universities also shows a definite increase of relationship attitudes in at least one other country.[59]

Specialization will increase, but it will be balanced by more team approaches to social problems. According to a report of the U.S. Department of Health, Education, and Welfare for February 1963, the number of master's degrees conferred during the twelve months ending June 30, 1961, represented a 21.2 per cent increase over those conferred in 1951, and the number of doctorates represented a 44.1 per cent increase over the same period.

The trend toward medium-size families among the professional classes will continue and family size among the lower classes will decrease.

There will also be stepped-up movement from urban to suburban—and perhaps on to rural nonfarm—living. Within the confines of its own quite small acreage, each family will have the opportunity to recapture some of the beauty and dignity that can spring only from family relations. There, each member will be able to find the security and courage to return tomorrow to the fray. Many have already found this to be the case. Bell describes it as a "quest for community."[60] The trend is unmistakable. The population of the United States as a whole gained 24.2

per cent from 1950 to 1965, but that of the large cities (those with 250,000 or more inhabitants) gained only 4.4 per cent, and many lost instead of gaining. Although annexation of surrounding areas helped some (mostly Midwestern) cities to grow, the eight largest cities in the Northeast all lost population. Cities in the South and West grow as people leave the small towns in the area to seek work in the new industrialized sections. The general movement even in the South and West is out of the cities into the suburbs.[61] The suburban population since 1950 has increased by 82 per cent.[62]

Figure 21-3. There is an increasing movement from urban to suburban to rural nonfarm living. (Courtesy of the United Van Lines.)

Tomorrow's technology promises transportation at incredible speeds on almost frictionless cushions of air. Large craft carrying hundreds of passengers will soon cross the entire continent in less than an hour and reach Europe in less than two hours.[63] Small craft will whisk individuals over shorter distances (as between home and the place of work) within seconds.

Summary

The family of today is no longer an isolated entity sufficient unto itself. Events in some far corner of the world may more drastically affect tomorrow's family than unemployment of the father affects the family of today. Change is an inevitable process, but through intelligence, interest, and ingenuity, individuals can play a tremendous part in their own destiny; this will then lead to an emphasis on the importance of human relationships. From this fresh awareness, there should arise fewer causes of wars and depressions; the more stable leaders developed through democratic families should be better able to conduct democracy throughout the world. Tomorrow's marriage and family life may not resemble today's but they promise to be even more rewarding for those who are properly prepared. The Age of Democracy in the fundamentals of marriage and family relationships is an inspiring and challenging time for youth to be preparing for marriage. It is not easy for the couple always to apply and practice the principles of democracy within their own personal lives at a routine, daily level, but it is essential if tomorrow's American family is to maintain the values of democracy in government.

> We must get rid of the false idea that we have arrived, and all that remains is for the rest of the world to catch up with us. . . . We have reached a precarious midpoint in the most rapid growth in the most radical economic and political experiment in man's history. To remain ahead, we must reach new peaks in the art of living together as individuals so that nations can also under law.[64]

Notes

1. Quoted in Benjamin C. Willis, "Vocational Education in the Years Ahead," *American Vocational Journal* (February 1963), 18–19.

2. Bernard Karsh, *The Nation* (January 31, 1959).

3. An address by Dr. James McCain, President of Kansas State University, on the significance of graduate study for the future (February 12, 1961); reconfirmed in an address by Dr. N. Fawcett, President of Ohio State University, at a special convocation commemorating the one-hundredth birthday of Kansas State University, the first land-grant college in the United States (February 16, 1963).

4. For an excellent discussion, see Arnold Toynbee, "We Must Pay for Freedom," *Woman's Home Companion* (March 1955).

5. See John H. Furbay, "The One World Is Here," *National Parent-Teacher* (October 1950).

6. Charles E. Bowerman and John W. Kinch, "Changes in Family and Peer Orientation of Children Between the Fourth and Tenth Grades," *Social Forces*, 37:206–11.

7. See a well-written analysis of the possibilities of automation in Floyd C. Mann and L. Richard Hoffman, *Automation and the Worker* (New York: Holt, Rinehart & Winston, Inc., 1960).

8. *A Report to General Electric Share Owners,* Board of Directors, General Electric Corporation, Sixty-Eighth Annual Meeting, 4–5.

9. *American Women,* Report of the President's Commission on the Status of Women (1963).

10. *Successful Farming* (July 1960), 15.

11. M. F. Nimkoff, "Biological Discoveries and the Future of the Family: A Reappraisal," *Social Forces,* 41:124.

12. Harriet F. Pilpel and Theodora Zavin, *Your Marriage and the Law* (New York: Holt, Rinehart & Winston, Inc., 1952), p. 255.

13. *Ibid.*

14. U.S. Department of Health, Education, and Welfare, *Vital Statistics,* Vol. 9, No. 8 (October 17, 1960), and Vol. 13, No. 7 (September 21, 1964).

15. See, for example, E. W. Burgess and Harvey J. Locke, *The Family: From Institution to Companionship* (New York: American Book Company, 1945), pp. 412–70.

16. *Today's Health* (September 1961), 61.

17. See annual report of Pinnellas County Juvenile Welfare Board, St. Petersburg, Fla.

18. Samuel Liebman, *Emotional Forces in the Family* (Philadelphia: J. B. Lippincott Co., 1959), p. 6.

19. G. H. Hodenfield, "U.S. Faces Education Woes," *Associated Press News Release* (March 1, 1963).

20. A fact presented by Judge George Edwards of the Michigan Supreme Court at the 1960 White House Conference on Children and Youth, *Today's Child* 8:5 (May 1960). The total 1960 White House Conference Report states that of every 100 young people of high school age, only eighty-seven enter high school, and less than sixty graduate. About twenty of these enter college, and only ten graduate.

21. Hodenfield, *op. cit.*

22. U.S. Bureau of the Census, Series P-60, No. 43, 1.

23. Alvin Eurich, "A Twenty-First-Century Look at Higher Education," *Current Issues in Higher Education* (1963), 39–46.

24. *Today's Child* (October 1961), 1.

25. Talcott Parsons, *Family, Socialization and Interaction Process* (New York: The Free Press of Glencoe, Inc., 1955), pp. 9–10.

26. Dale L. Womble, "A Declaration of Rights," *Marriage and Family Living,* 17:358.

27. *Today's Child* (October 1961), 2.

28. Milton J. Yinger, "The Changing Family in a Changing Society," *Social Casework,* 40:420.

29. Metropolitan Life Insurance Company, *Statistical Bulletin* (August 1961), 8.

30. Alton L. Blakeslee, "News," *Today's Health* (February 1963), 9.

31. *Associated Press News Release* (February 1960), quoting the *Journal of the American Medical Association.*

32. Francis Horn, "Forces Shaping the College of Arts and Sciences," *Liberal Education* (March 1964), 5–16.

33. U.S. Department of Health, Education and Welfare, *Bulletin* (January 1962), vi.

34. *Today's Child* (January 1963), 2.

35. Earl L. Koos, *Families in Trouble* (New York: King's Crown Press, 1948).

36. Kathryne Close, "Impressions of the White House Conference," *Children,* 7:88.

37. R. A. Littman, *et al.,* "Where Parents Go for Help," *The Family Life Coordinator,* 6:3–9.

38. Pending legislation in California would require persons under certain ages who apply for marriage licenses to attend and successfully pass a course in family-life education first.

39. Kenyon Scudden and Kenneth Beam, *The Twenty Billion Dollar Challenge* (New York: G. P. Putnam's Sons, 1961), p. 53.

40. Reuben Hill, Alvin M. Katz, and Richard L. Simpson, "An Inventory of Research in Marriage and Family Behavior," *Marriage and Family Living,* 19:89–92. According to a recently completed study by Yale University, there are now 80,000 technical journals in the world. The Yale authorities estimate that by the year 2000 the number will be about one million.

41. Donald Brieland, "Uses of Research in Recent Popular Parent Education Literature," *Marriage and Family Living,* 19:60–65.

42. Melvin J. Vincena, "Labor Under Review," *Sociology and Social Research* (September 1957), 10–17.

43. Robert W. Harvey, "Tomorrow Is Here," *Changing Times* (July 1964).

44. Klein Myrdal, *Women's Two Roles—Home and Work* (London: Routledge & Kegan Paul, Ltd., 1956), p. 196.

45. C. E. V. Leser, "Trends in Women's Work Participation," *Population Studies* (November 1958), 100–10.

46. Personal communication with author.

47. U.S. Department of Health, Education and Welfare, *Bulletin* (January 1962), vi; and *Today's Health* (April 1963), 10.

48. *Today's Health* (September 1962), 43.

49. Harvey, *op. cit.*

50. *Planning Committee on Population Trends, Social and Economic Implications, Background Paper on Population Trends* (Washington, D.C.: White House Conference, September 1960), pp. 3–5. There are presently 18 million Americans aged sixty-five and over, and there will be 25 million by 1980. See President's Message to Congress, *Associated Press News Release* (February 21, 1963), and *Statistical Bulletin,* Metropolitan Life Insurance Company (December 1964).

51. *Today's Health* (June 1962), 70.

52. Karl Menninger, "Reading Notes," *Bulletin of the Menninger Clinic* (March 1961), quoting William Vogt, *People! Challenge to Survival* (New York: William Sloane, 1960).

53. Beulah T. Coon, *Home Economics in the Public Secondary Schools—A Report of a National Study,* U.S. Department of Health, Education, and Welfare Bulletin 661 (1962).

54. June A. Bricker, "Education for Leadership in Tomorrow's World," *Journal of Home Economics* (June 1964), 383–88.

55. See *Recommendations: Composite Report of Forum Findings* (Washington, D.C.: Government Printing Office, 1960), p. 12.

56. From the *Reader's Digest* (January 1963), 20.

57. LeRoy Collins, "Higher Education in an Age of Revolutions," *Current Issues in Higher Education* (1962), 3–9.

58. Eurich, *op. cit.*

59. Ray E. Baber, "Attitudes of Japanese Students on Marriage and Family Matters," *Research Studies of the State College of Washington* (June 1956), 182.

60. Wendell Bell, "Familism and Suburbanization," *Rural Sociology* (September–December 1956), 276–83.

61. *Statistical Bulletin,* Metropolitan Life Insurance Company (March 1961), and (December 1964).

62. *Ibid.*

63. Harvey, *op. cit.*

64. Quoting Dr. Arthur Larson, Consultant to the U.S. State Department on United Nations matters, and formerly Director of the U.S. Information Agency, in Kennedy Lecture, Ohio University, Athens, Ohio, February 18, 1965.

Questions for further thought

1. To what degree is there an inborn drive for all men to be free, as interpreted within the American democratic philosophy?
2. Is the family system in a state of decadence?
3. Why is there often a difference between the legal cause and the real causes of divorce?
4. Are there any arguments in favor of divorce by mutual consent?
5. What community resources make the most or least positive contribution to the improvement of marriage and family life?
6. What are some of the most urgent needs in family research at present?
7. What loyalties compete, and often win, in a struggle with family ties today? Why?

Recommended film

The Family of Man (McGraw-Hill Book Company, Inc.).

Suggested supplemental readings

BOOKS

Allen, Frederick Lewis. *The Big Change.* New York: Harper & Row, Publishers, 1952.

Bassett, Marion. *A New Sex Ethics and Marriage Structure.* New York: Philosophical Library, Inc., 1961.

Bernard, Jessie. *Academic Women.* University Park, Pa.: Pennsylvania State University Press, 1965.

Blitsten, Dorothy. *The World of the Family.* New York: Random House, 1963.

Carter, Richard. *The Gentle Legions.* Garden City, N.Y.: Doubleday & Company, Inc., 1961.

Cohen, Nathan E. *The Citizen Volunteer: His Responsibility, Role and Opportunity in Modern Society.* New York: Harper & Row, Publishers, 1960.

Cousins, Norman. *In Place of Folly.* New York: Harper & Row, Publishers, 1961.

Drucker, Peter F. *Landmarks of Tomorrow.* New York: Harper & Row, Publishers, 1959.

Duncan, Beverly, and Philip M. Hauser. *Housing A Metropolis.* New York: The Free Press of Glencoe, Inc., 1961.

Ginzberg, Eli (ed.). *Values and Ideals of American Youth.* New York: Columbia University Press, 1961.

Jennings, Eugene E. *An Anatomy of Leadership: Princes, Heroes, and Supermen.* New York: Harper & Row, Publishers, 1960.

Schur, Edwin M. (ed.). *The Family and the Sexual Revolution.* Bloomington, Ind.: Indiana University Press, 1965.

Sullenger, Thomas Earl. *Neglected Areas in Family Living.* Boston: Christopher Publishing House, 1960.

Theobald, Robert. *The Challenge of Abundance.* New York: Clarkson N. Potter, 1961.

Walker, Charles R. (ed.). *Modern Technology and Civilization.* New York: McGraw-Hill Book Company, Inc., 1962.

Weil, Mildred W. *Marriage and The Family: Five Conceptual Approaches.* New York: Random House, 1965.

Zelomek, A. Wilbert. *A Changing America.* New York: John Wiley & Sons, Inc., 1959.

Zimmerman, Carle C., and Lucius F. Cervantes. *Successful American Families.* New York: Pageant Press, 1960.

ARTICLES

Babcock, Charlotte G. "The Contributions of the Family Agency in Meeting Community Problems," *The Social Service Review,* **32**:223–33.

Bass, Ralph. "How Will We Live Fifty Years From Now?" *Coronet* (December 1959), 82–86.

Commanger, H. S. "Brave World of the Year 2000," *The New York Times,* November 1, 1959, p. 24.

"The Fabulous Fifteen Years Ahead," *Changing Times* (January 1961).

Furbay, John Harvey. "The One World Is Here," *National Parent-Teacher* (October 1950).

Harrington, Michael. "Our Fifty Million Poor," *Commentary,* **28**:19–27.

Hurd, Helen G. "The Changing Society and Its Challenges," *Journal of Home Economics* (February 1963), 85–89.

Kephart, William. "Some Knowns and Unknowns in Family Research," *Marriage and Family Living,* **19**:7–15.

Landis, Judson T. "Values and Limitations of Family Research Using Student Subjects," *Marriage and Family Living,* **19**:100–105.

Menninger, William C. "How Community Forces Affect the Family," *Bulletin Menninger Clinic,* **14**:53–60.

Nye, F. Ivan, and Alan E. Bayer. "Some Recent Trends in Family Research," *Social Forces,* **41**:290–301.

Rose, Arnold M. "Automation and the Future of Society," *Commentary* (March 1956), 274–80.

Spaulding, C. B. "Changing Patterns of Family Life," *California Journal of Secondary Education,* **21**:28–35.

Tuttle, Elizabeth. "Serving the Unmarried Mother Who Keeps Her Child," *Social Casework,* **43**:415–22.

UNESCO Publications Center, New York, "Changes in the Family," *International Social Science Journal,* **14**:3 (1962).

Index